The CHICKAMAUGA Campaign

Glory or the Grave: The Breakthrough, the Union Collapse, and the Defense of Horseshoe Ridge, September 20, 1863

David A. Powell

SB
Savas Beatie
California

Library of Congress Control Number: 2015946032

ISBN 13: 978-1-61121-202-0 (hardcover)
ISBN 13: 978-1-61121-383-6 (First Paperback edition)
ISBN 13: 978-1-61121-203-7 (e-book)

SB

Published by
Savas Beatie LLC
989 Governor Drive, Suite 102
El Dorado Hills, CA 95762

Phone: 916-941-6896
(E-mail) sales@savasbeatie.com

05 04 03 02 01 5 4 3 2 1
First edition, first printing

MIX
Paper from responsible sources
FSC www.fsc.org FSC® C011935

RAINFOREST ALLIANCE CERTIFIED

Savas Beatie titles are available at special discounts for bulk purchases in the United States by corporations, institutions, and other organizations. For more details, please contact Savas Beatie, P.O. Box 4527, El Dorado Hills, CA 95762, or you may e-mail us at sales@savasbeatie.com, or visit our website at www.savasbeatie.com for additional information.

Proudly published, printed, and warehoused in the United States of America.

For my mother, N. Geraldine Powell,
who first encouraged my love of reading.

Table of Contents

Table of Contents (continued)

Table of Contents (continued)

Preface

"... for the purpose of preserving and suitably marking for historical and professional military study the fields of some of the most remarkable maneuvers and most brilliant fighting in the war of the rebellion."

— *Enabling legislation, Chickamauga and Chattanooga National Military Park, August 19, 1890*

This is the second installment of *The Chickamauga Campaign* trilogy. Volume 1, subtitled *A Mad Irregular Battle*, carried us from the crucial (but universally overlooked) Tullahoma Campaign (June 24 - July 4, 1863), which set the stage for all that was to follow, through the beginning of the Chickamauga Campaign in August 1863 through the end of the battle's second day, finishing with the close of the fighting on September 19, 1863. This volume, *Glory or the Grave*, opens with an examination of the councils of war held that night by the opposing commanders, and thereafter exclusively on the climactic events of September 20, 1863, the battle's final day. Ironically, much of this book was written years ago and before Volume 1 because it was intended to be a single volume study about the defense of Horseshoe Ridge. That project did not reach publication stage for several reasons, one of them being the book I wrote turned out to be far too long for the intended publisher at the time. I think things worked out for the best.

September 20 is the "big day" in terms of Chickamauga historiography. Two of the battle's three most infamous blunders—the Confederate failure to attack at dawn and the fateful Federal decision to pull a division out of the battle line at the worst possible time—took place that Sunday morning. The arguments generated by these errors have simmered ever since. Even today, after more than 150 years, they remain among the most well-known facets of Chickamauga. I realized early in the writing process that I could cover each of these incidents (as well as controversies spawned by similar, if lesser-known events) in one of two ways: a straight narrative based upon my best interpretation of the evidence, or through a more detailed exploration of the often-differing viewpoints of the numerous participants, concluding with what I think happened. Since the historiography of the battle interests me nearly as much as what actually occurred on the field, I settled upon the latter course (with its various threads and slight digressions). Readers will have to decide whether I chose wisely.

The third great "error" of the battle—the Confederate failure on September 21 to pursue their supposedly beaten Union foe—will find its place in the final volume of the trilogy. *Glory or the Grave* ends when nightfall brings Sunday's fighting to a wearied and very bloody close. Volume 3, *Barren Victory*, discusses that issue and more, comprehensively addressing the battle's aftermath. *Barren Victory* will also include several appendices designed to amplify aspects of the battle that don't necessarily fit into the main narrative. These include extended discussions of some of the other controversies, as well as topics such as logistics and the creation of the military park.

As first mentioned in Volume 1, the amount of material available describing actions on the third day of Chickamauga is simply staggering. Beginning almost with the cessation of shooting, thousands of participants would eventually try to describe what they experienced for their friends and families back home, and ultimately, for posterity. Some of them simply described their own role in the fight, while others left detailed regimental or brigade histories. Many wrote in remembrance of fallen comrades. Without those accounts, we would know very little about Chickamauga, and my own writing would be much the poorer for it. There is more material, frankly, than I could ever use even in a project of this length, but I hope that *The Chickamauga Campaign* collectively sparks greater interest in revisiting all their stories.

Describing the course of battle of September 20 was actually a bit easier than it proved to be for the 19th. Sunday's action is more straightforward. No longer are the Federals pushing back, counterattacking into wild confused melees in the woods. On this day it is the Rebels who possess the initiative, pressing home their assaults against largely static Union defenders. This is not to say there were not moments of breakthrough and horrific fighting—some of the most intense combat of the day resulted from such engagements. In general, the Union side of the line was reactive rather than proactive. Still, it is important to keep close tabs on the units and movements, and so I have included 37 maps to support the text, about all we could cram into the project. If you want an even more detailed cartographical look at the battle, you will have to turn to my earlier study (with David Friedrichs) entitled *The Maps of Chickamauga* (Savas Beatie, 2009).

Acknowledgments

Those folks I thanked in the preface to *A Mad Irregular Battle* are of course equally deserving of my gratitude in this volume. None of the installments of *The Chickamauga Campaign* would be as in-depth or as good without their contributions. In that regard, I wish to extend my thanks to everyone a second time.

Many thanks are due to my friend David Friedrichs for producing the outstanding maps that do so much to illuminate what would otherwise be a confusing and difficult narrative of the fighting.

I would also like to once again thank my publisher, Theodore P. Savas, and all the good people who work at Savas Beatie for their unswerving support and dedication to the creation and marketing of this work.

Further thanks go to Kenneth Bandy, especially for all his help concerning Harker's brigade and in particular, the 65th Ohio. Ken probably knows more about the 65th Ohio than any man alive, and is certainly a font of knowledge concerning Chickamauga.

I wish to also thank the readers who have taken the time to provide feedback on Volume 1. Your input has been invaluable, and very rewarding. This book is the better for it, as will be Volume 3. As ever, the mistakes are mine. I only hope they produce less controversy than did the "fateful order of the day."

I would be remiss if I did not thank Killian, my faithful research hound. The library is his domain.

* * *

A brief housekeeping note. Because this study is a trilogy, the full bibliography will appear in the third installment. Until then, readers will have to be satisfied with the extensive footnotes. Because of all the tactical detail in the first volume, a complete order of battle was included at the end of that book, and we decided there was no need to reprint the exact same lengthy accounting here.

David A. Powell
Chicago, IL
July, 2015

Prologue

The Battle Thus Far
September 18 and 19, 1863

The battle of Chickamauga began late in the morning on Friday, September 18, when Confederate infantry from Brig. Gen. Bushrod Johnson's Provisional Division encountered Brig. Gen. Robert H. G. Minty's Union cavalry brigade. The fighting first erupted near Peeler's Mill on Peavine Creek, along Reed's Bridge Road. Braxton Bragg, the troubled, temperamental commander of the Army of Tennessee, planned to insert a strong force of Confederates between Maj. Gen. William Starke Rosecrans's Army of the Cumberland and the city of Chattanooga. Once that was accomplished, Bragg intended to fall upon Rosecrans's left (northernmost) flank at Lee and Gordon's Mills, attacking and driving the Federals southward into the mountains of North Georgia, where they could be trapped and crushed.

This task was assigned to three Confederate infantry corps. Bushrod Johnson's force comprised the van of the newly arriving First Corps, Army of Northern Virginia, commanded by Lt. Gen. James Longstreet. Until Longstreet arrived, Maj. Gen. John B. Hood led the corps, only recently returned to duty after his wound at Gettysburg. Major Generals William H. T. Walker and Simon B. Buckner commanded another two infantry corps under Bragg. The entire force was supported by Brig. Gen. Nathan Bedford Forrest's cavalry. All told, it numbered nearly 30,000 Rebels, or roughly one-half of Bragg's combat power.

The day before the battle began, General Rosecrans set up his army's headquarters in the James Gordon mansion at Crawfish Spring. For the better part of a week, Rosecrans had been trying to extricate his troops from a trap. The Union XXI Corps was holding positions in and around Lee and Gordon's Mills, with the XIV Corps to its south. The soldiers of the XX Corps, meanwhile, struggled northward through the North Georgia mountains to rejoin their comrades from Alpine and Valley Head, Alabama.

West Chickamauga Creek divided the opposing armies, and if Bragg was going to execute his strategy as intended, he had to place those 30,000 men on the west side of that waterway first. Crossing Reed's Bridge, defended by Minty, and Alexander's Bridge, held by Col. John T. Wilder's famous "Lightning Brigade" of repeater-armed mounted infantry, was vital to the successful execution of this plan. Unexpectedly stubborn resistance from the Union cavalry foiled Bragg's plans for September 18. These two Federal brigades, all told fewer than 3,000 men, resisted Bragg's infantry all afternoon. Most of the Confederates did not cross the creek until well after nightfall. Two-thirds of Buckner's corps didn't cross until the morning of the 19th. While the casualty lists of September 18 were short by comparison to what was to come, the fighting that Friday afternoon, the true first day of the battle, shaped the course of the engagement's final two days.

The stubborn delaying actions waged by Minty and Wilder alerted Rosecrans to Bragg's movements and gave the Federals time to react. The Ohio army commander turned to his most trusted subordinate, Maj. Gen. George Henry Thomas, commanding the XIV Corps. Virginia-born, burly, taciturn, and capable, Thomas was a solid Union man despite his birth state, and easily the most competent of Rosecrans's subordinates. Having digested the intelligence of Confederates crossing Chickamauga Creek at a number of points beyond the Union left flank, Rosecrans and Thomas agreed on a countermove. Thomas would take the two of his four divisions most readily available under Brig. Gens. Absalom Baird and John M. Brannan northward. The La Fayette Road was Rosecrans's most direct link to the newly-captured city of Chattanooga, which was fast becoming his new supply base. Thomas would march north along the La Fayette Road to the Kelly farm, several miles above the army's current position. Thomas's remaining pair of divisions would follow as soon as they could be spared. Rosecrans trusted Thomas implicitly, and relied upon the XIV Corps commander to exercise his own judgment in blunting Bragg's thrust.

Sending Thomas north was feasible only because Maj. Gen. Alexander McDowell McCook's XX Corps divisions were finally arriving to take Baird's and Brannan's places in the Union defensive line. McCook's arrival also allowed Maj. Gen. Thomas L. Crittenden to shift his XXI Corps northward, extending his own left toward Thomas's new position.

Rosecrans's response, which entailed significant risk, required moving large bodies of troops laterally in the face of an aggressive opponent. The shifting of one contingent would open a gap in the line, which (if all things went as planned) would be immediately filled by the troops slated to replace the outgoing force. Precise timing was critical, and any unexpected delays or misunderstandings exposed the army to a potential disaster. Rosecrans was an experienced commander and surely weighed the consequences. But if he was going to stymie Bragg's movement, the Federals would have to sidle northward, and he ordered it done. His decision also meant that wearying night marches were in store for much of the Union army.

And it worked. The battle of September 19, a Saturday, began not at Lee and Gordon's Mills as Bragg intended but at a place called Jay's Mill, just west of Reed's Bridge. The fighting opened when two Federal brigades from the Union Reserve Corps encountered the Southern troopers of Brig. Gen. John Pegram's cavalry brigade, part of Nathan Bedford Forrest's command. The Federals had marched out of Rossville and then west along the Reed's Bridge Road at dusk the night before, belated reinforcements to help Minty in his fight to hold the crossing. They never found him. Instead, they captured a number of straggling Confederates near Jay's Mill. In response, Bragg ordered Forrest to reconnoiter the area, a move that triggered a heated skirmish where Bragg least expected Federals to be. Enemy troops there in strength threatened Bragg's right flank as his men readied to attack Crittenden's XXI Corps.

Those two Federal brigades soon departed, heading back to Rossville, but not before Col. Daniel McCook informed George Thomas that a lone Rebel brigade was ripe for capture near Jay's Mill. Reacting aggressively, Thomas ordered both of his two available divisions into the woods to investigate. Colonel John Croxton's brigade of Brannan's division soon ran into Forrest's men, and by 7:30 a.m. the battle was on.

When Forrest called for reinforcements, Bragg ordered William H. T. Walker's Reserve Corps to provide support. These developments changed the complexion of the battlefield and caused Bragg, suddenly gripped by uncertainty, to place his larger offensive on hold. From these humble beginnings, the conflagration spread of its own accord.

Walker reinforced the Rebel cavalry with two brigades of infantry that were quickly outmatched by the two Union infantry divisions in and around Winfrey Field. Walker's remaining division under Brig. Gen. St. John Liddell, however, flanked Baird's division and captured hundreds of prisoners and a number of cannon. By late morning, the confusing seesaw nature of the fighting induced both army commanders to commit more troops to the fight.

Both Bragg and Rosecrans made similar mistakes when each began feeding divisions into the growing fight piecemeal, with little or no regard for corps integrity. Bragg ordered his senior corps commander, Lt. Gen. Leonidas Polk, to take command of the fighting on the Confederate right, and reinforced him with Maj. Gen. Benjamin Franklin Cheatham's five-brigade command, one of the army's largest divisions. While Cheatham belonged to Polk's corps, the Bishop's remaining division under Maj. Gen. Thomas C. Hindman remained on the other side of Chickamauga Creek facing Federals at Lee and Gordon's Mills. As a result, Polk's corps would fight divided for the rest of the long battle. Rosecrans, meanwhile, augmented Thomas with two additional divisions, one under Maj. Gen. John M. Palmer of Crittenden's XXI Corps, and another under Brig. Gen. Richard W. Johnson of McCook's XX Corps—a decision that similarly disrupted Union corps integrity. Cheatham's, Palmer's and Johnson's troops collided in and around Brock Field, where the horrific fighting eventually settled into a bloody stalemate.

Bragg still had two infantry corps massed west of the creek, awaiting attack orders. John Bell Hood and his First Corps (consisting of Bushrod Johnson's Provisional Division and three brigades of the troops from Lee's Army of Northern Virginia) held their position in the timber south of Brock Field, while Simon Buckner's Corps of two divisions rested farther south on Hood's left. Together, these four divisions amounted to nearly 19,000 men, a powerful force indeed. Instead of committing them *en masse*, however, Bragg plucked Maj. Gen. Alexander P. Stewart's division out of Buckner's line and sent it north (marching behind Hood's line) to help Cheatham. This decision not only further eroded the chain of command, but also weakened Bragg's intended main blow.

On the other side of the field, Rosecrans continued to think aggressively. Unaware of the presence of Hood's and Buckner's troops, he sought an opportunity to outflank Cheatham's men from the south. After committing Richard Johnson's men to support Thomas, Rosecrans ordered Brig. Gen. Jefferson C. Davis into action about 1:00 p.m.; about the same time XXI Corps commander Tom Crittenden pulled two-thirds of Brig. Gen. Horatio Van Cleve's division away from Lee and Gordon's Mills to march north and support Palmer. Van Cleve would go into action in the woods east of Brotherton Field, where his troops encountered A. P. Stewart's Rebels. Jeff Davis's Federals entered those same woods south of Van Cleve near Viniard Field, with instructions from Rosecrans to find the

Rebel flank and strike it. This order unwittingly placed Davis's small division of two brigades on a collision course with Hood's entire corps.

Colonel Hans Heg's brigade, of Davis's division, stumbled into Bushrod Johnson's Confederates about 2:00 p.m. Both sides were surprised by the encounter, the Confederates perhaps more so than the Federals. Still, Johnson's command easily outnumbered Heg's line, which halted and fell back. Sometime after this initial clash, John Bell Hood ordered his entire corps into action.

Hood's advance was marred by a curious positional change that would impact the rest of the fighting that day. Evander Law's three brigades held Hood's right flank, while Johnson's three brigades were on the left, south of Law. Each division had two brigades in the front line and one in reserve. When they advanced, however, Johnson's command angled northwest, while Law's drifted southwest. In other words, their courses crossed. The result was two fractured Southern divisions. Neither would fight as a unified formation for the rest of the battle.

The fighting around Viniard Field now became general. Brigadier General William P. Carlin, leading Davis's other brigade, advanced into the field to support Heg's overmatched troops. General Crittenden reinforced Davis with Brig. Gen. Thomas J. Wood's division, adding two more brigades to the fight, bolstered a short time later by Col. Sidney J. Barnes's brigade, the last of Van Cleve's formations. Wood and Barnes had been left to guard the crossing at Lee and Gordon's Mills, but when Philip Sheridan's division of the XX Corps arrived to replace them, Crittenden lost no time summoning them north to join the spreading combat.

The action in Viniard Field was both the bloodiest and the most confused fighting of all of September 19. Wood's two brigades moved up behind Heg and Carlin, forming in the La Fayette Road. Crittenden initially intended Wood's men to move east, reinforcing Heg in the timber east of the road, until a threat from the north reoriented Wood's leftmost brigade under Col. Charles Harker.

The threat that turned Harker arrived in the form of two regiments from McNair's brigade of Johnson's division, which had crossed the La Fayette Road through a gap in the Union lines between Davis's men and the rest of the Federals fighting up around Brotherton Field. That thrust was turned back by some of John T. Wilder's men (who remained in position west of Viniard Field throughout the day on Saturday the 19th), but Wood decided to try and close this gap by sending Harker north along the corridor of the La Fayette Road.

In the meantime, Brig. Gen. Jerome Robertson's famed Texas Brigade, part of Law's command, moved into action. Half of Robertson's men engaged Heg while the other half collided with Carlin's Federals. Sensing an opportunity to turn Robertson's flank, Colonel Barnes led his Union brigade into Viniard Field as well, angling across Carlin's front. Barnes's attack might have routed Robertson, had not Barnes overlooked a threat to his own flank. While moving northeast across the field, yet another Rebel brigade had come up and occupied the tree line bordering the eastern edge of the cleared ground. These troops belonged to Col. Robert C. Trigg's brigade, part of William Preston's division of Buckner's Corps—sent forward to support Hood at Bragg's order. Trigg's men savaged Barnes's right flank, breaking their line. The subsequent Federal rout also swept Carlin's troops back.

Viniard Field played host to repeated swings of fortune that afternoon. Brigadier General Henry Benning's Georgians reinforced the Texans, only to be stopped by the devastating firepower of Wilder's mounted infantry and driven back in turn by the arrival of Col. Luther P. Bradley's Federals of Sheridan's division. One measure of the intensity of this action was the fact that the Rebels overran the 8th Indiana Battery not once, but twice, the guns recovered each time by Union counterblows. Only dusk brought an end to the action there.

Meanwhile, farther north in Brotherton Field, the Union center nearly collapsed around 4:00 p.m. when Confederate attacks from elements of Bushrod Johnson's and A. P. Stewart's troops outflanked the Federals opposing them. Horatio Van Cleve's line was routed out of the timber east of Brotherton Field by the first of these blows, and subsequently, Union Maj. Gen. Joseph Reynolds's scratch line in Brotherton Field was shattered in the same fashion. The Alabamians of Henry Clayton's brigade exploited this collapse by sweeping into Dyer Field, only to be rebuffed by fresh Federals from James S. Negley's division.

Similarly, William Bate's Rebels were shattered at the apogee of their charge into Poe Field, roughly half a mile north of Brotherton Field. Bate's Rebels were stopped by four Federal batteries in a stunning crescendo of close-range cannon fire. Clayton's and Bate's retreat marked the end of the action along most of the battle line.

The final act of September 19 played out in Winfrey Field, the scene of so much fighting that morning. During the day, Bragg shifted Lt. Gen. Daniel Harvey Hill's entire corps from the Confederate army's left flank, down near Glass Mill, to the far right. Bragg still hoped to find the Federal flank and interpose his troops between Rosecrans and the ultimate prize—Chattanooga. Hill's march consumed most of the afternoon.

Major General Patrick R. Cleburne's division led the movement, arriving near Winfrey Field just about dusk. Daylight was fast waning, but an attack was still expected, so Hill ordered one. Cleburne went into action. The result was a rare night engagement involving Cleburne's troops and the Yankees of Johnson's and Baird's divisions. Aside from adding to the casualty lists, the fight proved indecisive. When that last flare of combat ended, the day's battle ended with it. When darkness fell, so did the thermometer. The men, as they always do, suffered a long cold night, wondering what the morrow would bring.

Chapter One

Council of War:

Night of September 19-20, 1863

William Starke Rosecrans struggled to digest the fragmentary and often contradictory evidence that had been flowing into his headquarters throughout the long and exhausting day of September 19. Nightfall had ended the fighting in every sector except Winfrey Field. Combat had raged unceasingly for more than 12 hours, and by the time the sun set nearly every brigade in the army had seen action.

At 8:00 p.m., Rosecrans composed and dispatched a carefully worded telegram to Maj. Gen. Henry Halleck in Washington. "We have just concluded a terrific day's fighting, and have another in prospect for tomorrow," explained the commander of the Army of the Cumberland. "The enemy attempted to turn our left, but his design was anticipated, and a sufficient force placed there to render his attempt abortive." Rosecrans downplayed the damage his army had suffered and described the number of Union dead as "inconsiderable," but admitted the number of "our wounded [was] very heavy." Prisoners taken from no fewer than 30 Rebel regiments proved that the assault was no spoiling attack; General Bragg, concluded Rosecrans, was "greatly our superior in numbers." By now there was widespread recognition within both his own army's headquarters and Washington D.C. that Bragg had been reinforced from all quarters of the Confederacy. Captured Rebel troops—from Simon Buckner's command, from Mississippi, and others from James Longstreet's First Corps

A GROUP OF STAFF OFFICERS

CAPT. E. A. OTIS
CAPT. S. C. KELLOGG
CAPT. M. V. SHERIDAN
MAJ. F. S. BOND
LIEUT.-COL. G. P. THRUSTON
COL. ARTHUR C. DUCAT
MAJ. M. H. FITCH
LIEUT.-COL. A. VON SCHRADER

When the fighting ended, a commander's staff had much to do. These eight men served various Union generals. Bond and Ducat served on Rosecrans's staff. Von Schrader and Kellogg served Thomas, while Fitch worked under Baird (Thomas's XIV Corps). Thruston was McCook's XX Corps chief of staff, while the younger Sheridan served his brother Phillip. Otis worked for Horatio Van Cleve. *Archibald Gracie, The Truth About Chickamauga*

from Virginia, confirmed this. Some Union estimates of Bragg's strength exceeded 120,000 men.[1]

One persistent rumor had it that Gen. Joseph E. Johnston had transferred his entire army from Mississippi and was on the field in North Georgia. Other Federals mistook D. H. Hill's name for A. P. Hill from General Lee's army, which suggested the reinforcements from Virginia amounted to two infantry corps instead of one. Rosecrans did not blithely accept all these reports at face value, but he no longer needed to be convinced the Rebels could execute such a massive concentration of force without the authorities in Washington warning him in a timely fashion. The enemy was here, and in great numbers, and they had proven it this day.[2]

Despite what looked to be long odds, Rosecrans thought his army had fought well. In addition to minimizing casualties for the authorities back in Washington, he admitted only to losing 10 guns while capturing seven in return. In fact, Federal artillery losses had been closer to 20 pieces, but some of those had been recaptured and others claimed several times by different units. Sorting out the real numbers would take more than a quick evening tally. The next day's fighting would decide the contest. "The army is in excellent condition and spirits," reported Rosecrans, "and by the blessing of providence, the defeat of the enemy will be total to-morrow."[3]

The assistant secretary of war largely agreed with Rosecrans that evening. Charles Anderson Dana's missives reflected a similar spirit of confidence and included many of the same numbers, although he did pass on a preliminary estimate that put the army's wounded "as not exceeding 2,000." In fact, the day's losses had been very high and numbered between 6,000 and 8,000, with at least 1,000 killed. Still, the mood at army headquarters remained positive, and even upbeat. Despite thinking themselves badly outnumbered, everyone believed they had taken Bragg's best punch and stopped the Rebels in their tracks.[4]

1 U.S. War Department. *The War of the Rebellion: A Compilation of the Official Records of the Union and Confederate Armies*, 128 vols. (Washington D.C., 1880-1901), Series 1, vol. 30, pt. 1, 136. Hereafter cited as *OR*. All references are to Series 1 unless otherwise indicated.

2 Entries for September 12 to 18, "Summaries of the news reaching Headquarters of General W. S. Rosecrans," RG 393, National Archives and Records Administration. Hereafter NARA.

3 *OR* 30, pt. 1, 136.

4 Ibid., 192.

While the Army of the Cumberland had indeed repulsed Bragg's multitude of assaults, accomplishing that feat left the army in a jumble. Corps, divisions, and even brigades were interwoven with little regard to chain of command. XIV Corps commander George H. Thomas remained Rosecrans's primary field commander, controlling five of the army's 10 available infantry divisions. Thomas L. Crittenden's and Alexander McDowell McCook's spheres of authority were less clearly defined, since the army commander had cannibalized their commands throughout the day to feed the needs of the spreading battle. Nightfall brought with it the opportunity to re-order this confusion and draw up a plan for the next day.[5]

Rosecrans was still mainly concerned with the army's left flank and keeping his route to Chattanooga open. Thomas's night march on the 18th had stymied Bragg's effort to outflank the Army of the Cumberland on September 19, but Thomas's line ended just north of the Kelly farm—still eight miles short of Chattanooga. Major General Gordon Granger's three brigades defended Rossville, four miles distant. Brigadier General George Wagner's brigade of Crittenden's XXI Corps provided a garrison for the town itself, but if Bragg launched another flanking move, the main body of the army could still be cut off. Moreover, while Granger's men had not seen serious action on September 19, the day's sparring over Red House Bridge warned Rosecrans of the dangers of inattention there; the northern approaches had to be held.

Of less concern was the safety of Chattanooga itself. Wagner held the town with 1,438 infantry, six cannon, and the 3rd Indiana Cavalry battalion (numbering 159 sabers). In addition, some 1,000 men from the Pioneer Corps and several companies of the 1st Michigan Engineers were in town restoring bridges over the Tennessee River, all trained and equipped like infantry in the event of a fight. Even better, Brig. Gen. James Spears's brigade of East Tennessee Unionists had arrived in Lookout Valley that day, and was just a couple of miles from the city should it be needed. Spears's force included the 3rd, 5th and 6th Tennessee infantry, adding 1,300 more men to the town's available defenders. At 8:00 p.m. that night, Rosecrans instructed Granger to order Spears's men to move into Chattanooga the next day, bolstering the overall garrison to nearly 4,000. The city was also entrenched, thanks to the

5 This number does not include Gordon Granger's Reserve Corps of three brigades, which effectively constituted another division. Granger's force was an ad-hoc formation and not usually considered part of the main army.

labor of Bragg's infantry before they abandoned the place on September 8. Even now, those defenses were being turned to Federal use.[6]

One other reinforcement was expected to arrive on September 20. Major General Lovell H. Rousseau was returning to the army after a trip to Washington D.C., back from yet another effort pitching Rosecrans's idea of a mounted infantry force. Rousseau was not bringing any new troops with him, but he was a first-rate division commander, a tenacious fighter, and well-liked by his troops. He normally commanded the First Division of the XIV Corps, now led by Absalom Baird in his absence. Aware that a battle was imminent, Rousseau was hurrying to reach the front. Should unexpected trouble threaten Chattanooga, his presence there would be an important steadying factor.[7]

Protecting Chattanooga was imperative, but the issue of what to do on the field in front of Bragg's Army of Tennessee was of paramount importance. Rosecrans could not simply contract his lines northward and have the whole army fall back into Chattanooga. He still had substantial ties southward he could not afford to abandon. One major impediment to a sidle northward was the medical complex clustered around Crawfish Spring. No fewer than seven divisional field hospitals, each overflowing with wounded still arriving by the hundreds from the day's carnage, were concentrated there. These facilities essentially anchored the army's right flank into place, for they could not be easily moved, nor could they simply be abandoned to the enemy. Crawfish Spring, with its abundant source of otherwise scarce water, had been safely behind the army's center of mass that morning and was the logical place to establish the army's rear echelon. Few had fully anticipated the inexorable pull to the north that resulted from Thomas's march. Two exceptions were John Brannan's and Absalom Baird's divisional hospitals, which were established north of the field near Cloud Church on the La Fayette Road. As the battle of the morrow would demonstrate, however, they were equally vulnerable.

Now, however, Crawfish Spring was well south of the army's battle line, defended only by cavalry and in danger of capture. To some extent Rosecrans had to keep the army's right wing extended in that direction if he wanted to keep the water supply and massive hospital facility out of Rebel hands. This meant his main line of battle stretched from the intersection of the Reed's Bridge and

6 *OR* 30, pt. 3, 741.

7 Ibid., 745; Dan Lee, *Kentuckian in Blue: A Biography of Major General Lovell Harrison Rousseau* (McFarland & Co., 2010), 122-124.

La Fayette roads all the way south to Lee and Gordon's Mills, a length of four miles. This was simply too far to form a strong continuous front. Instead, divisions formed what amounted to isolated redoubts, with considerable gaps in between. Fortunately, Robert Mitchell's cavalry had closed up during the day, and could assume the responsibility for both establishing a picket line along Chickamauga Creek and for defending the hospitals. Their presence allowed McCook to shift the last of the infantry northward.

Nor were all of Rosecrans's forces yet clear of McLemore's Cove. Abandoning Crawfish Spring would have also had the unfortunate effect of exposing those columns to enemy attack. The most important of these forces was Col. Sidney Post's brigade, escorting the trains of Jefferson C. Davis's division, elements of the XX corps trains, detachments of sick and convalescent men, and some prisoners. Post was at Stevens's Gap, having reached that location late on the 18th after a difficult 23-mile march. Rosecrans ordered him to halt there and hold the gap "at all hazards" through the 19th. If pressed, Post was to send the trains into Chattanooga via Lookout Valley, "contesting the ground inch by inch."[8]

The only brigade still south of Post belonged to Col. Louis Watkins. On the morning of September 19, this brigade of cavalry (the 4th, 5th, and 6th Kentucky regiments) was still at Valley Head, site of the former XX Corps camps the week previous. Watkins was charged with bringing up the last vestiges of the army's presence around Alpine, which included some of the cavalry corps baggage train, another 400 sick Federals, and four captured Confederate officers.[9]

The vulnerability of both Post and Watkins weighed on Rosecrans even while the battle raged, as his periodic queries seeking reports of their progress north demonstrates. Their loss, together with the accumulated baggage and supply trains, would have been especially unfortunate given the lack of rail and river transport beyond Bridgeport. Rosecrans would need every wagon if he wanted to renew offensive operations once Bragg's Rebels were defeated on September 20.

Accordingly, Rosecrans ordered Mitchell's three available cavalry brigades to establish sufficient pickets along West Chickamauga Creek to prevent any unexpected forays by Rebel infantry or cavalry. Mitchell's troopers would take

8 *OR* 30, pt. 1, 507.

9 Ibid., 915.

responsibility for the bridge at Lee and Gordon's Mills, freeing up the last of Maj. Gen. Philip Sheridan's infantry brigades to move north, and defend the Glass Mill crossing in strength. They would not be able to stop a serious thrust if Bragg ordered a full-scale infantry attack, but would provide sufficient warning and the ability to delay and harass such a thrust.

As the fighting subsided, Rosecrans and his staff turned to the more mundane details of army management. One of the most pressing was water. As early as September 17, Rosecrans instructed members of the army's Pioneer Corps to collect barrels and casks in Chattanooga, assuming they would be needed to haul water to the front. On the 19th that work took on an added urgency when the first reports of the battle reached the city and the garrison braced for waves of wounded. At 6:00 p.m., Rosecrans also ordered General Mitchell to detail a cavalry regiment "to bring water along the line in buckets."[10]

After their brush with Rebel cavalry earlier that day, Colonel Harrison's 39th Indiana Mounted Infantry arrived at Crawfish Spring near sundown and was now available for this duty. Lacking buckets, however, they were forced to improvise. "We have orders to carry water in canteens and all available means to the front and there exchange a filled canteen for an empty one until we get them all supplied," Pvt. Will Ward told his diary. Fellow Hoosier John Klingaman noted in his journal that he and his comrades were at the work until midnight. Colonel Harrison reported the 39th delivered 1,000 full canteens to the battle line. Most of these went to the thirsty men of the intermingled XX and XXI Corps formations just west of Viniard Field.[11]

The painful business of assessing the day's losses and counting those still able to fight was also underway. At 6:00 p.m., with the fighting largely over in his sector, Lt. Col. Horace Newton Fisher, inspector general of the XX Corps, sent word to the divisional staffs that he needed their reports within three hours, "giving the exact number of men with their colors. . . . The object to know the minimum available for battle the next morning." Shortly after issuing those orders Fisher heard the fight between Johnson and Cleburne, and so expected Johnson's reports would be late. To his intense satisfaction, however,

10 Mark Hoffman, *"My Brave Mechanics": The First Michigan Engineers and Their Civil War* (Wayne State University Press, 2007), 168; *OR* 30, pt. 1, 744.

11 Entry for September 19, Williamson D. Ward Diary, Indiana Historical Society, Indianapolis. Hereafter InHS; Entry for September 19, John Klingaman Diary, InHS; *OR* 30, pt.1, 548.

all three divisional reports were in hand 10 minutes short of 9:00 p.m. Fisher tucked them in his notebook, confident they would be required at some point soon.[12]

One bit of important news at the end of the day for the Army of the Cumberland was that the bulk of the army's supply and baggage wagons were now either in Chattanooga or safely on their way there. With the exception of the Cavalry Corps trains, only ammunition and ambulance wagons remained with the army west of Missionary Ridge. The main baggage trains were either in Lookout Valley or beyond Rossville to the north, and so within an easy march of the relative safety of Chattanooga. Colonel John G. Parkhurst and his 9th Michigan, serving as the XIV Corps provost guard, spent all day on the 19th escorting Thomas's train to Chattanooga, where he "parked it on the bank of the Tennessee River" that afternoon. Similar movement would continue unabated through the night. Joseph Turner of the 10th Ohio, a provost at army headquarters, recorded that at "about dark . . . [we] were ordered with the train to Chattanooga . . . arriving about 3 o'clock in the morning." By moving the vast bulk of his transportation beyond immediate danger, Rosecrans secured a greater measure of operational freedom for the next day's fight while safeguarding critical assets.[13]

Sometime after 10:00 p.m., as the final sounds of the chaotic evening encounter between Generals Cleburne, Johnson, and Baird faded into fitful silence, Rosecrans called his senior officers together for a council of war. Lieutenant John J. McCook, youngest brother to corps commander Alexander, was serving on Tom Crittenden's staff and accompanied his boss that night to the meeting. "After we had made all necessary arrangements," explained Lieutenant McCook, "the gen'l and staff rode to Departmental Head Qtrs about a mile to the rear. Here we met gen'l McCook and staff, all of whom were well."[14]

12 Horace N. Fisher, "Memorandum of April 2, 1890," Chickamauga-Chattanooga National Military Park. Hereafter CCNMP.

13 Charles W. Bennett, *Historical Sketches of the Ninth Michigan Infantry* (Daily Courier Print, 1913), 35; Joseph Turner Papers, Swarthmore College, Swarthmore, PA.

14 "My Dear Sister," September 22, 1863, John J. McCook Letters, Gilder-Lehrman Collection, New York Historical Society. Hereafter NYHS. Rosecrans was commander of both the Department and the Army of the Cumberland. Hence, his headquarters was interchangeably referred to as one or both titles.

Charles A. Dana (left) recorded the most widely quoted description of General Rosecrans's late-night conference. He is pictured here, in Virginia, about one year after Chickamauga.

Library of Congress

Charles Dana was also present, granted entre (though doubtless grudgingly) thanks to his status as assistant secretary of war. Dana would later recall that some dozen or so men crowded into the Widow Glenn's cabin. Although he wrote that the divisional commanders were also invited, Rosecrans had in fact limited the conference to only his corps commanders and their most senior staff officers. In addition to McCook, Crittenden, Thomas, and their principal staffers, also present were chief of staff James Garfield and Brig. Gen. James St. Clair Morton, the army's chief engineer. Both had spent the day plotting the fight on maps and probably knew the larger picture as well as anyone else in attendance. Gordon Granger and Robert Mitchell did not attend. Granger remained at Rossville, while Mitchell, having just arrived at Crawfish Spring a few hours earlier, either did not get word of the meeting in time or decided he couldn't find army headquarters in the dark.[15]

Beyond Dana's account, almost no other detailed recollections of this important council of war were published. As a result, what took place during this oft-described meeting relies heavily on his original narration. "Rosecrans began by asking each of the corps commanders for a report of the condition of his troops and of the position they occupied; also for his opinion of what was to

15 Major General James Negley, a division commander in George Thomas's XIV Corps, may also have been present. On October 8, Maj. James Lowrie of Negley's staff reported that Negley paid a visit to departmental headquarters that night between 10:00 p.m. and midnight. Lowrie himself, however, did not accompany him, and Negley did not leave an account of the meeting or even note his presence there. Negley's illness prostrated him for a week or more after the battle, and his report lacks many details. Lowrie's report can be found at *OR* 30, pt. 1, 337-338.

be done," reported Dana. "Each proposition was discussed by the entire council as it was made." A couple of details stood out. According to Dana, Thomas contributed little. He "was so tired—he had not slept at all the night before, and had been in battle all day—that he went to sleep every minute. Every time Rosecrans spoke to him he would straighten up and answer," continued Dana, "but he would always say the same thing, 'I would strengthen the left,' and then he would be asleep [again], sitting up in his chair. Each time, Rosecrans made the same reply: 'Where are we going to take it from?'"[16]

Thomas was not the only thoroughly exhausted general in the room. Few if any of the men gathered that night had slept much in the past 36 hours. Rosecrans certainly had not. A bundle of nervous energy at the best of times, he tended toward freneticism while on campaign. David Stanley, who had observed the departmental commander since the summer of 1862 and had fought under him at Iuka, Corinth, Murfreesboro, Tullahoma, and through the opening of the current campaign, came to understand his boss well. "Rosecrans habitually used himself up badly in times of excitement," explained Stanley. "He never slept, he overworked himself, he smoked incessantly." In many previous times, "the stress of excitement did not exceed a week. His strong constitution could stand that," continued Stanley, "but at Chickamauga this strain lasted a month. . . . Rosecrans's health was badly broken."[17]

Crittenden, McCook, and the various others present were in little better shape. Like Thomas, they had gotten little or no sleep the night before. "As the whole army was in one valley, and that quite small," recorded Lieutenant McCook, "we had to move very slowly. We were up all night at work [on September 18]."[18]

Fortunately, Lieutenant Colonel Fisher, inspector general of the XX Corps, left one of the other detailed impressions of this critical conference. Fisher accompanied McCook, and at some point was asked into the room to present his status report on the corps' strength. Fisher's recollections differed from

16 Charles A. Dana, *Recollections of the Civil War* (Collier Books, 1963), 113-114.

17 William M. Lamers, *The Edge of Glory: A Biography of General William S. Rosecrans, U.S.A.* (Louisiana State University Press, 1999),336. It should be noted that Stanley had not been physically present with his boss since the first days of September. The cavalry and McCook's corps were far to the south between September 2-17, with Stanley falling sick and returning to Bridgeport by mid-month. He probably would not have had a chance to lay eyes on Rosecrans again until the latter was relieved in October and headed back north.

18 "My Dear Sister," McCook Letters, NYHS.

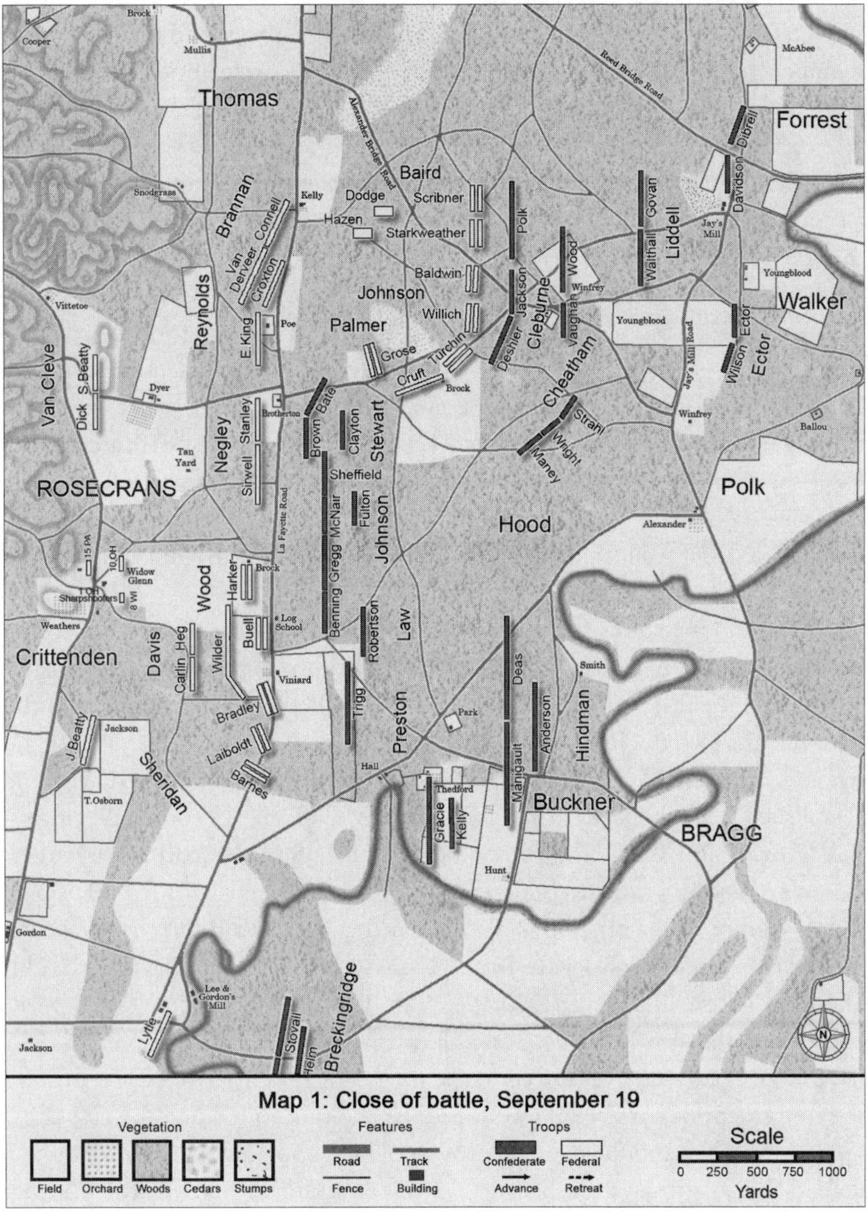

Map 1: Close of battle, September 19

Dana's in some particulars. When he entered the room, he remembered only Rosecrans, Garfield, Thomas, McCook, and Crittenden being present. "The General [Rosecrans] was lying on the cords of a rude bedstead at the right of the door; Thomas was standing in front of a big log-fire at the other end of the room . . . warming himself." Fisher did not mention Dana or any other officers, though at the very least Crittenden and Thomas must have had their own staff members along. Most strikingly, Fisher did not remember Thomas as inattentive, dozing in a chair, but as dominating the conversation.[19]

According to Fisher, the five senior men discussed the day's events for some time until Thomas summed up the situation: "We have fought desperately all day, we have had to put in line all our reserves, and though we are still ahead, the enemy have over-lapped us on both flanks while crowding us on our whole front; therefore it seems clear that we should move on to Rossville Gap, where we can avail of the strength of the position to make up for inequality of numbers." In effect, Thomas was calling for a controlled and deliberate retreat. Fisher's recollections are clearly accurate in this respect since they are corroborated by dispatches dated that evening. Unsure of the terrain around the gap, Rosecrans queried Granger via field telegraph. "What sort of a pass is Rossville to defend?" he asked, also wanting to know if the road could be commanded by artillery. "Yes," came the reply. The gap could be held as promised.[20]

After about an hour of discussion, a consensus was reached and Rosecrans put voice to orders for the following day. "The left flank movement," Fisher recalled, "should be continued as on Saturday, that Thomas should hold the Rossville [La Fayette] Road as the prize of battle, and be reinforced if it took the whole army to enable him to do so." A new army reserve would also have to be established. This all meant that the right flank would have to contract, swinging "back from Lee & Gordon's to the Crawfish Spring Road near Widow Glenn's." Thomas would continue to command the left with five divisions: Baird, Palmer, Johnson, and Reynolds on the line, and Brannan in reserve. McCook held the right with James Negley, Jefferson C. Davis, and Phil Sheridan. Crittenden, with Horatio Van Cleve and Tom Wood's men, constituted the army's reserve. The Crawfish Spring hospital complex would have to be evacuated over the course of the next day, a massive effort entailing the movement of some 3,600 wounded. In addition to holding the crossings, General Mitchell and the cavalry corps would cover that movement. "You will defend the hospitals at all hazards," stressed Chief of Staff Garfield in his

19 Horace N. Fisher, "Memorandum of April 2, 1890," CCNMP.

20 Ibid.; *OR* 30, pt. 3, 741. Fisher's account is especially interesting since it has Rosecrans, usually portrayed as restless and excitable, calm and laying down, while Thomas acts as facilitator.

written order, the last sentence of which reflected some worry about Mitchell's ability to get the job done. "The general [Rosecrans] is dissatisfied that you do not report oftener." General Stanley was not the only one harboring doubts about Robert Mitchell.[21]

Minty's reassignment to the northern flank meant that Granger should now be prepared to help Thomas, if possible. Since Granger's nearly 6,000 troops had yet to be seriously engaged, they could be a valuable addition to Rosecrans's combat power. Minty's cavalry was at Rossville, and would deploy forward to screen the crossings come dawn, the better to allow Granger to concentrate his infantry near the La Fayette Road and extend southward to connect with Thomas's left.

Colonel John T. Wilder's brigade also needed updated orders. Despite his relatively low rank and the fact that his brigade was still nominally part of Thomas's command, Rosecrans routinely treated Wilder as an army-level asset. He did so now. At 10:00 p.m., Wilder received orders to report to the commanding general. The war conference was under way when he arrived. He stayed but a few minutes, just long enough to report on the condition of his men and the situation on the army's right flank. "I . . . returned to my command at 11 o'clock, before plans for the following day were decided upon," he later noted. His men picketed the front of the Union lines, in some cases pushing as far forward as 500 yards east of the La Fayette Road, but no new orders arrived during the night. His previous instructions to remain on "the right fighting flank" of the army still held.[22]

Once Rosecrans was confident the general orders were fully understood, they were written out by Garfield and read aloud to all present. While this process took some time, it also made it more likely that everyone concerned would have a clear understanding of Rosecrans's intent, and a good grasp of the larger picture. It was midnight or after before the business of the day was concluded. Instead of dispersing, however, the assembled officers took a few minutes to eat. Private John Davis of the 15th Pennsylvania Cavalry remembered that he had to go all the way down to Crawfish Springs with a small keg in order to find water for coffee; the fare was sparse: "[Coffee,] a few strips

21 Fisher, "Memorandum of April 2, 1890," CCNMP; Francis F. McKinney, *Education in Violence: The Life of George H. Thomas and the History of the Army of the Cumberland* (Americana House, 1991), 236; *OR* 30, pt. 1, 137.

22 Wilder Revised Report, CCNMP.

of bacon, and a few scattered crackers constituted their rations for about forty hours."[23]

With the next day's plans complete and what little food that was available consumed, wrote Dana, the commanding general called upon General McCook to provide some entertainment. Noted for his fine singing voice, McCook chose "The Hebrew Maiden," a dark tune about lovers denied and unexpected loss. The refrain concluded with the phrase, "Bitter tears I shed for thee." The fact that untold bitter tears were being shed across the fields of Chickamauga on both sides of the line that night, soon to be replicated across the country, was likely not lost on anyone present. "McCook sang the song," recalled Dana, "and then the council broke up."[24]

The ballad's mournful lyrics notwithstanding, the mood among the senior commanders remained positive as they mounted their horses and rode back to their respective commands. Everyone faced a long night, for the new orders required a great deal of movement. Even Thomas, whose portion of the line was not contracting, wanted to shift his divisions into a more secure position around Kelly Field.

Generally speaking, Rosecrans's orders for September 20 were sound. He would contract his lengthy line of battle, reestablish a reserve, and restore some measure of corps continuity and command cohesion. The fact that the Army of the Cumberland had been caught wrong-footed by Bragg made continued retreat nearly inevitable, and Rosecrans and others believed they were badly outnumbered to boot. If so, Rossville was an ideal spot for an interim stand. It could still be outflanked by a superior force given enough time to maneuver, but it could also be made impregnable to a frontal assault.

At least one aspect of Rosecrans's orders, however, was not as efficient as it may otherwise have been. In assigning corps commander duties, it would probably have been better to have Crittenden and McCook switch places, since Crittenden had been fighting all day on the southern end of the field and almost certainly had a better grasp of the terrain and troop positions there than did McCook, who had spent most of the day moving northward or at army

23 Charles H. Kirk, *History of the Fifteenth Pennsylvania Volunteer Cavalry Which Was Recruited and Known as the Anderson Cavalry in the Rebellion of 1861-1865* (n.p., 1906), 240.

24 Dana, *Recollections of the Civil War*, 114. Peter Cozzens, *This Terrible Sound: The Battle of Chickamauga* (University of Illinois Press, 1992), 295; Peter Cozzens titled this piece "The Hebrew Maiden's Lament."

headquarters. Crittenden had done a first-rate job on the 19th, anticipating the need to support Thomas and sending most of his troops to that end of the field without waiting for orders from Rosecrans to arrive. Would McCook manage as well? Rosecrans tended to favor the portly Ohioan over Crittenden because McCook was a West Pointer and thus a professional soldier, while Crittenden was a lawyer and political general. Professional or not, McCook was assuming a battered hybrid command on largely unfamiliar terrain.

If the senior officers remained generally positive, the mood of some of the division commanders proved less upbeat. Like so many in the army, Maj. Gen. John Palmer of Crittenden's XXI Corps had experienced one of the most trying days of his life. Early in the fighting Palmer was detached from his corps to fight under another's command, attacked from multiple directions, had a good portion of his division scattered, and was nearly captured. By the time the sun set on the 19th, Palmer was feeling somewhat abandoned. Shortly after dark and a hasty supper, he rode to Rosecrans's headquarters "to obtain information and orders for the next day. I found the headquarters of the army, and was informed that I could not see either General Rosecrans or General Crittenden." Palmer eventually discovered that, because of "the difficulties of changing the positions of the troops, it was [again] expected . . . [that] my command would [still] be subject to the immediate orders of Major General Thomas." The nonplussed general rode back to his lines hoping to at least get some sleep. Like so many others, he had also been up for two days.

Palmer failed to record his feelings at this rebuff, though he did vent them to newspaperman William Shanks. The reporter was at army headquarters that night, though he did not witness or take part in the evening's conference. Shanks, who would never be accused of having much tact, recorded in frank terms what he heard that night. He was drafting a dispatch for his paper when Palmer arrived. "'Since I saw you this morning,' [Palmer] said, addressing me, 'I have got my troops together again. They are in good spirits, and ready for another fight. I have no hesitation in saying to you'—at this moment he saw Assistant Secretary of War Dana at the other end of the table, and would have liked to stop, but had gone too far, and so he added, 'and I have no hesitation in saying to you, Mr. Dana, that this battle has been lost because we had no supreme head to the army on the field to direct it.'"[25]

25 George Thomas Palmer and Lloyd Lewis, *A Conscientious Turncoat: The Story of John M. Palmer 1817-1900* (Yale University Press, 1941), 180; OR 30, pt. 1, 714; William F. G. Shanks, *Personal Recollections of Distinguished Generals* (Harper and Brothers, Publishers, 1866), 267. Shanks, no

Another malcontent, apparently, was Phil Sheridan. When they finally left the Widow Glenn's, both McCook and Crittenden rode together to the vicinity of Viniard Field. This made sense because their commands (each less one division shifted north to fight with Thomas) were intermingled, and Crittenden could also brief McCook on the relative positions of the new line he was tasked to oversee. One of their stops involved Phil Sheridan.

Sheridan's headquarters detail pitched the general's tent (a rare thing that night) behind the 73rd Illinois somewhere west of the Viniard woods, probably fewer than 1,000 yards from Rosecrans's headquarters. The men of the 73rd were a bit anxious. According to the rumor mill, they "were going to have the combined forces of Longstreet, [Joseph E.] Johnston, and Bragg to contend with . . . as well as the force of [Simon] Bolivar Buckner." In light of these unsettling reports, when the 73rd was called upon to provide some extra guards for Sheridan's camp, the corporal in charge of the detail, Amasa Hasty, attempted a little discreet eavesdropping. McCook's and Crittenden's arrival prompted "an animated and somewhat protracted consultation . . . General Sheridan grew still more restless and uneasy. He was greatly displeased at the rough usage his 3rd (Bradley's) Brigade had received . . . and . . . he was apprehensive that there would be more of the same . . . the next morning."[26]

In his memoirs, however, Sheridan offered a somewhat different description of events. Instead of being visited by McCook and Crittenden, he claims to have ridden to army headquarters, where he found "nearly all the superior officers of the army . . . and it struck me that much depression prevailed." There are several reasons to doubt Sheridan's recollections.[27]

The first problem with Sheridan's account is its timeline. Sheridan claimed he visited Rosecrans's headquarters after he received his new orders to pull back, and after his division had successfully retired to its newly assigned position. Those orders were issued as a result of the conference he claims to have witnessed, and could not have been issued before it concluded. It is

---

friend of Rosecrans, obviously used this incident to demonstrate the latter's unfitness for command. However, it has the ring of truth especially when matched with Palmer's memoir, which criticizes the army commander for bringing on the defeat by interfering with the corps commanders and sending too many orders directly to division leaders.

26 William H. Newlin, *A History of the Seventy-Third Regiment of Illinois Infantry Volunteers* (The Regimental Association, 1890), 231.

27 Philip H. Sheridan, *Personal Memoirs of P. H. Sheridan, in Two Volumes* (Broadfoot Publishing, 1992), vol. 2, 279.

possible Sheridan checked in at army headquarters after he moved his division, but by that time the generals had mostly departed to execute their own assignments, and he could not have judged their collective mood. Moreover, other accounts of that meeting suggest the senior commanders were not depressed at all, but cautiously optimistic about the next day's fight. Sheridan almost certainly confused McCook's and Crittenden's visit, assuming it happened at the Widow Glenn's and not his own campfire. The passage of time, and in this case a quarter-century, clouded his memory.[28]

The gloomy mood that characterized Palmer and Sheridan on the evening of September 19 was the exception rather than the rule amongst the army's senior officers. Like Palmer, the hot-tempered, bullet-headed Irishman had reason to be frustrated after seeing his division fed into the fight piecemeal and, in Bradley's case, entirely unsupported. But that didn't mean most other generals shared that opinion. Crittenden's actions throughout the day had been energetic, aggressive, and involved. While the fight was not without tactical setbacks, every Rebel attack had been foiled, every foray driven back. The army held its own despite the desperate odds nearly everyone thought they faced, which in turn gave reason for optimism and not pessimism.

One thing Rosecrans's orders guaranteed was another largely sleepless night for everyone. The extensive rearrangement of the battle lines he ordered would take hours to accomplish in the dark. George Thomas was in the process of taking up a new position before the conference, a movement rudely interrupted by Cleburne's night attack. Now Thomas returned to that business, focusing mainly on his left flank. His first priority was to bring Baird's and Johnson's divisions into line around Kelly Field. Even the simplest of movements proved exceedingly difficult, as Col. Benjamin Scribner's experience that night demonstrated.

In the wake of the firefight with Cleburne, Scribner left an aide, Lieutenant Devol, with his brigade and sought out General Baird, who was in turn looking for him. The two officers met somewhere in the gloom, but when they returned to Scribner's former position his brigade was gone. Fearing they'd blundered into Rebel lines, Scribner called out for Devol, who fortunately was still at his post, though all alone. The brigade, explained the staffer, fell back on concerns of "a flank movement of the enemy," but he remained as a guide for the general. After some fumbling, Scribner, Baird, and the faithful Devol located the rest of

28 Ibid.

the command. The entire force fell back into a large open field Scribner took to be the Kelly farmstead, though he wasn't sure. "Our movements in the night had so confused me," Scribner confessed, "that I did not know even the points of the compass. Lieutenant Devol was the only staff officer with me, the others having lost me in the darkness." Once he dispatched Devol to search for water, Scribner found himself entirely alone in the middle of a sprawling battlefield. He sat holding his horse's bridle and awaited the lieutenant's return—in vain as it turned out, for Devol got lost and did not reappear until morning. "My condition was indeed forlorn and miserable!" lamented the colonel.[29]

Eventually Scribner sought help from what turned out to be the 5th Indiana battery, part of Johnson's division. Its commander, Capt. Peter Simonson, recognized the brigade commander and helped him get settled and fix a makeshift camp, spreading his blanket next to a small fire. Even that creature comfort was not sufficient to allow Scribner to fall asleep. The day's events, ghastly and grim, played out in his head over and over as he huddled alone in the dark, waiting for dawn and almost certainly more of the same—or worse.

At least Scribner had a blanket. Many of the troops in the XIV Corps lacked even that small comfort. The men in Brannan's and Baird's divisions had dropped packs in the woods east of Kelly Field, now lost in the dark or overrun by Rebels and seized as plunder. The thermometer plunged again that night, and many soldiers spent the darkness shivering in anticipation of the morrow. Most Federals ignored the standing orders not to light fires for fear of revealing their positions, which in turned helped somewhat mitigate the ongoing misery of the night.

George Thomas remained concerned about his left flank. The new line he envisioned was supposed to run along a long open ridge parallel to and about 300 yards east of the La Fayette Road. This open spine, which ranged from south of the Poe farm to well north of the Reed's Bridge Road, was defined by a cedar glade, an open area edged with evergreens to form an elongated clearing as much as 150 to 200 yards wide. It was in many ways a perfect defensive position that caught Thomas's eye as he crossed it repeatedly during the morning's fight. Even now, Baird's Regulars sat upon this ridge astride Reed's Bridge Road, anchoring the army's left. After Absalom Baird had a chance to examine the position, however, he reported a problem. His division did not

29 Benjamin F. Scribner, *How Soldiers Were Made; Or The War As I Saw It Under Buell, Rosecrans, Thomas, Grant, and Sherman* (Blue Acorn Press, 1995), 149-151.

have enough men—especially after the day's losses—to fully man the line as far north as the Reed's Bridge Road. Another division would be needed to safely extend the line that far. Meanwhile, Baird pulled the Regulars back down toward Kelly Field and refused their left flank so their line faced northeast. At 2:00 a.m. Thomas sent word to Rosecrans, "requesting that General Negley be sent [to] me to take position on Baird's left and rear, and thus secure our left from assault." This note requesting Negley was the first small stone in what would eventually become an avalanche that visited disaster upon the army.[30]

At the other end of Thomas's position, Joseph Reynolds's and John Brannan's divisions had little need to move. Reynolds's scratched-together line along the western edge of Poe Field formed the nucleus of the next day's position. Turchin's four regiments had spent the day fighting amidst Palmer's command before falling back to the northern end of Poe Field at dark. Edward King's brigade broke apart during its fight east of Brotherton Field, but James Negley's arrival provided King with the bulwark behind which he rallied his troops. King's three regiments were largely reconstituted by 7:00 p.m. and camped in Poe Field alongside the 75th Indiana.[31]

Things were considerably less settled for Brannan's men. Most arrived on this part of the field at or near dark with little conception of where the fight was or what they were expected to do. Colonel John Connell of the 17th Ohio was still in command of the brigade. "We bivouacked in a meadow, hoping for a little sleep," he recalled, and even the "thunderous roar" of the Cleburne-Johnson-Baird engagement did little to disturb the men. "[A]t midnight we had to fall in and move to the left, and from then till daylight with drowsy steps, we changed position, at short distances, always moving to the left . . . at each halt [some] slept, and some threw up any kind of protection," continued Connell, until their course was clearly marked by "tolerable breastworks." The ongoing fitful moves characterized a larger uncertainty about where and how to deploy the division, an uncertainty that would manifest itself as considerable confusion in George Thomas's mind come daylight.[32]

30 *OR* 30, pt. 1, 251.

31 Edwin W. High, *History of the Sixty-Eighth Regiment Indiana Volunteer Infantry, 1862-1865, with a Sketch of E. A. King's Brigade, Reynolds' Division, Thomas' Corps, in the Battle of Chickamauga* (n.p. 1902), 67.

32 Charles T. DeVelling, *History of the Seventeenth Regiment, First Brigade, Third Division, Fourteenth Corps, Army of the Cumberland, War of the Rebellion* (E. R. Sullivan, Printer and Binder, 1880), 102.

After their consultation with Sheridan, meanwhile, McCook and Crittenden settled on a plan. The two men were responsible for five divisions, and all but one would have to be completely repositioned by dawn. Only James Negley's division, holding the woods at the western edge of Brotherton Field was to remain in place. McCook needed to move Jefferson Davis and Phil Sheridan a mile farther west in order to refuse the southern flank, while Crittenden shifted Tom Wood and Horatio Van Cleve about one and a half miles northwest onto the foothills of Missionary Ridge to form the army's designated reserve. Such a wholesale withdrawal in the face of an active and aggressive enemy was a dangerous undertaking, so orders were issued to reinforce the Federal picket line and leave it in place all night. No one would begin moving earlier than 3:00 a.m., and everyone had orders to be in their new positions by daylight.[33]

The upshot of these orders translated into agonizing hours for the men on the front lines. The most exposed men belonged to Col. Luther Bradley's brigade, part of Sheridan's division. After Bradley fell wounded, these four Illinois regiments spent the night in the low ground of Viniard Field just east of the La Fayette Road—within a handful of yards from where their advance had come to grief just a few hours earlier. Rebels lurked in the woods on the northern and eastern sides of the field, so close that here, at least, the orders prohibiting fires were scrupulously obeyed. Behind and around Bradley's Illinoisans rested intermingled elements of both Davis's and Wood's divisions waiting for the pre-dawn movement. Among them rode the water-bearing samaritans of the 39th Indiana. A thankful General Wood took a moment to note that these Hoosiers "brought to us some 400 canteens of good water," most of which was eagerly consumed by the parched infantrymen.[34]

The survivors of Horatio Van Cleve's division of the XXI corps enjoyed more shelter that night. Van Cleve, who was still short Barnes's brigade (which was camped with Wood near the Viniard farm), rallied his men on a low ridge west of the expansive Dyer farmstead about three-quarters of a mile north of the Widow Glenn's. By the standards of Civil War combat, where losses from a single firefight could approach one-half of a unit's engaged strength, Beatty's and Dick's regiments had not been hit hard, with casualties amounting to about 20%. They had, however, experienced significant straggling. Although many

33 *OR* 30, pt. 1, 579-580.

34 Ibid., 634.

other units had suffered heavier losses, they were among the most disrupted commands on the field. Both brigades had been all but routed twice, and both times in heavy woods. Stragglers multiplied their direct combat losses. "At first, only about one third of our regiment could be found," admitted Lt. Jason Hurd of the 19th Ohio of Beatty's brigade. "They had been so badly separated, and all other regiments seemed to be in the same condition." Fortunately, most of these stragglers rejoined their outfits during the night.[35]

By this time Van Cleve had recovered his composure, but Captain Murdock's loss, struck down at his side on the afternoon of the 19th, still weighed heavily upon him. Van Cleve's position provided a vista over much of the battlefield across the Dyer fields to the woods bordering the La Fayette Road beyond—a rare perspective for these Federals. Marcus Woodcock of the 9th Kentucky, Beatty's brigade, remembered viewing "after dark . . . one of the most magnificent scenes that is witnessed in any battle . . . a heavy musketry and artillery contest just a few hundred yards to the front." Although Woodcock and his comrades could not have known it at that time, they were witnessing Pat Cleburne's night attack.

Woodcock gathered what little information he could about how the overall fight had gone that day for the Army of the Cumberland. "Notwithstanding the fact that our Division had been roughly handled," he explained, "we were satisfied with the news we got from the rest of the army. It seemed that on almost every other part of the field our troops had come off victorious, and every passerby had a long story to tell about the great doings of his regiment or brigade." Interspersed with these heartening tales of success, however, were darker tidings, including descriptions of the masses of Confederates opposing them. "A forest of rebels charged upon Davis' Division," was how Woodcock vividly described an attack. Much of the talk was of Bragg being "largely reinforced."[36]

35 Entry for September 20, "Diary transcripts of Jason Hurd," 19th Ohio file, Combat Studies Institute, Fort Leavenworth, KS. Hereafter CSI. The 19th Ohio Infantry entered the fight with 384 men and reported a loss of 90, which suggests as many as 150 had become stragglers by the close of the first day's fight. This is a ratio of nearly two stragglers for every man killed or wounded.

36 Kenneth W. Noe, ed., *A Southern Boy in Blue: The Memoir of Marcus Woodcock 9th Kentucky Infantry* (U.S.A.) (University of Tennessee, 1996), 201. Van Cleve regarded Capt. Thomas Murdoch almost as a foster son.

Woodcock's fellow Kentuckian, David Claggett of the 17th regiment, was exhausted by the day's exertions and more concerned with the cold than speculating about the course of Union fortunes. "This was a cold night," he jotted in his diary, "and I slept without a blanket and slept well, except disturbed by the rattle of musketry."[37]

In addition to all the formal troop movements planned and executed during those dark hours, the battlefield seethed with other activity. All day long aid parties in both blue and gray had struggled to bring off non-ambulatory wounded and deposit them in the nearest field hospital. That laborious and heartbreaking work was nowhere near finished by the time night settled over the field. The battlefield was still carpeted with thousands of pleading injured—shouting, whispering, or waving for help of any kind. John Glenn of the 27th Illinois, Bradley's brigade, was manning one of the exposed positions in Viniard Field that evening. "[W]e remained all night on the ground when we quit fighting, among the dead and wounded of both armies," he wrote. "The wounded were taken away during the night, and large fires built to keep them warm. . . . Anyone who has seen a battlefield will never care to see another." Sergeant Benjamin F. Magee of the 72nd Indiana, part of John Wilder's brigade, was not too far from John Glenn that night. The Hoosier listened to the plaintive wail of an unidentified wounded man who pleaded, "O, for God's sake come and help me!" The repeated plea rattled a few men who finally decided to try and find the stricken soldier. Picket fire from the Rebels, however, quickly discouraged that idea and the men returned to their lines. The man's cry grew fainter each time it was uttered, until it eventually faded away.[38]

Despite the night's horrors, many had trouble keeping awake. Like the men of Connell's brigade in Dyer Field, many of the Hoosiers of the 72nd Indiana could not keep their eyes open. This presented something of a problem when it came time to man the picket lines. "As this was the second night without eating or sleeping," recalled Magee, "the men were so overcome with exhaustion that the skirmishers would go to sleep in spite of themselves and their critical and horrible surroundings." When volunteers were called for, Magee stepped forward. About 3:00 a.m., he and Cpl. William Wakeman slipped down into the

37 Entry for September 19, David M. Claggett Diary, 17th Kentucky file, CSI.

38 John A. Glenn Letters, Abraham Lincoln Presidential Library, Springfield, IL. Hereafter ALPL. Benjamin F. Magee, *History of the 72nd Indiana Volunteer Infantry of the Mounted Lightning Brigade* (S. Vater and Co., 1882), 183.

bloody ditch where Henry Benning's Georgia brigade had sought shelter from the flying metal that afternoon about 50 yards from the Viniard cabin. Once there, they again picked up the faint cry, "for God's sake come and help me!" "To this day that dying wailing petition is still ringing in our ears," admitted the sergeant.[39]

Despite the threat of nervous picket fire, men ventured out into no-man's land on their own hook. One of them was Lt. Henry Weiss of the 27th Illinois, who slipped out of the lines after dark to look for dead or wounded from his company. "I crept along examining the bodies as well as the dim and moonless night would permit," he wrote. "I found none . . . to my great satisfaction." Weiss did spot a dead Confederate wearing a revolver "of Colt's latest patent," and cut it off the dead man's belt, "resolved to try it out on our side." Weapons and military equipment might be fair game, but food, money, and personal effects were also there for the taking. Men from both armies were not above a bit of grave-robbing, and they too roamed the field that night.[40]

39 Magee, *History of the 72nd Indiana*, 183.

40 Letter dated October 16, 1863, "Battle of Chickamauga," excerpts of letters from Henry M. Weiss to his wife in Shipman, IL., 27th Illinois file, CSI.

Chapter Two

"Gang Aft Agley," Bragg's plans Miscarry

Night of September 19-20, 1863

The orders issued by William Rosecrans on the busy night of September 19 reshuffled the positions of a number of his divisions. Braxton Bragg, however, decided to reorganize his entire army.

Recent reinforcements had swelled the Army of Tennessee's strength to 70,000 men and swelled the table of organization to no fewer than seven corps—five of infantry and two of cavalry. This was too many to easily manage during a major battle in heavily wooded terrain. Bragg had already tried to informally simplify this structure several times, with uniformly unsatisfactory results. For example, Thomas Hindman had been given authority over his own division plus Simon Buckner's Corps on September 10, and the commanding general assigned four infantry divisions to Leonidas Polk during the course of the action on the 19th. Hindman had stumbled badly, overcome with undue caution, while Polk sent his divisions into action one at a time on what amounted to the sketchiest of details. Now, on the evening after the close of the first day of fighting, Bragg sought to implement a more official arrangement.

One reason for this restructuring was the arrival of Lt. Gen. James Longstreet. "Old Pete" was senior to every Confederate general on the field save Bragg himself, and his reputation as a fighting man loomed large in the fall of 1863. Short of Robert E. Lee, Longstreet might have been the most famous Rebel commander then alive. About one-half of Longstreet's First Corps from the Army of Northern Virginia was already on the field at Chickamauga and fighting well, but now the man himself was near at hand. With General Polk already commanding most of the units on the army's right, it only made sense to assign Longstreet to command on the left. Reordering the Army of Tennessee into two wings would dramatically simplify its already complicated command structure at a single stroke, while Gens. Joe Wheeler and Nathan Bedford Forrest continued to independently report from their positions on the army's flanks.[1]

Including reinforcements, Bragg's Tennessee army now counted 11 infantry divisions present or soon to arrive. These commands ranged in strength from Maj. Gen. Benjamin Cheatham's large five-brigade command of some 7,000 men to the rump of Maj. Gen. Lafayette McLaws's division from Virginia (led in the interim by Brig. Gen. Joseph B. Kershaw) with only two brigades available, all told some 2,800 rank and file. Bragg intended to divide these divisions roughly equally in an effort to maintain corps integrity wherever possible.

Unlike Rosecrans, Bragg did not call for a general meeting of his commanders. By this stage of the conflict Bragg had no great liking for councils of war. Many of his subordinate officers went on record in the spring of 1863 as having no confidence in their commander, which meant a formal conference might deteriorate into another such Bragg-bashing session. Instead, explained Bragg, "upon the close of the engagement [of the 19th] . . . the proper commanders were summoned to my campfire, and there received specific information and instructions . . . for the operations of the next morning." The "proper commanders" were Polk and Longstreet. Bragg expected the soon- to-be-appointed wing commanders to disseminate his orders to their newly assigned subordinates.

Simplifying the command process was a commendable goal, but adding a layer to the chain of command also introduced an added potential for confusion or misunderstanding. Longstreet's absence compounded the problem. He was not yet present on the field when the fighting ended and darkness fell, so Bragg did not meet with both generals simultaneously. His decision not to assemble

1 William Glenn Robertson, "The Chickamauga Campaign: Chickamauga, Day One," *Blue & Gray Magazine*, vol. XXIV, no. 6 (Spring, 2008), 50. Only Thomas "Stonewall" Jackson, martyred by death at Chancellorsville, eclipsed Longstreet's stellar reputation. The controversies surrounding his conduct at Gettysburg were still far in the future.

all, or at least most, of the army's senior officers would have unfortunate consequences on September 20.[2]

Bragg's headquarters at Thedford's Ford was buzzing with activity when the fighting drew to a close on the 19th. The mood among Bragg's immediate staff was cautiously optimistic. Diarist Taylor Beatty, who spent much of September 19 at army headquarters, recorded his impressions over the course of the day. "During [the] morning often carrying everything before us," he jotted, except on the "right [where] we were repulsed." Still, Beatty thought the arithmetic was breaking their way: "We have captured some 15 pieces of artillery and lost 5 . . . captured about 2000 prisoners and lost 1000." According to Bragg, "night found us masters of the ground, after a series of very obstinate contests." The army commander labored under one misconception: he thought his men fought all day "against largely superior numbers." Governor Isham Harris of Tennessee, who had very little of Tennessee left to govern, was present and acting as a volunteer aide. That night he sent a dispatch to the *Memphis Daily Appeal*, which was also in exile and being published in Atlanta. Harris thought the army had met with some success, but could not yet claim a decisive win. However, he added, "troops never fought better than ours. They are in high spirits, and ready to meet the enemy again tomorrow."[3]

It was Polk's front on the right that concerned Bragg the most. His plan all along had been to force the Yankees away from Chattanooga, and in order to accomplish this he would have to prevail on the right. The steady northward stream of Union reinforcements to George Thomas, however, had blunted each Rebel blow. Bragg's basic strategy remained sound, and he saw no reason to change his plans now.

Bishop Polk spent most of the day on or near the rise of ground where the ruins of the Alexander house smoldered. From there, he was centrally located to the fighting in both Winfrey and Brock fields. At 5:30 p.m., just as Pat Cleburne was deploying his division, Polk instructed Capt. W. J. Morris of his staff to

2 *OR* 30, pt. 2, 33; Such councils at Perryville, Murfreesboro, and Tullahoma proved inconclusive or resulted in precipitate retreats. Neither Bragg nor his reputation could bear any further retreats.

3 Entry for September 19, Taylor Beatty Diary, Leroy Moncure Nutt Papers, Southern Historical Collection, University of North Carolina. Hereafter UNC; OR 30, pt. 2, 32; Sam Davis Elliott, *Isham G. Harris of Tennessee* (Louisiana State University Press, 2010), 148. Bragg was mistaken. In fact, the armies thus far had been fairly evenly matched, and would likely be on the morrow. When Bragg's full force was available, he would have an advantage of fewer than 4,000 men over the Federals.

"locate his headquarters for the night at some central point in [the] rear." Seven hundred yards southeast across a long, open, and downward-sloping field, Morris spotted Alexander's Bridge. "I found the headquarter ambulance on the south side of the [creek]; and on the east side of the road, immediately at the bridge, I directed the driver to turn into the woods just to his right, and I located the bivouac within fifty yards of the bridge. A part of the staff slept on either side of the road," Morris recalled. Private Lucien Charvet of the Orleans Light Horse, which served as Polk's escort, remembered the main camp being a bit farther away, "about one-half or three-quarters of a mile" from the bridge, but that guides were posted at the turnoff to ensure no one could miss finding the headquarters in the dark. Charvet's comrade, Pvt. J. A. Perkins, stoked up a large fire at the bridge site "so as to attract the attention of anyone looking for General Polk." While these duties were being attended to, and once the fighting wound down, Polk himself rode to Bragg's headquarters, where he arrived about 9:00 p.m.[4]

By the fall of 1863, the adversarial relationship between Braxton Bragg and Leonidas Polk had come to define much of the Army of Tennessee's dysfunction. The generals first served together in the spring of 1862 during the Shiloh campaign, which left Bragg unimpressed with the latter's military skills. Polk was an 1827 graduate of West Point, but his decision to take up the cloth as an Episcopal minister meant he never served in the antebellum army. He flourished as a clergyman and rose to high levels within the church, elected Missionary Bishop of the Southwest in 1838 and Bishop of Louisiana three years later. By 1861 he was one of the premier Episcopalians in the country. In addition to his religious obligations, his duties required a great deal of practical administrative experience and allowed him to travel widely through the states of Mississippi, Tennessee, Alabama, and Louisiana—much of the area in which he would later command troops and be charged with defending. Polk also profited in more mundane spheres when he became a gentleman farmer with plantations in several states. The bishop was an extensive slaveholder and also the founder of the University of the South in Sewanee, Tennessee.[5]

4 William M. Polk, *Leonidas Polk, Bishop and General*, 2 vols. (Longmans, Green and Co. 1915), vol. 1, 254; *OR* 30, pt. 2, 58-59.

5 Joseph H. Parks, *General Leonidas Polk, C.S.A.: The Fighting Bishop* (Louisiana State University Press, 1992), 76.

It took the outbreak of rebellion for Polk to put down his Bible and unsheathe his sword. He was a close friend of Jefferson Davis from their days together at the military academy, and when Davis offered Polk a commission as a major general in June 1861, Polk accepted. In a single stroke an inexperienced Episcopal bishop became one of the senior generals in the budding Confederate army.

The military record Polk established from that day until the fall of 1863 was a rather unenviable one. His early military and diplomatic blunder of violating Kentucky's tenuous neutrality precipitated a Union occupation of much of the state. After the collapse of the Confederate northern perimeter, Polk led a corps at Shiloh, Perryville, and Murfreesboro without significant distinction. His disputatious relationship with his superiors, however, turned out to be much worse than his mediocre battlefield performance.

Polk regarded orders as suggestions, to be routinely ignored if he had a better idea. He took to behind-the-scenes intrigue like a Medici pope, and the focus of much of his art of deception was against Braxton Bragg. Polk had gotten on well with Gen. Albert Sidney Johnston until the latter's death at Shiloh. Bragg was a different matter entirely. Polk despised Bragg and secretly corresponded with President Davis in an effort to get him removed from command. After Perryville, Polk emerged as one of Bragg's most outspoken critics within the army and was at the center of the attempt to get Bragg removed from command in the spring of 1863. He was unsuccessful in his larger objective (Bragg retained command), but Polk's pernicious influence was the genesis of the current discontent seething within the Army of Tennessee as it embarked upon the Chickamauga campaign. Bragg would have liked nothing better than to see Polk cashiered, but the latter's friendship with Davis made that nearly impossible. Short of an egregious example of negligence on the bishop's part, Bragg was stuck with him. Despite his penchant for Machiavellian political maneuvering, Polk was genial in person and well-regarded by his troops. His personal bravery inspired men on the battlefield, and he was generally liked by his subordinate officers.

In light of their bitter and ongoing personal conflict, Bragg's decision to both expand Polk's authority and assign to him the primary offensive role on the army's flank seems at best misguided. The concept of seniority, however, was deeply imbedded in the officers of the old army, both North and South. Bypassing an officer or placing him under a junior was considered a grave insult, and sometimes viewed as tantamount to relieving him for cause. Simply put, Polk had the rank and would he receive the command that went along with it.

As for the importance of his mission, geography dictated that assignment. The wisdom of placing so much of the burden of success on the shoulders of Leonidas Polk had yet to be determined.

To carry out his assignment, Bragg reinforced Polk with D. H. Hill's powerful corps. Despite Pat Cleburne's night action, neither of Hill's two divisions (Cleburne and Breckinridge) had suffered significant loss on the 19th. Even better, Cleburne's division was already in close proximity to his intended position, and Breckinridge's troops were en route. Hill's six fresh brigades numbered about 9,000 veterans. Polk also retained control of Cheatham's division of his own corps (still 7,000 men strong, as noted above) and all of W. H. T. Walker's Reserve Corps. Walker's force currently numbered 4,000 men in five brigades, and one additional fresh brigade was expected hourly. During the night, Brig. Gen. States Rights Gist reached the field with his large 1,800-man command of Georgians and South Carolinians. Gist would augment Ector's and Wilson's mauled, decimated formations, and by right of seniority take command of that division. In light of their already heavy losses, both Walker's and Frank Cheatham's men would take a supporting role in Sunday's fight.

When he received his instructions for the morrow, Polk raised only one objection: D. H. Hill's rank. Hill was also a lieutenant general, albeit with a provisional appointment pending confirmation in the Confederate senate. According to Polk's son and later biographer, the bishop "saw in the arrangement an injustice and a needless affront" to the prickly Hill. Why not divide the army into thirds, with Hill on the right, Polk the center, and Longstreet on the left? Bragg's blunt response probably caught Polk by surprise: "Bragg was greatly irritated against General Hill for his failure to cooperate with Hindman in McLemore's Cove . . . [and by Hill's] querulous and insubordinate spirit in general."[6]

For most of those officers present and within earshot, this was the first intimation that relations between Bragg and Hill were so sorely strained. It should not, however, have come as a surprise. Bragg had his fill of argumentative subordinates, and no general was more argumentative than Daniel Harvey Hill. As noted historian William G. Robertson has pointed out, in McLemore's Cove, for example, Hill "never accepted his army commander's view of the overall situation and continued to press far too long for adoption of his own estimate." Most of the men involved in that debacle recalled Bragg's

6 Polk, *Bishop and General*, vol. 1, 255.

anger with Thomas Hindman, who bore the brunt of Bragg's verbal explosion on September 11, but at least some of Bragg's staff also recorded his displeasure with Hill. There would be no wing command for the North Carolinian. According to Polk's son, General Polk then pressed Bragg for more troops, asserting that there were more Yankees on his front than the army commander supposed, and that Granger's Unionists at Rossville posed a threat to Polk's right flank and rear. Once again Bragg demurred. Polk now had nearly 22,000 infantry and, as flank support, the 6,500 men of Nathan Bedford Forrest's cavalry. That force, concluded Bragg, was sufficient for the mission at hand.[7]

While Polk and Bragg conferred, other generals put in an appearance. After their morning engagement at Glass Mill, Maj. Gen. John C. Breckinridge's men shifted north to cover Lee and Gordon's Mills, replacing Hindman's command. Before they settled in, however, another order from Bragg arrived late that afternoon directing Breckinridge to follow Cleburne and take up a new position on the army's right. Breckinridge's troops reached Alexander's Bridge between 10:00 and 11:00 p.m. that night, halting in the large open fields just north of the creek. Sometime during the march north Breckinridge peeled away from his command and rode off to find someone to tell him what was expected of him. He was looking for Hill, but found Bragg's camp first.

Breckinridge was a wealthy Kentucky planter, lawyer, and politician from a family with deep roots in the Southern aristocracy. He had served in Congress, in both the House and the Senate, and was the youngest man ever elected vice president as part of the James Buchanan administration (1857-1861). His only prewar military experience was as a volunteer in the Mexican War, though his command never reached the fighting front. Breckinridge accepted a Confederate commission in November 1861 to lead a brigade. He rose to command the Reserve Corps (essentially a large division) at Shiloh, and led a daring assault on Baton Rouge, Louisiana, in July 1862. Despite his important Kentucky connections, he was unable to join the army in time for the Perryville campaign, though he did experience much of the fallout that littered the wake

7 William Glenn Robertson, "The Chickamauga Campaign: Bragg's Lost Opportunity," *Blue & Gray Magazine*, vol. XXIII, no. 6 (Spring 2007), 46-47; Thomas L. Connelly, *Autumn of Glory: The Army of Tennessee, 1862-1865* (Louisiana State University Press, 1986), 209; Polk, *Bishop and General*, vol. 1, 256. Connelly and other historians seem to regard William Polk's account of this discussion with some suspicion, given how partisan the son was to his father's memory. However, relations between Bragg and Hill were in decline by this part of the campaign, and there is plenty of reason to believe Bragg was displeased with D. H. Hill.

of that divisive operation. His dislike of Braxton Bragg, much of which originated with that officer's animosity toward the Kentucky block in the army, intensified when Bragg ordered his division to launch a bloody failure of an attack during the final hours of the battle of Murfreesboro. His lack of a military education or prewar experience notwithstanding, Breckinridge proved a capable field commander with an enviable combat record.[8]

While his men marched for the Confederate right on the night of the 19th, Breckinridge found Bragg's headquarters at Thedford's Ford, arriving just as Polk and the army commander were finishing. For reasons that remain unclear, he did not stay long nor, apparently, make his presence known to Bragg. He did, however, run into John Bell Hood, who had just arrived. As was the custom in Lee's army, General Hood rode to headquarters at the close of the fighting to give Bragg his report. Some of the men gathered there shared a grimmer mood than did Bragg, Taylor Beatty, or Governor Harris. "I there met for the first time several of the principal officers of the Army of Tennessee," recalled Hood, "and, to my surprise, not one spoke in a sanguine tone regarding the result of the battle." One of those pessimists was "the gallant Breckinridge . . . seated by the root of a tree." Bewildered by the former vice president's attitude, Hood remarked, "we would rout the enemy the following day." At that, Breckinridge "sprang to his feet, exclaiming, 'My dear Hood, I am delighted to hear you say so. You give me renewed hope. God grant it be so.'"[9]

Simon Buckner also reported in, though neither he nor Bragg left an account of what they discussed. Presumably Bragg informed Buckner that he would be reporting to James Longstreet and would receive further orders once Longstreet was fully briefed. While waiting for his boss, Maj. Henry Foote of Buckner's staff recalled meeting "one of [Bragg's] staff officers, who asked me how the day had gone. I told him I thought we had lost nothing; of this he seemed doubtful, until I said: 'Why, none of Longstreet's men have yet been in the fight, nor more than half of our infantry has been engaged.' He seemed relieved." No doubt Jerome Robertson's and Henry Benning's men would have been surprised to learn they hadn't yet been in a fight, given the bloodletting they experienced in Viniard Field, but Foote was not that far wrong. Evander

8 William C. Davis, *Breckinridge: Statesman, Soldier, Symbol* (Louisiana State University Press, 1992), 349-351.

9 John Bell Hood, *Advance and Retreat: Personal Experiences in the United States and Confederate States Armies* (Blue and Grey Press, 1985), 62.

Law's Alabamians had only been lightly engaged, Joseph Kershaw's and Benjamin Humphreys's brigades were still coming up and, except for the 6th Florida of Trigg's brigade, Brig. Gen. William Preston's entire division was still fresh.[10]

Buckner and Hood soon left to return to Buckner's headquarters. Hood, virtually destitute of "kit" (as Major Foote put it) shared a blanket with someone in Buckner's camp. Although Foote and at least one other officer would later claim that honor, Hood never specified his benefactor.[11]

Within a short time of Hood's exchange with Breckinridge, Polk emerged from his conference with Bragg and departed for his own headquarters near Alexander's Bridge. Breckinridge rode with him, discovering as he did so that he now reported to Polk. Breckinridge would spend the next several hours with Polk in conversation, which in turn made him a key witness to what was perhaps the most significant Confederate controversy to result from the fighting. Bragg's orders to Polk were verbal and not written, but this hardly mattered since no one disputed what was to be done. As Bragg later reported: "Lieutenant General Polk was ordered to assail the enemy on our extreme right at day-dawn on the 20th, and to take up the attack in succession rapidly to the left. The left wing was to await the attack by the right, and take it up promptly when made." The transmission of those instructions from Bishop Polk to D. H. Hill, however, would become a bone of contention large enough to wreck careers.[12]

Some time after leaving Thedford's Ford, Polk and his party met General Longstreet and several staff officers on their way to find Bragg. This encounter took place between 10:00 and 11:00 p.m. Longstreet had experienced an exasperating afternoon and, with much work ahead of him that night, exchanged a brief greeting with the Polk party before the two small groups went their separate ways. The roads were bustling with riders that night, and shortly after the exchange of greetings with Longstreet, Polk had a more important encounter with Lt. Col. Archer Anderson and Maj. A. C. Avery of D. H. Hill's staff, both on their way to find Bragg.

10 Henry S. Foote, *Recollections of the Chickamauga Campaign* (n.p., n.d.), 9.

11 See Foote, *Recollections of the Chickamauga Campaign*, 9; and Hood, *Advance and Retreat*, 62. J. Stoddard Johnson also claimed the honors in "A Personal Reminiscence of Chickamauga," *Montgomery Daily Advertiser*, October 1, 1905.

12 *OR* 30, pt. 2, 33.

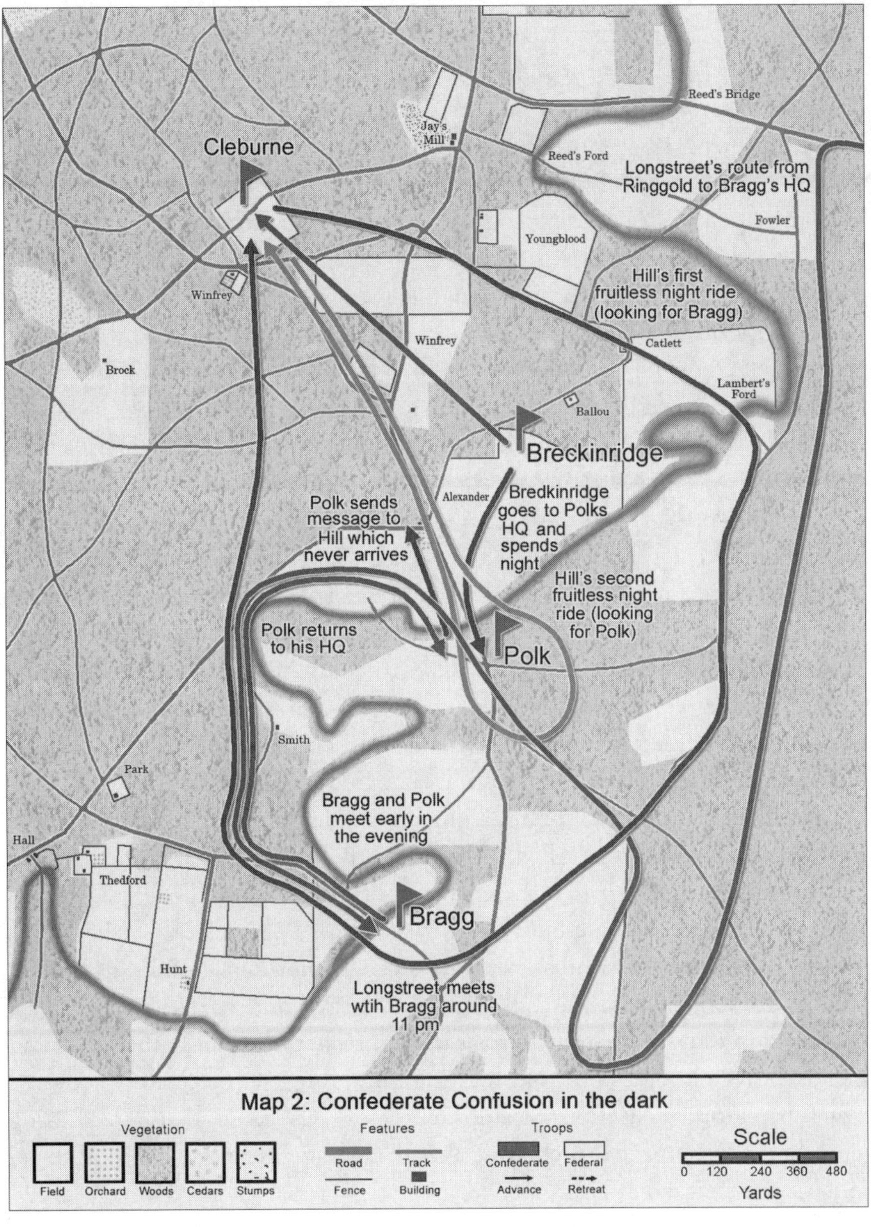

In the months to follow, who said what to whom would become a matter of some dispute. Polk and his staff later insisted they alerted both Anderson and Avery of the impending dawn attack, both during this encounter from horseback and in a subsequent meeting later that same evening. Hill and his partisans, however, denied that they had received any detailed information about an impending assault. All they got, or so they claimed, was a vague admonition to be ready for action the next morning. Breckinridge's presence, however, offered a more neutral perspective because he bore no share of the blame for the post-battle debacle and had no particular animosity toward either D. H. Hill or Leonidas Polk. Breckinridge's account of this meeting and of his own time spent at Polk's camp suggests Hill and his staffers were right, and the fault lay with Polk.

During the chance meeting on the road, recalled Lieutenant Colonel Anderson, Polk informed him that General Hill was now under Polk's orders, and to "tell Genl Hill I wish to see him tonight at my quarters as the fate of the country may depend on the attack tomorrow." The adamant Anderson insisted Polk never mentioned anything about launching that attack at first light, or that Hill's men were expected to kick it off for the entire army; Breckinridge's recollection corroborated this version of the discussion. With that, Anderson returned to Hill and Polk rode on to his camp near Alexander's Bridge.[13]

Polk arrived at his camp with Breckinridge still in tow around 11:00 p.m. and wasted no time instructing Lt. Col. Thomas Jack to "issue orders at once" pertaining to the impending assault. Jack wrote out the necessary copies and by 11:30 p.m. they were in the hands of couriers, who trotted off into the night. D. H. Hill's copy was entrusted to Pvt. John H. Fisher of the Orleans Light Horse, who was told Hill could be found at Thedford's Ford, the site of Bragg's headquarters. Fisher's claim raises some interesting questions. Why would he be informed Hill was at Thedford's Ford? Polk had just come from that location and knew Hill wasn't there when he left, and had told Hill, via Colonel Anderson, not to go there but to ride to see him (Polk) instead. Fisher's ride adds another layer of confusion to the story. Fisher initially rode north and stumbled upon Frank Cheatham's camp. The division leader told the private that he didn't know where Hill was camped. Fisher next wrote that he found General Breckinridge, who told him the same thing. Other credible sources place Breckinridge at Polk's campfire. Does this mean that after asking Cheatham, Fisher rode back to Polk's headquarters and made additional inquiries? Fisher didn't elaborate.[14]

13 Archer Anderson Memo, D. H. Hill Papers, North Carolina Department of Archives and History. Hereafter NCDAH.

14 *OR* 30, pt. 2, 57-58. Fisher's account was solicited by Polk, in anticipation of a future court of inquiry. It was dated September 29, 1863, only ten days after the events in question.Why Polk

The text of Polk's order was quite simple, and in keeping with Bragg's terse verbiage:

*CIRCULAR.**

HDQRS. RIGHT WING, ARMY OF TENN.

Near Alexander's Bridge, September 19, 1863-11.30 p. m.
1. Lieutenant-General Hill, on the right, will attack the enemy with his corps tomorrow morning at daylight.

2. Major-General Cheatham, on Hill's left, will make a simultaneous attack.

3. Major-General Walker's corps will act as reserve.

Corps and division commanders will see that their troops are amply supplied with ammunition before daylight.
By command of Lieutenant-General Polk
THOMAS M. JACK, Assistant Adjutant-General.

For reasons difficult to explain, neither Polk nor Jack showed these written orders to Breckinridge, who had by all accounts settled in at Polk's fire. Nor did Polk give Breckinridge his orders verbally, or otherwise inform him that his division would be spearheading a dawn attack in a few short hours. The two generals did converse in general terms about the next day's fight.[15]

Meanwhile, Privates Charvet and Perkins of the Orleans Light Horse, the unit serving as Polk's escort posted near Alexander's Bridge to direct people to Polk's camp, were also having a busy night. One of the first to trot out of the darkness was Lt. William E. Bertus of Breckinridge's staff, who showed up even before his boss and Polk returned. Polk and Breckinridge rode in next together, and within a few minutes, remembered Charvet, two of D. H. Hill's staff officers arrived looking for the general.

Charvet did not get the names of these two men, but the ensuing conversation (as recollected by the Louisiana private) suggested they were not

decided to send a private with these orders instead of one of his staff officers is another question that remains unanswered.

15 Ibid., 52.

Lt. Col. Archer Anderson and Maj. A. C. Avery. "Do you know if General Hill has been at General Bragg's tonight?" one of them asked. Charvet had no idea, but suggested that General Polk, who had just returned from Bragg's camp, might know. The private offered to direct them to Polk's fire, but the Hill staffer told Charvet to personally ask Polk. The Louisianan pointed out that he had been instructed not to leave his post, but everyone outranks a private and the officer insisted that he do as ordered. Charvet left to seek out Polk and returned a short time later with his reply: "General Polk's answer was, 'go and tell that officer that it is useless for him to go to General Bragg. . . . Tell him to come here, and I will give him all necessary instructions.'" With that, the two staff officers rode to see Polk. Charvet thought no more about them. He noted that "several [more] parties inquired" about Polk's camp that night, and that all of them found the camp without any problem.[16]

The identity of these two men and whether they found D. H. Hill before dawn remains a mystery. If these officers were Archer Anderson and A. C. Avery, then Charvet's account is inconsistent with all other descriptions of that earlier meeting between them and Polk which, according to Anderson, happened on the road between Polk's and Bragg's camps, and included a face-to-face discussion with General Polk. Also, if Anderson and Avery were the two men who Charvet encountered, then they would have now known where to find Polk's camp and could have guided Hill to it. Since these officers were not able to later find Polk's camp, it seems likely they were not Anderson and Avery. Hill's own description of his night's activities suggest Anderson and Avery never visited Polk in his camp that night. The identities of these other two officers remain unknown.

Sometime later Charvet went off duty and Private Perkins took over at the roadside campfire. Major General William H. T. Walker put in an appearance shortly after Perkins went on duty, probably around 11:30 p.m., just as Colonel Jack was finishing up Polk's attack orders. Jack recalled handing Walker's copy directly to the Reserve Corps commander. Frank Cheatham's written orders were also successfully conveyed. Cheatham was with his division no more than a mile distant, somewhere between the Winfrey and Alexander farms. The courier found him with no trouble, and returned soon thereafter with the signed envelope signifying his receipt. Private Fisher with D. H. Hill's copy had yet to return. After conducting Walker to Polk, Private Perkins returned to his fire,

16 Ibid., 58.

under orders to wait "an hour or so" for Hill. Perkins gave it another two hours, recalling that he left the fire in the hands of some infantrymen (probably Breckinridge's troops) about 2:00 a.m. No one from Polk's staff or the Orleans Light Horse thought to send a replacement for Perkins—a grave oversight.[17]

One last visitor, yet another of D. H. Hill's staffers, put in an appearance sometime around midnight. Lieutenant James A. Reid had been present with Hill during Pat Cleburne's closing fight, and about 11:00 p.m. rode with his superior when that officer set out to find Bragg. When Hill encountered some of Breckinridge's infantry along the way, he realized his other division was now close at hand and so ordered Reid to find the former vice president and guide him into position on Cleburne's right. Reid tracked Breckinridge to Polk's headquarters, apparently without much difficulty, around midnight. Breckinridge, however, demurred. He wasn't going to move immediately because his men were "greatly fatigued & [he] preferred to let them rest." Breckinridge assured Reid, however, that he "would have them in position before daylight." Polk interceded at this point to inform Reid that he was now in overall command of the army's right wing, and that he approved of Breckinridge's decision. The lieutenant, perhaps mollified, perhaps a bit uneasy, rode off to report to D. H. Hill.[18]

The most sought-after man in the Army of Tennessee that evening also spent much of the night in motion. Between 9:00 and 11:00 p.m. Hill was with Cleburne's men, helping that officer reorganize his division after the confusing night action. Hill, who was still acting more like a division commander than the head of a corps, noted that he conferred not only with Cleburne but each of his brigade commanders "individually." This was a task better left to Cleburne, but Hill could not resist. This was a mistake. Hill should have left Cleburne to handle these details and gone to see Bragg as soon as he could. Instead, it was not until 11:00 p.m. that he "left to find General Bragg at Thedford's Ford." Along the way, he detached Lieutenant Reid to locate Breckinridge. This left Hill and his chief engineer, Capt. Thaddeus Coleman, to continue on towards Bragg's camp alone.[19]

17 Ibid., 59.

18 James A. Reid Statement, Hill Papers, NCDAH.

19 *OR* 30, pt. 2, 140.

Despite the fact that Hill had met with Bragg at Thedford's just a few hours earlier, he had trouble locating army headquarters in the dark. "We lost the way," admitted Coleman, "and crossed the Chickamauga about a mile above." Coleman's statement suggests the two crossed at Dalton's Ford, though there were other unnamed places both upstream and down where they could have negotiated the banks. In any case, the pair spent a considerable amount of time wandering around in the dark. It was close to midnight when they located what they thought was Thedford's Ford, only to find the place deserted. There was no sign of either Bragg or a bustling headquarters. While there, Lieutenant Colonel Anderson and Major Avery rode up, bringing with them Polk's instructions for Hill to ride to see the wing leader at Alexander's Bridge.[20]

Hill's inability to locate Bragg's headquarters is yet another mystery. All of the officers now assembled (Hill, Coleman, Anderson, and Avery) were familiar with Bragg's camp at Thedford's Ford because they had been there that afternoon. An army headquarters was not a small affair. Wagons would have been parked nearby with tents dotting the immediate area. A variety of staff officers would have been coming and going, with escorts and pickets patrolling the road. Were Hill and his small party really at Thedford's Ford? If not, where were they, and how did two parties (Hill and Coleman, followed by Anderson and Avery) both get lost in a manner that carried them to the same deserted location at the same time of night?

By this time Hill was a very frustrated man. Alexander's Bridge was only a mile or so distant (closer if one cut cross-country on the east bank of the creek), but finding it would entail more riding in the dark. The men were debating their options when Lieutenant Reid reined in his mount. Reid reported to Hill that Breckinridge decided to rest his men rather than march immediately to Cleburne's right, and his subsequent promise that his infantry would be in position before dawn. Hill directed Reid to ride back to Breckinridge and to act as his guide for the movement.

This was another mistake. Hill should have gone with Reid at once to find Polk. Hill, however, also needed to rest. He often suffered from back pain, sometimes to the point of prostration. He was "much exhausted" that night from having been in the saddle since dawn, and he decided he could go no farther without at least a couple of hours of sleep. He did not, apparently, tell

20 T. Coleman Statement, Hill Papers, NCDAH.

Reid to inform Polk that he would be late in arriving. Hill estimated he and his party rested until 3:00 a.m.[21]

When their rest ended, Hill and his officers remounted to begin their search for Polk's camp. Sunrise on September 20 was at 5:47 a.m.—less than three hours away. The night was cold, and the fog rising along the creek bottoms made the ride that much more difficult. Coleman once again led the party. When they reached Alexander's Bridge, the promised guide was nowhere to be found. Privates Perkins and Charvet had both retired to their own blankets no later than 2:00 a.m., having done all they were ordered to do. The staff officers fanned out to search for a guide or the camp, to no avail. After several fruitless minutes Hill decided to return to Cleburne's division, detaching one more aide, Lt. R. H. Morrison (who had apparently found Hill sometime during Hill's rest) to remain behind and inform Polk of where Hill had gone if and when Morrison found the Right Wing command tents.

In a fitting coda to the entire confused affair, Private Fisher returned to Polk's campfire in the dead of night, Hill's copy of the all-important orders still undelivered. Fisher found Polk's camp deep in sleep, with only one man, a "Mr. McReady," still awake. McReady was Colonel Jack's civilian clerk, an overly officious man with instructions from Jack not to disturb him. Despite Fisher's protestations to the contrary, McReady refused to wake the colonel. Jack's directive is yet another perplexing piece of a very odd puzzle. The army was in the middle of one of the war's largest battles, General Polk had orders to open the second day with a major assault at first light, and his assistant adjutant general had issued blanket orders not to be disturbed? Fisher's inability to locate Hill and deliver the orders meant that Bragg's plans for the entire army were about to be thrown into complete disarray within a few short hours.

There was plenty of blame to go around. Bragg, Polk, and Hill each played a role in this sorry affair. Bragg should have sent Hill a written order informing him of Polk's new authority and his intentions to launch a dawn attack. Even worse, the slipshod approach to command procedures as demonstrated by both Polk and his staff is simply stunning. Polk personally failed to mention anything about the impending attack to Breckinridge, one of Hill's division commanders, nor did the wing commander mention the attack to any of Hill's officers with whom he spoke that night. His staff failed to ensure that guides were posted all night instead of just until 2:00 a.m., and did not follow through to confirm that

21 Hal Bridges, *Lee's Maverick General: Daniel Harvey Hill* (McGraw Hill, 1961), 209.

By the fall of 1863, Lt. Gen. James Longstreet was recognized as one of the Confederacy's best combat generals.
Library of Congress

Fisher had successfully delivered his envelope. As for Hill, he had no reason to meet and confer with every one of Cleburne's brigades at the close of the evening fight; that was Cleburne's job. Hill and his officers were also singularly inept at finding anyone at all, even though plenty of knowledgeable guides were available for the task. For one, Hill could have simply accompanied Lieutenant Reid back to Polk's camp; Reid seemed to have no trouble finding it.

This cascade of communications failures marked a performance nadir for the Army of Tennessee. Even Hill, who had been present little more than a month, seemed to not be the same man he was in Virginia, under Lee. Would James Longstreet fare any better?

Longstreet's introduction to the Western army was similarly unfortunate. When he arrived at Catoosa Station that afternoon, no guide or staff officer was waiting to lead the general and his two aides to Bragg's headquarters. According to Longstreet, he detrained about 2:00 p.m., but his horses did not arrive for another two hours. Lieutenant Colonel Moxley Sorrel, Longstreet's capable chief of staff, was indignant about the lack of an escort, fuming "we were left to shift for ourselves." Once the horses were unloaded and saddled, Longstreet, Sorrel, and Maj. Peyton Manning rode off to find Bragg.[22]

The ride was a lengthy journey of eight or nine miles, made longer by the unfamiliarity of the terrain. At one point Longstreet and his staffers almost rode into Union lines. Why no one was available to guide someone of Longstreet's rank and stature remains unknown. Longstreet's men had been arriving for several days, and about one-half of his corps was already present. While Bragg likely did not know the exact hour of Longstreet's arrival at Catoosa Station, another of Longstreet's aides, Maj. Osmun Latrobe, reached Bragg's headquarters on the 17th. Latrobe should have made arrangements to watch for his commander's appearance, but seems to have done nothing to arrange an escort for Old Pete.[23]

The lack of a guide notwithstanding, Longstreet and Sorrel did not step off onto a deserted siding. Despite its name, Catoosa Station was just a hastily built wooden platform alongside the track in the open fields just south of the Old Stone Church. It was also a large open-air depot and casualty station for Bragg's

22 James Longstreet, *From Manassas to Appomattox: Memoirs of the Civil War in America* (Blue and Gray Press, 1985), 438; G. Moxley Sorrel, *At the Right Hand of Longstreet: Recollections of a Confederate Staff Officer* (University of Nebraska Press, 1999), 183.

23 Entries for September 17-19, 1863, Osmun Latrobe Diary, Maryland Historical Society.

army. The place was swarming with men who had been coming and going from the battlefield all day long. In Ringgold, two miles west of Catoosa Station, some of Longstreet's own troops were acting as provost that Saturday afternoon. A constant stream of wounded, either trudging wearily or hauled in jolting agony by rolling stock of all sorts, moved eastward along the Ringgold-Reed's Bridge road—a stream of misery that marked the way forward to several division field hospitals, where directions to the command tents of Bragg, Polk, Walker, or any number of other general officers could be readily obtained. Longstreet, Sorrel, and Manning, however, did not take this road or secure a guide at Ringgold. The route they traversed is not known with certainty.

Besides the Reed's Bridge Road, two other routes headed more or less west. The first of these led southwest and would have eventually taken Longstreet to Leet's Tanyard, site of Bragg's headquarters on September 18 and an active staging area for the Army of Tennessee's supply trains. The second was the arterial Federal Road direct to Chattanooga via Red House Bridge and Rossville, both places now in Federals hands. Colonel John S. Scott's Confederate cavalry was theoretically picketing this route, but Scott's Rebels had thus far performed poorly, abandoning the bridge site altogether on the night of the 18th and blundering into a sharp fight with Whitaker's Federals on the afternoon of the 19th. It is more than possible that Scott failed to adequately reestablish his own pickets, and so left gaps through which Longstreet and Sorrel could inadvertently stumble into the Union lines.

The party managed to secure directions of a sort when someone told them "to follow the main road," Longstreet recollected, without specifying the name of the "main road." Unlike Virginia's variety of turnpikes and macadamized roadways, however, north Georgia had few improved thoroughfares. All those threading into and out of the battlefield were narrow dirt affairs with few bridges. The "main road" would have been recognized locally as the Federal Road running through Rossville to Chattanooga via the aforementioned Red House Bridge.[24]

As they rode along, however, the sound of the battle was clearly audible off to their right, recalled Longstreet, and men and wounded entered the road from the same direction. Wagons also rattled along, coming and going from Ringgold. If Longstreet and his aides were on the Federal Road, the sound of the battle and its detritus would have been coming from the left, not from the

24 Longstreet, *From Manassas to Appomattox*, 438.

right. This suggests someone had directed Longstreet toward La Fayette, via Leet's Tanyard.

"It was a bright, moonlit night, and the woodlands . . . were quite open, so that we could see and be seen," recalled the general, which added up to trouble when the officers stumbled into a picket post of unknown origins. When an unidentified picket asked "Who goes there?" the vague reply of "friends" did little to convince him. A further exchange revealed that the three Rebels had found a Federal sentry, for the challenger identified his unit with "the number of the brigade and the division" instead his brigade commander's name. The officers calmly bluffed themselves out of a potentially fatal situation and rode back the way they had come. Whatever route they took, they retraced their steps and found a safer way to cross Chickamauga Creek (probably at Alexander's Bridge, or perhaps as far north as Reed's Bridge) before getting directions to Bragg's camp.[25]

By the time Longstreet located friendly troops it was between 10:00 and 11:00 p.m. As described above, Longstreet briefly "met General Polk along the road. Polk had already received his instructions for the coming battle, and . . . . [was returning] to his [own] headquarters." According to Longstreet's estimate, he finally reached Bragg's camp at 11:00 p.m., but it was probably well after midnight. The army commander was resting when Old Pete arrived. Bragg awoke and the two generals immediately went into conference. Bragg sketched out the general positions of his troops and the plan of attack for the upcoming day. General Hood was already commanding the First Corps in Longstreet's absence, or at least the part of it that had reached the field, and he would continue in that role. Bragg informed Longstreet of his elevation to command the army's Left Wing, which meant he was now responsible for six infantry divisions. The attack would begin at daylight, continued Bragg, starting on the right. The offensive would progress from north to south until Longstreet's command was fully engaged. According to Longstreet, Bragg told him he "was not to take up the fighting until [Polk] had broken the line." The discussion lasted about an hour. When it finally ended, everyone took what little rest they could before daylight, unaware of D. H. Hill's ongoing tribulations or of the spreading confusion amidst Polk's command.[26]

25 Ibid.

26 "Interview with James Longstreet," *Cincinnati Enquirer*, April 1, 1883.

While their generals struggled, the rest of the men in the Confederate army tried to sleep, eat, or just pass the night as best they could under terrible circumstances. Unlike the Yankees, most Rebels had access to Chickamauga Creek, and so did not suffer as much from a lack of water. Like their Northern counterparts, however, they were not immune to the cold, insufficient food, and a lack of sleep.

Some troops were far enough behind the front lines to light fires. In Breckinridge's division, John Jackman of the 9th Kentucky, part of the Orphan Brigade, was one of them. "We stopped for the night in an old field" just after crossing Alexander's Bridge, he recalled. "We built a large fire, yet not having any blankets with me, I did not sleep any," he continued, doing his best to seek warmth wrapped in his "large overcoat." Not everyone was able to use the bridge. Some had to splash through the chilly creek during their march north. One of Jackman's comrades recalled that "the night was wet and cold and we had nothing to eat. The boys were wet and cold and spent most of the night trying to dry their clothes by what fires we were allowed to have."[27]

Just west of them, Cleburne's and Cheatham's men slept on their arms amid the carnage of their own battlefields. These men were prohibited campfires, though the woods themselves were burning in several places as a result of the earlier heavy artillery fire and musketry. Private William K. Pilsbury of the 5th Georgia, part of John Jackson's brigade, remembered that "on the night of the first day the woods took fire, and the cries of the wounded were dreadful to hear." Edwin Rennolds of the 5th Tennessee, Strahl's brigade, had some time to record the day's experiences in his diary and reflect on his own feelings: "We placed out pickets . . . stacked arms and bivouacked. The battle has not been general, but hot and stubborn, most of the time. . . . The 5th is not (as the generals say) eager for the fray, that is a humbug. [B]ut [we] are willing and not afraid to fight. I expected I would be afraid, but the firing soon brought on the old battle feeling and I heeded it not."[28]

Farther to the south and west, the Confederate lines were still considerably jumbled. The fighting that had raged around the Brotherton and Viniard

27 William C. Davis, ed., *Diary of a Confederate Soldier: John S. Jackman of the Orphan Brigade* (University of South Carolina Press, 1990), 87; Anonymous, "Reminiscences of War Times," *The Hartford (KY) Herald*, June 7, 1911.

28 W. K. Pilsbury, "The Fifth Georgia at Chickamauga," *Confederate Veteran*, vol. III, no. 11 (November 1895), 330; Entry for September 19, E. H. Rennolds Diary, Tennessee State Library and Archives, Nashville. Hereafter, TSLA.

farmsteads left the Rebels almost as disorganized as the Federals. Most gray-clad regiments and brigades simply fell back eastward across the La Fayette Road, coming to rest several hundred yards into the woods. More by accident than by design, these commands halted on or just behind a low ridge paralleling the La Fayette Road about a quarter-mile to the east. This was the southern extension of the same ridge George Thomas selected to anchor his new Union line around Kelly Field, which is why the Union battle line on September 20 would come to resemble a giant question mark. These Rebels included Bushrod Johnson's men, A. P. Stewart's division, and the three brigades of Law's (Hood's) division then on the field—nine brigades in all. They would comprise a large part of James Longstreet's new Left Wing, though they knew nothing of that yet. They would also require considerable untangling before any attack could get underway.

The irrepressible Captain Harder of the 23rd Tennessee, John Fulton's brigade, was one of those men. Harder and his company were ordered out on picket that night, but even that duty was insufficiently exciting for Harder. Once his line was established, Harder claimed he stole forward as far as the road, where he spied a Union artillery battery leading what the captain thought was a column comprising no fewer than 40 cannon, all moving north up the road. After a limited verbal exchange during which Harder passed himself off as a Federal officer, the daring captain slipped back to his own lines and badgered Colonel Fulton into taking him to see General Johnson so Harder could get permission to try and seize the guns by "a coup in the night." Johnson, however, was in no mood for stunts. "He only reprimanded me and ordered if I went to the front again he would order my arrest," griped the captain.[29]

These Rebels also suffered from the night chill. In the 32nd Tennessee of John Brown's brigade, Cpl. T. I. Corn noted, "by midnight the temperature had fallen low enough to bring a light frost; and some of the men, getting very chilly, stirred up some smoldering logs. The flames shot up suddenly and showed the enemy our position and brought on us an alarming fire of artillery and small arms . . . and causing a little excitement. General Brown rushed to the front and gave us a reprimand severe enough to settle the matter of having a fire." Frank Ryan of the 1st Arkansas Mounted Rifles, Evander McNair's brigade, recalled a similar incident. Shortly after the Arkansans halted for the night, Ryan

29 William Henry Harder Reminiscences, TSLA. While generally accurate, Harder's account is larded with self-serving accolades and almost certainly embellished.

remembered that he and two of his messmates slipped off behind the lines to what they thought was a sheltered spot. They built a small fire, he explained, just enough to "broil a piece of meat." They had trouble getting the wood to catch, and Ryan thought to kneel down and fan the feeble flame. He was still divesting himself of his belt and cartridge box, however, "when a shell came along and swept wood, fire, and all away." If the round had struck just a moment later, thought Ryan, "I . . . would probably [have] had my head torn from my shoulders." These incidents settled any additional questions about lighting a fire.[30]

Not everyone was able to rest. Captain Richard C. McCalla, who commanded a company of Simon Buckner's pioneer corps, "worked all Saturday night making forts [fords] and bridges" across the Chickamauga. Most of the Confederate baggage trains remained east of the creek, and with few crossings to use, getting rations to the troops on the fighting line was a slow process. Many of them went hungry or looked to morning before expecting any food. There was simply no room west of the stream to bring the army's supply trains that far forward. The critical ammunition wagons were kept as close to the crossings as possible. A sudden Rebel reverse with a vast congestion of wagons directly behind routing men on the west bank would bring about a disaster. The difficulties in getting rations forward, however, would also adversely affect Bragg's plans.[31]

* * *

For the past two days, 130,000 men had grappled for position in the woods and sparse fields alongside West Chickamauga Creek. Friday, September 18 had seen a handful of Union mounted troops foil Bragg's plans, setting the stage for the larger conflict. The fighting began again early on Saturday, September 19; the result was nearly 14 hours of brutal give-and-take as each side committed themselves to battle. Losses were heavy, but neither side gained a clear-cut advantage.

30 T. I. Corn, "Brown's Brigade at Chickamauga," *Confederate Veteran*, vol. XXI, no. 3 (March, 1913), 124. Likely this fire came from men of Negley's Union division defending Brotherton Field; Frank T. Ryan Reminiscences, Civil War Miscellany file, Georgia Department of Archives and History. Hereafter GDAH.

31 "My Dear Margaret," Richard C. McCalla to his wife, October 4, 1863, Speake-McCalla Correspondence, Auburn University, Auburn, AL.

Now, both armies prepared to resume the battle on Sunday, September 20. Each side expected the day to be decisive. For Bragg success was essential. After failures in 1862 and the summer of 1863, Bragg needed a definitive victory if he wanted to reverse the fortunes of the Confederacy, which were clearly on the wane. He also needed that victory for personal reasons. If he could not defeat Rosecrans and recapture Chattanooga it seemed likely that his own position as head of the Army of Tennessee was equally imperiled. For Rosecrans, even though his trains were now mostly safe and his army less at risk of piecemeal destruction, his army's circumstances were still precarious. The Union army was outnumbered and far from its base of operations. For both sides, then, the fighting on Sunday, September 20 would be desperate.

Chapter Three

Union Lines in Motion:

Sunday, September 20: Dawn to 10:00 a.m.

Charles Dana slept poorly. Unlike the vast majority of the tens of thousands of men bedded down in the surrounding woods and fields, he managed to make his bed indoors that night in the Widow Glenn's cabin, as did a number of other officers from army headquarters. Huddled together with Capt. Horace Porter, recalled Dana, "we would go to sleep, and then the wind would come up so cold through the cracks [in the floor] that it would wake us up, and we would turn over together to keep warm." Most of the staff managed a few hours rest, but for William Starke Rosecrans, none at all. Before dawn headquarters was stirring again.[1]

William D. Bickham, a reporter for the *Cincinnati Commercial*, was a longtime friend and observer of General Rosecrans. Also present that morning, Bickham observed Rosecrans in a rare moment of near-solitude. Watching, Bickham was struck with a flash of foreboding. Dressed in an overcoat, his trousers thrust into his boot-tops, and wearing "a light brown felt hat, of uncertain shape," Rosecrans strode out of the little house to stand near Bickham and the campfire crackling in the yard. Neither man spoke. "An unlit cigar" was clamped in Rosecrans's jaw. "I knew," continued Bickham, "for I had seen Rosecrans often

1 Dana, *Recollections of the Civil War*, 114.

under widely different circumstances, that he was filled with apprehension for the issue of that day's fight. . . . Rosecrans is usually brisk, nervous, powerful of presence, and to see him silent or absorbed in what looked like gloomy contemplation, filled me with an indefinable dread."[2]

Corporal John K. Ely of the 88th Illinois was nearby and also observed his commander in this moment of frankness. "About sunrise Rossie [sic] and his staff came out of the house. Rossie['s] countenance wore a heavy expression of care." Ely added, loyally, "but he has a noble self relying look and if there is a General in our armies that can win a victory here Rossie is the one. He held an unlit cigar in his mouth and rode slowly away with it [still] unlit."[3]

"We were all up early for various reasons," wrote Col. John Sanderson, "one of which was that the night was intensely cold," but also because "we expected an early attack." Alexander McCook arrived to report that his troops "were moving," but wanted advice on posting them. With the sharp overnight drop in temperature, fog now shrouded much of the battlefield. Contrary to everyone's expectations, things remained strangely quiet. "About six, the General [Rosecrans] and the whole staff mounted . . . most . . . without having a mouthful to eat and drink," and set out to survey the lines. Captain William Margedant of the Signal Corps recalled how still everything seemed. "General Garfield ordered the general staff officers to mount for the inspection of our lines. Major General Rosecrans led the cavalcade. It was one of those quiet, peaceful Sunday mornings enjoyed only in the country or the woods. There was no noise. [Even] speaking was done in a whisper."[4]

About the same time as Rosecrans was ready to depart, a dispatch arrived from Maj. Gen. George Thomas of the XIV Corps, via the field telegraph connecting the two headquarters. "Since my return this morning," wrote the burly Virginian, "I have found it necessary to concentrate my lines more." Next, Thomas recapped his comments of the night before, uttered at Rosecrans's council of war, asking for reinforcements. He reiterated that his left did not reach the Reed's Bridge Road, and he needed more men. "I earnestly request

2 Lamers, *The Edge of Glory*, 336.

3 John Ely Diary, 88th Illinois file, CCNMP.

4 *OR* 30, pt. 1, 966; Transcript of "Chattanooga, September 21, 1863," John P. Sanderson Letters, Ohio Historical Society. Hereafter OHS; L. W. Mulhane, *Major General William Stark Rosecrans: Hero of Iuka, Corinth and Stone River, and Father of the Army of the Cumberland* (n.p., 1908), 69-70.

that Negley's division be placed on my left immediately." With this repetition of the request for Negley, a second stone joined the slowly building avalanche.[5]

A lot had happened during the night. Two hours previous, Alexander McCook's and Thomas Crittenden's men began a quiet withdrawal from the Viniard Field line, completed successfully by first light. Brigadier General Tom Wood's two brigades along with Sidney Barnes's regiments all joined Horatio Van Cleve's division west of the Dyer house to constitute Rosecrans's designated reserve of five brigades. Captain T. J. Wright, commanding company H of the Union 8th Kentucky infantry, recalled that the redeployment was conducted "with such profound silence . . . that we on the skirmish line were not apprised of the move." About 4:00 a.m., Wright learned that his brigade was gone, but the officer of the day had not yet ordered him back, and he dared not abandon the line. Wright expected to be attacked at first light, but instead, "about dawn, a heavy fog arose from the river . . . under cover of this, the rebel skirmish line withdrew, probably with the intention of being relieved. At this time General Sheridan . . . passed in the rear of our little company of forgotten pickets." Catching the general's attention, Wright secured permission to fall back. Irritated and snappish, Sheridan grumbled "that such gross neglect in a field officer of pickets should be looked into."[6]

McCook commanded five brigades from his own XX Corps (Sheridan's three and Jeff Davis's two) as well as two more from Maj. Gen. James S. Negley's division of the XIV Corps. Sheridan and Davis fell back "to the forks in the road in rear of the Widow Glenn's house," while Negley held his position at the west edge of Brotherton Field. Loose ends still had to be collected. Negley was short Brig. Gen. John Beatty's brigade, which had stopped for the night at Osborne's farm for water, and John T. Wilder's men were now all alone in the Viniard Field area. A considerable gap now existed between Negley's right and Wilder's position. It was here that Rosecrans began the circuit of his lines.[7]

In Sheridan's ranks, the 36th Illinois spotted their army commander as he rode by. The 36th was without rations and obtained breakfast only through the generosity of their fellow Illinoisans in the 88th. As they were eating,

5 *OR* 30, pt. 1, 137-138.

6 T. J. Wright, "Battle of Chickamauga," *Estill County Historical and Genealogical Society Newsletter*, vol. XVII, no. 1 (May 1997), 5.

7 *OR* 30, pt. 1, 499.

"Rosecrans came round, accompanied by his staff and escort. He looked in bad plight," recalled regimental Chaplain William Haigh, "but his voice was ringing and cheery. 'Boys,' said he, 'I never fight on Sundays, but if they begin it, we will end it.'" Rosecrans rode on.[8]

Having eaten, Sheridan's division took up new positions. The regiments deployed in a line running south from the Glenn cabin, Col. Bernard Laiboldt's and Brig. Gen. William Lytle's men in line, with Col. Luther Bradley's regiments (now led by Col. Nathan Walworth since Bradley's wounding the evening previous) held in reserve. Behind them, also in reserve, were Davis's two battered brigades, formed on the hill just west of the Dry Valley Road.[9]

The morning fog obscured much, but Rosecrans, ever the perfectionist, made minor tweaks and adjustments all along the lines as he rode. He and McCook had a brief discussion about the intended location of Davis's division. McCook liked them on the hillside west of and overlooking the Dry Valley Road, from where they could repel and advance from either the south or east. That location might also keep them out of the worst of the fighting after their serious losses suffered the day before. Rosecrans disagreed. He thought that this put Davis too far to the west. The departmental commander wanted Davis's men down into the valley and placed in close columns of division—a formation better suited for quick redeployment rather than fighting. Now McCook objected, and Rosecrans demurred, leaving the "exact place to be chosen" to McCook's discretion. With that, McCook broke away to oversee his troops' deployment.[10]

It was still very early, probably a few minutes before 6:00 a.m., when the headquarters party turned northeast. The sun was now rising, "red and sultry," an effect of the ground mists and lingering smoke. To many, it seemed a bloody omen of things to come.[11]

Rosecrans next encountered Colonel Wilder, whom he passed on to McCook, "who would assign me to my position," recalled Wilder. That detail attended to, the group rode quickly up the Glenn-Kelly Road, passing behind

8 Lyman G. Bennett and William M. Haigh, *History of the Thirty-Sixth Regiment Illinois Volunteers, During the War of the Rebellion* (Knickerbocker and Hodder, Printers and Binders, 1876), 465.

9 Lytle Brigade Tablet, Widow Glenn House, CCNMP; *OR* 30, pt. 1, 951.

10 *OR* 30, pt. 1, 940.

11 Ibid., 57.

John M. Palmer (right) led a division in the XXI Corps, but as he had the day before, he would spend September 20 attached to, and fighting with, George Thomas's XIV Corps. Palmer's troops would help anchor the new defensive line around Kelly Field.
Battles and Leaders

Maj. Gens. James Negley's and Joseph Reynolds's divisions in line at the Brotherton and Poe farmsteads, respectively. Somewhere along the way the army commander took note of Maj. Gen. Tom Crittenden's XXI Corps, dimly visible to his left across the expanse of West Dyer Field, and situated too far to the south by Rosecrans's reckoning. He dispatched revised instructions to the XXI Corps commander whose wording was destined to become the theme of the day: move "farther to the left."[12]

Upon reaching Kelly Field, Rosecrans found Maj. Gen. John Palmer's division, and another bustle of activity. Palmer awoke before dawn from his first sleep in 48 hours and one of the first things he did was hunt up George Thomas. He would be reporting to Thomas again that day, and wanted to know what was expected of him. "Pap" Thomas "pointed out to me the position to be occupied by Baird's division . . . Johnson . . . moved and formed on Baird's right; my own division . . .came next; then Reynolds, on my right. . . . The sun was up before our lines were formed." As noted, next to Reynolds in line to the south was Negley, but that sector was currently McCook's responsibility.[13]

Here, too, Rosecrans adjusted things more to his liking. Thinking that Palmer's line needed to be more compact, he ordered that officer to close his line northward, moving Col. William Grose's brigade out of the front line and into reserve. In turn, this move shifted Reynolds leftward. With only two brigades, Reynolds had no hope of covering the resultant gap, so Maj. Gen. John Brannan, whose division up to that point had been behind the lines in

12 Ibid., 58, 949.

13 John M. Palmer, *Personal Recollections of John M. Palmer: The Story of an Earnest Life* (The Robert Clarke Company, 1901), 181.

Dyer Field, moved Cols. John Croxton's and John Connell's brigades up to fill the space opened between Reynolds and Negley.[14]

Who ordered Brannan forward into the front line remains a mystery. No one took credit for the movement and Brannan failed to identify the source of the order, reporting only that "during the night I was ordered to put two brigades into line, connecting Reynolds's and Negley's divisions." Brannan also noted that this redeployment was completed just before daylight, putting his recollection somewhat at odds with Palmer's memoirs and Rosecrans's own report. Rosecrans might have issued the order as part of his readjustments, but if so, leaving it out of his report would have been uncharacteristic for the notoriously meticulous army commander. A more likely candidate is Joseph Reynolds, who was senior to Brannan. Reynolds had taken overall responsibility for the Poe Field portion of the Union line the night before, which by the end of the action included Croxton's brigade, and might well have assumed this informal arrangement remained in force. Reynolds later denied giving Brannan any specific orders, but he did converse with Brannan early that morning and later suggested Brannan deployed on his own initiative. According to Reynolds, Brannan told him "that he had been ordered to that vicinity, but had received no orders as yet to go into action at any specific place, and as no troops were on my right, he thought it incumbent on him to join his command on to my right." Of critical importance, however, is that no one informed George Thomas of the new state of affairs, leaving Thomas to continue to think Brannan's entire division was in reserve and available to call upon if needed.[15]

At the moment, Thomas's attention was focused almost exclusively on what he felt to be the greatest vulnerability of his position: Brig. Gen. Absalom Baird's inability to cover the entire distance north as far as the Reed's Bridge Road some 800 yards north of Kelly Field. On September 19, when Brannan's men moved south to help deal with the break in the Union lines around Brotherton Field and Baird's division was shifted southward through the woods to support Palmer, Baird left his much-battered Regular Brigade under Brig. Gen. John King behind to guard this road. Rather than leave the Regulars there all alone, Baird during the night ordered them south to connect with the rest of his division. Once completed, King's men managed what sleep they

14 It is possible that Croxton was still in the front line, where he had ended up the night before, and only Connell moved up to fill in the newly created gap. The reports are unclear.

15 *OR* 30, pt. 1, 401; Joseph J. Reynolds Statement of September 20, CCNMP.

could until 3:00 a.m., when Baird roused all of his troops to start placing them in line at Thomas's direction.

The key to George Thomas's thinking was the long low ridge, much of it dominated by an open cedar glade, running parallel to and about one-half mile east of the La Fayette Road. This feature began at a point opposite Brotherton Field and ran north for roughly one mile until it tapered off just beyond the Reed's Bridge Road. Thomas had spotted the ridge's defensive potential on the 19th, and he intended to place his main line there. Unfortunately, south of Kelly Field the ridge was in Confederate hands, but beyond that the Federals made full use of the feature. By dawn, King's Regulars were holding Thomas's favored terrain where Alexander's Bridge Road crested the slope. King's troops also constituted the left flank of the entire army, which fell well short of Reed's Bridge Road, let alone Granger's people at Rossville. Confederates advancing up that road could easily interpose themselves between the left of the XIV Corps and Granger's men, or even turn the XIV Corps's left flank.

The Regulars were in dreadful shape after their ordeal the previous morning. Twenty-four hours earlier, John King's men entered these woods 1,375 strong. Just before the sun rose on September 20 they numbered about one-half that, or fewer than 700 muskets. The 1/16th and 1/19th U.S. had each lost so many men that Colonel King temporarily merged them for the day's fight into an ad-hoc battalion of about 200 soldiers, the amalgam commanded by the 19th U.S.'s Capt. E. L. Smith. Battery H of the 5th U.S. had been so roughly handled that even though its gunners had recovered all six of their pieces, every caisson had been lost. Two of the battery's three officers were out of action, as well as 42 enlisted men, and 65 horses were dead or wounded. The battery was obviously not ready for action.[16]

In later years, some veterans questioned the wisdom of placing the Regulars at such a critical point in the XIV Corps line, given that Thomas was worried about a threat from the left. Lieutenant Colonel Aquila Wiley of the 41st Ohio (Brig. Gen. William Hazen's brigade, Palmer's division), was one such critic. Baird's overall position lacked reserves, charged Wiley, and "worst of all his left brigade was the Regular Brigade. . . . It had been the worst cut up and demoralized of any brigade in our army in the previous day's fight." Wiley's argument echoed the criticisms of Col. Ferdinand Van Derveer's men, who

16 *OR* 30, pt. 1, 318, 323. The 1/16th reported five officers and 62 men present, the 1/19 with 12 officers and 124 men present.

witnessed the Regulars' discomfiture the previous morning near Jay's Mill, and his use of the word "demoralized" touched a nerve. "I admit we were badly cut up," wrote Bugler William J. Carson of the 15th U.S., "but deny most emphatically that we were demoralized, and worse things might have happened to Baird than to have had the Regulars at his left." Carson was correct, as events would bear out, and the bugler himself would play a prominent role in proving Wiley wrong.[17]

Thomas found Baird and Colonel King conferring amidst King's troops at first light. Accepting a cup of coffee from one of the Regulars doing provost duty at Baird's headquarters, Thomas discussed the importance of holding this flank with his two subordinates. The XIV Corps leader also instructed King to send Lt. Joshua Fessenden and the remnant of Battery H on to Rossville. Without any caissons the cannons had no ammunition and would be useless in any fight. As they were hashing out these arrangements, Rosecrans arrived. The army commander and corps leaders, their combined cavalcade of staffs in tow, rode up to the McDonald house sitting on another convenient rise along the west side of the La Fayette Road just a couple hundred yards south of the Reed's Bridge Road intersection.[18]

Thomas reiterated his request for Negley and after seeing the ground Rosecrans agreed, dictating two quick orders to Garfield. The first went to Negley "to report with your command to General Thomas at once." The second, to McCook, instructed the XX Corps commander "to fill the space left vacant by [Negley's] removal, if practicable." Written at 6:30 and 6:35 a.m., respectively, they went out immediately.[19]

Why Negley? Thomas's desire to reunite the elements of his corps made sense under normal circumstances, but Negley's men were holding a critical portion of Rosecrans's front line. Even worse, why call on McCook to fill the hole when Crittenden's men constituted the army's reserve? Both Rosecrans and Thomas knew two of Crittenden's divisions (Tom Wood's and Horatio Van Cleve's) were available for that purpose, and in Thomas's mind he still had Brannan to call upon as well. (Brannan was in fact not available to Thomas by

17 Aquila Wiley, "Gen. Hill Answered," *National Tribune*, May 19, 1887; William J. Carson, "A Bugler Replies to Gen. Wiley," *National Tribune*, June 23, 1887.

18 Mark W. Johnson, *That Body of Brave Men: The U.S. Regular Infantry and the Civil War in the West* (Da Capo Press, 2003), 397-398; *OR* 30, pt. 1, 324.

19 *OR* 30, pt. 1, 69-70.

this time, but Thomas still believed he was, and it was a significant consideration in Thomas's thought process that morning.) Since neither Rosecrans nor Thomas ever explained their thinking for calling upon Negley, the question remains unanswered. It does suggest, however, that both Thomas and Rosecrans were overly focused on the threat to the army's left, to the detriment of other parts of the line.

As the couriers bearing these dispatches dashed off, the combined party rode back south to the area of the Kelly farm buildings. By now the Union line was largely in place. The infantry line formed in the woods east of the field. Reserves, artillery, and ammunition wagons jammed the open space of the field itself. Had the generals looked at the line more closely, they might have noticed another oddity. It was imbalanced. Two-thirds of Thomas's available force was packed into the southern one-third of his line. Rosecrans's decision to contract Palmer's line was partly to blame. While condensing Palmer's formation allowed that officer to move Col. William Grose's brigade into reserve, Rosecrans failed to note that as a result, Brig. Gen. Richard Johnson's division's frontage was so short that he could only place one of his three brigades between the divisions of Palmer and Baird. Only Col. Philemon Baldwin's former brigade (now led by Col. William W. Berry of the 5th Kentucky since Baldwin's death the evening before) held a portion of the front. There was not sufficient space for Col. Joseph B. Dodge or Brig. Gen. August Willich. As a result, while all three of Baird's brigades were in the front line, only one of Johnson's and two of Palmer's brigades held any frontage. Moreover, in accordance with Casey's *Infantry Tactics* manual, each of the nine brigades formed with two regiments in front and the remaining two in support. This meant that in some places, especially on Johnson's front, the Union defense was six lines of battle deep. Neither Rosecrans nor Thomas noted the imbalance at the time, but Colonel Wiley of the 41st Ohio remembered it. In a rare criticism of George Thomas by one of his subordinates, Wiley later wrote that the lines of "the interior divisions of Palmer and Johnson were unnecessarily strong, and [Thomas's] flank failed to reach the point on which it was intended to rest, and was unnecessarily weak."[20]

Thomas, having just been promised Negley, must have felt it better to wait for that division to appear rather than start shifting his entire line or cannibalizing divisions by stripping out reserve brigades to send to other

20 Wiley, "Gen. Hill Answered."

sectors of the front. In the interim, however, Col. Joseph Dodge's brigade of Johnson caught the XIV Corps commander's eye. Finding no place in the line, Dodge had parked his regiments in Kelly Field amidst the wagons and reserve artillery. Thomas ordered him to march north and take up a temporary position on the left of King's Regulars. Last night's confused fighting had reduced Dodge's brigade to three effective regiments because much of the 79th Pennsylvania had been captured by Cheatham's and Cleburne's men. The surviving Keystoners were temporarily folded into Col. Allen Buckner's 79th Illinois. Once that shift was complete, Dodge left Buckner to exercise tactical command while he rode back and reported the movement to Johnson. Dodge and Buckner did not form facing east on Thomas's favored ridge. As the flank, the Regulars had refused part of their line to face northeast; Buckner extended this refused line with the 79th Illinois, 29th and 30th Indiana.[21]

Thomas was loath to start reshuffling his entire command because he expected a Rebel attack momentarily. Just about every Federal on the field believed Bragg would strike at dawn, and everyone was braced for the blow. When the minutes ticked past without an assault, the men in the ranks naturally cast about for ways to strengthen their positions. Impromptu breastworks made of fence rails, logs, rocks, and what trees they could cut down rendered a strong position even stronger.

Over time and in the memory of the old soldiers, the effort to strengthen the line became one of the critical moments of the battle, and General Hazen's men took great pride in initiating it. "At daybreak," reported Hazen, "a breastwork of logs and rails was commenced which was taken up on my right and left," eventually spreading to Johnson's, Reynolds's and Baird's commands. Hazen's two front line regiments, Wiley's 41st Ohio and the 9th Indiana, would eventually lay claim to the honor of first entrenching. In his memoirs, Hazen gave the credit to the Hoosiers. "Colonel [Isaac] Suman, of the Ninth Indiana, came to me and suggested a breastwork along our front, which no one before seemed to have thought of. I at once gave orders that one rank work at this while the other stood to arms." In 1887, in the same article that noted the imbalance in Thomas's deployment, Colonel Wiley claimed the credit. "'How do you like your position?'" Hazen asked of Wiley that morning. "'Well enough, if we are to attack,'" replied the Ohioan, but Wiley was less confident on the

21 Alan Buckner Rice, ed., *The Memoirs of Colonel Alan Buckner: Colonel of the 79th Illinois Volunteer Regiment in the Civil War* (The Michigan Alcohol and Drug Information Foundation, 1982), 21.

defensive. Wiley didn't like the trees to his front that choked off his field of fire and masked any attacker's approach until the last minute. "I would like to throw up some cover for my men," he continued, to offset that disadvantage. "Go ahead,'" replied Hazen. When Wiley's account saw print, Capt. Amasa Johnson of the 9th Indiana rose to defend his regiment's claim to the honor. Johnson insisted Suman had the idea before Wiley, and moreover, it was not immediately embraced. "Hazen at first objected to [t]his suggestion, saying that the enemy's artillery would throw shells into our works and cause many to be killed by [flying] rails." Suman, who had both Mexican War experience and service in this war since 1861, felt differently and persuaded Hazen to let the idea go forward.[22]

In fact, the idea of entrenching was germinating all across the Army of the Cumberland's front that morning. By this stage of the war experienced soldiers looked for any advantage in battle, and even a small barricade provided cover. Down at Brotherton Field, far beyond the influence of Hazen's men and well before first light, Pvt. James Fenton of the 19th Illinois of Col. Timothy Stanley's brigade (Negley's division) recalled that Negley's troops "threw up a slight breastworks of logs, rails and trash" when they halted the night before. In Poe Field, Sgt. Sam McNeil of the 31st Ohio described how Connell's brigade of John Brannan's division came into line a little after daylight. "A heavy mist or smoke hung over the field . . . so we could not see our own skirmishers," he recalled. "Stones, rails and logs were piled up to shelter our lines." Suman and Wiley might have been among the first to suggest the idea, but they were hardly alone in that impulse.[23]

Hazen's objection wasn't just Old Army fussiness. It had merit. The lack of proper tools in most of the regiments made it impossible to do any real digging, meaning that any protection would be comprised of what could be piled loosely upon the ground. Artillery fire could easily smash light works, sending debris

22 *OR* 30, pt. 1, 763; William B. Hazen, *A Narrative of Military Service* (Ticknor and Co., 1885), 129; Wiley, "Gen. Hill Answered;" Amasa Johnson, "Chickamauga: A reply to Gen. Wiley and a Defense of Gen. Thomas," *National Tribune*, June 16, 1887. In a speech given at the 9th Indiana's Reunion that same year, Amasa Johnson attributed the initial objection to General Johnson, not Hazen. See Amasa Johnson, *The Ninth Indiana Regiment at Chickamauga: An Address Given August 25th, 1887, during the Fifth Annual Reunion of the Ninth Indiana Veteran's Association.* (Watseka Republican Book Print, 1888).

23 Entry for September 19, 1863, James Fenton Diary, ALPL; Samuel A. McNeil, *Personal Recollections of Service in the Army of the Cumberland and Sherman's Army from August 17, 1861 to July 20, 1865.* (n.p. 1910), 16.

and splinters far and wide, which in turn could be more dangerous to the men sheltering behind them than having no works at all. Only well-dug strong earthworks offered an effective defense against artillery, and Hazen knew that no one in the Federal line had either the time or the tools to create such defenses.

By 1864, picks and shovels would be a regular part of any infantry regiment's field equipment, but in the fall of 1863 these items were scarce on the firing line. Captain Johnson of the 9th Indiana noted the men could only build "small works of rails and logs," most not even waist high to a standing man. Fortunately, artillery batteries regularly carried axes, which were freely employed by gunner and foot-soldier alike. Within minutes, the noise of their work echoed through the woods up and down the line. Despite their modest stature, the breastworks provided both physical protection and a boost in morale. They would prove surprisingly effective in stopping incoming small-arms fire, and they helped outgoing fire as well. "Our western men were protected by a breastwork of logs from which they could take aim, as if shooting turkeys," explained Sgt. John Kane of the 101st Indiana. The sound of those echoing axes also worked on Confederate nerves. Many of the men in gray and butternut would later recall the ring of sharp metal cutting into wood with a deep sense of foreboding.[24]

That same artillery contributed more than axes, studding Thomas's line with firepower from Poe Field all the way up to Baird's attenuated front. Twenty-eight cannon from five batteries dropped trail around Kelly Field, while 10 more pieces in two batteries covered the Poe farm. Baird, with two-thirds of his artillery already captured or so badly punished as to be ineffective, placed his remaining guns exceptionally well. Lieutenant David Flansburg initially commanded the 4th Indiana Battery, which had no better time on September 19 than did the rest of Baird's long arm. On Saturday, Govan's Rebels overran the Hoosier battery. Flansburg at one point lost five of his six guns, and was himself wounded and captured. Lieutenant Henry J. Willits took command and managed to recover all five pieces later in the day. However, unlike Battery H, Willits also recovered enough limbers and other equipment to restore two sections to working order, and had them in line now: two Napoleons and two

24 Johnson, "Chickamauga: A reply to Gen. Wiley and A Defense of Gen. Thomas;" Joseph E. Suppinger, ed., "From Chickamauga to Chattanooga, The Battlefield Account of Sergeant John M. Kane," *East Tennessee Historical Society Publications*, no. 45 (1973), 103.

re-bored bronze James rifles. His remaining guns, a pair of 12-pound howitzers, stood without limbers behind the battery prepared to serve as replacements.[25]

Taking advantage of a small bend in the ridge, Willits's guns were posted at the curve in Baird's line, between Scribner's and Starkweather's brigades, angled forward so they could shoot straight ahead and also sweep the length of the Union front north or south. Because of the cedar glade, "a clear space averaging 75 yards" in width, the Hoosiers's excellent field of fire extended laterally to the left as far as the Reed's Bridge Road. Any troops moving west against a Union line here would expose themselves to a flanking fire from a brace of Union guns. The 4th Indiana's gunners could also take heart from the proximity of the 1st Wisconsin infantry, just to their right, with whom they shared a close bond. At Perryville, where both units underwent their baptism of fire, the steadfast support of the Badgers had saved the 4th Indiana's gun crews. In thanks, the 4th presented the 1st Wisconsin with a new national standard inscribed, "Presented by the 4th Ind. Baty. to the 1st Regt. Wis. Inf. For Gallant Conduct at Chaplin Hills, Oct. 8th, 1862." That flag now waved lazily, and reassuringly, nearby in the slight morning breeze.[26]

Another quirk marked Thomas's line down at the south end of Kelly Field, where Joseph Reynolds had formed his two brigades in a staggered formation. John Turchin's command prolonged Hazen's right on Thomas's favored ridge, but that was as far as the Federal line could reach. Just a few hundred yards south of Turchin's right-most regiment, the 36th Ohio, Confederates claimed the ridge. There, Maj. Gen. A. P. Stewart's men went to ground on the east side of this same rise after their fight of the 19th, and now Rebel pickets occupied it.

Unable to prolong Turchin's line, Reynolds placed Edward King's brigade in a single line on the west side of Poe Field, facing east, about 300 yards west of and behind Turchin's flank. Forming what military science termed a *crochet*, the 68th and 101st Indiana were positioned directly behind the 36th, while the 19th Indiana Battery, 75th Indiana, and 105th Ohio all extended south along the west edge of the field beyond Turchin's advanced flank. Any Confederate advance that outflanked Turchin and turned north to roll up his line would expose its

25 Baird's other battery, A of the 1st Michigan, had also been all but destroyed the day before. The surviving crewmen had been sent to the rear, with most of their guns and limbers still in Rebel hands.

26 *OR* 30, pt. 1, 287; http://www.wisconsinbattleflags.com/units-flags/1st-wisconsin.php, accessed June 17, 2012.

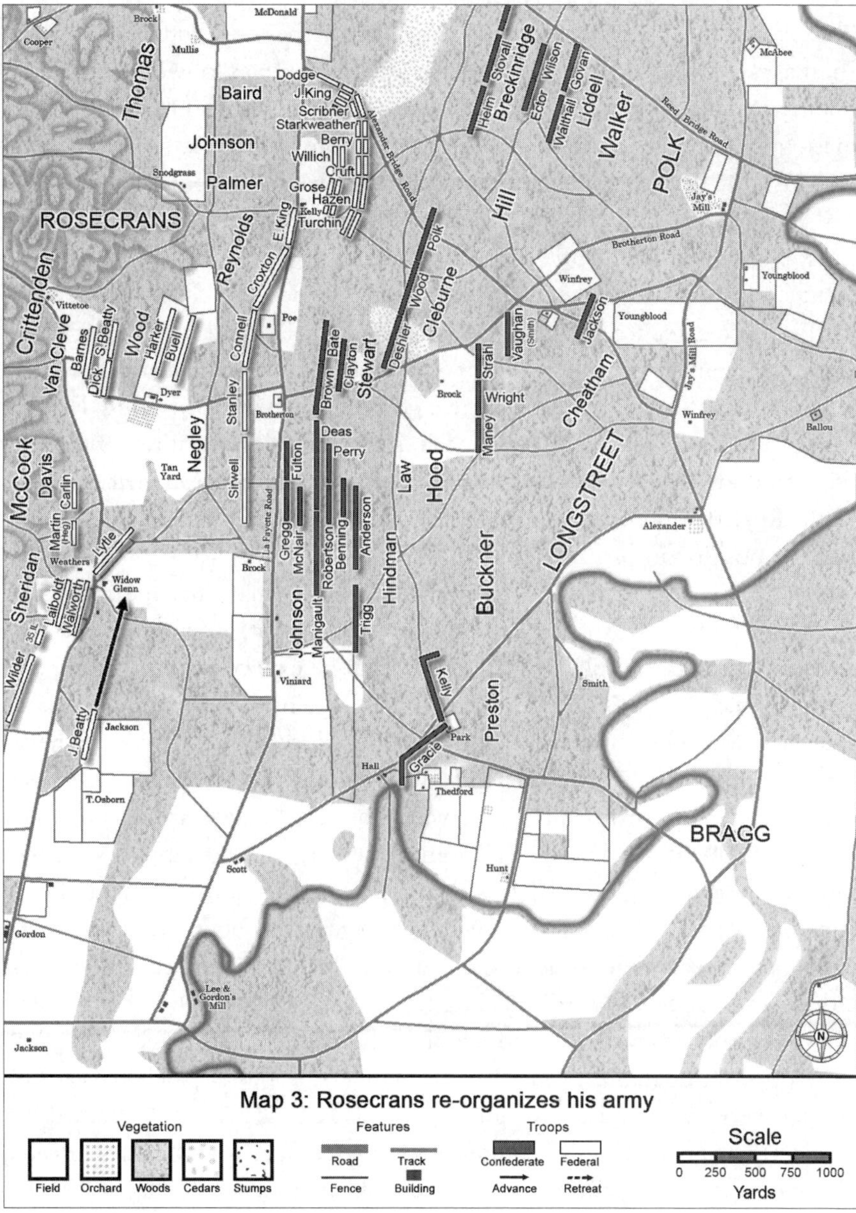

Map 3: Rosecrans re-organizes his army

own line to a deadly enfilade fire from King's men. Alternatively, if the Rebels moved directly against King's position by either wheeling part of Turchin's line back or by having the masked portion of King's line wheel forward, Reynolds could deliver a similar crossfire against them. While not as strong as a contiguous line, the *crochet* still placed an attacker on the horns of a dilemma.

Moreover, ample Federal reserves were on hand in the south end of Kelly Field. Thomas's overabundance of troops in this sector was obvious. The nine infantry regiments of Willich's and Grose's brigades (Johnson's and Palmer's divisions, respectively) and no less than four more artillery batteries (22 guns) were idling in the field and could be called up quickly if needed.

As noted earlier, it was probably Reynolds who ordered forward Brannan's division and used two of the Third Division's brigades to extend King's line. Connell's and Croxton's regiments, as well as their artillery, covered the rest of Poe Field and extended into the woods between the Poe and Brotherton farms, where they joined with Negley's left. Colonel Van Derveer's brigade filed in behind as Brannan's reserve. Brannan's portion of the line also fronted on the west edge of Poe Field, with the guns and troops deployed entirely within the strip of woods between that field and the Glenn-Kelly Road. On their way back south, Rosecrans's party rode past the rear of this line and on to General Negley's position in Brotherton Field.

Major General James S. Negley was a worried man that morning. The previous afternoon he rushed two brigades to the front, leaving John Beatty's command behind, and plunged right into what he expected would be a major fight. Instead, Negley's men pushed forward against evaporating resistance until they reached Brotherton Field. While the expected bloody contest never materialized, Negley remained concerned that his two brigades had been shoved so far forward without reserves, and were holding an extended line (wider than any other division in Thomas's sector) with no support on either flank. His connection on his left with Brannan was tenuous at best, and only some of Colonel Wilder's pickets remained to guard his right. Negley had only 2,400 men in six regiments deployed in a single line spanning nearly 800 yards, with no reserves. His two artillery batteries remained on the high ground behind him out in South Dyer Field, and not along his front.[27]

Negley's headquarters roused at 3:00 a.m., with aides dispatched to ensure the men were awake and alert in anticipation of the expected Confederate dawn attack. The Pennsylvanian's first concern was to retrieve John Beatty's brigade, still encamped at Osborne's farm a couple miles south. This was done promptly. "Before day break," recalled Adjutant Sharp of the 15th Kentucky,

27 In addition to lacking Beatty's command, the 74th Ohio of Col. William Sirwell's Third Brigade was detached as train guard, and Col. Timothy R. Stanley's Second Brigade contained only three regiments to begin with.

"we moved and joined our division at Brotherton's." Negley placed these new arrivals in the South Dyer Field behind his main line. Beatty's 1,191 men would serve as the divisional reserve. According to Sharp, the brigade was in place by 5:00 a.m., well before sunrise.[28]

When dawn passed with no attack, Negley reported that "a dense fog" precluded any action. Instead of by Rebels, the relative quiet of the early morning was disturbed by the first of a series of couriers. Around 7:00 a.m., Rosecrans's order directing that Negley's division join Thomas arrived. Negley promptly sent an aide to notify General McCook (his current superior) and another to Thomas, the latter rider with instructions to take some cavalry escorts and establish a courier line between Thomas's and Negley's headquarters in preparation for the march north. Additional officers were sent to the brigades, alerting them to be ready to move out at once. All that was needed were the promised replacements. Meanwhile, Negley began to be bombarded by a series of messages from various commanders, all urging haste.[29]

Thomas sent at least three different couriers within several minutes. By 7:00 a.m., the XIV Corps commander grew impatient with Negley's absence and sent Capt. John P. Willard to tell Negley to move "without delay." Willard arrived at Negley's command post within minutes of Rosecrans's original orders to join Thomas. Negley informed Willard he was complying as fast as he was able. Willard returned to Thomas to report that piece of good news. To ensure that no further delay resulted, Thomas sent Willard back to Negley, this time with instructions to lead the division into position on Baird's left. All told, Willard's repeated trips up and down the Glenn-Kelly Road probably consumed about half an hour.[30]

In the meantime, Negley also received Lieutenant Colonel Fisher of McCook's staff, who relayed the same instructions: go to Thomas's assistance. Fisher was sent by McCook when that general received his copy of Rosecrans's order. Impressed with the apparent urgency of these repeated instructions, and

28 *OR* 30, pt. 1, 360; D. N. Sharp Letter, 15th Kentucky file, CCNMP.

29 *OR* 30, pt. 1, 329, 357.

30 Ibid., 355. Most accounts have Willard carrying the 6:30 a.m. written order to Negley instead of one of Rosecrans's staff, but Willard's account contradicts this assertion. In an affidavit requested by Negley and dated October 9 1863, Willard clearly stated he carried a verbal order, not a written one, which makes this a different communication entirely.

since things on his front seemed quiet, Negley decided to join Thomas without waiting for the promised replacements.[31]

"I received orders from Major General Negley," reported Col. Timothy Stanley of the Second Brigade, "to withdraw from my position, and move off up the road to the left." Leaving his skirmishers behind, Stanley hastened to comply, followed by Col. William Sirwell. Beatty's men, back along the edge of Dyer Field, had yet to move. At this juncture, Rosecrans himself rode up on his way back from Kelly Field. Captain Alfred L. Hough of Negley's staff had the misfortune of being buttonholed by the army commander: "[Rosecrans] asked what troops these were. I replied, 'General Negley's division.' He asked what they were doing there. I replied, 'going to join General Thomas.' He asked if they had been relieved. I answered 'No.'" That response triggered Rosecrans's incendiary temper. Quickly, the angry army commander ordered Sirwell and Stanley back into the line, and, with a smarting Hough in tow, rode to see Negley. Even by his own admission, Rosecrans spoke "a little sharply" to Negley about the danger of withdrawing before he had been fully relieved. Hough would long harbor a considerable grudge against the army commander for that moment of reprimand.[32]

Rosecrans was right to be concerned. Private James Martin and the rest of Company H, 11th Michigan of Stanley's brigade, were selected for picket duty that morning and had already "skirmished with the rebs about two hours." Despite leaving Martin and his comrades in place, when Stanley's main body drew off, the Confederates sensed something was going on and pressed the Yankee pickets back toward their lines. When Rosecrans ordered him back into his works, reported Stanley, he had to drive back those aggressive Rebel skirmishers.[33]

On Negley's left, Colonel Sirwell also knew the enemy were stirring. Early in the morning his brigade adjutant brought word that "the rebels were massing a heavy force in my front." Sirwell added a section of Battery G, 1st Ohio to his line behind breastworks thrown up by his command overnight. His defenses, he thought, "were really quite formidable," and he was confident "it would have

31 Ibid., 342.

32 Ibid., 348, 378, 1014.

33 "Dear Parents," September 24, 1863, James A. Martin Letters, Bentley Historical Library, University of Michigan. Hereafter UMich; *OR* 30, pt. 1, 378.

been no easy task to dislodge" his brigade if attacked. Unfortunately, he would not have a chance to test those defenses.[34]

By now, 8:00 a.m. had come and gone. Negley was needed on Thomas's left without delay, but he could not leave Brotherton Field without being replaced. Faced with this dilemma, Rosecrans made an abrupt decision. Barking a quick command, Rosecrans instructed Negley to let John Beatty's brigade, still lying in reserve, follow Willard to the left immediately. The rest of the division could come later as soon as Rosecrans straightened things out with McCook. It was a Solomonesque decision, splitting the baby in half, but the best that could be done at the moment. Rosecrans set his spurs to find McCook, leaving a dismayed and chastened major general in his wake. Negley had no desire to see his command parceled out, brigade by brigade, all over the field. As he watched Beatty move off, the Pennsylvanian muttered to Captain Hough that he was most "anxious to keep [his] division together."[35]

As if to further stir the pot, within a few minutes of Beatty's and Rosecrans's departure, two more couriers arrived from Thomas. The first of these was Negley's own aide, Lt. Charles C. Cooke, whom Negley had earlier dispatched to establish the courier line with the XIV Corps. Once accomplished, Cooke returned with another verbal order from Thomas: the now-familiar "move immediately to the left and support of General Baird." Hard on Cooke's heels, Capt. John D. Barker of the 1st Ohio Cavalry rode up around 9:00 a.m. Barker commanded the XIV Corps escort company and had been sent by Thomas to find out what was taking Negley so long to reach him. The harried division commander explained that he still had not been relieved, but Beatty's brigade was at least on the way, and that Negley would be along with the other two brigades as soon as possible. Barker galloped back to Thomas with this news, which by now Thomas already knew, for Willard had appeared with Beatty's men in the interim. This wouldn't do. Thomas had been promised a division, not a brigade. The Virginian sent Barker back down the Glenn-Kelly Road to find Rosecrans to appeal to the highest authority he could to ensure Negley's speediest arrival.[36]

34 Ibid., 385.

35 Ibid., 348, 1014.

36 Ibid., 357. Barker claimed he did not leave Thomas on this mission until 9:30 a.m. This seems a little late. If true, he would have been present when Beatty arrived and would have

Once he left Negley, the army commander's focus shifted to Dyer Field. Intent on finding out what was delaying Negley's relief, Rosecrans made another snap decision along the way to finding McCook. During his ride south, Rosecrans once again caught sight of the massed brigades comprising Tom Crittenden's XXI Corps. Several hundred yards to the northwest were Cols. George Buell's and Charles Harker's brigades of Thomas J. Wood's division, resting quietly atop a ridge overlooking the Dyer farm from the west. Van Cleve's men were massed behind them. As of yet, Crittenden had no orders beyond serving as the army reserve. By now it was nearly 9:00 a.m., and many of Crittenden's troops were beginning to think the day might turn out to be anticlimactic. "We were calculating on a quiet day," recalled Lt. John McCook, of Crittenden's staff, when almost casually, an order arrived from Rosecrans instructing Crittenden to send Brig. Gen. Tom Wood's division to replace Negley and "to keep . . . Van Cleve in . . . supporting distance of . . . Wood." With a few dictated pen strokes, Rosecrans reshuffled his line.[37]

With Crittenden attended to, Rosecrans found General McCook. By this time the commanding general was visibly irritated with the morning's delays. McCook's circumstances didn't help matters. In Charles Dana's words, "McCook's line had been elongated so that it was a mere thread." Rosecrans's already short temper snapped again in another tongue-lashing. "Rosecrans was very angry, and . . . rebuked [McCook] severely," noted Dana, who thought the outburst unfair. Rosecrans's own orders, after all, were largely responsible for the poor deployment. Had the army commander forgotten that removing Negley left McCook with only five brigades, and of those, Jeff Davis's two were so badly bloodied they barely numbered one normal-sized brigade?[38]

The exact words uttered during this meeting are not known. The various accounts referring to it are to some degree contradictory. In addition to expressing his dissatisfaction with the holdup in relieving Negley, Rosecrans also found fault with Phil Sheridan's and Jeff Davis's deployments, which were

---

known about the lack of relief, via the message conveyed by Willard. Barker had to have left Thomas before Willard arrived. *OR* 30, pt. 1, 350.

37 "My Dear sister," McCook Letters, NYHS; *OR* 30, pt. 1, 609.

38 Dana, *Recollections of the Civil War*, 115. General McCook was also on the move. Earlier, when he first received the order from Rosecrans, Negley sent Capt. LaFayette Johnson to find McCook. Johnson talked to Sheridan and to General Lytle of Sheridan's Division, but could not find the corps commander. He reported his lack of success shortly after Rosecrans and Negley met.

still too far to the south. "Whatever might be the value of Sheridan's position, it was still more important that we should keep our line closed to the left," Rosecrans growled. After a few more sharply worded exchanges, Rosecrans sent McCook to set things to rights. "It is indispensable to close on the left," reiterated the commanding general, for "we cannot afford to have another Stones River." This last comment was a pointed reminder of the XX Corps's collapse during that previous battle, and the words surely cut the abashed McCook to the quick.[39]

The quiet morning, interrupted only by the usual fitful picket firing, ended between 9:30 and 10:00 a.m. when a sudden swell of distant firing from the north signified that the long-awaited Confederate attack had begun. And, as predicted, it began against Thomas. While details of the fighting were still lacking, the roar of gunfire added greater urgency to every order and communication.

As the testy exchange between Rosecrans and McCook concluded, it became Rosecrans's turn to be bombarded with couriers. First to arrive was Negley's man, Lt. William H. H. Moody. Moody carried the alarming report that Beatty's departure had left Negley's line very weak once again, bereft of reserves, and that the enemy was now "massing in our front." Rosecrans had Moody repeat the message before telling the young lieutenant to "go to General Crittenden and tell him I say to make that line strong and good." Rosecrans asked Moody if Wood had started arriving. "I know nothing of General Wood," confessed Moody as he galloped off on his errand to Crittenden.[40]

Next to arrive were two messengers from Thomas. The first was the aforementioned Captain Barker, and shortly afterward, the hard-riding Captain Willard yet again. Barker had come via Negley, who still had seen no sign of the replacement troops, and who reported that "the enemy were pressing [Thomas's] left . . . very hard, and asked for more troops." Rosecrans expressed surprise at this information, for he felt sure that by now Wood would have come forward. He was only a short distance to the rear. When Willard reported,

39 *OR* 30, pt. 1, 940. Rosecrans's testimony at the McCook court of inquiry contains some errors. Rosecrans claimed that he and McCook rode over to Sheridan's position at this time, after his return from Kelly Field, where they discussed Sheridan's deployment. All other accounts place this survey of Sheridan's lines at first light, before Rosecrans visited Thomas, and as described earlier in this chapter. Larry J. Daniel, *Days of Glory: The Army of the Cumberland, 1861-1865* (Louisiana State University Press, 2004), 324.

40 *OR* 30, pt. 1, 360.

he related that Wood's men did not yet have their new orders and were instead halted some distance behind Negley's front, per Crittenden's earlier instructions.[41]

Almost everyone else on the field seemed to be having a hard time following Rosecrans's game plan that morning. Perhaps the commanding general's directives were not as clear as he thought them to be. Since many of these orders were verbal, there is a sparse written record to check recollections against. Crittenden's instructions to Tom Wood are a case in point. Instead of moving up to replace Negley, Wood marched his men south and took up a position along the ridge behind Negley. This was the same location where Negley had deployed his men the night before prior to advancing, and where Rosecrans would later establish his headquarters. Willard, who was by now making what was at least his fourth circuit of the battlefield, rode past Wood's men on his way to Rosecrans. "I asked [Wood] if he had been ordered to relieve . . . Negley," Willard reported. "I am ordered to post my troops on this ridge," came the reply. Willard pressed the point, explaining that "General Rosecrans promised to send one of the divisions of Crittenden's corps to relieve General Negley."

Wood was equally insistent. His orders placed him on the ridge, and he couldn't move without additional instructions. Captain Hough had the same experience. Hough noticed Colonel Buell's brigade taking up a position on the ridge and, thinking relief had at last arrived, rode over. Were these the troops sent to relieve Negley? Buell repeated the same instructions Wood had quoted to Willard. He was ordered to hold the ridge, and nothing more. Hough attempted to induce Buell to go see Negley in person, hoping that might persuade the colonel to come forward, but Buell's orders, coming as they did from Wood himself, were unambiguous. He could do nothing without additional instructions and remained at least a quarter-mile behind Negley's front.[42]

When Willard reported Wood's apparent intransigence, Rosecrans sent one of his own aides, Capt. R. S. Thoms, directly to Wood with orders to replace Negley "at once." Next, Barker was sent back to George Thomas, and Willard to Negley, informing both men of these latest developments. On the way to

41 Ibid., 350, 355. Negley was repeating Thomas's information as it came to him.

42 Ibid., 348, 355-356.

Negley, Willard met Captain Thoms returning, who informed him that the revised orders to Wood had been successfully delivered.[43]

Before Thoms could report to the army commander, however, the impatient Rosecrans decided to intervene and straighten things out himself. Leaving McCook, the whole command party trotted over to Wood's new position, where Rosecrans and Wood exchanged words. It was a fateful meeting, and a great deal of controversy would arise from it in subsequent years. According to Rosecrans, when he found Wood on the ridge, "I inquired what he was doing there, and Wood said he understood Gen. Crittenden to direct him to form there. I told him, 'By no means; you are to replace Negley's division on the line, and I want you to do it as soon as the Lord will let you.'"[44]

There is little doubt that by now Rosecrans was in quite a temper. In the past hour he'd dressed down Negley for moving too recklessly, and publicly admonished McCook for his slowness and sloppy deployments. Even army staffer Henry M. Cist, one of Rosecrans's greatest partisans, would admit the army commander was visibly angry. "Rosecrans, impatient at the delay . . . expressed himself very forcibly to Wood, much to the dissatisfaction of the latter."[45]

The story grew in the telling. In a highly fanciful account written in 1936, author Edwin V. Westrate recreated a charged scene complete with invented dialogue: "'What is the meaning of this, sir?' [Rosecrans] shouted. 'You have disobeyed my specific orders. By your damnable negligence you are endangering the safety of the entire army, and, by God, I will not tolerate it. Move your division at once, as I have instructed, or the consequences will not be pleasant for yourself.' Wood, who had turned white with rage, was speechless."[46]

Wood's version of what transpired was quite different. Responding principally to Cist's account, in 1882 Wood wrote a lengthy letter to the *New York Times* explaining, "I was not reprimanded by Gen. Rosecrans on the

43 Ibid., 350, 355-356.

44 Rosecrans, "Chattanooga Campaign."

45 Henry M. Cist, *The Army of the Cumberland: Campaigns of the Civil War*, vol. VII (Charles Scribner's Sons, 1882), 220. Cist was back in Chattanooga and so not present for this exchange. His account is based on what other officers told him after the fact. Cist also had an additional motive for playing up Rosecrans's anger at that moment, as will become apparent later.

46 Daniel, *Days of Glory*, 324. Westrate offered no citation for this exchange.

morning of the 20th of September, 1863. The meeting was but for a moment and occurred as I was moving my division from its position in reserve to relieve Gen. Negley's division in the line of battle. Gen. Rosecrans asked me, without heat of language or manner . . . why I had not moved earlier. I replied that I moved promptly on receipt of the order." Rosecrans noted that the order had been issued "some time before," but Wood could only relate when it came to him from Crittenden. "Gen. Rosecrans made no further comment . . . and simply added: Hurry up and relieve Gen. Negley. . . . I certainly did not feel that I had been censured."[47]

Wood also pointed out that Cist was not present to witness this encounter. Cist "was not a field Adjutant-General," sneered Wood, but "a desk Adjutant-General" whose primary duties consisted of "filing away and preserving military communications." Since he was back in Chattanooga that morning, Cist relied upon hearsay and army gossip for his version of the "confrontation." All of this was important not just because two generals might have exchanged sharp words on a battlefield, but in light of later events. As Rosecrans put it, Wood's tardiness "subsequently proved of serious consequence." When Cist published his version of this contretemps, he was building a case that Tom Wood felt humiliated that morning, his dilatory movement to replace Negley was part of a pattern of sluggishness, and Wood's resentment was building toward a deliberate effort to sabotage the army commander—a storyline that would echo among historians. "For a third time since Lookout Valley," noted Rosecrans's biographer William Lamers, "Wood was having trouble with orders."[48]

Whatever the reasons for or consequences of the delay, at last troops were going to replace Negley. Wood's men started to arrive around 9:30 a.m. By now Negley must have also been equally frustrated, though he remained outwardly calm. Certainly some of his staff expressed their aggravation. In Lieutenant Moody's eyes, Wood's men deployed their skirmishers and advanced much too slowly considering the urgency of the moment. "They advanced very leisurely across the open field." Wood's men probably didn't take any longer to deploy than any other similarly sized command. Replacing one division with another in

47 Thomas J. Wood, "The Gaps at Chickamauga," *New York Times*, November 19, 1882. Wood's account was published within months of both Rosecrans's and Cist's versions appearing in print.

48 Rosecrans, "Chattanooga Campaign"; Lamers, *The Edge of Glory*, 341-342.

the battle line was no easy thing, and would naturally take time. However, in the past two hours Negley had received a half-dozen urgent messages, sent via four different couriers, all impressing upon him the need for haste. Initially responding with alacrity, he had been verbally rebuked by Rosecrans for planning to leave before being relieved, and then saw his division split up as Rosecrans sent Beatty's brigade ahead. Now the sounds of a fierce battle were clearly audible off to the north—a fight in which Negley's troops were supposed to take part. Probably no one could have moved fast enough to satisfy Negley or his staff.[49]

Wood's orders were to cover Negley's front and connect with Brannan's men to Negley's right. Negley, however, had formed his regiments in a single line in order to cover this distance. Wood's eight regiments were formed in a double line according to *Casey's Tactics*, and could not cover the whole of the space Negley occupied. Wood's two brigades only filled that portion of the gap formerly occupied by Stanley's brigade. Negley knew none of this as he took his place at the head of Stanley's column and started up the road. Behind Stanley marched Colonel Sirwell's brigade. Sirwell's four regiments had proceeded only a few hundred yards when word arrived that Wood's pair of brigades were not large enough to fully replace Negley's line, and that Confederate skirmishers had stepped forward into the gap just vacated. Negley had no choice but to dispatch Sirwell's troops back to their old breastworks, where they handily drove off the Rebels a second time. However, this movement finished fracturing his division, with Beatty gone ahead at least an hour previously, Stanley now on the march north, and Sirwell temporarily re-occupying his original position.[50]

Willard, acting as Negley's guide, was sent to General Crittenden to ask for more troops. Crittenden could act quickly and dispatched Col. Sidney M. Barnes's brigade of Van Cleve's division forward to extend Wood's line and allow Sirwell to depart once more. However, all of these travails meant that the thing Negley most feared—that his command would be split up and scattered about the battlefield—had come to pass.[51]

49 *OR* 30, pt. 1, 360.

50 George H. Puntenney, *History of the Thirty-Seventh Regiment of Indiana Infantry Volunteers: Its Organization, Campaigns, and Battles-Sept., '61-Oct., 64* (Jacksonian Book and Job Department, 1896), 56; Ward Journal, DePauw University, 139.

51 *OR* 30, pt. 1, 609.

Despite his Regular Army credentials, Tom Wood had come to respect and admire volunteer troops. After the fighting concluded on September 19, Wood visited Harker's headquarters fire. "This battle is not over yet," opined the divisional commander. "We will have to fight again tomorrow. If I were given my choice between Regulars and volunteers, I would choose volunteer troops. They can 'stick:' you can fight them as long as you please. . . . The Regulars are too sharp. They know when they are whipped," said Wood, who added with admiration, "but the volunteers don't: they will fight as long as they can pull a trigger." His eight regiments, all volunteers, would have ample chance to demonstrate that doggedness today. Wood's instructions when he assumed the new line echoed Rosecrans's overall defensive bent: "I was instructed not to invite an attack," wrote Wood, "but be prepared to repel any effort." The enemy's skirmishers were obviously present and aggressive enough to delay Sirwell, but Wood initially dismissed them. He remembered the handover as going smoothly, with the Rebel skirmishers putting in an appearance only after his own were thrown forward. After that, the steady popping of picket fire was largely ignored.[52]

Wood had two complaints concerning his new position. As noted, his original line was shorter than the space Negley occupied, and so he made a second appeal to Crittenden for another brigade, the request coming after Negley's and conveyed by Willard. Additionally, Wood sent word back "that it was useless to bring artillery into the woods." Crittenden had already ordered Van Cleve to loan Colonel Barnes's brigade to Wood, solving that dilemma. Mindful that Saturday's fighting in similar tree cover had cost the Federals a number of batteries, Crittenden agreed with Wood and cast about for some better use for his cannon. Accordingly, the XXI Corps commander ordered Major Mendenhall to collect any artillery otherwise unoccupied and post the guns on a high open ridge along the west edge of Dyer Field. It was an excellent position overlooking several hundred yards of open land to the east and south. Later, Crittenden reported (with hindsight) that "in the event of any reverse, these guns could cover our retreat."[53]

52 Wilbur F. Hinman, *The Story of the Sherman Brigade. The Camp, The March, The Bivouac, The Battle, and How "The Boys" Lived and Died During Four Years of Active Service* (Press of the Daily Review, 1897), 426; *OR* 30, pt. 1, 634.

53 Ibid., 609-610.

Barnes's men immediately went forward. "While trying to boil some coffee for breakfast," complained Captain Wright of the 8th Kentucky, "(our dusky cooks had not put in an appearance), we were ordered into line without the coveted coffee and 'ned.'" Barnes's new position was in the woods between Brotherton and Poe fields, connecting Brannan's right with Wood's left, where he settled in behind Negley's "slight and hastily formed breastworks, made of logs, rails, stone or anything that could be conveniently had." By now it was near 10:00 a.m., and the battle was raging in full force off to the north.[54]

About this same time, Rosecrans issued one other order that, had it been carried out, might have changed the entire battle. Horatio Van Cleve still had two brigades in hand, those of Brig. Gen. Samuel Beatty and Col. George Dick. Sam Beatty's First Brigade (not to be confused with John Beatty of Negley's command) numbered close to 1,100 men, while Dick mustered about 900 muskets. They'd both been handled roughly on the 19th, but the night's reorganization proved that many of their losses had been stragglers as a result of being flanked and routed, rather than combat casualties. These 2,000 men represented the last of Rosecrans's uncommitted reserves. The army commander decided, about the time Barnes was sent to Wood, to place them behind Tom Wood's formation as a support line.[55]

Potentially, this was not a bad decision. Barnes already belonged to Van Cleve, Wood was of the same corps, and Crittenden might have made himself useful here, coordinating the needs of his two divisions as well as the newly established gun line Mendenhall was building not far behind the infantry. Almost as soon as Van Cleve reached what he assumed was his intended position, however, the division commander was ordered to move again—and not for the last time.

54 Wright, "Battle of Chickamauga," 5.

55 *OR* 30, pt. 1, 58.

Chapter Four

Breckinridge Attacks:

Sunday, Dawn to 10:00 a.m.

Unlike General Rosecrans's activity-filled morning, General Bragg spent the early hours of September 20 at his headquarters waiting for something to happen. "Before dawn of day myself and staff were ready for the saddle," wrote Bragg, prepared to hear the sounds of battle. "With increasing anxiety and disappointment I waited until after sunrise without hearing a gun, and at length dispatched a staff officer to Lieutenant-General Polk to ascertain the cause of the delay." When he could not find Polk at the front, the staff officer, Maj. Pollock B. Lee, rode to Polk's headquarters on the east bank of the creek at Alexander's Bridge. Despite the fog, the major had no problem locating Polk's camp. His exchange with the bishop was anything but satisfactory. Lee returned to Bragg sometime after 7:00 a.m., bearing an infuriating tale.[1]

"I sent to Gen'l Polk," a still-enraged Bragg informed Davis on September 25, "and found him after seven o'ck two miles in rear of his line, in the house where he slept, and unable to account for the delay." In a letter to his wife, Bragg fumed that Polk "never gave his orders to any one, took up his lodging in a comfortable house across the river two miles in rear of his troops, [and] at 8:00 the next morning, after a most anxious time he was found by my staff [Lee], sitting in a rocking chair . . . after a most comfortable breakfast." Southern

1 *OR* 30, pt. 2, 33.

newspaperman-turned-historian Edward Pollard published an embroidered version of Major Lee's story in 1866. "Gen. Polk," wrote Pollard, "was noted for his fondness of military ostentation, and carried a train of staff officers whose numbers and superb dress were the occasions of singular remark." As Pollard explained it, Lee found the bishop-general seated at breakfast with those same "brilliantly dressed officers." Upon Lee's inquiry, "General Polk replied that he had ordered Hill to open the action . . . [adding], 'Do tell General Bragg that my heart is overflowing with anxiety for the attack—overflowing with anxiety, sir.'" Colonel Taylor Beatty witnessed Lee's return and the ensuing flurry of excitement and took a moment to jot in his diary (with considerable understatement), "Genl. Bragg impatient—[we] gallop to the front to find Genl Polk."[2]

It was now clear that Bragg's plan for a full-scale assault at first light was hopelessly derailed, and that Polk's complicity in that derailment was substantial. Major Lee's report, however, was nothing but slander. In fact, Polk was also up and moving before sunrise, waiting just as anxiously for sounds of the intended attack. As the morning brightened without the boom of cannon or the rattle of musketry, Polk's staff inaugurated a frantic search for the couriers responsible for delivering the prior night's order. Private Y. R. LeMonnier found Private Fisher first, warming himself before a fire. "Fisher, the general wants you," cried LeMonnier, who could not resist adding a dig: "You are going to catch hell." Once it was established that Fisher never located Daniel Harvey Hill nor delivered the orders entrusted to him, Polk scrambled to make amends.[3]

"Shortly after daylight (perhaps before sunrise)" Polk ordered Lt. Col. Thomas Jack to issue new orders, this time directly to Hill's division commanders, John C. Breckinridge and Patrick Cleburne. These new

2 "My Dear Sir," September 25, 1863, Charles Colcock Jones Papers, Perkins Library, Duke University. Hereafter DU; "Dear Wife," September 22, 1863, Braxton Bragg Papers, Missouri Historical Society, St. Louis, MO; Edward A. Pollard, *The Lost Cause* (E. B. Treat & Co., 1866), 450. Pollard was the editor of the *Richmond Examiner* during the war, and a harsh critic of President Davis, whom he viewed as a military despot. He was also not overly concerned with winnowing fact from fiction. Entry for September 20, Taylor Beatty Diary, UNC. There are several versions of this story. In 1873, Bragg recalled that Lee found Polk "an hour after sunrise . . . three miles behind the line." All versions are consistent in the main points, reporting Polk sitting on a porch, at breakfast, and reading a newspaper.

3 Y. R. LeMonnier, "Gen Leonidas Polk at Chickamauga," *Confederate Veteran*, vol. XXIV, no. 1 (January, 1916) 17.

instructions elucidated that Hill could not be found and that they must attack immediately. Polk called Capt. James F. "Frank" Wheless over: "I wish you to take these orders, find these officers as quickly as possible, and explain to them why the orders were not sent through their corps commanders. As you pass by Cheatham, inform him that you are going to order an immediate advance . . . instruct him to have his line ready to conform." Wheless galloped off, Polk's final injunction to "hurry, and do not spare your horse!" ringing in his ears. Hard on his heels, Capt. William J. Minnick took a duplicate set on the same mission. This time Polk would take no chances.[4]

Major Lee pulled up his mount shortly after Minnick left—just as Polk was mounting to ride forward himself. Polk explained the previous night's error, and that he had sent new orders. The general's son and aide, Capt. William Polk, witnessed this encounter. Major Lee departed, carrying with him a fanciful tale of breakfast, porch, and newspaper back to Bragg. Why Lee concocted that tale remains unknown, and perhaps unknowable. Lee never explained himself. According to William Polk, other members of Polk's staff confronted Lee two weeks after the battle, whereupon Lee denied making "any such report to General Bragg." This denial was a further lie, since Bragg's certainty in identifying Lee as the source of the tale is unambiguous and consistent. Recriminations would come later, however. With Lee gone, Polk and his staff rode to the front.[5]

In the meantime, Captain Wheless had done what seemed impossible just the night before: he located D. H. Hill. Wheless was a Tennessean, orphaned at age six, who had followed his older brother into the banking business in the 1850s. In 1861, he joined the 1st Tennessee infantry and saw action at Shiloh and Perryville. Wounded and captured in the latter battle, he was exchanged and offered a staff assignment with General Polk. He proved to be an excellent officer, and one about to become embroiled in the quarrels of the army's senior leadership.[6]

4 *OR* 30, pt. 2, 58; Janet B. Hewitt, Noah Andre Trudeau, and Bryce A. Suderow, eds. *Supplement to the Official Records of the Union and Confederate Armies*, 100 vols. (Broadfoot Publishing Co., 1995), vol. 5, 672. Hereafter *OR Supplement.*

5 William M. Polk, "General Polk at Chickamauga," *Battles and Leaders of the Civil War*, 4 vols. (Thomas Yoseloff, Inc., 1956), vol. 3, 663. William Polk dismissed Lee's version as "absurd." Polk, *Bishop and General*, vol. II, 266n.

6 W. W. Clayton, *History of Davidson County, Tennessee* (J. W. Lewis & Company, 1880), 434.

After leaving Polk, Wheless crossed the creek and found himself wrapped in a fog so thick he lost his bearings. The glimmer of the rising sun oriented him, however, and within minutes he reached Maj. Gen. Benjamin F. Cheatham and delivered the first part of Polk's instructions. From there, Wheless followed the battle line north until he stumbled upon Col. Archer Anderson and Lt. Cabell Breckinridge, another son serving on his father's staff. Anderson informed Wheless that Hill, Cleburne and the senior Breckinridge were all just a couple of hundred yards distant. Taking no chances, Wheless asked the two men to guide him. "The time consumed in reaching them," Wheless remembered, "was . . . not more than ten minutes—certainly did not exceed fifteen."[7]

"I have orders from General Polk," announced Wheless as he dismounted. Hill reached out to receive them. "These orders are for Generals Breckinridge and Cleburne," said the captain, who handed them to the division commanders. By way of explanation, and likely to stave off any nascent anger on Hill's part, Wheless outlined the fruitless efforts to locate Hill the night before.[8]

The orders perplexed Cleburne and astounded Breckinridge, who barely two hours earlier, shortly before 4:00 a.m., had departed Polk's camp. Polk had sent Breckinridge off with a cryptic statement, "a wish that the attack should be made as soon as possible . . . and a fear that the enemy would attack us." Nothing Polk said, however, indicated the former vice president's troops would be spearheading that assault.[9]

At dawn, Breckinridge's brigades were still clogging the road as they moved up from Alexander's Bridge. As a result, D. H. Hill's supply wagons had trouble coming forward through that press of troops. Now, Hill's infantry were just getting their rations, and some of these troops had not eaten in a full day. At least one of Breckinridge's regiments, the 1st/3rd Florida, was even farther to the rear. Colonel W. S. Dilworth's Floridians had been left to guard Glass Mill until John Wharton's cavalrymen appeared to replace them, which had not happened, reported Dilworth, "until 9:00 p.m." on the 19th. Thereafter, Dilworth's guide lost his way in the dark (an affliction common to Confederates that night), forcing the Floridians to march until dawn in an effort to find the division. At first light they were still unaccounted for, and the now-frustrated

7 *OR Supplement*, vol. 5, 674.

8 Ibid.

9 Breckinridge to Hill, October 16, 1863, Hill Papers, NCDAH.

brigade commander Marcellus A. Stovall had no idea where they might be. Since those 300 Floridians represented about one-third of Stovall's overall combat power, going into action without them was a less-than-pleasing prospect.[10]

The ground Breckinridge's men passed over offered a host of grisly sights, even for veteran troops. John Jackman of the Orphan Brigade, detailed to the brigade ambulance corps, left a vivid description. "The dead of both sides were lying thick. . . . I saw where six Federal soldiers had been killed from behind one small tree, and where eight horses were lying dead, harnessed to a Napoleon gun. Men and horses were lying so thick over the field, one could hardly walk for them. I even saw a large black dog lying mangled by a grape[shot]." Lieutenant Benjamin S. Williams, adjutant of the 47th Georgia, might have stumbled onto the same ghastly scene: "Lying dead very near each other in one place, I noticed six large gray horses, and close around were many dead blue artillerymen." The carnage indicated an intense fight, and seemed to confirm the warning passed on to Williams earlier by a wounded Rebel officer, who "gave me very discouraging news . . . 'You can't break their lines; they dispute and fight over every inch of ground and don't mind the bayonet; you'll catch h__l when you strike them tomorrow.'" Even the most enthusiastic troops might lose some of their ardor when confronting such stark reminders of their potential fate.[11]

In addition to Breckinridge being out of position, Hill had objections with Cleburne's current deployment. He and Cleburne had spent the predawn hour inspecting Cleburne's lines. As they passed by, Brig. Gen. James Deshler called for Cleburne's attention. Deshler's position on Cleburne's left was supposed to connect to Cheatham's right. However, Preston Smith's brigade of Cheatham's division (bereft of Smith, killed the night before) was formed at an almost perpendicular angle to Deshler's front. Things would have to be sorted out before anyone could advance. The next worry was about reserves. Hill intended to attack on a broad front, with all six brigades abreast, and felt he needed support. Moreover, Cleburne piped up, he and his men heard the Yankees

10 Connelly, *Autumn of Glory*, 218; *OR* 30, pt. 2, 233.

11 Davis, *Diary*, 87; William A. Bowers, Jr., *The 47th Georgia Volunteer Infantry Regiment* (Global Author Press, 2013), 20. The dead gunners, the abandoned Napoleon and the dead horses likely belonged to either Van Pelt's Battery A, 1st Michigan Light Artillery, or Flansburg's 4th Indiana Artillery.

"felling trees on his front all night," fortifying their position. For all these reasons, it would be at least an hour before Hill could strike.[12]

With increasing agitation Wheless waited about 10 minutes while Hill drafted all this into a note. While writing, Hill peevishly protested the lack of a courier at Alexander's Bridge as promised the night before. Captain Wheless defended his boss as best he could, stating that he knew for a fact that couriers had been posted, and remained until late in the night, but Wheless was forced to confess that he did not know when those guides were withdrawn. Once Hill's note was finished, Wheless headed back toward Polk's camp. Within a few minutes he met Captain Minnick bearing the duplicate orders, and diverted that officer to go tell Cheatham of the delay. Wheless discovered Polk and his party trotting toward him at the intersection of the Jay's Mill and Alexander's Bridge roads. The time was between 6:30 and 7:00 a.m.

Wheless dutifully explained his discussion with Hill, doing little to hide his irritation with the North Carolinian. "General," he burst out, "you notice General Hill says it will be an hour or so before he is ready to make the attack. I am confident that it will be more than two hours before he is ready." This statement was recorded in an official declaration Wheless drafted just 10 days after the battle. Polk "asked, with surprise, why I thought so. I answered, 'General Hill seems to me perfectly indifferent.' General Polk responded quickly and with decision. 'Well, Sir. Well Sir. I must go and see to this myself.'" After Polk dictated a quick note to Bragg outlining Hill's reasons for delay, the bishop ordered Wheless to stay put, establishing Right Wing headquarters on the spot, and rode off to find Hill.[13]

Not 15 minutes later, Bragg rode up and demanded Polk's whereabouts. Wheless explained all that had passed, outlining the previous night's confusion. He also emphasized Hill's delays, eager to deflect Bragg's obvious anger away from Polk and toward Hill. Bragg wasn't swayed. When Wheless repeated his story of the two-hour delay to the army commander, Bragg sarcastically inquired "how [Wheless] expected General Hill to make the attack before he received orders to do so." Flustered, Wheless only made things worse by

12 Cleburne to Hill, September 30, 1863, Hill Papers, NCDAH. In his note to Polk, Hill identified the offending brigade as Jackson's, not Smith's. *OR* 30, pt. 2, 61.

13 *OR* 30, pt. 2, 61. *OR Supplement*, vol. 5, 675. Wheless was even less circumspect when writing in 1867 to William Gale, another Polk family member and staffer. "Allow me to suggest that unless you go and in person give General Hill positive orders to make the attack," the frustrated captain vented in ink, "he will not begin it in *three hours*." *OR Supplement*, vol. 5, 675.

pointing out that when he (Wheless) left Bragg the night before he was under the impression that Bragg was going to issue orders to Hill in person, outlining the plans for the 20th. Polk's orders, averred the captain, were only confirming instructions that were supposed to have been already given "so that there could not possibly be any mistake." Wheless's not-quite-so-subtle effort to shift blame away from the bishop and this time onto Bragg himself only deepened the army commander's anger toward Polk and, by extension, Wheless. Sensing his blunder, Polk's staff officer quickly changed tack, steering matters back to the subject of Hill's recalcitrance. He stumbled again, however, when he added in the detail of Cleburne's remark about the Federals felling trees. "Well sir, is this not another important reason why the attack should be made at once?" snapped the incensed commander. Wheless agreed but added "it did not seem to impress General Hill in that way." Without another word Bragg rode on to find Polk and/or Hill, leaving the discomfited Wheless in his wake. By 7:30 a.m., the Confederate right was buzzing with angry generals, each surrounded by a sub-swarm of agitated staff officers. Despite the hive of activity and authority no attack was forthcoming.[14]

While Wheless quailed in the face of Bragg's withering sarcasm, Polk found D. H. Hill at Cleburne's headquarters among the wreckage of Battery A, 1st Michigan Light Artillery. For the first time on the field these two men, both critical to the proper execution of Bragg's plan, conferred face to face. Their meeting was brief. Accounts of what passed between them differ, based generally on the partisanship of who is telling the story. Cleburne's chief of artillery, Capt. Henry Semple, remembered Polk's arrival that fateful morning, noting the time as 7:25 a.m. Bypassing Hill, Polk turned directly to Cleburne to demand "why he did not advance" as previously instructed? Cleburne replied that "he was ordered by General Hill to issue the rations first." To that, "General Polk seemed to acquiesce." Hill concurred with Semple. Private Y. R. LeMonnier remembered the exchange differently: "'Sir,' said General Polk, 'this is not the time for eating; this is the time for fighting. Attack immediately; attack immediately.'" Then the bishop supposedly galloped off to issue similar orders on down the line.[15]

14 *OR* 30, pt. 2, 62. Bragg apparently harbored no lingering resentment against Wheless for this exchange and later offered him a position on his own staff.

15 See William Glenn Robertson, "The Chickamauga Campaign: The Battle of Chickamauga: Day 2, September 20, 1863," *Blue & Gray Magazine*, vol. XXV, no. 2 (Summer, 2008), 7, for the

LeMonnier's recollection was set to paper many years after the fact, and its accuracy is open to serious question. If General Polk did in fact ride the line ordering an immediate attack, it had no effect because no one attacked. Polk did ride away, and he did so certainly unhappy, but he also understood that a delay was inevitable. He would spend the intervening time inspecting the rest of his command.

Thirty minutes later, Bragg appeared and demanded to know why the dawn attack had not come off as planned. In a bizarre display, Hill feigned surprise. "I told [Bragg] that I was hearing then for the first time that such an order had been issued." How could that be? Hill was lying directly to Bragg's face. About two hours earlier, Wheless explained to Hill exactly why Polk's 5:30 a.m. orders were issued, and why they bypassed the corps commander. Not only did Wheless inform Hill of the original plan, but also that the new orders specified an attack as soon as possible. Issued and sent before sunrise, these follow-up instructions amounted to a reiteration of the original dawn attack order. Bragg's anger, however, was still focused on Polk. The frustrated army commander blurted out the Pollock Lee version of Polk's morning activities (breakfast, porch, and newspaper again) to Hill, who made no reply. Bragg rode on in search of Polk.[16]

Even if Hill had received his orders in a timely fashion the night before, launching a dawn attack would have been nearly impossible. No reconnaissance had been done the evening before, nor could one be done in the dead of night. Not only were Hill's men out of place, but so too were the rest of Polk's troops tasked to support them. W. H. T. Walker's Reserve Corps, (expected to act as an actual reserve for a change) had been badly battered on Saturday and spent the night resting and reorganizing. When day broke Walker's men were nowhere close to being ready to renew the fight. A great deal of work remained to be done before the Right Wing could launch a major assault. That work now began in earnest, while Cleburne's and Breckinridge's regiments wolfed down their breakfasts.

---

location of this meeting. H. C. Semple to Hill, October 13, 1863, Hill Papers, NCDAH; LeMonnier, "Gen Leonidas Polk at Chickamauga," 17. However, LeMonnier was a member of the cavalry escort company, which had been left with Wheless, and it is possible he wasn't even present at the meeting. William Polk, in his biography of his father, mentions this meeting only in passing and provides no details.

16 Daniel H. Hill, "Chickamauga: The Great Battle of the West," in *Battles and Leaders of the Civil War*, 4 vols. (Thomas Yoseloff, Inc., 1956), vol. 3, 653.

The first thing D. H. Hill did was send word to Nathan Bedford Forrest asking for support on his right. Unlike virtually anyone else in the Army of Tennessee that morning, Forrest's troopers were already in position for their expected mission. Brigadier General Frank Armstrong's two brigades were arrayed in a dismounted line several hundred yards east of and facing the La Fayette Road, a broad front stretching from the Reed's Bridge Road north as far as Cloud Church. Brigadier General John Pegram's division was again split, with Col. John S. Scott's brigade guarding the crossing at Red House Bridge, while Brig. Gen. Henry B. Davidson's brigade took up a reserve position east of Jay's Mill. At dawn, while the infantry generals were squabbling, Forrest sent Col. Daniel W. Holman and his 11th Tennessee Cavalry forward on a probe. Holman crossed the La Fayette Road near the McDonald house and moved as far west as the woods 600 yards beyond. All he discovered were a few disheartened stragglers "who had thrown away their guns." Holman's patrol might have yielded bigger booty, since the combined Rosecrans-Thomas party rode out as far as the McDonald house at 6:30 a.m., but the Tennesseans probably cleared the area at least 30 minutes before the Federal entourage appeared. Reporting back about 8:00 a.m., Holman outlined the exposed nature of the Federal flank and the demoralized condition of the Yankees.[17]

One-half hour later, Maj. Alphonso C. Avery of D. H. Hill's staff arrived with Hill's request for closer cooperation on the infantry's right flank. During the night, a gap opened between Forrest's left and Cleburne's northernmost brigade. Now, as Breckinridge's men started to fill that gap, Hill desired a tighter connection with Breckinridge's flank. Forrest agreed and passed Holman's findings back to Hill, including the critical detail that the Union line did not extend as far north as the McDonald homestead.[18]

Bragg and Polk, meanwhile, were scrambling to untangle the bulk of the right wing, though without much impact. Four of Frank Cheatham's five brigades were in line facing generally northwest; only Brig. Gen. John K. Jackson's brigade was in support. Despite the previous day's losses, Cheatham's command still numbered about 5,500 men holding a frontage nearly three-quarters of a mile wide. As noted, his right angled into and in front of

17 John B. Lindsley, *Military Annals of Tennessee. Confederate. First Series: Embracing a Review of Military Operations, with Regimental Histories and Memorial Rolls*, 2 vols. (Broadfoot Publishing Company, 1995), vol. II, 693.

18 A. C. Avery Statement, November 3, 1863, Hill Papers, NCDAH.

Hill's left. Polk and Cheatham met just before 8:00 a.m. near Turner's Mississippi Battery on a wooded rise 300 yards south of the Winfrey farmyard. Cheatham placed this meeting "around sunrise," which was much too early because he also noted they met only after Polk had visited Hill. The bishop seemed oblivious to Hill's concern regarding the overlap with Cheatham, for he made no changes to Cheatham's deployment.[19]

Bragg was in the area and may have also visited Cheatham, though none of the involved parties specifically mentioned such an encounter. He did finally meet briefly with Polk, likely an icy confrontation, but the damage was done and there was little left to say. The commanding general reiterated his attack orders to Polk, but now everyone had to wait on Hill.[20]

Polk did use this time to redeploy Walker's Reserve Corps. Originally, General Walker expected to take up a position behind Cheatham, and arrayed his line of battle with an eye toward that mission. Also containing five brigades, Walker's command was organizationally about the same size as Cheatham's, but after the previous day's damage Walker's "corps" numbered only about 4,000 rifles. Fortunately, Walker was expecting reinforcements momentarily.

States Rights Gist was a native South Carolinian and a Harvard-trained attorney. The 32-year-old brigadier general and one-half of his infantry command had detrained south of the battlefield at Ringgold on September 19, but only after making an extraordinary effort to reach the field. Originally stationed at Rome, Georgia, it was only on September 17 that Gist's 1,800 men were summoned to the front. Too few rail cars and delays caused by the unceasing flow of Longstreet's men also heading north meant that by the evening of the 18th, Gist and his men found themselves stranded in Kingston, Georgia, with only part of the brigade on hand and an exhausted railroad engineer unwilling to proceed farther.

This was simply intolerable. As his given name suggested, Gist hailed from a family of powerful Fire Eaters. His father Nathaniel was a wealthy planter and devotee of firebrand John C. Calhoun, South Carolina's most influential politician. One uncle had been a U.S. congressman, his brother Joseph was a state senator, and his cousin William Henry Gist was the governor who led South Carolina into secession in 1860. In addition to his law career, young

19 *OR* 30, pt. 2, 79.

20 Robertson, "Chickamauga: Day 2," 7.

States Gist had been elected a brigadier general in the state militia at the tender age of 24.[21]

Gist saw action at First Manassas in July 1861, where he acted with conspicuous bravery. Since then, as adjutant general of South Carolina, his main role had been administrative. Gist chafed at the lack of action and in 1862 secured command of an infantry brigade. Even then Gist remained in South Carolina, helping defend Charleston far from the fighting fronts of war-ravaged Virginia or Tennessee. It was not until the spring of 1863, when the Richmond government insisted troops be sent from South Carolina to reinforce Gen. Joseph Johnston in Mississippi, that Gist saw his chance. Department commander Gen. P. G. T. Beauregard had already promised another brigadier the coveted mission, but Gist pulled rank: he was the senior officer, and should be the one sent. Beauregard acquiesced. Action and glory proved frustratingly elusive. Gist's force reached Johnston's army in a piecemeal fashion, and half of his brigade was engaged at Jackson on May 14 under the temporary command of a senior colonel; Gist missed the fight entirely.[22]

The frustrated South Carolinian spent the rest of that summer with Johnston, but Vicksburg's surrender once again relegated him to garrison duty in a backwater theater. When the Army of Tennessee was assailed, troops were rushed to reinforce Bragg. Gist and his brigade, now serving under Walker, were among them. At the last minute the brigade was diverted to Rome, and the war seemed about to pass by yet again. Hope flared anew with the summons of September 17, and nearly flickered out at Kingston because of a recalcitrant railroad engineer. The thought of missing another impending battle was too much to bear. Colonel Clement H. Stevens of the 24th South Carolina took matters into his own hands by pulling a pistol on the stubborn railroad man. Stevens insisted he could find a crew, and told the engineer he must take them up to Ringgold or the hot-blooded colonel "would kill him" on the spot. The threat proved marvelously effective.[23]

By the afternoon of the 19th, Gist and 980 of his men in the 24th South Carolina, 8th Georgia Battalion, and three companies of the 46th Georgia detrained at Catoosa Station. The rest of the 46th and the entire 16th South

21 Walter Brian Cisco, *States Rights Gist: A South Carolina General of the Civil War* (White Mane Publishing, 1991), 38.

22 Ibid., 88-93.

23 Ibid., 100.

Carolina, another 800 men, would not arrive until much later and would follow when they could. Gist escorted an ammunition train to the battlefield, reaching Alexander's Bridge about sunrise guided by a Dr. Evans whom Gist had located in Ringgold. It was in Ringgold that Gist was told he would again be assigned to Walker, and further, as senior brigadier the ardent South Carolinian would be assuming command of Walker's former division—a limited honor considering the division consisted of Col. Claudius Wilson's and Brig. Gen. Matt Ector's now-battered brigades, each of which was now reduced to about 500 rifles. Gist spent much of the morning working his way through the heavy rear area traffic an army produces (including Cleburne's and Breckinridge's ration wagons), but at last he was moving to join his new command.[24]

In the meantime, someone—presumably Polk—redirected Walker to support D. H. Hill in answer to that officer's earlier concerns. "Between about 9 and 10," wrote Walker, "I was ordered, instead of supporting Cheatham, to support Hill's corps . . . [and] to form my reserve so as to *echelon* Breckinridge, who was on the right." This movement also took considerable time. Before it was completed, Hill attacked.[25]

* * *

While the Rebel brass squabbled, the Federals fortified. George Thomas fretted about his left flank, periodically firing off couriers to badger Negley, Rosecrans, or anyone else who might listen about that vulnerability. Brigadier General John Beatty's brigade, part of Negley's division, was the first fruit of those efforts.

Beatty was far from being a professional soldier. The Ohio banker was vehemently anti-slavery and a staunch Union man. By September 1863, he had been a soldier for 29 months and a general for 10. In April 1863, his brigade was transferred to Negley's division. Under Thomas and Negley, Beatty experienced the brilliant Tullahoma operation and the stealth crossing of the Tennessee River to open the current campaign. His quiet confidence marked him as a solid brigade commander, but no more of a standout than any of a couple dozen of his peers. His candid observations of military life and his

24 Robert Sparks Walker, "The Pyramids of Chickamauga: Peyton H. Colquitt," *Chattanooga Sunday Times*, October 4, 1936; *OR* 30, pt. 2, 245.

25 Ibid., 241.

John Beatty's original position was at the south end of McDonald Field, astride the La Fayette Road, facing north (towards the viewer). The cannon visible at the edge of the tree line marks the position of Bridges Illinois Battery. *Harvey Scarborough*

sometimes self-deprecating observations of his own foibles and those of his fellow officers were all recorded in his diary (later published as an invaluable gift to historians). That Sunday morning his day was already shaping up to be a bad one.

Beatty reached Thomas's location about 8:00 a.m., and was immediately dispatched onward to support Absalom Baird on the left. He initially deployed his brigade astride the La Fayette Road facing north toward the McDonald house. Beatty's 1,121 men and the fieldpieces of Bridges's Illinois battery were set up in the standard Federal deployment of a double infantry line with the guns in the middle. His right-most regiment, the 15th Kentucky, did not quite tie in with Col. Joseph Dodge's small brigade, still positioned alongside the Regulars. This gap between Dodge's left and Beatty's right measured about 150 yards, the length of a small brigade or a large regiment, and was further bisected by a shallow wet-weather drainage running toward an open field east of the McDonald farm. While this deployment did not satisfy Thomas's desire to cover the ground all the way to the Reed's Bridge Road, it did go a long way to securing Baird's exposed flank. Beatty thought his new position a strong one. Thomas felt otherwise. Very soon, Thomas's chief topographical engineer, Capt. W. B. Gaw, galloped up with an order instructing Beatty to move his brigade forward as far as the McDonald farm and face east, as originally intended. This was far too much space for Beatty's men to effectively cover, and Beatty protested. Gaw insisted the order "was imperative."[26]

Of course, Thomas expected the rest of Negley's division to arrive momentarily, but this was of little comfort to Beatty. In order to cover the expected distance, Beatty redeployed his four regiments into a long single line, with the 88th Indiana on the far left, and the 42nd Indiana and 104th Illinois extending the line to the brigade right, held by the 15th Kentucky. Once this was done, he swung his regiments, gate-like, to the northeast. As he moved, the distance between his two center regiments, the 42nd Indiana and 104th Illinois, widened to 250 yards. Half of Bridges's battery was left near the first line in a position where his guns could sweep the open expanse of the field in support of the infantry. The other half was posted on the rise alongside the McDonald house. Recognizing that he could do little to stem a real attack if it came, Beatty tried a bit of bluff by sending forward a reinforced skirmish line of two companies per regiment in order to fool the Rebels into thinking Beatty's line included an entire division. The brigade left managed to get into position without much opposition, but as the 104th advanced, its skirmishers ran into significant resistance and Beatty ordered three more companies of Illinoisans out to reinforce them. The 15th Kentucky, holding the right, ran into Rebels "almost immediately."[27]

By now it was a little after 9:00 a.m. Cleburne was aligned, and Breckinridge's three brigades were coming into position on the Arkansan's right. They deployed their own skirmishers, who promptly collided with Beatty's screen. On the Confederate left, Brig. Gen. Ben Helm's Kentucky Orphan Brigade faced a portion of Baird's line, and stiff opposition. A company from each of Helm's five regiments went forward, all under command of Lt. Col. John C. Wickliffe of the Confederate 9th Kentucky. "[We] soon developed the lines of the enemy, strongly posted and with works . . . of fallen timber and rocks," he reported. Things looked more promising farther north, though Beatty's reinforced line of blue-clad skirmishers put up a sizable scrap. On Breckinridge's right flank, Brig. Gen. Daniel Adams's mixed Louisiana and Alabama brigade included Maj. J. E. Austin's 14th Louisiana Battalion of

26 *OR* 30, pt. 1, 368.

27 Entry for September 20, Douglas Hapeman Diary, ALPL; William Wirt Calkins, *The History of the One Hundred and Fourth Regiment of Illinois Volunteer Infantry. War of the Great Rebellion 1862-1865.* (Donohue and Hennenberry, 1895), 135-136; *OR* 30, pt. 1, 368.

sharpshooters, two companies of picked men trained in light infantry fighting. Reinforced by an additional four companies drawn from the rest of the brigade, Austin pushed forward against Hoosiers from the 42nd and 88th regiments. "After moving about 700 yards," noted Austin, "I gained a position overlooking . . . the main Chattanooga [La Fayette] Road, along which the enemy's couriers, wagons and ambulances were thronging." The Louisianans opened fire, clearing the road for a time before Beatty's Hoosiers rallied, were reinforced in turn, and drove Austin back. In response, Adams sent forward the 145 men of the 32nd Alabama to bolster Austin's force.[28]

Hill, Forrest, and Breckinridge followed closely behind Austin's engagement and soon discovered Beatty's deception. The Union flank, observed Hill, "was covered for a great distance [only] by infantry skirmishers." Whatever else had gone wrong with Rebel planning that morning, nearly all of Breckinridge's division now overlapped the Federal left, just as Bragg originally intended.[29]

John C. Breckinridge's command numbered 3,785 men and 15 cannon. While it was among the smallest divisions in Bragg's army, it was a seasoned and well-led organization whose trio of brigadiers included Benjamin Hardin Helm, Marcellus A. Stovall, and Daniel W. Adams. Helm was the most prominent, a fellow Kentuckian and brother-in-law to Abraham Lincoln. He married Emily Todd, half-sister to Mary, and thus could claim a personal relationship with the man who was now chief executive of the United States. The balding 32-year-old was a member of the West Point class of 1851, and spent a year in the cavalry before resigning to pursue law and politics. Despite Lincoln's offer of a Federal commission, Helm's loyalties lay elsewhere. He rose to command the Orphan Brigade after fellow Kentuckian Robert W. Hanson was killed at Stones River on January 2, 1863. Despite his sometimes stern efforts to enforce discipline among the oft-rowdy Kentuckians, Helm was a popular replacement and much admired by his men. With nearly 1,400 in the ranks, Helm's command of five regiments (the 2nd, 4th, 6th and 9th Kentucky, as well as the 41st Alabama) was the largest in Breckinridge's division.[30]

28 *OR* 30, pt. 2, 141, 213, 220, 227. Reports from Breckinridge's division state the brigades were deployed anywhere between 5:30 and 9:00 a.m.

29 Ibid., 141.

30 This appointment came at the expense of the ambitions of Col. Marcus J. Wright, who ended up commanding a brigade in Cheatham's division. See David A. Powell, *The Chickamauga*

Stovall was from Augusta, Georgia. He enlisted in a volunteer company for service during the Seminole War of 1835, and pursued a military life. In 1836 he matriculated at West Point but was, according to one obituary, "compelled to return to the South on account of rheumatism contracted in the uncongenial latitude of a Northern clime." He remained interested in the life of the citizen-soldier, however, serving in various militia roles through the 1840s and 1850s. Much of the current campaign had unfolded over geography he found familiar, for in 1861 Stovall was a merchant and farmer with property near Rome. Upon secession he joined the war effort, initially as a colonel in the Georgia artillery. He saw service in East Tennessee and invaded Kentucky as part of Kirby Smith's column in the fall of 1862, but he and his men did not see action at Perryville. Stovall won considerable praise at Stones River, and on January 20, 1863, was promoted to brigadier general for his service in that battle. His brigade numbered only 897 men, and would have counted fewer than 600 if Colonel Dilworth's Floridians had not caught up in time. It was the smallest of the three in Breckinridge's division.[31]

Most of the 1,221 men in Breckinridge's final brigade under Daniel W. Adams were Louisianans, though Adams had been born in Kentucky. He practiced law and politics in Mississippi before moving to New Orleans in the 1850s. Politics was a full contact sport in the antebellum Magnolia State, and disputes were often settled by gunplay. In 1843, Vicksburg newspaperman James Hagan alleged in print that Adams's father, a federal judge, was taking bribes. Intent on defending his family's honor, the younger Adams confronted Hagan. The two grappled, during which Adams fatally shot Hagan. Acquitted in the ensuing trial, Adams went on to be elected to the Mississippi State legislature. Upon secession, Governor Thomas Moore appointed Adams to a three-man board commissioned to prepare Louisiana for war. From there Adams secured an appointment to lieutenant colonel of the 1st Louisiana Regulars, rising to command that regiment by the spring of 1862. His penchant for front-line leadership cost him the sight of his left eye at Shiloh, but won him a brigadier's braid. Adams took a second wound at Stones River, a shell fragment that tore into his left arm. "Old Pelican" (as the men took to calling

---

Campaign: A Mad Irregular Battle: From the Crossing of the Tennessee River Through the Second Day, August 22–September 19, 1863 (Savas Beatie, 2014), 374-376, for more detail on Wright's travails.

31 Marcellus Stovall, http://www.aug.edu/~liblsc/Grant/Stovall/Stovall_description.html, accessed 9/1/2011.

John C. Breckinridge (right), a former vice-president of the United States, led the Confederate attack on Sunday morning.
Library of Congress

him) returned to command in May 1863 while the brigade was in Mississippi, and returned to Bragg's army with his command that fall. Adams was an experienced veteran, toughened by war, with a good eye for the tactical advantage.[32]

By 9:30 a.m., Breckinridge's deployment was complete. "Gens. (D. H.) Hill, Breckenridge and Adams rode along the lines," recalled Lt. E. John Ellis of the 16th Louisiana, "but the troops were forbidden to cheer. Hill was not a remarkable man. . . . [H]e stooped in the saddle and there was an air of general negligence about his whole bearing. He appeared, however, entirely at his ease. Breckenridge looked all himself and glanced with evident pride along the ranks. . . . His broad, open brow bore no traces of care, his large eyes were full of light and confidence and a bland smile rested upon his face [which] slightly raised his inimitable mustache." Ellis was particularly impressed with the division commander's grooming, marveling that "Breckenridge had the finest mustache in the army." With Hill's assent and with skirmish fire still popping all along the line, Breckinridge ordered all three brigades into motion. Four hours late, Bragg's long-awaited attack was finally underway.[33]

Adams's Louisianans, comprising the right flank of Bragg's entire army, stepped off first. His main line consisted of five Louisiana regiments, converged by depleted numbers into three tactical entities. From north to south they included the 13th/20th, 16th/25th, and 19th. As the Pelicans moved through

32 M. Jane Johansson, "Brig. Gen. Daniel Weisiger Adams," in Bruce S. Allardice and Lawrence Lee Hewitt, eds., *Kentuckians in Gray, Confederate Generals and Field Officers of the Bluegrass State* (University Press of Kentucky, 2008), 10.

33 E. J. Ellis Diary, Louisiana State University, Baton Rouge, LA. Hereafter LSU.

the open cedar glade, Lt. John McGrath of the 13th glimpsed a look down the length of the brigade line. "It was a grand & exciting scene to witness the brigade moving through the open fields with a steady tramp, and with banners flying and aides-de-camp dashing along the lines," recorded the officer. As they swept forward Maj. John Kimball's 32nd Alabama, deployed forward earlier as reinforcements for Austin's men, fell in on the right, ordered by Adams to keep a careful eye on that flank. Complying, Kimball led the 32nd westward in column along the Reed's Bridge Road. Austin's skirmishers surged forward, still leading the brigade.[34]

Adams's attack first struck Beatty's 42nd Indiana skirmishers and achieved an early victory. Nearly all the Hoosier skirmishers were captured within minutes. The result was that when the blow fell against the main body of the 42nd, it came as almost a complete surprise and the regiment essentially collapsed. Lieutenant McGrath noted that the 13th Louisiana "advanced somewhat faster than the other regiments, [and] soon came to a skirt of woods in which were posted a body of yankees who as we approached gave a cheer and delivered a volley, which we answered with a shower of buck and ball that sent them flying with terror." Sixty Hoosiers were captured here and the few survivors fell back to the remainder of the regiment. An Indiana private named Rueben P. McCutcheon of Company A fell at the outset, shot in both hips, and now watched in mingled shame and horror as the gray tide of battle washed over him. "I remember that on that Sunday morning—September 20, 1863, I felt very little honor for any of the men. Why they ran away without any orders, and in such a hurry, and I asked myself, where were our officers, great and small?"

Desperate to escape capture, when Sgt. George Kirkpatrick stumbled across McCutcheon, the private pleaded that he could walk if only Kirkpatrick could cut his belt away. "I got down on my knees," recalled Kirkpatrick, "and I threw myself back to get my knife . . . just as I did that, a bullet cut me in both arms." The well-intentioned sergeant's blood splattered the prostrate private. "[H]e [McCutcheon] told me to go, [as] he was done for anyway, and it was better for one to die than two," continued Kirkpatrick.[35]

34 "September 24th, 1863," John McGrath Papers, LSU; *OR*, 30, pt. 2, 220.

35 Francis Carlisle Reminiscences, 42nd Indiana file, CCNMP; McGrath letter, LSU; George Morgan Kirkpatrick, *The Experiences of a Private Soldier of the Civil War* (Hoosier Bookshop, 1973), 30, 60.

The Louisianans now faced the remainder of the 42nd and their fellow 88th Indiana, whose combined line had come to rest northeast of the McDonald house, angled in that direction as if to refuse the brigade flank. Perhaps they sought to keep an eye on the Rebel cavalry operating to their north, though neither commander ever explained how their positioning came to be. This deployment, however, meant the 42nd Indiana's right flank was thrust out toward Adams's approaching line, vulnerable to a raking fire.

As he caught sight of the enemy's main line, Col. Randall Lee Gibson, leading the 13th/20th Louisiana saw his moment and ordered a charge. "We fell on him with such impetuosity that he broke in confusion," Gibson exulted, "the men throwing away their arms." The 42nd was overmatched. Once its skirmishers were disposed of, barely 200 Hoosiers were left in the main battle line. Gibson and Austin's sharpshooters combined brought 400 men against them, while other Rebel regiments were maneuvering to threaten their flanks.[36]

How long this fight lasted is open to debate. Hoosier Francis Carlisle noted the 42nd lost another 50 men here, cut down by fire, in as many minutes. Colonel Gibson did not provide a time estimate, but the fight was largely over before the rest of the Louisiana brigade caught up. When the wounded Sergeant Kirkpatrick ran by (he had fallen behind the Rebel advance, but avoided capture), he "passed by [the] regiment behind a barn and a pile of knapsacks about four hundred yards in the rear," already routed once and attempting to reform, but it was fruitless. Another survivor of the 42nd, Pvt. William R. Stuckey, bleakly offered up a stark assessment to his wife five days later: "They whomped the shit out of us."[37]

A captain with the 42nd Indiana, William M. Cockrum commanding Company F, was badly wounded here. His experience was much like McCutcheon's. Shot though the hip as the regiment crumbled around him, Cockrum later remembered how "I heard for the first time during my service the long, loud shout of victory by the rebels, and realized that I was doomed to remain a prisoner with a good prospect of bleeding to death."[38]

36 *OR* 30, pt. 2, 221.

37 Francis Carlisle Reminiscences, CCNMP; Kirkpatrick, *Experiences*, 31; "Dear & Darling Wife," Sept. 25, 1863, William R. Stuckey Letters, InHS.

38 William M. Cockrum Reminiscences, from *Oakland City Indiana Journal*, Sept. 10, 1894, http://freepages.history.rootsweb.ancestry.com/~indiana42nd/Chickamauga_Cockrum_Article.htm, accessed 9/7/2011. Cockrum was an ardent antislavery man, despite being from

On the rise by the farmhouse, the three guns of Bridges's half-battery were banging away with little obvious success. Austin's Sharpshooters mistook the several abandoned guns lining the La Fayette Road as the source of that fire. Sharpshooter Capt. William Q. Lowd "saw on the road two pieces of artillery, supported by perhaps a small company of infantry." That "company" was the 88th Indiana, and the cannon were pieces that had been dragged there overnight after being recovered from Saturday's fight.

The 88th Indiana's experience was even more chaotic than the 42nd's. The first warning of impending disaster arrived when Daniel Long, a member of the 88th, recalled catching a glimpse of a terrified deer "so badly scared it knew not where to go, running among the troops, first on one side and then on the other" before disappearing from view. The 88th's line was angled similarly to the 42nd's, about 100 yards to the north and a little west. These Hoosiers had no support. The next regiment in Beatty's attenuated line, the 104th Illinois, was 350 yards to the south and overwhelmed with troubles of its own.[39]

After its contribution to the reinforced skirmish line, the 88th numbered no more than 125 muskets—which explains why Austin's Louisianans mistook it for a detached company instead of an entire regiment. Gibson's impetuous rush pushed the 13th/20th Louisiana out past the 88th's southern flank, while at the same time the Hoosiers could see the 32nd Alabama moving up the Reed's Bridge Road, though still out of effective fire range. Even worse, as it collapsed, part of the 42nd ran through the anemic ranks of the 88th, just as Col. George Humphrey attempted to change front to his right in order to face Gibson's assault head-on.[40]

Witnessing the sudden disorder afflicting the 88th, Sharpshooter Captain Lowd and Lt. William Pierce both saw their chance. Rallying from skirmish order, Lowd took his company of the 14th forward in a rush and within minutes

---

southern Indiana, usually considered less hostile to slavery. Cockrum, however, helped organize the underground railroad in his part of the state (near Evansville) and at least once drove off a gang of slave-catchers in a violent confrontation. He survived his wound and returned to service, eventually earning promotion to lieutenant colonel of the 42nd Indiana.

39 Daniel E. Long, with Ken Wollenberg, ed., "My War Recollections From 1862-1865," *Indiana Journal of Military History*, vol. 12, no. 1 (January, 1987), 25.

40 Commissioners, *Indiana at Chickamauga, 1863-1900, Report of Indiana Commissioners, Chickamauga National Military Park* (Sentinel Printing Co., Printers and Binders, 1900), 263. At least some of the men of the 42nd Indiana first tried to retreat south, back the way they came and towards the safety of the XIV Corps position, instead of due west away from the Rebel attack.

"took possession of the guns, Lieutenant Pierce striking one of them with his sword, proclaiming the right of the battalion to have *crossed cannon* on its beloved flag." These guns did not belong to Bridges, who did not lose any pieces here. Instead, they likely belonged to Van Pelt's Battery A, 1st Michigan or Burnham's Battery H, 5th U.S., already captured and recaptured several times the day before. Now they were to be trophies again, and not for the last time.[41]

Overmatched and threatened from multiple directions, the 88th managed a moment of furious fire and then quickly dissolved. Its stand was just long enough to allow Bridges's three guns to limber, depart, and rejoin the other three pieces unlimbered at the southern edge of McDonald Field.[42]

Gibson's charge routed his immediate opposition and cleared Adams's brigade front. It also disrupted the brigade's formation. A courier arrived with orders instructing Gibson to halt and let the command reform. The cost had been relatively light: five killed and about 25 wounded in the 13th/20th, with another seven wounded from Austin's battalion, including Lieutenant Pierce, whose leg was shattered by a Federal bullet moments after celebrating his capture of the cannon. The halt allowed the survivors of both Hoosier regiments to fall back west, eventually reforming in the woods on the far side of McDonald Field one-half mile distant.[43]

Things were going equally poorly for the rest of John Beatty's men. About 9:30 a.m., the 104th Illinois's Lt. Col. Douglas Hapeman sent forward his skirmish line to try and connect with the 42nd Indiana's screen, but the effort was unsuccessful. Then, reported an alarmed Hapeman, "I discovered that the enemy was in large force in my front and on both flanks."[44]

The 104th's 23 officers and 276 men were facing Lt. Col. Richard Turner's 19th Louisiana (349 strong) and all of Stovall's 897 Confederates. From north to south, Stovall's line included the 47th Georgia, 60th North Carolina, 4th Florida, and on the brigade left, Col. Dilworth's combined 1st/3rd Florida.

41 Fannie A. Beers, Memories. *A Record of Personal Experience and Adventure During Four Years of War* (Press of J. B. Lippincott Co., 1891), 102. Federal troops dragged Van Pelt's guns out of the woods to the La Fayette Road the day before, where they were left for later easy retrieval. They were still there on the morning of September 20.

42 The 42nd lost 32% of its strength, including 53 prisoners. The 88th Indiana's losses were 20%, with only 16 missing or captured, suggesting a much more rapid departure.

43 *OR* 30, pt. 2, 221; Beers, *Memories*, 102.

44 *OR* 30, pt. 1, 372.

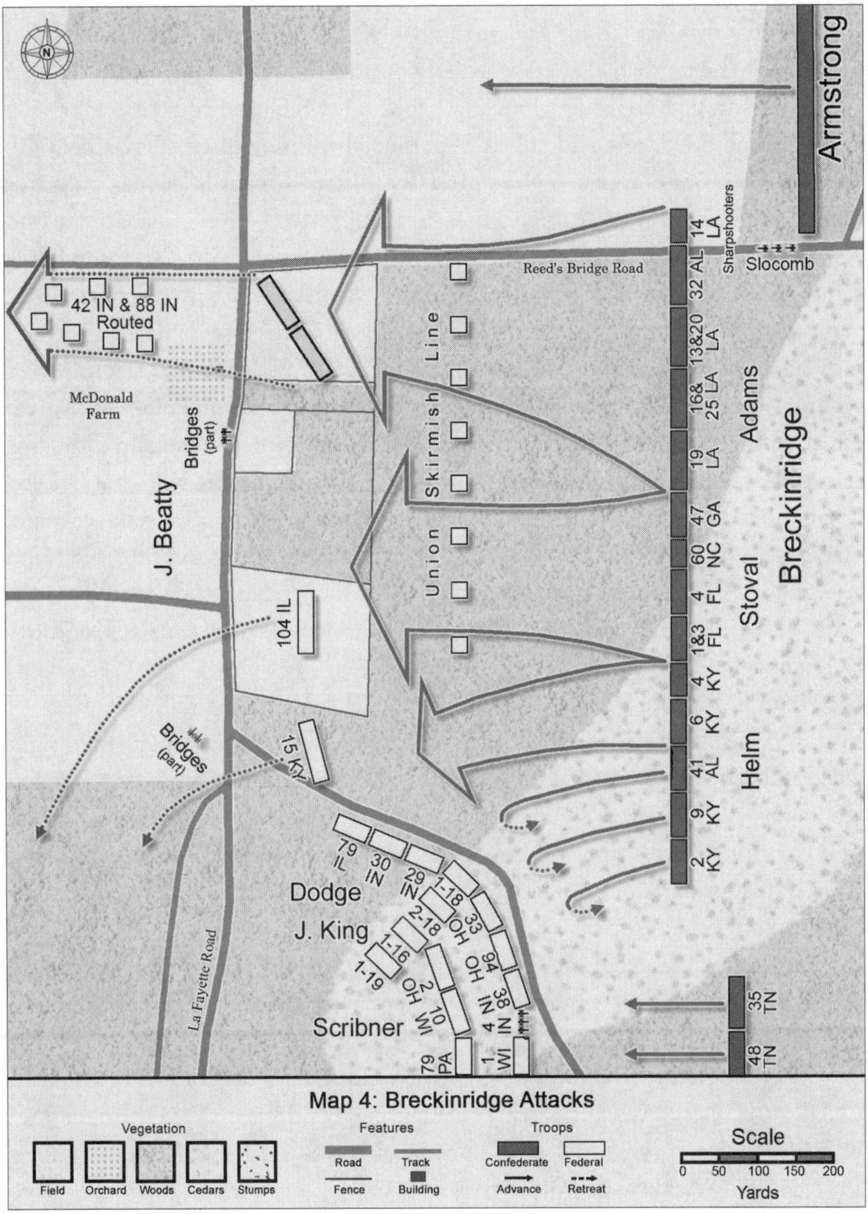

Hapeman's strength was already so dispersed that Stovall recalled only that his men encountered and easily drove "two distinct lines of the enemy's skirmishers."[45]

45 Ibid., pt. 2, 231.

The men of the 104th had no great liking for their circumstances that morning. "The fog had cleared away," recounted the regimental historian, "but clouds of smoke hung over the valley, through which the sun, red, as if with anger, shone down hot and sultry." As the skirmishing intensified, the 104th sent "three more companies, one after the other" forward, leaving only five companies in line. As elsewhere, this first line proved wholly inadequate and was brushed aside with impunity. Many of those men ran back to the supposed safety of the regiment, throwing it into some disorder when they appeared and jammed their way back into the ranks. The Rebels were close behind, in line and moving steadily forward. "At the order of Lt. Col. Hapeman," wrote Sgt. George Marsh in Company D, "we fired a volley into their solid ranks with great effect, but without stopping them in the least. They came on steadily with guns at a 'right shoulder shift' in spite of our fire, with their light wool hats pulled down over their eyes like men facing a storm." One volley was enough. Hapeman ordered his Illinoisans to "immediately fall back to the 15th K[entuck]y." The Union 15th, however, was already locked in a fight of its own, badly outnumbered and contending with two and a half regiments of Kentucky Orphans.[46]

Helm's brigade faced a more difficult task than did the rest of Breckinridge's battle line. While the 4th and 6th Kentucky on Helm's right faced only the Union 15th, Helm's left wing (the 41st Alabama, 9th and 2nd Kentucky) ran into Baird's Federals. Unlike Beatty's hastily sketched suggestion of a position, Baird's line was solid, the men deployed shoulder to shoulder, sheltered by rudimentary breastworks and supported by the guns of the 4th Indiana battery. As Helm advanced into the open cedar glade, the 4th Indiana's cannon opened an accurate enfilade fire along his line. Baird's infantry soon added in their fire, and it quickly became apparent that this part of the Union position would not collapse at the first contact.

When he first received the order to advance, Helm dispatched Lt. William W. Herr to Colonel Wickliffe, still commanding Helm's skirmishers, to instruct Wickliffe to "keep a hundred yards or more ahead of the line of battle . . . as long as he could." Wickliffe promised to do his best, but cautioned that "they were going into as hot a place as they had ever been in, as the Federals were entrenched on the hill." Wickliffe's gloomy assessment was borne out almost

46 Calkins, *One Hundred and Fourth Regiment*, 135; "War Reminiscences," Marsh Family Papers, ALPL; Entry for September 20, Hapeman Diary, ALPL.

immediately. A Bluegrass lieutenant named George R. Mattingly of the Confederate 9th recalled, "we moved forward and got within forty yards of their line; a second line appeared and they poured volley after volley into our ranks. We were ordered to lie down and fought them for some time." Wickliffe described the fire as "murderous." The sheets of lead struck down the 9th's Col. John W. Caldwell in the first few minutes, breaking the same left arm that had been shattered in 1862 at Shiloh. Wickliffe recalled his skirmish line and assumed command of the regiment himself.[47]

Like the 9th, the 2nd made no progress and also went to ground. The 4th and 6th Kentucky, however, faced unarmed scrub oak instead of Yankees and hurried to keep up with Stovall on their right. The 41st Alabama, the center regiment of the brigade, was being pulled in two directions, trying to keep contact with the regiments on either flank. When that proved impossible, the 41st split in two. When Helm saw the 41st's left wing unraveling, he ordered Alabama Col. Martin L. Stansel to hurry over and rally the four left-most companies. Stansel reformed them and closed up on Wickliffe's right, but in the meantime the 41st's other six companies under Maj. Jesse Nash pushed on west.[48]

The upshot of all this was that some 700 Orphans were now bearing down on Col. Marion C. Taylor and the blue-clad 15th Kentucky, which numbered only 305 rank and file. Some fire from Dodge's three Federal regiments, aligned on Baird's left flank and facing north, might have proved helpful in contending with those odds, but Dodge's line was about 200 yards south through the timber and had only the haziest notion of what was unfolding to their front. Like most of the other regiments in Beatty's brigade, Taylor's 15th Kentucky was angled, facing northeast rather than due east. They were also in the timber south of Alexander's Bridge Road rather than deployed in the open fields of the McDonald farm, and so did not have a full view of the approaching enemy. Thus, when the Confederate 4th Kentucky appeared on Taylor's right flank, in perfect position to roll up his line, it came as a bit of a shock. The 15th was game, however, and instead of panicking, Taylor wheeled his five available companies (the rest were still on the skirmish line) and charged into the teeth of the threat. The bold tactic might have stopped the 4th if these Confederates had

47 *OR* 30, pt. 2, 213; George R. Mattingly, "Reminiscences of the Nelson Grays," Kentucky Historical Society, Frankfort, KY.

48 *OR* 30, pt. 2, 207.

John Beatty (right) did not panic when his brigade was overwhelmed by the Rebel assault.
Miller, *Photographic History*

been alone. The Rebel 6th Kentucky, however, now materialized out of the timber to menace the 15th's left while Nash's portion of the truncated 41st Alabama enveloped Taylor's right. Taylor ordered a retreat.[49]

This is how Hapeman found things when he led the 104th Illinois south and west, trying to join with Taylor. Both regiments fell back precipitously, passing through and around Bridges's six guns, all of which were by now unlimbered back at their original position and firing at the plethora of Rebel targets spread out in front of them.

John Beatty observed all this from the perspective of Bridges's position. When the first attackers appeared Beatty knew instantly he was in trouble. He sent couriers scrambling. One went to Baird to ask that officer to "throw a force in the interval between their left and my right." Captain James S. Wilson dashed off to find General Negley to hurry up the rest of the division. Once these missives were sent Beatty could do no more than watch his brigade come apart. For a moment he thought Bridges's guns might check the enemy. A force of Rebels that thrust itself between the 42nd Indiana and 104th Illinois seemed to be driven back briefly by Bridges's fire, but the odds were too great. When Gibson's 13th/20th Louisiana launched its charge into the 42nd's flank, the big guns failed to check them a second time.

Very soon, Beatty focused his attention on Hapeman and Taylor. He was momentarily heartened to see the 15th Kentucky retreating "in good order, contesting the ground stoutly." The two regiments made a brief stand in the road, but then, considerably disorganized, fell back 300 yards into the timber behind the battery to the southwest. A few men of the 104th, noting a lack of

49 William P. McDowell, "The Fifteenth Kentucky," *Southern Bivouac.* New Series II (1886-7), 251; Kirk C. Jenkins, *The Battle Rages Higher: The Union's Fifteenth Kentucky Infantry* (University Press of Kentucky, 2003), 175-178.

gunners at some of the pieces, stopped to help crew the cannon and stem the Rebel tide.[50]

The varied career of Capt. Lyman Bridges and his battery began in 1861 when they were Company G of the 19th Illinois infantry and commanded by Russian expatriate John Turchin. The regiment was largely recruited in Chicago and included a number of members of the famed prewar Ellsworth Zouave Cadet Company, so the 19th was initially outfitted and drilled as one of those flashily garbed commands. In 1862, while at Nashville, General Negley ordered the company detached and trained as artillerymen. Their time as cannoneers was spent largely inside fortifications and not as field artillery. The men were returned to the 19th to fight as foot soldiers in time for Stones River. In January 1863, however, they were once again issued cannon and this time trained as a light battery. Chickamauga was their first serious action as red-legs.

Taylor's and Hapeman's retreat left Bridges's guns dangerously exposed, facing Stovall and Adams in McDonald Field, and with the 4th Kentucky coming up hard on their right flank. The 4th was the most immediate threat. Watching in dismay, Beatty saw the Orphans "advance through the woods to within 100 yards of my battery and poured into it a heavy fire." To Captain Bridges, who was more focused on hammering the Rebels near the McDonald farm, the 4th's attack came as a devastating surprise. "Some of my men and horses were disabled by a musketry fire from the woods upon my right. While under this fire General Beatty ordered me to retire." By the time Beatty issued that command, his men were falling at an alarming rate, including Lt. William "Billy" Bishop and 25 others killed, wounded, or missing. In all, Bridges lost nearly half of the crew manning the right-hand section.[51]

To the Orphans involved, the whole affair seemed one glorious rush. Kentuckian Fred Joyce in the Confederate 4th remembered that "such was the impetuosity of the charge that these lines were almost literally run over." And then the 4th was in amongst the guns of Bishop's section, capturing two of them, with the rest of Bridges's battery hastily retiring. Rebel Lt. Lot D. Young "seized the trunnion [he meant the cannon's trail] of one of the guns and with assistance turned it on" the fleeing Yankees, but "we could find no ammunition

50 John Beatty, *The Citizen-Soldier: The Memoirs of a Civil War Volunteer* (University of Nebraska Press, 1998), 335.

51 *OR* 30, pt. 1, 368, 374.

. . . and were deprived of the anticipated glory of firing on the enemy as they fled from the field."[52]

His battery wrecked, Lyman Bridges ordered the remaining four pieces to fall back to "the first available position" while he and Lt. Lyman White halted among the ranks of the 15th Kentucky, hoping a counterstroke might allow them to recover their two captured guns. Confederate Lieutenant Young watched all this in amazement, as a man he supposed to be "the captain commanding that battery . . . dashed into the road and past us, lifting his hat and waving us a salute that would have put shame to a Chesterfield or a Prince Rupert. The act was almost paralyzing," Young continued, "and not a man of the fifty or more who fired at him point blank touched him or his horse." Bridges might have escaped this dash unscathed, but not so his horse, which collapsed and died once Bridges reined it to a halt.[53]

The fight might have seemed easily triumphant to many of the Confederates, but it was far from a bloodless success. The 4th's commander, Col. Joseph Nuckols, took a wound in the right arm early in the affair and was forced to leave the field, leaving the regiment in the hands of Maj. Thomas W. Thompson. The 4th lost seven killed and 51 wounded in the assault. The 6th Kentucky escaped with less bloodletting, losing a pair of dead and 32 wounded, having not had to charge the Federals head-on. Both regiments, however, fared much better than their brethren holding the brigade's left. The other half of Helm's command was in a bad way, pinned down and taking heavy losses.

The 2nd and 9th Kentucky, along with the left half of the 41st Alabama, made no progress against Baird's fortified line. After some time under a heavy fire, they fell back and Helm met them. Lieutenant Herr remembered the general and all of his staff "were endeavoring to straighten out the lines" when Herr noticed a mounted officer to his right go down. It was Helm. Was he "hard hit?" queried Herr. "Yes," Helm replied, and "where it meant death—in the bowels." Within minutes, members of the ambulance corps bore their stricken commander out of the fight and eventually to the Reed cabin, where Helm would spend his final hours.[54]

52 Fred Joyce, "Kentucky's Orphan Brigade at the Battle of Chickamauga," *The Kentucky Explorer* (April, 1994), 29; Lot D. Young Memoir, 64, Western Historical Manuscript Collection, University of Missouri at Rolla.

53 *OR* 30, pt. 1, 375; Young Memoir, 65.

54 "Death of Gen. Ben Hardin Helm," William C. Lehen Papers, DU.

Word quickly traveled up the chain of command to Breckinridge, who took the news hard. "'Helm has been killed,' he told his staff with unconcealed emotion." There was little time for mourning, however, even for old friends. Breckinridge dictated an order to Col. Joseph Lewis, commanding the 6th Kentucky, instructing him to take command and reunite the brigade. Lieutenant John Cabell Breckinridge, the general's son (usually called Cabell to distinguish him from his father) carried the order to Lewis, who received it on the La Fayette Road as his men were celebrating their triumph amid Bridges's captured guns. The senior Breckinridge rode west into McDonald Field to find Adams and Stovall.[55]

In the meantime, the 2nd and 9th Kentucky delivered a second fruitless assault against Baird's line. When yet another of the Orphans's regimental commanders, the 2nd Kentucky's Lt. Col. James W. Hewitt went down with a mortal wound, Maj. James W. Moss assumed command. "We reformed and made a second charge," Moss reported. This time they "got within forty yards of the enemy's works; drove them out of their first line of entrenchments, but the enfilading fire from the left becoming so heavy, we were again forced back."[56]

Moss was deceived into believing he had driven the Federals, even momentarily. His line struck Baird's position just south of where the Regulars held the angle of the line, and just north of the 4th Indiana's artillery revetment. Despite their mauling of the day before, King and his men were hardly dispirited. King was alert to even the small nuances in his position, which he thought a strong one. His location marked the point where Thomas's line left the ridge to angle back toward the La Fayette Road, so that his front line had a good field of fire while the supporting battalions were sheltered by the falling ground to his rear. About 8:00 a.m., King ordered the 1/18th forward 50 paces, barricades and all, in order to improve even further upon that field of fire. King also threw out three companies of skirmishers across his narrow front, enough to give the Rebels the impression of a forward battle line.[57]

55 Davis, *Breckinridge*, 374; John B. Castleman, *Active Service* (Courier-Journal Job Printing Co., 1917), 46.

56 *OR* 30, pt. 2, 209. Hewitt died, and Moss was promoted almost immediately to lieutenant colonel to replace him, so the Official Records show Moss's rank as lieutenant colonel throughout. He was the regiment's major at the moment Hewitt fell, however.

57 Johnson, *That Body of Brave Men*, 400.

This skirmish line was still in place when Moss struck. The 41st Alabama's rupture had occurred opposite King's portion of the line, and so the initial Rebel attack passed either to the north of the Regulars or veered south to fetch up against Colonel Scribner's works. As a result, the fire of the 1/18th and their supporting skirmishers was directed mainly toward enemy flanks, and King's men suffered almost no losses in that first blow. In fact, it was fire from the Regulars in their advanced position that probably brought down Helm. This time, however, the Rebels hit them head on. King's heavy skirmish line retired, reforming on the main line, which King had by now reinforced with Capt. Henry Haymond's 2nd Battalion of the 18th U.S. "I Double Quicked my battalion a cross an open space in the woods," Haymond informed his father, "and formed on the crest of a slight declivity on the left of the 18th/1st."[58]

As the 2nd Kentucky came into action atop the ridge it met a fierce fire. In addition to that of King's men, the Kentuckians were also still exposed to a crippling flank fire from both the 4th Indiana artillery revetment and the men of Scribner's rightmost units. To Moss's right, Wickliffe and the 9th Kentucky fared no better. We "advanced in good style," he reported, but were exposed to a "terrible enfilading fire upon our left." The 9th broke and fell back. By now, recalled John Jackman, who was following along in the wake of his regiment looking for wounded to aid, "all of the little gullies were packed with straggling soldiers (but I saw none of our brigade among them) avoiding the shells."[59]

Colonel Stansel and the four companies of the 41st Alabama still under his direct command didn't even manage to join this second effort. When Stansel moved to the left at Helm's direction, he found his men pinned down facing Baird's line. Instead of breaking off directly to the rear, Stansel, worried about the same raking fire from the 4th Indiana's enfilading guns, fell back by the right flank, moving several hundred yards to the northeast. This took him and the 41st out of the fight for the rest of the morning.[60]

Battered and bloody, the 2nd and 9th still had to make one more effort. As Wickliffe was reforming his regiment a second time, Col. Leon Von Zinken

58 "Dear Pa," Sept. 24, 1863, Henry Haymond Letters, Pearce Civil War Collection, Navarro College, Corsicana, TX.

59 *OR* 30, pt. 2, 213; Davis, *Diary*, 88. Jackman was being charitable. Since his brigade was the only one in action here, it is highly likely that most of the stragglers he saw belonged to regiments of Helm's command.

60 *OR* 30, pt. 2, 207.

arrived bearing orders from Breckinridge. Von Zinken, normally the colonel of the 20th Louisiana, was detached and serving as Inspector General on Breckinridge's staff. The red-headed Prussian was considered a first-rate officer, "one of the best informed and educated officers in the service," according to his former corps commander Lt. Gen. William J. Hardee. Von Zinken brought with him grim instructions: "The balance of the brigade was again going in," he told Wickliffe, and the 2nd and 9th must make another charge. This attack, their third effort, met with no better success than the first two. "[We] again encountered the terrible fire, from which we had suffered so severely . . . [and] seeing the useless waste of life, I was compelled to order the regiment to fall back," penned Wycliffe.[61]

Sergeant Samuel B. Price of Company A, 2nd Ohio, had a front row seat for all three of these assaults. Initially in Scribner's supporting line, Price and the 2nd stepped up alongside the 33rd Ohio early in the action, adding to that "terrible fire" Wickliffe so feared. "On they came amid the showers of musket balls . . . pouring from our lines," Price recalled in a letter to his mother on October 19. "Oh, I could not but admire their bravery, although they were my deadly enemies. They came within 75 yards, but no troops could stand our fire, and finally they broke and fled in wild confusion. Oh, the cheer that we sent up, you should have heard it."[62]

It was now about 10:30 a.m. In less than one hour of fighting the Orphan Brigade was shattered, but Breckinridge was anything but done for the day. His other two brigades had entirely smashed Union resistance in and around McDonald Field, and were now poised to strike south down the La Fayette Road into Kelly Field and the deep Federal rear. George Thomas's worst fears were about to be realized.

61 Stuart Salling, *Louisianans in the Western Confederacy: The Adams-Gibson Brigade in the Civil War* (McFarland Publishing, 2010), 132; Daniel A. Bellware, "Colonel Leon Von Zinken" online essay, 2006, http://cvacwrt.tripod.com/zinken.html, accessed 10/2/2011; OR 30, pt. 2, 213-214.

62 Richard A. Baumgartner, ed. *The Bully Boys: In Camp and Combat with the 2nd Ohio Volunteer Infantry Regiment, 1861-1864* (Blue Acorn Press, 2011), 403.

Chapter Five

Longstreet Deploys, Thomas Reacts:

Sunday, Dawn to 11:00 a.m.

While Braxton Bragg struggled with recalcitrance and gross command inefficiency, Lt. Gen. James Longstreet was endeavoring to make sense out of the Army of Tennessee's haphazard command structure. By the middle of the morning, Longstreet had his jumbled command sorted out enough to assemble and organize a powerful attack column. While it was not organized precisely to his liking, it was poised to deliver a more powerful blow than any Rebel assault yet attempted at Chickamauga.

At first light, all six of the divisions assigned to him were scattered through the forest east of the La Fayette Road between Brock Field and Hall's Ford on the Chickamauga, and none were in a condition or position to launch an immediate attack. Like Bragg, Longstreet rose at "early dawn" and set out to find his command. He left army headquarters impressed with the need for quick action, for it was also his understanding that D. H. Hill would begin the battle at any minute. Initially it seemed as if Old Pete would not have time to implement an elaborate redeployment of his men.[1]

1 Longstreet, *From Manassas to Appomattox*, 439.

Newly assigned a force of roughly 27,000 men spread out over several miles of almost entirely forested front, the new Left Wing commander needed to organize a functioning headquarters. His staff was equally affected by the First Corps's slow and fitful journey across the sprawling Confederacy. On September 20, Longstreet had with him only Lt. Col. Moxley Sorrel, Maj. Osmun Latrobe, and Maj. Peyton Manning. Most of his staff, all his artillery, and three infantry brigades were still en route. Thomas J. Goree, who had been with Longstreet since First Manassas, "only reached the field just as the battle closed." Neither did Longstreet have with him cavalry to provide escorts, guides, or couriers.[2]

A further complication concerned Maj. Gen. John Bell Hood, who was commanding the veteran First Corps in Longstreet's absence. Hood would need at least some staff support in order to properly manage his affairs. Three companies of the 1st Louisiana Cavalry were detailed as escorts: Company A to Longstreet, and the combined force of Companies C and E to Hood. These troopers were more than just personal bodyguards and headquarters ornamentation; they would serve as couriers and guides to other officers as well, hazardous duty that would empty several Louisiana saddles during the course of the day.[3]

In addition to the rough map Bragg had given him the night before, Longstreet also had the benefit of a local guide named Tom Brotherton, a private in the 2nd Battalion, 1st Georgia (Confederate) Regiment. The Brotherton family cabin was barely 600 yards in front of Longstreet's line that morning, and was still home to Tom's father George, his mother Mary, and at least three sisters. Sarah, a fourth sibling, lived just a third of a mile north up the La Fayette Road at the Poe farm. Her husband was Larkin Poe, a teamster in Joe Wheeler's Rebel cavalry. Now, with thousands of men fighting back and forth across their farms, the civilians had fled. On September 18, Bragg sent word down through the ranks asking for local men who could serve as guides to create a pool of talent for use by the army's various commanders. Given the lack

2 William Miller Owen, *In Camp and Battle with the Washington Artillery of New Orleans* (Pelican Publishing Company, 1998), 264; Thomas W. Cutrer, ed., *Longstreet's Aide: The Civil War Letters of Major Thomas J. Goree* (University Press of Virginia, 1995), 112. Owen also lists Goree as present, but as noted, Goree did not reach the field until nightfall on the 20th, leaving Longstreet with only three aides throughout the day.

3 Howell Carter, *A Cavalryman's Reminiscences of the Civil War* (The American Printing Co., 1900), 88-89.

of grand vistas and generally limited visibility of the largely wooded battlefield, Tom Brotherton's intimacy with the neighborhood was invaluable.[4]

Longstreet completed his required complement of staff officers by effectively appropriating the headquarters of Maj. Gen. Simon Bolivar Buckner. The two officers were old acquaintances from their days together in Mexico and claimed a mutual friend in Ulysses S. Grant, the Union hero of Vicksburg. Buckner despised Bragg, but bore Longstreet no ill will and readily cooperated in the new command arrangement. Thus far Buckner had only been a spectator to the battle. Major General A. P. Stewart's division had been detached on the 19th and ordered into action independently by Bragg, but Buckner and most of Brig. Gen. William Preston's division remained in reserve.[5]

Stewart's commitment split Buckner's Corps, with Maj. Gen. Thomas C. Hindman's division and Hood's entire corps sandwiched between Preston and Stewart. Longstreet decided there was no time "to draw Buckner's divisions into reciprocal relations" so Stewart would remain on the line, with Preston's division once again held in reserve. As the army's left flank division, Preston was also the anchor while the rest of the Confederate line swept the Federals back toward Lee and Gordon's Mills. This mission left Buckner and his corps-level staff with nothing to do but supervise one division and some artillery.[6]

Next, Longstreet set out to locate each of his division commanders and obtain firsthand knowledge of their positions. Despite the uncertainty of the situation and the difficulties of the night before, he was calm and confident. General Hood was Longstreet's first stop. After the relentless negativity of Bragg's officers, Hood's spirits were buoyed by his old commander's optimism. When Hood confidently stated "we would rout [the Federals] before sunset," Longstreet answered "that *of course* we would whip and drive him from the field." Hood, who in just two days with the Western army had rubbed shoulders with more than enough gloomy senior officers, confessed that Longstreet "was the first general I had met since my arrival who talked of victory."[7]

4 Longstreet, *From Manassas to Appomattox*, 439. The 2nd Battalion was serving in J. K. Jackson's brigade, Cheatham's division.

5 Longstreet, *From Manassas to Appomattox*, 18-19; Arndt M. Stickles, *Simon Bolivar Buckner: Borderland Knight* (University of North Carolina Press, 1940), 17-19; *OR* 30, pt. 2, 357.

6 Longstreet, *From Manassas to Appomattox*, 440; *OR* 30, pt. 2, 33.

7 Hood, *Advance and Retreat*, 63.

By 1863, Longstreet had formed definite tactical ideas about how to properly assault an enemy line. At this stage of the war, he was one of the most experienced commanders on either side, having served at high rank under Gens. Joseph E. Johnston and then Robert E. Lee for more than two years. Longstreet directed large formations in some of the most significant battles of the war, including several corps-sized assaults. He believed every attack needed not only mass but depth and proper coordination. In a postwar letter to Porter Alexander, his former chief of artillery, Longstreet noted that Chickamauga "exemplified the evolution of [my] tactical views during the war." "I moved my troops into position for the assault with great care," he told another interviewer years later. "The number of men and the peculiar formation of the force that I sent against the Federal line in this battle could have and would have carried any position except a strongly fortified one."[8]

Longstreet favored deep attacking columns, with no division having a width of more than two brigades. Limiting frontage allowed divisional commanders to exercise better control over their lines, and also meant the immediate support line would be drawn from the same division. At Chickamauga, Longstreet wanted a central assault column supported by a division on each flank, and he would spend much of his morning trying to arrange exactly that.[9]

The column as it finally formed was not arrayed entirely to Longstreet's satisfaction. After the fighting of September 19, the Rebel infantry had fallen back haphazardly. Major General Bushrod Johnson's three brigades were just south of the Brotherton Road several hundred yards southeast of the Brotherton farm. Behind them, the three brigades of Hood's division, still commanded by Brig. Gen. Evander Law, were reunited after attacking on divergent axes the day before. A. P. Stewart's three brigades were in line north of Johnson facing the Brotherton and Poe farms, where they had fallen back after their previous engagements. Late in the day, Maj. Gen. Thomas C. Hindman's fresh division moved into the timber south of Johnson. Hindman halted and faced west, his overnight position somewhat to Johnson's left and

8 Jeffry D. Wert, *General James Longstreet: The Confederacy's Most Controversial Soldier-A Biography* (Simon and Schuster, 1993), 312; "Interview with James Longstreet," *Cincinnati Enquirer*, April 1, 1883.

9 In doing so, Longstreet was unwittingly echoing parts of Casey's Manual, newly adopted in Rosecrans's army.

rear. Finally, two more of Longstreet's brigades—comprising the one-half of Maj. Gen. Lafayette McLaws's division that reached the field in time for the fight—detrained the night before back at Ringgold and marched as far as West Chickamauga Creek. They spent much of the morning coming onto the battlefield and taking position behind Law's troops.

After leaving Hood, Longstreet rode to find his old West Point roommate, A. P. Stewart. The two had not seen each other in many years, but there was little time for reunion or reminiscence. Longstreet explained Bragg's plan, that Stewart was now reporting to him, and that Stewart's line marked the right flank of the Left Wing. This last part was important because Stewart would serve as the means of transmission for the implementation of Bragg's orders. When Polk's attack jumped off, it would be Stewart's observation of that movement that in turn informed Longstreet when to begin his own advance. This was all well and good, replied Stewart, but there was a problem: "There were no troops to [my] right, at least within a half mile."[10]

Longstreet tried to remedy that by ordering Stewart to move north a quarter mile. In addition to having Stewart's men close up with Polk's left to observe Polk's advance and signal Longstreet's attack, the move would allow Longstreet to open a gap between Stewart and Johnson to "make room for Hood in the front line." Longstreet was uncertain about the fighting qualities of the Western troops he had inherited, but he had no doubts about his own men, including the Texas Brigade, and he wanted them spearheading his attack.[11]

Had Bragg's attack jumped off at dawn as planned, there would have been no time to execute Longstreet's orders. However, confusion on the right at least granted the left time to make adjustments. "About 8 o'clock A.M.," recalled Lt. Terry H. Cahal of Stewart's staff, "we moved our lines about three hundred yards . . . thus placing us between Cleburn[e]'s Division on the right [the] second brigade of Johnson's division on our left." Like so many other Confederates that morning, Cahal distinctly "heard the enemy all Saturday night felling trees and getting artillery into position, so we knew we had a hot days work before us."[12]

10 Sam Davis Elliott, *Soldier of Tennessee: General Alexander P. Stewart and the Civil War in the West* (Louisiana State University Press, 1999), 129-130; *OR* 30, pt. 2, 363.

11 *OR* 30, pt. 2, 288.

12 "Dear Colonel," September 30, 1863, Terry H. Cahal Papers, TSLA.

Things did not go smoothly. Cahal's casual comment revealed the first error when he noted that Bushrod Johnson's division was still on A. P. Stewart's left. Longstreet intended to insert Hood's troops between Johnson and Stewart. That, however, did not happen. When he saw Stewart's shift to the right, Johnson followed suit, unwittingly frustrating Longstreet's intention to push Law's men to the front line. Because he was expecting the battle to open any minute, there was no time to reverse the mistake and Longstreet left Johnson in the front.

Johnson's front consisted of Brig. Gen. Evander McNair's and Col. John S. Fulton's brigades, with Fulton's left extended by three regiments borrowed from Col. Cyrus Sugg's (formerly John Gregg's) brigade. The rest of Sugg's command fell in behind as support. Law's men formed the third and fourth lines of Longstreet's main attack column. Sometime later McLaws's men, then under the command of Brig. Gen. Joseph B. Kershaw, filed in behind Law with his own (Kershaw's) and Brig. Gen. Benjamin G. Humphreys's brigades, also abreast, forming the fifth line.[13]

Despite the fact that it was not deployed exactly as Longstreet intended, his formation was formidable. In its final form, the main attack column comprised eight brigades massed into five lines, supported by a division on either flank. This formation would go a long way toward preserving continuity during the later stages of the fight, especially if the battle evolved differently than expected. He described his core concept years later when he explained, "our assaulting column was five brigades deep, and within easy supporting distance. . . . If one brigade faltered, another was there to take its place."[14]

Shifting A. P. Stewart north created yet another problem. Instead of connecting with Patrick Cleburne's division, Stewart's right inadvertently moved in front of Cleburne's troops and so masked Brig. Gen. James Deshler's brigade. This mishap occurred while Generals Bragg and Polk were trying to untangle Cleburne's and Frank Cheatham's divisions before the general advance sounded. Stewart's line was apparently several hundred yards farther west than Deshler, but no one noticed this new problem. Longstreet's intention

13 Since Kershaw was commanding the division in McLaws's absence, normal procedure would have him relinquish control of his own brigade to the senior colonel present, but Kershaw elected not to do that and decided instead to attempt to serve in both positions in the coming fight.

14 "Interview with James Longstreet," *Cincinnati Enquirer*, April 1, 1883.

Map 5: Longstreet assembles the Left Wing

in shifting Stewart north was sound, but flaws in its execution resulted in neither of the intended results being accomplished.

The cascading series of blunders that had delayed the attack on the far right side of the army left Longstreet and his subordinates waiting and wondering. For all they knew, an attack could come off at any minute. Sorrel recalled that "we waited with the utmost impatience for the guns, but no sound came." Focused as he was on getting Polk and Hill into action, Bragg apparently did not think to inform Longstreet of the delay, or the reason for it. As a result, Longstreet did not undertake a larger reorganization, lest he be caught unprepared if the battle suddenly commenced.[15]

As it had on September 19, happenstance once again conspired to put Bushrod Johnson in the center of the impending maelstrom. Johnson's was the command that circumstances dictated must lead Longstreet's advance. With the fight expected to open any moment, Longstreet believed he did not have the luxury of shifting Johnson's men out of the way to let his Eastern veterans take their place. It was a situation that Johnson, hungry for advancement, would again exploit to the fullest.

Most of the Rebel attacks delivered thus far at Chickamauga had been executed by single divisions entering the fight one at a time, usually with their brigades abreast and with each regiment on line. Reserve or support lines, assuming they were available, were from different divisions, often from completely different corps. Each division commander had to control a wide front, often with little idea of what lay ahead or behind. The most significant exception was that of Stewart's own attack on the 19th. His division entered the fight in a column of brigades, and was able to eventually tear a hole in William Rosecrans's center. Another problem was equally limiting: neither Bragg nor his corps commanders managed to get more than one or two divisions into action at one time. As one division was pulled out, another might be sent in, but integrated action by several divisions or multiple corps acting in concert had yet to be achieved. Stewart's attack once again serves as the example: his success near the end of the day on September 19 was rendered inconsequential, despite relatively large numbers of other Confederate troops in the area who could have provided assistance, because no overall commander was present to orchestrate a concerted effort to secure the fruits of Stewart's hard-won success.

Longstreet's attack was fundamentally different. Including the divisions on the flanks, he intended to send 14 brigades forward in one mass, using the power of five divisions simultaneously. Hood's main column would form the battering ram intended to crack through the Union position. To the north, A. P. Stewart's division deployed to guard this column's right flank, while Tom Hindman's command did similar duty on the left. If the Federals turned to take

15 Sorrel, *At the Right Hand of Longstreet*, 195.

Hood's column in flank, Stewart and Hindman would be positioned to stop them.

Bushrod Johnson's small division, now the attack's spearhead, had suffered significant losses on the 18th and 19th. Thus far, its casualties amounted to at least 25% of the force initially engaged. This reduction put Johnson's strength that morning at perhaps 2,700 men, and even fewer than that if its stragglers were still absent. In addition, another of his brigades was now led by a colonel. Cyrus A. Sugg stepped up from command of the 50th Tennessee to replace the wounded Brig. Gen. John Gregg, who was struck down near the end of the fighting the night before. Sugg was a farmer and just 29 years old when he was elected to command the 50th Tennessee in 1861. Despite his youth, Sugg was described as "cool and collected in the hour of danger; generally went into battle smoking his pipe, and never suffered himself to become excited during an engagement." September 20 would be his first time leading an infantry brigade in action.[16]

Bushrod Johnson placed Fulton's and McNair's brigades in the front with Colonel Sugg behind them. Fulton's brigade was aligned, from left to right, as follows: the 17th, 23rd, 25th, and 44th Tennessee regiments, about 600 officers and men. McNair's regiments included the 1st and 2nd Arkansas Mounted Rifles, 4th, 31st, and 4th Battalion Arkansas Infantry (consolidated into one command), 25th Arkansas, and 39th North Carolina, a total of another 1,000. Sugg's regiments included the 7th Texas and the 3rd, 10th, 30th, 41st, 50th, and 1st Battalion. Tennesseans all (with the exception of the 7th), Sugg's command numbered about 1,100 men. As noted, in order to augment Fulton's small line, three of Sugg's units—the 7th Texas, 50th Tennessee, and 1st Tennessee Battalion—shifted forward to extend Fulton's left by another 200 men. In all, Johnson had about 1,800 men leading the attack, fronting roughly 600 yards, with 900 troops behind in support.[17]

Evander M. Law's (Hood's) division manned the third and fourth lines. Law's own brigade had seen yet another command change. Colonel James L. Sheffield's fall from his horse at the start of the brigade's advance the previous day injured Sheffield so severely he could not resume command, which left the

16 Lindsley, *Military Annals of Tennessee*, vol. 2, 562.

17 David A. Powell, "Numbers and Losses in the Chickamauga Campaign," unpublished manuscript on file at CCNMP.

veteran brigade in the hands of Col. William F. Perry, the commander of the 44th Alabama.[18]

Evander Law was a proud and ambitious young South Carolinian. A graduate of the Citadel, South Carolina's famous military college, he pursued a career as an educator. He helped found a school in Alabama based on the Citadel's model, and was the superintendent there when war came. He was elected lieutenant colonel of the 4th Alabama in 1861, where his prewar military training proved instrumental in perfecting the regiment's skills. He and his men performed notably at First Manassas and, based on that record, Law was promoted to brigade command in April 1862. Law also cultivated good personal relationships with his superiors. Louis T. Wigfall, for a time a Confederate general and Law's commander, was now a powerful member of the Confederate Congress. Law was also one of John Bell Hood's protégés. Hood and Law shared a similar style. As noted by the brigade's modern historians, "both [were] fearless in battle, and their basic battlefield philosophy was the charge." Law performed well in brigade command, but his first experience with divisional leadership proved problematic. Hood's fall at the outset of the fighting on the second day at Gettysburg thrust Law into a confused tactical situation. He struggled to control the dispersed command in a difficult situation and with limited success. The fighting on September 19 saw similar problems, though this time Law at least knew beforehand he would be commanding the division. Still, his formation fractured badly on the 19th, though some of his brigades performed admirably.[19]

Now Law was once again the de facto divisional commander. His first command problem concerned his former brigade. Colonel Perry's elevation presented Law with something of a dilemma. Simply put, he did not trust Perry's courage or his ability to command. The day before, Law had come across Perry riding a gun limber to the rear, his entire regiment routed and running along behind it. Law reasonably assumed Perry was fleeing. In fact, the 44th had just run into an impromptu Federal ambush, and Perry was trying to get far enough ahead of his men to rally them, but Law would hear none of it. Instead of formally placing Perry under arrest, when Law discovered that Colonel Sheffield was still *hors de combat*, he turned to the next senior officer in

18 J. Gary Laine and Morris M. Penny, *Law's Alabama Brigade in the War Between the Union and the Confederacy* (White Mane Publishing Co. 1996), 157.

19 Ibid., 3, 10.

the brigade, Col. William C. Oates of the 15th Alabama, and placed him in charge. This off-the-cuff assignment injected Oates into an awkward position, especially since he was more sympathetic to Perry's version of events than Law. When Oates "suggested that he [Perry] be given an opportunity to redeem himself," Law acquiesced—but instructed Oates to "watch him, and if he goes to flickering today, you assume command of the brigade at once."[20]

With the command issue sorted out, the brigade formed. The Alabamians entered the fight on Saturday with 1,457 men, now pared down to 1,300 troops and 350 yards of frontage. In the column's fourth line, supporting Perry, was Brig. Gen. Jerome B. Robertson's Texas Brigade (1st, 4th, 5th Texas, and 3rd Arkansas) on the left, while Brig. Gen. Henry L. Benning's 2nd, 15th, 17th, and 20th Georgia regiments extended Robertson's right. Both brigades slogged through tough fights the day before. On this day they fielded a combined strength of 1,600 men behind the Alabamians. Their 450-yard line of eight regiments was only slightly longer than that held by Perry's five regiments.[21]

Kershaw and Humphreys, comprising the fifth line, were the last to move into position. Both brigades were large by Chickamauga standards, though still considerably weakened from their Gettysburg fight the previous July. Kershaw's brigade of six South Carolina units and Humphreys's four Mississippi regiments together massed slightly more than 2,800 men, with a frontage of just under 1,000 yards. In other circumstances, Longstreet might have chosen to place Kershaw and Humphreys at the head of his column. Besides being fresh, these regiments were among the doughtiest fighters in Confederate service, proven veterans of hard and reliable fighting on many fields. Fewer than three months previous, Humphreys's Mississippians, then led by William Barksdale, delivered a ferocious assault that shattered the center of the Union Third Corps position in the Peach Orchard. Time, however, precluded shifting them farther forward. Still, Longstreet was confident, as he later opined, "that no defenders without fortifications could withstand the pounding from successive waves of attackers."[22]

20 Ibid., 146-148, 157. Law's quote is from William C. Oates, "General W. F. Perry and Something of his Life in War and Peace," *Montgomery Advertiser*, March 2, 1902. Laine and Penny's work on Law's brigade provides an excellent detailed discussion of this incident, and of the brigade's fight at Chickamauga.

21 A few of Benning's losses were replaced by stragglers returning to the ranks that morning.

22 Wert, *General James Longstreet*, 310.

For his main thrust, Longstreet massed a dense but narrow column slightly wider at the base than at the front, but in general only about a half-mile wide. His support divisions, one on either flank bolstered that column and ensured its main strength would not be peeled away regiment by regiment on side missions. As noted, Stewart's three brigades fulfilled that role to the north. Stewart began the fight on the 19th with nearly 4,300 men, suffering roughly 1,200 casualties in a brutal afternoon's fighting. His 3,100 survivors would have to face a stubborn, well-positioned enemy defending the western edge of Poe Field, where many of William B. Bate's men had come to grief the previous evening. Despite several close calls, Stewart and all three of his brigadiers had escaped injury, leaving the divisional command structure intact. A number of its regimental officers fell, however, and the division's heavy losses had frayed morale somewhat. Stewart deployed Brig. Gens. John C. Brown and Bate in his front line, leaving Brig. Gen. Henry D. Clayton's Alabamians in reserve. Stewart fretted about his own exposed right flank, which remained unconnected to Cleburne's division or any other body of Polk's troops. Accordingly, he ordered Bate to extend his line "obliquely to the right and rear to prevent the enemy from turning our position."[23]

Stewart's men constructed breastworks of their own, perhaps hoping they might lure the Federals into attacking instead of having to go forward again. The gloomy, mist-shrouded light of dawn revealed to Lieutenant Cahal of Stewart's staff the high cost of yesterday's assaults as he hurried about on various missions. "The part of the ground over which our division fought was thickly strewn with our own dead, and where one yankee was found, there was thrible the number of Confederate dead. The division was terribly cut up, without inflicting apparently any severe loss upon the enemy."[24]

The other flanking division belonged to Maj. Gen. Thomas C. Hindman. Unlike Stewart's men, Hindman's three brigades were all fresh to the fight. Hindman's was a large command. Each brigade numbered close to 2,000 men, and with the supporting artillery, the division counted 6,350 rank and file that morning.[25]

23 David A. Powell and David A. Friedrichs, *The Maps of Chickamauga: An Atlas of the Chickamauga Campaign, Including the Tullahoma Operations, June 22-September 23, 1863* (Savas Beatie, 2009), 147; *OR* 30, pt. 2, 363.

24 Cahal Papers, TSLA.

25 Powell, "Numbers and Losses," CCNMP.

Hindman positioned Brig. Gen. Zachariah C. Deas's Alabamians alongside Fulton, with Brig. Gen. Arthur M. Manigault's mixed Alabama-South Carolina command extending Deas's front farther south. These two brigades occupied 1,400 yards of frontage. Centered between them and about 200 yards to the rear, Brig. Gen. J. Patton Anderson's Mississippians formed Hindman's support line.

Questions lingered about Hindman's fitness to command. Not only had he not performed well back in McLemore's Cove a week earlier, leaving his brigadiers to further regard him with a dubious eye, but he was now quite ill. Hindman took to an ambulance on September 16 with a raging fever, leaving Anderson in charge of the division. He resumed command at 3:00 p.m. on September 19, just as the division was ordered across Chickamauga Creek and battle seemed imminent. While "the enthusiastic shouts with which his men received him were perfectly electrifying," his health and command abilities remained an open question.[26]

Fortuitously, Hindman's line overlapped by a large margin the flanks of Union Brig. Gen. Jefferson C. Davis's two very battered brigades—the only Federals opposing him. With fewer than 1,400 Yankees, Davis was outnumbered more than four to one. While no Confederate in Longstreet's Left Wing fully grasped the extent of their advantage over Davis's men at the time, Hindman's tactical circumstances were much more promising than those facing Stewart's troops to the north.

Longstreet's remaining division under William Preston held the very southern end of the line, in the same position it occupied since crossing West Chickamauga Creek 24 hours earlier. With the exception of Col. Robert Trigg's brigade, Preston's men were unengaged on the 19th, and of Trigg's regiments, only the 6th Florida had been heavily involved. Longstreet did not intend for Preston to advance with everyone else. Instead, his men would act as Longstreet's reserve, to be committed as needed. Preston reported that the men erected "good field entrenchments," well supported with artillery, during the night.[27]

Before all these deployments were completed, battle erupted on the right. Longstreet recorded the time as "about 10 o'clock." Breckinridge had just gone in; Cleburne followed shortly thereafter. The din certainly hastened last minute

26 *Daily Huntsville Confederate*, October 1, 1863.

27 *OR* 30, pt. 2, 414.

preparations. But then, for an interminable time . . . nothing happened. "The battle seemed to rage with considerable fury, but did not progress as had been anticipated," Longstreet observed. "As soon as I was prepared, I sent to the commanding general to suggest that I had probably make my attack."[28]

* * *

Unbeknownst to Longstreet, time was working in his favor. Generals Rosecrans and Thomas continued to focus on the Union left, a worry only exacerbated when John Beatty's brigade was overrun. As the morning wore on, Thomas's calls for troops were re-doubled, and redoubled again once the action opened.

Thomas observed at least part of Beatty's fight, and at once understood that the lone Union brigade stood no chance of stopping Breckinridge's onslaught. His first reaction was to find more help for his endangered left. He once again thought of the large concentration of troops at the south end of Kelly Field. Thomas had already borrowed Dodge's brigade from Johnson's division at first light, dispatched to prolong the Regular brigade's flank. Now he noted Col. William Grose's brigade in the rear of Palmer's position, the regiments resting in column of division. When Rosecrans rode by that morning and ordered Palmer's line into a more compact deployment, Grose was squeezed out of line except for the 23rd Kentucky, which was loaned out to Hazen to fill out that officer's position. This left Grose with four regiments: the 84th Illinois, 36th Indiana, 6th and 24th Ohio, the whole numbering some 1,100 men. Batteries H and M of the 4th U.S. Artillery were also available, limbered and standing by in Kelly Field.[29]

Grose's men had idled away the morning. The 84th Illinois's quartermaster, Louis Simmons, recalled that the reserve ranks "had stacked arms" and were lying down. "The sun was slowly melting away the frost and sending a delicious warmth upon the limbs of thousands, who had shivered through the night."

28 Ibid., 288.

29 Hazen's brigade normally consisted of the 9th Indiana, 6th Kentucky, and the 41st and 124th Ohio regiments. The 6th Kentucky had taken so many losses among their officers on the 19th, however, that Hazen broke it up and parceled the companies out to the remaining three regiments. Grose, who had five regiments, loaned Hazen the 23rd in order to complete the latter's brigade deployment.

The slack time ended when the occasional crack of picket fire gave way to the sustained thunder of battle, and the fighting spread all along the front.[30]

Thomas ordered Palmer to send Grose northward. The situation was fluid, and the moment urgent. Grose understood little more than that he was to march to the left and support Baird's line. He knew nothing of Beatty's engagement, or even where Baird's line terminated. Even worse, from the troops' point of view the effort poured into constructing the breastworks, whose protection they now expected to enjoy during the day's battle, had been all for naught. "The brigade did not relish this movement," recalled Quartermaster Simmons, "but they were too good of soldiers to hesitate." "And the order came 'Left face, forward march,'" lamented Pvt. James Suitor, also of the 84th, "so we had to leave our strong position while other troops came in to fill our place." Grose hurried his four regiments northwest across Kelly Field until he struck the La Fayette Road, and then turned due north. Just short of the field's northern boundary Grose halted to form the brigade, placing the 36th Indiana and 84th Illinois in front and the two Ohio regiments behind them. Grose mistakenly believed his brigade was still masked by Baird's front, and was expecting to find a Union line of battle directly ahead of him. In fact, Beatty's men had already retreated to the southwest, while Dodge's line—which marked the left end of Baird's frontage—ended well short of the road.[31]

Behind and to Grose's left, moving up through the timber west of the La Fayette Road, were more newly arriving Federals in the form of Col. Timothy R. Stanley's men, the next of Negley's expected brigades. Stanley commanded only three regiments, or just more than 1,000 bayonets. Owing to the erratic nature of Negley's movements that morning (departure, recall, then departure again) Stanley's men were at least an hour behind Beatty, and thus too late to provide any help in McDonald Field. Stanley only started northward about the same time Beatty was first assailed, though Stanley had no way of knowing any of that. He could only hear the noise of battle swelling as he hustled along toward the army's left.[32]

30 Louis A. Simmons, *The History of the 84th Reg't Ill. Vols.* (Hampton Brothers, Publishers, 1866), 95.

31 Simmons, *84th Reg't Ill. Vols.*, 97; Entry for September 20th, James P. Suitor Diary, ALPL; *OR* 30, pt. 1, 781.

32 Negley places the delay at two hours, with Beatty going at 8:00 a.m. and Stanley departing at 10:00 a.m. *OR* 30, pt. 1, 330.

Just as Stanley started north, trouble erupted back at his original position. Negley was conferring with Stanley when word arrived (from either Col. William Sirwell, commanding Negley's third brigade, or Brig. Gen. Tom Wood, leading the replacing force) that Confederate skirmishers were pushing into the gap left by Stanley's and Sirwell's withdrawals. Negley ordered Stanley to continue on with the original mission while he rode back to investigate this new problem. Negley led Sirwell's brigade back to Brotherton Field in order to "assist in re-establishing my former line," as well as to "protect my ammunition train, which was passing at the time." The net effect of this reversal was to cast Stanley adrift, moving north with very little knowledge of the terrain or what was expected of him.[33]

Negley's final instructions to Stanley were vague—a hurried command "to push my regiments quickly into the woods to my right to support the forces then engaged there." Dutifully, Stanley deployed west of Poe Field, coming up behind Brannan's and Reynolds's men, but found no crisis or anyone in need of help. When he asked Joe Reynolds for guidance (whom Stanley identified only as the "officer in command") Reynolds merely directed him to move "farther to the left to report to whomsoever I found in command there." Further confusion followed. Farther north, Stanley found someone else (also unidentified in Stanley's report) who ordered him "into line at right angles with the front," but again, he found "nothing to do there." Leaving his men in line, Stanley finally found General Thomas, who at last gave him "definite and positive orders to advance to the support of . . . Beatty." Thomas apparently said nothing to Stanley about Grose's brigade, dispatched on the same mission.[34]

While Thomas was reacting to the growing crisis with firmness and alacrity, the details of the battle were also starting to slip from the big Virginian's grasp. Grose had only a vague notion of where to find Baird or how to help him. Stanley's search for orders and delay in reaching Beatty should have been unnecessary had Captain Williard, one of Thomas's other aides, or even one of John Beatty's staffers been tasked with bringing up the rest of the division when it appeared. Alternatively, the courier line established earlier should have enabled information to quickly flow between Thomas and Negley. Instead,

33 Ibid., 330.

34 Ibid., 330, 379.

Stanley's various deployments and movements consumed the better part of an hour during which Beatty's regiments faced increasingly desperate circumstances.

Thomas also sent a courier to inform Negley (who was still back in Brotherton Field with Sirwell) that the left flank had been turned, and to hurry along with the remainder of his division. Once he received this order, Negley immediately departed to take charge of Stanley and Beatty, leaving orders for Sirwell and the remaining divisional artillery to come on as quickly as they could. It was now close to 10:30 a.m.[35]

Thomas was far from satisfied. Significantly, he still believed John Brannan's division was lying in reserve near the Dyer house, and could be called on when needed. With the flank being turned the need was suddenly urgent. Yet another courier dashed southward to find Brannan.

Brannan, of course, was not in reserve. Instead, two of his brigades were prolonging Joseph Reynolds's line across Poe Field, connecting to Thomas Wood's (formerly Negley's) line at Brotherton's, called forward probably at the behest of Reynolds earlier that morning. "The battle, which commenced on the left of our army," recalled Reynolds, "reached Brannan's division and mine about nine-thirty or ten o'clock a.m. according to my estimation. I did not note the time by my watch." In reality, it was closer to 10:30, because Confederate troops were not only assailing the left, but also beginning their assault upon the rest of the Union line. (These attacks, delivered by Cleburne's and A. P. Stewart's Rebels, will be described in more detail later.)[36]

As it was, however, Reynolds noted that "while we were heavily engaged, Brannan came to me and said, 'I am ordered to the left.'" Joe Reynolds was flummoxed. "That is all very well," he exclaimed, "but you can't go[!] We are now hotly engaged and all that can be expected of us, is to fight hard in one place at a time, and heaven knows we have got our hands full right here." Brannan reassured Reynolds that he wasn't about to pull out in the middle of a battle, but he was worried about taking the responsibility (and the blame, should it come to that) for disobeying Thomas's orders. As senior officer Reynolds understood, and immediately assumed accountability for countermanding the order. As partial mitigation, Brannan suggested he could spare Col. Van Derveer, whose four regiments were in reserve and not needed to hold the line

35 Ibid., 330.

36 Reynolds Statement, CCNMP.

in Poe Field, which had so far easily repulsed all assailants. Reynolds concurred.[37]

Ferdinand Van Derveer's troops were positioned just inside the wood line east of the Glenn-Kelly Road, perhaps 150 yards behind Brannan's main line. Van Derveer took 1,643 men into the fight on September 19. On this morning just under 1,200 were still in the ranks. Colonel James George of the 2nd Minnesota noted he had 295 men ready for action, because in addition to his 49 casualties he was also missing another 40 men detached on picket and not yet recalled. There was no time for these troops to catch up. Once Brannan ordered him to the left to support Baird, Van Derveer "wheeled [the four] battalions to the left, deployed both lines, and moved through the woods parallel to the Chattanooga [La Fayette] Road, gradually swinging round my left . . . until I struck the road perpendicularly at a point just north of Kelly's house." Like Stanley's men, from there they were fed into the fast-developing battle. Rattling along behind came Lt. Frank G. Smith's Battery I of the 4th U.S. Artillery.[38]

Van Derveer's men departed with Rosecrans's knowledge and approval. In addition to the aide dispatched to Brannan, Thomas had also once again appealed to the army commander for help. "Two aides arrived successively, within a few minutes, from General Thomas, asking for reinforcements," reported Rosecrans. "The first was directed to say that General Negley had already gone and should be near at hand . . . and that Brannan's reserve brigade was available." This probably should have sufficed, but by now Rosecrans was overly focused on his endangered left, his attention repeatedly drawn there by the seemingly endless flow of requests from George Thomas. The second aide first found General Crittenden, who was busy with Van Cleve's troops at this time, and who sent him on to Rosecrans. When that second officer found the army commander and reiterated Thomas's latest appeal, as additional assurance, Rosecrans offered up the last arrow in his quiver: "The other [aide] was directed to say that General Van Cleve would at once be sent to his assistance."[39]

Thomas's attempt to bluff the Rebels with John Beatty's brigade had failed miserably, and disastrously so for Beatty's men. In response, the corps

37 Ibid.

38 *OR* 30, pt. 1, 429, 433. George did not explain where his detached pickets were located. They were likely somewhere in Dyer Field, or guarding the brigade ammunition wagons.

39 Ibid., 58-59. Van Cleve's activities will be discussed in more detail later.

commander reacted quickly, if instinctively, by pulling troops from wherever he could to rush northward, ignoring chain of command and organization tables alike. Thus, Stanley's, Grose's, and Van Derveer's brigades were plucked from other sectors of the Kelly Field-Poe Field line and sent hurrying leftward. Each movement was characterized by uncertainty and attended by a large degree of confusion. What was needed now was a controlling hand to stitch these various brigades and Beatty's fragments back into a cohesive defense.

In Thomas's mind, Negley was that man. He'd been intended for the left all along, as evidenced by that 6:30 a.m. order. Two of his three brigades were already committed to that sector. Once Sirwell caught up the whole Second Division would be re-united. Moreover, Negley was one of the senior divisional commanders in the army, and would have authority enough to command anyone sent to help him without any question of rank arising. Accordingly, while all of this activity was in swirling motion, Thomas dispatched Captain Gaw with yet one more order to Negley, carrying what should have been clarifying instructions. They proved to be anything but.

Gaw located Negley just as the Pennsylvanian overtook the rear-most regiment of Stanley's brigade. Thomas intended to extend his left as far as an open ridge approximately 900 yards west of Kelly Field, as far as the George Snodgrass homestead. Even better, the Snodgrass, Mullis, and McDonald farms all abutted, creating an expansive cleared area that offered one of the few excellent fields of fire for artillery in this heavily timbered, sparsely settled country. With an infantry line drawn solidly between Kelly Field and Snodgrass Hill, all supported by what amounted to an artillery battalion throwing enfilading fire down the ranks of the approaching enemy, the left flank should at last be secure. Accordingly, Negley was directed to "mass all the artillery at hand on [the] high ridge."[40]

Dutifully, Negley took his remaining cannon, Batteries G and M of the 1st Ohio Light, and deployed their 12 pieces atop the designated ridge. He also summoned Sirwell's four regiments, 1,729 men, to join him. At last fully disentangled from Brotherton Field, Sirwell's brigade hurried northwest. Captain Robert P. Findley, commanding Company K of the 74th Ohio, recalled that they "double-quicked in double columns thro' the brush and thick undergrowth and [across] the fields. While crossing [one] field a solid shot passed between our Regiment and the 78th [Pennsylvania] we double-quicked

40 Ibid., 330.

to wood and escaped other shots." Just as they had the night before, the men expected action at any minute, with the battle now raging to their north, east, and south. Instead, they found more waiting. After running about a mile, Sirwell reported, Negley instructed him to deploy "in an open wood, so as to cover any flank attack from the left." After a short time, Negley shifted the brigade "some 400 yards" to the right. "My line," Sirwell continued, "was now immediately in the rear of where the fiercest fighting was going on," but none of his troops became engaged. Once again they were spectators, not participants.[41]

Also nearby, hustling along up the Glenn-Kelly Road, were the four Napoleons of Lt. Frank Smith's Battery I, 4th U.S. Smith, of Brannan's division, was usually attached to Van Derveer, which is why he was following that officer now. He was heading toward Kelly Field when he was intercepted by Maj. James Lowrie of Negley's staff. When Negley rode for Snodgrass Hill, he dispatched Lowrie to find more guns and bring them to the same place. After all, Thomas instructed him to "mass all the artillery at hand." Lowrie soon spied Smith's guns trundling up the road, obviously looking for a mission and immediately commandeered them, citing Thomas's authority. Smith hurried his guns up the hill and planted them directly in front of the Snodgrass cabin.[42]

Negley's understanding of his new mission differed from Thomas's in one crucial respect. According to Negley, he was ordered to take position on "a high ridge facing the *south*." Thomas later reported that Negley failed to grasp his meaning. The XIV Corps commander intended for Negley to assume overall command of the left flank, bolstered by such other troops as he could find. The artillery anchoring that flank could only accomplish this mission if they were massed on the open slopes of Snodgrass Hill facing *north* or *northeast* in order to shred any attacker threatening the XIV Corps's rear. "Instead of massing the artillery near Baird's left," lamented Thomas, "it was posted on the right of Brannan's division, nearly in rear of Reynolds' right." Negley ultimately deployed all of his troops and artillery so as to face exactly the opposite of what Thomas intended. Even worse, instead of taking charge of the overall direction of the left flank and assembling a defense that would integrate with Baird's left, Negley merely watched the battle unfold before him. He misunderstood his

41 Theodore W. Blackburn, *Letters from the Front: A Union "Preacher" Regiment (74th Ohio) in the Civil War* (Morningside House, 1981), 150; OR 30, pt. 1, 385.

42 *OR* 30, pt. 1, 438.

intended role so completely that he would play no part in helping repulse Breckinridge's next assault.[43]

43 Ibid., 252, 330. Emphasis added. Note also that even at the time of the writing of his report, 10 days after the battle, Thomas still believed Brannan was being held in reserve at Dyer Field instead of being placed in line at Poe Field.

Chapter Six

Assailed Front and Rear:

Sunday, 10:30 a.m. to Noon

By 10:30 a.m., it wasn't just the left flank of the XIV Corps under attack but Thomas's entire line, beset by a series of determined Confederate assaults. Spearheading those efforts was the other half of D. H. Hill's Corps—Maj. Gen. Patrick R. Cleburne's powerful division.

Cleburne's men were deployed on the left of Maj. Gen. John C. Breckinridge's division in a similar formation with all three brigades abreast. The Irish general's command numbered roughly 4,900 infantry on the morning of the 20th. Despite the noise and confusion of the Winfrey Field action the previous evening, losses proved comparatively few. One-third larger than Breckinridge's division, Cleburne's line occupied a bit more than one mile of frontage, all of it in timber. Brigadier General Lucius Polk's brigade was on the right of the line, Brig. Gen. Sterling Alexander Martin (S. A. M.) Wood's brigade held the center, and Brig. Gen. James Deshler's Texans once again formed on the left. These men had bivouacked amidst the dead of both sides. Captain William E. Yeatman of the 2nd Tennessee in Polk's brigade discovered that "on awakening we found we slept with dead Federals thick amongst us, some of our men actually sleeping with their heads resting on the [bodies]." Hardened by war, the troops could make light of these grisly circumstances. In the 33rd Alabama of Wood's brigade, Pvt. Bob Watson awoke to similar circumstances. "Bully!" he exclaimed as the light revealed the immediate surroundings: "Two dead Yankees and a bull yearling." The dawn also brought a host of preparations for the coming day's trials. As the men fixed breakfast, ordnance sergeants made their rounds, making sure every soldier had a full cartridge box. Two men from each company were detailed to fetch water from Chickamauga Creek. Regardless of what they were doing, the troops could clearly hear the industrious Yankees felling trees to strengthen their front.[1]

While his men ate, Cleburne took the time to scout the Union position along his broad front. "I rode up and down my line more than once," confirmed the Irishman. What he saw dismayed him. The Union lines were well sited with breastworks in place—likely "too strong to be taken by assault." Another concern was the discovery that his front was not clear of friendly troops. In a confusing (and alarming) dispatch, General Wood relayed word up the chain of command that "it was probable" his line "overlapped troops on my left not of this division, and that some irregularity existed in the lines as formed."[2]

"Some irregularity" indeed. Wood's report remains difficult to interpret. The men on Wood's immediate left belonged to Deshler, but, as indicated, Wood meant men from another command, not Cleburne's own division. Additionally, Wood's phrasing seemed to be referring to troops behind his line, not to his front. He could have meant some of Cheatham's troops, but if so he was unclear on the attack plan, for Cheatham was supposed to be in support—it was perfectly logical for elements of Cheatham's division to be behind Wood's line. While Cheatham's formation would soon pose problems for Deshler's troops, they were not likely to affect Wood's advance. It was more likely that, despite the confused wording, Wood was referring to elements of Longstreet's wing.

In fact, there were troops masking Wood's line. They belonged to William Bate's brigade of A. P. Stewart's division, which had shifted north by Longstreet's order. Though they hadn't been there earlier when Cleburne scouted his intended position, they were certainly there now. Further, if Wood's front was masked then Deshler's line was also completely covered. Moreover,

1 William E. Yeatman Memoir, TSLA; William E. Preston Memoir, "The 33rd Alabama Regiment in the Civil War," Alabama Department of Archives and History. Hereafter ADAH.

2 Howell and Elizabeth Purdue, *Pat Cleburne, Confederate General* (Hill Jr. College Press, 1973), 22; *OR* 30, pt. 2, 161. Confusingly, S. A. M. Wood's report seems to refer to troops behind him, not in front of him, leaving it unclear if he meant Bate's men, Cheatham's troops, or someone else. Neither Cleburne's report nor any of Wood's regimental commanders' reports cast any additional light on the problem. It is probable that Wood was simply mistaken, misinterpreting a scout's report, or something similar. Wood's report was submitted on October 9, 1863. Very shortly thereafter Wood left the army for good, under a cloud for his performance on September 19, with Col. Mark P. Lowrey assuming command.

despite previous efforts that morning by both Generals Leonidas Polk and Bragg, no one had yet sorted out Cheatham's awkward deployment. In short, despite the hours of extra waiting, little if anything had been accomplished with regard to organizing a proper assault.

Fifteen minutes after Ben Helm's line stepped off farther north, and despite his misgivings, Cleburne ordered his own men into the fight. It was hard going from the start. "Owing to some mistake," complained brigade commander Lucius Polk, "I did not receive the order to advance until a few moments after General Breckinridge's Division had been put in motion." D. H. Hill later averred this was no mistake, but part of the plan explicitly ordered by Bragg—and in Hill's opinion a grave misjudgment. "The simultaneous advance of Cleburne's troops would have greatly relieved Helm, as he was exposed to a flank as well as a direct fire," complained Hill. This is a curious statement, for the orders to advance came from Hill himself, and he could have modified them if needed. Unfortunately, Hill failed to grasp the nature of the defense Helm faced. In addition to the curving nature of the Union line, which delivered that flanking fire, there was also a gap between the two divisions. Polk tried to close this gap by immediately obliquing to the right to close up on Helm's 2nd Kentucky. He never got there. Instead, Polk explained, "I encountered the enemy strongly posted." There was indeed blundering that morning, and much of the reason rested with Hill.[3]

Polk's line was facing the center of the Federal position atop the ridge earlier selected by George Thomas. A series of smaller, lower ridges paralleled the Union line to the east, rising like stair steps toward the Union defenses. This pattern continued westward through the Union position and beyond, with another such step along the alignment of the La Fayette Road, with the next being Snodgrass Hill, three-quarters of a mile farther west. From there, the stair steps became more dramatic—the steep hills of Missionary Ridge. For Pat Cleburne's men, however, the rise and fall was gentle, barely noticeable under normal circumstances, though each created a swale significant enough to offer considerable protection from enemy fire during their advance. Once they crested the final swell, however, Cleburne's Confederates confronted the barricaded Yankee line at a distance that varied between 175 and 225 yards. The ferocity of enemy fire that suddenly erupted from these works stunned the advancing Rebels.

3 *OR* 30, pt. 2, 177; Hill, "Chickamauga: The Great Battle of the West," 655; *OR* 30, pt. 2, 177.

In the center of Polk's line, the 2nd Tennessee faced the juncture between Baird's right and Richard Johnson's left, and so was opposed by the 24th Illinois and 93rd Ohio. The Tennesseans later remembered the Union position as a veritable Gibraltar: "Two lines of logs . . . rising in tiers on the hillside, the top of which was crowned with artillery." Those cannon belonged to the 4th and 5th Indiana batteries. The 4th Indiana's projecting revetment allowed the right-hand section to fire obliquely along Polk's right just as their comrades had done against Helm's left, while Captain Simonson's 5th Indiana fired frontally and angled northward. Working together, both batteries delivered a vicious crossfire into Polk's line. Lieutenant John M. Johnson of the 79th Pennsylvania, one of the supporting regiments in Starkweather's brigade, had a clear view of the bloody destruction: "Both our lines poured into them volley after volley, or rather one continuous volley, while the artillery on either flank (double-shotted with grape and canister) vomited its death-dealing discharges right into their faces."[4]

The effect was awful. Cleburne personally observed this movement and reported that Polk "encountered the heaviest artillery fire I have ever experienced. . . . A hurricane of shot and shell swept the woods from the unseen enemy in my front." Polk himself reported that the fire was "so terrible, indeed, that my line could not advance in the face of it." His brigade immediately went to ground and struggled to reply. Colonel William D. Robison of the 2nd Tennessee tried to induce a charge, but could be only "partially heard, and the yell with which we were wont to join battle was feeble, and roused little animation. Unfortunately, parts of the line began to fire, which occasioned a halt, and soon the firing became general. No further attempt was made to go forward."[5]

There was also still the matter of the gap between Breckinridge's left flank under Helm and Cleburne's right flank under Polk. Captain Robert Cobb commanded the five guns of the Kentucky battery attached to Helm's brigade. Enjoined by Helm to "follow . . . in the rear of the 2nd Kentucky," Cobb stumbled into the 300-yard space between the two commands, where he

4 Anonymous, "The Second Tennessee Regiment at Chickamauga," in Edwin L. Drake, ed., *The Annals of the Army of Tennessee and Early Western History* (May, 1878, Guild Bindary Press, n.d.), 56; John M. Johnston, "At Chickamauga: A Soldier's Story of the Battle," *The Lancaster New Era*, September 10, 1892.

5 *OR* 30, pt. 2, 155, 177; Anonymous, "The Second Tennessee," 56.

experienced the same storm of enemy fire. A small rise seemed to offer a place to bring his own guns to bear. The tree cover on the east slope of this hillock precluded moving his guns up via the limbers, so Cobb tried to have his men push several pieces into position by hand. Before he could site his guns, however, "a most terrible artillery fire with shrapnel was opened upon my left." At the same time, Cobb could see the 2nd Kentucky infantrymen breaking. Fearing sudden capture, the captain ordered a retreat. So too, did Capt. John Mebane, whose Tennessee battery was following Cobb with four 12-pound howitzers. Mebane was nominally attached to General Stovall's brigade (Breckinridge's division), but Maj. Rice Graves, Breckinridge's artillery chief, diverted Mebane toward the divisional left when it became apparent support would be needed here. Mebane briefly came into action on Cobb's right, facing "a bitter fire of all arms at short range," but followed suit when Cobb retired. Both batteries fell back about 500 yards.[6]

Lieutenant Thomas J. Key, commanding Calvert's Arkansas battery, had a similar frustrating experience. Key belonged to Polk and was following his infantry through the woods south of Alexander's Bridge Road looking for a place to engage when his gunners came under a punishing fire. Key pushed one section of his battery up into line between the 2nd Tennessee and 1st Arkansas "amid a shower of [musket] balls. Bravely they loaded and fired, but the underbrush and smoke made such a blank that their firing was extremely unsatisfactory." Quickly the gunners made to leave, but as they did so, "a shell severed the trail of one piece, and it was left to its fate." Key offered up no detail of this action in his report, noting only that a 12-pound howitzer was disabled "in the midst of the battle storm."[7]

With Polk stymied and bereft of supporting artillery, Cleburne rode south to check on the rest of his division and discovered that Wood's Brigade had also stumbled to a halt. Wood's Alabamians fell into disarray early. Initially, Polk's line crowded their right, so Wood "obliqued to the left to give room." When Polk later lurched right in his unsuccessful effort to re-connect with Helm, Wood's "brigade was at once ordered to follow this movement." Before the resultant gap could be closed, Wood's right, like Polk's own right, found itself facing the enemy's furious fire. Colonel Mark Lowrey, commanding the

6 *OR* 30, pt. 2, 217; Cobb's and Mebane's Tablets along Alexander's Bridge Road, September 20, CCNMP.

7 Anonymous, "The Second Tennessee," 57; *OR* 30, pt. 2, 186.

combined 32nd/45th Mississippi and 15th Mississippi Sharpshooters, was charged with keeping contact with Polk, so that general's sudden veer to the right placed Lowrey in a quandary. "I could not then unite with Polk's left without falling back and moving to the right and leaving my own brigade." Unsure of which course to follow, Lowrey's Mississippians lurched to a halt, losing contact both with Polk and the rest of their own brigade.[8]

Riding south, Cleburne found Lowrey's detachment. The Mississippians were still on line with Polk, but some distance to the south atop the same ridge and enduring the same hellish fire. Cleburne also found Wood here, who had come back looking for Lowrey. Wood quickly sketched out the difficulties encountered. His line, he related, was broken into three distinct segments, and intermingled with men from A. P. Stewart's division. When Lowrey tried to close to the right, Wood attempted to follow suit, but his brigade line fractured between the 32nd/45th Mississippi and the 45th Alabama. On Wood's other flank, Deshler's brigade was stuck behind Stewart's division and so lagging even farther behind. The hapless Wood seemed badly confused. When Cleburne told him to resume the attack, Wood expressed concern that both his flanks would be exposed. By this time Cleburne was losing patience with his subordinate and frustrated by how quickly his division had come apart. His worst fears about the strength of the Union line were being realized. It was time to change the plan. Cleburne curtly ordered Wood "to see to the left" of his brigade "and move forward." In the meantime, Cleburne intended to shift Deshler's Texans to the division's center to fill the newly created gap between Wood and Polk.[9]

Thus far, not a man in Deshler's brigade had fired a shot. Just as predicted, when Deshler stepped off he discovered that his way forward was blocked by other troops, though not initially any of Stewart's men. Deshler's front was masked by John K. Jackson's and Alfred J. Vaughan's (formerly Preston Smith's) brigades of Frank Cheatham's division. Cheatham's line was also advancing, but since the flaws in his deployment had never been corrected, his line was angling northwest across Deshler's front. The immediate result was that his Texans lost contact with Wood's left almost immediately. Deshler's men worked their way through this jam, only to discover their next obstacle: Stewart's men. Both Deshler and Cheatham (who had the same difficulty) halted in confused fashion. Cheatham sent word back to Bragg explaining the

8 Ibid., 161, 170.

9 Ibid., 155, 161.

mess, and received instructions to hold in place for the time being and serve as a reserve. Deshler awaited word from his divisional commander. When Cleburne found him, the young brigadier's entire line was halted several hundred yards east and south of Wood's position.[10]

S. A. M. Wood, meanwhile, returned to the rest of his command. In the brigade center, Col. Ephraim B. Breedlove led the 45th Alabama. Like the 41st Alabama in Helm's brigade, Breedlove faced the Federal line at an awkward place, where it jogged back westward to the far side of Poe Field. Lowrey, with the right wing of Wood's brigade, faced William Hazen's and John Turchin's Yankees no more than 200 yards to his immediate front, but Wood's left was still more than 400 yards short of the Federals (King's brigade of Reynolds's division) in Poe Field. If Breedlove turned north to support Lowrey, King's Federals could savage his regiment's left flank. If he kept going west, Turchin's men would enfilade his right flank. Stymied, Breedlove also halted. He and his men could see little, and Breedlove, who was no fan of wasting valuable ammunition, had already instructed his troops "to fire only when they could see the foe." With nothing obvious to shoot at, "they were ordered not to fire and did not." Instead Breedlove pulled the 45th back down behind the low rise in order to shelter them.[11]

Next came the Alabamians of the 16th regiment, already demoralized by their difficult action in Winfrey Field the night before. Once Maj. John H. McGaughy realized the 45th had stopped, he did the same. "We advanced nearly a mile . . . [until] within a short distance of the enemy, who held a very strong position," noted Capt. Frederick A. Ashford, upon whom it later fell to write the 16th's report. "Here [Major McGaughy] ordered [us] to lie down, and remained an hour under a heavy fire of shell, grape, and canister." Colonel Samuel Adams of the 33rd Alabama, next on the 16th's right, saw McGaughy stop and assumed the halt was ordered by Wood. Adams took his men another 15 paces forward to the shelter of a ravine that offered protection from the incoming artillery. "We moved up some 3/4 of a mile," noted Sgt. John H. Smith of Company H, 33rd Alabama, "and was ordered to lie down. We very orderly done so and while we were lying here [the] cannonading was very heavy

10 Ibid., 79. Had Deshler been able to continue moving forward, he would have also soon run up on Stewart's troops, but Cheatham's angled advance cut across his front before that occurred.

11 Ibid., 168.

at this place. Myself and 3 others of our company was wounded by the fragments of a shell."[12]

Lieutenant Richard Goldthwaite commanded Capt. Henry Semple's battery, tasked with supporting Wood. Goldthwaite came upon the 45th Alabama lying under cover, and seemingly alone. He unlimbered his four Napoleons and opened a slow, deliberate fire. The return fire included canister, which suggested that his opponents were perilously close, and he wondered where the rest of the brigade was. General Wood was wondering the same thing.[13]

Leaving Lowrey in place, Wood moved south through the timber, passing Breedlove's 45th Alabama to find the 16th and 33rd Alabama. He moved them into alignment with the right flank of John C. Brown's Tennesseans (of A. P. Stewart's division) whom he found in line nearby. Next he hunted up Brown. Wood explained his own orders, and asked Brown to join him in the attack in order to support his left. This was something Brown could not do without authorization, "but [he] would send to Major General Stewart for orders." Unable for the moment to garner Brown's support, Wood halted. Cleburne's attack was stalled.[14]

While Cleburne's effort was faltering, General Breckinridge was organizing a new assault. By 10:30 a.m., the destruction of John Beatty's Federals was nearly complete and Breckinridge's attention turned southward. Having ordered Col. Joseph H. Lewis to take charge of the Kentuckians in the wake of Helm's wounding and pull the Orphans back to reorganize, Breckinridge rode to the McDonald farmstead, where he conferred with Adams and Stovall. "It was now evident . . . that our line extended beyond the enemy's left," recorded Breckinridge, who determined to send his two remaining brigades south astride the La Fayette Road to envelop the exposed Federal flank. Breckinridge sent word to D. H. Hill informing him of this decision. He also asked for reserves, which were vitally needed to convert this local success into something more decisive. Hill "cordially approved" of the idea to "get in rear of the breastworks" rather than keep trying them frontally. Reinforcements, which in theory were close at hand in the form of William H. T. Walker's Corps, proved

12 Ibid., 164; John H. Smith Diary, 33rd Alabama file, CCNMP. In fact, the 16th Alabama's advance was closer to a half mile, amounting to no more than 700 or 800 yards.

13 *OR* 30, pt. 2, 174.

14 Ibid., 161.

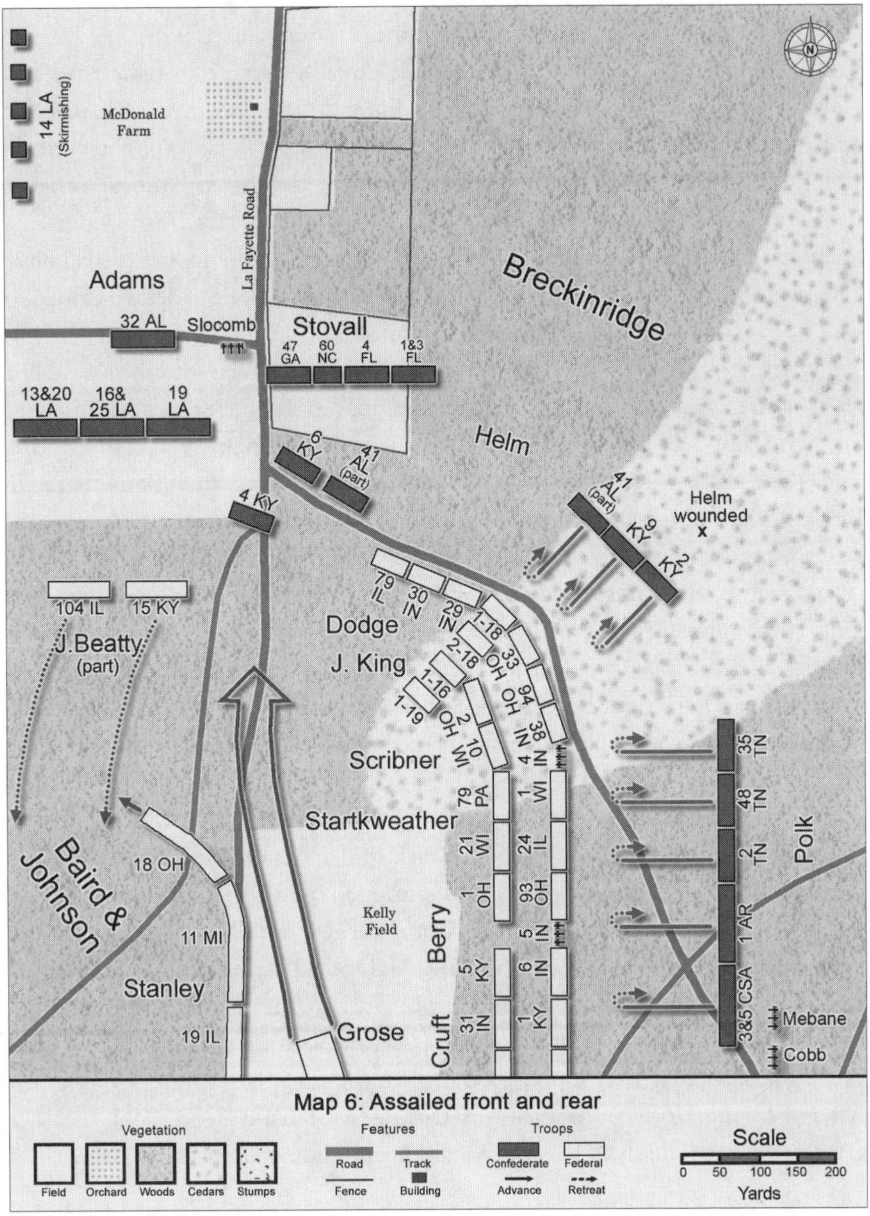

to be more problematic. For reasons that will become evident soon, it would be quite some time before D. H. Hill sent any additional troops forward to capitalize on John Breckinridge's success.[15]

15 Ibid., 199; Hill, "Chickamauga: The Great Battle of the West," 655.

Breckinridge would not wait. The opportunity to drive down behind the Federal line had to be seized. He aligned Stovall's men east of the road and placed Adams's Louisianans on Stovall's right. Adams left the 32nd Alabama and Austin's Sharpshooters behind to screen his right flank—the direction in which the 42nd and 88th Indiana had retreated—in case those Yankees reappeared. Adams then placed the 19th, 16th/25th, and 13th/20th Louisiana in line facing south. Even though the losses suffered in routing Beatty had been light, the absence of the Helm's Orphans and Adams's need to detach troops to watch his right greatly reduced Breckinridge's available combat power. Together, Stovall and Adams were leading about 1,800 men into the assault, or no more than one-half of Breckinridge's original strength. Perhaps surprise and momentum would compensate for the paucity of bayonets.[16]

Helm's loss struck an emotional chord with the demonstrative Breckinridge, but his composure appeared intact as he watched Adams and Stovall wheel into position. Lieutenant Mercer Otey of the Confederate Signal Corps marveled at Breckinridge "calmly sitting his beautiful bay, stroking that long, curling mustache . . . apparently as indifferent to the screaming shells then hustling the tree tops overhead as if he had been on dress parade. I never saw a more godlike hero than Breckinridge at that moment." John Beatty, who was frantically trying to rebuild some semblance of a Union line opposing this new threat, was also impressed. "Years later, when someone complimented [Beatty] on being the handsomest mounted figure he had ever seen, Beatty . . . replied: 'You certainly never saw . . . John C. Breckinridge on a horse.'"[17]

The only immediate support Breckinridge could offer his infantry came when Capt. C. H. Slocomb's 5th Company of the Washington Artillery unlimbered in the field just south of the McDonald farmstead. "[We] opened rapidly on the enemy that were in large force in the woods to the south," recalled Lt. Joseph Chalaron. Riding with Slocomb's gunners was the ever-aggressive Maj. Rice Graves, looking for the best place to employ his guns. After the tangle of woods that had frustrated Mebane's and Cobb's earlier efforts, the open fields of the McDonald farm seemed an ideal position.[18]

16 Powell, "Numbers and Losses," CCNMP.

17 W. N. Mercer Otey, "Story of Our Great War," *Confederate Veteran*, vol. VIII, no. 8 (August, 1900), 342; Davis, Breckinridge, 375.

18 J. A. Chalaron, "Vivid Experiences At Chickamauga," *Confederate Veteran*, vol. III, no. 9 (September, 1895), 278.

When all was ready, Stovall and Adams ordered their brigades forward. The Confederates believed they were entirely beyond the presence of any pre-positioned Union defenders. This assumption was correct as far as Adams's Louisianans were concerned, but Stovall's left faced the three small Federal regiments of Dodge's brigade, and his right was on a collision course with the four regiments of William Grose's command, recently plucked by George Thomas from the southern end of Kelly Field. Unfortunately for the Federals, Grose and his men were equally clueless about where, exactly, the Union flank ended.

After hustling across Kelly Field, Colonel Grose halted briefly astride the La Fayette Road, wondering what to do next. The 84th Illinois and 36th Indiana were in front, to the left and right of the road, respectively, with the 6th and 24th Ohio forming his second line. Artillery shells were dropping here and there and the general sound of battle swept in from all around him, but there were no immediate threats in sight. A few weeks later, an infantry officer from the 6th Ohio recounted what happened next. During the halt, he left the regiment and crept up the road a short distance through a skirt of trees until he could see into McDonald Field. "[T]o my astonishment," he wrote, '[I] saw the rebels forming scarcely two hundred yards from us. . . . I counted four columns of them, and saw two generals riding along the lines." The officer scrambled back as fast as he could to report his discovery to a highly skeptical brigade commander. "[Grose] said they were our troops, and I could not convince him to the contrary; he said they *must* be our troops, because there was at least one line ahead of ours."[19]

While the 6th Ohio awaited instructions, Lt. Harry Cushing's Battery H, 4th U.S. Artillery deployed behind the Buckeyes and began replying to Slocomb's incoming shells. Captain Wilbur Goodspeed's Battery A, 1st Ohio Light Artillery, followed suit. Before he realized it, Grose found his brigade in the middle of an artillery duel, with rounds screaming overhead in both directions. Cushing at least understood his business, however, and managed not to drop any shells among Grose's waiting troops. Captain Edward Grosskopff's 20th Ohio Battery, deployed farther south in Kelly Field, proved less

19 Ebenezer Hannaford, *The Story of a Regiment: A History of the Campaigns, and Associations in the Field, of the Sixth Regiment Ohio Volunteer Infantry* (Published by the Author, 1868), 466. Hannaford did not identify the officer from the 6th Ohio who first spotted Breckinridge's men forming.

discriminating. Grosskopff's gunners also opened fire, but mistook Grose's troops for Confederates. The situation for the hapless blue-clad infantry had gone from bad to worse. Grosskopff's gunners "began playing upon us with canister . . . notwithstanding our color-bearers bravely rode up and waved our flags to show . . . who we were," recalled the 6th's historian, Ebenezer Hannaford. When that failed, Maj. Samuel Erwin of the 6th Ohio sent a man back to relay the message personally. The damage was done, however. "We lost a number of men . . . [and] our regiment was much demoralized. . . . [We] could stand the rebel fire, but when it came to being shot by our own men, it was played out."[20]

Several of Colonel Grose's men remember a series of small movements or minor adjustments to their position during this time, which offer a description of the minutes just prior to Breckinridge's attack that collectively suggest a fair degree of uncertainty on Grose's part. The colonel was attempting to figure out where he should move next, still laboring under the false impression that he was supporting an existing Federal line in the woods somewhere just to his north. The last of these minor movements was cut short when the Confederates materialized in front and on the left flank of Grose's formation, with devastating results.

Grose's report omitted these adjustments: "Before we arrived at the intended position in the line, the enemy came upon Baird's Division, and consequently on my command, in fearful numbers. I formed the four regiments under a destructive fire . . . in a woodland covered with a heavy underbrush." Louis Simmons of the 84th Illinois remembered that he and his comrades "were speedily moving by the flank, when [we] came upon the enemy in strong force, so concealed by the brush . . . that the first intimation of their presence was a sharp volley. . . . A line of battle . . . was formed under a galling fire." The 6th Ohio was still in the reserve line, not yet moving and thus spared the worst of this initial collision. The Buckeyes managed to at least open fire. "We waited for the troops said to be in front of us to fall back," lamented an Ohioan, "but in vain—*there were none there*. . . . Suddenly a gray line burst into view, and before we were aware of it, fired into us a terrific volley. . . . Fortunately we were lying down, so that few were hurt."[21]

20 Ibid., 467. Hannaford never identified the battery, but the 20th Ohio was the only battery in the right place at the right time.

21 *OR* 30, pt. 1, 781; Simmons, *84th Reg't Ill. Vols.*, 97; Hannaford, *The Story of a Regiment*, 476.

Captain Winfrey Scott of the 19th Louisiana described that same moment from the other side of the front: "We then changed our line . . . and could see them very distinctly they were in an old field on a hill in tree lines lieing, kneeling, and standing with heavy batteries in their rear." When General Adams's attention was directed toward this new threat, "he replied with an oath, that we must take them . . . we marched on with rapid steps, when within one hundred and fifty paces, we opened a terrific fire upon them and loaded as we advanced."[22]

Surprised and caught deploying, Grose's regiments struggled to get into line and return fire. As their losses mounted, the lead ranks broke and scrambled for the rear in a rapid mass of confused rout. Colonel Louis Waters "had just formed" his 84th Illinois "when the enemy appeared well around our left flank." Worse, complained Waters, "the brigade at the works in our front as promptly disappeared, leaving . . . our men in a slaughter pen." Unbeknownst to Waters, there was no friendly brigade to his front. The 84th collapsed. Illinois Pvt. James Suitor admitted that "we were compelled to fall back, for we were nearly surrounded. . . . We became somewhat confused, and the regiments were considerably mixed, one with another."[23]

The 6th Ohio's Major Erwin, aligned behind the 84th Illinois, echoed Suitor. Erwin recalled being "forced back in some confusion." In fact, he continued, "my regiment became divided . . . and were for some time separated from me." The hammer-blow next struck the 36th Indiana and Grose's weakest reed, the 24th Ohio.[24]

That morning, after the grueling fight of the day before and having made a cold camp overnight, Col. David Higgins's rheumatism flared anew, effectively crippling him. Once again Higgins turned to Major McClure to take charge of the 24th since Higgins now found it impossible to keep up with the men. As a result, Higgins wasn't with his regiment during this phase of the battle and could only vaguely report that the 24th Ohio was "on the extreme left" when it "was crushed . . . and forced to give way, torn and bleeding at every part."[25]

22 Winfrey Scott to Mrs. E. C. Scott, Oct 3rd, 1863, http://www.louisianacivilwar.com/2010/02/19th-louisiana-at-kelly-field.html, accessed 2/15/2010.

23 *OR* 30, pt. 1, 787; "September 20th, 1863," James P. Suitor Diary, ALPL.

24 *OR* 30, pt. 1, 797.

25 Ibid., 798.

Directly ahead of the 24th was the 36th Indiana. The brush here was "so thick," noted an Indiana captain named David W. Chambers, "that although [the rebels] were within fifty feet of our left they could not be seen by [our] men on the ground. . . . They poured in the most destructive fire I was ever under." Mounted that morning to serve as one of the 36th's Indiana's field officers in the wake of the previous day's severe losses, Chambers caught more than his share of this deadly attention: "My horse was shot in the neck. I received two slight wounds—one on my throat, just grazing the jugular vein; the second on the left shoulder . . . about two inches long, and deep enough just to touch the bone."[26]

In scant minutes Grose's brigade was shattered and flying. Grose was at first mortified and then enraged, especially at the 24th Ohio, which he felt broke too easily. He later singled out Higgins and McClure as the significant targets of his ire; neither man would ever command the 24th again. Some members of the regiment agreed with Grose's assessment, casting an especially suspicious eye at Higgins's absence. "We are very unfortunate with our field officers, lamented Sgt. James D. Burnett of Company F. "At Stone River we lost our [first] Colonel and Major; they were brave men and both got killed. Here, our Colonel and Major were both cowards." Higgins, whose infirmities meant he never should have been with the regiment in the first place, would soon leave the army entirely when he resigned his commission on October 23 and went home. Fortunately for the Federals, a number of other Union regiments were headed directly for the dangerous breech left by Grose's collapse.[27]

John Beatty remained center stage for this drama. While Breckinridge was realigning his men to renew the assault, Beatty rallied the 15th Kentucky and 104th Illinois and posted them in the woods southwest of Grose's position. These two battered regiments, however, were not strong enough to stop the Rebels without a great deal of help and Beatty knew it. The brigadier ranged over much of Kelly Field looking for that aid (it was Beatty who induced Captain Goodspeed to open fire with the guns). Beatty, however, needed more than a few artillery pieces. Placing his rump of a brigade under the command of Colonel Taylor of the 15th Kentucky, Beatty recalled that he was riding "back to see General Thomas or Negley and urge the necessity for more troops" when

26 "Another Letter from the 36th," *New Castle Courier*, October 8, 1863.

27 "Letter from an old Democrat," *Western Reserve Chronicle*, October 28, 1863. The official roster is silent on McClure's fate.

he stumbled across Col. Timothy Stanley's brigade, a fellow command in Negley's division.[28]

Beatty immediately took charge, placing Stanley's men in line west of the road, and shifted his own two battered regiments into a supporting position on the left-rear of Stanley's command. The 700 men of the 18th Ohio and 11th Michigan formed Stanley's front line, with the 19th Illinois in support. Beatty ordered everyone to lie down. For Wolverine Sgt. James Martin of Company H of the 11th regiment, everything seemed to happen very quickly. As they went prone, the "line in front of us gave way and came tumbling over us, and on came the Rebels yelling like mad men." In the 18th Ohio, Sgt. James Verity recorded the same incident: "First Brigade overpowered and broken. We lay down and let them pass over." Once the front was clear, however, Stanley's men rose and delivered a powerful volley into the faces of the oncoming Confederates. The effect was dramatic, confirmed Sergeant Verity, who remembered "the ground was covered with their dead and dying."[29]

The bloody shock delivered against the onrushing Pelicans by Stanley's Federals claimed Adams as one of its first casualties. "[A] concentrated fire of the enemy was poured into our ranks," recalled a lieutenant named John McGrath attacking with the 13th Louisiana, and under this blast "Genl Adams fell wounded from his horse while gallantly leading us on." "Then a mistake was made," lamented Capt. John Ellis of the 16th Louisiana, "which altered the whole face of affairs and prevented the rout of the enemy. . . . Adams had fallen severely wounded and the command devolved on Col. [Randall] Gibson [of the 13th/20th Louisiana] who ordered the lines to halt. . . . The enemy rallied and reinforced their swaying line, poured in volley after volley."[30]

Although Ellis thought the halt was a blunder, Gibson checked the Rebel advance because his 13th/20th was already breaking for the rear. With nearly 900 men still in their ranks, Adams's men should have lapped Stanley's flanks, but Beatty's 15th Kentucky and 104th Illinois were not yet out of the fight. Stepping up to prolong Stanley's left, their additional muskets opened a flanking fire against Gibson's exposed right. The 13th/20th had become "scattered" in

28 Beatty, *Citizen-Soldier*, 337.

29 "Dear parents" September 24, 1863, James Martin Letters, Bentley Library, UMich; October 16th Journal entry, James Verity Journal, Clements Library, UMich. The routed Federals running through their ranks were men from Grose's brigade.

30 "Friend Dan," September 21, 1863, John McGrath Papers, LSU; E. J. Ellis Diary, LSU.

the fight with Grose, noted Gibson, and "while thus disordered received a terrific and unbroken volley from a second line that suddenly came up. . . . The whole line was checked." The Louisianans fell back about 100 yards, where Gibson grabbed the colors in an effort to reform his men and lead them back up to support the 16th/25th Louisiana's flank.[31]

It was while looking back south that Gibson realized Adams had been struck. The wounded brigadier, recalled Gibson, was "on foot" behind the other regiment "looking at his arm . . . but I presumed he was [only] slightly wounded." Within minutes, however, Col. Daniel Gober of the 16th/25th arrived with other news: Adams was badly hurt, and Gibson now had command.[32]

To Lieutenant McGrath of the 13th/20th, Yankee bullets seemed to cut a swath through the ranks. McGrath escaped injury, but his scabbard was "cut in pieces by a grapeshot." Captain Theodore Schneider, commanding Company D, immediately handed McGrath a replacement, taken from the just-stricken "Lieutenant Weistimer who was killed by a grape from the same gun. . . . I had scarcely buckled on the belt and turned to thank the captain," noted McGrath, "when I found him lying dead." The next to fall was "our Color Sergeant—poor McDevitt . . . he had been an english soldier and fought at Balaclava, Inkermann, and the Redan. . . . He fell holding to the breeze the flag of the 13th La."[33]

The Union fire intensified. On the Rebel brigade's other flank, Captain Winfrey Scott described "a most dreadful fire . . . [of] canister, grape and leaden balls, it would be vain for me to attempt to describe it. . . . [W]e got I suppose within 90 or 100 yards of them when our line ceased to advance and there was evidently some confusion among our troops." Here the 19th Louisiana was struggling. With Lt. Col. Leon Von Zinken detached and serving on Breckinridge's staff, regimental command was in the hands of Lt. Col. Richard Turner at the start of the day's engagement. Turner was wounded in the first action and forced to relinquish command, which left Maj. Loudon Butler in charge, though only for a few minutes. Butler, "the only officer in the brigade who dared to enter the charge on horseback, [had] his neck broken by a

31 *OR* 30, pt. 2, 221.

32 Ibid., 222.

33 Letter of September 24, 1863, John McGrath Papers, LSU.

Brigade commander Marcellus A. Stovall.
Library of Congress

grapeshot." His death thrust Capt. Hyder A. Kennedy of Company C into command. With the rest of the brigade wavering, Kennedy noticed that Stovall's right was more than 100 yards from his own regimental left, and also in distress.[34]

Marcellus A. Stovall's brigade was sweeping south along the eastern side of the La Fayette Road in an effort to keep pace with Adams's advance. Stovall, a tall man "of striking personal appearance" who like Breckinridge eschewed a full beard for a luxuriant black moustache, was trying to push his line forward into Kelly Field. The 47th Georgia and 60th North Carolina had a hand in wrecking Grose's formation, though Adams's Louisiana men did most of that damage when they turned Grose's left. Now, the Georgians and Tar Heels, along with the Floridians of the 4th regiment, were pushing through the timber directly into Kelly Field.[35]

Stovall's left-most regiment, the 1st/3rd Florida under Col. William S. Dilworth, did not accompany the rest of the brigade. Colonel Dilworth soon discovered that unlike Stovall's other regiments, he was facing a determined Union defense. Colonel Dodge's three Federal regiments, placed on the Regulars's left that morning, were still there, all but forgotten by almost everyone, even the Regulars. So far, most of the fighting on this flank seemed to pass them by. That now changed. Dodge's line was formed on a slight slope, "descend[ing] gradually for fifty or seventy five yards" and then "quite rapidly

34 Winfrey Scott to Mrs. E. C. Scott, October 3, 1863, *http://www.louisianacivilwar.com/2010/02/19th-louisiana-at-kelly-field.html*, accessed 2/15/2010; Salling, *Louisianians in the Western Confederacy*, 127; OR 30, pt. 2, 225.

35 C. L. Bragg, *Distinction in Every Service: Brigadier General Marcellus A. Stovall, C.S.A.* (White Mane Books, 2002), 163.

some twenty yards farther to the bottom of a little ravine and then ascended rather sharply" to mask the Union line from any distance. The effect was to create something of a slaughter pen in Dodge's immediate front. The only flaw was that the brigade's right was not in close contact with the 2/18th U.S. Regulars holding King's left. With Dodge spending most of his time in transit between the brigade and divisional headquarters, tactical leadership of the brigade devolved onto the shoulders of Col. Allen Buckner of the 79th Illinois. Buckner's line mustered only 700 men, but they were more than a match for Colonel Dilworth's 298 Floridians. "It became apparent that the right of the enemy extended far beyond my left," lamented Dilworth, "but the order to advance was positive, and we advanced up the hill at a double-quick under a galling fire." To Florida Pvt. Sam Pasco, the charge was nothing short of murderous: "nearly ninety men fell in about ten minutes."[36]

Curiously, the Regulars thought the Floridians's assault succeeded. The 2/18th U.S. was still on line with its brother 1st Battalion, having just helped repulse the 2nd and 9th Kentucky. The 2/18th's line was angled to face more west than north, however, and not firmly connected with the troops to its left. Captain Henry Haymond, commanding the battalion, was either unaware of Dodge's brigade's presence on his left, or mistook Grose's men for Dodge's troops and assumed that Grose's abrupt collapse rendered his own left flank dangerously exposed. "My position being flanked and the command being exposed to an enfilading fire," reported Haymond, "I fell back to the timber in the rear." Haymond elaborated in a private letter: "the brigade on my left gave way which enabled the enemy to flank my position and to pour on an enfilading fire. This we stood but a short time." Because they had been overrun the previous day, the Regulars were sensitive to any threats of flanking and fell back in considerable disorder. Had Colonel Buckner and his three small regiments been facing more than one Rebel regiment, additional Confederate troops might have been able to exploit the dangerous gap thus created, but the lack of immediate Confederate reserves allowed Haymond's retreat to go unnoticed by their opponents.[37]

36 Dodge, "The Story of Chickamauga, part two," *Northern Indianian*, February 11, 1875; *OR* 30, pt. 2, 233; Entry for September 20, Samuel Pasco Diary, 3rd Florida file, CCNMP.

37 *OR* 30, pt. 1, 321; "Dear Pa," September 24, 1863, Henry Haymond Letters, Pearce Civil War Collection, Navarro College. The 77th Pennsylvania, having lost so many men the night before, was now folded into the remaining regiments of Dodge's brigade.

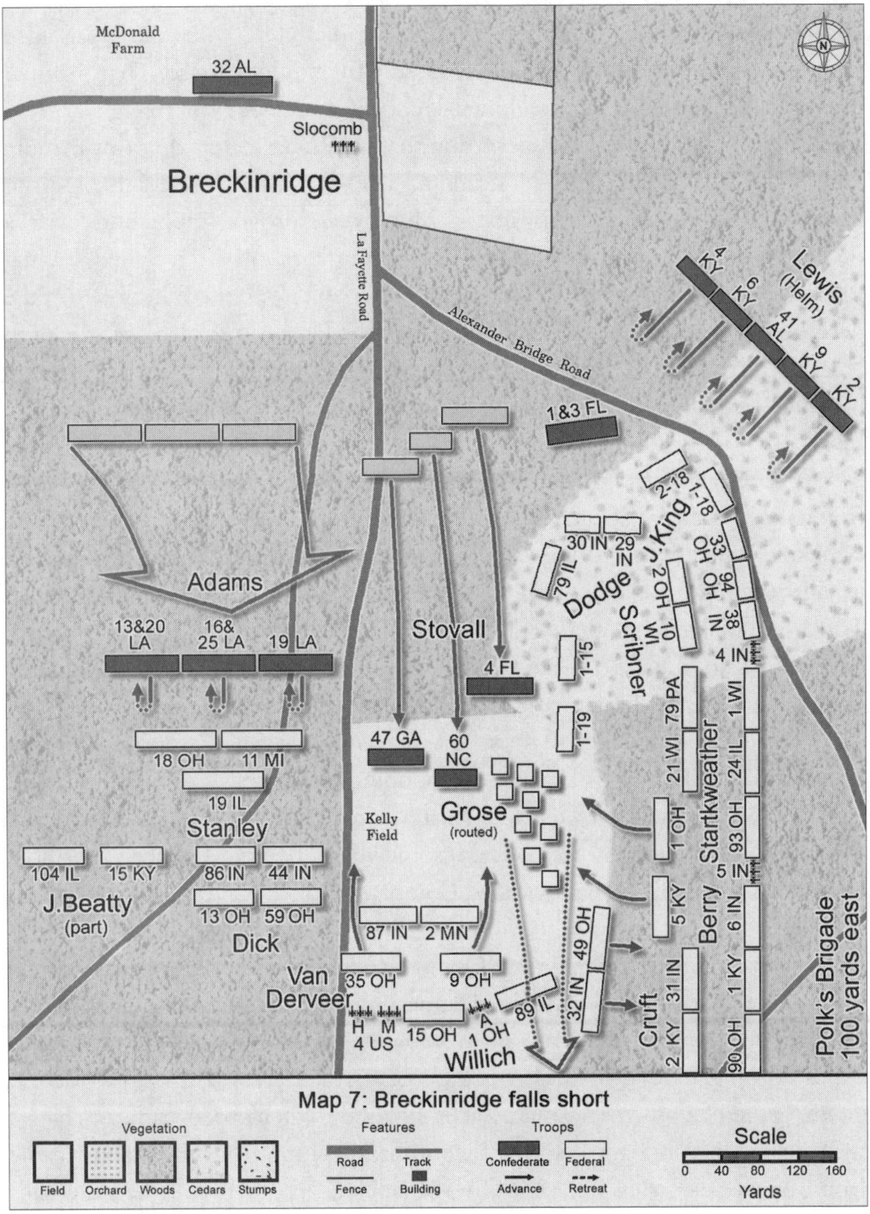

Map 7: Breckinridge falls short

Ignoring the discomfiture of the Floridians, the rest of Stovall's brigade moved south beyond Buckner's left flank. Anchoring Stovall's center was the 60th North Carolina. With only 168 men, the 60th was a mere skeleton of a regiment, and an unhappy one to boot. The command formed in the summer of 1862, most of them enlisting grudgingly under the threat of conscription. The men of the 60th cared little for secession or the Confederacy. Most of them came from the mountains of western North Carolina and if anything, harbored

Unionist sentiments. They were originally recruited with the misguided understanding that they would be used only for home defense. That promise was soon broken when the regiment left East Tennessee for Bragg's army, a move that triggered a wave of desertion that would ultimately drain away more than a third of the regiment's strength. The unit also suffered under poor leadership. Its first colonel, Joseph McDowell, proved inept and after a near-mutiny and disastrous performance at Murfreesboro he resigned, leaving Lt. Col. James Ray in charge. Ray was a better soldier, but could not stop the desertion. On September 10, 1863, Lt. Thomas Patton recorded that the 60th "lost over fifty men in the past week" alone. Those men still with the colors and moving south that morning were about to have their resolve tested to the fullest.[38]

Once clear of the trees, Stovall's men witnessed an awe-inspiring—and frightening—martial spectacle. "Moving into the open field," recalled Capt. Benjamin Williams of the 47th Georgia, on the 60th's right, "we were close and in full view of the parked batteries and massed columns of Rosecrans' left wing. The order was given to charge after our first volley and with fixed bayonets we swept on into the field." Stovall reported the moment, with considerable understatement, "I encountered the enemy in heavy force."[39]

A major component of those massed columns was comprised of Col. Ferdinand Van Derveer's brigade. Responding to Thomas's earlier summons, Van Derveer hustled into Kelly Field just before Grose was assailed. He initially deployed his regiments facing east somewhere behind Palmer's position. Lieutenant Jeremiah Donahower led Company E of the 2nd Minnesota across the road between the Kelly house and a "caved-in well in which we saw a half dozen wounded men" sheltering. Once in the field, the Minnesotans "began looking about for the enemy, whose appearance we expected in our front. . . . [instead] the air was suddenly filled with bullets and a line of gray smoke appeared on the edge of the woods on our left." "[We] had hardly got laid down," noted fellow Minnesotan, Sgt. Axel Reed, "when orders came to change front to the left and [we] had hardly got into position when the enemy came from the woods on us. The 9th Ohio which was in our front when the balls

38 James Carlisle Taylor, *The 60th North Carolina Regiment: A Case Study of Enlistment and Desertion in Western North Carolina During the Civil War.* Master's Thesis, Western Carolina University, 1996, 126-127, 134.

39 Benjamin S. Williams Reminiscences, Emory University; *OR* 30, pt. 2, 231.

whizzed over our heads like hail, came back in a rush and laid down behind us, when we opened a withering fire upon the rebels."[40]

Van Derveer's four regiments, with the 87th Indiana and 2nd Minnesota now in front and the 35th and 9th Ohio in support, confronted Stovall head-on. The mixed brigade of Federals were not alone. At least three batteries of Union artillery also fixed their attention on Stovall's line: four pieces of Cushing's Battery H, six guns from Battery A of the 1st Ohio, and six more from Battery M, 4th U.S. Brigadier General August Willich's brigade, which was in reserve and not called upon to repulse Cleburne's assault, supported this fight. Willich wheeled about his rear regiments, the 15th Ohio and 89th Illinois, to backstop Van Derveer's men confronting Stovall. Colonel William Berry, now commanding Baldwin's brigade (Richard Johnson's division) after Baldwin was killed the previous day, also demonstrated an agile tactical sense. Despite the fact that his two front regiments were then fully engaged fending off Lucius Polk's attacking Confederates, when more enemy dressed in gray and butternut appeared in his rear (Stovall's men), Colonel Berry adroitly refaced the 1st Ohio and 5th Kentucky of his supporting line so they could fire into Stovall's left flank.[41]

Due to the unusual depth of Col. John King's original deployment, two of his battalions, the 1/15th U.S. and 1/19th U.S., were perfectly situated to turn and face west and fire directly into the passing and wholly exposed flank of the 4th Florida at close range. Bugler William J. Carson of the 1/15th acquired a musket and roamed the rear of the battalion as a self-appointed provost guard. When Captain Haymond ordered the 2/18th U.S. to fall back, Carson witnessed the disorderly retreat and immediately recalled the disaster of the previous day. "I threw down my gun rushed out some 30 yards to the color bearer of the 18th and said. . . . 'Let us rally these men or the whole left is gone.' The brave fellow stopped and waved his flag. I sounded 'to the colors.' The men cheered. They rushed into line. . . . What a few minutes before seemed a hopeless, disastrous rout, now turned into a complete victory."[42]

40 Jeremiah Donahower Papers, Minnesota Historical Society, St. Paul, MN. Hereafter MinnHS; Judson W. Bishop, *The Story of a Regiment, Being a Narrative of the Service of the Second Regiment, Minnesota Veteran Volunteer Infantry, in the Civil War of 1861-1865* (North Star Press, 2000), 106; Entry for September 20, Axel Reed Diary, 2nd Minnesota file, CCNMP.

41 Powell and Friedrichs, *The Maps of Chickamauga*, 155; *OR* 30, pt. 1, 565.

42 Johnson, *That Body of Brave Men*, 403.

Despite the drama of the moment and Carson's colorful language, there was no "disastrous rout." In fact, Stovall's momentum was already faltering. The heavy fire of the 87th Indiana and 2nd Minnesota was savaging Stovall, whose embattled soldiers were doing all they could to return fire. The 2nd Minnesota's Lieutenant Donahower recalled how the Confederates "would rise to their feet, fire their rifles, and then drop down" again to reload. Responding in kind, "in about five minutes" Donahower and his fellow Minnesotans "made the position of the 60th North Carolina a dangerous one." On Donahower's left, the 87th was not only engaging the 47th Georgia but dropping men in the ranks of the 19th Louisiana. The left of the 87th and the 19th's left each stood in the La Fayette Road, blasting away at one another at close range. "Down the road about sixty yards," wrote Hoosier Sgt. Benjamin Brown, "I saw the rebels as thick as . . . pigeons on a newly sown wheat field. I got up then and went to work." When he perceived the enemy beginning to waver, Van Derveer ordered a charge.[43]

The 9th and 35th Ohio regiments comprised Van Derveer's support line. The 35th was lying prone, recalled its commander Lt. Col. Henry Van Ness Boynton, "until the first line should finish its fire; the second line then rose and charged, following the broken and retreating lines of the rebels." Similarly, "We loaded and fired," reported Sergeant Brown of the 87th Indiana, "until the 9th Ohio made a charge."[44]

To Colonel Kammerling and his fellow Germans in the 9th Ohio, the fighting was all in a day's work, or so the 9th's regimental history breezily recorded: "We charged at once with bayonets and cleaned out a stretch of the encircling forest." Behind the two regiments of Buckeyes, Van Derveer's original front line jumped up and followed suit, though perhaps not quite so enthusiastically. "We got orders to charge," recalled Capt. Horace Long of the 87th Indiana. "The rebels were there in front of us, two to one . . . but there was no backing out and nobody seemed to want to [go] forward. We went at the rebels at the command." To Long's relief, "It was more than they could stand, to have us come at them with cold steel; they broke and ran."[45]

43 Donahower Papers. MinnHS; "Letter By Sgt. Benjamin F. Brown, Co. D," *Rochester Chronicle*, October 15, 1863.

44 *OR* 30, pt. 1, 435; Letter of September 23, 1863, *Rochester Chronicle*, October 15 1863.

45 Constantine Grebner, *We Were The Ninth: A History of the Ninth Regiment, Ohio Volunteer Infantry April 17, 1861 to June 7, 1864,* trans. and ed. Frederic Trautmann (Kent State University

Colonel William Berry (heading up Baldwin's brigade) witnessed Van Derveer's charge and decided to help out. He retained the 1st Ohio to make sure his front line still engaging Polk had support, but sent his own 5th Kentucky slicing into the Rebels's left flank. Captain John M. Huston, now in charge of the 5th Kentucky, complied with a will, driving the Confederates a distance Huston estimated at "a mile and a half." The 5th also took "200 prisoners" though not without great personal cost to the captain. "My oldest son, Lieutenant Huston, was killed," he reported, adding, "He died like a soldier, with sword in hand, in the midst of a victorious charge upon a fleeing enemy."[46]

To Stovall's men, it must have seemed as if every Federal in the world was bearing down upon them. The 47th Georgia had pressed the farthest into the field, "75 or 100 paces" beyond the wood line, when Capt. William Phillips ordered his men to halt and lie down. The Georgians traded perhaps "a dozen or more rounds" with the Yankees, all the time waiting for the 60th North Carolina to catch up with them on their left. When that didn't happen, Phillips ordered his line back, just as Van Derveer was urging his men forward. At that moment Phillips went down, struck in the hip, leaving the command in the hands of Capt. Joseph Cone. It was too late for Cone or anyone else to do much of anything and the Georgia regiment dissolved into chaotic retreat. Lieutenant Benjamin S. Williams, the 47th's adjutant, recalled that the Georgians lost their second color-bearer of the day here: "Our flagstaff was cut in two and our colors riddled, but a young officer . . . caught up the flag [and] bore it safely to the rear, where a temporary staff replaced the old and polished one." Williams was struck in the midst of this retreat and knocked unconscious for a time.[47]

The 60th North Carolina hadn't pressed forward because the 4th Florida on its left also slid to a halt, savaged by a ring of Union fire from the aforementioned Regulars, the 1st Ohio, and 5th Kentucky, and at least some of the Minnesotans. For his part, Col. W. L. L. Bowen of the 4th Florida was still expecting fellow Floridians from the 1st/3rd to come up on his left. Instead, "The enemy poured a concentrated and effective fire upon us," lamented

Press, 1987), 143; "Letter From Captain Horace C. Long, Co. F," *Rochester Chronicle*, November 19, 1863.

46 *OR* 30, pt. 1, 570. Huston's report greatly exaggerated the distance of this charge, which in reality could not have been more than a few hundred yards.

47 Ibid., pt. 2, 237; Bowers, *The 47th Georgia*, 23.

Bowen, and "support failing to come up in due time, we were forced to yield." The Tar Heel commander, Lieutenant Colonel Ray of the 60th, also went down, felled with a hip wound. His injury thrust Capt. James T. Weaver into command. With the Georgians coming back on his right and the Floridians uncovering his left, Weaver had no choice but to order his own men to fall back.[48]

West of the La Fayette Road, John Beatty and Timothy Stanley were seized by the same idea: it was time for a countercharge. Stanley brought up the 19th Illinois to extend the brigade right, adding more rifle barrels against Adams's embattled 19th Louisiana. With Stanley's line hammering the Louisianans, recalled Beatty, the Rebels "wavered, I gave the order to advance, then to charge, and the brigade went forward with a yell." Down the line Stanley was doing the same thing, and the entire blue line lurched ahead.[49]

With General Adams down, Colonel Gibson was still struggling to come to grips with his new responsibilities when the Federals charged. Losses had mounted so quickly that effective command proved nearly impossible. "We began to give ground," admitted Lieutenant McGrath, "and were soon forced to fall back behind our battery, where we rallied amid a shower of shot and shell." Now feeling very alone indeed, Captain Kennedy of the 19th Louisiana reported, "I had no alternative left me but to order a retreat, which," he admitted, "was conducted somewhat disorderly." All of this occurred before Gibson even had a chance to communicate with the brigade's other officers. There was now little or no chance to reform the shattered command short of Slocomb's guns.[50]

Stanley's men vigorously pursued the Confederates, as did some of Van Derveer's command. The 11th Michigan of Stanley's brigade overran and captured the wounded Adams, laying the first of many boasts to that achievement. As many as six other regiments would eventually stake a claim to bagging Adams, noted Wolverine Capt. Borden Hicks, "but the best proof would say that I had his sword, other members of our regiment had his field glasses and revolvers, belt and so forth." Sergeant Major Washington Irving Snyder was the first to lay hands on the injured officer's sword. When he was

48 *OR* 30, pt. 2, 235, 258-259.

49 Beatty, *Citizen-Soldier*, 337.

50 McGrath Papers, LSU; *OR* 30, pt. 2, 225.

Confederate Brig. Gen. Daniel Adams, who was wounded and captured in McDonald Field.
Library of Congress

wounded in the left side soon thereafter, Snyder passed his trophy on to Captain Hicks, who rushed on after the Louisianans, "going into this charge with a sword in each hand, and looking as savage as a meat ax." Stanley conversed briefly with the downed Rebel general. When Adams asked for a stretcher, Stanley explained there was no time or help to spare. Soon thereafter Stanley's adjutant, Capt. R. J. Waggener, found Adams "reclining on his right side." When he inquired about the extent of his injuries, Adams replied, "I am wounded in the side and am bleeding profusely." Could he walk? "No," groaned the general. Waggener sent a man to fetch his horse and Adams made a painful saddle-borne journey to the rear.[51]

Adams was the most prominent capture, but not the only one. Various Federal reports claim a total of several hundred prisoners, which likely included many of the Rebel wounded. Stovall and Adams only reported a combined total of 150 or so missing, but the number of killed and wounded was high—especially given the short duration of the fight. Overall Rebel losses during this phase of the fighting amounted to 650, or just more than one-third of the 1,800 engaged. Yankee casualties are more difficult to extrapolate because the fighting here was not the only combat Van Derveer's and Stanley's men would experience during the battle. Almost certainly they were significant. Sergeant

51 Charles E. Belknap, *History of the Michigan Organizations at Chickamauga, Chattanooga, and Missionary Ridge, 1863* (Robert Smith Printing Company, 1897), 248. Originally reported as "slight," Snyder's injury proved fatal. The sergeant major died on October 5, 1863. Borden M. Hicks, "Personal Recollections of the War of the Rebellion," *MOLLUS*, vol. 31, 529; *OR* 30, pt. 1, 379.

Reed of the 2nd Minnesota noted that his regiment's losses here were the highest of the entire battle, and that every mounted officer lost his horse in the engagement. Lieutenant Colonel Judson Bishop of the 2nd Minnesota sent the sergeant back through the field to find his fallen mount and retrieve his pistols. Reed never did find Bishop's horse, but he did discover a grim sight that lingered with him to the end of his days: "I was soon on the ground where our regiment had fought," he recalled. "It was a horrible sight. . . . The men of my own regiment lying just as they were shot."[52]

Reed's comrades in the 9th Ohio moved up through the timber nearly to Alexander's Bridge Road. They swept past the left flank of Dodge's brigade, still overlooking their ravine and still apparently unnoticed by just about everyone. Then, recorded the 9th's regimental history, "a superior force of Rebels nearly surrounded us. . . . We barely saved ourselves with well-aimed shots and a slow, orderly retreat."[53]

Stanley's line broke cover at the northern edge of the woods and moved far enough out into McDonald Field to reclaim Capt. Lyman Bridges's abandoned artillery pieces from John Beatty's earlier fight. At that point a heavy fire by the Washington Artillery and reformed Louisiana infantry tore through the blue formations. Ohio Sgt. James Verity was one of those hit at the apex of Stanley's charge, a bullet smashing into his face, "severing his tongue and breaking both jaws" and knocking him unconscious. When he recovered his senses, Verity's comrades were gone and he had to make his own way to a field hospital. It would be a full day before he could find treatment for his disfiguring wound. Like Kammerling's Buckeyes before him, Stanley's line had to fall back because it had outrun any support. There was no time to recover the non-ambulatory wounded.[54]

Private James Fenton of Company K, 19th Illinois, part of Stanley's command, moved through the detritus of Bridges's battery, which had once been Company G of the same regiment. Fenton noted the guns had been removed before they arrived. The rest of the wrecked section was still there, however, including some old friends. "Lying by a caisson among the dead," he wrote, was his comrade "Lieutenant Billy Bishop, one of the old Zouave cadets,

52 A. H. Reed, "Van Derveer's Brigade at Chickamauga," *National Tribune*, October 16, 1924.

53 Grebner, *We Were The Ninth*, 143.

54 James Verity Journal, UMich.

in the agonies of death." Fenton took great pride in the 19th's Zouave panache. "No regiment in the Confederate [service] of anywhere near equal size had any business with the 19th Illinois at close quarters. It was the only regiment in the whole army drilled in the French bayonet drill . . . and this gave [us] a confidence nothing could shake." With Rebels fleeing before them, Fenton's boasting seemed to be borne out, for the19th's loss in the charge was trifling. Once in the open, however, casualties started to mount. "In a little while Company K alone lost one private killed" and five men "wounded so severely they never returned" to the ranks.[55]

John Beatty had largely stepped into the role Thomas intended for Negley by orchestrating Stanley's advance and arranging for reinforcements. Despite Stanley's success, Beatty understood the Union left was still threatened and was working hard to bring up still more troops. He managed to round up another brigade, which had rushed onto the field as the Federals surged northward.

This force, commanded by Col. George Dick (Van Cleve's division), was fresh from the Poe Field sector. Dick's experience was similar to Stanley's and Van Derveer's before him; a hurried move north, but with no accompanying details about where to go or what to do. Finally, wrote Dick, he halted his men behind Van Derveer. When he spotted "Colonel Stanley's brigade on the left . . . being . . . hard pressed, I went to his support." Dick's four regiments, the 44th and 86th Indiana, and 13th and 59th Ohio, were all small and had lost heavily in Saturday's fight. All told they now numbered fewer than 900 men.[56]

Stanley described falling back slowly, all three of his regiments now abreast. He did so until he halted his command in front of Dick's line, but informed Dick that if further pressed, he would fall back on his line. Off to the left were Beatty's 15th Kentucky and 104th Illinois under the continued direction of Colonel Taylor, who had supplied a manpower detail to Lyman Bridges. Bridges could not rescue his own guns, but he did find four more abandoned pieces lining the La Fayette Road and decided he could at least secure them. With the help of 30 Kentuckians, Bridges hauled the guns west toward Negley and the rest of his battery.[57]

55 Entry for September 20, James Fenton Diary, ALPL. Fenton also credited the 19th Illinois with capturing Adams.

56 *OR* 30, pt. 1, 824.

57 Ibid., 375, 379. The four cannon rescued by Captain Bridges were guns originally belonging to Absalom Baird's division, lost on the morning of September 19.

On the Confederate side of the field, meanwhile, uncertainty gripped General Breckinridge. The division commander had no idea whether the Federals would break off their pursuit after tearing apart the dual brigade assault. The former vice president had just suffered another difficult personal loss in what was turning out to be a disastrous morning for him. When Stanley's brigade seemed about to overrun the Louisianans and Slocomb's Washington Artillery, Major Graves fell badly wounded. An artillery round fired from Kelly Field "exploded in our midst, where Major Graves and Captain Slocomb stood mounted, side by side," recalled Lieutenant Chalaron of the Washington Artillery. "We saw them clasp each other, and then totter in their saddles. . . . Slocomb's horse was sinking to the ground, mortally wounded." Slocumb emerged unscathed. Graves's mount was untouched, but not so the major, who "was pierced by a shrapnel bullet from side to side through the bowels." The wound was clearly fatal. Graves was carried to such shelter as could be found, and Breckinridge sent for. When he arrived at the scene, the general "knelt by the side of Major Graves and showed emotion such as a father alone could feel for his child."[58]

Breckinridge had little time to mourn. All this transpired while Adams's men were stumbling into Stanley's line. Almost immediately, recalled Lieutenant Chalaron, "our attention was called by evidence of disaster to Adams' Brigade in our front. Now, with hanging bridles and frantic strides, the riderless horses of Gen. Adams and his adjutant, Guilet, came tearing to the rear . . . towards and past our guns." Hastily remounting, Breckinridge ordered Graves borne to the rear in the slim hope that a field hospital could save him, ordered the Louisianans to hang on as long as they could, and rode off to "bring up Liddell's Division."[59]

The mission proved in vain. Instead of arranging for support to sustain and exploit Breckinridge's success, Generals Hill, Polk, and Walker were squabbling like angry fishwives. No orders had been issued, and Brig. Gen. St. John R. Liddell's men lay quietly in line a mile or so to the rear. Instead of ready infantry Breckinridge ran into yet another aggressive artillerist, Capt. Charles Swett, formerly of Vicksburg, Mississippi, and the commander of the Warren Light Artillery from that city. Swett was acting as Liddell's divisional chief of artillery.

58 Joseph A. Chalaron, "Memories of Major Rice E. Graves, C.S.A.," *Daviess County Historical Quarterly*, vol. 3, no. 1 (January, 1985), 12-13.

59 Ibid.

Like so many in gray that morning, Swett was also experiencing more than his share of frustration. The 35-year-old son of a wealthy family had convinced his father to fund the raising of the Warren artillery in May 1861. Swett, two younger brothers, and a prominent local doctor named Harvey Shannon had all joined, with Charles elected as captain. Now Doctor Shannon was a first lieutenant running the battery while Swett commanded both the Warren artillery and Capt. William H. Fowler's Alabama battery. Shannon's pieces included two Napoleons and a pair of James rifles, while Fowler's complement consisted of four Napoleons. Swett was angry when Breckinridge found him, for he had just come from an unsatisfying encounter with D. H. Hill.[60]

Sometime earlier, Hill had ordered Swett to place his guns in line with Hill's own batteries (probably Cobb's and Mebane's) to support Breckinridge's attack. Perhaps having already seen the punishment doled out to those other batteries, Swett was not overly impressed with Hill's grasp of tactics: "'I'll be responsible for the loss of the guns,'" insisted the North Carolina general. "This rather amused me," noted Swett some years later. "At or about this time, he made what I thought was a very strange suggestion concerning what the art'y might do, which the assembly of officers not approving, I boldly expressed the opinion that in such a movement, all the horses, or most of them, would be killed; to which the Gen'l replied, 'We had better lose horses than men.' What would have happened to the men of the artillery while we were losing horses? I am neither a born, nor an educated soldier, yet will say this. On several occasions I considered the Gen'l's views to be very peculiar, to say the least."[61]

Instead, Swett thought to place his guns behind Breckinridge's men, now in full retreat, and let the infantry pass through. While he didn't think much of spending the lives of his men uselessly, he was not averse to risk if the reward were sufficient. "My idea," explained the Mississippian, was to let "Breckinridge's command fall back to the low ground. . . . His men could pass through the line of artillery . . . [which] would open with canister, and the mix-up would be pretty hot for a few minutes." That idea was quickly succeeded by another, when Swett noticed a shallow ravine running west to the

60 Family records in the old courthouse museum in Vicksburg claim Swett was an "honor" graduate from West Point serving as a U.S. Army lieutenant of artillery when the Civil War broke out. Neither West Point nor any other records confirm this.

61 Charles Swett, "A Brief Narrative of the Warren Light Artillery," http://www.perryville battlefield.org/html/ms-swett-charles-cs.html, accessed 5/28/2012.

Kelly Field was the high water mark of Breckinridge's attack. This picture of the Kelly farm is from the 1890s. *Indiana at Chickamauga*

north of his position. What if he took Fowler's four "splendid Napoleons" and ran them up this ravine to take the pursuing Yankees in flank? Breckinridge was dubious of the idea. "My men are falling back," he explained to Swett, and they would be in no position to offer support. Swett dismissed the danger, but Breckinridge remained unconvinced. The Kentuckian had just lost Helm and Graves, two men very dear to him; perhaps he could not bear the thought of sending yet another brave man to his death. "'You exercise your own judgment,'" Breckinridge replied, "and rode to the rear of his command."[62]

Swett's plan came to naught when a Liddell staff officer rode up with new orders: "Get out of here, and get out quick!" Liddell was preparing to attack and wanted his guns back. Swett complied. Once back with Liddell, he outlined the same plan but Liddell dismissed it as "too dangerous." It was also unneeded. The Yankees were breaking off pursuit and falling back to their own lines.

It was still short of noon, though not by much. The morning was gone, and seemingly the Confederate Right Wing had not accomplished much if anything toward Bragg's overall plan of driving the Union left south towards and across Longstreet's front. With Stovall and Adams in retreat, Breckinridge's entire

62 Ibid.

division was now out of the fight. Pat Cleburne's initial assault had been a disorganized and bloody failure. Breckinridge, who had come the nearest to success, identified the crux of that failure: "A good supporting line . . . at this moment probably would have produced decisive results." Considerable bitterness about that lack of support pervaded the ranks of Lucius Polk's brigade. One member of the 2nd Tennessee recalled that when they finally fell back, having been shot to pieces in front of the Union breastworks, the 2nd came across fellow Tennesseans in George Maney's brigade, of Ben Cheatham's division, lying down to the rear. "Maney's Brigade was upbraided by a Second Tennessean for not coming up to Cleburne's assistance." Maney's troops refused to accept blame, retorting they "were damned glad they didn't get into any such scrape."[63]

Still, fully one-half of Cleburne's men (Deshler and Wood) had not yet been engaged, nor had any of W. H. T. Walker's or Cheatham's men taken up the fight. Could the Rebel commanders directing affairs on this part of the field find a way to use these remaining troops more effectively?

63 *OR* 30, pt. 2, 200; Anonymous, "The Second Tennessee," 59.

Chapter Seven

Futility on the Right:

Sunday, 10:00 a.m. to Noon

September 20, 1863, was not one of Daniel Harvey Hill's better days. While his men were turning George Thomas's flank, Hill was focused on a different conflict, locked in a battle of wills with almost every other high-ranking commander in the Confederate Right Wing. His primary adversary was Maj. Gen. William H. T. "Shotpouch" Walker.

When Hill expressed earlier that morning his concern about the thinness of his own line, Right Wing commander Leonidas Polk directed Walker's Reserve Corps northward to support Hill's attack. Despite the hard knocks taken by the Reserve Corps the day before, Walker was still full of fight. Indeed, he was one of the most aggressive Confederates on the battlefield. But sidling 5,000 men a mile or so northwest took time, especially for States Rights Gist's just-arrived brigade, which was still trying to find its place in line. Before his men had finished redeploying, reported Walker, "I was sent for by General Hill."[1]

Walker ordered his corps to redouble its pace and rode ahead, accompanied by General Polk. When the pair found Hill, Walker reported that his corps was ready for action and awaited his instructions. Hill's response both surprised and confused Walker and Polk.

1 *OR* 30, pt. 2, 241.

Bearing in mind his earlier observation that if his line was "broken at one point [it] was broken at all points," Hill remained focused almost exclusively on the hole torn open between the divisions of Breckinridge and Cleburne when Ben Helm's shattered Kentucky command fell back. When he learned "that Gist's brigade was in our rear," explained Hill, "I sent a staff officer to bring it up in all haste to fill the gap. . . . This request was misunderstood," he continued in his official report, "for instead of getting this single brigade" Walker and Polk were bringing up Walker's whole corps. Few officers in the annals of military history have ever complained about receiving *too many* reinforcements.[2]

What followed could have been a farce written by Gilbert and Sullivan if it were not for the soldiers' lives being thrown away in the interim. "General Hill informed me . . . that he wanted a brigade," Walker reported, who went on to tell Hill "that there was one immediately behind him." Hill "remarked that he wanted Gist's brigade." According to Walker, he explained to Hill that Gist's men were at the rear of his corps column and just catching up, and so would take the longest to reach the front and go into action. Hill was adamant he wanted Gist, who was present during this exchange, having just reported to Walker and been informed that he was going to command Matt Ector's and Claudius Wilson's brigades as well as his own. Flattered by his expanded responsibilities, the South Carolinian noted that Hill insisted on "Gist . . . saying he had heard of that brigade." Walker reluctantly acquiesced, instructing Gist to report to Hill. Given his sudden elevation to division command, Gist explained to Hill that his brigade would be led by its ranking colonel, Peyton H. Colquitt of the 46th Georgia, who was now summoned to join the conference. Once Colquitt arrived, Hill explained what was expected of him.[3]

Throughout this exchange Polk, the senior officer present, remained mute. Not so the irascible Walker, who was growing more frustrated by the minute and not shy about expressing his anger. Various subordinates and staff officers watched the discussion with growing alarm. Walker's other divisional commander, St. John Liddell, was also present and surely recalled Walker's similar diatribe against General Polk just a week earlier on September 13. Walker, noted Liddell, "severely criticized and loudly found fault with the propriety of Hill's plans." Eventually, they hammered out an arrangement of

2 *OR* 30, pt. 2, 141-142.

3 Ibid., 241, 245.

sorts: Colquitt would go in to support Breckinridge's attack, coming up on what was thought to be Breckinridge's left-rear, in place of Helm. Gist would move the brigades of Ector and Wilson up to support Colquitt.[4]

Just as Gist's line was moving, however, the assembled generals received word of a new complication: Adams and Stovall had been repulsed. If Breckinridge was in full retreat, then who was Gist to support? Polk finally spoke up, ordering Liddell to use his division to "attack in place of General Breckinridge." As Liddell set off to bring up his 3,000 men, more grim news arrived: the stout Union defense had stopped brigade commander (and nephew) Lucius Polk's assault cold. Cleburne, too, had been unsuccessful. The bishop reacted immediately by personally detaching Brig. Gen. Edward C. Walthall's brigade from Liddell's command and, under the guidance of Major Ratchford of D. H. Hill's staff, sent Walthall to help Cleburne. This detachment reduced Liddell's effort to a single brigade numbering perhaps 1,500 men. It was another diversion of effort at a critical moment. Polk's interference infuriated Hill, who smarted over the incident for years thereafter. Archer Anderson, of Hill's staff, later grumbled that the whole affair was "ill planned and ill executed." That it was, but if Leonidas Polk had left things entirely up to Daniel Harvey Hill, nothing at all would have been done.[5]

This was the Army of Tennessee at its worst. Walker wanted to concentrate his command and use it *en masse*, while Hill and Polk seemed intent on trickling troops into the fight one brigade at a time. Hill was also being mulishly obdurate. Despite being granted almost complete control of the entire attack by Polk, Hill would later complain about how the assault was conducted, almost as if he was a spectator rather than its principal tactical commander. In his report Hill ranted at how useless the fight had been, railing against "the faultiness of our plan of attack" while waxing hyperbolic that "never in the history of war had an attack been made in a single line without reserves or a supporting force." Two decades later, writing for *Century Magazine*, Hill described the attack as a "desperate, forlorn hope." He also complained about faulty reconnaissance and suggested that if only more time had been taken to better understand the Union

4 Nathaniel Cheairs Hughes, Jr., ed., *Liddell's Record: St. John Richardson Liddell Brigadier General, CSA Staff Officer and Brigade Commander, Army of Tennessee* (Louisiana State University Press, 1985), 144-145; *OR* 30, pt. 2, 245.

5 *OR* 30, pt. 2, 253, 274; Archer Anderson, "Address of Col. Archer Anderson on the Campaign and Battle of Chickamauga," *Southern Historical Society Papers*, vol. IX, no. 7 (July, 1881), 414.

Major General William H. T. Walker commanded the Confederate Reserve Corps. He quarreled with D. H. Hill on the morning of September 20 about how best to use his men to support Hill's Corps.
Battles and Leaders of the Civil War

position, the morning's bloody frontal assaults need not have been conducted. Of course, it was Hill who made that reconnaissance, it was Hill who determined the alignment of his two divisions, and it was Hill who failed to grasp the extent of Breckinridge's success. It was also Hill who could have called upon Walker's entire corps as support, and Hill who initially refused most of that corps when it was offered to him.[6]

Walker's anger was fully justified. He later complained about the way D. H. Hill "disintegrated" his corps, arguing that if he had been allowed to mass both of his divisions (Gist's and Liddell's) behind Breckinridge, "the enemy's left would have been carried much easier then it eventually was." While there is no way of knowing that with certainty, an attack by three divisions numbering near 7,000 men into Kelly Field would have been a much greater threat than Breckinridge's two brigades. Leonidas Polk's lackadaisical attitude toward command, manifested on Saturday night in the faulty transmission of orders, carried through to their execution. His only intervention during the Hill-Walker argument was to further the disintegration of Walker's command by peeling Walthall's Mississippians away from Liddell at the last minute to send them into another fruitless assault against the strongest point in Thomas's line, simultaneously weakening Liddell's main effort.[7]

Meanwhile, the battle raged on. While Breckinridge's men were falling back, Pat Cleburne's division farther south went forward again. The Irish-born

6 *OR* 30, pt. 2, 143; Hill, "Chickamauga: The Great Battle of the West," 657.

7 *OR* 30, pt. 2, 242.

Arkansan had spent a considerable amount of time untangling his division, setting Wood's line to rights and trying to get A. P. Stewart's troops to join with him in attacking Poe Field. Finally, the bulk of his division was again in the fight.

When a courier from John C. Brown's brigade arrived at Stewart's headquarters conveying S. A. M. Wood's request for support in attacking Poe Field, Stewart demurred. He was worried about advancing prematurely. Stewart's division was part of Longstreet's Left Wing, and he knew nothing of Cleburne's orders. He could hear the heavy fighting raging to his north, where Cleburne was making no headway against the Kelly Field line, and painfully aware of the long reach of the Union artillery, which was now regularly dropping shells among his own men. "You will take your orders directly from me" had been Longstreet's parting words, and so Stewart felt he must wait. That all changed when General Bragg's staff officer, Maj. Pollock Lee, arrived.

Braxton Bragg's morning had not improved. After his meetings with D. H. Hill, Polk, and Cheatham, Bragg established a new field headquarters along Brotherton Road just east of the Winfrey cornfield. Like his opponent General Rosecrans, Bragg shifted to a location "immediately in rear of and accessible to all parts of the line" and waited out the morning's delays. Colonel George W. Brent of Bragg's staff noted that when the fighting commenced in earnest about 10:00 a.m., "it was equal to any thing I have ever heard." However, the sounds of battle did not progress, which indicated that far from driving the enemy, Polk's attacks were being repulsed. Nor was there sound from James Longstreet's sector—another sign the Federals were standing fast.[8]

Bragg was unaware of the unseemly squabble between Hill, Walker, and Polk, but by 11:00 a.m. he clearly understood his battle plans had been upended. The only thing left to do was order everyone into the fight. Major Pollock Lee was sent on his way to do just that, and A. P. Stewart was the first recipient of Bragg's new orders: all divisions were to "advance at once and attack." The initially reluctant Stewart explained to Lee his previous instructions from Longstreet. "General Bragg had directed [me] to pass along the lines," replied the major, "and give the order to every division commander to move upon the enemy immediately." In other words, trigger the *en echelon* attack, north to south, division by division. The new instructions were simple and clear.[9]

8 Ibid., 33; Entry for September 20, William Brent Journal, Braxton Bragg Papers, WRHS.

9 *OR* 30, pt. 2, 363-364.

Stewart responded by sending word back to General Brown to join S. A. M. Wood's proposed advance into Poe Field. Brigadier General Henry Clayton's Alabamians would, in turn, move up alongside Brig. Gen. William Bate's brigade, and together they would advance as well in support of Brown and Wood.

Brown's Tennesseans, the 18th, 26th, 32nd, and 45th regiment and the 23rd Battalion numbered fewer than 1,000 men. The organization had suffered at least 350 losses the day before while slugging it out for several hours with various Federals east of Brotherton Field. Despite these heavy losses, however, their morale remained high. Wood's brigade on Brown's right was considerably more disrupted. Wood had only the 16th Alabama and the combined 18th/33rd Alabama close at hand, all told perhaps another 1,000 men. His 15th Mississippi Battalion of Sharpshooters, the 32nd/45th Mississippi, and Col. E. B. Breedlove's 45th Alabama, however, remained a considerable distance to the right-rear clinging to the ridge in front of the Union Kelly Field line. In other words, these troops were out of immediate reach. Without making much attempt to round up the other half of his brigade, Wood ordered the 16th and 18th/33rd forward.

The 16th Alabama held the critical position, which was on the right of the 18th/33rd. The trajectory of its advance would carry the attack into the northern end of the Poe farmstead. With the other half of Wood's brigade stalled on the ridge, no one was protecting the 16th's right flank. Its advance would carry the Alabamians past the staggered Union defenses in the timber between Kelly and Poe fields. This area, it will be recalled, was the most awkward spot in the Union lines, the crochet Turchin described earlier. This was where General Reynolds had posted John Turchin's division to align with the Kelly Field front, but pulled back Edward King's brigade to the far end of Poe Field. Both King and Turchin faced west, but instead of being directly connected, King's left flank was some 200 yards farther west than Turchin's right.

The northernmost half of Wood's brigade (now led by Colonel Lowrey) halted when they confronted Turchin's line, while the other half pushed on. Once past Turchin's right, the 16th's right flank would be subject to enfilading as well as head-on fire. Cleburne later reported "that at a point opposite my center, his works formed . . . a retiring angle running in a westerly and somewhat oblique angle to the . . . La Fayette Road." Cleburne only knew that after the fact. Unfortunately for Maj. John McGaughy, his 16th Alabama, and the Rebel high command, the nature of the Union position was not obvious, but the consequences of the enemy alignment soon would be.[10]

An unidentified member of the 16th Alabama left a vivid description of the advance and the terrain:

> We advanced about 300 yards and came to a field about 200 yards across, the 1st 100 yards had a small undergrowth over it & and few rotten pine stumps and logs. The remaining 100 yards was an open field covered with broom straw. We . . . were just emerging from the bushes into the open field when the command charge was given; almost at the same moment the enemy opened a fire of small arms, shot, shell & canister, so well directed that it compelled our regiment to seek protection.

Instead of rushing to the slaughter, the 16th dropped to the ground, its members seeking cover behind the small bushes in the eastern half of the field. With such sparse shelter, noted the anonymous Alabamian, "[we] were killed by the dozen."[11]

Most of this fire came from their front, where Edward King's four regiments were formed in a single line about 400 yards long, centered on the 19th Indiana battery. Here, Wood's men faced the 101st and 68th Indiana, holding King's left. As noted, Wood's men were also taking fire from Turchin's forward line on their right. Those who looked to the south would have seen the entire Union line ablaze along the length of the Poe farmstead. Losses mounted quickly. The 16th Alabama had lost 129 people the evening before, and now numbered just 28 officers and 257 men. During this assault they suffered another 114 casualties, not including a number of lightly wounded who remained in the ranks.

Turchin's fire might well have been diverted if the other half of Wood's line had pressed a simultaneous attack, but the 32nd/45th Mississippi and 15th Mississippi did not advance. The fire from William Hazen's front line was simply too intimidating, and Wood seemed unable to coordinate both wings of his brigade. Colonel Mark Lowrey, the commander of the 32nd/45th Mississippi, reported that he lost fully one-quarter of his men while holding the ridge, even though he was at least 220 yards from the Federal position. Not only

10 *OR* 30, pt. 2, 155.

11 Unknown author to W. Bryce Wilson, Letter of October 2, 1863, Steiner Family Papers, Auburn University.

were the Federals fighting from behind breastworks, but they were doing so in double line, meaning they could shift regiments between the front and rear lines at will and so always maintain a fresh heavy fire. Unless the Confederates could turn a flank, this Union line was nearly impregnable. At the height of this engagement the barricades on the 11th Ohio's front briefly caught fire, but men from Company B dispersed the flaming timbers before they could ignite the rest of the works. Throughout, the 11th's rate of fire barely slowed.[12]

Colonel Breedlove and his 45th Alabama, part of Wood's brigade, did make an attempt to move forward but accomplished nothing. Breedlove's report paints a picture of complete confusion. All but abandoned by Wood, he initially attempted to move up and join the 16th Alabama before Wood and Brown launched their attack. That advance failed when Breedlove's left-most company reported the line on its left was falling back. In fact, this move was the 16th Alabama realigning with Brown's force. Breedlove, however, fell back and passed word up the line to Lowrey that the rest of the brigade was retreating. Somehow Breedlove also got the impression that Lowrey's Mississippians had retreated, so he ordered his 45th Alabama to do the same—only to immediately countermand that order when he discovered he would be leaving Semple's battery unsupported. Lowrey, of course, hadn't retreated at all, but with his men seeking cover it must have seemed to the commander of the 45th Alabama that the Mississippians disappeared.[13]

Breedlove's confusion increased when James Deshler's brigade line appeared on his left, where the 16th Alabama should have been, before shifting to a position behind him. Next, a courier from Wood arrived to inform Breedlove the 16th Alabama was about 100 yards in advance of his own 45th, and that Wood wanted him to come up and connect with the 16th's right, when all would then join in the impending attack. Breedlove sent the messenger back to Wood with a question: should he wait for Deshler to advance as well? Before he received an answer, Deshler and his men vanished. Deshler, of course, was already tasked by Pat Cleburne to close up on Lucius Polk's brigade.

Finally, after another courier exchange, Breedlove reported he led the 45th Alabama forward about 300 to 400 yards, though he never managed to connect with the 16th Alabama. In doing so, the 45th met "a murderous fire" and halted

12 *OR* 30, pt. 2, 171; Ibid., pt. 1, 480.

13 Ibid., pt. 2, 168.

to seek cover. When Breedlove saw troops falling back on his left (the apparently hard-to-find 16th Alabama), he ordered his own command to retreat back to Lowrey's position. For the men in the ranks, the entire affair was a confusing mess. The noise of battle was overwhelming—"a terrible discord" according to one correspondent, "reminding one more of Pandemonium than ought else which the mind can conceive. . . . We were ordered to move on, and in the confusion incident to such a crisis, and amid the multiplicity of orders, the regiment became divided."[14]

The exact movements recently described of Breedlove's 45th Alabama are untraceable. Its men and commander were probably just south of the right end of Turchin's line, but they almost certainly did not advance 300 yards, a distance that would have put them squarely in the middle of the northern end of Poe's cornfield, which was already occupied by the 16th and 18th/33rd Alabama. Nor did they strike Turchin's position with any determination. German-born Cpl. George Hechler of the 36th Ohio felt perfectly secure during this action. "Our position was behind breastworks made of old logs," noted Hechler, "so that we were safe from bullets as long as we were behind it." As for the Rebels, Hechler dismissed their efforts as nothing more than a feint. They "made several shows of attack, but came no nearer than 200 yards."[15]

When the 16th Alabama stalled at the brush-line, meanwhile, the combined 18th/33rd Alabama followed suit. Colonel Samuel Adams reported the command halted at the eastern fence line of Poe Field, about 275 yards short of the Union line. Like Breedlove, he too complained of a "very severe enfilading fire from the right."[16]

Wood contributed nothing to his brigade's fight here. Already reluctant to charge and with no brigade- or regimental-level leadership inspiring them to do so, the elements of Wood's left wing simply endured the murderous fire for as long as they could, suffering horrendous losses in the process. Retreat, however, would have even more dire consequences for A. P. Stewart's division, especially for Brown's Tennesseans, all of whom were now advancing across

14 Ibid.; "In Line of Battle near Chattanooga, September 24," *Daily Huntsville Confederate*, October 4, 1863.

15 Ken Hechler, *Soldier of the Union: Private George Hechler's Civil War Service* (Pictorial Histories Publishing Co., Inc., 2011), 179.

16 *OR* 30, pt. 2, 166-167.

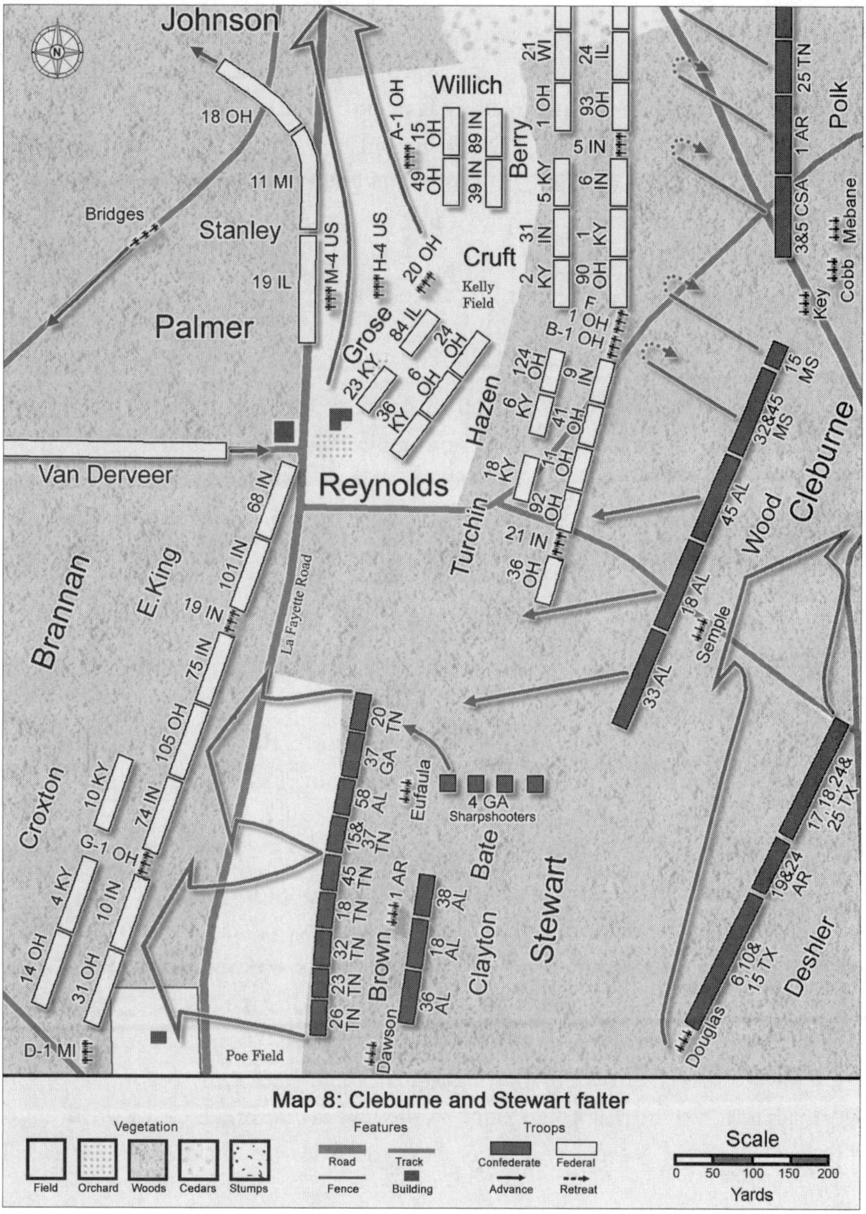

Map 8: Cleburne and Stewart falter

the southern end of the Poe Field line at S. A. M. Wood's behest and Bragg's dictate.

The Tennesseans advanced with considerably more gusto. Brown reported his line moved about 300 yards "through an open woods . . . when the brigade on my right (Wood) broke in confusion." The retreat of Wood's men left the

18th and 45th Tennessee, Brown's two right-most regiments, exposed to a "terrible crossfire" as they pressed forward into the field, closing to within 50 yards of the Union line. Private Jasper Hampton of the 18th Tennessee was in the middle of this maelstrom. "Our regiment marched off like clockwork, all elbow to elbow, until we came to a small field where there was an old house," recalled the private decades after the war. "We came in contact with about thirty pieces of artillery, heavily supported by infantry. . . . They threw such heavy volleys of musketry, grapeshot, and shells that we were compelled to fall back."[17]

Overwhelmed, the Tennesseans broke. Sergeant David B. Floyd of Company I, 75th Indiana, observed their bravery and recorded it: "The [enemy] Brigade advanced on solid columns on double quick, until it reached . . . within fifty yards of our improvised breastworks." When they broke, continued Floyd, their "officers with drawn swords and pistols threw themselves in front of the retiring crowd, and by every device which physical and mental nature . . . could invent, they tried to rally and reform the column . . . from the broken mass of humanity that was retreating over Poe's field." Each of these Tennessee regiments, 500 strong when they stepped off, endured awful punishment and fell back to its original position without pausing.[18]

Despite his personal intervention, wrote General Brown, "I found all effort to rally [my men] . . . short of the defenses in vain, and indeed, impracticable, under the storm of grape and canister which prevailed upon every part of the field." Another Hoosier, Pvt. James G. Essington of the 75th Indiana's Company D, was mesmerized by one particular Confederate battle flag: "Their officers did all that man could do to urge them to . . . stand and fight, but to move further forward they could not do. Down goes their flag . . . up it comes again, but in a moment, down it went. Up it comes, down it goes. . . . The enemy tried to rally but the air was too full of shot and shell."[19]

The left half of Brown's brigade did marginally better, driving in the Union skirmish line and moving smartly across the La Fayette Road. Colonel Edmund Cook, leading the 32nd Tennessee, took these Union skirmishers for a full

17 Ibid., 372; N. J. Hampton, *An Eyewitness to the Dark Days of 1861-65* (n.p., 1898), 32.

18 David Bittle Floyd, *History of the Seventy-Fifth Regiment of Indiana Infantry Volunteers, Its Organization, Campaigns, and Battles, 1862-65* (Lutheran Publication Society, 1893), 158.

19 *OR* 30, pt. 2, 372; Entry for September 20, James G. Essington Diary, InHS. This flag was probably that of the 18th/33rd Alabama, who moved up to support Brown, see below.

defensive line and reported driving them off handily; his situation quickly deteriorated thereafter. Cook was across the road directing his regiment against the 17th Ohio of Col. John Connell's brigade when he took note of "an enfilading fire from the enemy's battery on our right . . . caused by that portion of the brigade to my right falling back." The collapse of the 18th and 45th Tennessee had exposed the rest of Brown's line to a similar metal shellacking. The 32nd received "a murderous fire" and the regiment "fell back in somewhat of disorder." Rebel Cpl. Thomas Corn was almost killed here when a shell buried itself in the ground directly in front of him. When it detonated, he recalled, "the solid earth seemed suddenly to sink from under our feet, and I was hurled violently to the ground. . . . I was knocked senseless, and when I came to myself I was lying in a ghastly heap of dead and wounded." Corn soon realized the rest of his fellows were gone, and as quickly as he could he hurried after them. He found Colonel Cook trying to reform the regiment in the road bed for another effort when Brown rode up and countermanded the order. Instead of another attack, Brown instructed Cook to fall back into the sheltering woods on the east side of the field.[20]

Farther to the left, the 26th Tennessee crossed the La Fayette Road near the Poe cabin directly opposite the 4th Michigan battery and the 31st Ohio, also of Connell's command. Blasts of canister fire from the Michigan guns set the Poe house on fire, creating a landmark referred to thereafter by almost every observer as "the burning house." The resultant smoke may have helped hide the Tennesseans, for the Wolverine gunners did less damage to the 26th, which emerged relatively unscathed from this charge, at least compared to the rest of Brown's regiments. The quick action of Maj. Richard Saffell, who ordered a rapid retreat as soon as he observed the rest of the brigade falling back, helped his men escape the worst of the crippling enfilading fire that ravaged Brown's other regiments. Saffell reported a loss of 25 out of 172 engaged, as opposed to the 32nd's loss of 82 from 278. The raw 23rd Tennessee Battalion under Capt. W. P. Simpson emulated Saffell's example and also emerged from the assault with light casualties (24 out of 136).

Despite the initial audacity of Brown's advance, his momentum had broken quickly and, thought the Federals, with comparative ease. Indeed, the defenders in this sector found this fight one of their easiest of the entire war. They suffered little from Rebel fire, which in turn allowed them to mow down each

20 *OR* 30, pt. 2, 378-379; Corn, "Brown's Brigade at Chickamauga," 124.

Rebel formation as it appeared. Private Sam McNeil of the 31st Ohio believed that "with plenty of ammunition and food . . . [we] could have held that position just so long as the enemy came up on our front."[21]

At least one of Wood's regiments essayed another effort. When he saw the Tennesseans pouring into the field, Colonel Adams of the 18th/33rd Alabama tried to support them with an advance. His effort failed to stir much enthusiasm within his own ranks. Adams recounted that he crossed the road and reached a point near the burning cabin. "At this point," he lamented, "I found myself with but 60 or 70 of my own men, and but very few if any of the other two brigades." An Alabama private named William E. Preston recalled that charge as pretty hard going: "Coming on a clearing, [we] pushed off opposite corners of the rail fence and went across the field with a yell. However, we were getting enfilading fire from the woods to our right . . . [and] the line wavered. Colonel Adams took the colors with a broken staff from [Color Sgt.] Neal Godwin and urged us on." It was no use. Under the "enfilading fire," admitted Preston, "we broke and ran back . . . into the woods, leaving our dead and some badly wounded in the field." The men of the 18th/33rd understood, perhaps better than their leadership, the deathtrap that Poe Field represented. Adams's engaged strength numbered 513 officers and men on September 19, and he suffered 33 losses that evening in the botched assault. The butcher's bill for this day, September 20, was much higher. Another 149 men fell dead or injured in the charge across Poe Field.[22]

Finding that most of his own regiment had failed to advance, that the 16th Alabama hadn't budged, and that Brown's men were already retreating, Adams ordered the handful of men still with him back posthaste. Returning, he discovered the bulk of the 18th/33rd was gone, having already fallen back even farther to the ravine that had sheltered them earlier. Adams set to work restoring order. The attempted sortie left the 16th Alabama feeling completely isolated. Major McGaughy was wounded by this time, leaving Capt. Frederick A. Ashford in command. Ashford stubbornly clung to his position for some time, bereft of orders and now seemingly all alone.

While S. A. M. Wood's and John Brown's troops were attempting to storm the Poe Field line, Patrick Cleburne struggled to get the remainder of his division into action. Brigadier General James P. Deshler's Texans and

21 S. A. McNeil, "The 31st Ohio at Chickamauga," *National Tribune*, February 9, 1888.

22 *OR* 30, pt. 2, 166; William Preston Memoir, ADAH.

Arkansans had yet to enter the action. As noted, Cleburne was concerned about the gap between Lucius Polk's and Wood's men. Deshler's 1,693 troops would fill that hole nicely.[23]

Born in Alabama to parents of Pennsylvania origin, the 30-year-old Deshler was a West Pointer, class of 1854, who had already served in nearly every theater of the war. He was wounded in western Virginia in December 1861, commanded artillery during the Seven Days' Battles outside Richmond in June 1862, and later that summer transferred to Arkansas along with his boss, Maj. Gen. Theophilus T. Holmes. There, Deshler was promoted to colonel and given command of a brigade of Texans. He and his men were part of the garrison at Arkansas Post when it fell to a Federal army under Maj. Gen. William T. Sherman in January 1863. Exchanged a few months later, Deshler's command was sent to the Army of Tennessee. He was promoted to brigadier general on July 28, 1863, while in Chattanooga. Chickamauga was his first action as a general officer.[24]

Thus far, Deshler's morning had been one of delay and frustration. Blocked by Cheatham's and Stewart's formations, Deshler's line was at a standstill when Cleburne located it and led the brigade into its new position behind Colonel Lowrey's ridge (thereby adding to Breedlove's confusion as described earlier). Cleburne intended to bring Deshler into action north of Lowrey, on Lucius Polk's left flank, to restore the integrity of the divisional line.

Nothing worked as planned. By the time Deshler's men were ready to move up the ridge and engage, Polk's brigade was already retreating, unable to face the sheets of Union lead and iron ripping through its ranks. By the time Cleburne realized this, however, he was already well to the south, on his way to check up on Wood. Deshler moved out alone.

Once amongst Wood's command, Cleburne discovered more bad news in the form of Colonel Lowrey, who explained the recent bloody fiasco on his front. Lowrey had charge of his 32nd/45th Mississippi, the 15th Mississippi Sharpshooters, and for a time, Breedlove's 45th Alabama. According to Lowrey, fully 25% of his men had been cut down "in a very short time." His troops were running low on ammunition, except perhaps for the 45th Alabama,

23 This is Deshler's engaged strength on September 19. The figure should probably be lower for September 20, but only by a handful. His losses during the night action were very light.

24 Anne Bailey, "James Deshler," in William C. Davis, ed., *The Confederate General*, 6 vols. (National Historical Society, 1991), vol. 2, 66-67.

which had been ordered not to fire. In fact, the regiments were beginning to unravel as men slipped off the ridge singly and in small groups to seek better cover and cartridges. Lowrey was attempting to address these problems when he discovered "nearly the whole number [of] the Forty-Fifth Alabama on my left, began to fall back." Breedlove's men were returning from their earlier abortive attempt to find and connect with the 16th Alabama, but were not doing so in good order. Their fear proved infectious, and Lowrey's Mississippians were beginning to abandon their own position in ever increasing numbers.[25]

It was into this budding rout that Cleburne rode. He immediately understood that Lowrey had no choice but to fall back and regroup, and he ordered him to do so. About this same time, Cleburne learned not only that the rest of Wood's brigade had been repulsed, but also of Lucius Polk's bloody retreat. Instead of renewing the attack with the power of his full division, as he thought he was doing, Cleburne had unwittingly just dispatched Deshler into a frontal attack alone with no support on either flank.[26]

"We were thus moved to the right under fire in this sort of hot haste to fill a gap caused by Wood's Mississippi brigade giving way," recalled Lt. Robert M. Collins of Company B, 15th Texas. "This was the outfit that had poked so much fun at us Texas fellows, and the boys seemed to enjoy it as a good joke on the mud-heads." The jest ceased to be funny once the Texans topped the ridge. "As we reached the crest . . . we struck the same sawyer that had knocked Wood's brigade out at the first round. The rain of lead that the Federals poured into our line was simply terrific." Sergeant Jim Turner of the 6th Texas agreed: "Besides the infantry fire," explained Turner, "eighteen Napoleon guns poured a deadly fire of grape and canister into our advancing ranks."[27]

Deshler's line stumbled to a halt and its members scrambled for whatever cover they could find directly opposite and about 175 yards distant from Union Brig. Gen. William B. Hazen's line. Hazen's section of the Kelly Field line was probably the single strongest part of Thomas's entire position—well-sited, with plenty of reserves and supported by numerous batteries. Hazen, ever the

25 *OR* 30, pt. 2, 171.

26 Ibid., 155.

27 R. M. Collins, *Chapters from the Unwritten History of the War Between the States* (Morningside House, 1988), 158-159; Deanne Labenski, ed., "Jim Turner Co. G, 6th Texas Infantry, C.S.A., From 1861 to 1865," *Texana*, vol. 12, no. 1 (Spring, 1974), 164.

meticulous Regular Army man, controlled his men's fire with disciplined volleys, crisply delivered, and now they engaged Deshler's force with redoubled fury. There was no chance for a further advance. "We were ordered to lie down and commence firing," reported Col. Roger Q. Mills, commanding the combined 6th/10th/15th Texas. The men flattened and began to fire back, but they found little protection on the hill. Forced to endure what Lt. Col. Thomas S. Anderson of the 6th described as a "severe and disastrous fire," Deshler's losses spiked.[28]

With both Polk and Wood effectively out of action, however, only Deshler was left to maintain any pressure on the Federals. Accordingly, Cleburne made a difficult choice, ordering Deshler to hold his position despite the mounting casualties. Captain Samuel T. Foster, commanding a company in the 17th/18th/24th/25th Texas, recorded his own grim impressions of the fight: "Old Pat Cleburn orders us in to stay and we stay . . . but we are too close to the Yanks who have made works in the night. . . . We are so flat on the ground that we don't make much show. They shoot at us, but we don't return it."[29]

Some of Deshler's troops must have been returning fire, for within a half hour or so, reports filtered up the chain of command that the men were running out of rounds. "About 12 m. [probably closer to 11:00 a.m.] our supply of ammunition began to give out," reported Colonel Mills, "and I sent a courier to Brigadier General Deshler to inform him of that fact, and to ask where we could get more." In response, Deshler began working his way along the firing line, examining the men's cartridge boxes. He was about "40 paces" from Mills when the general was "struck by a shell in the chest and his heart literally torn from his bosom." Within minutes of this horrific event, Mills discovered that the next ranking colonel, Franklin C. Wilkes of the 24th Texas, had just been wounded and was leaving the field. Mills was now in command of the brigade. Deshler's loss was deeply mourned. Private Isaiah Harlan, Company G, the 10th Texas, lamented in a letter home that "our noble brigadier, a noble a fellow as ever lived, was killed in the action."[30]

Mills went about trying to set the brigade to rights, ordering ammunition culled from the boxes of the fallen so that each man had at least one round. He

28 *OR* 30, pt. 2, 188, 192.

29 Norman D. Brown, ed. *One of Cleburne's Command: The Civil War Reminiscences and Diary of Captain Samuel T. Foster, Granbury's Texas Brigade, CSA* (University of Texas Press, 1980), 52.

30 *OR* 30, pt. 2, 188-189; Isaiah Harlan Letters, Hill College, Hillsboro TX.

happily discovered that the left four companies of his own regiment (including Sam Foster's, no doubt) had not been firing much and still had a plentiful supply. Moving those men to his center, Mills readied the command for a possible Federal countercharge. About this time he received further word from Cleburne: Mills was not to try and advance, but "must not retire if it were possible to hold my position." Wisely, Mills eased the bulk of the brigade a few yards back to the lee of the ridge, sheltering them from incoming fire, leaving behind only a thin skirmish line to pick at the Yankees. Cleburne's mismanaged assault was stalled.[31]

A. P. Stewart's first effort to drive the Federals proved an equally bloody failure. Unlike Cleburne's division, however, Stewart still had two uncommitted brigades he could call upon. He and his staff were observing the fight as best they could from a short distance behind Brown's brigade line, though the timber prevented a direct view into Poe Field. Had Stewart been able to view the initial repulse more completely, he might have halted his next line short of the carnage in the cornfield. However, Stewart was one of the more capable officers in the Army of Tennessee, and—a rarity among high ranking officers in that army—knew how to follow orders. Currently, those orders called for an assault. Without much of a pause, Clayton's and Bate's brigades surged forward in a second effort.

Bate's pitifully shrunken formations followed Wood. Leaving his sharpshooter battalion behind to screen his right flank, Bate led the 58th Alabama, 37th Georgia, 15th/37th and 20th Tennessee into action. These four formations, only about 700 men in total, had been cut to pieces (many of them in this same field) the evening before. Bate was especially concerned about his right because both the 20th Tennessee and 37th Georgia had lost veteran commanders the day before. Choosing to supervise their movements personally, Bate had but limited attention to spare for the 15th/37th Tennessee in his center, while Col. Bushrod Jones and the 58th Alabama on the brigade's left were entirely on their own.[32]

Like Colonel Breedlove of the 45th Alabama, Bate was aware of Deshler's presence. Earlier, Deshler's troops had formed on Bate's right. Bate expected that relationship to continue when his men were called to go into the fight, a

31 *OR* 30, pt. 2, 189.

32 Ibid., 386.

hope that was dashed when the Texans moved off to the north. Word arrived soon thereafter that Deshler was dead.

Bate and his men faced the same deadly arc of fire ringing Poe Field. Once again it was the right flank that faltered first. "My right," reported the brigadier, "became hotly engaged almost the instant it assumed the offensive . . . subject to a most galling fire . . . from my right oblique and front, cutting down with great fatality the Twentieth Tennessee and Thirty-Seventh Georgia at every step." Once out in the field, Bate realized the full nature of his exposure. An appeal to Cleburne yielded no help. The messenger came back bearing word that the Irishman had no troops left to give. Reluctantly, Bate ordered the two regiments back to their starting point.[33]

Their departure left the 15th/37th Tennessee and 58th Alabama to press on alone. Farther south, and thus initially less exposed to the crippling crossfire, both units pressed as far as the brush line at the eastern edge of the field. Once the right wing recoiled, however, it was the left portion's turn to be badly raked. "In this charge," recalled a member of the 58th, "we were cross fired with grape, canister and musketry from every direction save our rear. . . . We advanced to within 100 yards of the fortifications, and there stood and fought until it seemed almost suicide to remain longer." Colonel Jones felt that "if the [rest of the] brigade had been on line with me and in good order," the effort might have managed to take the Federal works, but as things stood, a successful assault was simply impossible. Jones hung on for a few minutes, his men and the 15th/37th dispersed and returning as best a fire as they could manage. When no support appeared, Jones ordered a retreat. The entire attack was "badly planned," mourned the 58th's correspondent, who concluded that "Gen'l Stewart ordered it in ignorance as to the enemy's position."[34]

Sergeant Richard M. Gray of Company K, 37th Georgia, agreed. Gray stepped out into the field just about a quarter-mile north of where he and his comrades had encountered Hazen's gun line the previous evening. That night, after the regiment had reformed, "General Bragg issued an order of thanks to be read to his army for their gallant bearing on the first day and promised us a complete triumph" on Sunday. It was not to be, at least not here, and not yet. "We fought for hours in the attempt to dislodge them," concluded the

33 Ibid., 385.

34 "58th Alabama Regiment," *Daily Huntsville Confederate*, October 4, 1863; OR 30, pt. 2, 390.

embittered Georgian, "but failed in every effort. Our gallant men threw away their lives by the hundreds without meeting with the success which [their] sacrifice warranted."[35]

This attack wrecked Bate's brigade. Already fragile from its previous losses, formation after formation shattered like dropped glassware. The 15th/37th all but disintegrated as a combat unit. Its commander, Lt. Col. R. Dudley Frayser, went down with a severe leg wound, leaving command to Capt. R. M. Tankesley of Company D, who'd been serving as the unit's acting major. The colors of the 15th Tennessee (the consolidated outfit carried the flags of both the 15th and 37th regiments into action) were almost lost when their color-bearer was killed at the apex of the advance. Members of the all-but-forgotten 16th Alabama, from Wood's brigade, helped rescue the 15th's banner, which was passed back to the Tennesseans once they had reached the shelter of the woods.[36]

At the southern end of Poe Field, meanwhile, Henry D. Clayton's Alabama brigade faced a similar ordeal tracking in the wake of Brown's Tennesseans. Clayton's three regiments now numbered about 1,100 men and, after their bloodletting of Saturday, could be considered green no longer. By the time they reached the open field they could also no longer be considered fresh. Major Peter F. Hunley of the 18th Alabama reported that the charge "commenced . . . too soon. The men were exhausted before the point was reached where the charge ought to have [begun.]" Once across Brown's own hastily constructed breastworks, now sitting empty, the Alabamians advanced in what soldier-correspondent Capt. Ben Posey of the 36th Alabama called "a mad, reckless charge. We were in a dense woods and could not see the enemy, but we felt him terribly, for our men fell by scores." Clayton's line became further disordered when it met Brown's survivors in full retreat seeking the cover of their own defenses.[37]

With little chance to directly observe the overall assault, Stewart and his staff had only a limited understanding of the fight. Ten days afterward, Lt. Terry Cahal remained confused about exactly what had occurred. "Brown's brigade," he reported, "carried the [Union] position most gallantly, but from some panic which the men themselves are even unable to account for they fell back,

35 R. M. Gray Reminiscences, UNC.

36 *OR* 30, pt. 2, 164, 397.

37 Ibid., 405; "Clayton's Brigade at Chickamauga," *Montgomery Daily Advertiser*, October 23, 1863. Captain Posey used the pen name "Ben Lane."

throwing Clayton's brigade . . . into confusion." Of course Brown's men had not carried any Federal position; they had only driven in the first line of skirmishers before being stopped cold well short of the main enemy line. Clayton's men faced the same unyielding defenders. Once in the field, and unable to hear even shouted commands, the brigade plunged into "a sheer slaughter pen." Artillery raked them from the flank not 200 yards off. Captain Posey estimated that out of the entire brigade, barely 100 men crossed the road "and gathered about a little log house . . . which soon caught fire." Pinned there by a hailstorm of fire, the attack faltered, though the small band of men hung on while Posey stubbornly refused to order a retreat. "Finally some of the men dropped off to the rear, and it became contagious, until all the living and unwounded men sullenly retired." Clayton's effort was over.[38]

By 11:30 a.m., Stewart's and Cleburne's attacks were unequivocal failures. Stewart's second effort likely cost an additional 700 casualties, while Cleburne's losses more than doubled that figure, bleeding away about 1,500 men. All along the line, Federal losses were slight. William Hazen attributed this lopsided success to the breastworks he had initially been reluctant to construct, noting that "my loss [while] behind it . . . was only 13 men during a period of more stubborn fighting than at Shiloh or Stones River, when the same brigade at each place lost more than 400 men." For that matter, just the day before, unprotected fighting in Brock and Brotherton fields had cost Hazen's regiments nearly 500 losses. Breastworks, however rudely and hastily constructed, would be a feature of Union battle positions wherever possible from now on.[39]

At first glance, this pounding against Thomas's line seems entirely one-sided and a clear-cut defeat for the Confederate Right Wing, producing absolutely no military advantage. Viewed dispassionately after 150 years, however, we can discern at least one militarily significant benefit. The constant pressure of these assaults was holding the Army of the Cumberland's attention, from the lowliest privates pulling the triggers to their senior commanders making the critical decisions. The two most important men in Union blue that morning—William Starke Rosecrans and George Thomas—were both entirely fixated on what was happening along the northern half of the Union line. That fixation might still hand Braxton Bragg a chance for victory.

38 "Dear Colonel," September 30, 1863, Cahal Papers, TSLA; "Clayton's Brigade at Chickamauga," *Montgomery Daily Advertiser*, October 23, 1863.

39 *OR* 30, pt. 1, 763.

Chapter Eight

"To draw up the Right": Sunday, 10:00 a.m. to Noon

Between first light and 10:00 a.m., William Rosecrans set a large part of his army in motion. While most of those moves were relatively minor tweaks to his overall defensive scheme, a number of them were substantial, especially on the right. Each of the four divisions still under Alexander McCook's and Tom Crittenden's authority occupied at least two positions that morning. Much of this activity arose from the need to replace James Negley, but there was also a good deal of confusion among his subordinates in divining the army commander's intent. This confusion, in turn, affected Rosecrans's mood, leading the snappish and intemperate general to rebuke several of his officers over the course of the morning.

McCook bore the brunt of Rosecrans's ire. While Negley certainly came in for a measure of his sharpness, and much (perhaps too much) would later be made of an exchange between Rosecrans and Tom Wood, the dressing-down borne by McCook was both public and scathing, especially in its reference to the disaster at Stones River. McCook was not likely to forget that his XX Corps broke there, to the rest of the army's dismay. Accordingly, McCook hustled to set matters right, redeploying his troops to positions more in keeping with Rosecrans's purpose. However, the exchange clearly rattled McCook, and his subsequent actions reflect some degree of confusion as a result.

McCook's first act after Rosecrans left was to hunt up Brig. Gen. Philip Sheridan, whose infantry division McCook intended to use to replace Negley.

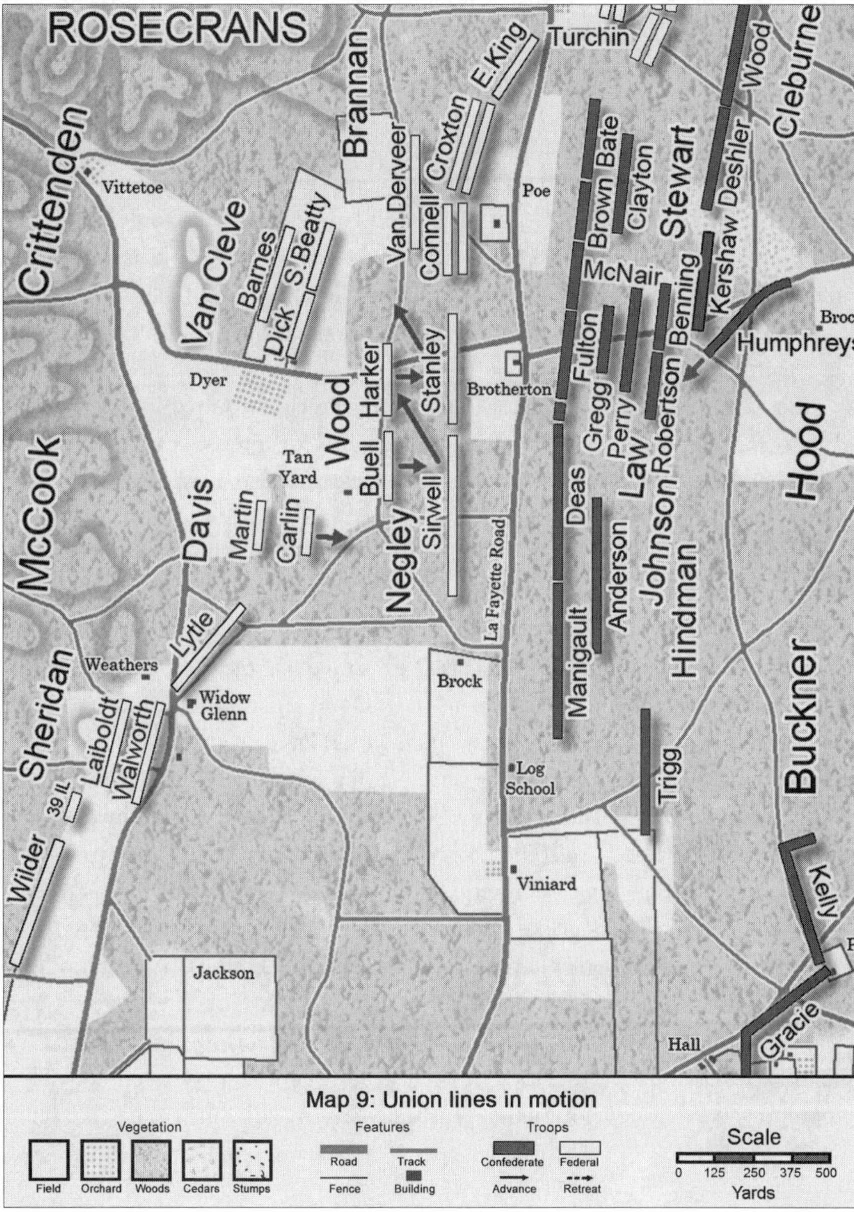

Map 9: Union lines in motion

Both men rode forward to Brotherton Field where, to their surprise, they found Tom Wood's division of the XXI Corps already filing into place. Either Rosecrans had not informed McCook of the decision to move Wood up during their earlier meeting, or McCook misunderstood. In any case, Sheridan's men were not going to be needed there.[1]

At dawn that morning, Col. John Wilder informed McCook that two of his Spencer-armed mounted infantry regiments were screening Negley's right flank south of the timber dividing Brotherton and West Brock fields. As they watched Wood deploy, McCook and Sheridan realized he would not have enough manpower to connect with Wilder's screen. McCook assumed the initiative by ordering Sheridan to bring up Col. Bernard Laiboldt's mixed brigade of Illinois and Missouri troops and place them on Wood's left, plugging that potential hole.[2]

Sheridan galloped off. McCook departed as well, presumably to see about Jefferson C. Davis's men—the other subject of Rosecrans's wrath. The portly Ohioan had barely covered 100 yards before he met Jeff Davis riding toward him, his foot division trailing behind.

Davis was having an equally baffling morning. His division had already been a particular bone of contention between Rosecrans and McCook several times. At 7:00 a.m., after Rosecrans's and McCook's first discussion, McCook ordered Davis's men out of reserve "to move to the left and close on Crittenden's right." This instruction, as both Davis and McCook understood it, was not to move onto the front line (which would have been on Negley's right), but move into a support position behind Negley somewhere out in south Dyer Field. Dutifully, Davis rode north until he met Tom Wood, whose division was at that time still in reserve, also behind Negley. After a conversation with Wood, Davis returned to his own command. By the time Davis organized his troops and returned Wood was gone, departed Davis knew not where. (Wood had advanced to replace Negley.) Instead, Davis found elements of Horatio Van Cleve's division moving into Wood's former position. The exchange of Van Cleve for Wood did not negate his own orders, however, so Davis posted his two brigades on the forward slope of what would eventually be called Lytle Hill, in column, to await developments. "I [then] sent my adjutant-general, Captain

1 *OR* 30, pt. 1, 489; The following February, at McCook's court of inquiry, Rosecrans would insist he did inform McCook of Wood's mission, but admitted that "several orders were sent . . . the hours of which and the substance of which I cannot fully give from memory." Ibid., 940.

2 Ibid., 489.

Morrison, to either General Rosecrans or McCook to see if we were in the right position," noted Davis.[3]

Morrison found Rosecrans easily, just 150 yards to the north. The army commander immediately informed Morrison that things were not right at all. Just as with Wood, Rosecrans elected not to wait for McCook to straighten things out. The General explained Wood's new mission, and directed Davis to move forward and form on the left of Wood's new position. This was a significant deployment change, moving Davis from a reserve position, supporting a strong front line, to taking up the right flank of the entire Union army. McCook encountered Davis while the latter was executing this most recent order.

Davis's new position was exactly where Laiboldt was supposed to go. McCook, however, was by now not about to override a direct order from the commanding general, regardless of how much discretion he might nominally have as a corps commander. McCook and Davis rode forward to discuss Davis's deployment, sending word back to Davis's troops to hustle forward with all haste.

Brigadier General William P. Carlin led Davis's column, his four regiments now numbering no more than about 700 men. Carlin was to connect with Col. George P. Buell's command. Buell's men occupied the western edge of Brotherton Field, holding works earlier constructed by Negley's troops. Placing the 21st Illinois, 81st Indiana, and 101st Ohio in a single line alongside Buell, Carlin also found similarly hastily constructed defenses ready to use. The 38th Illinois was held in reserve, about 80 yards back from the main line. Carlin's position was entirely in the woods south of the field. While his men were deploying, Carlin reconnoitered. "I rode out to the front about four hundred yards, crossing the La Fayette Road. . . . I could neither see nor hear any signs of an enemy." With no sign of a threat in his front, Carlin returned to his brigade. Within a few minutes, restless and expecting trouble, Carlin repeated the exercise. This time he rode out about 300 yards, just beyond his own picket line. Once again he found no Rebels.[4]

3 Ibid., 951. While "Lytle Hill" is postwar nomenclature, I use it here for clarity's sake. The hill had no prewar name of note.

4 Robert I. Girardi and Nathaniel Cheairs Hughes, Jr., eds., *The Memoirs of Brigadier General William Passmore Carlin, U.S.A.* (University of Nebraska Press, 1999), 101.

Carlin wasn't the only uneasy Yankee in his brigade. That morning, Sgt. William W. Hensley of the 21st Illinois was seized with a sudden attack of nerves. Back on the ridge near the Widow Glenn's cabin, Hensley was overcome with a certain dread: "Such feelings as I had then was such as I never had before or since. . . . I was so unnerved I thought I would act the coward and disgrace myself." Nearly a year earlier at Perryville, Hensley saw the blackened faces of the Rebel dead, an image that stuck. "I was told that [they] had been given whiskey with gunpowder in it to make them brave. I did not have the whiskey," reasoned Hensley, "but I did have the gunpowder, so I ate a cartridge." The first one didn't seem to work, but while in position on Lytle Hill, a second seemed to do the trick. His nerve restored, Hensley and the rest of Company C moved out past the breastworks to establish a picket line in the woods ahead of the regimental line. They, too, took note of the apparent absence of any Confederates.[5]

Colonel Hans Heg's former brigade, now under Col. John Martin of the 8th Kansas, was in even worse shape. The brigade numbered 1,218 men when it entered the fight the previous day, but now Martin's four regiments fielded just 600, with the 15th Wisconsin mustering fewer than 100 bayonets. Initially, the brigade was to form on Carlin's left, but Buell's troops were in their place. Davis directed Martin to form his line in reserve behind Carlin's 38th Illinois, with instructions "to lie down in a small ravine."[6]

This change placed Davis's small battered division on the army's extreme right. Carlin fretted, and rightly so, that no one supported his right flank—not even mounted videttes, for Wilder's regiments had been withdrawn to the ridge on the west side of the Dry Valley Road. With a combined strength of only some 1,300 men, the entire division was now the strength of an average brigade, and a weak reed upon which to secure the army's southern flank.[7]

In fact, there was a skirmish line to Carlin's south, posted by Sheridan before dawn. These men were left in place when Sheridan was ordered away to the northwest, and did not immediately follow suit. They remained in position

5 William Wallace Hensley Autobiography, 19, Virginia Polytechnic Institute and State University, Blacksburg, VA. Hereafter VPI.

6 OR 30, pt. 1, 530.

7 Wilder pulled his whole command back to the Widow Glenn ridge and formed on Sheridan's right following his earlier orders to "form on the right fighting flank" of the army. Wilder was apparently not informed of Davis's shift forward, and McCook did not request that he leave any troops to screen Davis's flank.

to the south and east, extending down into Viniard Field. Beyond them were deployed eight companies of Col. Smith D. Atkins's 92nd Illinois Mounted Infantry. Atkins's men were in their saddles early, their picket line connecting the last of Sheridan's screen with the Union cavalry holding Lee and Gordon's Mills. Atkins's orders were to "hold the ground" formerly occupied by the whole of Wilder's brigade "until pressed back," whereupon they were to retreat to Wilder's new position south of the Widow Glenn's. None of this was of any comfort to Carlin, for he had no idea they were there. The failure to connect the skirmish lines lay with the corps staff, where an officer of the day normally had such duty. There had been too much shifting of troops by now, however, and attention to detail was slipping.[8]

While Davis was deploying, Sheridan returned to his own command and ordered Colonel Laiboldt forward, as previously instructed. As his troops marched up the Glenn-Kelly Road, Laiboldt rode on ahead to see where he was needed. He was only the latest commander to discover a problem with his assignment, finding Martin and Carlin already in place, exactly where he had been ordered to form. Confused, Laiboldt halted and sent word of his dilemma to Sheridan. The fiery Irishman ordered Laiboldt to fall in behind Davis "on a very strong ridge to his rear . . . so as to prevent Davis's flank from being turned." Once apprised of these changes, McCook seemed satisfied and said no more about it.[9]

Bernard Laiboldt was a German-American, born in the Grand Duchy of Baden in 1827. His family immigrated to the United States in 1833, settling in St. Louis. He served in the Mexican War and joined the current conflict in August 1861 as lieutenant colonel of the ethnically German 2nd Missouri infantry. He proved to be an able and aggressive soldier. Laiboldt assumed command of his brigade at Stones River after friend and fellow German-American (also from the 2nd Missouri), Col. Frederick Shaefer, fell mortally wounded. Rosecrans commended Laiboldt for his "skill and courage" under fire. The open hillside behind Davis on September 20 struck Laiboldt as an ideal position to deploy in depth, and he posted his brigade accordingly.[10]

8 *OR* 30, pt. 1, 456.

9 Ibid., 580.

10 Ibid., 20, pt. 1, 203.

Laiboldt formed his four regiments into a column, each unit in line, one behind the other. The 73rd Illinois was in front, with the 15th Missouri, 44th Illinois, and 2nd Missouri finishing out the order. Numbering 1,100 troops, Liaboldt's brigade was comprised of well-led veteran troops who had previously distinguished themselves in combat. The men were pleased with a position that offered good fields of fire—a rarity so far in this battle. "We formed three [four] columns deep," recalled Missouri Pvt. Maurice Marcoot of the 15th. "It was a position without fortifications but one we thought we could hold until doomsday against all attacks from the front." They were also only about 600 yards from Carlin's front line and readily available if the need arose.[11]

Sheridan's other two brigades remained in position near the Widow Glenn cabin. Even if Rosecrans was unhappy with their choice of position, they believed it was a good one. "We threw up barricades of logs and rails," wrote Maj. Seymour Chase of the 21st Michigan, "expecting if we . . . had a fight at all that day, it would be there, as we were the extreme right of the army." Chase's regimental commander, Col. William B. McCreery, "was cheerful and in good spirits." He wandered over to Chase, and both men surveyed the defenses. "They can't drive us from here," said McCreery with evident satisfaction. While the officers conversed, Cpl. John Ely of the 88th Illinois, with nothing to do at the moment, took a practical approach. I "layed down to get what rest I could. . . . I slept for two hours or more. . . . A solder that has seen much service," mused the corporal, "Learnes to enjoy a moments rest whenever he may be placed."[12]

In a decision echoing Wood's advice, Davis elected not to bring either the 2nd Minnesota or 8th Wisconsin batteries into the woods with his infantry. Instead, Davis ordered Capt. William A. Hotchkiss to post both batteries to cover the Dry Valley Road near the Widow Glenn cabin, back near their first position of the day. Laiboldt was accompanied by Battery C, 1st Illinois Light Artillery, but even it was posted far to the rear at the top of Lytle Hill, some 200 yards behind and above Laiboldt's infantry. Unlike Thomas's sector, where the heavy guns studded the very forefront of the Union defenses, Federal artillery support was essentially nonexistent here in McCook's sector.[13]

11 Maurice Marcoot, *Five Years in the Sunny South: Reminiscences of Maurice Marcoot* (n.p. n.d.), 37.

12 "Dear Sir," Chase to Mr. McCreery, October 15, 1863, McCreery Family Papers, Bentley Historical Library, UMich; John Ely Diary, CCNMP.

13 *OR* 30, pt. 1, 504, 803-804.

Thomas L. Crittenden was also struggling to divine Rosecrans's intentions. With Wood taken from him, the only remaining command left to the corps leader was Maj. Gen. Horatio Van Cleve's division, and even Van Cleve had been stripped of Sidney Barnes's brigade, loaned out to fill Wood's line. Sometime between 9:30 and 10:00 a.m., Van Cleve was ordered to fall in behind Tom Wood and support him. Van Cleve moved his remaining brigades promptly, intending to form on the same open ridge west of the Glenn-Kelly Road that Negley had used the night before, and where Wood himself first deployed. Once again, a disputatious Rosecrans found fault with that arrangement. Rosecrans informed Van Cleve that he "was much too far in the rear to give immediate support to the main line of battle." Rosecrans ordered the Minnesotan "to form my regiments in double column on the center, move rapidly to the foot of the hill, cut roads through the woods for my artillery, and there hold myself in readiness for any emergency." Van Cleve hastened to comply, moving his line up close behind Wood's. Next, Rosecrans met Crittenden in the Dyer Peach Orchard after returning from overseeing Wood. He reiterated his instructions by ordering Crittenden "to move Van Cleve at once down the hill to a better position," even repeating the instructions on how to form the individual regiments, "for fear that General Van Cleve would not understand them fully." This adjustment proved minor, advancing Van Cleve no more than 200 yards. With that, the army commander rode up the slope Van Cleve had just vacated to establish army headquarters there on the open knoll.[14]

Rosecrans's various interactions with McCook, Crittenden, Davis, Wood, and Van Cleve reflect a significant degree of micro-management. Corps commanders McCook and Crittenden were bypassed multiple times. Rosecrans simply communicated directly with their various division commanders and informed their respective corps leaders of changes only after the fact—or, as McCook and Sheridan discovered upon finding Wood already in position, didn't in some cases inform them at all. Wood's instructions were originally passed through Crittenden, but then Rosecrans also intervened directly in that process. The army commander's interaction with Van Cleve showed an even greater degree of meddling. He shifted Van Cleve's men a mere regimental frontage, and that was done before Van Cleve had even settled into his initial location. Rosecrans further dictated how Van Cleve was to form his individual

14 Ibid., 803-804.

regiments. These were not the types of minor decisions an army commander was supposed to concentrate upon.

Much of this peevishness on Rosecrans's part can be explained by his intense focus on what he viewed as the most pressing threat: the fighting on his left along Thomas's front. With Thomas, Rosecrans's style was entirely different and virtually hands-off. After his early morning reconnaissance, the commanding general did not visit the XIV Corps sector again that morning, relying instead upon Thomas to handle everything there. Thomas's solution to every threat, of course, was to send a courier—and sometimes several at once—to ask for more men.

These requests for reinforcements intensified when Confederate brigades began to pound the entire arc of Thomas's line from the McDonald farmstead in the north to Poe Field farther south. Except for Breckinridge's temporary success on the far left none of those repeated Rebel attacks achieved anything, and most were quickly repulsed with dreadful slaughter. The continued threat of more, however, suggested to George Thomas that the Confederates had a great deal of force ready to hurl against his line, and sooner or later they would manage another breach. Accordingly, Thomas continued to press for additional troops.

By 10:00 a.m. the Union right at last settled into a sort of quiet, with most of its formations arranged to the commanding general's acceptance, if not outright satisfaction. Rosecrans rode to the knoll that would host his headquarters group for the next few hours. This elevation, the northern spur of Lytle Hill, terminated about 200 yards south of the Dyer Road. It overlooked the Dyer farmyard and orchard, and presented Rosecrans one of the few vistas available on the wooded battlefield of Chickamauga. The Dyer property consisted of a series of cleared fields stretching nearly a mile from north to south between the Glenn-Kelly and Dry Valley roads, bisected by the Dyer farm lane. This terrain offered both an outstanding view and rapid communications with the southern half of his command, with Thomas's sector only a slightly longer gallop to the north.

The stabilization of his right did little to settle Rosecrans's nerves: the battle now raging in full fury around Kelly Field remained uppermost in his mind. Accordingly, once the new headquarters was established the first thing Rosecrans did was to send a written confirmation of his discussion with McCook in order to ensure that the XX Corps commander fully grasped the situation and his expected role:

Headquarters, Department Of The Cumberland,
In the field, September 20, 1863 - 10:10 a.m.

Major General McCook,
Commanding Twentieth Army Corps,

General Thomas is being heavily pressed on the left. The general commanding directs you to make immediate disposition to withdraw the right so as to spare as much force as possible to re-enforce Thomas. The left must be held at all hazards even if the right is withdrawn wholly back to the present left. Select a good position back this way and be ready to start reinforcements to Thomas at a moment's notice.

J. A. Garfield
Brigadier General, and Chief of Staff.[15]

Given his location at this time, Rosecrans's instruction to "select a good position back this way" is particularly significant. It evidences that Rosecrans was already preparing to shorten his line by a considerable margin—at least 1,000 yards and perhaps more—and draw McCook to the north.

If he was going to reinforce George Thomas with more men, refusing the army's right was the only practical alternative. With the return of Negley, the XIV Corps commander now controlled six of the Army of the Cumberland's 10 infantry divisions (not counting Maj. Gen. Gordon Granger's three brigades at Rossville: Brigadier General Whitaker and Colonel Mitchell, of Steedman's division, and Col. Dan McCook's independent brigade). This left Alexander McCook with the divisions of Jeff Davis, Tom Wood, and Phil Sheridan to protect the Union right, and Tom Crittenden with only Van Cleve's two brigades still under his control. At first glance Rosecrans had already sent the big Virginian managing the left of his army all the men that could be spared. If more were to be found, they had to be pried loose from McCook's line.

Starting about 10:15 a.m., the fleeting stability that had settled upon the Union right was shattered anew by a series of rapid-fire orders pouring out of army headquarters. During the next half hour, Rosecrans once again threw his right wing into complete disarray, sending formations scurrying about like

15 *OR* 30, pt. 1, 489. The timing of this order, while internally consistent with other communications sent by Rosecrans's headquarters, does not synch up with the times used by the Confederates. The Rebels put Breckinridge's step-off time as 9:45 a.m., and Cleburne's as 10:00 a.m. This order was probably sent around 10:30 a.m. by the Confederate clock, meaning the crisis in Kelly Field was already fully developed and Cleburne's assaults were hitting all along Thomas's line.

insects boiling out of a disturbed anthill. And by doing so, he unwittingly set the stage for disaster.

The first of these orders was sent to General Van Cleve via Tom Crittenden. Shortly after 10:00 a.m. Crittenden joined Rosecrans on the knoll after placing Van Cleve's line. Captain Percival P. Oldershaw of Crittenden's staff noticed "some smoke which we all saw rising in the front and a little to our left." The smoke could only have been A. P. Stewart's Confederates striking the Union position in Poe Field. To everyone observing, the powder smoke suggested another major assault on the Federal line. Rosecrans reacted promptly. As Crittenden recalled it, "I was now ordered to move General Van Cleve directly to the front to take part in the battle now raging in that direction." These orders disposed of the last troops under Crittenden's direct control. Under the assumption that they would soon be in combat, the XXI Corps leader asked Rosecrans if he could accompany them. Rosecrans agreed.[16]

Crittenden galloped to join Van Cleve with Captain Oldershaw in tow. To Lt. Marcus Woodcock in the Union 9th Kentucky, the sudden flurry of activity signaled impending action: "the bugles sounded *attention*, and we were moved a few yards towards the front—Staff officers were now flying in all directions." Crittenden ordered Van Cleve "to move forward and engage the enemy wherever I should find an open space in our front lines." Because he advanced directly forward, it only took a handful of minutes before Van Cleve's men ran up against the back of Tom Wood's division. Brigadier General Samuel Beatty sent back word that he had stumbled into Col. Charles Harker's brigade, and "that there were two lines of our troops before us." There was no "open space" for Van Cleve to "find."[17]

Crittenden briefly pondered the report before directing Van Cleve to "take ground to the left, to pass through the first interval he could find, and engage the enemy." It was an intriguing order—and one largely overlooked by historians—because it demonstrates that Crittenden was thinking offensively. Perhaps he was hoping to accomplish what he had tried so hard to achieve the day before—the striking of an enemy flank while the Rebels were engaged with other Yankees to their front. If so, it did not come to pass.[18]

16 *OR* 30, pt. 1, 609, 988.

17 Noe, *A Southern Boy in Blue*, 204; *OR* 30, pt. 1, 804, 809.

18 Ibid., 804.

Alexander McDowell McCook had already been dressed down by Rosecrans once on the morning of September 20 when he received two communiques—the 10:10 and the 10:30 a.m. orders—from Rosecrans, alerting him to the fact that Rosecrans intended to close the army to the left. With these directives in hand, McCook scrambled to comply. *Library of Congress*

The dutiful Van Cleve sent Beatty sidling left, moving north "until I should find an opening." Moving a brigade-length brought Beatty up behind Sidney Barnes's portion of the line. There was still no gap to attack through. His first instructions frustrated, Van Cleve directed Beatty to once again move left "and support any weak place in the line." This next move placed Beatty behind John Connell's brigade of Brannan's division, which was heavily engaged in beating back John Brown's and Henry Clayton's attacks. Connell did not appear to need any help, so Beatty ordered his men to lie down, still in column of division, until they were needed. Van Cleve's remaining brigade under Col. George Dick followed suit, falling in on Sam Beatty's left behind John Croxton's portion of Brannan's front. Unwittingly, both of Van Cleve's brigades now occupied the same position recently vacated by Ferdinand Van Derveer's brigade (Brannan's division), which had been sent just a few minutes before to Kelly Field.[19]

Back on the army headquarters knoll, meanwhile, Rosecrans continued issuing orders. His next directive of consequence was to McCook at 10:30 a.m., which the corps commander took for an "order of execution" supplementing the previous "order for preparation" (the 10:10 a.m. order reproduced earlier). This instruction read as follows:

> Headquarters, Department of the Cumberland,
> In the field, September 20, 1863 - 10:30 a.m.
>
> Major General McCook,
> Commanding Twentieth Army Corps,
>
> The General commanding directs you to send two brigades of General Sheridan's division at once and with all possible dispatch to support General Thomas, and send the third brigade as soon as the lines can be drawn in sufficiently. March them as rapidly as you can without exhausting the men. Report in person to these headquarters as soon as your orders are given in regard to Sheridan's movement. Have you any news from Colonel Post?
>
> J. A. Garfield
> Brigadier General, and Chief of Staff.[20]

This directive stripped Rosecrans's entire right flank of his last reserves. Moreover, Rosecrans specifically directed that Brig. Gen. William Lytle's and Col. Nathan Walworth's brigades were to move immediately with Col. Bernard Laiboldt to follow as soon as McCook could send him. Rosecrans had just consigned his only remaining uncommitted force—Van Cleve's pair of brigades—to action in his immediate front. Even Rosecrans was a bit uneasy, for as he admitted later, "I deemed the wording of the order too precipitate for events, but [was] unwilling to have it rewritten." Instead, Rosecrans "intended for General McCook to report to me in person, presuming he would arrive before the troops would move, intending to give him [more] specific directions." Rosecrans was right to be worried, but what he did next only compounded the problem. Before McCook even received the 10:30 a.m. order,

19 Ibid., 809.

20 *OR* 30, pt. 1, 489. Colonel Sidney Post, it will be recalled, was escorting trains out of McLemore's Cove and had not yet reached the army.

let alone acted on it, Rosecrans further tilted the army's balance toward Thomas by sending Horatio Van Cleve northward.[21]

While Van Cleve was probing for a place in the line to make his men useful, Crittenden encountered another of George Thomas's ubiquitous couriers, Lt. Col. Alexander von Schrader. Thomas was "pressed on the left," explained the messenger. Crittenden sent von Schrader on to Rosecrans. Within minutes Rosecrans sent von Schroder galloping back down the hill and across Dyer Field to buttonhole General Crittenden, bearing the following missive:

Headquarters, Department of the Cumberland,
In the field, September 20, 1863 - 10:45 a.m.

Major General Crittenden
Commanding Twenty-first Army Corps,

The General commanding directs you to send General Van Cleve's command to General Thomas's support with all dispatch. General Van Cleve will put his force in on Thomas's left as quickly as he can do so without exhausting the men too much.

J. A. Garfield
Brigadier General, and Chief of Staff.[22]

"I gave the order immediately to General Van Cleve and its execution was at once begun," reported Crittenden, with the added injunction "to occupy any gap or interval he might find in the lines." Crittenden demurred with his commander on one point: the Kentuckian's impression was that Thomas's right, manned by Brannan's division, needed the help, not the left. He would comply for the moment, but Crittenden also sent Captain Oldershaw galloping back to the knoll to convey this opinion to the army commander. Along the way, Oldershaw met von Schrader and questioned him again: which was it—the XIV Corps's right or its left? The right, replied the German, affirming Crittenden's opinion. Oldershaw reported this revised estimate to Rosecrans, and once he returned, he did the same to Crittenden. Still, Rosecrans's order was peremptory, and so Crittenden had Van Cleve start Col. George Dick's

21 Ibid., 943.

22 Ibid., 71.

brigade up the Glenn-Kelly Road immediately, headed for Thomas's left. For the moment, Sam Beatty's men remained in place.[23]

Like several earlier movements, Colonel Dick's was also marked by confusion. Dick's orders were vague: "To move on the double-quick by the left flank to the support of some artillery said to be in position in the woods." When he complied but found no artillery, Dick sent a courier back to Van Cleve with that information. No matter, replied the division commander, who instructed Dick to simply keep on until he found someone who needed his help. A short while later Dick found himself behind Van Derveer's command, where he halted.[24]

Samuel Beatty was anything but happy with his current position. He had been left behind to grope for a position in the line where he could make himself useful and, as discussed earlier, his four regiments had gone to ground behind Brannan's right flank at the Poe house, pressed up so close on John Connell's brigade that his men were "but a few yards" to Connell's rear. So close, in fact, that "the four lines more resembled a column in mass" than a combat formation.[25]

Captain Oldershaw also brought one more piece of news that surely confused Crittenden: "General Rosecrans," said the captain, just "ordered General Wood to leave his position and move to Thomas's assistance as soon as he was relieved by General McCook." Now, to General Crittenden, this information also suggested Rosecrans was commencing a wholesale shift to the north. While Rosecrans's order to Alexander McCook demonstrated this was exactly what the army commander intended (though Crittenden was apparently not privy to that order transferring Sheridan, and thus could not know what was going on in McCook's sector), the order to Wood was not part of that overall plan.[26]

23 Ibid., 610, 988. This small confusion probably explains why, when Col. George Dick's brigade was sent up the Glenn-Kelly Road immediately in Stanley's and Van Derveer's wake, Van Cleve and Sam Beatty did not immediately follow suit. Neither Crittenden nor Van Cleve later explained why they did not have Beatty's regiments fall in directly behind Dick, or why neither of them accompanied Dick on his move north. If Crittenden was observing the fighting in Poe Field at this time, it would not be unreasonable to conclude that the greater threat was unfolding right in front of him. Retaining Beatty hedged a bet.

24 Ibid., 824.

25 Ibid., 809.

26 Ibid., 988.

Also at roughly 10:30 a.m., while Rosecrans was dictating the missive to send Sheridan north and ordering Van Cleve to do the same thing, George Thomas sent yet another aide-de-camp on a troop-finding mission. Captain Sanford T. Kellogg rode south, looking for John Brannan. The 21-year-old Kellogg joined Thomas's staff in March 1863, directly commissioned as a captain. His only previous military experience was as an enlisted man in the 37th New York militia, a three-month regiment called up in the summer of 1862 but which saw no action. Kellogg was also Thomas's nephew on his wife's side, prominent residents of Troy, New York. Kellogg had been schooled in Switzerland and worked in banking before joining his uncle. While his military qualifications were not extensive, he was bright, educated, energetic, and courageous—all the hallmarks of a first-rate aide-de-camp.[27]

An hour or so earlier, when Thomas had initially requested John Brannan's troops, Brannan and fellow division commander Joseph Reynolds agreed they could spare Ferdinand Van Derveer's brigade. With this second call for troops, Brannan once again rode to find Reynolds. "I am again ordered to the left," explained Brannan. "Do you think you can maintain your position without me? Kellogg is here and says the call is urgent." Given that this request arrived amidst repeated Rebel attacks, Reynolds must have thought he had matters well in hand, for he replied, "Well, perhaps Thomas needs you more than I do . . . and I believe I can hold here. So go along and good luck to you."[28]

Kellogg added that General Thomas was under the impression (as worked out the previous night during the council of war) that John Brannan's division was in reserve. Reynolds said he understood, but that Brannan was in the front line. He asked Kellogg to convey all this information to Rosecrans in the hope of getting someone to replace Brannan's troops. "My right flank had been in the air during all the previous day's fighting," explained Reynolds, and if Brannan departed, "my right flank would be entirely exposed" once again. "If [Rosecrans] had any troops lying around loose . . . I would welcome them and probably be able to give them a job." Curiously, neither Reynolds nor Brannan mentioned Crittenden, Van Cleve, or either of Van Cleve's available brigades—

27 Cist, *Army of the Cumberland*, 206, made no mention of Kellogg or this mission. Cist identified von Schrader as the man who reported Reynolds's flank was uncovered, and triggered the later confusion with Wood. Cist wrote that Brannan's division went unnoticed by von Schrader, hidden as it was in the woods. Cist was apparently unaware of Kellogg's mission at the time he wrote his history.

28 Reynolds Statement, CCNMP.

all of whom were close by while the two generals were conferring with Kellogg. Either Brannan and Reynolds assumed Van Cleve's men were already spoken for and heading for Thomas, or were simply unaware of the latter's presence.[29]

With that, Kellogg rode off to find Rosecrans as the battle raged along that part of the front. Kellogg must have passed through Van Cleve's men, who were at that time shifting about on the road directly behind Brannan's line, but seems to have taken no notice of them. His mission was urgent; once Brannan moved, the Union line would be broken.

Almost immediately, a new Rebel attack jolted the line. This was almost surely A. P. Stewart's second effort, launched by William Bate and Henry Clayton after Brown's repulse. Once again everyone was heavily engaged. Colonel Connell's brigade held Brannan's right, tied in with Col. Sidney Barnes's brigade (attached to Wood's division) on Connell's right. Brannan had already issued the departure orders to his subordinates. "I received orders to move to the left, following [John T.] Croxton's brigade, and passing to the rear of Reynolds' division," recalled Connell, "but before the movement was executed the order was countermanded." Much later, Connell elaborated further: "I was then engaged, my battery in action and fully served, skirmishers in from the front and firing all along the line." He could not up and leave with at least a brigade of Rebels assaulting him. "If I obeyed," he added, "I would destroy this perfectly formed line." Connell then spied Reynolds, who had ridden down the length of Brannan's front, probably to see for himself just how vulnerable Brannan's departure would leave his own command. Connell sent his adjutant to him to convey that he had "decided not to obey, if he [Reynolds] would approve my decision." No longer as sanguine about holding on by himself, Reynolds heartily approved, "begging Connell" not to go.[30]

Brannan must have concurred, for Croxton also remained in place. Since both brigades remained in the line, there was no longer the need for Kellogg to ride and inform Rosecrans of Reynolds's anticipated plight. As long as Brannan remained in place, Reynolds's flank would not be exposed. However, neither Reynolds nor Brannan thought to send another rider after Kellogg, who had already left to inform Rosecrans. The oversight would prove fatal to the army.

Within a few minutes, Kellogg arrived at army headquarters and outlined Brannan's intended movement, and relayed Reynolds's concerns about his

29 Ibid.

30 *OR* 30, pt. 1, 409; DeVelling, *Seventeenth Regiment*, 103.

exposed right flank. Rosecrans, who had no way of knowing that none of this was in fact transpiring, reacted quickly. "Tell General Thomas our line is closing towards him and to hold his ground at all hazards and I will reinforce him with the entire army if necessary." Kellogg was also instructed to "tell Brannan to obey Gen. Thomas's orders." Army chief of staff James Garfield was already busy drafting the earlier order intended for Crittenden and Van Cleve, so Rosecrans dictated the next instruction to Maj. Frank S. Bond, as follows:

Headquarters, Department of the Cumberland,
September 20, 1863 - 10:45 a.m.

Brigadier General Wood,
Commanding Division,

The General commanding directs that you close up on Reynolds as fast as possible, and support him.

Respectfully,

Frank S. Bond
Major, and Aide-de-camp[31]

Once written, the order was handed to Lt. Col. Lyne Starling of Crittenden's staff for delivery. In the meantime, A. P. Stewart had been repulsed and another lull settled over the field. "There was no firing, and no evident need of support for anyone, and I hesitated," Starling later testified, "not understanding the object of the order." Garfield was busy drafting the other dispatch, but he was also paying attention to this latest development. He now spoke up: "The object . . . was that General Wood should occupy the vacancy made by the removal of Brannan's division, Brannan having been ordered to General Thomas's left."[32]

There are two other factors worth noting in Starling's February 1864 recollection. First, despite Starling's assertion that Crittenden was present for this exchange, the XXI Corps commander was almost certainly not there. As both the order Garfield was then writing and Captain Oldershaw's testimony demonstrates, Crittenden had already ridden off to catch up with Van Cleve's

31 Rosecrans, "Chattanooga Campaign," *National Tribune*, March 25, 1882; *OR* 30, pt. 1, 635.

32 Ibid., 983.

northward bound troops. At this time Crittenden was likely just west of Poe Field in the immediate vicinity of Brannan, Reynolds, and Wood. He could easily have informed Rosecrans that there was no gap in the line to fill—had he known what was transpiring. If he had been granted the authority, the XXI Corps leader could also have orchestrated a more coordinated redeployment of the various commands if Rosecrans insisted more troops be sent to Thomas. By this time, however, Rosecrans had largely bypassed both McCook and Crittenden, to Rosecrans's own and the army's detriment. Second, Starling noted that there was no firing at the time the order was drafted. It is possible that 10:45 a.m. marked the lull between A. P. Stewart's first and second assaults on the Poe Field line, but even if that were so, it could only have been a short interlude, with more attacks expected any minute. After all, Van Cleve's men had been sent forward to join in that very action. The sense of urgency, even crisis, seemed palpable. The order was marked "gallop." Starling, his confusion resolved, dashed off towards Brotherton Field to find Tom Wood.[33]

Meanwhile, what of Alexander McCook? The highest ranking member of the "fighting McCooks'" was on the move a great deal that morning, and proved a hard man to track. Couriers bearing both the 10:10 a.m. order to shorten the right, and the 10:30 a.m. directive committing Sheridan to the left were about to have an even greater impact than perhaps even Rosecrans intended. McCook, busy with first Sheridan and then Davis, did not receive either of these communiqués until just shy of 11:00 a.m., when both appeared almost simultaneously. "The difference in time could not have been more than six minutes," testified Gates Thruston, McCook's chief of staff. "The . . . officers carrying these orders . . . following each other almost immediately."[34]

After reading them both, McCook, who was with Davis, grasped that he now had several things to do at once. He reacted quickly. First, he sent Capt. Beverly Williams to find Sheridan and relay the order dispatching that officer to reinforce Thomas. A second courier, Maj. Caleb Bates, rode to find Colonel Wilder and alert him that the army's right flank was shifting. Chief of Staff Thruston was sent to find and inform the Union cavalry commander, Brig.

33 Lamers, *The Edge of Glory*, 343.

34 *OR* 30, pt. 1, 955.

Gen. Robert Mitchell, of what was about to transpire and that he was to follow the shift northward as best he could.[35]

Despite his quick compliance, the orders dismayed the beefy Ohioan. All through the morning McCook had been growing increasingly anxious about the security of the Union right flank; these new orders only compounded his anxiety. "Rosecrans is mistaken," he fretted to his staff. "A very formidable attack" was coming, and his remaining troops "were not sufficient to hold the line."[36]

Next, McCook rode north to tell Tom Wood the right flank was being drawn up. Once he finished with Wood, presumably McCook intended to ride to Rosecrans's headquarters and report in as ordered. It might have been better if McCook had visited Rosecrans first before reacting, but given Rosecrans's current mindset, the overall outcome would likely have been the same. Whatever McCook wanted to discuss with Wood was soon forgotten. As soon as the XX Corps commander rode up and dismounted to talk to the division leader, Lieutenant Colonel Starling arrived with the order to "close up and support Reynolds."

Wood's men had been holding their current front for less than an hour, and were still settling into Negley's breastworks. Wood's position ran along the western edge of the Brotherton farm below the crest of the ridge that dominated the middle of the field. As a result, Wood's infantry were sheltered from long range enemy fire by what amounted to a reverse slope defense, but they could not see anything beyond their immediate front—not even the La Fayette Road a mere 200 yards to the east. Skirmishers fanned out to provide advance warning of any enemy activity. Like William Carlin's earlier reconnaissance, Wood's skirmishers initially reported that everything was quiet. Wood must have still been in considerable pain from his fall and resultant groin injury the day before, but his bearing displayed nothing of it.

Opposite Wood, about 400 yards east of the La Fayette Road, waited James Longstreet's Confederate Left Wing. Longstreet's massive pile-driver of a formation needed only the orders necessary to be set in motion. Initially, Longstreet's skirmishers remained well short of the Union skirmish line, which explained the lack of contact. That soon changed. By 11:00 a.m. Wood's pickets

35 Ibid., 938.

36 Ibid., 958.

were engaged in "desultory skirmish firing," according to Chaplain John J. Hight of the 58th Indiana, but it did not amount to much more than routine picket squabbling.[37]

The 58th Indiana belonged to Col. George Buell's brigade, which was holding Wood's right adjacent to and just north of Carlin's position. Buell's command was still trying to recover from its bloody ordeal of the 19th in Viniard Field, where the brigade suffered brutal losses and had their battery overrun. Now, each of his four regiments numbered no more than 200 men, holding a front that stretched them thin. The 26th Ohio formed on Buell's right, with the 100th Illinois on its left. The 13th Michigan and Buell's own 58th Indiana comprised the second line, massed in column of division. The 8th Indiana battery remained limbered behind them. The fortunes of war had allowed the Hoosier artillerymen to retrieve their overrun guns during the night, refit, and rejoin the brigade. Still, the men were shaken and the battery was not functioning at its best.

While in line in Brotherton Field, one of Buell's regiments launched what amounted to a unilateral attack against the massed central column of Longstreet's Wing. Shortly after deploying, Buell discovered that Col. Frederic Bartleson had led his 100th Illinois in a reckless plunge across the La Fayette Road into the woods beyond. The thrust kicked up such a hornet's nest of activity that Bartleson called for support. Buell supposed that he had somehow missed a general order to advance and sent the 26th Ohio up to the crest of the ridge midfield, but the Buckeyes were to go no farther until he could discover what it all meant.[38]

The men of the 26th Ohio had seen plenty of hard fighting at Stones River and again the previous day, but their choice of a nickname derived from another skill: digging. They called themselves "the Groundhog Regiment" because of, as one regimental reunion booklet noted, "the facility with which the regiment could bury itself with a bayonet and a half a canteen, or a spoon, and the expedition with which it could construct a line of more elaborate field works." In the spring of 1863, the 26th was detailed to help construct the massive fortification at Murfreesboro known as Fortress Rosecrans. The labor required the movement of a great deal of dirt. They had just settled comfortably behind

37 John J. Hight and Gilbert R. Stormont, *History of the Fifty-Eighth Regiment of Indiana Volunteer Infantry, Its Organization, Campaigns, and Battles from 1861 to 1865* (Press of the Clarion, 1895), 189.

38 *OR* 30, pt. 1, 656.

the works constructed by Negley's men that morning when the order arrived calling them to move up to the crest of the ridge and lie down.[39]

On Wood's personal orders, Colonel Bartleson had led the 100th on a desperate foray on the 19th in an effort to save the embattled guns of the 8th Indiana. Perhaps Wood was thinking specifically of the 100th when commenting the night before about his preference for volunteer troops over Regulars. This time, Bartleson charged on his own initiative. That idea, a member of the 100th named George Woodruff wrote with some understatement, "turned out to be an unfortunate movement."[40]

Bartleson's initial objective was the Brotherton farm, standing just over the rise and along the west side of the La Fayette Road. Confederate sharpshooters had been using this position to pick off and generally annoy the Illinoisans. After having secured the farm buildings, however, Bartleson continued across the road toward the main Confederate battle line, sending back the regimental bugler to belatedly inform Buell of his aggressive actions. Moving across the road proved a disastrous decision. "We were led right on a masked battery, which opened up on us with grape and canister," wrote one member of the 100th Illinois, Pvt. J. C. Lang of Company D, in a letter home. "The regiment gave way and fell back behind the breastworks [except for] most of our company and company F. We rallied behind a picket fence; Colonel Bartleson was with us."[41]

Once he was satisfied there was no general order to advance, Buell left Lt. Col. William Young and the 26th Ohio midfield to cover the 100th's retreat, but refused to send Bartleson any other help. After about 30 minutes, Buell watched as blue soldiers retreated toward the main line. Satisfied the 100th had pulled back, Buell ordered Young to leave four companies on the crest as a reinforced skirmish line and pull the rest of his Buckeyes back to the western fence line.[42]

39 Association of the Regiment, *Roster of Survivors of the Twenty-Sixth Ohio Veteran Volunteer Infantry* (The Office of the Ohio Soldier, 1888), 2; Jeffrey A. Hill, *The 26th Ohio Veteran Volunteer Infantry: The Groundhog Regiment* (Authorhouse, 2010), 184.

40 George H. Woodruff, *Fifteen Years Ago: Or the Patriotism of Will County* (Joliet Republican Book and Job Steam Printing House, 1876), 285.

41 Frank E. Hills, "Chickamauga," *National Tribune*, November 26, 1891; J. C. Lang letter, *Joliet Signal*, Joliet, IL., October 27, 1863.

42 *OR* 30, pt. 1, 672.

Buell was mistaken. Bartleson never got back to the brigade line. When his regiment met the masked battery and tumbled back in disorder, he rallied the two companies around the Brotherton farm, apparently intending to hold it as a strongpoint until help arrived. Bartleson took a wound soon thereafter and sought shelter in the cabin with about a dozen other injured men. His incapacitation further complicated matters. Unable to find Bartleson, Maj. Charles M. Hammond took charge of the regiment and led most of the men back to the western side of the field. Buell observed this retreat and the regimental colors flying above the withdrawing men and assumed the 100th Illinois was back with the brigade line. Colonel Bartleson, the other wounded from his regiment, and Companies D and F, however, were still in the farmyard, for all intents marooned between the lines.[43]

McCook and Wood met shortly after all this occurred, about 150 yards or so west of the Brotherton cabin. The fighting Bartleson had provoked also triggered a reaction in the 3rd Kentucky of Harker's brigade, which was still back at the wood line along the west edge of the field. Colonel Henry C. Dunlap reported a "severe fighting of skirmishers" in which his men drove the Rebels "under cover of heavy timber . . . [where] they added canister to the rapid musketry." Colonel Dunlap nearly emulated Bartleson when he ordered the main body of his regiment to move out into the field. The advance was quickly checked by Harker, who ordered Dunlap back to his defenses. Chauncey Woodruff, the 43-year-old adjutant of the 65th Ohio, watched all this actively with a close eye and reported, "Gen. Wood seeing this retrograde movement . . . mistook it for a [general] retreat and rode up quickly to check it." The skirmishing soon subsided, but Wood remained close by, allowing Woodruff to observe all that happened next.[44]

It was here that Lieutenant Colonel Starling found Tom Wood, Alex McCook, and delivered his order. Little did any of them know that the exchange that followed would become infamous. This incident, however, which directly led to the subsequent Union disaster, is the single most famous issue of the entire battle of Chickamauga. Accordingly, each of the participants and their various partisans developed considerably different versions of what actually transpired that morning.

43 Hills, "Chickamauga," *National Tribune*, November 26, 1891.

44 *OR* 30, pt. 1, 700; C. Woodruff, "Chickamauga," *National Tribune*, December 3, 1891.

As Starling would later testify, "I gave the orders to General Wood, told him the object of it, and he stated that General Brannan was in position, and that there was no vacancy." Startled by the reply, Starling shot back, "Then there is no order." The staffer turned to ride back to Rosecrans (who was only some 800 yards to the rear) for clarification.[45]

The order troubled Tom Wood. "My God!" he exclaimed, "I can't pull out of here. The very moment my troops commence to move, the Rebels will bulge right through." Adjutant Woodruff of the 65th Ohio overheard this exchange. Wood, he recalled, "in his sharp, crisp way" protested against "opening the line till other troops were provided to take the place of his." However much he might protest, though, Wood was unwilling to simply ignore Rosecrans's directive. Instead, he decided to wait until Starling returned with clarification. This is when McCook stepped in. Perhaps he was still smarting from Rosecrans's earlier dressing-down, but whatever the reason he would brook no delay. Neither McCook nor Wood, insisted the XX Corps commander, knew what was happening with Thomas, and "there was no time to lose." "You could be court-martialed for not obeying it," McCook added emphatically. Wood agreed, noting that "the order was so imperative and peremptory that I must obey it immediately." McCook offered up the final persuasive argument: besides, McCook declared, "We can move in as fast as you can move out." The obvious solution was to shift Jefferson C. Davis's division northward. Major William J. Richards, the XX Corps provost marshal and the head of McCook's escort, was also present. Richards recalled that Wood, who was still worried about moving too quickly, suggested a measure of camouflage: "Mack [McCook], I'll move out by the right flank and rear, to hide my move from the enemy." Even that was too slow for McCook. "No Tom . . . just march out by the left flank and I'll order Jeff [Davis] to close your gap." With that, and despite his deep misgivings, Wood prepared his men for departure.[46]

45 *OR* 30, pt. 1, 983-984.

46 Charles and Barbara Whalen, *The Fighting McCooks: America's Famous Fighting Family* (Westmoreland Press, 2006), 228; Woodruff, "Chickamauga," *National Tribune*, December 3, 1891; Robertson, "The Chickamauga Campaign: September 20 1863," 28; Thomas J. Wood, "The Gaps at Chickamauga," *New York Times*, November 19, 1882; William J. Richards, "Rosecrans and the Chickamauga Campaign," *MOLLUS*, vol. 24, 475. Dr. Robertson's sources include a number of letters from Wood's aides, all of which agree that Wood was initially reluctant to move. Dr. Robertson has done more than any other student of the battle to present a fair and balanced portrait of Tom Wood on September 20, 1863.

Rosecrans and his supporters would blame Wood for the defeat that followed by constructing a narrative in which Wood, supposedly still shamed and smarting from Rosecrans's earlier upbraiding, deliberately chose to obey an order he knew was wrong to spite the commanding general. Captain Henry Cist, in his 1882 history of the Army of the Cumberland, portrayed Wood as remarking that "he was glad the order was in writing, as it was a good thing to have for future reference." Rosecrans's version of the event outlived him and took on a life of its own. The language, and the accompanying villainous flourishes, grew more dramatic over time. One version, relayed to Rosecrans in June 1864, has Wood ostentatiously declaring, "Gentlemen, I hold the fatal order of the day in my hand and would not part with it for five thousand dollars." With that, he supposedly tucked the incriminating document into his pocketbook for safekeeping. By the 1930s, Wood was supposed to have stated, "I am certainly happy to have this in writing." An "incredulous" staff officer pointed out the gap the move would create. "'I can't help that, [Wood] exclaimed, his eyes gleaming with fury, 'I shall obey my orders. General Rosecrans will never have another opportunity to speak to me as he did this morning. I have my order here—in writing—. . . and I couldn't think of disobeying an order in writing—not when it comes from General Rosecrans." The most extreme language comes out of McCook family lore, which has Wood supposedly sneering, "I'm glad that Catholic son-of-a-bitch put it in writing. I'll ruin him now!" According to the various accounts, Wood had so many things to say about the order and General Rosecrans that one imagines him holding forth in a Shakespearian soliloquy, verse after vitriol-laden verse.[47]

47 Cist, *Army of the Cumberland*, 220; Frank P. Varney, *General Grant and the Rewriting of History: How the Destruction of General William S. Rosecrans Influenced Our Understanding of the Civil War* (Savas Beatie, 2013), 199; Cozzens, *This Terrible Sound*, 363. Varney and Cozzens present contradictory views of Colonel Starling's actions after delivering the order. Varney, based on Starling's testimony at the Crittenden court of inquiry, has Starling returning to Rosecrans and informing the army commander that there was no gap and thus Wood was not moving. Cozzens has Starling begging Wood to wait before moving while he rode back to get clarification—a request that Wood peremptorily refused. Since Rosecrans was surprised by the breakthrough, the former account is likely more accurate. E. V. Westrate, *Those Fatal Generals* (Kennikat Press, Inc., 1936), 224; Whalen, *The Fighting McCooks*, 228. The source for this last quote is oral history, passed from Alexander McCook to his grandson. Obviously, a great number of alternative versions of Wood's reaction abound. I consider most of them to be, at the very least, highly embellished. In reality, it is likely Wood did call the dispatch "the fatal order," since language to that effect appeared in newspapers as little as two weeks after the event—though the phrase was almost surely uttered after disaster struck, and with a much different context. As for the rest of Wood's more venomous outbursts, their provenance makes them highly doubtful.

This image of a bitter, spiteful Thomas Wood has largely persisted into the present day. In 1992, author Peter Cozzens certainly found much to criticize: "Wood let petty bitterness get the better of him. . . . A true professional would have considered another reprimand a small price to pay where so much was at stake." In 2007, though historian Larry Daniel shifted a greater burden of error onto Rosecrans's shoulders than did Cozzens, he also still faulted Wood by accusing him of being "blinded by hatred."[48]

The order itself posed problems, obviously. In his later writings Rosecrans insisted he originally told Major Bond to have Wood "close to the left," instead of the more vague terminology "close up." Unfortunately, Major Bond wrote the latter, and Rosecrans did not review the phrasing before Starling rode off. This, Rosecrans insisted, was the root of the mistake. Starling's testimony, however, belies this argument. When he asked for verbal clarification, Starling was made to understand perfectly what Rosecrans intended and should have been able to explain that to Wood.[49]

In later years, James Garfield partisans and some subsequent historians have also argued that Bond was the wrong man to write the order. If Garfield had been the author, he would have understood that Brannan was still in place, or at least made the instructions conditional upon Brannan moving. There is no evidence that Garfield's understanding of the battle at that moment was any different than Rosecrans's, or by extension, Bond's. As noted in Starling's account, Garfield was the one who clarified things by explaining Brannan's supposed departure. The problem was not with Major Bond, who after all was merely the scribe, but with Rosecrans's and Garfield's overall grasp (or lack thereof) of the tactical situation.

Much has also been made of the order being self-contradictory. "Close up" meant that Wood needed to shift to his left and connect with Reynolds, while "support" meant falling in behind Reynolds's line. In a curiously perverse effort to blame the recipient instead of the author, Rosecrans found great fault with Wood for attempting to obey the instruction in the first place: "Without seeking explanations from Brannan or Reynolds, and without notifying me (I was . . . not 600 yards from him) he drew his command out of the line." Henry Cist concurred with this assessment. "General Wood was a graduate of West Point,"

48 Cozzens, *This Terrible Sound*, 368; Daniel, *Days of Glory*, 328.

49 See Rosecrans, "Chattanooga Campaign," *National Tribune*, March 25, 1882; and "The Campaign for Chattanooga," *Century Magazine*, May, 1887, 133.

wrote Cist, "had been in the army all his life, and knew the full meaning of all the technical terms used to describe military movements. . . . He knew he could not execute the order literally as given, and from the wording of it must have known there was some mistake about it. Instead . . . he chose to give it a meaning that it was never intended to convey."[50]

In 1876, Brig. Gen. John Turchin wrote his history of the battle, wherein he undertook one of the earliest efforts to explain the whole affair. As both a brigade commander in Reynolds's division and a European-educated professional soldier, Turchin saw things much the same way as Rosecrans: "According to the phraseology accepted in military language the order had no sense; one part of it was contradicting the other part. Why then not to ascertain the meaning of it from the person who wrote the order before moving?"[51]

The overlooked player in this whole drama, of course, has been XX Corps commander Alexander McCook. Just a few minutes before the delivery of the fatal dispatch, McCook had received two earlier orders from the commanding general in quick succession. Each suggested Thomas was under heavy pressure, that the entire army was going to begin closing to the left, and that time was of the essence. In fact, as described above, some witnesses insist Wood *did* want to wait until Starling returned with clarification, but McCook was adamant that he move at once. After the fact, however, McCook attempted to conceal his role in the controversy. "Much to my surprise," McCook later reported, "Wood's division left the position it held in line of battle on Davis' left, marching by the left flank, leaving a wide gap in the line." Surprise? It should have been no surprise at all because Wood did exactly as McCook insisted he do.[52]

Part of the reason McCook is often overlooked stems from Wood's own version of the affair. Cist charged that Wood attempted to use McCook (and Thomas as well) as cover for his actions; in other words, Cist accused Wood of passing the buck and the responsibility for executing the order onto shoulders other than his own. This charge cut Wood to the quick, for it suggested a lack of moral courage. Wood accordingly and repeatedly denied the responsibility for following the order belonged to anyone but himself. In an article that appeared in the *New York Times* following the publication of Cist's book, for example,

50 Rosecrans,"The Campaign for Chattanooga," *Century Magazine*, May, 1887, 134; Cist, *Army of the Cumberland*, 222.

51 John B. Turchin, *Chickamauga* (Fergus Printing Company, 1888), 113.

52 *OR*, 30, 1, 490.

Wood heatedly wrote: "referring to the fact that General McCook happened to be with me when I received the order . . . he charges that I attempted to shift the responsibility for the movement on Gen. McCook. This is a wholly gratuitous fling. Gen. Cist (a post-war rank) knows I never sought to throw my responsibility on anybody's shoulders." In doing so, Wood inadvertantly diminished Alexander McCook's part in the mess.[53]

There is a larger issue at play, however, than a mistaken order or the actions of a willful subordinate. Wood's division was not moving alone, and Wood, McCook, et al., were not operating in a vacuum. The real problem was that in the space of a quarter of an hour, General Rosecrans set virtually the entire Union right wing in motion. He did so in the face of a powerful enemy already attacking his left wing, and who at that moment was preparing to attack his right wing. Colonel Emerson Opdycke was the colonel of the 125th Ohio, Col. Charles Harker's brigade, Wood's division. Opdycke (a strong supporter of Wood) provided one of the best assessments of the convoluted command problem: "Rosecrans, in the short space of fifteen minutes—10:30 to 10:45—ordered to his left Van Cleve, from the reserve, and Sheridan, from the extreme right; and, by the blunder of an aide in wording an order, sent Wood out of line . . . while McCook was to move Davis by the left flank into the position vacated by Wood. These disconnected and fatal movements . . . were [all] in progress . . . when Longstreet attacked. . . . Disaster was the immediate and inevitable result." By 11:00 a.m., the single stone dropped early that morning by Thomas's first request for Negley, had become an avalanche.[54]

On Monday, September 21, the day after the battle ended, Union generals Tom Wood and Joseph Reynolds encountered one another at Rossville. "I want you to understand one thing," said Wood to his old friend Joe Reynolds. Referring to Rosecrans's original order to close up and support Reynolds's division, Wood explained that "no man ever tried to find another harder than I did to find you yesterday." This admission bewildered Reynolds, for it was the first he heard of any such order. After all, Brannan stayed put and Reynolds only learned of the order to Wood long after the fact.[55]

53 Thomas J. Wood, "The Gaps at Chickamauga," *New York Times*, November 19, 1882.

54 Emerson Opdycke, "Notes on the Chickamauga Campaign," *Battles and Leaders of the Civil War*, 4 vols. (Thomas Yoseloff, 1956), vol. 3, 670.

55 Reynolds Statement, CCNMP.

Shortly after 11:00 a.m., Wood's first two brigades pulled out of line without incident. Colonel Sidney Barnes's four regiments led the way. Riding with them up the Dry Valley Road, Wood noticed an unidentified Union force of "about a brigade" occupying "one of the spurs of Mission Ridge" but took little note of it at the time. Barnes soon ran into more immediate difficulties. "I double-quicked my command a mile or more," he wrote, and "sent aides-de-camp in every direction in quest of General Reynolds, but could find neither him nor his command." Barnes sent word back to Wood, leaving both officers confused. Wood ordered Barnes to halt while he figured things out.[56]

And then Thomas appeared. He was riding south himself, impatient and on the lookout for the troops Rosecrans had promised him to bolster John Beatty's front. When Wood inquired about Reynolds's location, it was Thomas's turn to be surprised. Based upon Captain Kellogg's earlier exchanges with army headquarters, the XIV Corps commander was expecting either the rest of Van Cleve's men (Sam Beatty's brigade and Van Cleve himself, both of whom were still holding fast behind Brannan), the van of Sheridan's division (promised to him half an hour earlier), or the remaining two brigades of Brannan's division, under Cols. John Croxton and John Connell. Nothing in Thomas's exchanges with Rosecrans said a word about Tom Wood or his men. In fact, shortly after Kellogg returned, Thomas turned his nephew back around and sent him to find Sheridan to hurry that command along.

That morning, Thomas had made 13 separate demands on Rosecrans for help in defending the army's left. Now here was Wood, coming not to help with that mission, but to move to support Reynolds, on the XIV Corps's right. Reynolds, as Thomas informed Wood, did not need support. Wood's order, however, was specific: go to Reynolds. Would Thomas take the responsibility for changing it? Thomas would and promptly did so. Led by one of Thomas's staff, Wood sent Col. Sidney Barnes's troops to Brig. Gen. Absalom Baird at the northern end of Kelly Field. For the moment, Wood and his next brigade, under Charles Harker, would hold fast and await further instructions.[57]

56 *OR* 30, pt. 1, 840, 1019-1020; Barnes was loaned to Wood from Van Cleve's division.

57 McKinney, *Education in Violence*, 244; *OR* 30, pt. 1, 635.

Chapter Nine

The Reserve Corps Falters:

Sunday, 11:00 a.m. to 12:30 p.m.

Almost nothing was going as planned on the right side of the Army of Tennessee. While D. H. Hill, Leonidas Polk, and W. H. T. Walker bickered, significant opportunities slipped through an unclenched Confederate fist. By 11:00 a.m., General Breckinridge's promising effort to turn and crush Rosecrans's left flank had failed. A. P. Stewart's and Pat Cleburne's infantry divisions had shed much of their blood in a failed effort to launch coordinated attacks, fighting and dying to little apparent purpose against the southern half of George Thomas's XIV Corps line. The Confederate Right Wing, however, was not ready to concede defeat. Late in the morning, the scene shifted back northward, where Walker's Reserve Corps was finally brought into action. They did so amid a backdrop of simmering anger still evident between the senior commanders involved.

Colonel Peyton H. Colquitt and his brigade were about to pay the price for continued Confederate ineptitude. Colquitt was just about two weeks shy of his 32nd birthday and along with the other colonels in States Rights Gist's brigade, had worked hard just to reach the battlefield. Colquitt was the son of Walter T. Colquitt from Columbus, a Georgia state representative, senator, and noted antebellum "Fire-Eater." He was also the younger brother of Confederate Brig. Gen. Alfred Colquitt, who had already seen extensive action in Virginia.

Like Gist, Peyton Colquitt hungered for military recognition in his own right. He spent a year with the class of 1853 at West Point, but did not graduate with his fellow matriculants who included John Hood and Henry Davidson, both of whom were serving elsewhere on the same field. His experience running a paper provided a springboard for following his father into politics as a state senator, but war intervened. He enlisted early in the 2nd Georgia Battalion and was promoted to command the 46th Georgia in March 1862, a new outfit stationed in South Carolina. The result was that he had seen little action since joining Gist's command. With the unfolding Vicksburg crisis, however, Colquitt and his fellow Georgians were at last moving to center stage. Colquitt's first combat command came when he led part of the brigade into the fight at Jackson, Mississippi on May 14. Heavily outnumbered and commanding what amounted to a forlorn hope, Colquitt and the 46th were roughly handled, suffering 88 casualties—three-quarters of whom were captured or missing.[1]

Colquitt "was certain he had an appointment with destiny" in the coming combat. He might also have been looking for a measure of redemption. According to Sgt. James E. White of the 46th, General Gist was openly critical of Colquitt's conduct at Jackson, though no one else questioned his performance. That fight had been a foregone conclusion, a rear guard action against overwhelming numbers. Now, here in North Georgia, a second chance was in the offing. Despite almost missing the entire affair and having to leave seven of his regiment's 10 companies behind, Colquitt was at last on the field of a major battle, and once again unexpectedly thrust into brigade command.[2]

Colquitt had only the vaguest notion of where he was needed. Despite Ben Helm's and Lucius Polk's earlier fight, no ranking Confederate was able to tell Colquitt how to align his brigade, which included only the 24th South Carolina, the 8th Georgia battalion, and three companies of the 46th Georgia. With the 24th South Carolina on the left, Colquitt deployed his line facing west and set off toward the La Fayette Road, duplicating Helm's earlier advance. He, too, unwittingly exposed his left flank to the same sort of enfilade fire that had earlier ripped through the unsuspecting Kentuckians. As the 24th moved past the salient held by King's Regulars and the 4th Indiana battery, the Yankees opened on the South Carolinians with deadly effect.

South Carolina Lt. Col. Ellison Capers of the 24th provided a graphic description of the result: "About 11 or 12 we catch it. [Adjutant Joseph C.] Palmer & I were riding together in front of left center, [Colonel Clement H.]

1 *OR* 24, pt. 1, 787.

2 Joe Griffith, "Smashed Against 'The Rock of Chickamauga,'" *North Georgia Journal* (Spring, 2000), 22; James E. White Reminiscences, 46th Georgia file, CCNMP.

Stevens up on right of regt. [Maj. Jesse S.] Jones in front of left, when a tremendous fire opens, right on our left & down our line! Stevens gallops down on his blooded stallion, sword in hand, and sings out 'Change front forward on 10th Co. by companies left half wheel." Captain John H. Steinmeyer of Company A later recalled that the 24th was unable to complete this maneuver. "There was necessarily some confusion resulting, first in the attempt to change front to storm the works that were discovered to our left, and from which a murderous fire was enfilading and even reaching us from our rear, and then in consequence of the loss of nearly every field and staff officer."[3]

Adjutant Palmer was killed almost immediately. As Colonel Stevens whirled about, the boyish Palmer, an 1861 Citadel Graduate, exclaimed "Gee Whiz, Colonel, ain't this hot!" shortly before a musket ball "struck him just below the left eye and exited the back of his head." Colonel Stevens was unhorsed at the same moment. He rose unscathed and cast about for a second mount. On the left, Major Jones fell with a serious wound to his right shoulder, leaving Lieutenant Colonel Capers as the only functioning field officer in the regiment. Capers brought the two leftmost companies into action against the Federal line, lying prone and struggling to return the hail of incoming fire, the "men crowded around me in some confusion." Colonel Stevens, mounted anew, returned to the action and worked to bring up the remaining companies. Capers's relief proved short-lived. Within seconds, Stevens's second horse was cut down. Someone handed Stevens the reins to Adjutant Palmer's mare, but as the colonel swung into his third saddle within 10 minutes, another bullet struck him in the back. Capers was once again in charge.[4]

Affairs were in a ghastly tangle. The 24th was not untried, having seen action at Secessionville, South Carolina in early 1862 and taken 105 casualties at Jackson, but these Palmetto State soldiers had never faced anything like this. Dozens of men were falling. Of the 410 carried into action just a few minutes before, 191 fell killed, wounded, or missing. Many of those were officers or NCOs whose fall shattered any chance the regiment had at effective command control for the rest of the battle.

3 Ellison Capers Memoranda, 24th South Carolina file, CCNMP; Extracts of John H. Steinmeyer Diary, The South Caroliniana Library, University of South Carolina.

4 Eugene W. Jones, Jr., *Enlisted for the War: The Struggles of the Gallant 24th Regiment, South Carolina Volunteers, Infantry, 1861-1865* (Longstreet House, 1997), 120; Capers Memoranda, CCNMP; Jones, *Enlisted for the War*, 121.

With his command cut to pieces and regimental leadership essentially decapitated, Capers sought help from the rest of the brigade. He left his struggling line to return the Yankee fire as best as it could to ride north, looking for Colquitt. Unfortunately, Colquitt had no help to give. The failed West Pointer was also already down with a mortal wound.

Lieutenant Robert J. Redding of Company B, 46th Georgia, was bewildered by the savagery of the initial onslaught. "Many of our men were killed & wounded by this enfilading & concealed fire," he later recalled, admitting "I did not see a [single] Federal soldier, so thick were the woods." Sergeant James White of Company A had just been detailed "to keep every man in line or bayonet him." And then "the Billies opened fire on us. What a position. Oh how I felt, I cannot describe." At the first swell of firing, Colquitt rode south to investigate. "With hat off and sword in hand," Colquitt was riding along the line "when a canister shot struck him in the breast and hurled him from his horse." Sergeant White thought the colonel exposed himself to the point of recklessness, and he knew the reason: "If Brigadier General S. R. Gist had not criticized . . . Colquitt in [that] first fight at Jackson," White lamented, "Colquitt might not have bin killed at Chickamauga." The frightfully wounded Colquitt would live another 30 hours, but his destiny was met within minutes of advancing.[5]

Capers, meanwhile, had barely started for the left when it was his turn to be struck. "Hardtimes [Capers's mount] got a shot through his neck, & my sword was shot out of my hand. One of Co. I handed it to me, and as I sheathed it a canister shot struck it midway of the scabbard & in a moment more I got a bad wound in my left thigh." Capers turned command over to Capt. D. F. Hill of Company F and attempted to go to the rear, but passed out from blood loss. Capers would know nothing more of the regiment's fate until he woke up much later in a field hospital surrounded by wounded and dying Kentuckians from Helm's brigade.[6]

Watching their opponents collapse into chaos, the Federals did a surprising thing: they counterattacked. When King ordered his front line forward, both

5 R. J. Redding Letter, October 24, 1894, 46th Georgia file, CCNMP; White Reminiscences, CCNMP; "Death of Col. P. H. Colquitt," *Daily Columbus Enquirer*, September 26, 1863; White Reminiscences, CCNMP. Colquitt's wound has been variously reported as being from either canister or a minie ball. He died on September 22, 1863.

6 Capers Memoranda, CCNMP.

battalions of the 18th U.S. scrambled out of their works and dashed up to the Alexander Bridge Road and opened fire. As described by the Regular brigade's modern historian, "a devastating volley slammed into the enemy line" followed by an immediate charge. What was left of the 24th South Carolina broke for the rear. For a brief moment the Yanks were actually among the retreating South Carolinians, and then, as the surviving Rebels scrambled rearward, the Regulars halted, reloaded and delivered a parting volley into their fleeing foes. Union Capt. George Smith, commanding the 1/18th, estimated his men advanced 600 yards. King considered the "charge the most gallant act of that day's engagement."[7]

The Union counterattack and the firestorm that followed was too much for the 24th, which dissolved in headlong flight. Captain Steinmeyer was leading one fragment when he stumbled into General Gist, who calmly directed him to keep making for the rear, where the regiment was attempting to reform. General Walker also met the fleeing survivors, though less calmly, cursing in his trademark manner: "Oh what hard and rough beneaming language Gen. Walker did use to these S. Carolinians," recorded Sergeant White. "[I]t would not do to think of starting Sunday School with." When they took stock of their situation, in addition to the serious casualties, Steinmeyer recalled "nearly . . . every man could show the effect of a ball or fragment of shell on his clothing."[8]

Gist blamed D. H. Hill for the slaughter. "Colonel Colquitt did not reconnoiter the position," Gist alleged, "as he was instructed that our troops were in his front." In less than half an hour, "one third of the gallant command was either killed or wounded." Gist hastened to bring up Claudius Wilson's and Matt Ector's men to protect Colquitt's retreat. Advancing more cautiously, both formations stepped within rifle range and opened a covering fire. Even this action, thought Colonel Wilson, was "a very unsatisfactory fight." The 18th U.S. spotted Wilson's Georgians approaching, fell back into the breastworks, and opened fire. Neither Ector's nor Wilson's small brigades made any impression on Brig. Gen. Absalom Baird's line. Realizing the futility of

7 Johnson, *That Body of Brave Men*, 410; *OR* 30, pt. 1, 311.

8 White Reminiscences, CCNMP; Steinmeyer Diary, University of South Carolina. Sergeant White's word choice is rather unusual. "Beneaming" certainly isn't a word in any dictionary I checked. However, it is clear that Walker was roundly cursing and swearing at the retreating men.

renewing the assault, once Colquitt's remnants were safely disengaged Gist ordered the two latter commands back as well.[9]

Meanwhile, Edward C. Walthall was bringing his five Mississippi regiments into action. Earlier, it will be recalled, General Polk had detached Walthall to march to the aid of Lucius Polk's brigade (Cleburne's division). Major James Ratchford was ordered to guide Walthall's men into position. He led the Mississippians by the left flank in an effort to insert Walthall's 1,500 bayonets between Colquitt's advancing left and Polk's stationary right. Unfortunately, Polk's regiments were already pulling back. The Mississippians started to take indiscriminate fire almost immediately. Once he reached an approximation of his intended position, as best could be determined, Walthall fronted his line, which included, in order from north to south, the 24th, 27th, 29th, 30th and 34th Mississippi. As he later reported, "I pressed forward 200 or 300 yards under this fire through dense undergrowth until the enemy opened fire on my left flank from the angle of his fortifications just opposite."[10]

The left half of Walthall's line faced the 4th Indiana's deadly salient, with his right extending northward to a point roughly opposite (but still east of) the scene of Helm's and Colquitt's disastrous assaults. Most of Walthall's line was exposed to an angled fire from the Hoosier cannon, and every step forward increased the degree of enfilade. Wisely, Walthall hesitated and soon found he had no one to support. With Colquitt shattered and Polk retreating, Baird's Federals could devote their full attention to this new threat. It did not help matters when panicked soldiers from the 24th South Carolina began running through Walthall's ranks, yelling at his Mississippians that Walthall's right "had fired into our own friends." This accusation Walthall later determined to be false, but for the moment the damage was done. Now his men were exposed to this same shredding Federal fire and feeling helpless.[11]

Walthall found no sign of the junior Polk, and elected not to press the issue. As a result, his losses here were lighter than Colquitt's, though not inconsequential. The hardest hit was the 34th Mississippi on the brigade's left, already reduced to a mere 177 officers and men. In the absence of the regiment's field officers and several of the more experienced captains, Lt. Col.

9 *OR* 30, pt. 2, 246, 248.

10 Ibid., 274.

11 Ibid.

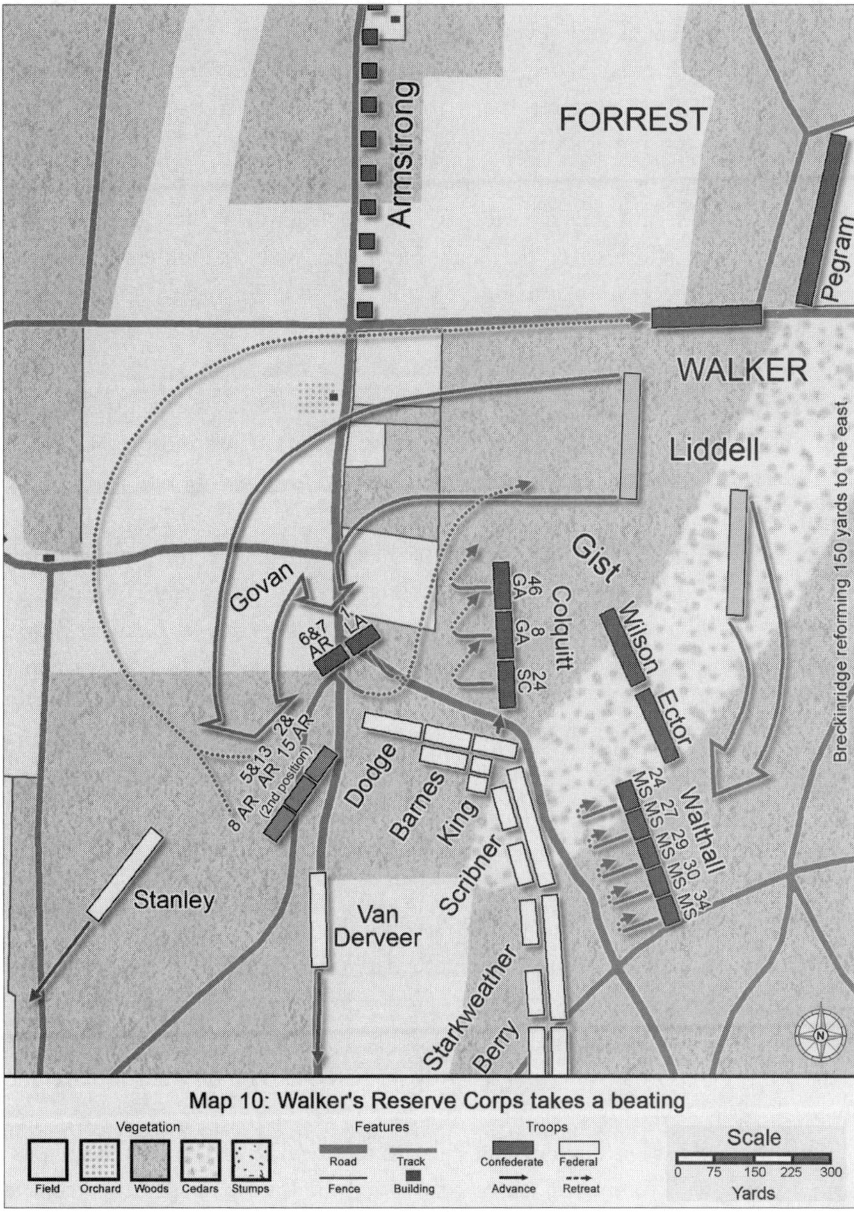

Map 10: Walker's Reserve Corps takes a beating

Hugh Reynolds of the 30th Mississippi had been assigned command of the 34th. The promotion was short-lived, for Reynolds was mortally wounded during the short engagement. "No braver man or better soldier fell upon the field of Chickamauga," lamented Walthall. Other casualties soon followed. Corporal John H. Freeman noted that his Company F, 34th Mississippi suffered a man killed and several more wounded in this place; a significant percentage of the small outfit's surviving manpower. Leaderless and feeling exposed, the 34th began to retreat. With the "left . . . driven back, the right was ordered to cease firing, and the [whole] brigade then retired."[12]

All morning, the key to the Yankee defense in this area proved to be Lt. Henry J. Willits's 4th Indiana battery. While other Union artillery fired fast and furiously farther south along the Kelly Field line, Willits's gunners served the only effective pieces remaining in Baird's division. Their projecting salient allowed for them to deliver a crippling iron crossfire up and down the length of the open cedar glade. If the Confederates were ever going to prevail here, Willits's guns would have to be silenced. Breckinridge's divisional artillery (the batteries of Cobb, Mebane, and Key) each made some effort to do so, with little effect. A more coordinated response was needed, but it would be a long time coming.

Not quite finished throwing men into the grinder to no effect, yet one more Rebel brigade aligned its ranks and blundered ahead. Frank Cheatham's division, it will be recalled, had been designated as a reserve by General Bragg. Cheatham's five brigades had thus far sat out the fight while Stewart and Cleburne tried repeatedly to crack the Federal defenses. About 10:30 a.m., however, when word reached Bragg that Hill needed a brigade on his front (a request ultimately filled by Gist and Colquitt), the army leader ordered Cheatham to send one of his formations up to help out. Cheatham complied with alacrity, ordering Brig. Gen. John K. Jackson forward. Jackson started to move to the right, sending two staff officers ahead to find out from General Hill where his men were most needed. Upholding the finest traditions of the Army of Tennessee, however, both officers returned to inform Jackson that they were unable to locate General Hill. This was sometime after 11:00 a.m., for shortly thereafter Jackson bumped into a thoroughly irritated wing commander in the form of Leonidas Polk, who had recently departed D. H. Hill's headquarters in abject disgust.[13]

Bishop Polk at least knew what Hill wanted, having spent most of the past hour arguing with the man. Jackson, explained the bishop, was needed on the right of "Brigadier General [Lucius] Polk's brigade and to move forward at

12 Ibid., 275; Entry for September 20, John H. Freeman Diary, TSLA; Walthall's Brigade Tablet near Alexander's Bridge Road, Noon, September 20, CCNMP.

13 *OR* 30, pt. 2, 84-85.

once." Strangely, Polk failed to inform Jackson that he had just assigned Walthall to the same mission. Nor did Polk attempt to redirect Walthall to rejoin St. John Liddell's division now that another brigade could take Walthall's place.[14]

Jackson's command was a small one, having entered the fight on the 19th with 1,300 men and left at least 400 of them on the field. Only Brig. Gen. Marcus Wright's brigade had suffered a higher casualty percentage among Cheatham's formations. Jackson felt his way forward cautiously, leading with the four companies of the 2nd Georgia Battalion Sharpshooters under Maj. Richard H. Whiteley. Like most of the Confederate Sharpshooters, the 2nd was formed in 1862, using handpicked men selected from the other commands in the brigade. The 2nd Battalion originally included six companies commanded by Maj. J. J. Cox., which boldly styled themselves as "Cox's Wild Cats." Chronic bronchitis and a persistent cough, however, forced Cox to resign in March 1863, but the battalion proudly retained the moniker. Now consolidated from six companies into four, Whiteley deployed his men across the length of Jackson's front. Before long, they encountered a line of blue skirmishers about 100 yards distant on the far side of what one Georgian described as "an old open field."[15]

While the sharpshooters deployed, Jackson managed both to locate Polk's brigade and establish contact with Hill, who sent one of his officers forward to show Jackson where to deploy. Moving up and to the right, the staffer directed Jackson "to fill up a gap between [Walthall's] brigade and . . . Cleburne's right." At the same time, reinforcing Whiteley with two companies from the 2nd Battalion, 5th Confederate, Jackson ordered his sharpshooters to drive off the Yankee skirmishers.[16]

"To have to charge across that open space of 200 yards, with the enemy in ambush in front of us, required more than ordinary courage," confessed a sharpshooter known to history only as "Charlie." However, things went more handily than expected, for the Federals, a picket line in front of Baird's main line, had no intention of holding their ground. "They were in such a hurry,"

14 Ibid., 85.

15 Anonymous, by CHARLIE, "Camp in the field near Chattanooga," September 24, 1863, unidentified newspaper clipping, 2nd Georgia Sharpshooters file, CCNMP. The "old open field" referred to is the cedar glade.

16 *OR* 30, pt. 2, 85.

crowed Charlie, "that they left their blankets, haversacks and other things on the field."[17]

The Wild Cats's elation was short-lived. Once across the glade they discovered Baird's real position, striking it just south of the 4th Indiana salient, where Brig. Gen. John Starkweather's Federals gripped their weapons and waited for them to step into killing range. Whiteley halted his skirmish line to assess this new obstacle and sent word back to Jackson that "he could not dislodge the enemy . . . they were in strong force." For the next hour or so, the Georgians and the Federals settled into a fitful exchange of small arms fire until Jackson, concerned that his small brigade still did not fill up the space between Polk and Walthall, shifted Whiteley's men to his right flank to keep Yankees from creeping into that gap. Jackson's losses were few, but his arrival further complicated an already convoluted Confederate command situation. Walthall, Jackson, and Lucius Polk were from three separate divisions, from three separate corps, with no single officer exercising overall control. As a result, while all three commands operated in the same general area, opposite Baird's position and the 4th Indiana Artillery salient, they did so separately, never acting in a coordinated manner or managing to form a single line. Each brigade took up an individual position in the woods, with Jackson's men some distance in advance of Polk and Walthall, and closest to the Federals. It was an additional example of what can happen when a general simply dispatches brigades willy-nilly in a fashion that had so angered W. H. T. "Shotpouch" Walker.[18]

* * *

Out on the far left of the Union line, John Beatty was experiencing a similar frustration. Beatty was working hard to weave together a line anchoring the Union left flank in the woods south of the McDonald farm. He was only a brigadier, and his authority extended only so far. As a fellow brigade commander in Maj. Gen. James Negley's division, Col. Timothy Stanley willingly accepted Beatty's authority, but Beatty could only cajole, not compel, support from other commands. Colonel George F. Dick's brigade (of Van Cleve's division) had come up behind Stanley's line, but both Stanley and Beatty

17 "By CHARLIE," CCNMP. In reality, the abandoned gear probably belonged to Brannan's men, dropped the day before when the battle opened and never retrieved.

18 *OR* 30, pt. 2, 85.

thought Dick's men appeared nervous and uncertain. If the Rebels came again, Beatty reasoned, more reliable help would be needed.

Ferdinand Van Derveer's brigade would have been ideal in this role, but Van Derveer was not aware of Beatty or his needs. After repulsing Brig. Gen. Marcellus Stovall's Rebel thrust, Van Derveer marched his men back to the southern end of Kelly Field. They halted near the barn on the west side of the La Fayette Road and took stock of their losses. Casualties had been frightful; details were assigned from each of Van Derveer's four regiments to gather in their wounded. Van Derveer looked for someone to tell him what to do, but he could not find either Maj. Gen. Joe Reynolds or Baird, whom he had initially been ordered to support.[19]

Appealing to the highest authority he could find, John Beatty took his case for help directly to George Thomas, who had observed his earlier fight against Breckinridge. "General Beatty came to me for fresh troops, in person, stating that most of those I had sent to him had gone back to the rear and right," reported the XIV Corps commander. Thomas assured Beatty help was on the way in the form of Maj. Gen. Phil Sheridan's division, which Thomas just learned was en route. Mollified, Beatty rode back to his own lines while Thomas dispatched Capt. Sanford Kellogg to hurry Sheridan along. Beatty had not yet reached Stanley's position when Capt. James S. Wilson of Beatty's own staff appeared with verbal orders from Negley. Had they been followed, Thomas's left would have been thrown back into crisis. According to Wilson, Negley wanted Beatty to bring both his own and Stanley's brigades back to his own position on the open hill near the Snodgrass cabin. Beatty, who understood the disaster such a move would create, wisely demurred "until I could see General Negley and explain to him the necessity of maintaining the line and reinforcing it." Before Beatty could do so, the storm broke again in the form of Govan's Rebel brigade attacking Stanley's position.[20]

Daniel Govan led the second of two brigades in Liddell's division (the other being Walthall). He began his movement facing west, tracking Daniel Adams's and Marcellus Stovall's original deployments, with Peyton Colquitt's brigade on his left. Initially unopposed, Govan's Arkansans reached the eastern edge of the McDonald farm before spotting any Federals. Both Liddell and

19 *OR* 30, pt. 1, 430.

20 Ibid., 252, 369.

Govan were increasingly alert to trouble on their own left flank. The sudden swell of firing that marked Colquitt's entry into the battle had caught their attention, and at some point Liddell ordered "Colonel Govan to change direction to the left." However, Gist's advance and repulse had happened so quickly that no one in higher authority had time to fully inform Liddell or Govan what had transpired. While his command was moving forward in a looping left wheel, groping for either Adams's brigade (which Govan mistakenly believed was still somewhere ahead of him) or their blue-clad opponents, one of Leonidas Polk's aides galloped up with word of Gist's difficulties. Help was needed at once, and Govan was directed to provide it. As might be expected, details were lacking. "The officer could only give me general direction as to where General Gist's brigade was engaged," Govan complained. Dutifully, he changed his direction farther to the left and pressed forward. Govan's regiments entered the fight the previous day numbering just shy of 2,000 men, but lost roughly one-quarter of that number by the time their fighting had ended. His was still a powerful command holding a front nearly 400 yards wide.[21]

Once at the eastern wood line of the McDonald farm clearing, Govan's van spotted a Union skirmish line at the edge of the woods bordering the southern end of the same field. Wheeling even farther to the left, Govan's formation was now reoriented to face due south. This placed the line of Arkansas troops astride the La Fayette Road, with the 6th/7th Arkansas east of the artery, moving to oppose the Yankees of Col. Joseph Dodge's brigade, while the 2nd/15th Arkansas, 8th Arkansas/1st Louisiana, and 5th/13th Arkansas all drifted south on the west side of the road, opposing Stanley. All the marching and wheeling attenuated Govan's line, with noticeable gaps opening between several of the regiments.

Lieutenant Colonel Peter Snyder, heading up the 6th/7th Arkansas, was feeling especially isolated. After turning south his line drove in Dodge's skirmishers, but "owing to the heavy loss sustained and the want of support to our left, we were unable to drive him any farther." Outnumbered roughly two to one, Snyder's Razorbacks went to ground about 100 yards from Dodge's line and made no additional progress in the ensuing fight.[22]

21 Ibid., pt. 2, 253, 259.

22 Ibid., 267.

The rest of Govan's command on the far side of the road included three formations totaling approximately 1,200 bayonets, all opposing Stanley's line, which now numbered perhaps 800 men. Implementing the plan he had earlier worked out with Colonel Dick, Stanley began a slow, deliberate retreat back toward Dick's position. Stanley intended for his men to fall back through Dick's four regiments, and while the Arkansans contended with that fresh Union battle line, regroup to bring his three regiments back into the fight on one flank or the other. Combined, Dick and Stanley should be able to mass about 1,700 Federals, and in theory this would have been more than a match for Govan's brigade. Stanley's plan—trying to effect a passage of friendly lines while conducting a controlled retreat pursued by an aggressive foe—was a risky business.

And it did not happen. "Upon looking around," decried a furious Stanley, "I found the support had disappeared and we were left to our own resources." John Beatty was equally angry. "The unknown brigade . . . retired with unseemly haste, and without firing a shot." Dick's men had bolted, unnerved by the sight of Stanley's retreat.[23]

Colonel Dick, naturally enough, attempted to minimize his brigade's sudden collapse. "Colonel Stanley's brigade . . . being soon hard pressed, I went to his support, but after firing a short time his line gave way in confusion, and retreated in disorder over my command lying on the ground." Dick continued: "This uncovered my line and caused it to become somewhat confused, but having partially recovered, I gave the enemy a galling fire for more than fifteen minutes. I was soon overwhelmed . . . and fell back in some disorder." Little of this was accurate. In fact, Dick's men broke quickly and his regiments fragmented. The commander of the 44th Indiana, Lt. Col. Simeon C. Aldrich, was more forthcoming and freely admitted that Stanley's retreat "caused a panic with most of our brigade." In his diary, Cpl. Thomas McCain of the 86th Indiana described the affair as a wholesale stampede: "At last we are driven, routed. Our brigade is scattered to the four winds. Fall back. We know not where the men are." Dick's brigade would not reform or fight again this day as a unit, although pieces of the several regiments would remain on the field. Their

23 Ibid., pt. 1, 379; Beatty, *Citizen-Soldier*, 338. Exercising discretion, neither Stanley nor Beatty positively identified Dick's brigade by name. In his report, Stanley believed he knew who they were, but was not certain enough to name names and trigger opprobrium that might not be justified. In his report, Dick obviously knew he was supporting Stanley, since he mentioned Stanley by name.

precipitate collapse could not have come at a worse moment for Stanley or John Beatty.[24]

Dick's rout was problem enough, but now the 15th Kentucky and 104th Illinois—that half of Beatty's brigade that had managed to remain on the field under the command of Col. Marion Taylor of the former regiment—were suddenly nowhere to be found. They should have been in place to help support Stanley's left flank. Earlier, Beatty placed Taylor to the left and rear of Stanley's line, aligned roughly with Dick's formation. Even with Dick's troops in wild retreat, Taylor's two regiments should have closed up and supported Stanley's left. Taylor and his men, however, had vanished.

Beatty was "greatly provoked" at Taylor's mysterious departure, but the 15th's colonel had little choice for he was ordered off the field. During Stanley's first charge, Beatty directed Taylor to recover Capt. Lyman Bridges's lost cannon. A detachment of the 15th Kentucky returned with not only Bridges's pieces but three more guns (from Baird's division) lost during the fighting on the 19th and dragged to the La Fayette Road overnight. While these five guns were being hauled off toward Snodgrass Hill, Taylor took up his position on Stanley's left rear, as directed. Before Govan's Rebels appeared, Negley staffer Maj. James Lowrie arrived bearing orders from Negley, who was trying to gather in all his wayward troops. Just as Captain Wilson relayed to John Beatty, Lowrie ordered Taylor to take both regiments back to Snodgrass Hill. Beatty, it will be recalled, had sent Wilson back to Negley a short while earlier to explain the dangerous situation and prevent such a withdrawal. Later, Beatty admitted that Taylor could not simply ignore a direct order from the major general commanding the division, so off Taylor went.[25]

George Thomas's left flank, which a half hour before had seemed secure, was now anything but. Lacking overall direction, several brigades' worth of troops, perhaps 3,000 men melted away like ice in a hot summer sun, leaving Beatty and Stanley alone and outnumbered. Having little other choice, "my brigade continued to fall back slowly, halting and firing at intervals," reported Stanley. Eventually Govan's Arkansans stopped pursuing, though neither

24 *OR* 30, pt. 1, 824, 828; Richard K. and Geraldine M. Rue, eds., *In Song and Sorrow: The Daily Journal of Thomas Hart Benton McCain, 86th Indiana Volunteer Infantry* (Guild Press of Indiana, 1998), 91.

25 Beatty, *Citizen-Soldier*, 339; Jenkins, *The Battle Rages Higher*, 182-183; Beatty, *Citizen-Soldier*, 339.

Beatty nor Stanley could explain why. It was enough that the Confederates had halted. Beatty took stock of the situation, and at last decided he had better report to Negley. "Stanley's brigade, considerably scattered by the last furious attack . . . was gathered up by its officers, and retired to the ridge on the right and rear of the original line of battle." In doing so, Beatty was violating Thomas's earlier instructions, given at 8:00 a.m., and leaving Thomas's flank even more vulnerable than it had been that morning. However, like Colonel Taylor, Beatty had new orders from Negley and felt he could no longer ignore them.[26]

The Rebel decision to halt couldn't have come at a more opportune time for John Beatty, but there was nothing mysterious about it from Govan's perspective. Even as the opposition weakened to his front, Govan, already worried about the apparent loss of Lieutenant Colonel Snyder and the 6th/7th Arkansas, which had failed to keep up, became aware of a new threat to his left flank, one that cut Govan and his remaining three regiments off from the rest of the Confederate army and threatened to bag the entire command.

Colonel Sidney M. Barnes's brigade (the 35th Indiana, 8th Kentucky, 51st and 99th Ohio) was now on the scene. By this time Barnes was getting used to fighting independently, having had to make his own way into Brock Field yesterday and been loaned out to Tom Wood's division that morning. Now he was supposed to reinforce Absalom Baird's division. Barnes's four regiments numbered about 1,050 officers and men, having lost about 150 people the previous day. Barnes was leading Wood's column when Thomas changed Wood's orders, so Barnes was dispatched to help Baird.

Leaving his men to catch up, Barnes and one aide "galloped forward . . . to be shown my position." Once he ascertained where to deploy, Barnes thundered back to his command "through a shower of balls" to bring up his two leading regiments (51st Ohio and 8th Kentucky) into position on Baird's left "behind a barricade." Interestingly, just as the Regulars seemed oblivious to Dodge in the earlier fight against Stovall, Barnes made no mention of Dodge's brigade even though his command went into line between Dodge's men and King's Regulars. Within minutes of arriving, Barnes observed Stanley's and Dick's difficulties: "The enemy drove back a body of our troops, apparently a brigade, in disorder through the open field on my left." Baird, who was also

26 OR 30, pt. 1, 370, 379.

present, knew what to do, as Barnes related: "I was then ordered to change front, charge the enemy, and drive them back."[27]

Barnes's other two regiments, the 35th Indiana and 99th Ohio, had fallen behind during the approach march, and he decided he could not wait for them to catch up. Without hesitation, Barnes ordered Col. Richard W. McClain of the 51st Ohio to take charge of his own command and the 8th Kentucky, and move immediately into the attack while he brought up his missing units. "We entered a cornfield that had lately been laid waste, we being in column by companies," recalled Kentucky Capt. Thomas Wright of the 8th. "The exulting rebels . . . were pressing forward, but not in very good order, though their bullets were making the cornstalks rattle in a most unpleasant manner." Swinging into line at the double-quick "with as much precision as we ever did on the drill field," Wright continued, once the last of the retreating Federals cleared their front, "our boys opened 'fire at will.'" Colonel McClain ordered both regiments to charge, and with a cheer the 51st Ohio and 8th Kentucky rushed forward due west behind Dodge's line to strike at Govan's exposed left flank.[28]

A sergeant named Israel A. Correll in Company A of the 51st Ohio remembered hearing: "'Fix bayonets!' We all knew what this meant—we were to make a charge; and charge we did, and the way the Rebels scattered was a caution." Lieutenant Colonel Charles H. Wood of the 51st reported Govan's men "broke in great confusion, throwing away their arms and accoutrements. We charged them three fourths of a mile, killing, wounding, and capturing many." Sergeant Correll took special note of a captured "Rebel battle-flag," which the company retained as a trophy (a banner Colonel Wood mistakenly identified as belonging to the 26th South Carolina).[29]

McClain's counterattack caught Govan's brigade in the flank, not the first time these Razorbacks had endured that particular peril in this battle. This time,

27 Ibid., 840.

28 T. J. Wright, *History of the Eighth Regiment Kentucky Volunteer Infantry During Its Three Years Campaigns Embracing Organization, Marches, Skirmishes, and Battles of the Command, With Much of the History of the Old Reliable Third Brigade, Commanded By Hon. Stanley Matthews, and Containing Many Interesting and Amusing Incidents of Army Life* (St. Joseph Steam Printing Co. 1880), 192-193.

29 *New Philadelphia Democrat*, October 2, 1863; *OR* 30, pt. 1, 847. This flag remains unidentified. The 26th South Carolina was not present at Chickamauga. It might have belonged to the 24th South Carolina of Gist's brigade, which was on the field and fairly close, but that regiment did not report losing its colors. Most likely the Ohioans captured a company flag or guide marker from the 24th, which somehow got dropped earlier or got caught up in the retreat of Govan's men.

with the 6th/7th lagging well behind, facing off against Dodge, the brunt of McClain's fire tore through flesh belonging to the 2nd/15th Arkansas commanded by Lt. Col. Rueben S. Harvey. Govan watched his brigade unravel one regiment at a time, a circumstance he attributed to the usual Confederate complaint at Chickamauga: a complete lack of support. "Gist's brigade, which I had not succeeded in finding, had fallen back about the time I had engaged the enemy," he complained, so "I was thus completely isolated from our line. . . . The enemy massed in heavy force behind his breastworks and . . . made a vigorous attack upon my left and succeeded . . . in breaking it."[30]

The Arkansans's most direct path of retreat—east or northeast—was now blocked. Not only were Barnes's two leading regiments driving in Govan's left flank, but by now the rest of Barnes's brigade was coming up. Barnes deployed the 35th Indiana and 99th Ohio in Kelly Field, readying them to make a second charge and finish the work so successfully begun by McClain.

Confederate Lt. Col. John Murray, commanding the 5th/13th Arkansas, first knew of the trouble on his left when Colonel Harvey stumbled into Murray's ranks to breathlessly report that not only was the 2nd/15th shattered by a Yankee charge, but the Federals were now in his rear! Murray decided the Yankees to his front (Stanley's brigade) were no longer much of a threat, and proposed to simply have his command about-face and charge back north to cut his way through to Confederate lines. Somewhat to Murray's shock, however, his men took a dim view of this idea. "Finding the men were opposed to this, and somewhat demoralized on account of the enemy's being behind them," he explained, "and thinking that if I attempted to cut my way through I might be fired upon . . . by our friends . . . I concluded it was best to move by the right flank."[31]

Murray, together with Harvey and at least some of Harvey's men in tow, moved west until they bumped into Maj. Anderson Watkins heading up the combined 8th Arkansas/1st Louisiana. Watkins was equally shocked to discover Yankees "in force on my left and also in my rear." By now all three commands had been driven some distance, and no one knew where Govan might be found. After a hurried council of war, the three regimental commanders decided "not to advance any farther, but if possible, to rejoin our

30 *OR* 30, pt. 2, 259.

31 Ibid., 265.

division." The only way out of this fast developing trap seemed to be to move even farther west, then turn north and eventually head back east, circling completely around McDonald Field. Fortunately, a member of Maj. Gen. Nathan Bedford Forrest's cavalry found them not too long into this journey and helped guide them "by the most practicable route."[32]

Barnes did not follow. Once the Rebels were checked and moving off, he returned his regiments to Kelly Field and took up his previously assigned position next to King's Regulars. However, the Arkansans's circumnavigation of McDonald Field did not go unremarked. General Negley, still perched on the open hill of the Snodgrass farm roughly 1,000 yards to the southwest, observed a number of Confederate troops moving west, apparently across the La Fayette Road. Negley's interpretation (and exaggeration) of this movement would have important consequences a short while later.

Govan and his remaining regiment, the 6th/7th Arkansas, had in the meantime fallen back from in front of Dodge's line. For some time Govan had no idea what happened to the rest of his brigade, apparently swallowed up by the Yankees in Kelly Field. When the missing regiments eventually reappeared, Govan moved the survivors of his brigade back to reorganize and take stock of their losses. The serious combat on the northern end of the battlefield, at least for now, was over.

32 Ibid., 269.

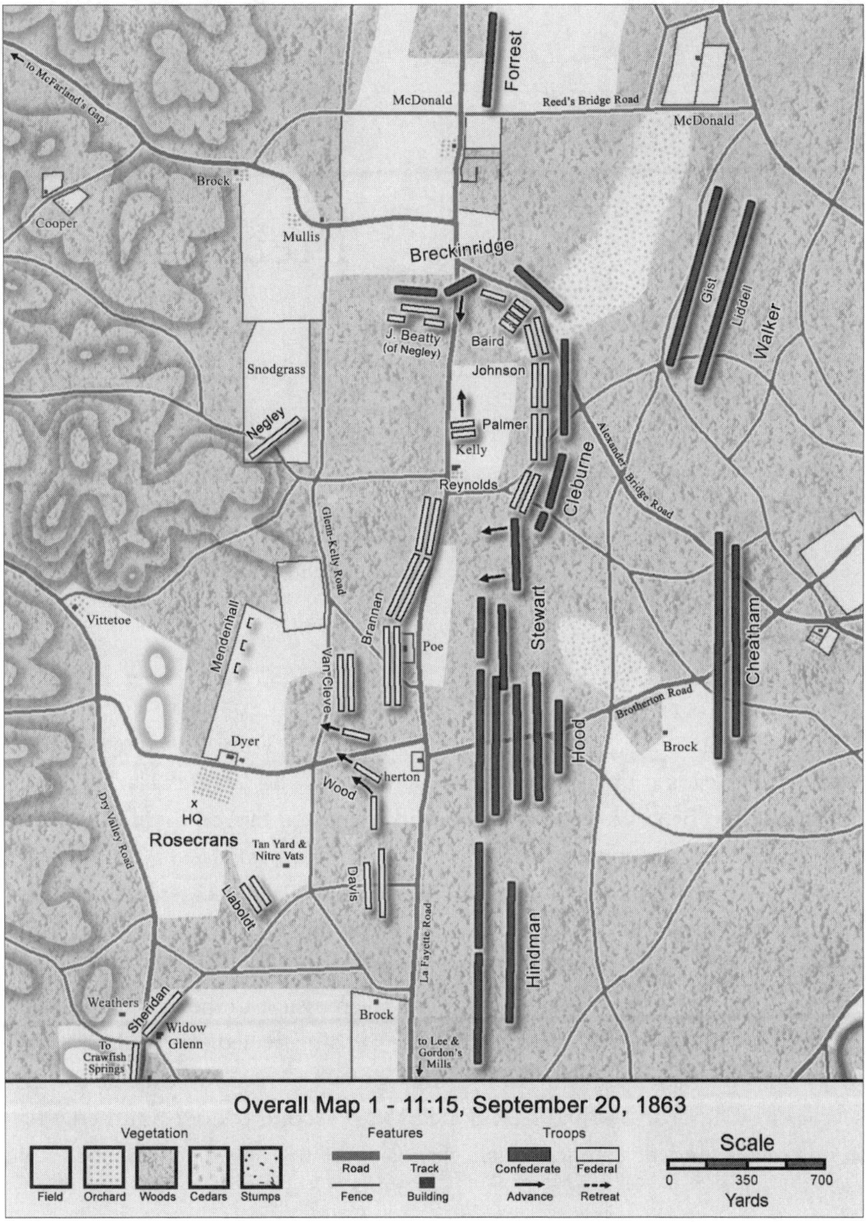
to McFarland's Gap
McDonald
Forrest
Reed's Bridge Road
McDonald
Brock
Cooper
Mullis
Breckinridge
Gist
Liddell
Walker
J. Beatty
(of Negley)
Baird
Johnson
Snodgrass
Palmer
Negley
Kelly
Reynolds
Cleburne
Alexander Bridge Road
Glenn-Kelly Road
Brannan
Stewart
Cheatham
Vittetoe
Mendenhall
Poe
Van Cleve
Brotherton Road
Hood
Brock
Dyer
Wood
HQ
Rosecrans
Dry Valley Road
Tan Yard &
Nitre Vats
Davis
Liaboldt
La Fayette Road
Hindman
Weathers
Sheridan
Widow
Glenn
To
Crawfish
Springs
Brock
to Lee &
Gordon's
Mills
Overall Map 1 - 11:15, September 20, 1863
Vegetation
Field
Orchard
Woods
Cedars
Stumps
Features
Road
Track
Fence
Building
Troops
Confederate
Federal
Advance
Retreat
Scale
0
350
700
Yards

Chapter Ten

Breakthrough!

Sunday, 10:30 a.m. to 11:30 a.m.

"Tell the general that my skirmishers are actively engaged," Col. George P. Buell insisted to a courier, "and I cannot safely make the move." Buell's division commander, Tom Wood, managed to ease his two leading brigades under Sidney Barnes and Charles Harker out of position at the Brotherton farm without incident and moved them north until they were eventually commandeered by George Thomas. Moving his third and final brigade was a bit more difficult. The directive flabbergasted Buell, who almost refused to follow it and delayed pulling out of line for as long as he could. The colonel had an inkling the enemy line he was about to unmask was strong and harbored aggressive intentions. His message to the general revealed his anxiety with the move. Wood, however, had already had this argument with Maj. Gen. Alexander McCook of the XX Corps (who was responsible for that sector of the line) and would hear none of it. A second courier returned a few minutes later and threatened Buell with a court martial if he did not move immediately.[1]

Buell's instincts were sound. Eight hundred yards to the east, James Longstreet was growing more impatient by the moment. His earlier courier to Gen. Braxton Bragg, asking for permission to attack, had not yet returned when

1 Woodruff, *Fifteen Years Ago*, 285-286.

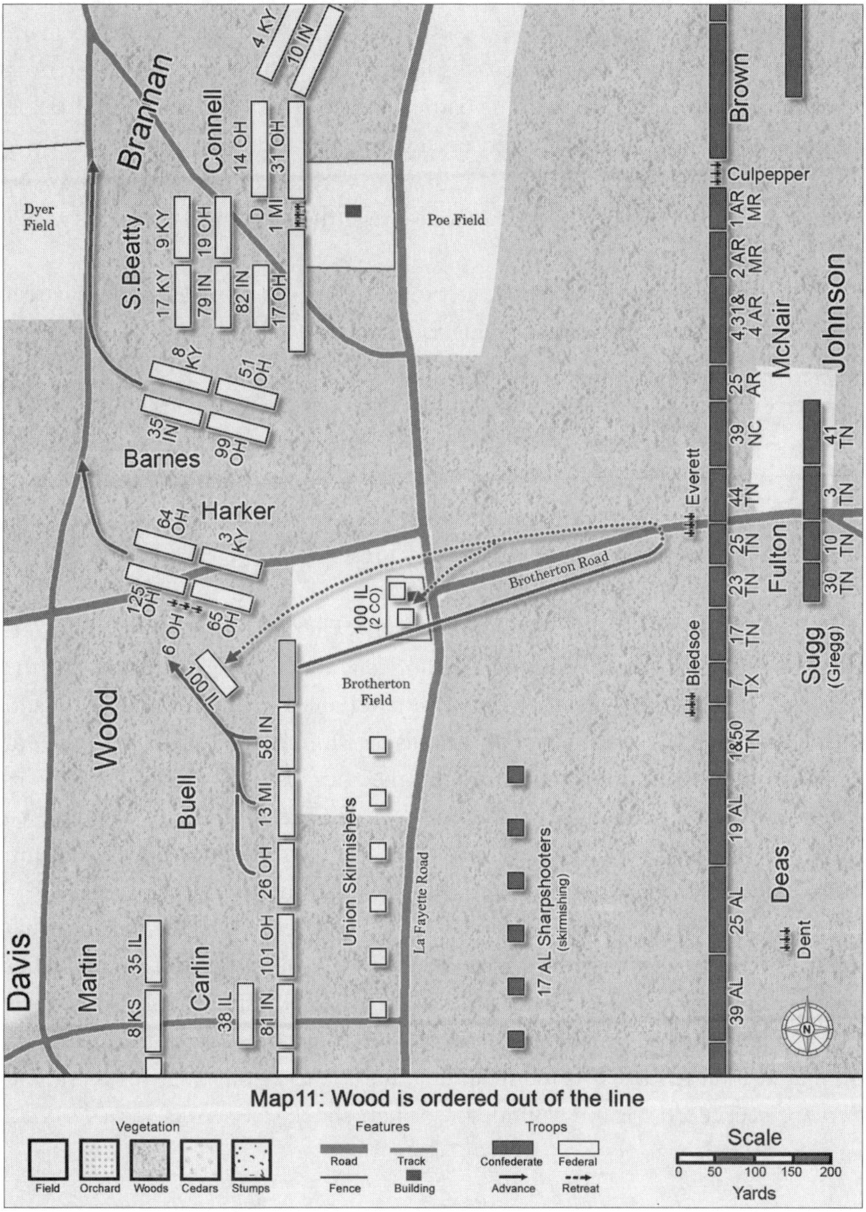

Map11: Wood is ordered out of the line

a messenger arrived from Maj. Gen. A. P. Stewart explaining that officer's sudden (and to Longstreet, seemingly unauthorized) assault. With Maj. Pollock Lee now riding the line to order every division forward at once, per Bragg's frustrated instructions on that score, the entire Confederate army was lumbering into the attack, with Buell's brigade squarely in the crosshairs.

Longstreet believed in the power of mass. He had witnessed too many piecemeal, poorly coordinated assaults in this war, and Bragg seemed intent to implement more of the same. "The battle had been put in the hands of division commanders," he fumed, still angry even years after the fact. It was ironic, then, given his earlier impatience to attack, that the very next order he issued was to instruct Maj. Gen. John B. Hood to hold—regardless of the instructions Major Lee brought.[2]

The pause was a fleeting one, just long enough to ensure that Longstreet could get the rest of his wing moving in a coordinated fashion. It was too late for Stewart, who had already attacked and been repulsed by the time Longstreet ordered the rest of his wing forward. When he did, roughly 17,000 Confederates in the form of Hood's three-division column plus Maj. Gen. Thomas Hindman's large command bore down on the Union right, the attack centered squarely against Brotherton Field. Only Maj. Gen. William Preston's 4,862 officers and men were held back as a reserve.

With great reluctance, Colonel Buell complied with Wood's orders and pulled out of battle line. It was 11:15 a.m. Leaving his skirmish line in place, Buell rode off at the head of his two leading regiments, the 58th Indiana and the battered 100th Illinois—the latter shy two companies and its commander—and hurried to catch up with the rest of Wood's division. Behind them came the 8th Indiana battery, bumping along through the rock-strewn woods. The battery could not keep up and its slow progress retarded the two rearmost regiments, the 13th Michigan and 26th Ohio. Within a few minutes Buell's column fragmented, its front two regiments pulling away from their trailing comrades.[3]

Not everyone marched away. Colonel Frederick A. Bartleson, lying wounded in the Brotherton Cabin, needed help along with a dozen other casualties from the 100th Illinois's reckless foray. For a short while Companies D and F held the farmstead, but then Pvt. J. C. Lang and some of the remaining uninjured men fell back to the main line, hoping to rejoin their regiment and perhaps secure aid for the wounded. To their shock, the works were deserted and the brigade was gone.[4]

2 Longstreet, *From Manassas to Appomattox*, 447.

3 *OR* 30, pt. 1, 656; Captain Welden Kelly, *A Historic Sketch, Lest We Forget—Company "E" 26th Ohio Infantry in the War for the Union 1861-65* (n.p., 1909), 15.

4 J. C. Lang, "Letter from a Soldier," *Joliet Signal*, October 27, 1863.

The slight crest in the center of Brotherton Field limited the Union view into Brotherton Field. This view, taken from Buell's brigade position looking eastward, shows both the Brotherton Cabin and the masking nature of that crest. *Harvey Scarborough*

Lang and his comrades reached the abandoned line just minutes after Buell's departure, while the 26th Ohio and 13th Michigan were probably not more than 10 yards to the northwest. It was perhaps 11:20 a.m. It was at this moment, with the brigade recently away and Private Lang and his handful of comrades standing in their just-abandoned line, that the Confederates of Bushrod Johnson's division emerged from the trees east of the La Fayette Road. Buell would later report that his command had "scarcely moved one brigade front when the shock came like an avalanche" against his right flank.[5]

Sweeping forward in the face of scattered skirmish fire, Col. John S. Fulton's brigade cleared Brotherton Field easily. Leading the 25th Tennessee, Lt. Col. R. B. Snowden captured the Brotherton house and its occupants, including the impetuous and now injured Colonel Bartleson. Snowden and his officers immediately appropriated the swords, belts, pistols, and other accoutrements of Bartleson and several other Yankee officers for their own use.[6]

The southern half of Buell's brigade, the 13th Michigan and 26th Ohio, was directly in Fulton's path and struck hard. Lieutenant Colonel William H. Young, commanding the 26th, heard the tumult to the east, and trotted his horse back

5 *OR* 30, pt. 1, 656.

6 Ibid., pt. 2, 490.

from his position at the head of the regiment to the left rear just in time to watch the brigade skirmishers come pouring through his ranks in a disorganized mob. The stampede pushed back the 26th another 50 yards or so before Young halted the Ohioans and met the oncoming Rebels as best he could. Young's intent was to buy enough time for the 8th Indiana battery to escape capture a third time. The 13th Michigan fell in on the 26th's left and for a few minutes both commands maintained a desperate fire.[7]

As the 8th Indiana dashed away, Colonel Young ordered the "Groundhogs" to fall back. "It was useless sacrifice to do otherwise," explained Capt. Welden Kelly. Young and his men gave ground stubbornly, halting when they could to make brief stands to retard Fulton's Rebels. The commander of the 13th Michigan, Maj. Willard G. Eaton, realized the approaching peril and felt he had two choices: "to surrender or fall back fighting. Surrender," he scoffed, "I could not think of, and to fall back seemed certain death . . . but I determined to try." With a different logic, however, Eaton first "ordered a charge, hoping to drive the enemy's front line back and thus gain time." Dutifully, just as the 26th was scrambling westward, the Michiganders charged east into the teeth of Fulton's oncoming line. The 13th had already suffered about 70 casualties in the previous day's fight and had left a company on skirmish duty that morning. When it threw itself against the advancing Tennesseans, it fielded no more than 130 bayonets. Despite these sparse numbers, Eaton's bold tactic pushed Fulton's men back almost to the road, buying time for both the 13th and 26th to get away. Eaton next implemented the second part of his plan and slowly withdrew the 13th through the woods and into the large Dyer Field beyond, halting three times to turn and fire at their opponents. The 25th Tennessee's Lt. Col. R. B. Snowden gave no details of this struggle in his report, noting only that "we drove [the Federals] slowly through a densely wooded thicket." In this fashion, Young and Eaton independently moved their regiments to the far end of Dyer Field, where they halted near a line of Union cannon crowning a high ridge at the western edge. Their momentary escape was aided by the fact that Fulton's Confederates paused to reform when they emerged from the tree line on the east side of the same field.[8]

7 Ibid., pt. 1, 667, 673.

8 Kelly, *A Historic Sketch*, 16; Letter to "Brother Rice, September 30, 1863," William G. Eaton Papers, Western Michigan University, Kalamazoo, Michigan. Hereafter WMU. Powell, "Numbers and Losses," CCNMP; *OR* 30, pt. 2, 490.

Meanwhile, the rest of Buell's brigade moved northward. When the attack broke on his flank, the only regiment Buell could locate in the initial excitement was his own 58th Indiana, led by Lt. Col. James T. Embree. The 100th Illinois was there as well, now under the direction of Maj. C. M. Hammond, but after being so battered from the morning's activities, Buell did not recognize it by name in his report, referring to them only as "some stragglers of other regiments." Buell was far enough ahead of the rear half of the brigade that he had no idea what happened to the 13th Michigan and 26th Ohio. Embree noted that "all the Federal forces within view of [my] regiment fell back before this [enemy] host." Buell did not attempt to return to his original position or launch a counterattack. Instead, he marched the 58th Indiana out into Dyer Field and put the Hoosiers in line, hoping to rally the rest of his brigade upon this thin blue wall. The 58th waited patiently while Buell tried to locate his remaining troops, to no avail. He returned a few minutes later and marched the regiment toward a prominent knoll overlooking the northern end of the field, held by an unknown Union battery.[9]

Buell's halt and subsequent departure all happened very quickly, while Eaton and Young were trying to conduct their fighting withdrawal through the timber separating Dyer and Brotherton fields. Certainly Buell's retreat northward was made in great haste as he next tried to find Wood or someone from the division. Along the way, the 100th Illinois tried to keep up. One of the Illini recalled the whole afternoon as little more than a blur: "we continually rallied and retreated until at last it became a general rout towards Chattanooga," related Capt. Harlow B. Godard, commanding Company H. The 100th fell behind and soon lost sight of Buell and the 58th. Major Hammond led them even farther north, fetching up near the Snodgrass cabin.[10]

Driving Buell's regiments ahead of them, Fulton's Rebels emerged into Dyer Field. Lieutenant Colonel Snowden and his 25th Tennessee, the officers newly re-equipped, advanced through the epicenter of the gap in the Union line. The 25th was one of the first Rebel units to reach the eastern edge of Dyer Field, where for the first time Snowden could see more than just a few yards. "Here was presented to the eye the most magnificent scene of the day, brigade

9 *OR* 30, pt. 1, 656, 663.

10 Letter from Captain H. P. Godard, *Joliet Signal*, October 6, 1863; *OR* 30, pt. 1, 660. Hammond noted only that he ended up with the troops of General Negley, who was near the cabin at that time.

after brigade emerging *en echelon* from the woods." Snowden also learned that "the line on either side of us had not kept up with [our] rapid advance," forcing the brigade to halt. Fulton had broken through the center, but the rest of Bushrod Johnson's men still had to deal with Federals on either side of the breach.[11]

Just to the south, Jefferson C. Davis's Federals were caught in the act of redeploying when Longstreet's wave fell upon them. Alexander McCook convinced Tom Wood to move by promising to immediately fill the resultant gap. If Wood didn't hurry, McCook asserted, his men would get tangled up with their replacements. Just who McCook intended those replacements to be remains an open question. Davis had only two brigades, and with Brig. Gen. William Carlin on line extending Wood's right, only Col. John Martin's handful of the mortally wounded Col. Hans Heg's survivors, perhaps 600 muskets, were immediately on hand to take the place of the nearly 4,000 men comprising Wood's vacating division. Lieutenant George K. Shaffer, one of Wood's aides, remembered McCook promising to bring up Phil Sheridan's division to fill the gap. Several of Wood's other officers also recalled mention of Sheridan, though they at least thought this was because Sheridan, not Davis, was on their right flank. Captain Cullen Bradley commanded the 6th Battery, Ohio Light Artillery and also served as Wood's chief of artillery. Writing in 1906, Bradley mistakenly recalled that Sheridan was present with McCook and Wood that morning. These accounts were all provided many years after the fact, and each contains small discrepancies. All, however, suggest that at least initially, McCook intended to use Sheridan to replace Wood.[12]

But how could that be? McCook had to know Phil Sheridan was already committed to Thomas, and had in hand his new marching orders. It is possible that McCook intended to only use Col. Bernard Laiboldt's brigade of Sheridan's division, although this command, too, was supposed to head north when it could.

This left only Jeff Davis, or more specifically, only Colonel Martin's men. At his court of inquiry, even McCook understood the problem, pointing out the impossibility of filling the gap with the paltry force left under his command. "There was not only no time to fill the space," he testified, "but I had no troops

11 *OR* 30, pt. 2, 490.

12 Whalen, *The Fighting McCooks*, 228; Cullen Bradley, "Chickamauga: The Story of the Break in the Line," *National Tribune*, September 20, 1906.

to fill it with, unless a small brigade could cover a division interval." What then, was McCook promising to do when he left Wood?[13]

The answer lies in Wood's testimony in that same inquiry, which, when coupled with General Rosecrans's order of 10:10 a.m., makes it clear McCook was not intending to extend Davis to fill the entire gap. Instead, explained Wood, McCook intended to "move Davis' division toward the left, or up, so as to cover the interval."[14]

In other words, just as Wood was supposed to sidle left, so too would McCook move Davis northward at the same time, making sure there was no gap while simultaneously (and dramatically) shortening the Union right as Rosecrans had outlined in his earlier orders. From his hilltop position to the rear, Colonel Laiboldt could anchor the new flank until Wilder took over that task, and then move on to rejoin Sheridan's command. Colonel Wilder had already been alerted to move accordingly. While the idea had obvious risks—putting yet another Union division into motion at a critical moment being just one of them—had McCook succeeded, much of Longstreet's attack might have initially brushed past the southern (right) end of the new Union line and punched into thin air instead of catching about one-third of the Union army in motion. While XX Corps Chief of Staff Col. Gates Thruston was perhaps being overly optimistic, he later thought it all came down to a question of timing: "Thirty minutes earlier Longstreet would have met well-organized resistance. Thirty minutes later our marching divisions could have formed beyond his column of attack." In reality, a successful redeployment would not have put the Union right out of danger. The southern end of McCook's line would have still faced heavy frontal and flanking attacks simultaneously. That was not a recipe for victory, but it might have mitigated the ensuing disaster.[15]

As a result of all this, General McCook did not immediately ride back to report to Rosecrans after leaving Tom Wood. Instead, thinking an additional order to shorten the line might even then be galloping his way, McCook rode south to find Davis and put into motion what he assumed were Rosecrans's wishes. Davis was not far off, and had just learned via courier from Colonel Buell that Wood's line was ordered northward. This news could not have been

13 *OR* 30, pt. 1, 968.

14 Ibid., 944.

15 Gates P. Thruston, "The Crisis at Chickamauga," *Battles and Leaders of the Civil War*, 4 vols. (Thomas Yoseloff, Inc., 1956), vol. 3, 664.

welcome, for it meant Davis now had no support on either flank. McCook's arrival brought with it the order for Davis to move Martin out of reserve and into Buell's position.[16]

Colonel John A. Martin was young, only 24 years old that September, but he was already a proven leader and soldier. Born in Pennsylvania, Martin learned the printing trade, but as an abolitionist was drawn to Kansas by the troubles brewing there in the 1850s. He bought a pro-slavery broadsheet in Atchison, boldly renamed it *Freedom's Champion*, and steered it through an abrupt editorial course change, making it into a strong Free-Soil publication. His unabashed stance as a Free-Soiler won him acclaim and a political career, which in turn secured his appointment as lieutenant colonel of the 8th Kansas infantry. Martin, however, was not some bumbling political figurehead, promoted beyond his years and experience. He took well to soldiering. He soon rose to regimental command, and under his tenure the 8th became one of the best drilled regiments in the army. He was personally brave and an effective officer, and by 1863 a proven combat veteran. Colonel Heg's death in the predawn hours of September 20 thrust Martin into brigade command, though heading up a much-reduced formation, now little stronger than a single regiment.[17]

With so few men, Martin deployed his regiments in a single line, hoping to cover as much of the gap as possible. The 25th Illinois took up position on the brigade right, connecting with Carlin's 101st Illinois. Then came the 15th Wisconsin, 8th Kansas, and 35th Illinois. Martin had almost completed this movement, with only the 35th still hurrying to come on line alongside the Kansans, "when the enemy rose up from the tall weeds in front and advanced on us four columns deep."[18]

After ordering Hood into action, Longstreet, Simon Buckner, and their combined headquarters party rode south along the line of battle until they reached Brig. Gen. Zach Deas's large brigade, 1,932 infantry in five regiments

16 *OR* 30, pt. 1, 500.

17 According to the Kansas Historical Society, the original paper, *The Squatter Sovereign*, was "the most notorious of the Kansas pro-slavery papers" until it was bought by a financial backer of the New England Emigrant Aid Company, who then sold it to Martin. http://www.kshs.org/p/kansas-territorial-newspapers/13875, accessed 10/13/2013; Adjutant General's Office, *Report of the Adjutant General of the State of Kansas*, 2 vols. (Kansas State Printing Company, 1896), vol. 1, 120.

18 *OR* 30, pt. 1, 530.

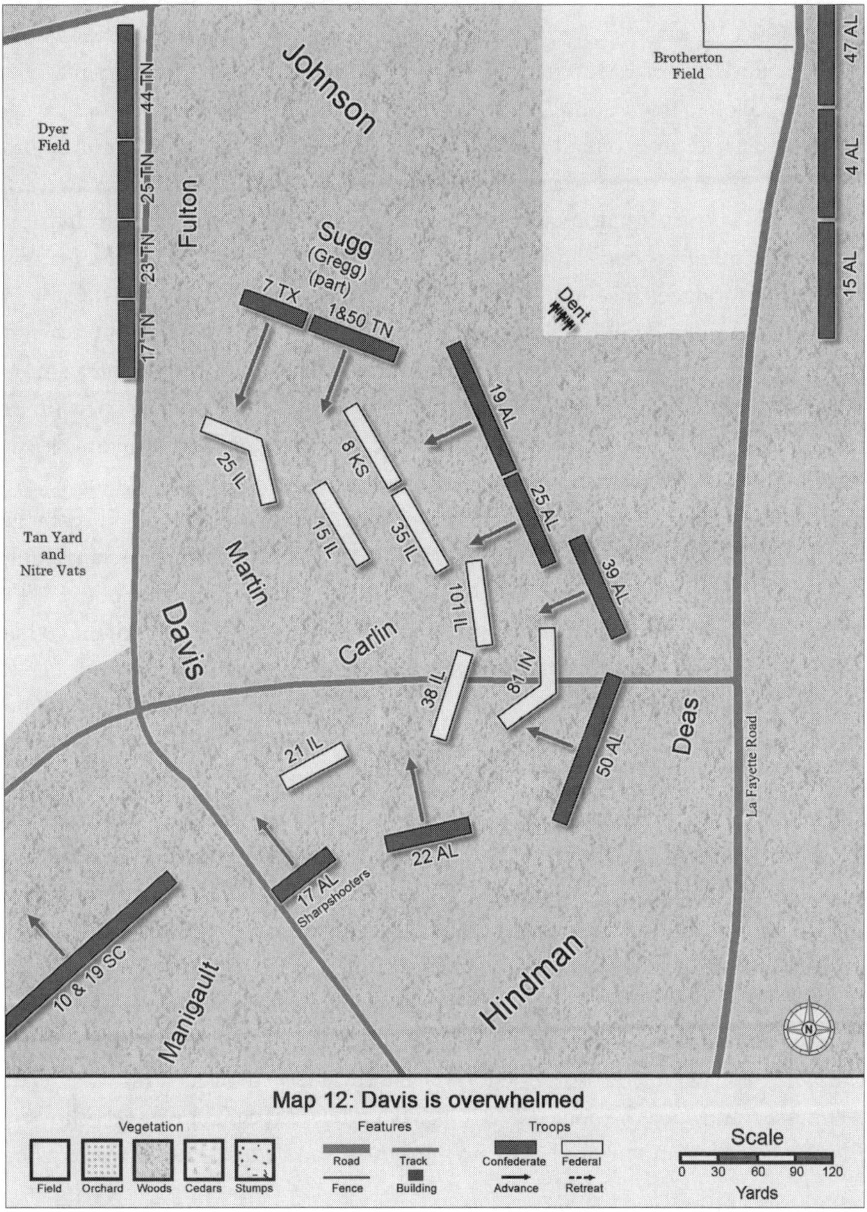

and a sharpshooter battalion, Alabamians all. Here Lt. James H. Fraser of the 50th Alabama got his first view of the famous eastern general: "Longstreet is the boldest and bravest looking man I ever saw. I don't think he would dodge if a shell were to burst under his chin." Deas was also present to greet his new commander: "'General Longstreet I presume?' 'Yes sir.'" came the laconic reply. Once pleasantries were exchanged, Longstreet ordered the whole division into action. Lieutenant William B. Moore of the 25th Alabama was digesting a letter from home, just received that morning, when the order came. "I . . . barely had time to read and destroy it when Gen. Deas gave the command 'Forward, Guide Center, March!'"[19]

Deas's command alone outnumbered Jeff Davis's entire Federal division by roughly 500 bayonets, and to Deas's left was Brig. Gen. Arthur Manigault's even larger brigade, another 2,025 Rebels marching into action against Carlin's unprotected right flank. Facing such overwhelming odds, Davis's men stood little chance, but the initial clash, at least, did not all go the Confederates's way. Some of the men on Bushrod Johnson's left watched the resultant collision as Deas and Martin ran headlong into each other. Lieutenant Colonel Watt Floyd, leading the 17th Tennessee, met with a "terrific" fire as the regiment crested the ridge in the center of the field, but almost immediately the Federals directly in front fled. This fire was delivered by the last of Buell's skirmishers, a parting shot before they bolted to find their brigade. Before Floyd could order the 17th to pursue, he caught sight of the 8th Kansas fronting along the wood line to his south, and the 35th Illinois coming into line just to his southwest.[20]

At almost the same moment, the 19th and 25th Alabama burst out of the woods east of the La Fayette Road and crested the small ridge mid-field, just as Floyd's Tennesseans had done. Instead of facing the departing shots of a Union skirmish line, however, the Alabamians faced a stunning fire delivered by Martin's incoming Federals. "At the first fire," wrote Col. Samuel McSpadden of the 19th Alabama, "so unexpected and near, my regiment exhibited a momentary hesitancy and wavering." Martin recalled the volley's devastating impact: "Our men stood steady, firing coolly, taking deliberate aim, and mowing down the rebels like chaff. . . . Their line broke and wavered."[21]

Seeing Deas's Alabamians recoil, Floyd directed his men to fire obliquely to the left, engaging Martin's Federals. Sandwiched between Floyd's 17th Tennessee and Deas's men, the 7th Texas and 1st/10th Tennessee followed Floyd's targeting and poured their fire into the same Federal line. Major Kleber

19 James H. Fraser Letter, "September 24, 1863," *Montgomery Daily Advertiser*, October 8, 1905; William Moore, "Writing Home to Talladega," *Civil War Times Illustrated*, vol. XXIX, no. 5 (November/December, 1990), 71.

20 *OR* 30, pt. 2, 482.

21 Ibid., 334. "Letter from Col. Martin," *Freedom's Champion*, October 1, 1863.

Van Zandt led the 7th Texas, who inherited command when the regiment's colonel fell wounded the day before, recalled moving through the orchard near the Brotherton cabin: "We went over the rail fence, driving the enemy."[22]

At the time Van Zandt had no idea who he was fighting. However, years later the fortunes of business brought him and an old opponent together. When Martin rose to command of the brigade, Lt. Col. James L. Abernathy took over the 8th Kansas. In 1896, Abernathy returned to the field for the opening ceremonies of the National Military Park, and saw Van Zandt's name on the park tablet marking the Texans's position. He realized that he held stock in Van Zandt's bank in Fort Worth. On his next business trip, Abernathy made a point of looking up the former Rebel: "'Major' he said, 'they tell me you and I got pretty close together in the war.' 'I know where I was,' [replied Van Zandt.] 'If you know where you were it will not take long to settle the question. Do you know where the Brotherton House was? And the grove of timber? Where were you?' [Abernathy] replied, 'I was in the timber.' 'Well, I was in the orchard,'" answered Van Zandt. "'We were pretty close together sure enough.'"[23]

All three of these three regiments pushed past the 8th Kansas's left flank to engage the 35th Illinois, which was still trying to come onto line. Pummeled in the act of deploying, the 35th Illinois could only fall back farther. Suddenly, to the rest of Martin's men, it seemed a Rebel force was now directly in their rear. At that moment, the newly rallied 19th and 25th Alabama reentered the fight. Floyd's flanking fire distracted the Federals, ensuring Deas's success. Advancing without stopping to fire, Deas's men gained the works and routed Martin's thin line, capturing many prisoners. "We were engaged with the enemy hid behind strong breastworks," crowed Lieutenant Moore, "from which we drove them with great slaughter. . . . It was the most ludicrous thing I ever saw in my life. As we ran forward over the breastworks scores of the Yankees came tumbling over the other side 'like turtles off a log.'"[24]

The Federal flank turned, disaster progressed down the Union line. Lieutenant Colonel Ole Johnson commanded the Scandinavian 15th Wisconsin. Initially he thought things were progressing rather handsomely, a

22 "Letter from Col. Martin," Freedom's Champion, October 1, 1863; Sandra L. Myres, *Force Without Fanfare: The Autobiography of K. M. Van Zandt* (Texas Christian University Press, 1968), 102.

23 Myres, *Force Without Fanfare*, 103.

24 *OR* 30, pt. 2, 336; Moore, "Writing Home to Talladega," 71.

nice contrast to the hard fighting of the day before. "The enemy came up and endeavored to carry the position by storm, but we had a splendid range, the ground in front of us was open, and we drove them back with great slaughter." Then, said Johnson, "I looked toward the left . . . [where] the 8th Kansas was already some distance to the rear and the rebels getting over the breastworks. . . . On looking towards the right I saw that the [25th Illinois] had also given way, and that we were almost surrounded." Johnson, having barely survived yesterday's fighting, was captured here.[25]

The 25th Illinois was falling back because, even while Martin's left flank was being turned from the north, William Carlin's brigade was experiencing much the same sort of trouble off to the south. This left the 25th in dire straits. A mournful Cpl. George D. Barnett of Company D discovered later that his brother Amos, also a corporal, "was wounded . . . [and] limpt part way off the field [but] the enemy was pressing us so close that Amos could not keep up and fell into the enemies hands." Few Northerners escaped capture. A handful of days later, Corporal Barnett confessed, "I am one of the loneliest there is since the fight you ever saw. Amos and all of the boys from the heart of the timber is missing from the company." Unfortunately, George never saw his brother again. Although Amos survived his wound, he lived to perish in Andersonville a year later.[26]

Colonel Martin managed his escape, but was heartsick and angry over his brigade's ordeal. A month later on October 18, he wrote with no little bitterness that "there was bad Generalship on our side (not on 'old Rosey's' part, but by some of his subordinate commanders) and our Right . . . was simply *crushed* by overwhelming numbers. Our little Division, reduced by the first day's fight to less than 1,200 men, was confronted on the second day by at least *two full divisions* of the enemy's army, and both its flanks were left exposed by some one who moved the troops on our left away."[27]

The sudden appearance of Thomas Hindman's Rebels sent a shockwave through Carlin and his brigade, and for good reason; neither Carlin's

25 Ole C. Johnson Letter, Wisconsin Historical Society, Madison, WI. Hereafter WHS

26 George D. Barnett Letters, http://www.douglascountyil.com/images/1_CW_MORE_LETTERS.pdf; accessed 9/4/2011.

27 Martha B. Caldwell, ed., "Some Notes on the Eighth Kansas Infantry and the Battle of Chickamauga; Letters of Colonel John A. Martin," *Kansas Historical Quarterly*, vol. XIII, no. 2 (May, 1944), 143.

skirmishers nor his own personal reconnaissance missions found "the least sign of the enemy" in his front. The first harbinger of trouble came when Carlin "heard the pickets fire one round. Immediately I discovered that they were coming back to the line in haste." Sergeant Samuel C. Broughton of the 21st Illinois had been too ill to fight the previous day, and only rejoined the regiment that morning. Still being "somewhat sore and weak," he was allowed to fall out behind the regiment to rest. Broughton was sitting behind the battle line when disaster struck. "The pickets said there were no Rebels in front," he recalled, "but the skirmish line had hardly been sent forward when the Rebels came charging in our front, four lines deep. We were on the extreme right and only one line without any support."[28]

"Almost simultaneously, volleys of musketry broke forth in front and on my right flank," Carlin wrote. "There were some large pine trees near me, and the needles from these pines commenced falling in showers to the ground. . . . Then the rebel battle flags began to show themselves at the breastworks on my right." The men of the 21st Illinois, manning Carlin's right, leveled their rifles and fired in a desperate effort to stem the tide against the surging 22nd Alabama of Deas's brigade. Alabama Pvt. John Goodwin was, in the words of his friend Jim Martin, "pierced with 12 bullet holes; he was literally shot to pieces." Captain H. R. Toulmin of the 22nd Alabama described the firing as "heavy volleys," but the Illini effort failed to check the attack. Without stopping to deliver their own fire, the Alabamians "gallantly charged the works, capturing some 250 prisoners and a piece of artillery, and putting to flight the remainder of the line." Illinois Sgt. Samuel Boggs of Company E recalled little more than moments of vast confusion. "There was a crashing roar; the air seemed full of bullets, dust, and Rebel yells. Men went down on all sides of me; we were in a hand-to-hand encounter. Some of our men had saved themselves by timely flight, but [for the rest] our retreat was cut off; it was either surrender, or foolishly throw our lives away."[29]

28 *OR* 30, pt. 1, 517; Carlin, *Memoirs*, 102. Samuel Broughton Memoir and Journal, http://www.rootsweb.com/~ilcivilw/scrapbk/broughtjourn.html, accessed 9/4/2011.

29 Girardi and Hughes, Carlin Memoirs, 102; Jim R. Martin Letter, 22nd Alabama Regiment, http://geocities.com/~bobjones/22nd_docs.htm. Accessed 9/4/2011; *OR* 30, pt. 2, 336; Samuel S. Boggs, *Eighteen Months A Prisoner Under the Rebel Flag: A Condensed Pen Picture of Belle Isle, Danville, Andersonville, Charleston, Florence and Libby Prisons from Actual Experience* (S. S. Boggs, 1887), 8. The artillery piece remains unidentified. None of Davis's batteries had been brought up to the line in Brotherton Field.

With 371 men, the 22nd Alabama had the edge over the 300-man Illinois regiment and overlapped Carlin's flank to the south. Even worse, the 63 men of the 17th Alabama Sharpshooters, who had been serving as the brigade skirmish line until the fight was joined, reformed and fell in to the left of the 22nd. The unopposed sharpshooters swung around well into the 21st's rear, dooming Lt. Gen. U. S. Grant's former command.[30]

Sergeant Broughton, still resting just behind the Illinois battle line, heard Col. John W. S. Alexander utter his final words—an order for the regiment to fall back; Alexander was cut down immediately thereafter. Broughton watched with horror as most of the regiment fell into enemy hands. The sight helped him gain his feet and he take to flight, his aches and weariness forgotten. He stumbled for the rear ignoring calls to "halt, you damned Yankee!" Broughton covered about a mile of ground and found General Sheridan's division trying to make a stand. When that defensive effort fared no better, he again joined the general retreat, passing Rosecrans's headquarters along the way. The sergeant finally fetched up at Rossville that night, where he found the remnants of the 21st Illinois: 60 men under a captain.[31]

The house-of-cards effect continued. Now came the turn of the 81st Indiana (still under the able command of Maj. James Calloway of the 21st Illinois), facing the 50th Alabama of Deas's brigade. The 50th closed quickly to within a few yards of the breastworks. Calloway was not only aware of the collapse of his former regiment to his right, but could hear tremendous firing off to his left and rear (the beginning of the disaster being visited upon Martin's men). With the enemy about to leap the works and with both flanks giving way, Major Calloway ordered the 81st to retreat. "As there was no support behind us," wrote the regimental historian, "it was . . . impossible to form anything like a line," so the regiment retreated by squads, firing as it fell back.[32]

On Carlin's left, the 101st Ohio had a more optimistic first encounter, at least initially. Facing the 39th Alabama, Maj. Bedan B. McDonald and his Buckeyes fended off the 39th's first charge. "With deliberate and deadly aim," recalled Ohio Sgt. Louis Day, "[we fired] into their ranks not two hundred feet

30 OR 30, pt. 2, 340.

31 Samuel Broughton Memoir and Journal, http://www.rootsweb.com/~ilcivilw/scrapbk/broughtjourn.html, accessed 9/4/2011.

32 George W. Morris, *History of the Eighty-First Regiment of Indiana Volunteer Infantry in the Great War of the Rebellion, 1861 to 1865* (Franklin Printing Co. 1901), 59.

away. They staggered, halted, hesitated, and before they were aware of it received another volley, which sent them flying." A second effort, however, did the trick. The 101st's Ohio's collapse, when it came, came quickly. Confronted by "three divisions . . . fresh from Virginia . . . there was one of two things to do, run or be captured in toto. It was needless to say that we ran," admitted Sgt. Ben Strong of Company A. "It is said that we had orders to do so, but if we did, some did not have the orders, and were a little slow in getting started." Sergeant Strong proved to be one of the holdouts, breaking away from the line only when Rebels began crossing the barricades. He only made it about 30 yards before a ball took him in the arm halfway "between the wrist and the elbow," sending him sprawling. Before he was up again, he was a prisoner.[33]

Carlin's brigade line was shattered. "[W]ith the attack in front and on both flanks simultaneously it was impossible for my troops to hold their position," he concluded. "The line melted away." Carlin tried but failed to orchestrate a more controlled retreat in an effort to "reform on a rocky ridge . . . about 400 yards" to the west. "[Only] one field officer . . . succeeded in getting away . . . [and] but few company officers: I believe nearly . . . all of them were killed or wounded," he concluded. Carlin's leaderless front line had been either completely routed or captured in place.[34]

The 38th Illinois, barely 100 men strong, serving as Carlin's only reserve behind the center of his line, was too weak to alone salvage the situation. Carlin ordered Lt. Col. Daniel H. Gilmer to get his regiment away—fast. The order, however, arrived too late. "The line in front came over us," reported Capt. William Harris of the 38th, "the men fired one volley and retired." Colonel Gilmer and Maj. Henry N. Alden were both cut down, the former's wound a mortal one. The 38th's survivors joined the general westward stampede.[35]

Despite watching his command break for the second time in two days, Jeff Davis remained outwardly calm. His orderly, Charlie Dennis, had been moving steadily back and forth between the divisional ammunition train and Davis's location, periodically updating the general on the status of the train. Early in the fight Dennis found Davis on the move, "seeking a better place of observation," trailed by the divisional headquarters flag, "a blood red square of bunting-about

33 L. W. Day, *Story of the One Hundred and First Ohio Infantry* (The W. M. Bayne Printing Co., 1894), 173; Benjamin T. Strong, *3 Years or During the War* (Charles R. Green, 1913), n.p.

34 William P. Carlin, "Military Memoirs," *National Tribune*, April 16, 1885; *OR* 30, pt. 1, 517.

35 *OR* 30, pt. 1, 522.

four or five feet square-with a black star in center. . . . We were all the while under a pretty sharp fire." The sight of the flag-bearer, a man named Ruger, "folding up" the banner, rattled Dennis, who just a moment earlier had a bullet pass through his cap and raise "a welt on his head." When Davis saw the flag being furled, however, "the language he applied to that orderly would have made a dog smart . . . suffice to say that flag was unfurled pronto."[36]

To Davis's way of thinking, the collapse of his command was all but inevitable given the circumstances. "The absence of any support . . . made my position little better than an outpost and perfectly untenable against the overwhelming force coming against it," he later wrote. "Nothing but precipitate flight could save my command from annihilation or capture." Davis tried to save what he still could—his trains and his artillery. The next time Dennis found his boss, "[the general] did not seem to be very badly frightened, and only told me to keep the train well in hand and watch carefully the noise of battle." If the fight turned north, said Davis, the orderly should "take the train into Chattanooga and behind the works there." When Dennis rode to safeguard the ammunition, Davis rode back to find Captain Hotchkiss and the division's artillery. Davis ordered Hotchkiss to take both the 2nd Minnesota and 8th Wisconsin out of immediate danger before making an effort to rally his men.[37]

The heady wine of success helped many Alabamians overlook its cost and the initial stubborn resistance they met. "As we came in sight [of the Union line] the boys all took the run and everyone shouted and shot as fast as he could," wrote Lieutenant Fraser of the 50th. "Their first line gave way like nothing, so did their second and third. . . . It is reported that General Longstreet . . . never saw anything more beautifully done." With Martin and Carlin both swept away, Hindman's Confederate division was free to move deep into the Union rear. Left in the wake of Hindman's success were a large number of Deas's wounded and killed Alabamians—the first of a series of many bloodlettings to come.[38]

Davis and the Army of the Cumberland's right flank might be gone, but the fight was far from decided. North of the break, Union Brig. Gen. John Brannan and his division faced a similar crisis. Whether they would fare any better remained to be seen.

36 Charles B. Dennis Memoir, Rutherford B. Hayes Presidential Library, Fremont, OH.

37 *OR* 30, pt. 1, 500; Dennis Memoir, Hayes Library; OR 30, pt. 1, 504.

38 James H. Fraser Letter, "September 24, 1863," *Montgomery Daily Advertiser*, October 8, 1905.

Chapter Eleven

Brannan's Retreat:

Sunday, 11:30 a.m. to 12:30 p.m.

Brigadier General John Brannan's decision not to heed XIV Corps commander George Thomas's latest request for reinforcements may have unwittingly sown the seeds of disaster farther down the Union line. The events unfolding in Poe Field, however, justified Brannan's decision.

Unleashed by General Bragg's abrupt, everyone-into-the-fight attack order, A. P. Stewart's men pounded the Federal breastworks. "For several hundred yards both lines pressed on under the most terrible fire it has ever been my fortune to witness," Stewart wrote. "[Men were] . . . mowed down at every step." Stewart's effort was in vain, which pleased Federal division commander Maj. Gen. Joseph Reynolds. "I . . . felt greatly relieved by the fact that one brigade could then be spared, as we thought, from our position to go to the left," he reported, "[while] attack after attack was delivered by the Confederates and repulsed by us."[1]

Brannan's division, less Col. Van Derveer's brigade, consisted of but eight regiments. Colonel John Connell's brigade included the 82nd Indiana, and 31st and 17th Ohio (the 38th Ohio and Col. Edward H. Phelps were still serving as train guard). The Buckeyes of the 17th held the brigade's right. On its left were six guns of Capt. Josiah Church's Battery D, 1st Michigan Light Artillery,

1 Reynolds Statement, CCNMP; *OR* 30, pt. 2, 364.

equipped with a pair each of 10-pound Parrott rifles, James rifles, and 12-pound smoothbore howitzers. Church unlimbered in the brigade's first line directly west of the Poe cabin and farmyard. The 31st Ohio formed on the left of the guns. The Hoosier 82nd formed Connell's support line about 60 yards behind the 17th Ohio.

Brannan's remaining brigade, Col. John T. Croxton's five regiments, lined up north of and on the left of Connell's command. Croxton placed the 10th and 74th Indiana on his front, with the 4th and 10th Kentucky in support. The 14th Ohio also formed in the second line, but behind Connell's left (the 31st Ohio). Since Connell only had three regiments, and Croxton five, both brigades formed with four regiments in the front and four in support. Unlike Connell, Croxton initially stationed his artillery, Lt. Marco B. Gary's Battery C of the 1st Ohio Light Artillery—four James rifles and a pair of Napoleons—in the second line. Once the action began, Gary moved his guns to the front.

Both brigades saw action the previous day, though Croxton's large brigade suffered much more severely than did Connell with a staggering 750 casualties. Connell's command numbered about 1,100 men; with Church's guns, it held a frontage of about 300 yards. Croxton's counted about 1,250 infantry and covered roughly the same distance. Brannan's 2,350 men and a dozen guns stretched across the southern two-thirds of Poe Field.

Connell's men were not in the best of moods that morning. They dropped their packs in the woods east of Kelly Field prior to entering Saturday's fight and, through the vagaries of combat, lost them to the enemy. They spent that cold night shivering and seeking comfort in haystacks, imagining Rebels enjoying their captured blankets. Colonel Moses T. Walker of the 31st Ohio was the brigade's ranking officer, but he was under arrest (for a trifling affair) and serving on Brannan's staff. This left Colonel Connell in command. Brannan closely supervised Connell on the 19th , parceling out his three regiments to his division's other two brigades to let more experienced men exercise tactical control.[2]

The Federal line here was strongly posted behind breastworks and well supported. The only aspect of his position that bothered Connell was his right flank. When Connell first deployed, Col. Timothy R. Stanley's brigade anchored

2 McNeil, *Personal Recollections of Service*, 15. Colonel Moses B. Walker was placed under arrest before the battle by Colonel Phelps of the 38th Ohio, the brigade's ranking officer. However, Phelps and his regiment were assigned to guard the trains, and were not present either, leaving Connell in command. Moses B. Walker Report, George Thomas Papers, RG 94, NARA.

his right. Around 9:00 a.m., however, Stanley's men pulled out. For a time, Connell's right lay naked. Things were set right when Sidney Barnes's brigade replaced Stanley. Barnes's men were still present after 10:00 a.m., when Connell absorbed A. P. Stewart's first two assaults. That fighting opened on Connell's left and swept down the length of Poe Field to wash up on his front when John Brown's Tennesseans swept out of the timber. Captain Church's Michigan battery, reported Connell, "opened a continuous, rapid, and deadly fire, which was kept up . . . for more than an hour." Brown was easily repulsed. A second attack by Henry Clayton's Alabamians fared no better.[3]

It was during Clayton's assault that Samuel Beatty's brigade halted in the timber behind Connell. As noted earlier, General Beatty's men were there more by accident than by design. They, too, were in a foul mood after losing heavily as the unfortunate recipients of a disastrous flank attack on Saturday. In the 19th Ohio, Lt. Jason Hurd recalled the morning as "hazy and cold." Breakfast was slim fare, just some bacon and hardtack, eaten without enthusiasm. Hurd noted that "anxiety had banished our appetite and the horrors of battle worked heavily upon our feelings." The early morning quiet, he thought an "ominous stillness." To Hurd, "it was an actual relief, when at 8:00 [a.m.] the first few shots of skirmishing rang out." Shortly thereafter, Horatio Van Cleve's division moved forward to the front looking for a place to enter the fight.[4]

Sam Beatty deployed the 19th Ohio and 79th Indiana in his front, the 9th and 17th Kentucky behind them. They were lying down directly behind Brannan's position. The men were not in line, but formed in "closed column of division," with each regiment in a block two companies wide by five deep, making it in Beatty's words "more a column in mass than supporting lines." Handy for movement or rapid redeployment, it was not intended as a combat formation, but was often used by regiments in support. However, the typical interval for a supporting line was at least 100 yards between regiments of the same brigade, or 200 yards between brigades—room enough so that the units could form battle lines as needed. Unfortunately for Beatty's men, they were parked only a handful of yards behind Connell's second line.[5]

3 *OR* 30, pt. 1, 409.

4 Entry for September 20, Jason Hurd Diary, CSI.

5 George W. Parker, *History of the Seventy-Ninth Regiment Indiana Volunteers Infantry in the Civil War of Eighteen Sixty-One in the United States* (The Hollenbeck Press, 1899), 91; *OR* 30, pt. 1, 809.

Not surprisingly, Beatty's men were unhappy with this state of affairs. During Clayton's attack, Pvt. J. A. Reep in the 19th Ohio remembered that "our close proximity to that front line brought us under their fire without any opportunity of replying to it. . . . The moment was one of intense suspense." Of course, neither General Van Cleve nor XXI Corps commander Maj. Gen. Tom Crittenden intended them to remain there for more than a few minutes—Beatty's men were supposed to soon follow Col. George Dick's brigade on a march to the army's left flank. Private Reep recalled how their unease increased when he and his comrades noticed "the hurried movement of large bodies of troops in our rear," which proved to be yet more Federals marching behind them up the Glenn-Kelly Road.[6]

Though Reep had no way of knowing it, these troops consisted of Col. Sidney Barnes's brigade, followed at an interval by Col. Charles Harker's troops, both commands moving under Tom Wood's instructions to find Reynolds's division. Both brigades continued moving north without stopping. Reep would have been even more alarmed had John Brannan acquiesced to George Thomas's second request for help, which would have stripped away the solid line of defenders to Reep's front in yet another scurry northward.

"I received orders to move to the left following Croxton's brigade, and passing to the rear of Reynolds's division," reported Connell, "but before the movement was executed the order was countermanded." And so Connell remained in place and Reep and his comrades suffered less anxiety—for the moment. A few minutes later, however, the troops on his right vanished when Wood's men pulled out of line, leaving Connell "without any support either in my rear or upon my right flank." The colonel sent word to Brannan about his now exposed right flank and prepared for the worst. "I . . . threw out flankers to my right, under command of Major [Paul] Slocum, of the Eighty-Second Indiana . . . and gave orders to the commanders of the regiments to front by the right flank as soon as the enemy appeared." For reasons that remain unclear, everyone seems to have overlooked Beatty's brigade immediately behind the 82nd Indiana. Brannan and Connell were either unaware of its presence, or understood Beatty was also tasked to leave momentarily and so dismissed this brigade from the equation.[7]

6 J. A. Reep, "Guttmachrala, or Four Years at the Front as a Private," 19th Ohio file, CSI.

7 *OR* 30, pt. 1, 409.

The Confederate battle lines opposing Brannan's division did not square off, brigade for brigade, to their Union opposition. Brown's and Clayton's brigades (in that order) struck Brannan's line at the seam between Connell and Croxton, subjecting them to the frontal fire of Frank Church's cannon and a crippling, raking fire from Gary's guns. A good part of the south end of Connell's line (at least the distance of the 17th Ohio's regimental frontage), remained unengaged because A. P. Stewart's left ended short; just north of Connell's right. The Rebels in line with Stewart to the south belonged to Brig. Gen. Evander McNair's brigade, part of Maj. Gen. Bushrod Johnson's division. As part of General Hood's central attack column, none of Johnson's men had received orders to attack, and would not do so until after Stewart's division had already shot its bolt.[8]

When Evander McNair's brigade did step off, a good many of its members faced that same solid Union defense. McNair's five regiments deployed in a single line about 300 yards long. At least one-half of that line faced not the yawning gap of Wood's vacated position, but Connell's 17th Ohio and Church's rightmost section of artillery. Well before any attacks had begun that morning, General Hood rode along McNair's line, his left arm still in his sling from his Gettysburg wound. The acting corps commander was examining not only his front, but the men about to go into action under his command for the first time. Observing from the ranks of the 1st Arkansas Mounted Infantry was a private in Company B named Frank T. Ryan. Hood's instructions, recalled Ryan, were to "capture all the ground in front of us we could . . . by all means hold all we got, keep going ahead, but never back." Shortly after that, Ryan watched as one of the division's artillery pieces was pushed forward toward the Federal line and opened fire with the intent, thought Ryan, of inducing the Yankees to charge first. When the blue-coated fish failed to take that bait, the order to advance finally arrived.[9]

Private Ryan stepped off with the rest of the brigade and after a few minutes caught his first sight of the Federal line—"a solid line of breastworks, one log piled on top of another to the height of a man's waist." The Union line blazed with fire. Almost immediately Ryan was shot, and then shot again, badly wounded in the leg. He crawled behind a tree to watch the rest of the brigade

8 This situation was explained in detail in Chapter 10.

9 Ryan Reminiscences, GDAH.

press home its attack. "The Minnie balls were coming thick and fast, the cannon balls were cutting away the limbs of the trees, and they were falling all around me," wrote the private. "For the time being, our line was wavering, staggered by the galling and deadly fire." The heavy defensive fire, at least for a short time, stymied McNair's attack. One of the opposing Federals, Jacob H. (Harry) Allspaugh, 1st sergeant of Company F, 31st Ohio (Connell's brigade), remembered firing "a number of rounds into the heavy columns in our front." Fighting alongside Allspaugh in Company F was Pvt. Sam McNeil, who wrote that "with plenty of ammunition and food, and with a continuous line on our right, the 17th and 31st Ohio could have held that position just so long as the enemy came up on our front." Within a short while, however, Allspaugh noted an ominous development: "troops at a right shoulder shift moving obliquely to the right past our front." Connell's line was about to be flanked.[10]

While Private Ryan was watching his comrades hurl themselves fruitlessly forward against the Federal position, Confederate Col. Cyrus A. Sugg brought up John Gregg's brigade behind McNair. Sugg watched as McNair's men "first wavered, then halted in considerable confusion" short of the Federal line. After rallying, a renewed effort by McNair fared no better, halting "a second time in the face of a heavy force of the enemy, strongly posted behind breastworks and fallen timber." McNair's formation fell into disarray. Seeing no point in repeating failure, Sugg—after a quick conference with McNair—led his men closer to the front and around McNair's left to work his way around Connell's flank.[11]

Suddenly, the space just vacated by Barnes yawned like a chasm. The 82nd Indiana's Lt. Col. Henry Davis spotted "the enemy pouring in through the opening" and hastened to alert his regimental commander, Col. Morton Hunter, that "we were being flanked on the right." Hunter ordered him to take Companies A and C, reinforce Major Slocum's thin line of flankers, and try and hold the Confederates at bay.[12]

10 Ryan Reminiscences, GDAH; H. Allspaugh, "Chickamauga," *National Tribune*, October 7, 1886; McNeil, "The 31st Ohio at Chickamauga," *National Tribune*, February 9, 1888; Allspaugh, "Chickamauga," *National Tribune*, October 7, 1886. Frank T. Ryan lost his leg as a result of his wound. Note that the 31st Ohio's fire was actually angling into McNair's flank, since Stewart's men were already repulsed, but their accounts make it clear that Allspaugh and Mcneil viewed Brown's, Clayton's, and McNair's efforts all as parts of the same assault.

11 *OR* 30, pt. 2, 495.

12 Lt. Col. Davis Letter, 82nd Indiana File, CCNMP.

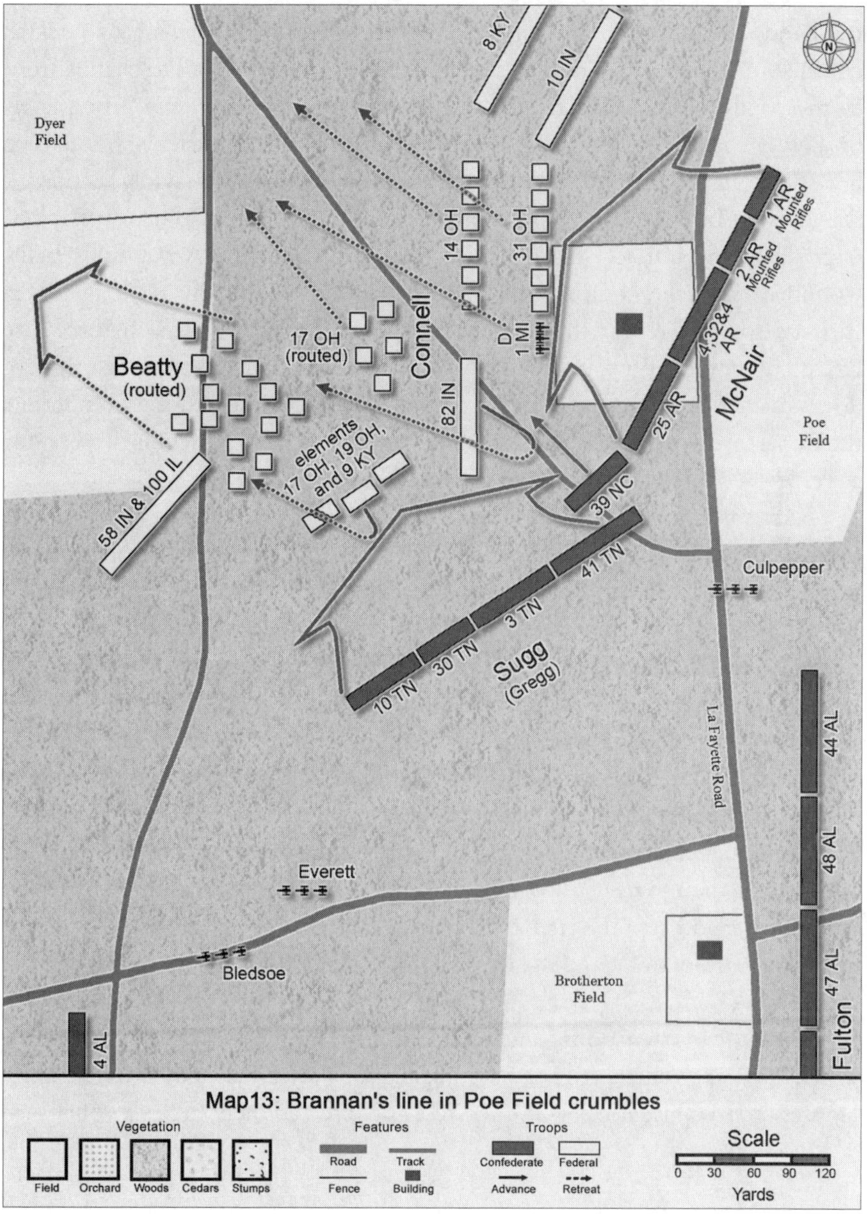

Map13: Brannan's line in Poe Field crumbles

Two companies of blue infantry had no hope of stemming such a tide. Within minutes Sugg's Rebels were enfilading Connell's first line. In the ranks of the 17th Ohio, Sgt. Alanson Gierhardt noticed the enemy pouring "a most destructive fire down the line of our regiment. . . . I had emptied the contents of my Springfield at the Johnies [sic] and in return, got the sight shot off close to my hand." The deadly flanking fire had the effect of "throwing us back in confusion." Lieutenant Colonel Durbin Ward ordered the 17th to change front to the south. In its effort to do so, however, the regiment was "completely broken on its right wing." Three days later in a letter to his hometown newspaper in Lancaster, Ohio, Capt. James W. Stinchcomb vividly recounted the disaster. Initially, Company A of the 17th tried to file by the right flank to oppose this new attack, he explained, but Capt. John H. Arney fell, "badly wounded" and the company broke. Next in line, Company F's Capt. Ezra Ricketts tried to repeat the maneuver, only to be struck dead in turn. The horrified Stinchcomb watched "company after company break; I cast my eye down the line and find my company the only one left; the battery is limbering; the Rebels are close enough to use the bayonet. . . . The Regiment is running for cover."[13]

Sixty yards to the rear, in command of the 82nd Indiana's Company A, Capt. Allen W. Brown gaped, astonished at the sight. "My attention had all been taken up with what had occurred in the front and I did not see the flank of Rebels coming down on us," wrote Brown. "I did not know what the 17th was running for." In their haste, the men of the 17th ran right over Brown's Hoosiers, who were still lying prone.[14]

The 17th's Ohio's rout triggered a domino effect. Church's guns were the next to fall. Battery D had been throwing shells all morning, their latest fire helping to check McNair's attacks. Suddenly, Church noticed the Buckeyes of the 17th struggling to change front, and before long breaking for the rear. "The enemy were then so near," he wrote, "I ordered the pieces to be double-shotted with canister and kept the enemy back for a short time." Church wanted to turn his whole battery to face to the right, but too many friendly troops were in the way.[15]

These "friendly troops" included Colonel Hunter and the 82nd Indiana, which now entered the fight. As panicked Buckeyes crashed through them, Hunter ordered his Hoosiers to their feet and directed them to fire a volley into

13 A. L. Gierhardt Recollections, OHS; OR 30, pt. 1, 409; "Letter from Captain Stinchcomb," *Lancaster Gazette*, October 8, 1863.

14 Roger D. Ruddick, *From the Hayfields to the Battlefields* (n. p. 1986), 161; Alfred G. Hunter, *History of the Eighty-Second Indiana Volunteer Infantry, its Organization, Campaigns and Battles* (Wm. B. Burford, Printer and Binder, 1893), 66.

15 *OR* 30, pt. 1, 413.

friend and foe alike. Once the volley ended, Hunter ordered a charge and the 82nd jumped forward through the "flying ranks" of the 17th Ohio. The 82nd Indiana's counterattack took them all the way back to the original line of breastworks, driving the Rebels before them. The cost was high: crossing just 60 yards killed and wounded 92 men—nearly half of those who began the charge.[16]

Regaining the original works bought a little extra breathing room for Church's gun crews, but did nothing to solve the problem of Rebels enveloping Connell's right flank. The Hoosiers of the 82nd found themselves in the same trap the Buckeyes of the 17th had just left. Captain Brown realized the peril: "We raised the yell when we raised to our feet and we went to the breastworks and held our ground for fifteen minutes, [in] a perfect storm [of] laden hail. I turned my eyes to the right when the bullets commenced coming in behind me and not more than 100 yards off here, two soiled lines of battle were moving." Company K's Cpl. Benjamin Mabry agreed: "We made a charge on them and drove them, but they got around on our right flank and comensed a cros fire on us."[17]

Lieutenant Colonel Davis and his two companies of Indianans could not stop Sugg's entire line of battle. "For a short time [we] checked the advance of the enemy," Davis recalled, "but they soon discovered that it was only a skirmish line in their front and commenced advancing. . . . We commenced falling back from tree to tree until we reached an open field in our rear." Colonel Davis did not yet know it, but while he was busy on the brigade right, his son, Pvt. Henry P. 'Peeler' Davis, fell wounded during Hunter's countercharge. The young man took what appeared to be a serious but not overly dangerous wound to the foot. It left him unable to walk and he remained on the field for more than 24 hours; the wound festered. Henry died a week or so after the battle. Heartsick and devastated, Colonel Davis resigned on October 1, 1863. "The death of our brother broke the spirit of our father, and he wanted to get back home to his family," explained Davis's second son, William.[18]

16 Ibid., 409; *Hunter, History of the Eighty-Second Indiana*, 66.

17 Ruddick, *From the Hayfields to the Battlefields*, 162; Verle Proctor Sutton, ed., *Benjamin Benn Mabry, Yankee Soldier* (Crown Printers, 1978), 81.

18 Lt. Col. Davis Letter, CCNMP; "Details of Col. Davis's resignation," The Indiana Civil War Message Board, http://www.history-sites.net/cgi-bin/bbs62x/incwmb/webbbs_config.pl?md=read;id=796, accessed 12/11/2011.

By this time the barricade was a lonely place, and Hunter was feeling abandoned. "I looked around, and not a single man in the Union army, outside of the 82nd Indiana, was to be seen." He expected the 17th Ohio to rally and make the charge with him, but as Pvt. D. L. Glenn of Company K saw things, "Col. Hunter doubtless did not realize the situation." Hunter had little choice but to order the 82nd to retreat, though he did so stubbornly, halting to fire about every 50 yards. Captain Brown recalled a more chaotic retreat: "The regiment was thrown into confusion by the near approach of the Rebels and by some not hearing the order to fall back. We were pretty badly scattered." Private Glenn was too busy to notice any instructions. "I had fired a shot or two," he wrote, "when Captain [Harrison] McAllister waved his sword and gave some order. I kept on firing. Looking around soon after, I had found the regiment all gone but me and comrade Jackson, of our company. 'Lafe,' said I, 'we must get out of this.'" Just then, Glenn was shot in the wrist, the ball lodging between the bones under the skin. Decades later Glenn still carried the bullet, a permanent reminder of the bloody day.[19]

Hunter might have felt all alone, but he was mistaken, doubtless overwhelmed by the lethal circumstances swirling about him. Battery D was still engaged fewer than 100 yards to his left, even if unable to fire to its right because of Hunter's presence. Beyond the artillery, the 31st Ohio and Col. John Croxton's brigade were still very much in the fight. For his part, as Captain Church watched the 82nd fall back he knew his own disaster was imminent. Still, the 82nd Indiana's charge bought Church a few precious minutes with which to save at least some of his guns. With Rebels pressing too closely to limber the cannon, the Michigan captain ordered his men to withdraw the pieces by hand, hauling them through the brush about 50 yards. Only four of the six pieces could be dragged away in time.[20]

Church's battery was on the verge of being completely surrounded. With losses in both men and horses mounting, the captain had some hard choices to make. Two guns were left on the original line because there were not enough men left to haul them out of harm's way. A third piece was abandoned at the

19 Hunter, *History of the Eighty- Second Indiana*, 66; D. L. Glenn, "The 82nd Ind. at Chickamauga," *National Tribune*, December 9, 1915; Ruddick, *From the Hayfields to the Battlefields*, 162; D. L. Glenn, "Indiana Veteran Saw Much Action in Campaign around Chattanooga," *Washington Times*, December 29, 1938.

20 *OR* 30, pt. 1, 414.

line of limbers, for by now the battery had lost nearly 40 horses and there were not enough animals left to pull even the four surviving cannon to safety. Sergeant S. W. Allen defended one piece almost to the last, firing his pistol at the oncoming Rebels until he was nearly run through by Confederate bayonets before falling back. Church reported that Allen's piece could not be saved because he had already ordered the rest of Allen's crew to haul off a different gun. Even the battery's rear-most echelon was threatened when Church came near to losing his forge, battery, and headquarters wagons until a quick-thinking saddler named Harry Bartlett intervened, leading the three wagons off through a rapidly shrinking gap in the closing Rebel net. According to Bartlett, at one point the Michigan gunners were "completely surrounded by the Rebs." With his last three pieces in tow, Church fell back through the woods to the high open knoll about a half mile to the northwest, south of the Snodgrass house. Once there, he reported to the next senior officer he could find, Maj. Gen. James S. Negley, who put what was left of Battery D into position next to Capt. Frederick Schultz's Battery M, 1st Ohio Light Artillery.[21]

With Church's abrupt departure, of Connell's front line only the 31st Ohio remained. Behind the 31st was the prone 14th Ohio, loaned out to support its fellow Buckeyes. This time, however, because of the flanking nature of the enemy attack, the 14th was the first to be struck and to give way, in the same manner as the previous units had tumbled. From their prone position these men had watched the 31st Ohio engage and drive back McNair's Confederates, until, as Pvt. B. B. Jackson explained, "the Rebels came pouring in upon us far superior to us in numbers, and a flank movement was made upon us at the same time."[22]

The 14th Ohio had already seen more than its share of fighting at Chickamauga. The regiment was heavily engaged on September 19, so much so that when Capt. William H. Eckles of Company G arrived on the morning of the 20th to rejoin his command after several days on detached duty, he was shocked to discover his company numbered but 14 men out of the 51 rank and file present the morning before. Here in Poe Field, Eckles wrote his wife, "bullets and grape were flying almost as thick as hail, and the poor boys were

21 *OR* 30, pt. 1, 414; "Dearest Ma & Eugene," October 1, 1863, Harold J. Bartlett Letters, Bentley Historical Library, UMich.

22 "Beloved Wife and Family," Letter of September 27, 1863, B. B. Jackson Papers, Bowling Green State University, Bowling Green, Ohio. Hereafter BGSU.

hugging the ground almost as flat as adders," unwilling even to raise their heads as they reached up to shake hands with their returning captain.[23]

The commander of the 14th Ohio, Lt. Col. Henry D. Kingsbury, reported that his regiment "held the position until the right was so far driven back . . . that we were forced to retire." As was his custom, Kingsbury was still toting his signature rifle instead of an officer's sword. Private Augustus C. May noted with no little admiration that his commander "did not go into the fight like some officers do—swinging his sword in the air—but he went in on foot . . . with musket in hand." The 14th splintered into fragments during the retreat. The separate pieces Kingsbury and Maj. John J. Wilson later rallied on different parts of Snodgrass Hill would fight apart for the rest of the afternoon.[24]

The retreat of Church's battery and the collapse of the 14th Ohio made the 31st Ohio's position wholly untenable, and its retreat inevitable. Harry Allspaugh recalled that by this time the Buckeyes of the 31st were taking both infantry and artillery fire from the right, and he and his comrades "thought it best to get out of that, without orders, if necessary." Sam McNeil also remembered the sudden onslaught of Confederates attacking the 31st from the rear, and the command to leave: "Lieutenant J. J. Miller gave the order to our company to retire from that position." The 31st fell back in a jumble, all formation lost.[25]

Some of Connell's men made one last effort to restore the line. Lieutenant Colonel Durbin Ward was a lawyer and Democratic politician with no previous military or even militia experience in 1861. Nevertheless, he entered the war in the first rush of patriotic enlistment. He was said to be the first volunteer in his county. He chose to enter service as a private in the 12th Ohio believing that, despite his political connections, his service as a common soldier would demonstrate his commitment to the Union cause. Once he proved his military virtues in a three-month regiment, Ward accepted a major's commission in the newly organized 17th Ohio. He was an effective and tenacious soldier, qualities he now demonstrated in full.[26]

23 "Dear Wife," Letter of September 27, 1863, *Paulding Independent*, October 22, 1863.

24 *OR* 30, pt. 1, 425; "The Fourteenth at Chickamauga," *Toledo Commercial*, October 17, 1863.

25 Allspaugh, "Chickamauga," *National Tribune*, October 7, 1886; McNeil, *Personal Recollections of Service*, 16.

26 Elizabeth Probasco Ward, *Life, Speeches and Orations of Durbin Ward of Ohio* (Hann and Adair, 1888), xvii.

Not yet ready to cede the field, Ward tried to rally the 17th behind Colonel Hunter's countercharge. That effort failed, and the whole mass fell back another couple of hundred yards. Here, however, a second rally succeeded when Ward gathered about 250 men of the 17th into an ad-hoc line. He was aided in this effort by Lt. Jacob M. Ruffner of Company B, who was acting that day as the brigade provost marshal. With his line reformed, Ward essayed one more effort to restore the position. As Captain Stinchcomb reported, "double-Quick [we] went into the same strip of woods we were driven from . . . and fought for 15 minutes . . . [to] within 50 to 75 yards of the breastworks, but it got too hot and we had to retreat again." The 17th almost lost one of its flags in the bold venture when Rebel rounds shattered the staff and dropped the national colors to the ground. Lieutenant Ruffner dashed forward, reaching the prize just ahead of a squad of enemy soldiers eager for the trophy. Grabbing the flag in his left hand, Ruffner drew a revolver with his right and emptied its six chambers into the very faces of the lunging Confederates. His work unfinished, the lieutenant produced a second pistol and managed five more shots. With the enemy at least temporarily checked, Ruffner raced back to join the battered 17th—though not unscathed. Ruffner, according to one eyewitness, "was wounded in back of the neck; had his sword struck, one of his pistols hit twice, besides several holes in his clothing." In recognition of his incredible display of reckless courage, eight days later he was promoted to First Lieutenant and made regimental adjutant. The 17th Ohio's withdrawal ended the last effort by Connell's brigade to stem the breakthrough. Its retreat also stripped away the last vestige of support for Colonel Croxton's brigade, which would now have to deal with the rapidly deepening crisis on its right flank.[27]

Potentially, Samuel Beatty's Federals stationed directly behind Connell's line could have had a significant impact on the Rebel advance. Instead, Beatty's men barely played a role in the engagement. Their awkward formation, close-packed ranks, proximity to the Federal front line, and overall lack of coordination between the various commanders conspired to shatter Beatty's brigade before it fired a shot. Beatty's two front line regiments, the 19th Ohio and 79th Indiana, were the most disrupted. Lieutenant Colonel Harry G. Stratton mournfully reported that his 19th Ohio was stationed directly behind

27 "Stinchcomb," *Lancaster Gazette*, October 8, 1863; "Obituary of Jacob M. Ruffner," *Lancaster Gazette*, August 18, 1864. Ruffner was killed in the trenches outside Atlanta on August 9, 1864.

"two lines of troops and a battery," which subsequently "retired in confusion, the battery breaking through and disorganizing my line. My men became confused and scattered as a consequence, and I did not succeed in rallying them again in a body until evening." Describing the 79th Indiana's experience, Cpl. Leander Munhall of Company C complained, "we were just literally tore to pieces and scattered in every direction." Munhall's commander, Col. Frederick Knefler, also bemoaned the awkward deployment, noting that his regiment lay only "a few yards" behind the 82nd Indiana. When the crisis came, Knefler lamented that his regiment could have stood fast, had only there been "sufficient space to deploy." Like the 19th, the 79th would not reform as a unit for the rest of the day.[28]

Lying with his comrades in the 9th Kentucky, Lt. Marcus Woodcock described the mess as it descended upon him: "Presently the front line [Connell's brigade] broke and back they came in helpless confusion, running over us as we lay. . . . Next came the front line of our Brigade, which was so badly demoralized by the issue of the contest in front, and by the unearthly yells of the now rapidly approaching and victory-flushed Rebels." Most damaging by far were the limbers and caissons and of Church's battery, which cut a swath right through Beatty's prone ranks. Private Reep of the 19th Ohio recalled watching Connell's troops struggling to form a new line to the right and Beatty's ranks spontaneously coming to their feet, only to be ordered to lie back down. "Almost simultaneously," Reep recalled, "we were thrown into confusion by the caissons and limber boxes of a battery of artillery plunging obliquely into our ranks. . . . Several of the brigade were seriously hurt." "This was more than human nature could bear," concluded Woodcock. In an instant, the brigade had dissolved as an effective combat force.[29]

However, like Ward's Buckeyes, the men of the 9th Kentucky were not yet ready to quit the field and made one last gallant effort to restore the situation. According to Col. George Cram, the 9th fell back "some 25 yards, when we rallied and moved forward at the double-quick about 150 yards." The partial rally of the Kentuckians for the countercharge carried the regiment all the way back to Connell's forward breastwork line, putting Cram's men on line—at least temporarily—with Hunter's 82nd Indiana to their left and the last guns of

28 *OR* 30, pt. 1, 819; George A. Smyth, III, ed., *Leander Whitcomb Munhall's Letters Home, 1862-1865* (George A. Smyth Publishing Co., 1992), 45; *OR* 30, pt. 1, 812.

29 Noe, *A Southern Boy in Blue*, 205; Reep, "Guttamachrala," CSI.

Church's battery on the regimental right. Twenty-year-old Lt. DeWitt C. Downing of Company I mistook the recaptured works for the enemy's. In a letter home four days later, Downing told his family, "we charged on the Rebs and drove them from a log breastwork they had put up." Woodcock also recalled reaching the breastwork. He thought the Kentuckians, augmented by a small fragment of the 19th Ohio, charged nearly 200 yards, reaching what he called "a small barricade." The fragment of the 19th was mainly comprised of Company F and the color guard carrying the state colors, but counted no more than 35 men. It took a brief position on the right of Battery D, 1st Michigan, just as the last of Church's men departed.[30]

Lieutenant Woodcock witnessed the final struggle for Battery D, recalling how there were only enough men left to work two of the big guns. With all their horses dead, he continued, "it was impossible to haul off the pieces." The 9th Kentucky started the day with 213 men, but no more than 150 (including the attached Ohioans) rallied to make the determined counter-assault. The effort was doomed, but like the 82nd Indiana's charge, it helped buy some additional time for Battery D. In any case, the 9th did not linger long at the front for it too was taking fire from the right flank. Colonel Cram, "after an unsuccessful effort to change front" southward, ordered the regiment back. They retreated about a half a mile. Woodcock recalled crossing a small gully "literally filled with men who were so cowardly they would not raise their heads." Anger flashed through him at the sight of those huddled stragglers, so much so that Woodcock made a point of deliberately stepping down hard on one slacker's back as he passed.[31]

While Connell's and Beatty's men were struggling against McNair and Sugg/Gregg, John Brannan was seeking help for his crumbling line. He first dispatched Lt. Ira V. Germain up the Glenn-Kelly Road, hoping to find support. Germain stumbled upon Col. Charles G. Harker's brigade of Tom Wood's division, halted just north of Dyer Field while Wood and Thomas conferred. Germain burst into this discussion with the alarming news that Brannan's flank was turned and Van Cleve's division "broken." Thomas immediately ordered Wood to take Harker and move back south.[32]

30 *OR* 30, pt. 1, 814; "Dear parents," Letter of September 25, 1863, DeWitt Clinton Downing Letters, Western Kentucky University, Bowling Green, KY; Noe, *A Southern Boy in Blue*, 206; Reep, "Guttamachrala," CSI.

31 Noe, *A Southern Boy in Blue*, 207; *OR* 30, pt. 1, 814.

32 *OR* 30, pt. 1, 694.

Brannan's next thought was to find a rallying point for his crumpling right wing. Though Poe and Dyer fields were relatively flat, 1,200 yards to the northeast the ground abruptly rose where a spur of Missionary Ridge projected eastward to form Snodgrass Hill. Atop this spur sat James Negley's division of Thomas's XIV Corps. Though Thomas had originally sent Negley there in order to help defend against other threats, Brannan reasoned the location would be an excellent point upon which to rally his own command.

Meanwhile, back in Brotherton Field, Bushrod Johnson's Confederates had swept all opposition from their front and cleared both immediate flanks. The course of the fight altered Johnson's dispositions slightly. His initial success realigned his three brigades on a single long front, formed in a westward-facing arc. Fulton's brigade (the 1st/50th Tennessee and 7th Texas still attached) held the left and faced southwest, having helped Hindman's Confederates crush Jeff Davis's division. The rest of Sugg's men, once they passed through McNair's ranks, comprised the division's center, facing nearly due west astride the Dyer Road. McNair's brigade was still angled to the northeast, having had to battle its way through Connell's position.

The scene confronting these Confederates when they emerged into Dyer Field was nothing short of breathtaking. Mobs of Union soldiers were running in every direction. Here and there small clusters of Federals marked the remnants of units attempting to retreat in better order. Lieutenant Colonel Daniel H. Reynolds, commanding the 1st Arkansas Mounted Rifles, recorded that he "reached an open field through which the enemy were retreating in great confusion." To Bushrod Johnson the scene was "unspeakably grand." As far as he could see to both his right and his left, long lines of Confederate troops moved from the shadows of the timber into bright sunlight as Federals fled before them. It "made up a battle scene of unsurpassed grandeur." Lieutenant Colonel Snowden of the 25th Tennessee remembered the moment as the "most magnificent scene of the day, brigade after brigade emerging *en echelon* . . . and sweeping across [the field] with a wildness of enthusiasm." On the far side of the field, only a line of about 20 Union cannon appeared to offer any real resistance. The guns opened fire soon after the Rebels appeared. "Here," Johnson wrote, "General Hood gave me the last order I received from him on the field, 'Go ahead, and keep ahead of everything.'"[33]

33 *OR* 30, pt. 2, 457; "Sept. 20, Sunday," Daniel Harris Reynolds Diary, University of Arkansas, Fayetteville, Arkansas; *OR* 30, pt. 2, 457-458, 490.

Johnson's advance still left half of John Brannan's Federal division hanging on in Poe Field. It fell to the next echelon in the Rebel column, Hood's division commanded by Brig. Gen. Evander M. Law, to deal with this threat. Colonel William F. Perry of the 44th Alabama, in command of Law's brigade of Alabamians, comprised General Longstreet's third line of battle. The steady veterans moved along in the wake of Johnson's successful attack, passing over ground littered with casualties and the general detritus of battle. One member of the 4th Alabama took note of an odd sight: iron ramrods imbedded in tree trunks, fired by nervous or overly hasty soldiers who forgot to remove them after loading. According to Perry, his line stepped off at a slow pace that gradually increased as the excitement level rose and the Alabamians hurried to catch up with Johnson's line. They crossed over the first Union position (marked clearly by the rudimentary breastworks and numerous casualties) with "no perceptible resistance." As the brigade worked its way through the strip of timber bounding Brotherton Field on the west, however, Perry's formation increasingly lost cohesion until the brigade was little more than an "indiscriminate surging mass."[34]

About this time Perry noticed a threat to his right flank in the form of an unidentified Union regiment sweeping back westward in Poe Field. This unit (probably the amalgam of the 9th Kentucky/19th Ohio) was at least 200 yards to his north and posed only a limited threat, so Perry detached just his own 44th Alabama to deal with the potential problem while the rest of the brigade followed Johnson. Under the command of Lt. Col. John A. Jones, the 44th faced north and delivered several volleys through the timber in the direction of these Federals who, after an effort to change front to the south, promptly retreated. And there the 44th halted, seemingly forgotten. Jones neither moved north nor tried to rejoin the brigade. There was a long bloody day ahead, but the regiment would end it after suffering only six men wounded. While understandable, Perry's decision to detach the 44th weakened his own line and removed the regiment from the battle for the rest of the day.[35]

34 Robert T. Coles, "History of the 4th Regiment Alabama Volunteer Infantry, CSA," ADAH; William F. Perry and Curt Johnson, eds., "A Forgotten Account of Chickamauga," *Civil War Times Illustrated*, vol. XXXII, no. 4 (September-October, 1993), 55. Colonel Sheffield was injured in a fall from his horse the previous day.

35 Laine and Penny, *Law's Alabama Brigade*, 164. Laine and Penny identify this Union unit as the 17th Ohio, based on Colonel Connell's official report. However, it is more likely to have been the 9th Kentucky/19th Ohio. The timing of the 9th/19th's advance fits better with

Brig. Gen. Henry Louis Benning (right), former associate justice of the Georgia Supreme Court, commanded a brigade in Hood's division.
Miller, Photographic History

Perry's error was compounded by Col. William C. Oates. While Perry was dealing with the threat to his right, Oates's 15th Alabama holding his left lost contact with the 4th Alabama in the timber and drifted left until Oates emerged from the trees well south of the remainder of the brigade. By the time his command arrived in Dyer Field, Perry's brigade was off to another inauspicious beginning, similar to the previous day's action. His original five-regiment line of battle had broken into three distinct pieces, each of which would act independently of the others for the balance of the day.

Brigadier General Henry L. Benning, leading his four Georgia regiments in the line behind Perry, was also alert to threats from the right. Benning had orders to follow the Alabamians at an interval of 300 to 400 yards, but when Perry's speed increased Benning fell behind. He was hurrying to catch up when firing off to the north (the 44th Alabama) caught his attention. "I immediately changed the direction of march . . . so as to face this enemy," Benning reported. His regiments came on line at the north end of Brotherton Field, facing north, and advanced through the timber toward Poe Field. The 2nd Georgia anchored Benning's right flank, with the 17th, 20th, and 15th Georgia filling in the line to the left. Benning's command had also been hard hit on Saturday, and even though some stragglers caught up overnight, his was still a much-reduced formation. The Georgians stepped off this morning between 600 and 700 strong, holding a frontage of 150 yards. Across the length of the Poe farmstead,

Perry's own movements, and as noted, Colonel Cram specifically made an effort to change facing to the south before withdrawing, suggesting the 9th was the target of the 44th's fire. Laine and Penny also note that a section of a Confederate artillery battery halted here, as well, though it is not identified. These guns, which probably belonged to one of the three batteries attached to Bushrod Johnson's division, did not linger in the area for long.

250 yards distant, elements of John Croxton's Federal brigade were turning to face them.[36]

The breaking of the 14th and 31st Ohio regiments fully alerted Colonel Croxton to the danger threatening his right flank. During the earlier fight with A. P. Stewart's Confederates, Croxton moved Lt. Marco Gary's Battery C, 1st Ohio Light Artillery forward, adding Gary's firepower to his forward line, and instructed his supporting regiments to lie down in a small ditch about 100 yards to the rear. When Church's battery was overrun, Gary—who had been targeting enemy troops about 600 yards to his front—turned his attention to the right. Rebel infantry reached within 100 yards of his rightmost piece before falling back in the face of double canister. This attempt was made by some of McNair's or Sugg's men, now departed and heading west into Dyer Field. To support Gary, Croxton brought his two reserve regiments forward, intending initially to reoccupy Connell's breastworks and reestablish the line south of his position. However, as the 10th Kentucky moved, it discovered the breastworks were in flames, the smoke and heat rendering them unusable, and the primary threat was still to the right, not out in front. Colonel William H. Hays, commanding the 10th, halted his regiment facing south. The 4th Kentucky came into line alongside Hays's right. Together, both regiments put about 500 Federals into the fight against Benning's Georgians.[37]

Benning went right over to the attack. The brigade's adjutant, Capt. Ben Abbott, recalled that general placed himself at the head of the 2nd Georgia and sent Abbott to do the same with the 15th Georgia on the left. The Poe house, fully ablaze now, lay between the Georgians and Hays's Kentuckians, billowing even more smoke into the already murky atmosphere. "The old rebel yell broke out from every throat," noted Abbott, only to be met by a "volcano of fire." Abbott's and Benning's horses were both quickly struck, pitching both men to the ground. Their fall did not deter the Georgians, who ran right through the remnants of Church's battery and the handful of Federals trying in vain to save the remaining guns. Within a short time they were overwhelming Gary's pieces and Hays's newly formed line. Private Sherman Hendricks, sweating profusely as he worked one of Gary's pieces, took initial notice of this new attack when he and the other gunners saw fire "coming from our right." The Georgians

36 *OR* 30, pt. 2, 518.

37 Ibid., 426; I. B. Webster, "Chickamauga," *National Tribune*, July 2, 1891; *OR* 30, pt. 1, 423; Powell, "Numbers and Losses," CCNMP.

managed to close to within "two rods [about 11 yards]" of the Union field pieces. The desperate gunners were trying to haul the trails around when Confederate fire ripped through their position. Hendricks was one of those struck down.[38]

Just after Hays redeployed his line to the south, and while leading the 4th Kentucky into position alongside the newly reoriented 10th Kentucky, Croxton went down with a severe leg wound. Hays assumed brigade command and remained focused on the developing fight with Benning's Georgians. The Federal brigade's two remaining regiments, the 10th and 74th Indiana, still faced east, separated from Hays and the other half of the brigade by Battery C. Hays also noticed that more Confederates were behind the Georgians and streaming into Dyer Field.[39]

Despite the more distant threat, the odds immediately facing Hays were roughly equal. The Georgians couldn't extend their line farther west in order to overlap the Union right without opening gaps in their own front. Lieutenant Colonel Jones, who might have added the 44th Alabama's strength to Benning's line and provided the Rebels with a decided advantage, instead held his ground. The Rebels Colonel Hays saw moving past the 4th Kentucky's right belonged to yet another Confederate brigade pushing its way into the gap between Perry's and Benning's formations. Brigadier General Jerome B. Robertson's Texas Brigade began its advance on Benning's left behind Perry. After Benning peeled away, Robertson pushed westward following Perry's men. That changed once the Texans reached the eastern limit of Dyer Field, where Robertson heard the roar of musketry marking Benning's fight, and observed that a "considerable space" now separated his command from the Georgian battle line. Accordingly, Robertson wheeled his 1st, 4th, 5th Texas, and 3rd Arkansas to the right and advanced to support Benning's left.[40]

The fighting between Benning and Hays was intense and confusing. At one point an unidentified Rebel officer rode into the ranks of the Bluegrass soldiers of the 10th regiment, urging them to cease fire under the mistaken belief he was

38 Letter of September 26, 1863, Ben F. Abbott Papers, GDAH; Rev. S. Hendrick, "Chickamauga," *National Tribune*, November 5, 1891. Hendricks's name is incorrect in the *National Tribune* article. His wound was not severe, for he returned to duty within a month and was promoted to corporal on October 31, 1863.

39 *OR* 30, pt. 1, 423.

40 Laine and Penny, *Law's Alabama Brigade*, 164-166; *OR* 30, pt. 2, 511.

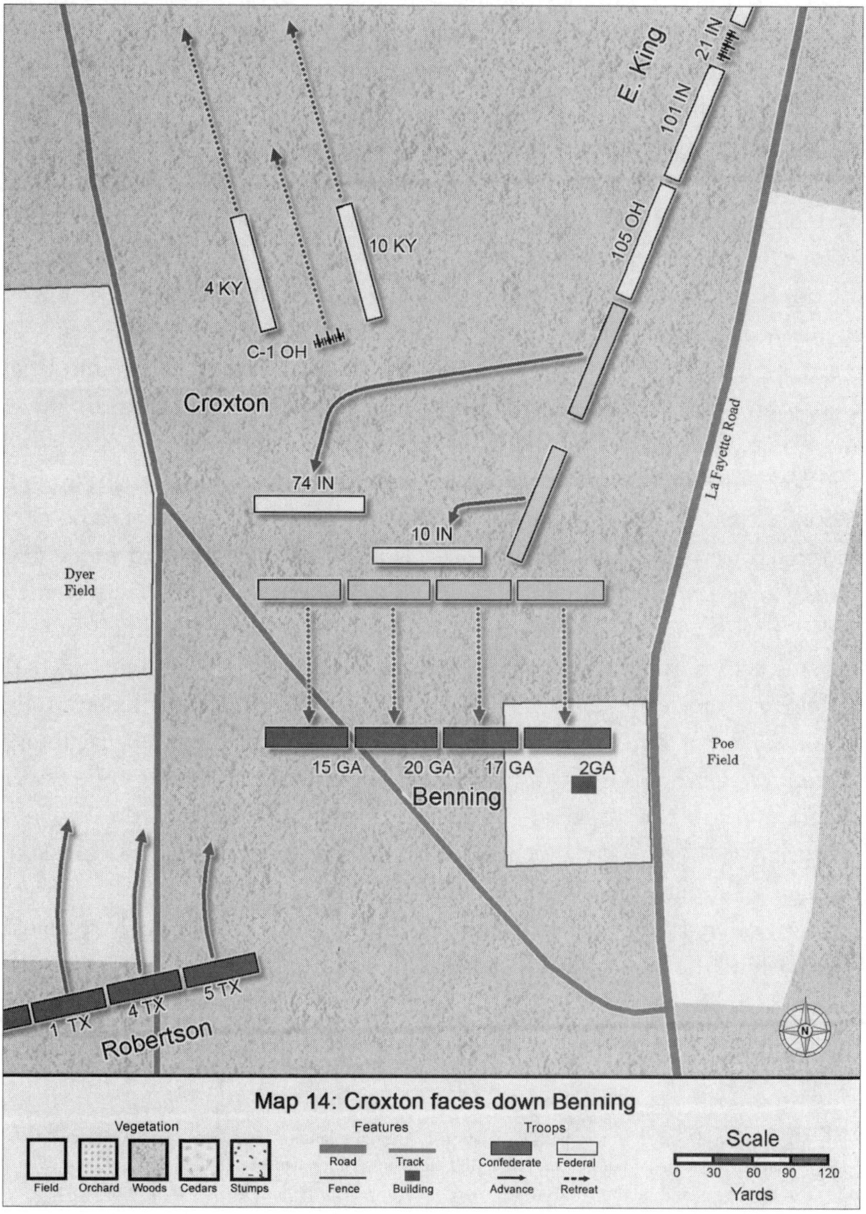

Map 14: Croxton faces down Benning

amidst a friendly command firing upon his friends. Two of the Kentuckians, Sgt. Richard Boyle of Company E and Capt. I. B. Webster leading Company I lived to recall the moment. Boyle and Webster mistook the man for a Federal officer and ordered their men to cease firing, but the troops protested that the soldiers on the far side of the field were most certainly shooting at them. This settled the matter as far as the 10th was concerned, and they continued firing.

The mystery officer, apparently realizing his blunder, turned back toward the Georgians, only to be shot down on his way.[41]

With the threat to his right immediate and potentially lethal, Hays decided to fall back: pushing past Benning's left, Robertson's Texas Brigade, about 1,000 strong, had rendered Hays's position untenable. The 4th and 10th Kentucky retreated northeast, but their withdrawal was far from orderly. When Colonel Hays directed the 10th to fall back toward Snodgrass Hill, Company E did not hear the order and found itself trying to hold the line alone. Seemingly abandoned, Sergeant Boyle formed the company, now numbering perhaps 40 men, and fell back behind the 10th and 74th Indiana. There, he ran into Brig. Gen. John Turchin of Joe Reynolds's division, next in line to the north. Boyle and Company E fought with Turchin's men the rest of the day.[42]

With his infantry support gone, Croxton down, and Hays caught up in a chaotic retreat, Lieutenant Gary could find no one to tell him what to do next with his battery. When Benning's Georgians closed once more to within 100 yards, Gary decided his foremost duty was to preserve his guns. Thirteen men and 25 horses had already been cut down, and Gary believed it "impossible to save the battery" unless he acted immediately. Accordingly, "without orders [I withdrew to the] left and rear." The 4th Kentucky had an even harder time of it. Major Robert Kelly, temporarily commanding the 4th, reported that things started to go wrong almost from the first. His command began its process of disintegration when he tried to change front: "the line was thrown into confusion and . . . very much scattered by the retreating troops breaking through it," admitted Kelly. Some in the 4th Kentucky stopped to help Gary get his guns safely away, further fracturing the regiment. Finally, Kelly retreated north behind the 10th and 74th Indiana. He reached that point with his colors, about 25 men from his regiment, and a handful of soldiers from other organizations.[43]

41 Richard Boyle, "Chickamauga," National Tribune, January 10, 1907, and Webster, "Chickamauga," *National Tribune*, July 2, 1891. Benning's men had been issued new uniforms on the way to Georgia with jackets of a dark steel gray. Webster and Boyle were not the only Federals deceived by their appearance. At this remove, it is impossible to identify the rider. Very few reports from Benning's brigade survive, and the toll on their officers was especially high.

42 *OR* 30, pt. 1, 423; Boyle, "Chickamauga," *National Tribune*, January 10, 1907.

43 *OR* 30, pt. 1, 427, 1062; Kelly was the divisional inspector, and Brannan assigned him to command the 4th after Lt. Col. P. Burgess Hunt was badly wounded on the morning of the 19th.

This series of Union retreats exposed the right flank of the 10th Indiana. Hoosier Pvt. Samuel F. Thompson had been watching with admiration as Gary's cannoneers "poured a terrible fire onto the Rebels for several minutes, unsupported." With Gary in trouble, Lt. Col. Marsh B. Taylor, commanding the 10th Indiana since the death of Col. William B. Carroll the night before, reacted instantly. "In that shrill, piping voice, [Taylor gave] the command, 'About face, fix bayonets, to the left oblique, charge!'" As the 10th Indiana rushed to meet Benning's men, Gary asked for help dragging his guns out of danger. Captain Thomas A. Cobb's Company A helped pull five of Gary's six pieces rearward where they could be limbered. They had to leave one gun behind, but not before a pair of quick-thinking sergeants, Theodore Stoughton and Barnhart Reichart, dismounted it from its carriage and threw the linchpins away, escaping "just as the Johnnies were on the point of laying hands on them."[44]

Ohio Pvt. Silas M. Childs was serving one of Gary's rifled six-pounders that early afternoon. He vividly recalled the moment years after the event: "The Confeds charged en mass [and] captured the 4th Mch Battery [Church's] just to the right. . . . Turning the same on [us] . . . cutting down men and horses by the dozen. We had but two rounds of ammunition left in our limber chests [before] being ordered back. We knew it to be a critical moment. . . . Our gun was trained on the captured gun and fired, striking it direct in the muzzle, dismounting it and throwing it in the air, killing several of the enemy." It was at that point, continued Childs, "I was stricken down with the last shell in my hands and left on the field for dead." Once away, Gary met General Brannan, who confirmed his decision to withdraw and ordered him toward the Snodgrass house.[45]

The 250 men of the 10th Indiana drove Benning's right back some distance. Benning, worried these new Federals might turn the right flank of his remaining line, ordered the rest of his men to fall back through Church's abandoned guns. Next, Lt. Col. Myron Baker brought the 74th Indiana up from behind and to the right of Taylor's 10th, extending the new Union line all the way out to the Glenn-Kelly Road. From there, the men of the 74th could see well into Dyer Field, and so more fully observe the true scope of the unfolding

44 Entry for September 20, 1863, Samuel F. Thompson Diary, WHS; James Birney Shaw, *History of the Tenth Regiment Indiana Volunteer Infantry, Three Months and Three Years Organizations* (Burt-Haywood Co., 1912), 233-234; Hendrick, "Chickamauga," *National Tribune*, November 5, 1891.

45 S. M. Childs Personal History, CCNMP. Childs was knocked unconscious for a time, but when he came to he found his way back into Federal lines later that day.

Union disaster. Captain Orville Chamberlain, adjutant for the 74th Indiana, described a chilling scene: "[I]mmense bodies of rebels in the field to the west and south." The nearest of these were Robertson's Texans and Arkansans tramping north and only a few hundred yards away.[46]

Despite their success repulsing Benning, Lt. Cols. Taylor and Baker quickly realized, as had Colonel Hays before them, that they could not hope to hold their new position for long. Nor could they figure out where the rest of Croxton's command had gone. When Hays took charge of Croxton's brigade, Col. Charles W. Chapman assumed command of both his own 74th Indiana and the 10th Indiana. Soon after, Chapman's horse was shot from under him, collapsing both man and animal into a heap. The fall broke Chapman's arm and knocked him out of action for the rest of the battle. Hays, meanwhile, had already disappeared with the Kentuckians. Taylor now took command of the Indiana regiments and fell back through the woods in a northeasterly direction, coming to rest somewhere behind Reynolds's line. Even that short retreat proved confusing. Samuel Thompson, after laboring to save Gary's artillery, "lost the regiment," and with several other stragglers eventually ended up on Snodgrass Hill.[47]

Benning's regiments suffered severely in this fight. They had already shed copious amounts of blood on the 19th, and on the 20th suffered just as severely. Though the brigade's combat strength on either given day fluctuated, in total Benning brought about 900 men into action during the battle of Chickamauga. Of those, 492 became casualties. Nearly 300 of those fell on Saturday. Even with another 100 to 150 late arrivals joining the brigade overnight, Benning took fewer than 700 men into action on the 20th. Losses in the 17th and 20th Georgia were especially severe, approaching a casualty rate of 60%. Officer casualties were cripplingly high: 17 of 23 fell in just the 20th Georgia alone. Benning's regimental organizations were already all but wrecked at the start of the day's fight, and when pressed by the Hoosiers, the brigade fell back in considerable confusion. Benning and Abbott both remounted on freshly captured artillery horses cut free from the traces but still in their harnesses, but neither officer could stem the retreat of the Georgians; they could only follow their men rearward. According to one account, Benning himself was completely

46 *OR* 30, pt. 2, 518-519; "Gen. H. V. Boynton," November 26, 1895, Orville T. Chamberlain Letters, 74th Indiana file, CCNMP.

47 Ibid; Entry for September 20, 1863, Thompson Diary, WHS.

distraught by the unexpected turn of events. Lieutenant Colonel Moxley Sorrel, General Longstreet's capable and always outspoken chief of staff, watched the bluff Georgian riding down the road with his new mount's "harness flying." According to Sorrel, Benning blurted out, "I am ruined; my brigade was suddenly attacked and every man killed!" Realizing the unlikelihood of an entire brigade being wiped in such a manner, Longstreet calmly reassured the brigadier all would be well, and instructed him gather the scattered remnants of his command.[48]

The final stroke against Benning was delivered by Maj. George Perkins's 105th Ohio of Col. Edward King's brigade. With Brannan's division gone, Joe Reynolds faced the same tactical problem that had bedeviled Brannan: a collapsing right flank. Reynolds's two brigades under King and Brig. Gen. John Turchin were deployed at the northern end of Poe Field in a staggered formation, both facing east. When Croxton's brigade started to unravel, he reported that fact to Reynolds, probably just before Croxton fell wounded and left the field. Reynolds rode over to take a personal look—just in time to witness Colonel Hays's retreat. The sight convinced the division leader to set his spurs and gallop back to his own lines, where he found Major Perkins and his 300 Buckeyes of the 105th in reserve. Without hesitation, Reynolds ordered Perkins to charge Benning's Rebels.[49]

The 105th was about to embark on one of the oddest adventures of the day. Many years later, Pvt. Charles Radcliff remembered Reynolds riding up to Perkins, pointing toward the enemy, and ordering the major to "have your men fix bayonets and charge right down thru there!" The men realized the effort was a forlorn hope, a desperate tactic that would likely result in their injury, death, or capture. Despite this grim prospect, Lt. Albion Tourgee of Company G, who would one day become the regiment's historian, proudly stated that not a man hesitated. What happened next amazed everyone who lived to tell the tale.[50]

No one was more surprised by the 105th's audacious charge than Benning's Confederates. "When we struck their flank," explained Tourgee, "they were

48 Powell, "Numbers and Losses," CCNMP; *OR* 30, pt. 2, 518; Letter of September 26, 1863, Abbott Papers, GDAH; Sorrel, *At the Right Hand of Longstreet*, 203.

49 *OR* 30, pt. 1, 441.

50 Charles K. Radcliffe, "Battle of Chickamauga," *National Tribune*, September 1, 1921. Albion W. Tourgee, *The Story of a Thousand: Being a History of the Service of the 105th Ohio Volunteer Infantry, in the War for the Union from August 21, 1862 to June 6, 1865* (S. McGerald and Son, 1896), 223.

already blown by their long charge through the woods. Startled by our bold assault, they scattered; many surrendering." According to one Ohio soldier-correspondent in Company K, the 105th took "about as many prisoners as there were men in the regiment." Not all of Benning's men were so quick to give up. As the 105th charged into and through their scattered ranks, a number of Georgians threw themselves on the ground and, after the Ohioans passed, fired into their rear. One of these shots struck Major Perkins in the leg and knocked him out of action, but the Buckeyes drove on a half-mile or more before halting near the Brotherton Road. For the moment there were no Rebels to be seen in any direction, but they knew plenty of angry Confederates were waiting behind them. Their amazing success thus far, however, left the Yankees full of confidence. "As we had cut through," wrote Charley Caley of Company F, "of course we could cut our way out again and did so."[51]

The 105th Buckeyes moved by the right flank, heading west through the timber. The path they followed remains one of the battle's lingering mysteries. Tourgee insisted they stayed in the cover of woods the whole time, reaching the Dry Valley Road somewhere west of Horseshoe Ridge before joining the general retreat of the Union XX Corps and XXI Corps toward Rossville. If so, they did it after Longstreet's attack turned north to strike at the Union forces coalescing on Horseshoe Ridge, which in turn allowed the small band of the 105th to pass through Longstreet's rear unnoticed. Another claim, however, further obscures the matter of their escape route. At some point during this odyssey Tourgee recalled meeting the wounded Confederate Brig. Gen. Daniel W. Adams and rescuing him from a couple of Union stragglers intent on robbery. Adams, it will be recalled, was wounded and initially captured in McDonald Field by members of the 11th Michigan of Colonel Stanley's brigade. The 105th, however, did not come anywhere near that part of the battlefield on September 20; where and how Tourgee was able to come upon General Adams remains unknown. For Reynolds's part, he did not see the

51 Ibid., 224; "Dear Friends at home," Letter from 'Wes' September 29, 1863, *Ashtabula Weekly Telegraph*, October 17, 1863; Tourgee, *Story of a Thousand*, 225; Letter of September 24, 1863, Caley Family Correspondence, University of Notre Dame, South Bend, Indiana. The distance from the 2nd Brigade Tablet on the west side of the La Fayette Road to the 105th Ohio stone marking the apex of the charge, just north of the Brotherton Road, is about six-tenths of a mile.

105th again that day and assumed the worst until, during the general retreat of the army that evening, he and the 105th met up again by chance at Rossville.[52]

Regardless of their route back to safety, the 105th Ohio's charge accomplished its purpose. With Benning in retreat, Reynolds had time to shift his two brigades into a defensive posture facing south, well supported with artillery. Joined by the 10th and 74th Indiana from Croxton, Reynolds now had nine regiments with which to anchor the southern end of Thomas's line. The Union right flank was finally stable, if not wholly secure.[53]

The same could not be said for the troops south of the breakthrough, where Alex McCook's men were facing disaster.

52 Tourgee, *Story of a Thousand*, 226, 238. Tourgee's account of his encounter with General Adams is corroborated by "Wes" of Company K, who also noted capturing General Adams. See "Dear Friends at home," *Ashtabula Daily Telegraph*, October 17, 1863. Adams had been carried to the rear by a litter party, hastily treated for his wound, and was in the process of being evacuated to the rear when apparently, the Federals carrying him left him propped against a tree. They may have learned of the disaster and abandoned their charge to escape capture.

53 The two Indiana regiments made no mention of Reynolds, but they did fall in behind William Hazen's brigade on Reynolds's immediate right, effectively replacing troops Reynolds shifted westward across the La Fayette Road.

Chapter Twelve

The Fight Comes to Sheridan:
Sunday, 11:30 a.m. to 1:00 p.m.

The exact moment Alexander McCook realized disaster was upon him is not known, but it could only have been a very short time after he left the side of Jeff Davis. The XX Corps commander had just sent his chief of staff, Lt. Col. Gates Thruston, south to find Brig. Gen. Robert Mitchell and the Union cavalry at Crawfish Spring with an order for the troopers to close up on his left as the XX Corps sidled northward. According to Capt. Isaiah McElfatrick, McCook's topographic officer, the XX Corps command group was due west of Davis's position, "about a half mile north of the Widow Glenn's" when Longstreet's blow landed. McCook estimated the time as 11:30 a.m., perhaps no more than 15 to 20 minutes after Longstreet's men crossed the La Fayette Road. It was time enough for their formations to give way, pursued by line after line of Confederates.[1]

With Davis's collapse, McCook's remaining command was reduced to exactly one brigade: Col. Bernard Laiboldt's. The rest of Phil Sheridan's men, it will be recalled, were already executing their orders to join Thomas's XIV Corps farther north. Even Laiboldt's availability was conditional; once the army completed the shift northward, Laiboldt was supposed to join the march to Thomas. Now, however, Laiboldt was the last uncommitted brigade in the corps, and McCook needed him. The XX Corps commander spurred his horse

1 *OR* 30, pt. 1, 956.

toward Laiboldt's position on what would come to be called Lytle Hill. As Laiboldt was soon to discover, a multiplicity of generals and their entourages were converging on his position.

The first to arrive, ahead even of McCook, was Jefferson C. Davis. Realizing his own men could not hold for long, Davis went in search of aid within moments of the attack. "If [Laiboldt] was there for the purpose of supporting my troops," barked Davis upon his arrival, "then it must be done immediately." Before the flummoxed colonel could even offer a reply, however, a breathless Lt. Horace N. Fisher of McCook's staff pounded up. Fisher was riding north along the Glenn-Kelly Road on some errand for the general behind what he thought was Tom Wood's position when, "to his utter astonishment," he spied Fulton's Rebels moving unopposed through the narrow band of timber towards him from the east. The bewildered Fisher galloped back to Laiboldt "and most strongly urged him to throw his brigade into the gap."[2]

Laiboldt was in a quandary: too many missions and too few troops. By now many of Davis's stragglers were visible. His division was clearly breaking, but was the greater danger there, or in the gap left by Wood? Formed as it was in a column of regiments, whatever must be done the brigade had to first redeploy to gain a wider frontage. Colonel Laiboldt was issuing the necessary redeployment orders when McCook rode up.

McCook's demeanor would later be cause for considerable debate. Some charged that the portly young corps commander was overwrought, even frantic. Members of McCook's staff would later loyally affirm their boss remained as calm as circumstances would admit, though his earlier anxiety had proved fully justified. However calm his outward manner, his next decision was clearly one made in haste: he ordered Laiboldt to immediately advance down the hill into the timber and drive back the Rebels. "Laiboldt suggested that we deploy," recalled Capt. J. L. Morgan of Laiboldt's brigade staff, but McCook's order was "peremptory. . . . To charge as we were."[3]

2 Ibid., 500. Fisher was not in good health. His horse fell on him back in August, crushing a vertebra. The resulting nerve damage produced a growing paralysis in his bowel and lower extremities. One side effect of this was that he was having trouble digesting food, and thus losing weight. By the time he left the army in October, his weight had fallen from 145 pounds to just 92. Horace Newton Fisher Papers, Library of Congress. Hereafter LOC.

3 *OR* 30, pt. 1, 950, 956, 958 all bear on McCook's demeanor; Henry A. Castle, "Sheridan with the Army of the Cumberland," *National Tribune*, October 25, 1900.

The lead regiment, the 73rd Illinois, was raised by Col. James F. Jacques in 1862. Jacques, a minister of the First Methodist Church in Springfield and a good friend of Illinois Governor Richard Yates (hence the 73rd 's nickname "Preacher Regiment") conceived the idea of raising an all-Methodist command when Lincoln called for more troops that second summer of the war. By end of August, the 73rd was departing for Kentucky and the war with a number of clergy in the ranks and Jacques's 12-year-old son William outfitted as a drummer boy. Its assignment to a brigade full of beer-drinking German Free-Thinkers was a bit of a culture clash. The "Preacher Regiment" eventually won acceptance, especially after its first hard fight at Stones River, where the Methodists stood up well in combat.

The men of the 73rd got little sleep the night before, plagued as they were by the cold and a lack of rations. Even worse, noted the regiment's commissary sergeant Riley Hoskinson, were the ominous tales being spread by confident and cocky Rebel prisoners: "They intend to give us the severest fight yet . . . as they have come prepared to meet 110,000 men." Reinforcements from all over the South were apparently on hand. "How much of this is truth, remains to be seen," concluded the sergeant.[4]

That morning drummer Willie was standing next to his father in "a good position . . . and had we been allowed to hold [it] until reinforcements . . . arrived, the history of the Battle of Chickamauga might have been differently written," he wrote years later. Unbeknownst to young Willie, Union reinforcements were a scarce commodity at the southern end of the battlefield that Sunday; the 73rd Illinois and its comrades were sorely needed and would have to advance alone into the teeth of the Rebel onslaught. Alexander McCook's order to "immediately advance" was greeted with dismay in the ranks. "The officers and men saw that this would be suicidal," recalled the younger Jacques, "but orders are orders, and the charge was made."[5]

The rash order to charge proved a grave mistake. Captain Tilman Kyger, commanding Company C of the 73rd Illinois, left a vivid description of what happened next. The "Preachers" led the brigade down the hill, passing just to the north of the Dyer tanyard (a collection of soaking pits, nitre vats and small shacks alongside the Glenn-Kelly Road) and entered the fringe of pine trees

4 Riley Hoskinson Journal, ALPL.

5 William G. Jacques, "Account of my experiences in, and capture in the battle of Chickamauga," Lilly Library, Indiana University, Bloomington, IN.

edging the eastern side of Dyer Field. There, Kyger recalled, "[we met] the advancing foe, coming eight lines deep toward us." The 73rd opened fire "amid a shower of balls flying from our front, right and left." Color Sergeant John Lewis fell almost immediately, "wounded in the leg . . . . The flag was taken up by [another] of the color guard," and then another, as each man went down in turn.[6]

In addition to this crippling enemy fire, the advancing Federals encountered yet another problem as they reached the tree line. As Laiboldt's men "rushed into the thicket," they were met by fleeing knots of Davis's panicked stragglers. The Illinois troops now checked their fire lest they hit their friends, and worse, Laiboldt's regimental lines were "thrown into confusion by the fleeing troops." Within a few minutes the 73rd was swamped. Each of the other three regiments, stacked one behind the other, watched as the unit in front melted into chaotic confusion in its turn. In dismayed frustration, the helpless Colonel Laiboldt could do nothing other than watch his brigade dissolve.

Behind the 73rd, Col. Joseph Conrad of the 15th Missouri attempted to correct this problem by halting to wait until the Illinois men opened enough space between themselves and his own line. Once that happened, he put his Missourians into a half-wheel to the right to shift out from behind the "Preachers." Before he could complete this maneuver, however, Conrad reported that the Rebels closed "in on our flanks, keeping up a heavy fire."[7]

The ranks of Zach Deas's brigade represented anything but parade-ground precision given their initial repulse, the breaking of the Union first line, and lengthy pursuit through the woods. But Deas's Alabamians retained enough cohesion to inflict serious damage on Laiboldt. "Their first line gave way like nothing," boasted a giddy Lieutenant Fraser, and soon thereafter "so did their second and third."[8]

General William Carlin was attempting to rally his own men in the open fields just to the north, and witnessed Laiboldt's collapse. Advancing in close order, thought Carlin, proved to be "a fatal error. . . . I saw the poor fellows struggling . . . but the enemy was too close at hand to permit Laiboldt to

6 Newlin, *Seventy-Third Regiment*, 225.

7 *OR* 30, pt. 1, 590, 592-593.

8 James A. Fraser Letter, "September 24, 1863," *Montgomery Daily Advertiser*, October 8, 1905.

deploy." Rebel bullets scythed through "the compact, almost solid mass of men only a few steps distant. The loss . . . was very great." Employed properly, thought Carlin, Laiboldt's men might have made a real difference. "If his brigade had advanced in line instead of in close column of divisions, it would have been a most opportune arrival and might have exerted a decisive influence on the battle." While hindsight suggests that this was unlikely given the odds they faced, they still could have at least limited the breakthrough, which might have allowed for a more orderly retreat for the rest of the attenuated right wing. Formed as they were, they accomplished nothing.[9]

The sudden turn of events shocked Maurice Marcoot, a member of the 15th Missouri. "[We] never had, up to this time, been repulsed in a charge," he recounted, "and . . . did not believe [we] could be. . . . Perhaps it might have been better had we awaited their coming." Once they entered the woods, explained Marcoot, "a withering volley" cut through their ranks. Before having "the opportunity to fire a single shot . . . the fight now became a desperate hand to hand encounter with bayonets and clubbed muskets." Nearly surrounded, Marcoot and his comrades fought their way out before breaking into "a fair footrace with our jubilant opponents."[10]

The 73rd Illinois and 15th Missouri were decimated, their survivors bolting rearward as best and as fast as they could. Farther back, the 2nd Missouri and 44th Illinois fared no better. The 44th was an unusual unit, including as it did two companies of Michiganders and one from Ohio; like the 2nd and 15th Missouri, it contained enough Germans to give it an unmistakably ethnic flavor. The men of the 44th were veterans, but none had faced quite this kind of crisis before. "It was the hottest place we have ever been in," opined Illinois Pvt. James Frazee in a letter to his sister that marveled at his escape: "how I got out as well as I did was a mercy, as men was killed and wounded at my very side. The Rebels outnumbered us greatly."[11]

General Rosecrans was just 400 yards north of Laiboldt's position when McCook issued his destructive order. The Army of the Cumberland's headquarters was a sizable affair that included not only Rosecrans's immediate staff, but the 438 officers and men of the 15th Pennsylvania Cavalry and the

9 Girardi and Hughes, *Carlin Memoirs*, 102.

10 Marcoot, *Five Years in the Sunny South*, 36.

11 "Dear Sister," September 29, 1863, James Frazee Letters, ALPL.

three companies of the 1st Ohio Sharpshooter Battalion, another 154 troops. The sharpshooters fit right in with Rosecrans's concept of elite, specially armed troops. In the wake of Col. Hiram Berdan's celebrated success in raising two regiments of United States Sharpshooters, a number of similar efforts began across the country. Various companies of sharpshooters were recruited in Ohio in 1862, including Capt. Gershom M. Barber's 5th Company. Sent to Nashville in the spring of 1863, Rosecrans enthusiastically welcomed them. Barber's 5th was combined with the 6th and 7th companies to form the special battalion. The men were armed with Spencers, drilled and trained as elite skirmishers, and given blue uniforms with green trim (instead of the infantry's traditional light blue facings) to distinguish them from other infantry. Rosecrans retained them with his headquarters guard, to utilize as he saw fit. On this day, at least two companies were nearby, along with the cavalrymen of the 15th Pennsylvania, sheltering in the small valley just west of the knoll Rosecrans claimed as his command point.[12]

Also present were civilians Charles T. Dana and the junior senator from Oregon, James W. Nesmith. Senator Nesmith, a War Democrat who strongly supported President Lincoln, served on the Senate Military Affairs Committee and was charged with overseeing the Federal Conscription Act. He also had prewar militia experience with active service against Indians in the Pacific Northwest, where he was befriended by a number of Regulars, some of whom were now serving in Rosecrans's army. One was Gordon Granger, who served in Oregon with the Mounted Rifles during the 1850s. Senator Nesmith's exact reason for visiting the Army of the Cumberland at this time was obscure, but likely he was serving as another set of independent eyes and ears for both his comrades in the Senate and for the administration. He arrived in Rossville on September 17 and joined Rosecrans's headquarters at Crawfish Spring the next day. Nesmith was a distance north of the knoll, perhaps a half mile to the north, "standing near a couple of batteries posted on a slightly elevated ridge," which must have been the guns Major Mendenhall placed at General Crittenden's

12 Hiram G. Berdan was a New York engineer and a celebrated target shooter before the Civil War. At the conflict's outbreak, Berdan proposed to recruit a regiment (later expanded to a pair of regiments) of sharpshooters, proven shots from all over the country who would be specially armed and equipped. Within a short time, similar elite formations were being proposed across the North. For more information, see C. A. Stevens, *Berdan's United States Sharpshooters in the Army of the Potomac, 1861-1865* (Press of Morningside Bookshop, 1984), 2-7.

earlier direction. Both Nesmith and Dana had front-row seats for the events now unfolding.[13]

Pennsylvanian Charles Kirk of the 15th Cavalry, the regimental adjutant, recalled that his unit was feeding its horses just before the break came: "My attention was attracted by flocks of small birds flying among us and over our heads from the battle line." This sudden flush of avian confusion "was so unusual," continued Kirk, "that I went to the brow of the hill." There, a thunderous roar of musketry, artillery fire, and thousands of human voices mingled into a magnificent din. Kirk climbed the rise just in time to witness Col. George Buell's rout and the first dramatic appearance of Bushrod Johnson's Rebels at the edge of Dyer Field. Rosecrans and his staff now had a similar panoramic vista that had so awed Johnson, though they were more distressed than impressed. Rosecrans's first thought was to halt the incipient panic beginning to grip his army. He turned to Col. William Palmer, the commander of the 15th Pennsylvania Cavalry, and directed him to "stop those stragglers!"[14]

In an unwitting imitation of the thousands of birds flushed moments before, the entire headquarters group rushed into action in every direction. Dana, who had been dozing in the grass, awoke with a start. His first sight as he blinked into wakefulness was of Rosecrans making the sign of the cross. "Hello," thought Dana. "If the General is crossing himself, we are in a desperate situation." Dana mounted his horse and looked about. "I saw our lines break and melt away like leaves before a wind," he wrote. It was then Dana discovered that "the headquarters around me had [similarly] disappeared."[15]

Bullets and shellfire passed over the heads of the fragmenting headquarters group, with some dropping low enough to find flesh. James St. Clair Morton was wounded here, a shell fragment ripping into his hand and shredding his sleeve. "We mounted and galloped off down the hill & up the other under a shower of shot & shell that was far from agreeable," remembered Colonel Sanderson. Rosecrans led the way, not waiting for the rest of his staff to ride with him. He rode south down the far side of the ridge behind cover, intent on finding either McCook or Sheridan.[16]

13 "Letter from the Seat of War," *Oregon Statesman*, November 9, 1863.

14 Kirk, *Fifteenth Pennsylvania Volunteer Cavalry*, 235-236.

15 Dana, *Recollections of the Civil War*, 115.

16 Entry for September 20, Sanderson Letters, OHS.

Senator Nesmith was left behind to make his own way out of danger as best he could. The senator was momentarily mesmerized by the sight unfolding around him. "The first intimation we had of an attack in that quarter was our troops flying through the cornfield pursued by immense masses of rebel troops," he wrote. With his attention focused on Dyer Field, Nesmith failed to notice Rosecrans's departure. He would not see the army commander again that day.[17]

Rosecrans's reaction was precipitate, but not unthinking. Grasping that Sheridan's division represented the last force available to him to try and set things right, the army commander's first instinct was to seek out those troops. Fortunately, the orders dispatched 40 minutes earlier forwarding Sheridan on to Thomas had been delayed sufficiently so that Brig. Gen. William Lytle's and Col. Luther Bradley's brigades were not yet beyond reach.

Rosecrans and his XX Corps commander, Alexander McCook, met on the Dry Valley Road just west of Lytle Hill. McCook assured his commander that "he had just ordered in Laiboldt's brigade . . . which he thought would soon set matters to rights." To Rosecrans, this optimistic assessment sounded like a glimmer of good news, especially if Sheridan's other two brigades could deploy against the Rebel flank at the same time. Either McCook was too flustered to say, or Rosecrans too overwrought to hear, that McCook had already sent orders to Sheridan to the same effect. No longer trusting middlemen, Rosecrans told the befuddled McCook, "I would go to see the other two brigades" personally, and departed. Like Crittenden before him, McCook was now fully usurped. Rosecrans later admitted, "I gave [McCook] no special orders" before riding away.[18]

Since his view was blocked by Lytle Hill, the commanding general could not see—and hence did not realize—Laiboldt's travails. Others did. Trailing the general at some length, Colonel Sanderson and the majority of the staff were suddenly awash in fleeing soldiers from Carlin's, Martin's, and now Laiboldt's shattered commands. The experience completely overwhelmed Sanderson. "In that brief moment," he wrote, "so many things occurred, that it is impossible to describe with any kind of accuracy." He did recall "the hill rapidly filling up with stragglers who broke from the center and fled." Their progress impeded,

17 "Letter from the Seat of War," *Oregon Statesman*, November 9, 1863.

18 *OR* 30, pt. 1, 941.

Sanderson and the others lost sight of their commander. By galloping south in such haste, Rosecrans effectively cut himself off from the machinery of army command.[19]

Senator Nesmith was caught up in this rout, much to his dismay and growing anger. "I was first at the point where the enemy pierced our lines," he informed his cousin Harriet, "and did not leave until everybody else did, and then rode slowly over an open space of a quarter of a mile under a most terrific fire, all the while extemporizing bad words at the cowardice of most wearing shoulder straps."[20]

Captain Horace Porter, an ordnance officer and 1860 graduate of West Point, was equally appalled. His horse stepped on a nail and he was prying it out with his saber-tip when a flood of refugees surrounded him. Remounting, Porter rode up to the crest of the hill just west of the Dry Valley Road and met former classmate James P. Drouillard. "I was going no farther," declared Porter emphatically, "as long as we could hold ten men together." Both officers struggled to restore order. Over and over they assembled a squad or small company, only to have the men melt away when a shell burst too close for their comfort. One stampeded soldier threatened Porter with a bayonet. Once the men were over their initial panic, however, Porter's and Drouillard's entreaties took effect. Within a short time they scraped together an impromptu battalion of rattled men capable of fighting to protect the Dry Valley Road and the Union path of retreat.[21]

More by accident than design, Phil Sheridan was already executing Rosecrans's intended plan. Lytle's and Bradley's (Walworth's) brigades were just beginning to move up the Glenn-Kelly Road at the double-quick on their way to Thomas when Longstreet's assault fell against the Federal right. Ahead of his column, Sheridan witnessed Laiboldt's disaster and, about the same time, received McCook's "most urgent order to throw in my other two brigades." Sheridan's mood had not improved from the previous night. Earlier that morning he had chewed out William Lytle for taking the time to make sure his brigade got its rations, his short-tempered dressing-down of the poet

19 Entry for September 20, Sanderson Letters, OHS.

20 "Dear Cousin Harriet," Nashville, September 23, 1863, James W. Nesmith Papers, Oregon Historical Society.

21 "Dear Sister," October 3, 1863, Horace Porter Papers, LOC. In 1902, Porter's efforts would be recognized with the Medal of Honor.

The "Poet-Soldier," William H. Lytle (left), was mortally wounded near the crest of the hill that would later bear his name.
Battles and Leaders

attributable to frayed nerves. When Laiboldt's men were flung recklessly into action by McCook's foolish order, unsupported and with little hope of success, the directive to throw in his other two brigades struck Sheridan as a repeat of the tactics that led to Bradley's mauling the previous afternoon. Bad generalship was the cause, and Sheridan was not shy in expressing his opinion on the matter. The Irishman accosted Laiboldt and, within earshot of Captain Morgan, used "language more forcible than polite regarding the manner of our going in." Laiboldt's losses might have been even worse had Lytle's brigade not appeared in a timely fashion.[22]

William Haynes Lytle could have served as the prototype for the ideal Victorian. He was from a prominent family, a proven soldier in both the Mexican War and the current struggle, and yet possessed a sensitive side. Lytle was a poet of note. His most famous work, "Antony and Cleopatra," was published in 1859 and gained him a measure of national repute. Like the stereotypical poet, he had his moody aspect. Lytle was often his own worst critic, destroying some of his best work before it ever saw print when he thought it did not measure up to his exacting standards. Some of the work that did reach the public did so only through the intervention of friends. He once proposed to a young lady, only to be rebuffed, after which he carried an air of unrequited and tragic love. Bouts of depression debilitated him, and many of those closest to him thought he lacked focus, despite his many talents. In war, however, Lytle found his niche. Simply put, he was a superb leader. When the

22 *OR* 30, pt. 1, 580; Henry A. Castle, "Sheridan with the Army of the Cumberland," *MOLLUS*, vol. 43, 172.

Civil War broke out, he wasted no time securing a commission as colonel of the 10th Ohio in May 1861.[23]

Lytle proved capable of both enforcing discipline on raw troops, and retaining their respect. He drilled the 10th into a superb regiment, leading them into their first action at Carnifex Ferry in September 1861. Wounded there, he next commanded a camp of instruction at Bardstown while he recuperated. Upon returning to field service, he was assigned a brigade in Maj. Gen. Ormsby M. Mitchel's division of Maj. Gen. Don C. Buell's army, serving in that capacity through the summer and fall of 1862. In the arduous march from Alabama to Louisville, when Buell's force was racing to catch up to Bragg during the Kentucky campaign, Lytle commanded the rear guard. For this duty, according to Ohio newspaperman Whitelaw Reid, "he received from General Buell the warmest commendations." At Perryville, the 10th Ohio (one of the regiments in his brigade) proved their mettle. Surprised and outflanked by two Confederate brigades, Lytle and the 10th attempted to organize a counterattack. The regiment suffered brutally, losing 50% of their complement; but retreated only grudgingly. Of their fight John Fitch, one of the earliest historians of the Army of the Cumberland, wrote glowingly that "surrounded . . . by masses of the enemy, their numbers diminishing at every step, the regiment cleared its way" back to the main line. When Rosecrans took command of the army that October, in recognition of the 10th's discipline and fortitude, he reassigned them to act as the army's provost guard.[24]

War might have been Lytle's forte, but it extracted a hefty price. In addition to the severe leg wound Lytle suffered at Carnifex Ferry, in his next combat at Perryville he was once again wounded. This time he was struck in the head and left on the field for dead. Even he thought he was done for, managing a suitably Victorian epitaph when he told a fellow officer to leave him: "'You *may* do some good yet, I can do no more, let me die here.'" Fate thought otherwise. Instead of dying, Lytle was captured. He recovered, was eventually exchanged, and rejoined the army in the spring of 1863. At Bridgeport that August, the men of the 10th Ohio presented their former commander with a jewel-encrusted

23 Ruth C. Carter, ed. *For Honor, Glory & Union: The Mexican & Civil War Letters of Brig. Gen. William Haines Lytle* (University Press of Kentucky, 1999), 15-20.

24 Whitelaw Reid, *Ohio in the War: Her Statesmen, Her Generals, and Soldiers*, 2 vols. (Robert Clarke Co., 1895), vol. 2, 881; John Fitch, *Annals of the Army of the Cumberland* (Stackpole Books, 2003), 241.

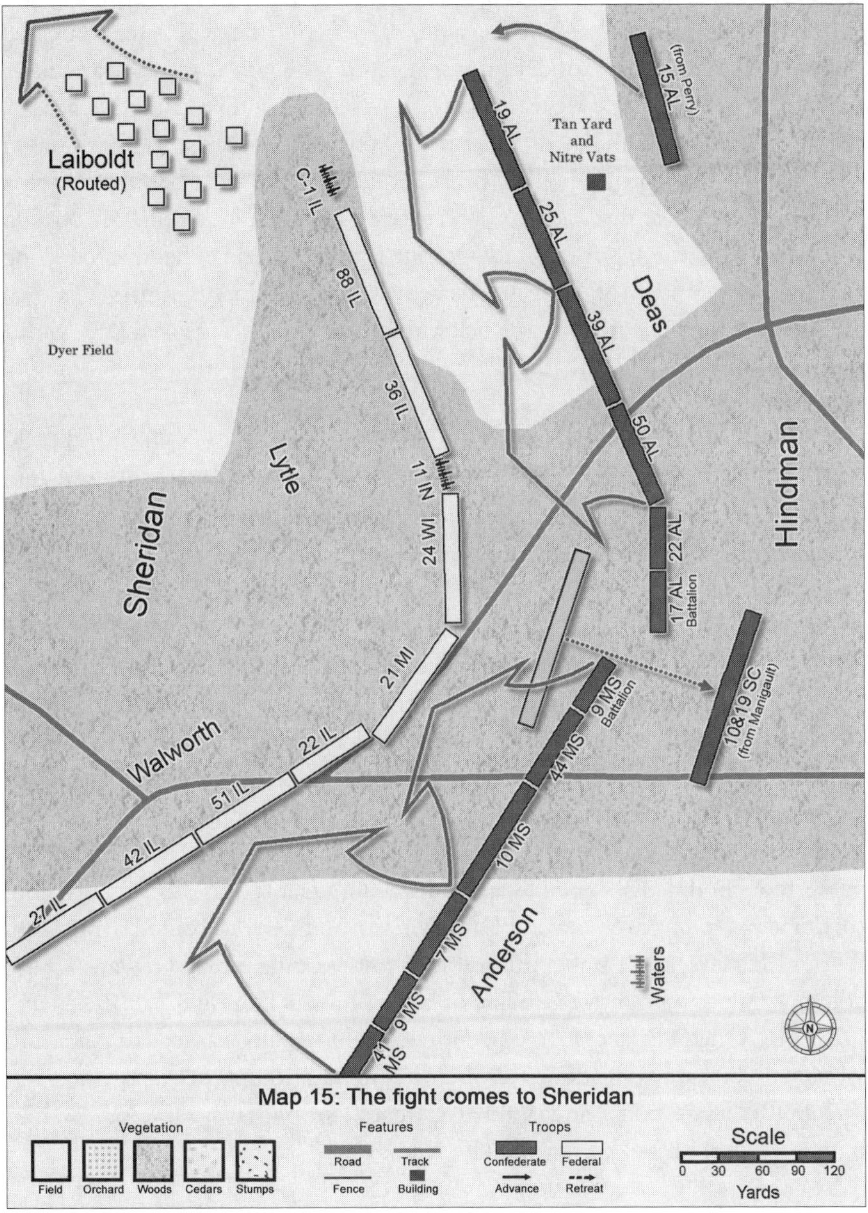

Map 15: The fight comes to Sheridan

brooch in the form of a Maltese Cross, adorned with Gaelic symbols (the 10th was an Irish regiment) as a token of their esteem for their old colonel.[25]

25 Kenneth Noe, *Perryville: This Grand Havoc of Battle* (The University Press of Kentucky, 2001), 269; Carter, *For Honor, Glory & Union*, 222-223.

Lytle was idolized by his young aide, Lt. Alfred Pirtle, who later confessed "how I did love Lytle . . . under his warm exterior he was as warm hearted as a woman." Pirtle regarded the general as a second father, and the general reciprocated. That 20th day of September, however, Lytle rose in a dark mood that alarmed his protégé. The brigadier and Pirtle were sitting under a convenient tree near the Widow Glenn cabin when Lytle inquired, "My boy, do you know we are going to fight two to one today?" Sheridan had passed along the unwelcome news of Longstreet's arrival, and, no doubt, a bit of his own gloomy perspective. Pirtle must "stick with him to the last," insisted Lytle with a note of finality that left the lieutenant shaken. Had the general felt a premonition?[26]

Sheridan had been right about the odds. Lytle was moving his brigade up the Dry Valley Road, each regiment in column of companies with the 36th and 88th Illinois in front. The four Napoleons and two 3-inch rifles of Capt. Arnold Sutermeister's 11th Indiana battery came next, followed by the 21st Michigan and 24th Wisconsin. On the 19th Lytle mustered 1,556 infantry, but his numbers were a bit smaller now. Even though the brigade had taken no losses yet, so quickly had come the order to move that one company from each regiment had been left behind on picket, to catch up as best they could. Now the brigade numbered about 1,400 bayonets. Heading as they were for Thomas, there was no immediate expectation of combat. Suddenly, Lt. John Turnbull of Company C, 36th Illinois, dashed up in a lather. Turnbull had just come from the brigade skirmishers, not yet recalled from the right flank. There, he had witnessed Hindman's Confederates advancing against Jeff Davis's division, their line extending well beyond Carlin's right. With Carlin routed, Brig. Gen. Arthur M. Manigault's Rebel brigade was now heading directly toward Lytle's column. "We should move into line of battle," urged Turnbull, "for the enemy [is] close." One of Rosecrans's unidentified aides, detailed earlier as a guide and who had left army headquarters before the disaster struck, "laughed" at Turnbull's suggestion "and intimated that Turnbull was scared." Within minutes, Turnbull's distress would be vindicated.[27]

26 "Dear Pa," September 23, 1863, Alfred Pirtle Papers, Filson Historical Society, Louisville, KY; Alfred Pirtle Memoir, "Leaves of my Journal," Lytle Family Papers, Cincinnati Historical Society.

27 Lyman G. Bennett and William M. Haigh, *History of the Thirty-Sixth Regiment Illinois Volunteers, During the War of the Rebellion* (Knickerbocker and Hodder, 1876), 467-468.

The swell of combat and Sheridan's revised orders came almost simultaneously. While Laiboldt was charging in the wrong formation down the hill that was soon to bear General Lytle's name, Lytle's brigade was moving up it, the 88th Illinois in the lead. The 36th Illinois followed. Behind them, Lytle sent Pirtle with orders for the 11th Indiana to move up and unlimber so as to fire up the Glenn-Kelly Road into Dyer Field. Behind Sutermeister's guns, the 21st Michigan and 24th Wisconsin struggled to extend Lytle's right. For the moment both units were falling a bit behind, slowed by the deploying cannon.

Sergeant Austin Stebbins was with Company D of the 88th Illinois. "Looking up on a hill 30 or 40 rods away, we saw a battery unlimbering. . . . [W]e supposed it was our battery, and we were going up to support it." Suddenly, the 88th saw a shower of stars: "Rosecrans, McCook, and [Sheridan] came riding down from the direction of the battery. . . . Rosecrans rode through our regiment and came up to the rear of our colors. . . . I remember just how he looked and how his voice rang out. "Fix Bayonets—Forward—Double-Quick—Charge!" "They took us into a very hot fire," marveled fellow Illinoisan Capt. Daniel Barnard, commanding Company K. "We double-quicked to gain a ridge and form our line to meet the shock," recalled Cpl. John Ely, a member of Barnard's company: "[T]he bullets began to whiz and the men commenced falling."[28]

The battery the 88th Illinois was racing to support was not their own. Captain Mark Prescott's Battery C, 1st Illinois Light Artillery, had been placed atop the hill earlier by Captain Hescock in support of Laiboldt. When Laiboldt's men charged down the hill and into the teeth of disaster, no one told Prescott what was happening. Prescott tried to engage, but his targeting was hindered by Laiboldt's disintegrating formation. "[M]en were coming through my battery in such a confused mass," reported Prescott, "that it was impossible to fire without killing our own men." The Rebels were laboring under no such compunction. Battery C, noted Prescott, was receiving "showers of bullets from both my front and left flank, I thought it prudent to withdraw." Some of those bullets, fired by enemy sharpshooters, struck with unerring accuracy. Confederate Lt. William Mead commanded a small detachment of nine men,

28 A. E. Stebbins, "A Daring Movement," *National Tribune*, October 19, 1899; "Dear Sister," September 21, 1863, Daniel E. Bernard Letters, Newberry Library, Chicago, IL; Entry for September 20, Ely Diary, CCNMP. Stebbins originally said Crittenden was present as well, but based upon my research, I assume he meant Sheridan. Crittenden was nowhere nearby at the time.

hand-picked for marksmanship and armed with imported English Whitworth Rifles. Mead and his section moved forward when the division stepped off. Until they reached Dyer Field, Mead had little chance for useful employment. But now, with Prescott's guns outlined on the distant crest, they went to work. "I got within 500 yards of this battery . . . and poured a fire into it for twenty minutes," wrote Mead. Surveying the damage after the fight, the lieutenant reported with satisfaction that his fire had been highly effective.[29]

Lytle brought the 36th Illinois in on the 88th Illinois's right, extending the line down the slope towards Sutermeister's cannon. "By company, into line," he barked, the order echoing down the ranks of the 36th. The newly arrived men from Illinois "were falling on every hand, thick and fast," lamented its regimental history, "but they formed a good line and moved rapidly to the crest." Laiboldt's "dead and wounded obstructed the way, while men, horses and artillery were scattered in great confusion." This pandemonium was augmented when one of Prescott's battery wagons, "swinging round with almost lightening speed struck a dead tree, which caused the top to break off, coming down into Company F and injuring two men."[30]

Lytle's sudden appearance checked the Confederate onslaught. Deas's Alabamans were by now out of breath and, as Deas later admitted, "somewhat scattered." The appearance of two fresh blue-clad regiments brought them to a halt well short of the crest, which allowed the last of Laiboldt's stragglers to make good their escape. The 19th Alabama, holding Deas's right, had further reason to halt; the regiment was taking rounds from the rear. That fire was not coming from men in blue, but from Rebels, and from fellow Alabamians to boot.

Colonel William Oates and his 15th Alabama were having their second difficult day in a row. Evander Law's brigade had suffered both multiple changes in command and significant tactical fragmentation on September 19. Law himself was aghast that his old brigade was experiencing such difficulties, and said as much to Oates that very morning when he warned the latter to watch Colonel Perry, lest he go "to flickering" again. Perry wasn't "flickering," but now it was Oates's turn to disappoint. The 15th Alabama stepped off on Perry's left. "When we crossed the [La Fayette] road," Oates recollected, "it raised a tremendous dust and soon after I could see only a few scattering men of

29 *OR* 30, pt. 1, 600; William L. Mead Report, Braxton Bragg Papers, WRHS.

30 Bennett and Haigh, *Thirty-Sixth Illinois*, 468.

the Union army running away." As Perry's line advanced through Brotherton Field and into the belt of timber, the 15th somehow lost the guide completely, broke contact with the 4th Alabama on its right, and drifted southwest. Now, nearly 800 yards south of where he should have been and effectively alone on the battlefield, Oates spotted some fighting off to his left front, where "Federals in solid phalanx . . . were beating the Confederates back down the slope through the open field."[31]

While hurrying to help, a shell fragment struck Oates a glancing blow on the left hip, tearing his coat and knocking him to the ground. Badly bruised and stunned, he took a minute to regain his feet. His 15th Alabama, however, had surged onward without him. The Alabamians were still in the timber directly behind the 19th Alabama of Deas's command when, in the confused excitement of the moment, Oates's men leveled their rifled muskets and opened fire directly into the backs of their comrades. "The 15th . . . began a heavy enfilading fire upon me," reported an angry Col. Sam McSpadden of the 19th, which he headed off by the expedient of sending his own colors to the field's edge and having the bearers wave them prominently. That did the trick. The 15th ceased fire and moved up onto the 19th's right flank.[32]

A mortified Oates would later insist that his men did not fire into the 19th Alabama. Even though he was hobbling along well behind his men, Oates claimed that his shouted cry of "'Don't fire, Fifteenth, until you are ordered!'" was fully obeyed. He admitted that the two regiments did intermingle some when a pair of companies on the 15th's left passed through the two rightmost companies of McSpadden's line, but Oates insisted "there was not a shot fired by the Fifteenth until after it passed the Nineteenth." The allegation troubled Oates even years later, when he stated, "how Colonel McSpadden could make all these statements in his official report I am unable to see."[33]

Oates was wrong. The 15th did indeed fire on the 19th, though how much damage it inflicted can never be ascertained. Perhaps the 15th fired a full volley, perhaps only a scattering of shots, but the sudden appearance of the 15th was an

31 William C. Oates, *The War Between the Union and the Confederacy and its Lost Opportunities with a History of the 15th Alabama Regiment and the Forty-eight Battles in which it was Engaged* (Neale Publishing Company, 1905), 255-256.

32 *OR* 30, pt. 2, 334.

33 Oates, *The War Between the Union and the Confederacy*, 256.

Zachariah C. Deas (right), a brigadier general from Alabama. *Library of Congress*

additional distraction that, added to the appearance of the pair of Federal regiments to his front, helped check Deas's advance, if only briefly.

Zach Deas's line was now also taking a battering from the 11th Indiana. With two regiments atop the hill, Lytle sent his Hoosier gunners into action on their flank. Captain Sutermeister was having trouble finding suitable ground to deploy all six guns, and the enemy was working forward at dangerously close range. His 1st and 2nd Sections (the four Napoleons) unlimbered, but had trouble finding targets. Accordingly, Sutermeister sent his 3rd Section of 3-inch rifles under Lt. Henry M. Williams "still farther into the woods" in an effort to enfilade that part of Deas's line visible out in Dyer Field. "Here," noted Williams dryly, "our active work began."[34]

The 22nd Alabama, holding the brigade left, received a heavy dose of this artillery fire. Alabama Capt. Harry Toulmin noted that Lytle's brigade was doing considerable damage, "obstinately contest[ing] every foot of ground. . . . Here took place a terrible conflict, which lasted about 20 minutes, and in which we lost many brave spirits." One of those "brave spirits" was the 22nd's commander, Lt. Col. John Weedon, who was killed attempting to storm Lieutenant Williams's guns. Weedon fell within just a few paces of the smoking fieldpieces. The regiment's second color-bearer of the day, Lt A. B. Renfro also fell with a shot through the head. Weedon's fall thrust Captain Toulmin into command.[35]

The 22nd was further discomfited by the entry of Lytle's other two regiments into the fray. The 24th Wisconsin arrived first, coming into action on

34 John Otto, *History of the 11th Indiana Battery* (n.p. 1894), 10.

35 *OR* 30, pt. 2, 336.

the right of the 36th Illinois and Williams's rifles. Moving up by column of platoon, the Badgers rushed into the fight "amid a pall of dust that almost smothers the men," recounted Pvt. Daniel Davis of Company I. By this time Lytle was back down at the foot of the hill after placing his left. The poet-general halted the Badgers in battle line. "Stand firm, boys," he urged. "Stand like iron." Again the bevy of senior commanders was recognized. Sergeant Eugene Comstock of Company B was shocked to see Sheridan, McCook, and Rosecrans all there, and all urging the 24th to "go in, Badger Boys, go in Wisconsin, give it to them, 24th!"[36]

When the 24th surged over the southwest shoulder of the hill, it encountered Deas's men at an extremely close range. One Badger recalled the enemy as being "only two musket lengths" away, or nearly muzzle-to-muzzle. The Alabamians buckled at the unexpected blow, falling back in some disorder. "We drove their first line and maintained our position," bragged Wisconsin Lt. Robert Chivas, also of Company I, "keeping up a steady and destructive fire on the enemy."[37]

The 21st Michigan slammed into place alongside the Wisconsin men with equal fervor. Wolverine Maj. Seymour Chase described the movement: "The Col. gave the order, 'forward into line' and the whole reg't came into line as handsomely and steady as if on battalion drill. . . . We advanced in line . . . some twenty rods to the crest of the hill." There, continued Major Chase, when the men from Michigan discovered some of Laiboldt's stragglers still to their front, Colonel McCreery "ordered the men to lie down, as the bullets were whistling thick and fast." The officers dismounted. McCreery turned his horse over to the bugler and let the stragglers pass through. Then, added Chase, "the Col. gave the order to 'rise up,' and 'ready, aim, fire,' rang out clear and strong. It was a fearful odds against us, but we checked them," concluded the officer with evident pride.[38]

36 *Daily Wisconsin*, October 19, 1863; William J. K. Beaudot, *The 24th Wisconsin Infantry in the Civil War: The Biography of a Regiment* (Stackpole Books, 2003), 233. A column of platoons put a regiment in a wide column, with a half-company front, one behind the other. A full regiment would have 20 lines in column.

37 *Milwaukee Sentinel*, October 10, 1863.

38 "Dear Sir," Seymour Chase to Mr. McCreery, McCreery Family Papers, UMich. It is very likely that, given the 21st's Michigan's position, many of those stragglers were from Carlin's brigade.

Lytle's arrival might have been enough to break Deas's attack—had the Alabamians been unsupported. The bulk of Thomas Hindman's division, however, had yet to weigh into this action.

Arthur Manigault's large brigade included his own 10th/19th South Carolina and three more regiments of Alabamians, the 24th, 28th, and 34th. His brigade was the largest in the division, counting 2,025 men in his ranks. Formed in a single line, this also left Manigault to contend with a large, unwieldy frontage of at least 500 yards. Initially Manigault's men faced no serious opposition, for their entire front was well south of Carlin's right flank, but they did move through several hundred yards of timber, and as they advanced their exuberance got the better of them. "When we had gone about three hundred yards," noted Lt. Joshua Callaway of the 28th Alabama's Company K, "our skirmishers encountered those of the enemy, and as soon as the firing commenced all order and control was lost, the men raised the 'War Whoop,' 'the yell,' 'the Battle Cry,' and away they went like a gang of mad tigers or demons. . . . [T]he enemy fled as if Old Scratch had been after them."[39]

Calloway and his comrades were driving Sheridan's pickets (including Lieutenant Turnbull, who tried to give warning) left in place to screen Carlin's flank. This was a normal procedure, designed to hide the movement of large bodies of troops from enemy scouts until they were safely away, but now it left a mere scattering of Federal skirmishers to oppose Manigault's 2,000 troops. Given the lack of any troops backing those skirmishers, it is no surprise that the Yanks scrambled rearward on the run. Further excited by the precipitate chase, however, Manigault's line became badly disordered. On the brigade right the South Carolinians advanced largely through the timber dividing the Brotherton and West Brock fields, while the course of Manigault's three Alabama regiments carried them through the large open expanse of West Brock Field. The combination of dust, smoke, trees, and heedless enthusiasm split the brigade into multiple pieces.

In an attempt to correct the organizational chaos, Manigault ordered a halt. In the center of the brigade, the 24th Alabama and the left half of the 10th/19th South Carolina complied. However, Col. James F. Pressley and roughly half of the large 10th/19th South Carolina—350 men—failed to hear the bugles signaling the command. Attempting to keep pace with Deas and therefore

39 Judith Lee Hallock, ed., *The Civil War Letters of Joshua K. Callaway* (University of George Press, 1997), 136.

guiding to the right, Pressley angled his line northward, emulating the 22nd Alabama's movement. On Manigault's other flank, the 28th and 34th Alabama also failed to heed the halt order. The 28th lost contact with the 24th Alabama's left sometime during the charge, well before Manigault called a halt. As a result, both the 28th and 34th regiments pushed west, oblivious to Manigault's stop order.[40]

This confusion left only Pressley's northernmost half of the 10th/19th South Carolina supporting Deas's brigade. Lagging a bit, the Gamecocks came into action first against the 21st Michigan as the Wolverines were savaging Deas's 22nd Alabama. Part of Pressley's line also struck the first of the four Illinois regiments in Colonel Walworth's (formerly Bradley's) brigade, the last of Sheridan's troops to enter the fight. Effectively unsupported, the South Carolinians would be overmatched if Walworth could get his whole force into action, but this disadvantage was initially offset by the fact that Pressley's line took Walworth's men by surprise.

Colonel Nathan Walworth was hustling his brigade up the road, following Lytle just as ordered, when, he reported, "we were assailed by a heavy fire of musketry." The 22nd Illinois was in the lead and Walworth "immediately ordered [it] to face the enemy and check them if possible." The 22nd, numbering only about 225 men, faced some 350 South Carolinians (less those engaging the 21st Michigan), and was further disadvantaged by being strung out from the flank march. The men went into action in a loose line of battle—there was no time to properly form. Before the 22nd Illinois could be overwhelmed, however, Walworth hurried up the 51st Illinois and placed them on the 22nd's right.[41]

Sergeant George Pratt of Company A, 51st Illinois, found himself in the thick of this fight. With growing alarm, he realized the Rebels "gained a lodgment in the timber, and were moving around the left of the brigade firing on us from three directions. Just at this time Generals Rosecrans and Sheridan rode up to the line of the 51st and by the hardest of fighting we checked the advance of the enemy for a few minutes." The 51st was in no better shape than

40 William Lee White and Charles Denny Runion, eds., *Great Things are Expected of Us: The Letters of Colonel Irvine C. Walker, 10th South Carolina Infantry, C.S.A.* (University of Tennessee Press, 2009), 195.

41 *OR* 30, pt. 1, 595. The full 10th/19th numbered 676 officers and men, but only half were engaged here.

the 22nd. After their 94 casualties of the previous day, and with a company still away on skirmish duty, the 51st now numbered fewer than 190 officers and men. Together, however, the 22nd and 51st, combined with the 21st Michigan's fire, proved sufficient to halt Pressley's South Carolinians.[42]

Walworth intended to bring up the 42nd and 27th Illinois behind the 22nd and 51st, re-forming his brigade into the standard combat deployment per Casey's *Manual*, but before he could do so Alexander McCook intervened once more. McCook led the 42nd into line alongside the 51st, and the 27th followed suit on its right. The net result was that Walworth's entire line of roughly 1,000 men now stretched more than 500 yards through the woods all the way back to the Widow Glenn's, where Lt. Gustavus Schueler's Battery G, 1st Missouri, was still deployed. This was too much frontage for too few men—about twice what was normal. More than four times the number of men Walworth had would be needed to hold this frontage using Casey's tactics, but there was little other choice. By now at least two more Confederate regiments were visible in West Brock Field (more of Manigault's men) and it was clear the Rebel front extended far beyond Walworth's right flank. Walworth augmented his line by moving three of Schueler's guns up to support the 22nd Illinois, where his left joined Lytle's 21st Michigan. Battery G was Captain's Hescock's own command, and he placed himself with this half of the battery for the coming fight.[43]

Fortunately for the Federals here, Manigault's faltering offered something of a respite. Had Manigault's entire brigade advanced *en masse*, Walworth's anemic suggestion of a line would not have been able to withstand the blow. A collapse at that time would have taken Lytle's right flank with them. But Manigault had his own problems. In addition to trying to rein in his over-excited command, he was now worried about his own left. At any moment he expected Brig. Gen. William Preston's Confederate division to advance with him. Manigault was badly misinformed, for not only was Preston not part of the general advance, but he had orders not to move because General Longstreet intended to hold the division in hand as a reserve. When it became obvious no

42 Recollections, George O. Pratt Papers, ALPL. Pratt's orientation was to the north, thinking that the 51st was going into the fight facing that direction. The curved nature of Lytle's line led Pratt to conclude that the men of the 51st were entering the equivalent of a cul-de-sac with Rebels on three sides.

43 *OR* 30, pt. 1, 595.

one was pacing him on the left, the South Carolinia brigadier, at least temporarily, abandoned any plan for bold offensive action.

When the 28th and 34th failed to heed his stop order, Manigault sent an aide galloping after them. This did the trick, and both regiments stopped some distance ahead of and to the south of Manigault's current position with the 24th. All three regiments consumed precious minutes reforming. Once they finished, Manigault ordered the rest of his brigade forward with the intent to join the attack against Walworth's extended line. Out on the brigade left, meanwhile, the 28th and 34th Alabama resumed advancing, albeit much more slowly.[44]

The woes plaguing Manigault's brigade were not over. Major John N. Slaughter, commanding the 34th Alabama on the brigade's extreme left, was approaching the Union line atop the small ridge where sat the Glenn cabin when Slaughter found what he thought was an ideal position: "a ravine, and short, low bluff in front, over which the men could rise and fire and be protected while loading." Slaughter left his men there while he personally moved forward to reconnoiter. Slaughter, however, was supposed to be attacking, not looking for defensive cover. This ill-considered decision influenced Manigault at the worst possible moment.[45]

With the 34th having unexpectedly gone to ground in the natural trench, Manigault ordered Col. John C. Reid's 28th Alabama and Col. Newton N. Davis's 24th Alabama (along with the rump of the 10th/19th) to halt. Lieutenant Charles Watkins, who had charge of Water's Alabama Battery, unlimbered in West Brock Field and opened fire on the Federals. This delay would cost Manigault's men dearly, for while it kept the brigade out of the fight for Lytle Hill, it also provided time for Colonel Wilder's Federal mounted infantry brigade to weigh into the fight a short time later.[46]

With Manigault's command stalled, it fell to Patton Anderson's large Mississippi brigade—five regiments and a sharpshooter battalion numbering 1,865 officers and men—to bolster Zach Deas's attack. Anderson's command was Hindman's support, his line originally centered about 250 yards behind and

44 Ibid., pt. 2, 348.

45 Ibid., 352.

46 Ibid., 348. Neither Davis's report nor Manigault's own writings specifically note this second order to halt, but nothing else can explain why Manigault's line was the last to engage, and how Anderson's Mississippi brigade entered the fight before Manigault's command.

between Deas and Manigault. Realizing Deas's left was now exposed because Manigault's command had fragmented, Anderson shifted his line to come into action on the 22nd Alabama's left, replacing the 10th/19th South Carolina. He moved promptly into the attack, this new blow falling against Lytle's right and the northern two-thirds of Walworth's thin battle line. Anderson's timely arrival derailed any hope, however faint, that Rosecrans, McCook, or Sheridan might harbor of taking the Confederate assault column in flank.

Facing this new onslaught, Walworth's Federals could not hold. Lieutenant Colonel Samuel B. Raymond commanded the 51st Illinois. "Before we had time to halt and form," noted Raymond, "we were met by our retreating troops, hotly pursued by an eager foe who poured into us a deadly fire on front and flank." Utter chaos was the result. "We had scarce time to deliver one volley before they were upon us," reported the mortified colonel, "and notwithstanding the most energetic efforts on the part of myself and [my] officers we had to give way." The 22nd Illinois suffered similarly, "compelled to give ground which they contested strongly until their left flank was exposed" by the 51st's collapse. The gunners of Battery G, the 1st Missouri, would have concurred. Lieutenant Schueler reported the half-battery "came into action under a most destructive fire of musketry" and was nearly overrun. Captain Hescock was taken prisoner but the guns got away, though they did lose two limbers.[47]

The 42nd Illinois suffered a similar fate. Private Merritt J. Symonds was badly wounded here: "Many of our brave boys fall. I am struck in the right leg just above the knee, shattering the bone some. I try to get off the field but cannot." Crippled but conscious, Symonds lay on the field and painstakingly recorded the dead and wounded of his company lying all around him. "We all lay here together," he scrawled, "God only knows how many more fall after this. . . . [W]e are repelled and driven back." Private Symonds would lay in that spot for the next six days, helpless and unable to walk, but faithfully recording each day's passage in his pocket diary.[48]

47 Samuel B. Raymond Report, George O. Pratt Papers, ALPL; *OR* 30, pt. 1, 505, 593. The "retreating troops" mentioned by Raymond must have been either some of Laiboldt's men, or the retreating skirmishers from Sheridan's division. Rebels reported they also captured the 1st Missouri's guns, but they must have confused other captures for them; Battery G reported that all of its guns got off the field safely.

48 Entry for September 20, Merritt Symonds Diary, Northern Illinois University, DeKalb, IL.

To Anderson's men, the collapse of the Federal opposition seemed almost too easy. Colonel William H. Bishop of the 7th Mississippi, one of Anderson's more capable regimental commanders who would later be struck down at Franklin, hit the 51st head-on: "I attacked the enemy in my front, drove them from their position, capturing three pieces of artillery, and pursued them nearly a mile," he reported. Bishop's losses amounted to only two killed and about 10 wounded, out of 291 officers and men entering the fight. On the brigade left, Col. William F. Tucker reported that his 41st Mississippi became somewhat disrupted moving through Manigault's troops (part of the 10th/19th South Carolina) but that once through, "they dashed at the enemy, who immediately fled." Not everything went Tucker's way. Even as the enemy to his front broke, the 27th Illinois and the other half of Battery G raked his line from the left, inflicting his highest losses of the day. Tucker turned his regiment and, along with a portion of the 9th Mississippi, faced this new fire head-on. He later blamed Manigault's failure to press home his own attack for the punishment his line suffered here.[49]

Walworth's collapse exposed Lytle's flank and rear to a horde of yelling Mississippians. Deas's brigade, joined and aided by the wayward 15th Alabama, had renewed its attack against the open, east-facing slope of Lytle Hill. The embattled General Lytle, meanwhile, continued riding the lines of his brigade, encouraging his men as the battle for the hill that would soon bear his name rose to a renewed crescendo. Down the slope toward Lytle's right, Wisconsinite Dan Davis recalled the intensity of that moment. "Soon all firing was blended in one general roar," Davis marveled. Both sides were now trading fire at close range, "volley for volley and ball for ball . . . sand, gravel, choking dust, balls and shells render objects almost indistinguishable. Almost half the men on our part of the line are killed or wounded. . . . 'How long shall this continue?'" fretted Lytle in Davis's hearing, observing the growing strain on his men. It was at this moment a bullet struck Lytle, the first of several wounds he would take in rapid succession.[50]

After placing the guns of the 11th Indiana, Lieutenant Pirtle returned just in time to witness the first injury to his beloved commander. Initially, Pirtle had no idea Lytle was injured, for he showed no outward sign of distress. He could see

49 *OR* 30, pt. 2, 321, 326.

50 *Daily Wisconsin*, October 19, 1863.

Lytle trying to tell him something, but the noise was too great to distinguish the words coming from his moving lips. The lieutenant leaned forward in his saddle, and this time caught, "'Pirtle, I am hit.' For an instant I cannot speak," continued the young Ohioan, "my heart almost ceases to beat . . . 'Are you hit hard, General?' 'In the spine—if I have to leave the field you stay here and see that all goes right.'" For the moment, Lytle was determined to remain in action, despite his injury.[51]

The 21st Michigan was the first of Lytle's regiments to pay the price of Walworth's collapse. Major Chase was on the left, near the juncture with Sutermeister's cannon and the 24th Wisconsin. He was fully preoccupied with his own fight until he noticed "a heavy column of the enemy marching past our right flank." Within minutes, Colonel McCreery, Lt. Col. Morris B. Wells, "and the entire right wing of the regiment" were retreating. Chase scrambled to follow suit. Sergeant John C. Taylor of Company K thought it was time to leave. "We were on a slight crest of ground, and might possibly have held the position for a time," he recalled, "but for the fact that the enemy was flanking us on both sides. . . . When this was discovered we did not linger, and on the order . . . the men broke and moved back with speed." The senior leadership of the regiment was hard-hit: Lieutenant Colonel Wells was struck down, and Chase was injured, though not seriously enough to prevent his escape.[52]

To the 21st's immediate left the 24th Wisconsin was standing fast, but Taylor was not wrong about being flanked on both sides. Farther up the ridge, both the 36th and 88th Illinois were being pounded by Deas's men. With the addition of the 15th Alabama, the two Prairie State regiments were now outgunned nearly two to one, their 800 men facing at least 1,500 attacking Confederates.

As they went up the hill the first time, Corporal Ely of the 88th Illinois heard General Sheridan "cheerfully telling us to keep cool and we should surely check them." Ely had his doubts even then. "[Laiboldt's] brigade was the best and largest in our div[ision] composed entirely of old troops . . . and until then had never been repulsed." How could the 88th hold where Laiboldt did not?

51 Pirtle Memoir, Cincinnati Historical Society.

52 Chase Letter, McCreery Family Papers, UMich; John C. Taylor, *Lights and Shadows in the Recollections of a Youthful Volunteer in the Civil War* (Ionia Sentinel-Standard, n.d.), 13. Chase's injury was unspecified, but it was sufficient to lead him to resign on October 20, 1863, due to "disability."

When the Alabamians did stop, Ely was momentarily heartened. Perhaps the 88th could hang on. Ely's vantage from the top of the hill provided the defense with a substantial tactical advantage, and also gave him a panoramic view to the north, where Ely and his comrades could see wave after wave of Rebels, all moving seemingly unopposed toward the Dry Valley Road And then Deas's men came on again, overlapping the 88th's left. "We had nothing to oppose them," lamented Ely, so "slowly we fell back to the foot of the hill." Doing so exposed the 36th's left flank in turn, and now the bulk of Deas's punishment fell upon them.[53]

The 36th Illinois was also known as the "Fox Valley Regiment," hailing from Kane and McHenry counties just west of Chicago. By now, these men had seen more than their full share of war. Mustered in August 1861, the regiment saw its first combat at Prairie Grove in Arkansas. Limited service followed at Perryville, but the men were in the thick of things at Stones River, where their magnificent stubborn defense helped save Rosecrans from disaster—and cost the regiment 212 casualties (50% of its strength). Now they found themselves in the thick of it once more. "Our left three companies were nearly annihilated," lamented Lt. Leonard Mann of Company A in a letter to the hometown folks a week after the battle. "To rush right in where men and artillery were flying to the rear was no trifling thing to do. We think we were poorly managed," he bitterly concluded. Major George Sherman admitted the 36th Illinois gave way here, having taken yet another frightful bloodletting and having seen "a second line" (probably a reference to Oates's 15th Alabama) come up to renew the attack. Stubborn to the end, the 36th and 88th regiments fell back only far enough to reform, and then returned to the crest. Their renewed effort proved futile. "We . . . rallied and charged [back] up the hill," recalled Ely, but once there, "[We] were again flanked and forced by the mere power of numbers to fall back."[54]

For a time, Lytle did not know his left was being overpowered. He was still behind the 24th Wisconsin and, despite the distraction of his wound, still trying to exercise effective command. He saw the 21st Michigan break and fall back. "For God's sake, bring up another regiment!" he yelled to Lt. Charles Boal, who couldn't hear the general over the roar. This time Pirtle heard the command,

53 Entry for September 20, Ely Diary, CCNMP.

54 "Letter From Lieut. Mann," *Elgin Gazette*, October 7, 1863; "Letter from Maj. Geo. Sherman," *Elgin Gazette*, October 14, 1863; Entry for September 20, Ely Diary, CCNMP.

and Lytle sent him off up the hill toward the 36th Illinois. Within seconds, Lytle, Boal, and Capt. Howard Greene followed Pirtle.

The reason for Lytle's sudden move to the left remains a mystery. There were no other regiments to be had. Did he ride that way expecting to shift either the 36th or the 88th Illinois down the hill to bolster his crumbling right? Did he see the 36th wavering, and ride to rally it? Lytle was confronting too many crises with far too few men. Greene and the others could only follow their commander.

Captain Greene was new to Lytle's staff, having the week before been a line officer in the 24th Wisconsin. A foot rubbed raw from marching almost sent him to the rear on the sick list, for he was unable to keep up with the rest of his men. The captain was a determined young man, however, who despite his background as a Quaker and after much soul-searching believed he had no choice but to enlist in the defense of his country. When he displayed a dogged determination to remain with his men, Lytle intervened and made him a temporary aide, now mounted. Once horsed, Greene managed to keep up. Fate placed him at the very center of the brigade's maelstrom.[55]

When he reached the 36th Illinois, Lytle halted near its colors. "He drew his sword . . . and was apparently about to give orders to charge, when he was struck in the head with a bullet," recalled Captain Greene, who was close to the general's side. "He had just turned to give me an order when the ball struck him in the mouth, passing through his head and coming out near his eye." Greene slid from his saddle in time to catch the stricken poet-general "by the head and shoulders . . . his blood spurting all over me." Lytle wasn't dead, but he was the next thing to it. Choking on the blood, he was unable to speak. Both Greene's and Lytle's animals, freed from their riders, bolted. A cluster of other aides rushed to help and moved the stricken commander a short distance to the rear.[56]

By now, the entire brigade was collapsing and the party was in danger of being overrun. Moving Lytle any farther, however, would certainly kill him. Greene recalled that Col. Thomas J. Harrison appeared on the scene. Harrison commanded the 39th Indiana Mounted Infantry, the quasi-independent regiment that had supplied canteen after canteen of much-needed water the night before. Harrison's men had halted on Lytle's right, southwest of the hill,

55 Beaudot, *24th Wisconsin*, 231.

56 Bennett and Haigh, *Thirty-Sixth Illinois*, 469; Beaudot, *24th Wisconsin*, 237.

while Harrison sought instructions on where he could best help. Spotting the stricken general, Harrison lent a hand and urged the others to "carry him, or we will be taken prisoner." Just then Lytle convulsed in what Greene interpreted as his death spasm. "He gave me one embrace," mourned the Milwaukeean, and then "his limbs immediately relaxed, his eyes rolled up into his head, and he fell over limp and lifeless." With that, Harrison and Greene abandoned Lytle's body.[57]

A few minutes later, riding up the southeastern slope of the hill, Colonel McCreery of the 21st Michigan discovered his fallen commander and tried to organize an evacuation. According to McCreery, the badly wounded general was still conscious, though speechless. Lytle was coherent enough to wave McCreery away, but McCreery insisted, collecting several men of the 21st and 24th to help him carry Lytle off the field. After much effort they managed all of four paces before a shell burst nearby. Its fragments killed one man outright, shattered a second's leg, and struck the colonel in the shoulder. The unharmed survivors bolted, leaving both Lytle and McCreery to their fates. McCreery would be captured, sent to Richmond as a prisoner, escape from the notorious Libby Prison the next spring along with Col. Thomas E. Rose of the 77th Pennsylvania, and live a long and prosperous life. Lytle would not.[58]

With Lytle down, command of the brigade fell to Col. Silas Miller of the 36th Illinois, who inherited only disaster with his new responsibilities. The 88th had broken a second time, pulling the 36th along with it. Both regiments were melting away despite efforts to hold them in place. Losses were staggering. In barely half an hour the 36th suffered 20 killed, 101 wounded, and 20 missing out of 358 engaged—a casualty rate of 39%. Many more had light wounds or "touches" to their person or gear. The 88th suffered fewer losses but still incurred a 20% casualty rate with 88 men down.

The 24th Wisconsin and 11th Indiana Battery were now all but doomed, but they did not yield easily. The situation might have appeared hopeless, but the Badgers had something to prove and stubbornly held on past the point of prudence. The 24th's first combat came at Stones River, and while its overall performance was credible, a number of men panicked in this first action. The regiment suffered 174 casualties, of which 98 were recorded missing—a total

57 Greene Letter, Lytle Family Papers, Cincinnati Historical Society. The 39th Indiana, detached and mounted like Wilder's men, was serving as cavalry for McCook's XX Corps.

58 Beaudot, *24th Wisconsin*, 237.

much higher than any other regiment in the brigade. Whispers of cowardice dogged them in the months that followed. Accusations and recriminations found their way into the hometown Milwaukee newspapers, fomenting further discontent.

The 24th also suffered leadership problems. Regimental commander Col. Charles Larrabee was conspicuous by his repeated absences, and had yet to prove himself in combat. Larrabee missed the fight at Stones River and would eventually resign in August 1863, and Maj. Elisha Hibbard, who commanded the 24th in Larrabee's absence, was already gone, resigned as of March 1863. Hibbard did so in poor health, but was heartily disliked by many of the men. These departures cleared the way for a new man—Lt. Col. Theodore West, former adjutant of the 5th Wisconsin and a veteran of the Army of the Potomac. West assumed command of a demoralized 24th that spring. By all accounts it was a welcome change. A month after his arrival, noted one Wisconsinite, West was considered "the best tactician in the division . . . universally loved and respected by all . . . and has shown himself to be both a soldier and a man, in every sense of the words." A change of arms also improved the men's moods when they turned in their older Austrian .54 rifles for new English Enfields.[59]

West's tactical skills were about to be sorely tested. As the 36th fell back, Deas's Rebels directed their fire against the 24th's exposed left. In response, West refused the two left companies, who "poured an effective fire" into the Alabamians. This measure, however, was only a stop-gap effort for nothing could be done about the right flank, where Mississippians, having broken the Wolverines, were now turning their attention against West's beleaguered Badgers. Faced with twin simultaneous disasters, West had no choice but to order a retreat. Stubborn and mindful of the previous stain of disgrace, even then some of the Milwaukeeans refused to go, but Dan Davis recalled that "the murderous crossfire . . . soon caused [even] the most determined to retire."[60]

West almost certainly intended to execute a controlled retreat, but that was impossible under the circumstances. Instead, small groups of Badgers fell back slowly, firing as they went. Color Sergeant John Borth was waving the 24th's National Colors with a bold defiance when a shell burst stripped the banner from the pole. Borth scooped up the shredded remnants as West grabbed the

59 Beaudot, *24th Wisconsin*, 210-211, 217.

60 *OR* 30, pt. 1, 587; *Daily Wisconsin*, October 19, 1863.

barren flagstaff, "rapped . . . [it] with his saber and rallied two or three companies." When the attempt proved futile, West ordered the men to "scatter as much as possible and 'rally on the reserve,'" assuming there was any reserve to find. He was about to affect his own escape when another shell burst flattened the colonel and paralyzed his left hip; he was seized by the Rebels and, along with McCreery sent east to Libby Prison. West, too, would make his escape with McCreery via Colonel Rose's tunnel.[61]

General Sheridan's earlier cheery facade may have been for the sake of his men's spirits, but that mask was slipping now. In the midst of the rapidly deteriorating tactical situation, Sgt. Charles Brough of the 15th Pennsylvania rode up looking for Brig. Gen. Jeff Davis. Well before any of the current catastrophe unfolded, Rosecrans had dispatched Brough with an order for Davis, but the sergeant had been having the devil's own time finding the recipient. Initially Brough had ridden to the far right of the line, where he was informed (correctly) that Davis had moved off, and (incorrectly) that Davis's men had been sent to the far left to join Thomas. Riding north, Brough was told by someone on Thomas's staff that this wasn't so, and as far as they knew, Davis and his men were still on the right flank. The frustrated Brough spurred his mount southward at the gallop, only to be caught up in the rout of Van Cleve's division about 11:00 a.m., taking a wound to his hand in the process. Finally, Brough came across Sheridan and asked him of Davis's whereabouts, proffering the now long-out-of-date order. "'I don't know, my boy; but it's too late. Let me see it,'" snapped the Irishman. "He tore it open and read it, saying 'Too late! Too late!'" At that moment, the last of the line collapsed. Sheridan grabbed the division standard from an orderly and, flag in hand, made a final effort to arrest the panic. It failed. He snarled, "'it's time for us all to get away from here.'"[62]

Singlehandedly, Lieutenant Pirtle was doing his best to buck this outgoing tide, growing increasingly alarmed about Lytle's whereabouts and condition. Pirtle was still with Colonel Miller and the 36th when he "saw General L's horse gallop past without his rider and I thought the General had been thrown." Fearing the worst, the distraught lieutenant rushed back toward the last spot he had seen Lytle, but failed to find him. Lytle had been carried at least twice by

61 Beaudot, *24th Wisconsin*, 241.

62 Kirk, *Fifteenth Pennsylvania Volunteer Cavalry*, 269-270.

this time, and could have been anywhere on the hill. As Pirtle drew close, all he could see were Rebels. "I started for the rear rallying the men, by twos and threes whenever I could, the enemy pursuing us and keeping up a brisk fire." Pirtle stumbled on Colonel Harrison, who "seized a flag and waved it before [the men] calling on them by everything in language to rally, but it was in vain." When Harrison rode on, Pirtle ran behind in an attempt to keep up with the mounted colonel until exhaustion overtook him. When he informed Harrison that he could go no farther, the officer turned around and, despite Pirtle's protests, "lifted me into the saddle and on foot he ran ahead of me up the hill amid a shower of balls." Several hundred yards to the rear, the entire brigade came to rest on the rugged hill complex west of the Dry Valley Road.[63]

Captain Sutermeister and his 11th Indiana cannoneers paid a bloody price for their forward deployment, especially those in 19-year-old Lt. Henry Williams's section. "Finding . . . that our infantry was nowhere supporting us," reported Sutermeister, "I ordered the battery to limber up and retreat." The two sections of Napoleons managed a clean getaway, but no one told Williams, who was deeply absorbed in his work. "All was going well," Williams thought, "when . . . to our great amazement, the infantry to the left of us retired . . . and the enemy were soon in their places, almost touching our elbows." Williams dismounted, personally sighted one of the rifled pieces, and fired. For a moment it seemed like the line could be restored, continued the young officer, but "our infantry on the right was . . . in full retreat." Under "a rapid galling fire rapidly cutting down men and horses," the 3rd Section had no choice but to flee. Williams took a bad wound to the wrist that severed an artery. Corporal Fred May was bandaging the injury when he was mortally wounded. Williams fainted from the loss of blood, borne off the field by the appropriately named fellow gunner Edward Schell. Casualties in the 3rd Section amounted to 60%. Both guns were left on the field.[64]

Rosecrans, McCook, Sheridan, and Jeff Davis were all caught up in this rout, though not in a group. The Federal survivors all moved west, and like Pirtle, came to rest on the hill complex west of the Dry Valley Road, where order slowly began to be restored. This effort was aided by the fact that, once the Union line was broken, Thomas Hindman halted the Rebel pursuit. He did

63 "Dear Pa," September 26, 1863, Pirtle Papers, Filson Historical Society, Louisville, KY.

64 *OR* 30, pt. 1, 588; Otto, *History of the 11th Indiana Battery*, 10-11. Williams survived, mustering out with a disability on November 23, 1863.

so for two reasons. First, Hindman believed Sheridan's and Davis's commands were so badly mauled that, as General Deas reported, the Rebel attack "scattered the enemy in our front so effectually that they never rallied or reformed again during the day on this part of the field." Second, in contrast to Anderson's and Deas's success, Manigault's men did not achieve anything remotely similar. In fact, Manigault's men were being driven back in disorder, which appeared to confirm both Manigault's and Hindman's fears about their exposed left flank. Instead of a vigorous continued pursuit, Hindman set about regrouping his brigades and restocking ammunition.[65]

65 *OR* 30, pt. 2, 330.

Chapter Thirteen

Ruin and Retreat:

Sunday, 12:30 p.m. to 4:00 p.m.

While Sheridan's men were fighting for their lives, the XX Corps's chief of staff, Lt. Col. Gates Thruston, was on his way back from Crawfish Spring. Having delivered Alexander McCook's pre-crisis dispatch to General Mitchell and the Union cavalry, Thruston was now looking to rejoin his commander. Instead, while riding north along the Dry Valley Road, Thruston came upon "the 39th Indiana . . . a full, fresh regiment, armed with Spencer's repeating rifles." Colonel Thomas Harrison of the 39th, who had just departed the dying (or dead) Lytle's side, described the unfolding disaster around Lytle Hill to Thruston and put himself at Thruston's disposal. Immediately, Thruston and Harrison "led the regiment at a gallop to the Widow Glenn's."[1]

The former site of Rosecrans's headquarters was fast becoming a focal point of growing Federal strength. In addition to Harrison's 581 Hoosiers, Col. Jonathan R. Miles's 27th Illinois, the last of Colonel Bradley's regiments (the brigade now fighting under Colonel Walworth) was still in line there and willing to fight. Thus far, the men of the 27th had been relatively lucky, suffering lighter losses than the rest of their comrades both in the previous day's combat and in this day's action. Numbering 463 when it entered the fight, the Illinois unit was the largest regiment in the brigade by half again as many. The 27th lost two

1 Thruston, "The Crisis at Chickamauga," 664.

killed and 48 wounded on Saturday, and now had about 360 in the ranks. So far, the fighting had not reached their front. J. Patton Anderson's Mississippians, of Hindman's division, broke Walworth's other three Federal regiments with relative ease when they entered the fight against Sheridan, but the Mississippi battle line did not extend as far south as the 27th's front, leaving Miles's command so far unscathed. Miles's regiment became a rallying point for stragglers from the rest of the division, seeking somewhere to reform.[2]

Sheridan's divisional skirmishers also augmented Colonel Miles's firepower. Prominent among these were Companies B and H of the 21st Michigan (of Lytle's brigade)—just 37 men in all, commanded by a lieutenant shockingly young for his position. Charles E. Belknap was still a month shy of his 17th birthday, but he had revealed a positive talent for command, infused with boyish enthusiasm for combat. Like several other Michigan regiments, the 21st carried Colt revolving rifles, and that morning, before being ordered out as skirmishers, Belknap was instructed to make sure there was more than enough ammunition for the Colts. His detachment hit the skirmish line with 200 rounds per man, the extra cartridges stuffed in pockets and haversacks. Eyeing the Widow Glenn cabin after Rosecrans's entourage decamped, Belknap decided it would make a pretty good fort, and set his men to work knocking the chinking out from between the logs to create firing slits. Shortly thereafter, he and his comrades were ordered out on picket.[3]

Some hours later Belknap and his fellow Wolverines watched as the 24th, 28th, and 34th Alabama worked their way across West Brock Field. In response, the Federals fell back. "When I reached the Glenn House," recalled the boy lieutenant, "to my surprise the brigade was gone." No matter, Colonel Miles was there, and now, "coming in from every angle of the front were the [divisional] skirmishers." Belknap estimated these men augmented Miles's force by as many as another 300 men, adding what amounted to an extra regiment to the burgeoning Yankee line.[4]

Miles also had the advantage of artillery support in the form of the remaining half of Schueler's Battery G, 1st Missouri Light Artillery. Like the 11th Indiana, Battery G had four Napoleons and two rifled pieces (in this case,

2 In addition to stragglers from his own brigade, men from both Sheridan's and Laiboldt's commands joined Miles here.

3 C. E. Belknap, "Chickamauga," *National Tribune*, April 6, 1893.

4 Ibid.

10-pound Parrotts). Half the battery had advanced northward to support the main fight and was caught up in the subsequent rout, but the Parrotts and one Napoleon remained with the 27th Illinois on the brigade right. From there, Schueler's guns dueled with Waters's Alabama Battery (attached to Manigault's brigade, under Lt. Charles W. Watkins) out in West Brock Field, and also threw shells northward into Patton Anderson's flank and rear. Soon, however, they would have a much more immediate target in the form of Manigault's three Alabama regiments, which were at last moving forward to the attack.[5]

Arthur Manigault was still having great difficulties coordinating his brigade. After Anderson's brigade moved up and through his line, Manigault reunified the 10th/19th South Carolina and sent it off in the wake of the Mississippians before turning his attention to his three regiments of Alabamians. With Col. Newton Davis's 24th Alabama on the right, the large 28th under Col. John C. Reid in the center, and Major Slaughter's 34th on the left, Manigault intended to send these 1,300 men forward in a belated attack in support of Anderson's left. "Thus we charged fully half a mile across an old field," noted Lieutenant Callaway of the 28th, "then across a skirt of woods then another old field and into another skirt of woods." Once through that second belt of timber, the Alabamians found themselves "in a cornfield perfectly exposed to the enemy's small arms and artillery." Harrison's Hoosiers, Miles's 27th Illinois, and every other Federal on the ridge had opened fire.[6]

Dramatically, Col. John T. Wilder and his large brigade now appeared on the scene. Wilder arrived because he was hurrying to comply with his orders to stay on the "right fighting flank" of the Union army. Shy only the 92nd Illinois, which was still off to the south on picket duty, Wilder brought with him the 18th Indiana battery and the better part of four regiments of mounted infantry. About 11:30 a.m., Wilder marched his command—his infantry all dismounted—north about half a mile intending to close on what he thought would be Alexander McCook's new position. During the early minutes of this move the Federals exhibited no urgency, admitted Sgt. Benjamin Magee of the 72nd Indiana, moving only at "common time." That changed when Capt. A. S. Burt of McCook's staff reined in his lathered horse carrying electrifying news: the infantry was broken and Wilder must "interpose [his] command in Sheridan's rear." This news set them moving at the double-quick. The pace

5 *OR* 30, pt. 1, 597.

6 Hallock, *The Civil War Letters of Joshua K. Callaway*, 136.

redoubled again when they drew near the fast-developing fight around Lytle Hill. Here Wilder wheeled everyone into line and moved rapidly eastward.[7]

The Glenn house stood on a small rise that not only provided an excellent defensive position for Harrison and Miles, but masked Wilder's approach. While Wilder's infantry were deploying into line on the move, Capt. Eli Lilly dashed ahead, planting his six wrought-iron rifles on the forward slope of that same ridge several hundred yards south of the Glenn farmstead. Once unlimbered, they immediately opened fire. Within a few minutes, the aggressive Lilly hustled two guns even farther forward, placing the section just south of the widow's domicile on the 27th Illinois's right flank within barely 100 yards of Manigault's fast-approaching Rebels.[8]

Had Wilder's infantry not been closing rapidly, Lilly's tactic might have been a foolhardy move. With the rest of the Lightning Brigade close by, however, Lilly had little fear of losing his guns. The first of Wilder's infantry to crest the rise was the 98th Illinois, Spencers blazing. They came up between the sections of Lilly's divided battery. The 98th numbered about 400 men after accounting for losses and detachments, but surprise and the rapid fire of their repeating rifles magnified their numbers into a veritable lethal force.

Until their dying hour, this encounter would loom large in the collective memory of Wilder's troops as both a dramatic war story and a pivotal moment in the battle. Dozens of written accounts from brigade veterans and observers dissected the affair with vivid word-portraits of the event. The Glenn cabin was ablaze, previously ignited by artillery fire. (It was a good thing Lieutenant Belknap and his comrades did not hole up in the log "fort.") Noting a gap between the 98th Illinois and Harrison's 39th Indiana, which was simultaneously coming into the fight between Miles's 27th and Lilly's advanced section, Wilder directed his 72nd Indiana farther north and into line on the 98th's left, passing through Belknap's polyglot skirmisher force as they did so. The 39th and 72nd added nearly another 1,000 well-armed Federals into the combat, every man firing as rapidly as he could lever the action on his rifle.[9]

7 Magee, *History of the 72nd Indiana*, 185; John T. Wilder, "Preliminary Movements of the Army of the Cumberland Before the Battle of Chickamauga," *MOLLUS*, vol. 7, 269.

8 *OR* 30, pt. 1, 467.

9 James Fisher, "Wilder's Brigade at Chickamauga," *National Tribune*, May 13, 1886; Belknap, "Chickamauga," *National Tribune*, April 6, 1893. Belknap recounts a dramatic tale in which he fights, entirely surrounded, repelling numerous charges from all directions, until at last Wilder

The 24th and 28th Alabama of Manigault's brigade bore the brunt of this assault. To these Alabamians, it seemed as if the very ground had suddenly erupted. "We had scarcely gotten in range when they opened on us with a continuous sheet of fire," recalled Lt. Col. Benjamin F. Sawyer of the 24th Alabama. "We were in the very jaws of the monster." Sawyer thought the 24th's regimental commander, Col. Newton N. Davis, had no choice but to press home the attack; turning back now would only expose the men to an even worse slaughter. "Never before had I . . . seen such terrible execution in so short a time." Private Joel H. Puckett of the 24th's Company C was certain he was doomed. "Mary, here I bid you good bye forever," he confessed to his wife a few days later.[10]

Just south of the 24th, matters were even worse. With more than 600 men in line, the 28thAlabama was by far the largest of Manigault's three Alabama regiments. They lost nearly one-third of that strength here, in an exchange that lasted no more than a quarter-hour. Colonel John Reid reported that the 28th "fought determinedly" for some time until Manigault ordered him to retreat, which, Reid admitted, "was not done in the best order." Lieutenant Callaway had a more vivid description of the retreat: "The carnage was awful. . . . Men were shot down all around me. . . . We fought them thus close I suppose about ten minutes when, as if by command, our whole line gave way and down the hill we went like a gang of sheep."[11]

Reid's men suffered heavily in part because once again, Maj. John Slaughter and the 34th Alabama did not advance. Slaughter was still reconnoitering, the 34th still sheltering in its convenient ravine when the 28th Alabama lurched forward into disaster. This kept the 34th's losses down; they suffered only 38 casualties, or about 12%, out of the 329 engaged. Their absence, however, allowed more of Wilder's deadly Spencer-armed infantry to tear into the unfortunate 28th's exposed left. The men of the 34th clung to their cover and watched while the 28th bolted rearward.

---

arrives. Belknap mentions neither Colonel Miles and the 27th Illinois, nor Colonel Harrison's 39th Indiana, and has the Glenn cabin being used as a hospital, when in fact it was burning down. His version is a trifle fanciful.

10 Benjamin F. Sawyer, "Chickamauga," *Battles and Leaders of the Civil War*, vol. 5 (University of Illinois Press, 2002), 427. "Dear Mollie," September 24, 1863, Joel H. Puckett Letters, Briscoe Center for American History, University of Texas at Austin.

11 *OR* 30, pt. 2, 348; Hallock, *The Civil War Letters of Joshua K. Callaway*, 137.

When the 28th Alabama broke, Federal attention shifted northward to rip into the 24th Alabama. "The regiment came under a heavy cross fire," reported Colonel Davis, and "it being discovered that we were being flanked on our left, the order was given to fall back." The open ground directly to the rear made retreating due east (which Lieutenant Colonel Sawyer thought suicidal even before the 28th collapsed) a bad option. Instead, Davis elected to try and fall back northeast into the timber recently cleared of Federals by Patton Anderson's brigade. Sawyer confessed that this movement began "instinctively and without command," the men moving "by the right flank . . . [and] doubling upon Anderson's" Mississippians. Even weeks later, Colonel Davis was too overwhelmed to leave a detailed description of the slaughter. He could only thank "Almighty God" for his survival, admitting that "it was the most terrific firing that I ever heard."[12]

Manigault was observing the bloody affair when his horse was shot down. The same bullet that killed his mount smashed his sword scabbard and clipped his trousers. An inspection of his uniform revealed several more "touches" by Yankee projectiles, though none drew blood. Manigault was not too distracted by this close call to immediately notice Wilder's 123rd Illinois and 17th Indiana regiments extending the Union flank south. He later discovered that, "As far to the left as I could see, the enemy overlapped us, and there were no troops . . . opposing him." An urgent message from Major Slaughter served to confirm Manigault's worry: the Federals were working their way into Manigault's rear. "Our position was becoming critical," concluded Manigault. "I was reluctantly compelled to retire the whole line." The general ordered Slaughter and Reid to fall back about 600 yards. Once Reid rallied his 28th Alabama, directed Manigault, he was to assume charge of both regiments. Manigault next instructed the 10th/19th South Carolina and 24th Alabama to fall back about half that distance, intending to reform the entire brigade facing south against the looming Federal threat. He also sent word to division commander Brig. Gen. William Preston appealing for at the very least the release of Col. Robert Trigg's brigade, which had been on Manigault's left just before the advance began.[13]

12 *OR* 30, pt. 2, 346; Sawyer, "Chickamauga," 427; "My Dear Bettie," October 11, 1863, Newton N. Davis Letters, ADAH.

13 R. Lockwood Tower, ed., *A Carolinian Goes to War: The Civil War Narrative of Arthur Middleton Manigault* (University of South Carolina Press, 1983), 98-99, 108.

The Federals on this sector of the field were elated, even awed, at the carnage they inflicted. Captain John Glenn, commanding Company F of the 27th Illinois, had a front row seat for the grand event: "Our regiment was not in as bad a place as many others," he wrote, "we got on their flank where they could do us but little damage while we were killing them as fast as they could fall. It was awful to see one of our batteries, our Regt, [and] a battalion of mounted infantry with seven-shooters mow them down." "Their line melted away in a few minutes," marveled Pvt. Williamson Ward of the 39th Indiana. "It appeared to me like we had slain all of them."[14]

For once, Union losses were slight. Colonel John J. Funkhouser of the 98th Illinois fell with a leg wound, but his injury was a rarity. Wilder lost fewer than 25 men here, with no casualties at all in the 72nd Indiana or among Lilly's gunners. The 39th Indiana lost 40 men, the 27th Illinois 41, and an unknown number of Belknap's skirmishers (but they were engaged for a longer time and, except for the 39th, lacked the benefit of that stunning repeater fire to keep their opponents' heads down).[15]

Among Wilder's regiments, the elation of a heady victory translated into a vigorous pursuit of Manigault's retreating regiments at least as far as West Brock Field. "We unfurled our banners, leaped over the works, & swept down the hill like an avalanche," exulted William H. Records of the 72nd Indiana. "They run," boasted a fellow Hoosier private named Alva Griest. "Now Wilder orders a charge and leaping the works we take a host of those daring Texans [sic] prisoners." The Federals estimated they captured as many as 200 Rebels. Conversely, Manigault's brigade reported very few men missing or captured; only 28 fell into that category from the 34th Alabama (the 28th did not report their losses in detail). Almost certainly, many of those prisoners were also wounded.[16]

Whatever the number of Confederates captured here, all were promptly turned over to Colonel Gates Thruston. Unable to locate McCook and resume

14 "Dear James," September 29, 1863, John A. Glenn Letters, ALPL; Entry for September 20, Williamson D. Ward Diary, InHS.

15 Richard A. Baumgartner, *Blue Lightning: Wilder's Mounted Infantry Brigade in the Battle of Chickamauga* (Blue Acorn Press, 1997), 291.

16 Entry for September 20, Records Diary, InSL; Alva C. Griest Journal, 101, InSL. Griest rewrote his diaries into a more coherent narrative after the war, and likely confused the Alabamians for Texans when he did so. His 72nd Indiana engaged Gregg's Texas Brigade the previous day.

his staff position, Thruston commandeered a detachment from the 39th Indiana to help him march his captives rearward as quickly as possible. Thruston later complained that the prisoners took a great deal of prodding to get off the field; they realized the longer they lingered, the greater chance they had of being liberated. Thruston's band passed within 300 yards of another Confederate line—presumably one of Anderson's Mississippi regiments—but there were so few blue uniforms bobbing in the sea of prisoners that Thruston concluded the group looked like fellow Confederates from that distance. The Yankees also recovered the pair of field pieces of Battery G, 1st Missouri Light, overrun earlier and, much to Colonel Davis's chagrin, the colors of the 24th Alabama.[17]

The loss of his colors was something Davis found especially shameful. The 24th's Color Sergeant, George W. Moody, fell severely wounded during the retreat and dropped the flag. In the confusion no one noticed. After the regiment rallied and things quieted down, the flag was discovered missing. Lieutenant Andrew Young volunteered to lead a detail to try and recover it. When the effort proved unsuccessful, someone voiced that Sgt. George B. Ackerman of Company G was the last one seen with the flag—"but going toward the enemy's lines." "It is supposed he deserted," concluded Davis, "as he has not been heard from since." Davis's supposition was correct. After snatching up the banner, Ackerman discovered a party of Union stragglers under Lt. Thomas Cummings of Company D, 51st Illinois, and immediately gave himself up. Lieutenant Cummings proudly bore his trophy rearward, the capture allowing General Sheridan to report its seizure as some small measure of success in the midst of the overall disaster. On March 29, 1864, Ackerman took the oath of allegiance at Camp Douglas in Chicago, and became once again a free and loyal citizen of the United States.[18]

While Ackerman and his presumably more reluctant fellow prisoners were hustled off the field, the rest of Manigault's men fell back to the La Fayette Road. Their rout was not surprising given the stunning volume of enemy fire they had faced. Colonel Wilder later described his preferred method of fighting: "I trained my command to hold their rapid fire until our opponents were within 300 yards, when our rapid fire with aim never failed to break their charge." He

17 Thruston, "The Crisis at Chickamauga," 665.

18 *OR* 30, pt. 2, 346; Raymond Report, George O. Pratt Papers, ALPL; *OR* 30, pt. 1, 580.

would never encounter a better chance to implement that tactic than here, at the Widow Glenn's.[19]

Wilder's men did not pursue beyond the La Fayette Road. "My command was still moving forward," reported Maj. William T. Jones, commanding the 17th Indiana, "when the order of recall was received." Initially, stopping the pursuit was the last thing Wilder intended. He knew both Generals Davis and Sheridan had been routed, but he was so ebullient at his men's success that he conceived of a much more ambitious attack. Manigault's Rebels might have also broken, but large numbers of Confederates were still between him and George Thomas's Federal line farther north. Dust and distant noise from that quarter of the field made it clear that Thomas's battle was far from over. Moreover, Wilder had been reinforced. At the close of the fight with Manigault, the last of Wilder's regiments under Col. Smith Atkins reported in with eight companies of his 92nd Illinois. Fresh off picket duty, Atkins's men had fallen back with Sheridan's skirmishers and had finally joined their parent brigade.[20]

Years later, Atkins would report that he was standing with Wilder near the blazing remnants of the Glenn cabin, where "we could both see the long column of Confederate regiments doubled on the center, and [Wilder] instantly conceived the bold idea of charging with his brigade through the center of the confederate column, taking their regiments in flank, and pushing for Thomas on the left." And what did Atkins think? "It was a desperate and bold movement," he told the colonel, "but his Brigade of Spencer Repeating Rifles could do it . . . and might entirely change the result of the battle." Writing in 1888, Wilder explained, "[I] prepared to move my whole command in column of five regiments towards the heavy firing, thinking to strike the enemy in left and rear, believing that my five lines of Spencer Rifles could break any line on earth."[21]

Wilder's idea was to put the brigade into a hollow square, with the 72nd Indiana and 98th Illinois in front, the 17th Indiana and 123rd Illinois on the flanks, Lilly's limbered guns in the center, and Atkins's regiment bringing up the rear. Over the years both Wilder and Atkins provided multiple descriptions of this moment, eventually claiming that they went so far as to actually form the

19 John T. Wilder tactical notes, Author's collection.

20 *OR* 30, pt. 1, 462.

21 Anonymous, *Dedication of the Wilder Brigade Monument on Chickamauga Battlefield* (The Herald Press, 1900), 28; Wilder Revised Report, CCNMP.

Colonel John T. Wilder (left) would later claim that Charles Dana's sudden appearance headed off a daring counter-attack that might have changed the course of the battle.
Library of Congress

brigade up as described (in a square). Reality, however, was something very different. None of the many official reports—the documents prepared closest to the actual event—filed by Wilder or his regimental leaders (including Atkins) describe the proposed attack or even describe organizing such a formation. Indeed, no other contemporary accounts even suggest it. If Wilder did conceive of this plan at that moment, the idea died aborning.[22]

The reason the grand plan died so quickly had to do with the sudden appearance of a wild-eyed Charles A. Dana, who stumbled into their midst with his red hair askew and his head hatless. According to Wilder, the panicked Dana announced, "'our troops had fled in utter panic; that it was a worse rout than Bull Run; that General Rosecrans was probably killed or captured;' and strongly advised me to fall back and occupy the passes over Lookout Mountain." This description, perhaps even then a little embellished, first appeared in Wilder's official report penned two months after the incident. By 1888, Wilder cast Dana in an even more hysterical light: Dana insisted "'the army was routed and fleeing in panic' and . . . the firing heard was 'the enemy pursuing Thomas and killing his men.' That my brigade 'was the only portion of the army left intact' and that 'General Rosecrans was either killed or captured. . . . I must take my command and escort him to Chattanooga.'"[23]

Wilder was now stricken with uncertainty. He offered Dana the escort of some of his scouts, "who knew every foot of the ground and could get him

22 Wilder, "Preliminary Movements," 269.

23 *OR* 30, pt. 1, 449; Wilder Revised Report, CCNMP.

through . . . in much less time than it would take the brigade," but the colonel insisted his larger duty "was to reach Thomas" with his men. Dana supposedly would have none of it: "He ordered me to move immediately to Chattanooga and take possession of Lookout Mountain. I was a young volunteer," Wilder recalled in yet a third version of the incident, "and did not know what to do, but concluded that if he [Dana] could order Rosecrans to do his bidding I had better obey him even against . . . my better judgment." With that, all thought of a grand charge into Longstreet's left flank ended.[24]

Atkins, a newspaperman by trade, strongly opinionated, and devoted to both the memory of Wilder and the brigade to which he belonged, summed up the affair even more forcefully. "Wilder was daring and desperate; Dana, a coward and an imbecile."[25]

Of course, Dana had a much different view of the incident. His version was first set down in 1896—more than three decades after the battle. By then he'd had plenty of time to choose his words carefully, especially regarding his alleged issuing of an order to a commander on a battlefield, something no civilian, even an assistant secretary of war, had the authority to do. His version of events unfolded thusly: "'Mr. Dana,' asked Colonel Wilder, 'what is the situation?' 'I do not know,' I said, 'except that this end of the army has been routed. There is still heavy fighting at the left front, and our troops seem to be holding their ground there yet.' 'Will you give me any orders?' [Wilder] asked. 'I have no authority to give orders,' I replied; 'but if I were in your situation I should go to the left, where Thomas is.' Then I turned my horse, and, making my way over Missionary Ridge, struck the Chattanooga Valley and rode to Chattanooga."[26]

The two accounts differ dramatically, but neither paints a completely accurate picture. One hatless and distraught civilian did not change the course of the battle. Other information, all of it worrisome, was also influencing Wilder's decision.

When the mounted infantry of the 72nd Indiana returned to the hill, they discovered their mounts were gone, along with Companies D and F. "During

24 Joseph A. Scott Reminiscences, InHS.

25 Anonymous, *Ninety-Second Illinois Volunteers* (Journal Steam Publishing House and Bookbindery, 1875), 112.

26 Dana, *Recollections of the Civil War*, 116. Not only had Dana time to reflect on his version of the encounter, but he was probably aware of recent discussion of the affair given the amount of interest in creating the park during the mid-1890s.

the absence of the regiment," noted Magee, "a squad of rebel cavalry had dashed in from the right . . . killed five or six horses, and stampeded the rest." The two guard companies chased off the Rebels, but had to ride "several miles" rounding up their animals. Wilder had to be aware of this situation, which took more than an hour to rectify. Would he have willingly abandoned the 72nd's invaluable horses to pursue his attack, and risk losing them for good? Moreover, how would he protect his own flank and rear as he advanced? He had no idea how many Confederates still lurked in the woods to the east or south, and if they could return in much greater strength.[27]

Additionally, no one else was willing to accompany the brigade on what could easily turn out to be a death ride. Private Henry Tutewiler of the 17th Indiana, one of Wilder's orderlies, recalled seeing an unidentified infantry regiment "behind our brigade and a little to our left. . . . [T]heir uniforms were clean and new, and they had evidently not been engaged." The colonel dispatched Tutewiler to ask for the regiment's support in the impending attack. "I don't believe I am taking orders from Colonel Wilder today," was the haughty reply. "Damn his cowardly soul. I'll see him later," snapped Wilder.[28]

What was the identity of this phantom regiment? It could only be one of two: Col. Thomas Harrison's 39th Indiana (independent) or Col. Jonathan Miles's 27th Illinois (Bradley's brigade). Tutewiler places this incident before Wilder's initial engagement, but since both the 39th and 27th joined in and supported that effort, Tutewiler's recollection of the timing of the refusal seems mistaken. However, if the refusal came in the context of Wilder's contemplated grand stroke, it makes much more sense. The initial encounter at the Glenn cabin was much more limited in scope, and one in which the Federals present had very little choice. Striking northward to join Thomas was a much more ambitious movement.

Whatever its timing and despite Tutewiler's recalled outrage, the unnamed colonel's response was not inappropriate. Both Harrison and Miles had other duties, and they belonged to other commands. Miles had with him roughly 1,000 men who belonged to Sheridan's division, and he urgently needed to rejoin that division commander. As for Harrison, who reported directly to McCook's XX Corps, "at that juncture we were ordered to take a train, which

27 Magee, *History of the 72nd Indiana*, 186.

28 Baumgartner, *Blue Lightning*, 285. Tutewiler recounted both this and another incident to Wilder in 1889.

was also cut off, and make our way in the direction of Lookout Mountain." Harrison could not have simply ignored his instructions and joined a grand attack in the opposite direction on the whim of John Wilder.[29]

It is also important to note that Wilder's last instruction from General McCook was to protect Sheridan's flank and rear—which he had done admirably by appearing at the Widow Glenn's in so powerful and timely a fashion. Were not those instructions still in effect? Sheridan and Davis were still trying to reform their commands on the hills to the west. Protection while this effort was underway would be necessary, and Wilder's command was the best situated to do so. Moreover, Lt. Col. Gates Thruston of McCook's staff was present and "advised [Wilder] that I had better fall back to Lookout Mountain."[30]

After Thruston's final words of advice to Wilder he departed, prisoners in tow. It would have been better had he remained at the front. Thruston was, after all, the XX Corps's chief of staff, and as such he carried at least nominal authority to issue orders in McCook's name. He could have helped orchestrate a more coordinated response by what amounted to some 3,500 Federals, or roughly the strength of an unrouted division.

There was also one, and probably two, communiqués from Sheridan. During Wilder's initial fighting with Manigault, he dispatched a small party to locate the division commander. The group, including Private Tutewiler and Lt. Jacob R. Harding, found Sheridan "surrounded by a half dozen staff officers." Harding reported that "Wilder's brigade was in good fighting order and ready to join his command, or receive any order he might be pleased to give. . . . Little Phil answered, 'By God, I have no command.' Turning to his orderlies the general added, 'Here is my command. You tell Wilder he better get his brigade into Chattanooga as quick as he possibly can.'" Harding and Tutewiler carried this news back just as Wilder was reforming his brigade in the wake of Manigault's repulse. The information surely dampened everyone's mood.[31]

Years later, in a story that almost certainly benefited from hindsight, Wilder recalled that he sent another courier to Sheridan after the repulse, bombastically "asking him to rally his men and come to my aid, and I would lead an attack on

29 *OR* 30, pt. 1, 548. These orders probably came from Thruston.

30 Ibid., 449.

31 Baumgartner, *Blue Lightning*, 290.

the enemy." The messenger—identified only as "Lieutenant Smith", soon returned with a similarly disheartening reply: "Sheridan was falling back to Rossville and had sent me orders 'to get out of there,' as the army was 'routed.'" At the time Sheridan's men, Wilder noted with some scorn, were 'three-fourths of a mile in my rear and still falling back in disorder . . . though unpursued."[32]

These factors almost certainly exerted a more significant cautioning influence on John Wilder's actions than did Dana's words, hysterical or otherwise. It is also likely the tale of the incident "grew in the telling," becoming an old war story to repeat at reunions and as Wilder rode around the battlefield with veterans from both sides, each of whom stoked the idea of how decisive Wilder's "grand attack" might have been. By the 1880s, Wilder was convinced "the charge . . . would have resulted in the rout of Longstreet's corps. . . . I have lived in Chattanooga for eighteen years and have gone over Chickamauga field with a great many ex-rebels, who all admit that had I been allowed to attack as I wished, it would have been fatal to Bragg's army."[33]

While Wilder agonized over his course of action, other Union generals struggled mightily with their own decisions. These officers included General Rosecrans (and with him, James Garfield), McCook, the above-mentioned Sheridan, and Jeff Davis. Each of these men ended up leaving the field. Despite their very close proximity to one another, each departed singly, each man apparently unable to locate any of the others.

By the time Rosecrans reached Lytle Hill only a handful of his staff remained at his side: Garfield, Frank Bond, a couple of orderlies, and, fortunately, Capt. W. B. Gaw of George Thomas's staff. Gaw, the XIV Corps's topographic officer, had been on one of his seemingly endless shuttle missions between Thomas and Rosecrans when the breakthrough occurred. His expert knowledge of the surrounding countryside would soon prove helpful.

A number of men in the ranks recalled Rosecrans's presence among them. Someone in every regiment in Lytle's brigade had a recollection of the army commander cheering them on as they went into action. Rosecrans lingered there a while, observing the disastrous outcome. Lytle's riderless horse galloped

32 Wilder, "Preliminary Movements," 269; Wilder Revised Report, CCNMP. Despite the more self-serving language, this account by Wilder essentially matches previous accounts of Wilder's attempts to contact Sheridan, and is probably, at its core, accurate.

33 George S. Wilson, "Wilder's Brigade of Mounted Infantry in Tullahoma-Chickamauga Campaigns," *MOLLUS*, vol. 15, 67. Wilder took up residence in Chattanooga after the war, becoming both a businessman and its mayor.

past him—a harbinger that both Lytle's and Bradley's (Walworth's) brigades had been "shattered." Rosecrans lent his hand at rallying the men, to no avail, and was swept along in that tide of chaotic rout until all reached the hills west of the Dry Valley Road. The main mass of men halted there to begin the painfully slow process of coalescing back into companies, regiments, and finally, brigades.[34]

Lieutenant William H. H. Moody found Rosecrans here shortly after noon. Moody was one of two couriers dispatched by General Negley seeking reinforcements and further orders. It had been no easy task to find the army commander. "I was compelled by the presence of the enemy to make a circuit in rear of the ridges, supposing that General Rosecrans was on the right," he later wrote. Moody first found the bulk of the staff and the army escort, all "endeavoring to stop the stragglers, who were coming back in great confusion and in great numbers." Another 500 yards on, Moody found Rosecrans, apparently all alone. "The yell of the enemy could be heard to the right and front and very close," Moody recalled, so he and the general "rode a short distance to the rear" with Moody relaying his mission while they rode. "'It is too late: I cannot help [Negley],'" was Rosecrans's only reply. Moody spurred his mount away bearing those grim words. Within minutes Negley's second courier, Capt. Alfred L. Hough, appeared with the same request. "I have just sent him word that I could not help," reiterated the army commander.[35]

According to Rosecrans's own recollections, he decided to join Thomas on the left in the hope that the imperturbable Virginian was holding out. Like Wilder, Rosecrans could also hear the steady roar of combat off to the north, signifying that at least some Federals were still in the game. "I left directions for Sheridan to form his men as soon as possible . . . and Davis's division to halt and form on the ridge." Once regrouped, Rosecrans intended for both commands to fall back and cover the Dry Valley Road.[36]

With that Rosecrans and his small party (Garfield, Bond, Gaw, and the handful of escorts) rode north until gunfire from a Rebel brigade positioned on "the verge of the field occupied recently as my headquarters stand" killed one of

34 Rosecrans, "Chattanooga Campaign," *National Tribune*, March 25, 1882.

35 *OR* 30, pt. 1, 1011-1012.

36 Rosecrans, "Chattanooga Campaign," *National Tribune*, March 25, 1882. Later critics would make an issue of how certain Rosecrans was of Thomas still holding out, charging that at the time Rosecrans believed the whole army had been routed.

Gaw's orderlies and drove the party farther west. The group of riders used the shelter of the intervening hill complex to shield them from enemy eyes as they continued their journey. Rosecrans intended to strike a road that would take him to either Rossville or the Dry Valley Road, and from there find his way back to George Thomas. Captain Gaw's knowledge proved invaluable in this regard, for the XIV Corps's topographer had a firm grasp of the region. The area swarmed with stragglers and military vehicles of every description, but once out of immediate threat the panic subsided. Large numbers of these men belonged to Van Cleve's division, mostly Sam Beatty's brigade. Rosecrans urged them to find Sheridan and join the rear guard.[37]

This hill complex, part of the larger eastern face of Missionary Ridge, was broken by a series of small valleys and hollows. The next major valley to the west was that of Chattanooga Creek. As they rode along, Rosecrans and his party could hear the battle but could see nothing. Eventually they struck the Dry Valley Road again, which carried them up to McFarland's Gap and from there, the road to Rossville. When the riders reined in their mounts around 2:00 p.m., Gaw pointed and said, "'General, this is the direct road to Chattanooga. I trust you will permit me to return to General Thomas?' 'Certainly,'" Rosecrans responded. The momentous discussion that followed triggered a controversy that is ongoing to this day because the two principals involved, Rosecrans and Garfield, each recalled that pivotal event very differently.[38]

While on his way back to Washington, D.C. a month after the battle, Garfield met with Brig. Gen. Jacob D. Cox at the latter's headquarters in Cincinnati, Ohio. Cox, a good friend and political ally, eagerly sought out Garfield's account of the Chickamauga fighting. According to Garfield, by the time Gaw rode away, "mental and physical weakness seemed to overcome the general [Rosecrans]. He rode silently along, abstracted, as if he neither saw nor heard." Even Rosecrans would admit to his brother Sylvester, a fellow convert and an ordained priest, that he had suffered a crisis of confidence. "It was possibly one of the most trying and anxious periods of my life." His solution, as ever, was found in his faith. "But in the midst of it all I prostrated myself in

37 Rosecrans, "Chattanooga Campaign," *National Tribune*, March 25, 1882; Lamers, *The Edge of Glory*, 353. The Rebels encountered could have been from Hindman's division, either from Anderson or Deas; or just as likely, men from Bushrod Johnson's division.

38 John Beatty, "The Diary of John Beatty," *Ohio History*, vol. 58, no. 4 (October, 1949), 413. Beatty recorded this information in his diary entry of Tuesday, March 3, 1884, after a discussion with Thomas Van Horne, who was quoting Gaw.

spirit at the feet of our Crucified Lord and implored his most Sacred Heart to pity us." Whatever the cause of his outward silence—exhaustion or spiritual contemplation—Rosecrans had little to say during the first part of the ride away from the battlefield.[39]

Now, however, there was much to do. The McFarland's Gap Road was also clogged with troops and trains heading back to Chattanooga. The rear of any army in the wake of a reverse is never a breeding ground for optimism, and September 20 in North Georgia was no exception. Rumors abounded. "The whole army was defeated," announced the stragglers. "Rosecrans and Thomas were both killed, and both McCook and Crittenden were prisoners." While Rosecrans knew he, at least, was very much alive, men from the 42nd and 88th Indiana of John Beatty's brigade informed their commander that "Negley's division was knocked all to pieces." Negley, of course, had been sent to Thomas and the extreme left. If that was true, as historian and Rosecrans staffer Henry Cist later reasoned, then "the whole army was a broken mass." This tale also seemed to jibe with the earlier reports from Lieutenant Moody and Captain Hough that Negley needed reinforcements urgently if he was to hold firm.[40]

Seeking confirmation of Thomas's status, Garfield and Rosecrans dismounted and prostrated themselves, ears to the ground. They could hear small arms fire, but little or no artillery. Cist asserted that the lack of cannon fire and only "a scattering fire of musketry" convinced Rosecrans that Thomas had also been overwhelmed. However, Garfield thought he could hear the crash of more regular volleys, signifying a sustained fight: "the sound . . . seemed to indicate that [Thomas] was not yet broken."[41]

And then came the crucial choice: Chattanooga or Thomas? If the whole army was indeed shattered, Rosecrans must return at once to Chattanooga to rally the returning commands and prepare for the city's defense. If Thomas was still holding on, then just as it had been at Stones River, Rosecrans's presence would be invaluable. Perhaps victory could still be snatched from the yawning jaws of defeat. According to Rosecrans, his mind was now awhirl, calculating all the orders that needed to be issued if the army had to fall back to Chattanooga.

39 Jacob Dolson Cox, *Military Reminiscences of the Civil War*, 2 vols. (Charles Scribner's Sons, 1900), vol. 2, 10; William S. Rosecrans to Sylvester Rosecrans, October 9, 1863, William Starke Rosecrans Papers, University of California, Los Angeles. Herafter UCLA.

40 Cist, *The Army of the Cumberland*, 224.

41 Ibid.; Cox, *Reminiscences*, vol. 2, 10.

"In view of all the interests at stake I decided what must be done," exampled Rosecrans. "I said to General Garfield and Major Bond, 'By the sound of the battle over to the southeast, we hold our ground. Our greatest danger is that Longstreet will follow us up the Dry Valley Road. Post, with all of our commissary stores, is over the ridge, not more than two or three miles. . . . If Longstreet advances and finds that out, he may capture them. This would be fatal to us." And then, in what must have seemed a startling burst of energy, Rosecrans began to rattle off orders:

> *First*, Sheridan and Davis must have renewed orders to resist the enemy's advance on the Dry Valley Road.
>
> *Second*, Post must be ordered to push all our trains into Chattanooga.
>
> *Third*, orders must go to Mitchell to extend his cavalry line . . . [to] connect with Sheridan's position . . . and cover Post's train from the enemy until they are out of danger.
>
> *Fourth*, orders must go to [Brigadier General James] Spear's brigade, now arrived near there, to take possession of the Rolling-Mill bridge across Chattanooga Creek, put it in good order, hold it until Post arrives with his trains, then turn the bridge over to him and march out on the Rossville Road and await orders.
>
> *Fifth*, Wagner in Chattanooga must have orders to park our reserve artillery defensively, guard our pontoon bridge across the Tennessee, north of the town, and have his men under arms ready to move as may be required.
>
> *Sixth*, General Thomas must be seen as to the conditions of the battle and informed of these dispositions.[42]

If Rosecrans's account is accurate, Garfield, Bond, and Gaw likely all stared at him, agog at this sudden outburst. Certainly the barrage overwhelmed Garfield. "Can you give these orders?" Rosecrans barked at his chief of staff and future president of the United States. Stunned, Garfield confessed they "are too many and rather too complicated for me." Instead, he offered, "I can go to General Thomas and let you know how things are going there."[43]

Rosecrans's most detailed accounts of this exchange appeared after Garfield's untimely death by assassination in 1881, and benefited from hindsight. In reality, and under those conditions, he would not have been

42 Rosecrans, "The Campaign for Chattanooga," 134. For a slightly different and more abbreviated list of these instructions, see Rosecrans, "Chattanooga Campaign," *National Tribune*, March 25, 1882.

43 Rosecrans, "Chattanooga Campaign," *National Tribune*, March 25, 1882.

capable of summarizing the tasks at hand with such clinical efficiency. Just as they had with his orders that morning, his subordinates had trouble following his train of thought. Here then, according to Jacob Cox, was Rosecrans's "fatal defect" which prevented him from being a great general: "The liability to be swept away by excitement and lose all efficient control of himself and of others in the very crisis when complete self-possession was the essential quality" needed. In reply to this verbal barrage, "Garfield asked a number of questions," recalled Major Bond, "and evinced a hesitancy in undertaking the great responsibility."[44]

In contrast to Rosecrans's recollection, Garfield remembered an entirely different general, one still dazed from the morning's disaster. The army commander, he wrote, merely "assented listlessly and mechanically" to Garfield's request that he be allowed to go to Thomas and discover what had befallen the army's left. Garfield never personally criticized his superior in public, but in private he described Rosecrans as a beaten man, incapable of such an astounding recitation. Such whispers from a man who was his chief of staff had a way of becoming common knowledge. Ever alert to the political winds, Garfield claimed to be worried about "the official and personal propriety . . . [of] turning their backs upon the battlefield . . . without any knowledge of the fate of the greater portion of the army." However, he continued, Rosecrans "yielded" only reluctantly to Garfield's "urgent plea for permission to set out in quest of Thomas." As a strong Rosecrans partisan, Henry Cist perhaps saw a darker motive underlying Garfield's request. Garfield, he noted, argued that it was Rosecrans's "duty" to go back to Chattanooga, especially if the rest of the army had also been routed. He was the only one who could "possibly save the army from complete destruction." With the benefit of hindsight, Cist understood this as a grave error, and one that would cost Rosecrans dearly, but to the mentally exhausted departmental commander it seemed a logical choice at the time.[45]

44 Cox, *Reminiscences*, vol. 2, 9-10. Frank Bond Recollections, CCNMP. Also quoted in James R. Gilmore, "Garfield's Ride at Chickamauga," *McClure's Magazine*, vol. 4 (1895), 358.

45 Cox, *Reminiscences*, vol. 2, 10. Henry Villard, *Memoirs of Henry Villard, Journalist and Financier, 1835-1900*, 2 vols. (Houghton Mifflin and Co., 1904), vol. 2, 157; Cist, *Army of the Cumberland*, 225. Villard had been with the army from May until July (through Tullahoma) and was a familiar figure at headquarters. Taken ill, he returned to Ohio in August just in time to cover the aftermath of Morgan's Ohio Raid. He started back to rejoin the Army of the Cumberland on September 29, reaching Chattanooga on the morning of October 5, 1863. While not present on

There is some corroboration for the idea that Rosecrans lacked his usual energy, lapsing back into a brooding silence. Journalist Henry Villard reached Chattanooga a few days after the battle and interviewed a great many officers about the events in question. According to members in the party, wrote Villard, "General Rosecrans continued his mournful ride from Rossville to Chattanooga in gloomiest despondency." Once there, even the ever-loyal Cist admitted that Rosecrans was so enervated that he "had to be helped from his horse into the house" serving as headquarters, and "that he had the appearance of one broken in spirit."[46]

One other aspect of Rosecrans's decision to head for Chattanooga must be considered. Once again, Rosecrans's urge to personally manage the army's every affair and detail interfered with his primary duty of command. Rosecrans routinely interfered with, and became involved in, mundane details better left to competent staff officers. The result was an inevitable degradation in the efficiency of those officers. As one student of the army's staff pointed out, this "produced [a] distracting doubt in the commander. This lack of confidence in his coordinating staff compelled Rosecrans to depart the battlefield for Chattanooga in order to ensure the completion of necessary tasks" that could and should have been capably handled by those same staff officers.[47]

Phil Sheridan was neither morose nor lethargic. Instead, he was boiling mad. As one biographer described it, "anger, disgust, and . . . outrage that hundreds of his troops had fallen in futile counter-attacks against overwhelming forces" blackened his demeanor at that moment. He was so angry, in fact, that he verged on insubordinate. When his brigades under Walworth and Lytle fell into chaos on the back side of Lytle Hill, Sheridan was in the thick of things attempting to rally the men. The division commander was aware of Rosecrans's presence, but paid the commanding general scant

---

September 20, he had ample time to discuss the dramatic moment with any number of eyewitnesses.

46 Villard, *Memoirs*, vol. 2, 165; Cist, *Army of the Cumberland*, 226. See also Varney, *General Grant and the Rewriting of History*, 209-219. Varney examines the various eyewitness accounts and historical treatments of Rosecrans's demeanor in great detail, noting a number of contradictions. Though he erroneously places Cist with Rosecrans at the time of the breakthrough (Cist was in Chattanooga at that hour) in all other respects his exploration of the various accounts brings clarity to a very confusing episode.

47 Robert D. Richardson, *Rosecrans' Staff at Chickamauga: The Significance of Major General William S. Rosecrans' Staff on the Outcome of the Chickamauga Campaign.* MMAS Thesis, U.S. Army Command and General Staff College, Fort Leavenworth, Kansas, 1989, 173-174.

attention. He even refused a direct summons: "During these occurrences," recalled Sheridan, "General Rosecrans passed down the road behind my line, and sent word that he wished to see me, but affairs were too critical to admit of my going to him at once." Rosecrans didn't linger. After sending orders to Sheridan via courier, he departed as described above. If he had waited, grumbled Sheridan, "the delay would have permitted him to see that matters were not in quite such bad shape as he supposed."[48]

At first, things were every bit as bad as anyone supposed. The initial rout proved hard to arrest. Private Marcoot, one of Laiboldt's men, remembered a line of officers making "strenuous efforts to stop our fleeing commands," but Sheridan himself rode by "on his big black charger and shouting at the very top of his voice, said: 'Let them go! Let them go for their lives, and rally beyond the hill.'"[49]

The retreat was chaotic, but thanks to Wilder, free of Confederate interference. Officers began organizing ranks out of the retreating morass. Sheridan came across one such effort when he found Lieutenant Turnbull of the 36th Illinois, who "had got about one hundred men in line. . . . Gen. Sheridan . . . rode up and said, 'You are doing a good work: have the men fall back to the next ridge and gather up every straggler.'"[50]

Men began to compare notes and marvel at their close calls. During the heat of the action, Cpl. Charles Ayers of the 36th Illinois had rushed to take the place of a fallen corporal in the color guard. Ayers counted no less than "forty bullet holes through his blankets and uniform." Nearby, when Sgt. John Taylor of the 21st Michigan met fellow Wolverines Adjutant Allan B. Morse and Lt. Thomas Stevenson, all three embraced "as a sign of mutual congratulation and gratitude for our escape." Realizing Morse was the senior surviving unwounded officer, they set about gathering in the rest of the regiment.[51]

Wilder's two messengers, Lieutenant Harding and Private Tutewiler, must have found Sheridan early in this process, before much of the rebuilding had begun and when Sheridan was in the blackest of moods. By the time the entire force had fallen back to the second line of hills and was in considerably better

48 Richard O'Connor, *Sheridan the Inevitable* (Konecky and Konecky, 1994), 117; Sheridan, *Memoirs*, vol. 1, 283.

49 Marcoot, *Five Years in the Sunny South*, 37.

50 Marcoot, *Five Years in the Sunny South*, 37; Bennett and Haigh, *Thirty-Sixth Illinois*, 472.

51 Bennett and Haigh, *Thirty-Sixth Illinois*, 472; Taylor, *Lights and Shadows*, 14.

order, things looked a little less dire. While "Little Phil's" anger hadn't abated, the troops were beginning to feel like they might yet be a fighting force. "Before we had gone a mile to the rear, the whole division was reformed," wrote Maj. George D. Sherman, also of the 36th Illinois, "and there, even though we were forced back, three times three cheers were given for the old flag, which made the woods ring."[52]

Colonel Miles, with the 27th Illinois and the rest of his scratch force, were unable to rejoin Sheridan here. Having been cut off, "we were very dubious about escaping," explained Lt. Henry M. Weiss, "but succeeded finally by making a detour thro' the woods and over hill and hollow." Miles reported that his column marched three miles until he stumbled on the divisional ammunition and ambulance trains. The ammunition was much needed, and Miles's men happily refilled their cartridge boxes. The teamsters informed Miles that Sheridan was only a mile and a half to the north. Here among the wagons Miles also found Capt. William E. Merrill of Rosecrans's staff, who suggested he couldn't leave "the heavy and valuable train" unguarded. "I acted on said advice," Miles reported, and escorted the train to a point five miles short of Chattanooga, where he halted at 6:00 p.m.[53]

In place of Miles, Sheridan added most of Davis's division to his strength. Carlin's brigade, absent its brigadier and almost every one of his regimental commanders, was now Maj. James Calloway's responsibility. Major Calloway had once again performed heroically in extricating the 81st Indiana from its predicament that morning, and had even personally saved the 81st's colors. Calloway was now the senior brigade officer present overseeing about 400 other officers and men. The brigade had been reduced to the size of a regiment.[54]

Similarly, Col. John Martin brought in Heg's brigade, which was in even worse shape. As the surviving senior man in the 15th Wisconsin, Capt. Mons Grinigar reported how he and the men "made a hasty retreat to the hill on the north [west] side of the Chattanooga road, in which the battalion soon became scattered." Ultimately the brigade loss would top 57%. Even with the lightly

52 *Elgin Gazette*, October 14, 1863.

53 Henry M. Weiss Letters, CSI; *OR* 30, pt. 1, 598.

54 Morris, *Eighty-First Regiment*, 59.

wounded refusing to leave the ranks, the whole command now numbered fewer than 300 bayonets.[55]

Sheridan was in a quandary. He apparently never received Rosecrans's intended orders for him to act as the army's rear guard, for he never mentioned them. He had no knowledge of the whereabouts of his corps commander, McCook, or of fellow division commander Jeff Davis. Lieutenant Colonel Thruston was close by, but in the general confusion he and Sheridan would not meet until much later near Rossville. Moreover, he noted, "I here learned positively what I had before partially seen, that the divisions still farther on to my left had been driven, and that I was completely cut off." In the absence of any better instructions, "I then determined to connect myself with the troops of General Thomas."[56]

Fortunately, wrote Union Capt. J. W. Hill when describing the moment to his friends back home in Winnebago County, Illinois, "The General [Sheridan] is an ardent, practical student of roads" who made a regular practice of personally familiarizing himself with his surroundings. Hill recollected that in the past couple of days Sheridan and his staff made a point of reconnoitering the various routes to Rossville that might be needed in a pinch, knowledge that now paid off.[57]

The missing man in all this disorder was Alexander McDowell McCook. He was both a corps commander and in charge of the Union right. His responsibilities embraced not just Sheridan and Davis, but the connection with the Union cavalry and the protection of the army's field hospital complex at Crawfish Spring. John Wilder's "Lightning Brigade" was his to use as needed, as was Harrison's 39th Indiana. While his command had been overthrown, broken, driven, and battered, it had not yet been destroyed. The men would fight on, if properly led. Where was that leadership?

Brigadier William Carlin supplied part of that answer when he reached Sheridan's position an hour or so later. When his men broke, Carlin sent most of his staff back to rally them (the force that joined Sheridan) while he did what he could at the front. Carlin observed Laiboldt's destruction, and thereafter the balance of Sheridan's division. However, he also noticed a strange thing:

55 *OR* 30, pt. 1, 534.

56 Ibid., 581.

57 "The Battle of Chickamauga," *Rock River Democrat*, October 7, 1863.

"Where I was standing, the enemy were not advancing." Carlin was observing the effect of Wilder's intervention, and Confederate Maj. Gen. Thomas Hindman's ensuing caution. Though he likely didn't know the cause, he quickly grasped the implication: "It did not seem to me a very serious or at least irreparable state of affairs. . . . It was here," continued Carlin, "that Major General McCook rode up to me and asked me what ought to be done."[58]

If Carlin was shocked at this query, he did not say so. Instead, pointing to the ridge to his rear (which must have been the scene of Sheridan's first rallying point) Carlin "said to General McCook that if he would take his position on that ridge with his staff and corps flag, I thought we could rally our men . . . [in] a new line and hold it." McCook made no reply. Instead, "he rode away." Carlin could only watch him leave.[59]

Alexander McCook was not a coward. Colonel Thruston once loyally observed that he "was wholly without fear in battle." He was not afraid of the front line, as he proved on several bloody fields (he had a horse shot out from under him at Stones River). However, he lacked that particular quality Napoleon Bonaparte valued so highly in a solder—luck. McCook's corps was attacked and effectively routed three times during the course of the war. At Perryville, his troops fought alone and unsupported while the bulk of the Federal army watched, largely because a trick of atmospherics hid the sound of the fighting from his army commander at the time, Don Carlos Buell. At Stones River, he was struck by the main weight of Braxton Bragg's assault, but the army was again slow to come to his aid. Now, at Chickamauga, his men were being driven from yet another bullet-swept field.[60]

Despite Carlin's implication, McCook wasn't fleeing the field. Instead, he deployed his cavalry escort as a picket line to stop straggling, and set his aides to trying to restore order. However, the scope of this new disaster mentally flummoxed McCook, a condition that explained his seeming unresponsiveness. This distress persisted for some time, perhaps for several hours. A short while after that first meeting with Carlin, McCook returned, staff in tow, to tell Carlin

58 Girardi and Hughes, *Carlin Memoirs*, 103.

59 Ibid.

60 James Harrison Wilson, "Alexander McDowell McCook," *Thirty-Fifth Reunion of the Association of Graduates of the United States Military Academy* (Seeman and Peters, 1904), 98. Oddly enough, Rosecrans intended for McCook to be attacked at Stones River, but Bragg struck with much greater strength than Rosecrans anticipated.

that "we couldn't do anything with our men." For his part, Carlin reiterated his idea of rallying on the same distant ridge. Didn't Carlin see "the rebel cavalry coming?" asked McCook plaintively. Carlin saw no Confederates at all. Once again McCook rode away, leaving Carlin alone and fuming.[61]

With that Carlin finally made his own way west, crossing the now-empty ridge to find his way to Sheridan and, with the Irishman, his own troops. Most of Jeff Davis's staff officers were also present, including Orderly Ruger and the divisional pennant, though no one knew Davis's whereabouts. Rumor had it that he was dead or a prisoner. Carlin assumed command of what was left of the division, placed himself under Sheridan, and presumably outlined his previous encounters with the hapless corps commander.

The two generals and surviving field officers held an impromptu council of war, with Sheridan addressing the group. His knowledge of the road network paid dividends. "'We are cut off from the main army and must reach Gen. Thomas with the least possible delay," insisted Sheridan. "This, I think, from my field notes, is ——— Ridge, and if I am right, by following it we shall come to a crossroad where, I hope, we can communicate with the General.'"[62]

Sheridan's reckoning proved correct. The column moved north, collecting more stragglers as it went. The group rode roughly three miles before striking the Dry Valley Road, and then followed that to McFarland's Gap. Though they had yet to find Thomas's XIV Corps, they did meet up with a very much alive and uncaptured Jeff Davis, who resumed command of his division; Colonel Thruston, who still had not located McCook; and Maj. Gen. James S. Negley, bearing what turned out to be mistaken news of the Union left.

McCook was not part of that meeting because by this time he was on his way to Chattanooga, though that was not his intended destination. Unlike Crittenden, Thomas, or for that matter Sheridan, McCook was completely unfamiliar with the terrain. Both the XIV Corps and XXI Corps had spent much of the past week marching back and forth over the surrounding countryside (and a fortnight in Crittenden's case). Their maps were updated and their staffs familiar with the road network. McCook's XX Corps had just arrived on the scene after its hard march up from Alpine. As a result, McCook

61 Girardi and Hughes, *Carlin Memoirs*, 103-104.

62 Bennett and Haigh, *Thirty-Sixth Illinois*, 473. The name of the ridge, if it ever had one, did not survive into print. Sheridan might have been simply referring to Missionary Ridge.

hadn't managed to find time to duplicate Sheridan's efforts and familiarize himself with the neighborhood—more of that ill luck that dogged him.

McCook's first inclination, like nearly everyone else, was to join up with George Thomas. After leaving Carlin, McCook rode north toward the Vittetoe house. He found Jeff Davis rallying a few stragglers. Davis, like Carlin, recalled that McCook "expressed fear of the enemy's cavalry getting around in our rear." For his part, Davis was finding it impossible to rally his division, and he told McCook he needed to fall back to have the time and space to do so. McCook agreed and left Davis to his work. A few yards farther north McCook's party met Capt. Michael Sheridan, younger brother and aide to Phil, who informed McCook that Sheridan's troops were rallying off to the southwest. McCook left the younger Sheridan with orders for his brother to fall back on Rossville, and set out in that direction himself.[63]

Along the way, McCook met a number of staff officers from both Crittenden's and Rosecrans's headquarters. Determining the exact sequence of these chance encounters is impossible, but they all happened between 1:00 and 2:00 p.m. while McCook was seeking a path that would take him to Thomas. One of the first he met was Brig. Gen. James St. Clair Morton, the Army of the Cumberland's Chief Engineer. Morton was in some pain from his arm wound, but asked to be placed temporarily in McCook's service until he could reconnect with Rosecrans. According to Morton, McCook seemed "perfectly composed, and . . . deeply sensible to the reverse the army sustained."[64]

Senator James W. Nesmith and another Rosecrans staffer, Col. John Sanderson, were also present when Morton and McCook met, though they did not join McCook's party. Both groups met near a road jammed with stragglers and transport of every description. Sanderson and some other staff officers were engaged in trying to untangle that mess when McCook rode by and Morton attached himself to the XX Corps's headquarters group. Shortly thereafter rumor buzzed that Rosecrans was alive and not a prisoner; Sanderson and others headed toward Rossville to find him. Realizing that as a civilian he was of little help in the crisis, Senator Nesmith was seeking a safe route back to Chattanooga, and from there intended to head on to Bridgeport. The senator's opinion of McCook was less charitable than Morton's. "I fell in with McCook's

63 *OR* 30, pt. 1, 952, 959.

64 Ibid., 950. For details of Morton's wound, see Chapter 12.

column," wrote Nesmith, which was "demoralized and broken up and rode on their left for an hour and a half, and saw enough of cowardice and imbecility to disgust any . . . man. McCook," concluded the disgusted politician, "ought to try some other business besides fighting."[65]

Sanderson also took note of one other person riding with Morton and (subsequently) McCook—local civilian John McDonald. Pressed into Federal service as a guide, McDonald had lived in the area for 17 years and his doorstep and yard were now littered with the human detritus of the Sabbath morning slaughter. McDonald, who was with Rosecrans when the Union line broke, fell back in the confusion and stuck to Morton. Now his services were desperately needed. McCook explained they wanted to reach Thomas, but everyone understood the direct route was impossible; could McDonald find a safer path?

What followed was a disaster for McCook's subsequent career and reputation. McDonald set off to the southwest, leading the group on what ultimately proved to be a 10-mile diversion. Captain Alexander McClurg of McCook's staff observed that "when we were following the guide, he kept bearing toward the left." The farther they rode, the more uneasy McCook became. "Several times the general expressed the opinion we were going too far to the left: two or three times he rode to the right himself, stopped, and listened to the artillery fire." At one point McCook halted. "That [firing] was certainly General Thomas' guns, and . . . we should keep more to the right, and not in the direction the guide was taking us." McDonald insisted his route "was the only feasible one." By now, many of the riders were growing suspicious of McDonald. McClurg quietly asked another officer "whether the guide was reliable." Was he guiding them into Rebel lines?[66]

Once they crossed Missionary Ridge and debouched into Chattanooga Valley, Morton knew they had gone wildly astray. The wounded engineer took up a map and "prismatic compass" in an effort to track the dust and smoke rising from what was now a distant battlefield. Morton concluded that "the whole army was in retreat for Chattanooga." The group moved on and soon passed a part of General Thomas's XIV Corps ammunition train under the

65 "21 September 1863," Sanderson Letters, OHS; "Dear Cousin Harriet," September 23, 1863, Nesmith Papers, Oregon Historical Society. In another letter, written on the 29th, Sanderson described an unnamed general and his staff "running away from [the battle] like a scared hare." This is almost certainly a reference to Alex McCook.

66 *OR* 30, pt. 1, 958.

command of Maj. John Levering, one of Maj. Gen. Joe Reynolds's staff officers. By now McCook was highly agitated and Levering was not favorably impressed. "[We] had proceeded 6 miles (1/2 way to Chattanooga) when we were overtaken by Gen. McCook and staff on a rapid retreat. They reported 'our whole force cut to pieces and flying in all directions.' After McCook's staff and escort passed, no more seemed to be following. . . . Looked very much like a run on the part of McCook."[67]

McCook's anger was mostly directed at civilian McDonald. Trooper John M. Davis of the 15th Pennsylvania Cavalry watched as, "with his revolver almost under the man's nose," McCook raged, "if you guide us into Rebel lines I will blow your head off! The general [then] used some additional adjectives." The damage was done, however, for they were now miles away from where they intended to be. Riding north along the Chattanooga Valley Road carried them to the intersection with the Rossville Road. There, they met Unionist Tennesseans from Brig. Gen. James Spears's brigade, newly arrived from Bridgeport. McCook was four miles north of Rossville and less than two miles from Chattanooga. Spears also informed McCook of Rosecrans's presence in Chattanooga. With the city and the army commander so close, McCook decided they had best first ride into town and consult with Rosecrans before riding back to Rossville. It was about 4:00 p.m. when the XX Corps commander and his entourage drew rein in front of Rosecrans's new command post.[68]

It is impossible, from this distance in time, to know whether John McDonald deliberately led McCook astray, or if he was simply overwhelmed by events and got lost. If the latter, then once again bad luck plagued Alexander McDowell McCook, whose absence during that critical Sunday afternoon would not pass unremarked. The XX Corps had been effectively decapitated at a stroke, and the leadership void would continue to be evident for the rest of the day.[69]

67 Ibid., 950; Entry for September 20, John Levering Papers, University of Virginia, Charlottesville, VA.

68 Kirk, *Fifteenth Pennsylvania Volunteer Cavalry*, 242; *OR* 30, pt. 1, 959, 985.

69 McDonald did have sons in the Rebel army, but so did many other Unionists in the area. It is worth noting that McDonald was at Rosecrans's headquarters in Dyer Field at the moment of the breakthrough, but did not use that confusion to try and slip away. Instead, he stuck close to James St. Clair Morton.

Chapter Fourteen

West Dyer Field:

Sunday, 12:30 p.m. to 2:00 p.m.

By 12:30 p.m., virtually all organized Union resistance south of the Dyer Road except for Wilder's command had been swept away. Senior Confederate officers pondered their next moves. At the forefront of the advance was Bushrod Johnson. With John Bell Hood's order to "stay ahead of everything" still ringing in his ears, Johnson focused on the next obvious target: the Union artillery pieces lining the ridge on the far side of Dyer Field. Bereft of infantry support, these cannon offered a tempting prize to an aggressive general.

This gun line was the tactical brainstorm of Maj. Gen. Thomas L. Crittenden and his chief of artillery, Maj. John Mendenhall. Crittenden had spent much of the morning watching while his troops were parceled to various sectors, leaving him in the position of something of a supernumerary.

When Tom Wood entered the timber around the Brotherton house and reported his new position offered no good place for artillery, Crittenden, mindful that Saturday's fighting in similar tree cover had cost the Federals a number of batteries, cast about for some better use for the guns of his XXI Corps. He instructed Mendenhall to collect any pieces otherwise unoccupied and post them on the west edge of North Dyer Field, a high ridge overlooking the Dyer farmhouse and outbuildings. It was an excellent position with open fields to the east and south, though there was timber to the north and west. Crittenden also reported (perhaps indulging in a bit of hindsight) that "in the event of any reverse, these guns could cover our retreat." A short while later

Crittenden asked General Rosecrans if he could accompany the last of his command, Horatio Van Cleve's troops, into action.[1]

Van Cleve's unassigned artillery formed the nucleus of Mendenhall's line. The young Mendenhall rode to the rear of Van Cleve's infantry line, which had temporarily halted in Dyer Field, and found there the 7th Indiana, 26th Pennsylvania, and 3rd Wisconsin batteries. Their crews were already somewhat irritated by the repeated shifting of positions, and the new orders did not change their disposition. "As usual," grumbled Wisconsin Pvt. Joseph Brenling, "we charged about from place to place."[2]

Together the batteries numbered 16 guns. Captain Alanson J. Stevens's 26th Pennsylvania was reduced to four tubes after suffering a net loss of two pieces in the woods the day before. Captain George R. Swallow's 7th Indiana and Lt. Courtland Livingston's 3rd Wisconsin batteries still numbered six guns apiece. Taking charge, Mendenhall led them west to the new position.[3]

From there, the gunners had a splendid view of the battle equal to Rosecrans's own. Lieutenant Livingston, who had assumed command of the 3rd on September 13 when Capt. Lucius Drury was severely wounded, placed his four 10-pound Parrott rifles and two older 12-pound brass howitzers at the southern end of the new line. The ground directly behind them was heavily timbered. "The underbrush directly behind us," noted Private Brenling with some unease, was thick enough "to make a retreat straight back impossible." Swallow deployed four Parrotts and two brass Napoleons at the northern end of the line, where the trees covered both his rear and his left flank. Between them, Stevens positioned his four surviving guns, a pair of smoothbore six-pounders and two James rifles.[4]

As evidenced on September 19, like the wounded Captain Drury, Stevens was not afraid to fight his guns at the forefront of an action, and the battery paid a high price in the tangled woods east of Brotherton Field. In addition to the two six-pounders lost there, the 26th suffered significant casualties in men and

1 *OR* 30, pt. 1, 609-610. See chapter 8 for the previous discussion of Crittenden and his movements.

2 "Dear Friend," September 29, 1863. Joseph Brenling Letters, 3rd Wisconsin Battery file, CCNMP.

3 Stevens actually lost four guns, but recovered one and replaced the other with a captured Confederate six-pounder from Carnes's Tennessee battery.

4 "Dear Friend," September 29, 1863. Joseph Brenling Letters, CCNMP.

animals. Stevens was the nephew of one of the most powerful politicians in Washington, D.C.: Pennsylvania Congressman Thaddeus Stevens, Chairman of the House Ways and Means Committee, perhaps the most radical of all Radical Republicans. Alanson and his brother Thaddeus Jr. were also wards of their famous uncle, their own father having died when they were young. The elder Stevens demanded much of his two nephews.[5]

Congressman Stevens was not just a fervent abolitionist but embraced the idea of full equality between the races. He wished nothing more than to see the war prosecuted with all possible vigor. In one letter, the Congressman vented his anger over the war's interminable length by offering this blood-drenched solution: "The slaves ought to be incited to insurrection and give the rebels a taste of real civil war." That sanguinary attitude did not extend to his own kin. Uncle Thaddeus was not happy to see his wards in uniform, believing their talents were wasted on mere soldiering. When they enlisted anyway, he did what he could to further their careers. Instead of seeking a staff position, Alanson Stevens first went to war as a private in the 2nd Pennsylvania infantry, a three-month regiment. In October 1861 he joined the 26th Pennsylvania Battery as an artillery lieutenant and ably led the guns at Stones River. He received permanent command with a promotion to captain on January 5, 1863.[6]

Alanson's embrace of army life alarmed Thaddeus, who worried that the prospect of further promotion might induce Alanson to extend his service: "If you should be made a Col. or Lut. Col. [Lieutenant Colonel] . . . would you not expect to stay for another three years? I had supposed that if you got safely through this term, you might think you had done your share," asked the elder Stevens.[7]

From their position on the ridge, the Federal gun crews spent the next hour or so observing the fighting raging a mile to their front. The obscuring timber masked the details of the action, leaving the guns wanting for useful targets. The 3rd Wisconsin's historian remembered the scene with some foreboding, watching Van Cleve's infantry shifting from position to position behind Wood and Brannan, all the time moving steadily to the left, until, with Wood's departure, there seemed to be no troops at all directly in front of the guns.

5 *OR* 30, pt. 1, 820.

6 Beverly Wilson Palmer and Holly Byers Ochoa, eds., *The Selected Papers of Thaddeus Stevens*, 2 vols. (University of Pittsburgh Press, 1997), vol. 1, 397.

7 Ibid.

During a lull, Captain Stevens took the time to pen a few lines to his friend John Sweney, who managed his uncle's iron works in Pennsylvania: "We have been fighting for three days. I have lost four of my guns and Several of my men but I am unhurt yet[.] We are resting our division and expect to be engaged shortly."[8]

One other Union battery was in position to sweep Dyer Field—Capt. Frederick Schultz's Battery M, 1st Ohio Light, emplaced on an open knoll about 250 yards to the northeast. Schultz's six cannon included four brass James rifles and two of the more modern three-inch ordnance rifles. Battery M's guns faced to the southeast, perfectly sited to provide effective crossfire with the guns on Mendenhall's line, though the positioning was accidental, not intentional.

Schultz's men were there because of Thomas, who ordered James Negley to the open ground near the Snodgrass cabin. Negley subsequently shifted Schultz's battery to the knoll it now occupied in order to protect his southern flank. Other artillery remained in place near the cabin, ready to support the XIV Corps line in Kelly Field.[9]

While these dispositions were being settled, fighting erupted all along the Federal line. Timber obscured direct observation of the fight, so the gunners could only judge the progress of the action by sound and the stream of wounded and stragglers passing rearward. Lieutenant Eben Sturges, a section commander in Battery M, thought the number of wounded officers seemed unusually heavy—a fact that struck him as ominous.[10]

While Mendenhall was placing cannon, Crittenden was trying to find a place in the line for Van Cleve's infantry. After much fruitless shifting about, the orders sending Van Cleve to Thomas arrived and Colonel Dick's brigade promptly moved north. Crittenden left Van Cleve (who was still with Sam Beatty and Beatty's prone brigade behind Connell's line) and was riding toward Mendenhall while trying to decide whether to have the batteries follow their division when, in his words, "my difficulty was suddenly removed by the enemy." Masses of routed men poured out of the trees behind him, "suddenly

8 Anonymous, *History of the Services of the Third Battery, Wisconsin Light Artillery in the Civil War of the United States, 1861-65* (Courant Press, n.d.), 29; Palmer and Ochoa, *Selected Papers*, vol. 1, 412. Two of the four guns Stevens referred to were returned to service. See footnote 4, above.

9 *OR* 30, pt. 1, 330; Entry for September 20, Eben Sturges Diary and Letters, U.S. Army Heritage and Education Center, Military History Institute, Carlisle, PA. Hereafter AHEC.

10 Entry for September 20, Eben Sturges Diary and Letters, AHEC.

and unaccountably thrown into great confusion." Longstreet's attack had broken the Union right.[11]

Despite the fact the resistance put up by the divisions under Brannan and Davis lasted upwards of one hour, the woods hid the full nature of the crisis until the final break came. Until that rupture, all that could be seen of the fighting was the smoke rising from the timber in dense clouds, the casualties headed rearward, and the frantic activity of the staff officers. When the collapse did come, it manifested itself with hordes of routed Federals tumbling out of the trees all at once. The shock was immediate and severe. Riding with Crittenden, Capt. John J. McCook recalled that suddenly "our staff was . . . surrounded by stragglers." Most of them were Sam Beatty's men, who were all but trampled in the first rush. "While awaiting further orders," lamented Van Cleve, "their right was uncovered and a brigade of our army with a battery driven by the enemy passed diagonally through them, injuring and crippling some of my men, and throwing them into confusion."[12]

Beatty's four regiments would be among the most badly disrupted of any Federal troops that morning, despite not being engaged when the rupture came. Beatty reported that "the penetration of our lines separated me from the major part of my command and a part of my staff," which helps to account for the extreme confusion now rampant among his regiments. Beatty's front line regiments, the 79th Indiana and 19th Ohio, were shattered beyond recall and would not fight as intact formations again that day. These two commands broke through Beatty's second line, sweeping up panicked and confused men as they did so. One portion of the brigade fell back northwest toward Snodgrass Hill, while another fragment, together with both Beatty and Van Cleve, fell back west directly toward Mendenhall's guns.[13]

Beatty's second line fared slightly better than his two forward regiments. The coalescing agent here seems to have been Col. George Cram and his 9th Kentucky. After the desperate attempt at a counterattack to restore Brannan's line, Cram led about half of the 9th back toward Snodgrass Hill where, "with the fragments of several other regiments," he and his Kentuckians would join the defense there. Colonel Alexander Stout and at least some of the 17th

11 *OR* 30, pt. 1, 610.

12 "My Dear Sister," September 22, 1863, McCook Letters, NYHS; "My Darling Wife," October 7, 1863, Horatio Van Cleve Letters and Papers, MinnHS.

13 *OR* 30, pt. 1, 809. See Chapter 11 for a detailed description of Beatty's misfortunes.

Kentucky also made it back to Snodgrass Hill. Stout noted that the press of stragglers and pursuing Rebels made it impossible for him to change front, and taking fire from his right flank, he had no choice but to retreat northward. He also likely benefited from Cram's charge, which drew off enough Confederate attention to allow him to move off as a regiment rather than as a mob. Still, the 17th did not escape without loss. Lieutenant Colonel Robert Vaughn and Sgt. Maj. David Duncan were both badly wounded and borne off the field. "With the major [David M. Claggett], adjutant [Edmund L. Starling], and colors, and about 100 men I moved to the left and rear, several times halting and firing a volley at the enemy," reported Stout.[14]

Lieutenant Sturges in Battery M watched all these events unfold from his vantage on the knoll. Despite the hellish chaos, he discerned "some batteries and regiments coming out in tolerable good order." (He must have witnessed Stout's efforts as well as Cram's retreat, since both formations were coming his way.) Sturges could also see other troops headed toward Mendenhall's line of guns, though he could not actually view Mendenhall's batteries from his position.[15]

The friendly artillery ranged on the hills above Dyer Field drew retreating Federals like a magnet. Captain Estep and the 8th Indiana battery arrived first, their escape made possible by the stand of the 13th Michigan and 26th Ohio. Estep unlimbered his six guns on the right flank of the 3rd Wisconsin. As he did so, Lt. Col. Lyne Starling rode up and told him not to start firing until his front was free of friendly troops: currently the field below was alive with Union stragglers. Mendenhall's next reinforcement came from farther afield. Lieutenant Harry C. Cushing's Battery H, 4th U.S. Regulars belonged to Maj. Gen. John Palmer's division of Crittenden's XXI Corps, attached since the previous day to Thomas. Cushing had already been in one hard fight, repulsing the Confederate breakthrough into Kelly Field. Out of ammunition and with one gun temporarily disabled, Thomas had personally ordered Cushing to leave and refit. During that action to repulse Breckinridge, however, someone else ordered his caissons out of Kelly Field, which required a lengthy chase to hunt them down. Cushing eventually located them "back on a hill" somewhere far in the rear. While refilling his limber chests and fixing the disabled gun, Cushing

14 Ibid., 814, 816.

15 Entry for September 20, Sturges Diary, AHEC.

While neither the unit nor the scene are related to Chickamauga, note the spacing between the guns (Battery D, 2nd U.S. Artillery), supposedly in action near Fredericksburg, Virginia. This image offers an excellent idea of the frontage needed for a 6-gun battery. In this case all the guns appear to be 12-pound Napoleons. *Library of Congress*

met Major Mendenhall, who ordered him to Dyer Field. Cushing complied, finding space for his four pieces between the 3rd Wisconsin and the just-emplaced 8th Indiana, his teams under fire even as he swung his guns into place.[16]

Tom Crittenden arrived as well, and from the high ground managed to get a more complete view of the situation. It was both alarming and awe-inspiring. "Here we had a view of the whole field," wrote Lieutenant McCook. "The extreme Left nearly steady, the Centre falling back and the Right trying to reform on the ridge to our right and rear."[17]

The Federal artillery drew more than friendly attention. While these new arrivals swelled Mendenhall's force to five batteries comprising 26 pieces, he still lacked much in the way of infantry. Large numbers of Rebels were beginning to show themselves at the edge of the timber, 400-600 yards distant, their attention directed toward the gun line. When a Confederate battery appeared and unlimbered opposite the 3rd Wisconsin, the Badgers seized upon the target and opened fire. Almost as quickly Crittenden ordered the artillerists to cease fire, for he was still concerned about killing and wounding retreating

16 *OR* 30, pt. 1, 678, 800, 851.

17 "My Dear Sister," September 22,1863, McCook Letters, NYHS.

Union men. The brief but rapid shooting by the Wisconsin men, however, was apparently accurate enough to force the Rebel guns back into the woods.[18]

In the strip of timber just west of the Union guns, meanwhile, Van Cleve and Sam Beatty attempted to rally some of their men. Crittenden rode back and forth between them and the gun line three times, outwardly calm but obviously concerned. He had already sent most of his staff down the reverse side of the slope and off to the left and right in the hope they would rally as many stragglers as possible. Theirs was a meager success. "I went to the left . . . about a quarter of a mile," recalled Maj. Louis M. Buford, "picked up some mounted men and tried to rally the men," but the effort proved fruitless.[19]

Shortly after Captain Estep's guns arrived, one-half of Buell's brigade put in an appearance, sans its brigade commander. The first component to arrive was the 26th Ohio. Having "held its organization under as trying circumstances as war produces," the 26th went into line in front of and down slope from the 3rd Wisconsin battery. The next to arrive was the 13th Michigan, which halted in front of the muzzles of the 8th Indiana. According to the 13th's commander, Maj. Willard Eaton, he made "three separate rallies" in the open field before reaching the ridge where the artillery stood with only "a few of the brave men who started out." This small force, now perhaps no more than 100 men in each regiment, was woefully insufficient to face even one of the multiple Confederate brigades now emerging into Dyer Field. As of yet, the effort to rally some portion of Van Cleve's men failed to produce any organized force worthy of the name.[20]

The threat to the gun line was immediate and palpable. "The rebel infantry seeing the batteries," noted Lieutenant McCook, "quit shooting at the soldiers under the hill and devoted their whole attention to the artillery." Now the guns opened in earnest, any thought of avoiding hitting their own men forgotten. McCook saw at least one "blue flag with a gold star," similar to the standard carried by King's brigade of Regulars in Brig. Gen. Absalom Baird's division, which gave some of the gunners a moment's pause until "when they were out of the woods, seeing their uniforms, all guns opened on them." The noise was simply overwhelming. "The concussion from the artillery was so great," wrote

18 Anonymous, *History of the Services of the Third Battery*, 29.

19 *OR* 30, pt. 1, 975.

20 Kelly, *A Historic Sketch*, 16; Letter to "Brother Rice, September 30, 1863," Eaton Papers, WMU.

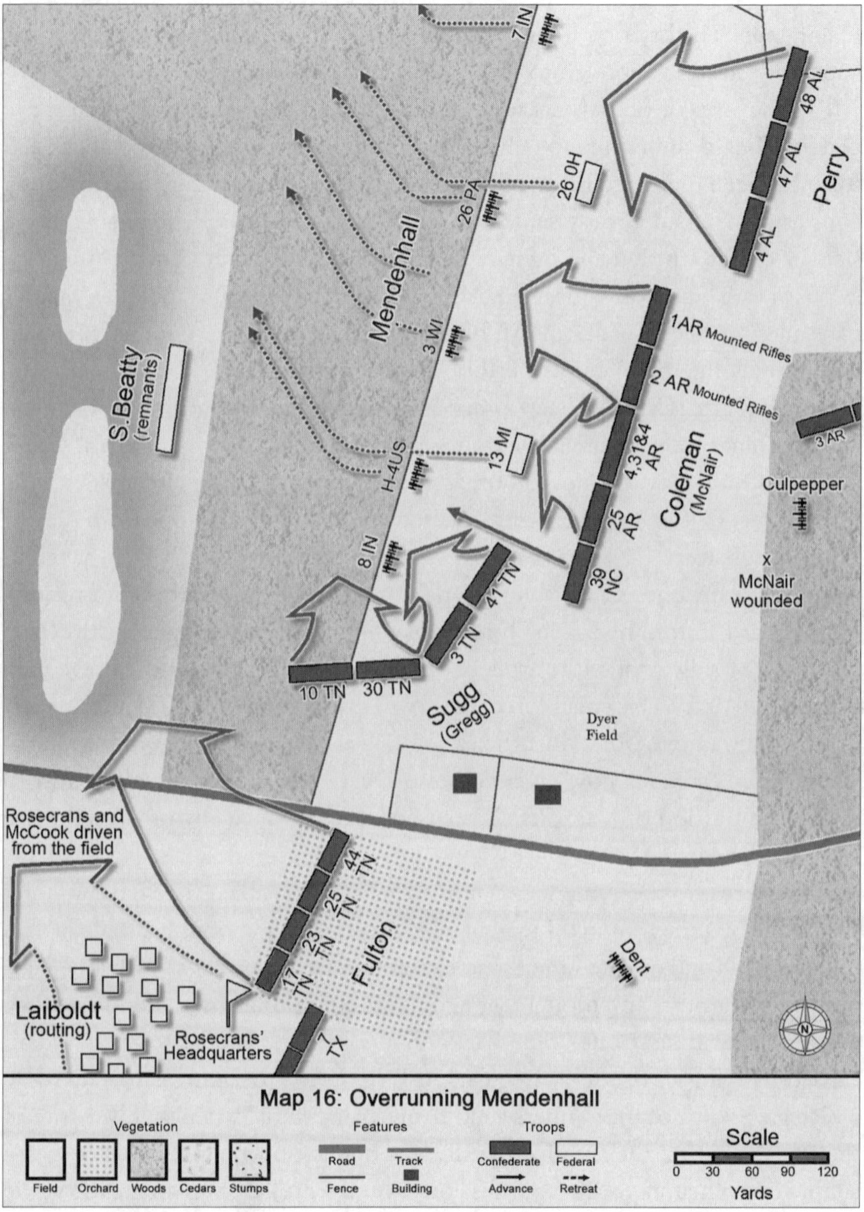

one Union eyewitness, "That several [Union] officers were unhorsed" by the shockwaves.[21]

21 "My Dear Sister," September 22, 1863, McCook Letters, NYHS; *OR* 30, pt. 1, 978.

The view from the far side of the field was an enticing one. There, Bushrod Johnson was working hard to bring his entire division to bear on this thinly manned Yankee line. When Col. John Fulton's brigade emerged into the field, his Tennesseans saw just how little opposition they faced. With no Federals of consequence in their front, Lt. Col. Watt Floyd of the 17th Tennessee pointed out the guns and exclaimed, "Boys, do you see that battery?" His words were met with a cheer. "That's ours!" On Fulton's right, Colonel Sugg (leading Gregg's Tennesseans) formed the center brigade of Johnson's division. The Texans saw the same vision. Also unopposed to their front, Sugg's brigade "emerged from the timber into a cleared field of considerable extent, gradually sloping down from the farther edge, where the enemy had posted a battery of eight guns."[22]

Evander McNair's men burst out of the trees a little farther north, more directly opposite the Union cannon, and suffered accordingly. In the 1st Arkansas Mounted Rifles, Lt. Col. Daniel H. Reynolds recalled the fields filled with Yankees "retreating with great confusion," but even as McNair's men fired into the running enemy, Mendenhall's guns "played upon us effectively." The artillery fire was so effective that Reynolds soon found himself commanding the regiment. Artillery fire wounded both General McNair and Col. Robert W. Harper of the 1st Arkansas Mounted Rifles, the latter mortally. Colonel David Coleman of the 39th North Carolina stepped into McNair's shoes, while Reynolds replaced Harper. Also drawing fire were Lt. William S. Everett and his Company E of the 9th Georgia Artillery (York's Battery). Everett followed Johnson's advance, seeking ways to bring his guns into the fight, but the fluid situation made it difficult.[23]

Everett's Rebel gunners managed to get off 18 rounds when Col. Frederick Bartleson of the 100th Illinois made his earlier ill-advised advance back in Brotherton Field, but had not fired a shot since. The open expanse before him offered tantalizing possibilities, and Everett optimistically moved his three guns into Dyer Field. It was his trio of pieces that the 3rd Wisconsin had engaged so enthusiastically. "Here," Everett reported, "we encountered a heavy cross-fire from the enemy's batteries." A Badger agreed when he remembered, "Our

22 Elijah Wiseman, "Tennesseans at Chickamauga," *Confederate Veteran*, vol. 2, no. 7 (July, 1894), 205; *OR* 30, pt. 2, 495.

23 "Sept. 20, Sunday," Daniel Harris Reynolds Diary, University of Arkansas, Fayetteville, Arkansas. Hereafter UARK; *OR* 30, pt. 2, 500.

battery was trained on them so speedily and severely" that, after managing to get just one piece unlimbered, the Confederate guns "rushed back to cover of the woods."[24]

Bushrod Johnson intended to outflank the Yankees. Riding up to the brigade that until a week earlier was his sole command, Johnson instructed Colonel Fulton to move due west along the Dyer Road at the double-quick and, once into the woods on the far side of the field, turn north behind the enemy cannon. Next, Johnson ordered Sugg's brigade to move west and then wheel to the right, "leaving" as Sugg reported, the Union artillery "on my right." Once in the trees, Johnson intended that Sugg's men would also flank the artillery from the south. Sugg complied, though he fretted about whether there was enough space between his command and McNair's (now Coleman's) to leave his own brigade "unsupported on my right flank." The hardest work belonged to Coleman's troops. From their position along the tree line, Johnson directed them to move directly against the Union position across the field, and into the muzzles of those 26 Yankee guns.[25]

Unbeknownst to Johnson, the better part of yet one more brigade joined in this attack. Shortly after Coleman's men began their advance, Col. William Perry arrived on Coleman's left with his three remaining regiments (the 4th, 47th, and 48th Alabama). Colonel Oates's wayward 15th Alabama was still wildly off course bedeviling Deas's troops, and the 44th Alabama was still back near Brotherton Field. Perry's men must have arrived just as the last Federal cannon were deploying, for he recalled that the Federal gunners "were making the utmost exertion to unlimber and open upon us. One or two of them were already beginning to fire."

Despite stumbling into line alongside the division he was supposed to be supporting, Perry seems to have made no effort at all to find Johnson or anyone else in authority. With that ominous line of artillery trained upon his men, Perry decided "the boldest policy was the safest": he would charge. Perry's decision may well have been driven by his recollection of the previous day's embarrassment in front of General Law. The three new regimental arrivals added roughly 700 men to Johnson's attack, which, combined with Johnson's own numbers, meant that more than 3,000 Confederates were bearing down on Mendenhall's exposed position. In addition to Mendenhall's flaming guns,

24 *OR* 30, pt. 2, 494; Anonymous, *History of the Services of the Third Battery*, 29.

25 Wiseman, "Tennesseans at Chickamauga," 205; *OR* 30, pt. 2, 495.

barely 300 Federal bayonets were in position to oppose roughly 10 times their number.[26]

This area of Dyer Field was not a single open field but rather a patchwork of smaller cultivations bisected by a series of farm fences overgrown with weeds and brush. At least one fence ran through the middle of the field on the north-south axis, with another fence bisecting it east to west, carving the area into a minimum of four separate distinct plots. The fencing proved both a blessing and a curse. Since no one had time to knock them down, they were movement obstacles that hindered the Confederates more than the Federals. They also provided a measure of cover for troops sheltering behind them, another advantage to the defending Yankees rather than the attacking Confederates. The corners of these same fence lines, however, were choked with tall weeds and thick brush that tended to channel the vision of the Federals, so that they focused more on what was happening in front of them rather than on their flanks.

Johnson's attack, well and speedily planned, succeeded brilliantly—though at a high cost. The Federals initially focused on the most immediate threat: Coleman's onrushing line. The 13th Michigan and 26th Ohio faced the first onslaught. Matters quickly became confused for the Federals. Colonel Young of the 26th Ohio made no mention of the 13th Michigan on his right, and was apparently unaware of Major Eaton's presence. Young had not seen his brigade commander, Colonel Buell, since before leaving Brotherton Field. One of Buell's staff officers, Capt. William Baldwin, was present but did not know Buell's location. Far away to the left, too far to provide any support, an unidentified Union "regiment" was visible near Schultz's battery. While this unit cannot be positively identified, it was probably not a regiment at all but an ad hoc force of Federal stragglers. In any case, while its presence might have been symbolically comforting, it was too far away to lend any real help. From Colonel Young's and the 26th Ohio's perspective, they were the only Federal regiment currently in action on this part of the field. In reality, Major Eaton's remnant of the 13th Michigan was also still in the fight, but there must have been a considerable gap and an intervening fence line between the two regiments. This fence obscured the Michiganders from Young's Groundhogs. Despite these circumstances, the 26th Ohio fought tenaciously. According to

26 Perry and Johnson, "A Forgotten Account of Chickamauga," 56.

This image shows the area of Johnson's attack on Mendenhall, from the perspective of Sugg's brigade. The trees on the right are where McNair's and Perry's Confederates deployed. The tree line on the left, rising in the distance, is where Mendenhall's artillery dropped trail. While this area is one large open field today, at the time of the battle farm fences crisscrossed this expanse. *Harvey Scarborough*

Young, he managed to hold the Rebels in front of him back for about "fifteen minutes."[27]

Eaton's 13th Michigan was feeling similarly alone. Once at the artillery, Eaton "hoped to find support," but none seemed at hand. Eaton subsequently reported that he was ordered "to take position at a fence about midway in the [Dyer] field . . . [where] we held the enemy in check for about twenty minutes." (Eaton did not identify who gave him that order, although it could have been General Crittenden, who was likely present, Colonel Starling, or possibly even Major Mendenhall.) Here, Eaton's Wolverines found themselves in the vortex of the storm, taking fire not only from Coleman's men but from Bushrod Johnson's belching artillery. With the Federal guns focusing more attention on the gray infantry, Lieutenant Everett's Georgia gunners re-engaged. In just a few short minutes the 13th's colors were shot down, their bearer killed on the spot, and the flag "literally demolished by a shell passing through it," recalled one eyewitness. The fragments of that flag would later be borne off the field

27 *OR* 30, pt. 1, 673.

with the men, ripped into easily hidden squares should the regiment be captured.[28]

The Federals tried to give as good as they got, and returned a furious fire, both from the two infantry regiments—the 13th and 26th—and from Mendenhall's massed cannon. Facing this stubborn opposition and intense shellfire from the Union guns, Coleman's Rebels also suffered severely. Coleman's report omitted much that took place here, noting only the brigade "charged furiously." In fact, their initial attack faltered. Both Eaton and Young recalled holding for about a quarter-hour, suggesting a much more stubborn contest than Coleman admitted to. Other observers noted this check to Coleman's advance. A member of Sugg's command remembered passing Coleman's men, who "had just charged this battery in front . . . [and] were driven back." Coming up from behind on Coleman's right, Pvt. Theophilus F. Botsford in the 47th Alabama recalled the "line we were to support [was] lying in the fence corners firing upon two batteries of the enemy's artillery." This did not constitute more than a temporary stumble, however. Coleman changed tactics. The fence between the 13th and 26th offered a more protected avenue of advance. Young soon discovered the Rebels working their way around his 26th's right flank using the weeds and brush along this fence line to conceal their approach until the last minute, when they opened fire at close range. Young ordered his Groundhogs to fall back to the fence line in their rear (probably the same fence line Eaton's Wolverines were already defending), and there again made a stand.[29]

Young and Eaton had more than they could stand when Perry's Alabamians entered the picture. For a short time the 4th Alabama halted at the foot of the hill while Perry took stock of the situation. "The slope . . . was bare," noted Adj. Robert Coles, "and on its crest, in full view of us were two batteries supported by infantry, a very difficult position to assault and capture." For a few minutes the new arrivals remained stationary, pouring fire on the Federals and receiving their share in return. But not for long. A galvanizing moment was at hand, and Capt. Lee Terrell seized it. Formerly a member of the 47th but now

28 Letter to "Brother Rice, September 30, 1863," Eaton Papers, WMU; *OR* 30, pt. 1, 667; "Dear Mother," *Allegan Journal*, October 5, 1863.

29 *OR* 30, pt. 2, 500; John T. Goodrich, "Gregg's Brigade in the Battle of Chickamauga," *Confederate Veteran*, vol. XXII, no. 6 (June, 1914), 264; T. F. Botsford, *Memories of the War of Secession* (Paragon Press, 1911), 11; OR 30, pt. 1, 673; Hill, *The 26th Ohio Veteran Volunteer Infantry*, 269.

serving on the brigade staff, Terrill was riding the length of the brigade line when he stopped his mount next to the 4th Alabama's flag. Adjutant Robert Coles of the 4th watched in admiration as "Terrell snatched the colors, wheeled his mount toward Dyer field, and yelling at the top of his voice, spurred his horse toward the Federal batteries." At first only the 4th followed, but soon thereafter the rest of the brigade lurched into the attack. Alongside, Coleman's troops abandoned caution and joined in. The attack was renewed in one wild, if staggered, rush.[30]

To Colonel Young and his Buckeyes, everything seemed to happen at once. Still worried about the problem of the Rebels threatening his right, the Ohio colonel viewed this renewed frontal assault with alarm. Even worse, the Federal "regiment" far to his left (the unknown fragment supporting Schultz's battery) was retreating before another line of advancing Rebels. Worst of all, however, was the disquieting commotion behind him. The blue-clad gun crews seemed to be limbering their pieces and departing. Young faced a grim choice: stand in place and be destroyed, or risk losing control of his command by ordering a retreat. Captain Kelly of the 26th recalled Rebels creeping up through the timber to the north and south, threatening to encircle the regiment. Finally, he confessed, "we were compelled to abandon our position." It was more than time to go. Private Thomas N. Cantwell of the 26th's Company D recorded that the regiment suffered severely during its stand here: "Held them for a while, were charged by four times our number, fell back to a fence where the rebels flanked us, got a cross fire on us, capturing and killing a great many."[31]

Eaton's heavily overmatched 13th Michigan had done an equally impressive job holding back the Confederates in its front. Fully occupied with Coleman's attack, Eaton was unable to do anything about Fulton and Sugg on his right. Indeed, Eaton never realized what was happening as these Rebels reached the trees behind Eaton's right-rear, where they turned north to enfilade the artillery line, forcing the collapse of the entire Union position.

Tom Crittenden was turning away to leave, once again in search of General Van Cleve to bring up any troops he could find, when several battery officers asked him "where they should go in case they were driven from their position.

30 Coles, "History of the 4th Regiment Alabama Volunteer Infantry, CSA"; Laine and Penny, *Law's Alabama Brigade*, 167.

31 *OR* 30, pt. 1, 673; Kelly, *A Historic Sketch*, 16; Hill, *The 26th Ohio Veteran Volunteer Infantry*, 269.

He expected to find support," reported Lieutenant McCook, "so he told them they must not be driven." This was slim comfort. Even "before he left," continued McCook, "a good many of the horses and some of the men had been killed, the enemy being so near upon them." Lieutenant Cushing was one of these embattled artillerymen. His guns were just getting into position, but already the young officer could see disaster unfolding to his right. "You are not to retire at all, but hold your position," Crittenden insisted. The bantam gunner dutifully returned to his guns. Within "a short time," recalled Colonel Starling, Cushing was back telling Crittenden "the enemy had got to our rear and was firing upon us." No one doubted Cushing's courage, for he had already proved himself time and again on this field in North Georgia. If he thought the situation dire, then it was so.[32]

Even so, Crittenden had a hard time grasping just how quickly affairs had deteriorated. "It was impossible" that the enemy could be behind the gun line, he told Cushing, before riding off to see for himself. Finding proof didn't take long. "We were on our horses between two of the guns looking at the enemy's line advancing, when at one volley every horse at the guns were killed. This was the 'hottest' place I was in," confessed Lieutenant McCook, "and . . . I was not sorry to see the general ride toward the rear."[33]

This hammer-blow fell first and hardest upon the 8th Indiana battery. Sugg's brigade advanced unopposed into the cover of the woods just behind and south of the 8th's position, delivered a crippling fire, and charged. Hoosier Pvt. Perry Hubbard recalled that the left-most piece was still firing double canister into the teeth of the oncoming Confederates (McNair's men) even as the right section was being overrun. In their haste to get away, the drivers cut some of the surviving horses loose from the limbers. For the third time in two days, the 8th Indiana battery was about to fall into the hands of the enemy. This time, Estep managed to save only one gun, abandoning the rest amidst a cluster of writhing, dying horses.[34]

This disaster at the gun line was already unfolding behind him when Major Eaton ordered the 13th to retreat. They started back in the nick of time. The 13th Michigan passed through some of the 8th Indiana's abandoned pieces just

32 *OR* 30, pt. 1, 977, 984.

33 "My Dear Sister," September 22, 1863, McCook Letters, NYHS.

34 P. L. Hubbard, "The Capture of the 8th Ind. Battery," *National Tribune*, June 6, 1907.

before Sugg's exultant Tennesseans laid claim to their new trophies. "My heart ached as I passed a line of Parrott guns which stood silently pointing towards the enemy, having been deserted by their gunners," confessed Eaton. Given the circumstances, the major's judgment was unrealistically harsh, though understandable.[35]

Gun by gun, the rest of the line was rolled up. Harry Cushing's 4th U.S. Regulars were next. The frustrated and helpless Cushing watched as more Rebels poured through where the 13th Michigan had been deployed, below him on the slope to his right. The last battery to arrive, Cushing's pieces were still limbered, ready to drop trail. By now it was too late. Cushing recalled giving the order "Action Front, [and] a volley shot all the horses on my right piece." He sent the other three guns away and spent a few moments trying to rescue his stranded cannon, to no avail. Most of Cushing's battery was saved because it was limbered. The 3rd Wisconsin was not nearly so fortunate. Private William Plackett, a driver, remembered that Sugg's crossfire wreaked havoc on the gun crews, dropping men and horses all through the battery's position. Plackett wheeled his limber up to his gun and glanced down the line to the right. He remembered "Horses rearing and plunging, seemingly trying to extricate themselves from their fallen mates. Nothing short of a miracle could save the battery." No miracle was forthcoming. Fellow Badger Joe Brenling, serving one of those guns, recalled the bullets striking "the gun carriage as fast as a drummer can beat his drum." The battery lost 30 horses trying to limber, and left four of their six guns on the line. A fifth was dragged a short way back into the woods, before having to be abandoned.[36]

The 26th Pennsylvania lost two of its remaining four guns here, along with Capt. Alanson J. Stevens, leaving Lt. Samuel McDowell to report the action. Even though Mendenhall had cautioned them not to open fire until they could positively identify the Rebel columns coming out of the woods, the 26th expended its entire supply of canister during the few minutes of this intense engagement. And then the same "galling fire" from the right raked their line, forcing the artillerists into a desperate retreat. One gun was successfully limbered, and another retired by prolonge with the aid of some infantry stragglers, but the other two could not be withdrawn. Stevens was killed trying

35 Letter to "Brother Rice, September 30, 1863," Eaton Papers, WMU.

36 *OR* 30, pt. 1, 800; Anonymous, *History of the Services of the Third Battery*, 29; "Dear Friend," September 29, 1863, Brenling Letters, CCNMP.

to save them. As the left-most section was leaving, the captain called for volunteers to help him go back for the remaining pieces. A bullet pierced his left breast, and he died quickly. There was no time to collect his body.[37]

The 7th Indiana battery escaped relatively intact, deployed on the northern flank when the Rebel attack struck from the south. There, the Hoosier guns were banging away at Perry's Alabamians when Capt. George R. Swallow noticed Stevens's gunners, adjacent on his right, taking fire. Swallow's short ride south to the Pennsylvanians put him in the midst of several infantrymen, all of whom were aiming northward along the line of the Union guns. "What are you shooting at our own men for?" demanded the shocked artillery officer. His answer arrived when the muzzles of five Confederate muskets swung toward him. Realizing his error, Swallow turned to gallop away, leaning over in his saddle to use his horse as shelter. Riding back through the 7th Indiana, he yelled, "Limber up and get out of here!" Somehow all of the guns managed to limber, though one piece became irretrievably wedged against a stump and was abandoned.[38]

While Sugg's men were flanking the gun line from the south, Perry's and Coleman's troops crashed into the batteries from the front. Rushing up the hill in Coleman's brigade was Capt. John Lavender at the head of Company F of the 4th Arkansas. The Yankees, recounted Lavender, "made a Desperate Stand . . . but they could not Depress the Guns Enouf to hurt us without hurting their own men." Private Botsford, of the 47th Alabama, remembered Union gunners running up the elevating screws as fast as they could, trying to depress the guns enough to deliver a point-blank fire at the onrushing Rebels, "hoping to wipe out the line with one volley." The gunners over-compensated and fired too low, allowing the Alabamians to press on unscathed, swarming forward "with clubbed guns" to capture the 3rd Wisconsin. Any doubts of Perry's performance had been dispelled, for he was at the forefront of the desperate

37 *OR* 30, pt. 1, 820-821. See Palmer and Ochoa, *Selected Papers*, vol. 1, 413, and Albert G. Chadwick, *Soldiers' Record of the Town of St. Johnsbury, Vermont* (C.M. Stone & Co., 1883), 178 for details on Stevens's death. Later efforts by Thaddeus, Jr. to find his brother proved fruitless. Captain Stevens was hastily buried on the field, and almost certainly was later reinterred as an unknown soldier in the National Cemetery created the following year in Chattanooga. A prolonge was a rope attached to the gun carriage that allowed the gun to be moved short distances by dragging it.

38 O. H. Morgan and E. R. Murphy, *History of the 7th Independent Battery Indiana Light Artillery* (n.p., 1895), 24.

charge, urging his men on amid "hatfuls" of canister. His *sang froid* under fire "gave to everyone the liveliest assurance of his courage and capacity to command."[39]

All told, the Confederates captured 14 guns on the bloody slope. Competition was fierce for credit. Sugg's men claimed the greatest honor and the largest share of the spoils, sending nine pieces to the rear, several pulled along by captured Union drivers and teams. Sugg's role in the attack had been nearly bloodless, "taking three batteries with very little loss," boasted Lt. James Thompson, the 3rd Tennessee's assistant surgeon. Lieutenant Clarence Malone of the 10th Tennessee described the charge in a matter-of-fact manner: "Out in an open field they had a battery of eight guns. We started at it. The [Federal] infantry ran but the cannoneers fired until we got within thirty yards. They were nearly all killed or captured."[40]

By contrast, McNair's brigade (under Coleman) suffered significantly. The men claimed 10 captures (including some of the same guns seized by Sugg), but reported sending only eight pieces to the rear immediately—two guns tangled up in the woods were not recovered until after the battle. Perry's men made no specific claims, though Perry noted that "every piece of artillery, and a few of the horses, fell into our hands." Botsford settled for more mundane loot. He lost his hat in the charge, but a brief search turned up a new one, complete with ostrich feather. Sugg's and Coleman's brigades began quarrelling over who captured which guns almost immediately, an argument that festered for decades. Their lively and very public disagreement obscured Perry's role in the attack. The park tablets eventually resolved the matter by attributing the joint capture of 15 cannon to Sugg and Coleman—without mentioning the Alabamians at all.[41]

39 John W. Lavender, *They Never Came Back: The Story of Co. F. Fourth Arks. Infantry C.S.A (Originally Known as the Montgomery Hunters) as Told by Their Commanding Officer* (The Perdue Co., 1956), 80; Botsford, *Memories of the War of Secession*, 11. Perry and Johnson, "A Forgotten Account of Chickamauga," 56; Oates, "General W. F. Perry and Something of his Career in War and Peace," *Montgomery Advertiser*, March 2, 1902.

40 *OR* 30, pt. 2, 497-498; Robert W. Ikard, "Lieutenant Thompson Reports on Chickamauga: A Comparison of Immediate and Historical Perspectives of the Battle," *Tennessee Historical Quarterly*, vol. 44, no. 4 (Winter, 1985), 427; "Dear Florence," September 28, 1863, Clarence C. Malone Letter, Martha Harper Clayton Papers, DU.

41 *OR* 30, pt. 2, 500; Perry and Johnson, "A Forgotten Account of Chickamauga," 56; Botsford, *Memories of the War of Secession*, 12; Park tablets refer to either "nine cannon" or "fifteen cannon," but in fact, a close reading of the Union battery reports makes it clear that the five

General Crittenden was not present at the gun line when it fell to the Confederates. Instead, he was struggling to bring Van Cleve, Beatty, and their handful of men forward. "About 100 yards to the rear," recounted Lt. Col. Lyne Starling, we "met General Van Cleve bringing about 75 men to try and support the battery." While so embarked, "Major Mendenhall rode up and said that the batteries had been taken." There was no choice now but to retreat farther west across the Dry Valley Road to a second hill, where another 100 or so stragglers were gathering. Other survivors fell back northwest through the woods to eventually arrive at Rossville.[42]

Crittenden, like Alex McCook, would soon face a great deal of condemnation for his subsequent actions, and eventually a court of inquiry. He was at a loss about what to do next. Unlike General McCook, Crittenden effectively had no command at the moment of disaster, for all of his troops had been parceled out to fight with George Thomas. Rosecrans was gone, the knoll formerly occupied by army headquarters completely overrun. The Dry Valley Road was an impassible mess, jammed with abandoned vehicles and threatened by advancing Rebels. Stragglers roamed the hills, many showing little interest in sacrificing themselves as a rear guard or in a forlorn effort to retake lost gun tubes. After a half-hour, and when "stragglers had ceased to pass . . . Crittenden remarked, 'I believe I have done all I can.'" Turning to his staff, the corps commander next asked, "'Can any of you make a suggestion?'"[43]

Crittenden's query touched off a short debate. Most everyone believed Rosecrans and McCook were either dead or prisoners, and no one knew anything about what was happening on Thomas's front. Starling ventured the opinion that "if General Crittenden regarded public opinion or newspaper reports, that he had better try to go to Thomas . . . 'You know I care nothing of that kind,'" shot back the corps commander. "'My whole object is to do my duty as an officer.'" In that case, Crittenden's "proper position was in Chattanooga, to reorganize the scattered troops for further operations." Crittenden's reasoning appeared sound, so the entire party rode north cross

batteries involved lost 14 guns during the fight, as delineated above. The "nine" clearly refers to Lt. Beaumont's report, from Sugg's brigade, describing the removal of nine guns. See *OR* 30, pt. 2, 498. Mendenhall reported that all six guns of the 8th Indiana were captured, instead of five, which explains why most accounts peg the loss at 15. *OR* 30, pt. 1, 623.

42 *OR* 30, pt. 1, 984.

43 Ibid.

country toward the Dry Valley Road on the far side of McFarland's Gap. This path would take them as far as Rossville. From there, they could either turn back south to join Thomas or go on to Chattanooga.[44]

A mile or so on, the party came upon Col. John G. Parkhurst and the 9th Michigan infantry. Parkhurst and his men were serving as the XIV Corps's provost guard. On the previous day, the 9th escorted some of General Thomas's wagons back to Chattanooga. Early on the 20th, before the fighting began anew, Parkhurst and eight companies of the 9th started back toward the battlefield escorting a train of medical supplies. The Wolverines were approaching McFarland's Gap from the west when Sgt. Charles R. Brand of Company G witnessed a dismaying sight: "Cannon driven at full speed, army wagons, ambulances, horsemen, footmen, able and disabled all rushing to the rear."[45]

There could not have been a more timely appearance of a provost guard. "I had seen one stampede & succeeded in checking it" at Stones River, recalled Parkhurst, and "I thought I could do the same again . . . so [I] put my regiment in line of battle across their path—bayonets fixed." The quick-thinking Parkhurst ordered his men to halt everyone who tried to pass, separating those actually injured from those simply panicked; letting the former pass and putting the latter back into some semblance of a line. "Most dismaying of all," observed Sergeant Brand, "was the number of officers begging or demanding to be let through. . . . A Colonel drew sabre on one of our . . . boys because he would not allow him to pass, but cooled down quickly when told a bayonet would pass through him."[46]

Before long, Parkhurst had formed enough men into companies to constitute an ad hoc regiment, which he placed under the direction of Maj. William C. Janney. A number of cannon were also collected, which Parkhurst turned over to Capt. William A. Hotchkiss of the 2nd Minnesota. Hotchkiss had come through the gap under trying circumstances, extricating his battery while being shelled by Rebel guns that made the roadway all but impassable.

44 Ibid., 985. Lieutenant Colonel Starling, testifying before the official court of inquiry for Crittenden, larded his account with dialogue calculated to place his boss in the best possible light before the board.

45 "Friend Lizzie," September 28, 1863, Charles R. Brand Letters, 9th Michigan File, CCNMP.

46 "My Dear Sister," September 29, 1863, John G. Parkhurst Letters, Bentley Historical Library, UMich; "Friend Lizzie," September 28, 1863, Brand Letters, CCNMP.

Abandoned and broken vehicles blocked passage, forcing Hotchkiss to untangle the jam "by drawing them out in columns, piece by piece, on either side of the road."[47]

By the time Crittenden's party appeared, Parkhurst had perhaps 1,000 men gathered up, including his own regiment and the supporting artillery. Parkhurst, a 39-year-old lawyer from Coldwater, Michigan, cut an imposing figure on horseback with his full dark beard, but he was not a professional soldier. And because he was not, the colonel offered Crittenden command of the scratch force. Crittenden complimented Parkhurst on his quick thinking and good work but declined the offer. The general's exact words, however, at least as reported by Parkhurst, were unsettling: "This . . . is no command for me," snapped the Kentuckian. Taken aback, Parkhurst responded, "The force . . . collected . . . was too much of a command for me." "You have done marvelously well and you had better keep command," Crittenden rejoined hastily, seeking to reassure the officer. Next, Crittenden inquired about Rosecrans. Parkhurst knew nothing for sure, and could only pass on a rumor that Rosecrans had gone either to Chattanooga or Rossville.[48]

Crittenden's refusal to assume the responsibility was abrupt and off-putting, but it was also the correct decision. At that moment, he still did not know whether McCook or Rosecrans were alive, unhurt, or prisoners of war. Going on at least as far as Rossville made sense for the corps commander; from there, he could establish contact with Generals Thomas or Granger, and hopefully better assess the overall situation. However, not leaving a general officer behind to take charge and help Parkhurst was much less excusable. Both Horatio Van Cleve and Samuel Beatty were either present with Crittenden, or nearby rallying their own men. Since he had just been with them, Crittenden certainly knew where they were. Why neither general was tasked with this mission remains yet another unanswered question.

Leaving Parkhurst with orders to slowly fall back toward Chattanooga, guarding the retreating trains as he did so, Crittenden rode on to Rossville. After a mile or so he met two of Rosecrans's staff officers, who give him the first definite news of the army commander's whereabouts. Rosecrans, they assured him, had ridden on to Chattanooga. About 2:30 p.m. Crittenden reached

47 *OR* 30, pt. 1, 264, 505.

48 Ibid., 264-265, 989. Colonel Parkhurst later described the straggler contingent as "a small regiment." Sergeant Brand thought they had more, estimating the stragglers at some 2,000 men.

Rossville, where this information was confirmed by a number of other officers, including Lt. Col. Arthur Ducat of Rosecrans's staff. The Kentuckian should have halted here, where he could have taken control of the chaotic situation in the army's rear and established contact with Thomas. Senior leadership was in short supply at Rossville, and Crittenden's presence could have made a real difference. Instead, Crittenden rode on to Chattanooga, which he reached about 4:00 p.m.—the same time as General McCook. It was a fatal decision.[49]

The Confederates also had decisions to make. In addition to securing the fruits of victory in the form of hats and field pieces, Bushrod Johnson pondered his next course of action. Fulton's and Sugg's brigades had suffered little and were still in good shape, but they were short of ammunition. To Johnson, the next obvious position to hold was an open ridge about 600 yards southwest of Mendenhall's gun line, ground that commanded the Dry Valley Road. Once there, Johnson deployed his command in an L-shaped line, with Sugg's brigade facing north and Fulton's men facing west overlooking the narrow valley leading north toward the Vittetoe home. Lieutenant Everett's Georgia battery (three guns) unlimbered in the 100-yard gap between Fulton's right and Sugg's left. From this line, Fulton's skirmishers could descend into the valley (referred to as "the hollow" or "the cove" in some reports) toward the panicked and retreating Yankees visible below. About this time, Johnson also discovered that Coleman's brigade was missing after becoming separated from the rest of the division during the attack. Johnson sent an urgent appeal to Longstreet for more troops, and especially artillery, to exploit the enemy's confusion.[50]

Only Everett's three pieces had kept up with the advance. Johnson's other two batteries (Bledsoe's Missourians under Lt. R. L. Wood and Capt. James F. Culpepper's South Carolinians, a combined eight guns) fell behind early in the attack and would not fight with their division for the rest of the day. A thankful Johnson received an unlooked-for replacement when Capt. Samuel H. Dent's Alabama battery, with six first-class Napoleons, rolled up to his new position. Dent belonged to Thomas Hindman's division and started the attack behind Zach Deas's brigade. He had tried several times to unlimber, each time firing only a few rounds before the tide of battle swept away from him. Before long he lost track of his division. When he heard firing to the northwest, Dent rolled his

49 Ibid., 265.

50 Ibid., pt. 2, 458-459.

guns in that direction and stumbled upon Johnson. He unlimbered to add his firepower to Everett's trio of pieces.[51]

While Everett and Dent were going about their deadly business, Fulton's skirmishers descended down into the hollow. Instead of organized opposition, they met the detritus of an army fleeing for its life. A large number of vehicles crowded the narrow valley, including wagons, ambulances, artillery limbers, and caissons competing for road space in the defile. When Dent's and Everett's shells began dropping among them, more panic set in. Vehicles recklessly driven overturned, others jammed between trees when anxious drivers sought ways around the blockage, and many more were simply abandoned. Lieutenant R. W. McCullough of the 17th Tennessee discovered Rosecrans's field telegraph line snaking along the road, which he was immediately ordered to cut.[52]

Only minutes before, that same telegraph line was humming with messages. A Federal telegrapher remembered the moment Rebels appeared here and opened fire:

> My office at one p.m. Sunday was a spring by the side of the road, which ran through a narrow gorge immediately back of our right center. The road was crowded with retreating ambulances, artillery, wounded soldiers, etc. . . . The enemy . . . came up to within less than one hundred yards and poured their fire in and through the gorge. Several were killed immediately around me, and before I could get out my instrument and mount my horse, I was very near being crushed in the melee. I changed my base! For a mile and a half up the gorge we were exposed to a fire of shell from a battery planted immediately where my office had been. Unpleasant, very.[53]

Not every Yankee was in full retreat mode. Captain William Hotchkiss ordered his 2nd Minnesota battery to throw a few shells in the direction of the Confederate guns. Everett responded the this fire by moving one Rebel gun down into the valley to open a raking fire up the defile, wreaking havoc on the vehicles trapped there. Everett's other pair of guns were brought to bear on the Minnesotans. One of Everett's six rounds broke the axle of one of the Union cannon, which sent the rest of the battery's guns and artillerists packing. With

51 Ibid., 465-466; Dent's Alabama Battery Tablet, CCNMP.

52 *OR* 30, pt. 2, 459, 482.

53 Anonymous, "From the Chickamauga," *Missouri Democrat*, October 8, 1863. Rebel soldiers cut lengths of wire from the telegraph line as souvenirs.

the last Union opposition dissolved, Johnson moved to take possession of the spoils.[54]

The bounty was rich. Ordnance wagons provided enough cartridges to resupply both Fulton's and Sugg's brigades. Several cannon were captured, including one Napoleon originally taken from Capt. Charles L. Lumsden's Alabama battery the day before. Two limbers from the Federal Battery G of the 1st Missouri were also captured, further crippling that command. Battery G's commander and Sheridan's acting chief of artillery, Capt. Henry Hescock, had been captured earlier near the Widow Glenn house along with two of his pieces. Although the guns were soon recaptured, Hescock remained in Rebel hands. The entire area yielded a tremendous haul in personal effects. Rows of Union knapsacks marked Van Cleve's first position that morning when his men dropped them in what was assumed to be the rear before going into action. All of them were appropriated by the victorious Rebels. Captain William Harder of the 23rd Tennessee thought them an odd sight: the knapsacks lined up neatly, but no "men or rifles." Blankets, clothing, personal possessions, even food—all were fair game now.[55]

While Fulton's and Sugg's troops were sorting through these spoils, Coleman's and Perry's men were retreating because they were unable to locate General Johnson and they worried about a Federal counterattack. "With our forces reduced by our rapid advance," Coleman reported, "our ammunition nearly exhausted, it was necessary at once to abandon our position." The retreat was a rather disorderly one and reduced the cohesiveness of the command. The 1st Arkansas Mounted Rifles, admitted Lieutenant Colonel Reynolds, had been "badly cut up and scattered by the enemy's batteries." Reynolds rallied a portion of the 1st, but, unable to locate Coleman, attached his battered regiment to the right side of Brig. Gen. Joseph Kershaw's South Carolina brigade, which was just arriving in Dyer Field. The rest of Coleman's men retired all the way back to

54 *OR* 30, pt. 2, 460. If this battery was the 2nd Minnesota, Hotchkiss reported no damaged guns, so the damage must have been quickly repaired.

55 George Little, *A History of Lumsden's Battery, C.S.A.* (R. E. Rhodes Chapter, United Daughters of the Confederacy, 1905), 18; *OR* 30, pt. 2, 460; Harder Reminiscences, TSLA. Hescock's capture created some confusion amongst the Confederates. Both General Johnson and Colonel Sugg reported the guns of the Union 1st Missouri artillery were turned over to Bledsoe's Confederate 1st Missouri battery. The Union 1st Missouri, however, was not part of Mendenhall's artillery line, and it reported no permanent gun losses during the battle (just the two limbers were lost).

Brotherton Field, found some fresh ammunition there, and settled in for some rest.[56]

Perry had similar concerns. He wanted to attack when he spotted a Union force a couple of hundred yards into the woods (likely Van Cleve and Beatty's scratch force), but the disorganized state of his command gave him justifiable pause. His brigade was intermingled with Coleman's command, and his Alabamians were also low on ammunition. "About this time," wrote Perry, "I observed a body of Confederates on our left, moving in good order." The colonel rode over to the commander of this force (whom Perry did not identify, but who had to be Bushrod Johnson) and proposed a plan: Johnson's men could flank the Federals again, while his Alabamians hit them head on. Since Johnson was already attempting something very similar, he agreed.[57]

Perry returned to his men. Once there, however, he witnessed another Rebel line to his right-rear in hasty retreat. "I have never understood what caused it," he later wrote. He was observing Jerome Robertson's Texans falling back in the face of a Union counterattack. When Coleman's men started back as well, Perry's regiments were left alone at the scene of the recent triumph. Thinking a general retreat had been ordered, Perry followed suit. On the way east he passed General Hood, who was attempting to rally the Texans, and halted his troops inside the trees on the east side of Dyer Field. Just a few minutes later Hood passed Perry, this time badly wounded and being borne off the field in a litter. Hood's fall triggered confusion in the Confederate ranks, and Perry's troops would be largely forgotten.[58]

With the exception of William Oates's 15th Alabama, Perry's other regiments were essentially finished fighting for the day. The battle for Horseshoe Ridge, however, was just beginning.

56 *OR* 30, pt. 2, 500; Entry for September 20, 1863, Reynolds Diary, UARK.

57 Perry and Johnson, "A Forgotten Account of Chickamauga," 56.

58 Ibid.

Chapter Fifteen

North Dyer Field:

Sunday, 12:00 p.m. to 2:00 p.m.

At noon, Tom Wood and George Thomas were on the Glenn-Kelly Road a couple hundred yards southeast of the Kelly farm. On Thomas's orders, Wood had just dispatched Sidney Barnes's brigade to the north end of Kelly Field to support Absalom Baird's division. Wood and the XIV Corps commander, along with Charles Harker's brigade, were waiting for George Buell's four regiments to catch up. Buell failed to show.

Buell, of course, had been struck mid-move by Bushrod Johnson's attacking Rebels. The collapse of Jeff Davis's division was also under way, with Phil Sheridan's fate soon to be sealed thereafter. Neither Thomas nor Wood had any way of knowing any of this, or that the entire Union right flank was collapsing. Another fight, much closer to home, was drawing their attention: combat along the front of John Brannan's division had swelled to a cacophony.

Brannan's line was only 600-700 yards to the south, and Wood ordered Harker to move his brigade back that way to see if Brannan needed help. Harker was just beginning to move when the agitated Lt. Ira Germain of Brannan's staff arrived. Brannan did indeed need help, and he needed it quickly. Wood soon confirmed with his own eyes the extent of the looming crisis when he looked back toward his former position: "I found the valley [to the] south . . . swarming with the enemy."[1]

1 *OR* 30, pt. 1, 635, 694.

That "swarming" enemy—the Texans and Arkansans of Brig. Gen. Jerome B. Robertson's brigade—crossed the La Fayette Road on the left of Henry Benning's brigade and behind William Perry's five Alabama regiments about 11:30 a.m. The previous day's bloody fight in Viniard Field had knocked about one-quarter of Robertson's 1,300 troops out of the ranks, leaving a battle line this day of about 1,000 men.

They might have started out in reserve, but Robertson's troops were veteran enough to know, in the words of Pvt. James M. Polk of Company I, 4th Texas, that "we would soon have another big killing." Private Polk's comrades took advantage of minutes before the fighting to indulge in a little gallows humor. Pulling Polk close to him, Pvt. Jack Massie joked, "you get by the side of me. When you fall I want that watch." Another soldier, Sgt. Bob Crawford, could not resist chiming in: "I want his boots." Less than 30 minutes later they were in line tramping toward the eastern edge of Dyer Field. Polk's expectations of a "big killing" were about to be met.[2]

As described earlier, Colonel Perry's brigade (minus the 15th and 44th Alabama) merged with Bushrod Johnson's division in the assault against Mendenhall's guns. Simultaneously, Benning peeled away his brigade to the right to roll up John Croxton's Federals in Poe Field. These movements opened a broad gap of about half a mile between Perry's right and Benning's left, a dangerous chasm Robertson felt obliged to fill. The brigadier wheeled his line to the right, changing "front forward on the first battalion" until his line faced north. Once properly aligned, or so Robertson believed, he resumed his advance, moving parallel to Benning on the Georgian's left, perpendicular to (and behind) Perry's line.[3]

Thus far, other than the odd stray shot, Robertson's men had not suffered at all. They represented Hood's fourth line, so by the time the Texans crossed the La Fayette Road any Union defenders there had long since been driven off. They moved through the now-abandoned Union position on the far side of Brotherton Field and across the Glenn-Kelly Road, where Robertson decided to turn north.

Once reoriented, Robertson and his men found themselves chasing a broken foe. Many Federal stragglers were coalescing around a battery of Union

2 J. M. Polk, *The North And South American Review* (Press of Von Boeckmann-Jones Co., 1914), 36.

3 *OR* 30, pt. 2, 511.

artillery on a high hill on the far side of an open field several hundred yards wide. The Ohio guns belonged to Capt. Frederick Schultz's Battery M, where Lt. Eben Sturges of the same battery was watching the drama unfold. Robertson's advance was not without problems. The 5th Texas, lagging behind its three sister regiments, soon lost sight of the brigade in the belt of timber during the wheel to the right. The 5th Texas had also lost its regimental commander, Maj. Jefferson C. Rogers, the day before to a severe wound. That injury thrust Capt. John S. Cleveland into regimental command. Temporarily adrift, the 5th halted. On Cleveland's right, Benning's Georgians were falling back (in the face of a counterattack by the 10th and 74th Indiana). Captain Cleveland interpreted Benning's retrograde as a general order to retreat and followed suit for about 100 yards before realizing his mistake. The untimely error, however, deprived Robertson of nearly 30 percent of his effective strength at a critical moment.[4]

While Captain Cleveland and the 5th Texas were falling back, Robertson's remaining three regiments (from left to right, the 3rd Arkansas, 1st and 4th Texas) moved north, though the grand wheel had disordered their normal parade-ground cohesion. The 3rd Arkansas's Col. Van Manning on Robertson's left, for example, was concerned about the "deranged condition of the line" during the change of front. Unaware of the temporary loss of the 5th Texas and despite the disordered condition of the rest of his line, Robertson decided to press on rather than halt and reform. Federals were gathering around Schultz's guns, and any delay might prove fatal.[5]

A large number of Union troops were now reaching Schultz's position. The three surviving guns of Church's Battery D, 1st Michigan arrived and unlimbered on Schultz's right. Captain Church, it will be recalled, lost half his battery in the fight for Poe Field when Col. John Connell's brigade line was flanked and overrun. Church sent these three pieces back to find a place to deploy while he attempted to recover the three abandoned guns. Church himself appeared shortly thereafter, on foot after losing his mount in that attempt. The Michigan gunner arrived to a familiar scene: Rebels threatening the front and right flank of this new line. Elements of Connell's infantry were rallying here too, in the form of bits and pieces of the 31st Ohio, Sgt. Harry

4 *OR* 30, pt. 2, 517. Major Rogers would never return to field duty. Permanently disabled, he resigned his commission on October 24, 1864.

5 Ibid., 513.

Allspaugh among them. Members of the 17th Ohio were also present, mixed in with Allspaugh's fragment of the 31st. One of these was Cpl. Alanson Gierhardt of Company K, who was shocked to see his friend Pvt. Henry Shirts standing there. "[I] stepped up to him," wrote Gierhardt, and said, "'Henry, I thought you got shot down in the edge of the woods?' 'I did,' said he, 'look here,' taking hold of the U.S. plate on his cartridge box, he showed me the point where the ball had struck and glanced off." The bullet had bowled Shirts over and knocked the wind out of him, but did not inflict any serious harm; Shirts recovered a few minutes later and legged it out in time to avoid capture.[6]

More of Connell's brigade fetched up farther north, halting near the Snodgrass house to rally amidst Maj. Gen. James Negley's command. Later, Sergeant Allspaugh would discover that the 31st's commander, Lt. Col. Frederick Lister, the regimental colors, and about 125 more men reformed there. Allspaugh would not see them again until the next morning.[7]

Also present on the knoll were Colonel Buell and Lt. Col. James Embree with the 58th Indiana. The Hoosier regiment maintained its organization during the retreat and, with a portion of Maj. Charles Hammond's 100th Illinois attached, stopped at the tree line on the right of Schultz's guns. The 100th might have already lost its colonel, a pair of companies, and a number of casualties, but the survivors were still game. Illinois Sgt. George W. Holmes of Company G lingered behind a tree firing at Confederates until he noticed he was alone. "[A]fter going through a cornfield, [and] up a hill," he wrote, "I [found] the major [Hammond] rallying the men on the brow."[8]

Some of Sam Beatty's men were also present, including the 9th Kentucky's Marcus Woodcock. "Our regiment was so badly scattered that no man could have decided which way it was going, and by some means I had lost sight of the colors," Woodcock confessed. His odyssey makes for a colorful episode. After trodding angrily on a fellow Federal laying prostrate in a gully, Woodcock ran into Dyer Field, where he briefly fell in with a regiment he thought were his comrades of the 9th Kentucky, only to discover the men were complete strangers. When this unknown unit dissolved, Woodcock observed "the rebels charging on one of our batteries . . . on the crest of a hill." Scrambling toward

6 Entry for September 20, Harrison Allspaugh Diaries, University of Iowa; *OR* 30, pt. 1, 414; A. L. Gierhardt Recollections, OHS.

7 Entry for September 20, Harrison Allspaugh Diaries, University of Iowa.

8 Hight, *Fifty-Eighth Regiment*, 193; Woodruff, *Fifteen Years Ago*, 291.

the Union defenders, Woodcock "found a gallant band of near 500 men who seemed to have been gathered from all regiments." This scratch force would do its best to defend Schultz's and Church's combined battery of nine guns, but its members would need more substantial help if Robertson was going to be repulsed.[9]

Robertson was also looking for support. A series of aides galloped to the units on his right and his left seeking help during his northward drive, but he got no takers. The division was acting without a guiding hand. No one in Benning's, Perry's, or Robertson's brigades mentioned seeing or interacting with division commander Evander Law during this phase of the battle. Bushrod Johnson, even then confronting a similar tactical situation just a few hundred yards away in west Dyer field, was successfully coordinating his three brigades in a combined frontal and flanking attack against Mendenhall's line. By contrast, Law seems to have lost control of his division. Benning changed front to attack the Poe Field line of his own volition. After shedding two of his five regiments, Perry joined Johnson's attack on his own initiative. Robertson saw a gap in the front line and moved his brigade into it without orders, and when he saw a Union line off to the north, changed front and requested help from Benning and Perry (to no avail). Law, who should have been orchestrating all of this, was notable by his absence.[10]

Part of Law's problem may simply have been the continued lack of horseflesh. Adjutant Robert Coles of the 4th Alabama noted that all of the horses had to be left behind in Virginia, something that triggered comment among the western Rebels. By this time, however, most of the field officers had secured mounts by some fashion. Colonel Perry borrowed his horse. General Benning, who led his command off the train at Catoosa Station on foot, rounded up horses for himself and at least some of his staff before the battle started that morning. Unfortunately, Law left no report or even a postwar

9 Noe, *A Southern Boy in Blue*, 208-209. The battery was clearly Schultz's Battery M, 1st Ohio Light. Woodcock's first "regiment of strangers" remains unidentified. However, his recollection fits with the 26th Ohio's Lt. Col. William Young, who mentioned an unknown Federal unit well off to his left. (See chapter 12.) The "regiment of strangers" was probably another conglomeration of stragglers and not a full regiment. The "gallant band" Woodcock joined was the same force Sergeant Allspaugh described, and included elements of the 17th and 31st Ohio, 100th Illinois, the bulk of the 58th Indiana, and a scattering of individuals from a number of other units.

10 *OR* 30, pt. 2, 511.

account of his actions during the battle, so his movements during this phase, or even whether he was mounted, remain unknown.[11]

Despite this lack of help, Robertson pressed on, leaving the 5th Texas to catch up as best it could. Manning's 3rd Arkansas was still on the brigade left, the 1st Texas to Manning's right, and—with the absence of the 5th—the 4th Texas on the brigade right. In the 4th, Sgt. Valerius Giles remembered briefly halting at the edge of a woodlot before the charge. This tree line was the northern limit of the same large belt of timber that concealed Bushrod Johnson's men as they readied themselves to assault Mendenhall's gun line. Looking north, the Texans could see open ground rising toward Schultz's knoll, as well as a much smaller woodlot about 200 yards distant on the flat ground below the rise. "The Federal batteries beyond the old field were making our position a veritable hell on earth," Giles remembered thinking. Hell or not, the brigade went forward, even as Robertson sent out second and third appeals for support. All went unanswered. The Texans angled northwest, making directly for the knoll crowned by Schultz's battery.[12]

The unsupported attack "advanced to the top of the hill and drove the enemy from it," reported Robertson. Captain James T. Hunter, in charge of the 4th Texas (by the end of the day, all three Texas regiments would be led by captains) concurred: "On our gaining the height they deserted it."[13]

This was not quite so. During the Rebel advance, a mistaken order created the impression of another Union rout. According to Lieutenant Sturges, "the enemy kept getting nearer, owing to the absence of support on our right. [I] heard an order given to 'get that battery out of there.' Looked to the left and saw that the captain with the other four guns was already some distance in the rear. [I] limbered to the rear and started after him." Sturges never learned who gave the order. Perhaps it came from one of Negley's aides, sent to collect the guns on Negley's order. In any case, the instruction nearly proved disastrous. Witnessing this commotion and now sure of success, the Texans surged forward.[14]

11 Coles, "History of the 4th Regiment Alabama Volunteer Infantry, CSA," ADAH; Coles, "Letter of September 26, 1863," Abbott Papers, GDAH.

12 Mary Lasswell, ed., *Rags and Hope: The Recollections of Val. C. Giles, Four Years with Hood's Texas Brigade, Fourth Texas Infantry 1861-65* (Coward-McCann Inc., 1961), 203.

13 *OR* 30, pt. 2, 511-512, 515.

14 Entry for September 20, Sturges Diary, AHEC.

The Confederates sensed a significant tactical victory at hand, but John Brannan disagreed. At that critical moment, the Union division leader galloped into the middle of Schultz's guns and ordered the gun crews to move back into place. Brannan's own brigades were rallying on the next ridge north, and he needed time to weave a new line out of the wreckage. By the time the field pieces returned to their positions to unlimber, however, Robertson's Confederates were already retreating. Another blow, equally unlooked for, had just landed.[15]

The Texas Brigade was on the verge of likely success when small arms fire began zipping up and down the line—from both flanks. The frustrated Robertson believed other Confederates were doing the shooting, including those who had previously declined to help him. A private in the 4th Texas named Lawrence Daffan also believed it was friendly fire, and that it was a result of mistaking the 4th for Federals because of their "new, neat, and standard uniforms. Bragg's army had never seen a well-uniformed Confederate Regiment before," he sneered. The new uniforms drawn by so many of General Longstreet's men while still in Virginia included wool jackets so dark they "appeared more blue than gray." Some of this fire may well have originated from confused Confederates, but there were also plenty of Yankees still in the fight.[16]

The initial pressure came from Robertson's right flank. With the 5th Texas still lagging, Robertson called them forward, relaying the news that the brigade had overrun three Federal guns and needed help. Captain Cleveland hastened the 5th across the field. During his advance, Cleveland's formation received a volley from a Union line concealed in the timber to its east. There, Hoosiers from the 74th Indiana fired from a position near the blacksmith shop. Captain Cleveland wheeled the 5th Texas to his right and fired back, a volley Capt. Tacitus Clay claimed "proved so fatal that they scattered and fled." In reality the Hoosiers were already retreating, having merely fired a parting shot before falling back toward Kelly Field. Mindful of Robertson's instructions, the Texans did not follow. Instead, Cleveland left Clay with a skirmish line to guard this flank while he hurried with the balance of the regiment to reconnect with

15 Ibid.

16 *OR* 30, pt. 2, 512; Kate Daffan, *My Father As I Remember Him* (Press of Gray and Dillaye, 1907), 41; Col. Harold B. Simpson, *Hood's Texas Brigade: Lee's Grenadier Guard* (Landmark Publishing, 1999), 324.

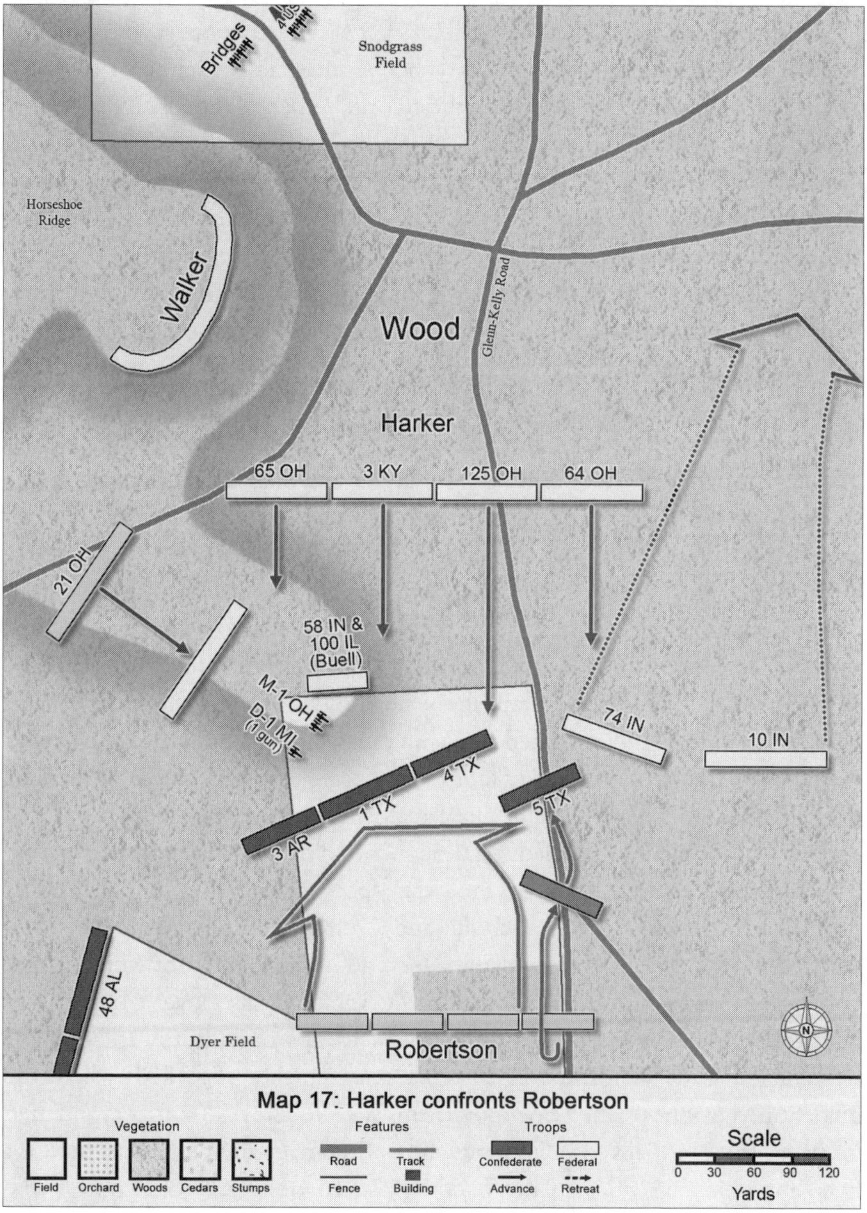

Robertson. By the time he reached the battle line, however, the rest of the brigade was already falling back.[17]

17 *OR* 30, pt. 2, 517.

The incoming fire striking Robertson's left was much more severe. Many of these rounds probably came from other Confederates—either Perry's or Coleman's brigades could have been the culprits. When Mendenhall's survivors retreated, any Confederates firing at them would also be shooting in Robertson's general direction. However, there was also a new large Union regiment just moving to join the fighting here. This regiment—the 21st Ohio—belonged to Col. William Sirwell's brigade of James Negley's division, part of George Thomas's XIV Corps. These Ohioans had been loaned out to John Brannan while he was casting about for troops to help hold his new line. Brannan's mission for them was vague: move out on his right and defend the ridge.[18]

From its position in the lane east of the Snodgrass house, the 21st Ohio moved through the chaos unfolding atop Horseshoe Ridge. The Buckeyes shifted "south and west, about one fourth or three eighths of a mile," recalled Capt. Isaac Cusac, and "the first man I saw that I recognized was Colonel [Moses] Walker, of the 31st Regiment O.V. I., who was making a great effort to rally the broken lines." Captain Cusac met up with Walker on what would come to be called Hill One of Horseshoe Ridge, and there he and the rest of the regiment helped the colonel establish the beginnings of a new line on the south slope of the ridge. "We remained there but a short time," continued Cusac, and then moved farther south to "a flat, or low piece of ground" at the foot of the ridge. "Although we had to fight our way down the ridge, the enemy appeared very careful and slow to attack us, as though they did not know what was in their front." Several descriptions of the "flat spot" match the spur extending southeast to the knoll where Schultz and Church were deployed. This new location offered the Buckeyes of the 21st a good position from which to fire into the Texans's left flank. Initially, the Ohioans also had trouble with uniforms. First, they identified the body of troops moving toward them as retreating fellow Unionists. That idea was quickly dispelled when the unidentified troops opened fire upon them. With roughly 500 officers and men on hand, the 21st packed quite a punch, its firepower augmented by the Colt five-shot repeating rifles in the hands of seven of its ten companies. The regiment was also well supplied with nearly 100 rounds apiece. The volume of

18 Silas S. Canfield, *History of the 21st Regiment Ohio Volunteer Infantry, in the War of the Rebellion* (Vrooman, Anderson and Bateman, 1893), 116.

return fire coming from this body of men would have greatly worried any field commander, and Jerome Robertson was no exception.[19]

All of these threats conspired to further disrupt Robertson's already disordered line. Colonel Manning reported his 3rd Arkansas "engaged the enemy but a few minutes before the entire line gave way under the apprehension that our position was being turned by a flanking party of the enemy." Manning's sense of being outflanked is easily explained: in addition to the 21st Ohio appearing on his left front, his Arkansans also suffered under a crossfire from friendly troops in his left rear. That scenario is exactly what Capt. R. J. Harding of the 1st Texas, next in line to Manning's right, reported when he wrote, "At this point we received a very destructive fire from some regiment not known, but supposed to be friends, on our left and the rear." By this time there was nothing Robertson could do. "Before I could stop it," he reported, "my line had been thrown into confusion, and I found it necessary to fall back to reform." Fortune's smile had suddenly reversed, and the Texans now tumbled rearward several hundred yards.[20]

Captain Cleveland, who had just caught up to Robertson with the bulk of his 5th Texas, also fell here. Cleveland received (as reported by Captain Clay, who had just inherited command of the 5th, though he did not know it yet) "a severe wound in the fleshy part of the thigh." The 5th, momentarily leaderless, fell back with the rest of the brigade.[21]

At just this moment a fresh Union line weighed in and converted the Texan retreat into a rout. At George Thomas's direction, General Wood and Colonel

19 Ibid.; George E. Dolton, "Chickamauga," *National Tribune*, November 9, 1893; *OR* 30, pt. 1, 390; Canfield, *History of the 21st Regiment*, 141, 144. Dolton was not a member of the 21st, but instead served in Battery M, 1st Illinois, which did not reach the ridge until more than an hour later. In later years Dolton studied this part of the battle in minute detail, corresponding extensively with men of the 21st about every aspect of their experience that fateful Sunday. Unfortunately the bulk of his papers are not in any public repository, if they even still exist, but we do have several examples of his writing on the subject. The number 539 was the strength given by Maj. Arthur McMahan in his report. Bradley Quinlin, the 21st Ohio's outstanding modern historian, places the number a little lower (around 500). Bradley Quinlin and Joshua Haugh, *Duty Well Performed, the Twenty-First Ohio Volunteer Infantry in the Civil War* (Little Miami Publishing Co., 2011), 49.

20 *OR* 30, pt. 2, 512-514.

21 Ibid., 517. Captain John S. Cleveland would never return to the regiment. He spent the fall of 1863 at a Confederate hospital in Selma, Alabama, and when released, made his way back to Texas for the rest of his recuperation. As of March 1865 he was still disabled, detached to the Department of Trans-Mississippi and capable only of light duties.

Harker were moving south when Wood realized the field before him was full of Rebels. The division commander ordered Harker to change front to the rear, extending all four of his regiments to form a single line. This line, from left to right, included the 64th Ohio, 125th Ohio, 3rd Kentucky, and 65th Ohio. Once deployed, Wood rushed the men forward to reinforce Buell's remnant holding on to the east slope of the knoll.[22]

Harker's brigade numbered slightly more than 1,200 men, holding a frontage 300 yards wide. They moved steadily south until Wood could clearly see the Texans trying to reform in Dyer Field. The Rebels were still 500 yards distant, the two sides separated by the fence sketching the northern boundary of the field. Wood turned to the 125th's commander, Col. Emerson Opdycke, and ordered him to charge. Mounted on his horse Barney, Opdycke eased his way to the front, ordering "fix bayonets" and "Forward at the double-quick" as he did so. "The steel rattled in answer," Opdycke proudly wrote his wife. "Barney galloped forward, and the 125th came after, with a yell that rose above the din of battle." The rest of Harker's men surged after them.[23]

Confederate bullets were already finding their mark by the time the men of the 125th made it to the fence line and threw themselves to the ground, pulling the rails into a rude breastwork. Having seized the fence by a *coup de main*, the Buckeyes opened a deadly fire on Robertson's men. The 64th Ohio came up on Opdycke's left and the combined fire of the regiments further paralyzed the Texans. The Ohio 65th and 3rd Kentucky fell into line on Opdycke's right, with the 65th also connecting to Colonel Embree's detachment and the rump of the 17th/31st Ohio, forging a new battle line that now ran from the Glenn-Kelly Road all the way up to and over the knoll where Schultz's cannon were just returning to their position at Brannan's exhortation. Offset to Schultz's right-rear, the large 21st Ohio still lurked in the trees.[24]

22 Ibid., pt. 1, 708.

23 *OR* 30, pt. 1, 636; Glenn V. Longacre and John V. Haas, eds., *To Battle for God and the Right: The Civil War Letterbooks of Emerson Opdycke* (University of Illinois Press, 2003), 100; Charles T. Clark, *Opdycke Tigers: 125th O.V.I. A History of the Regiment and of the Campaigns and Battles of the Army of the Cumberland* (Spahr and Glenn, 1895), 107; Longacre and Haas, *To Battle for God and the Right*, 100. Harker reported 1,346 men present on the 19th, and lost 71 men on the first day. However, two companies of the 3rd Kentucky had been detached as skirmishers in Brotherton Field, and had not yet rejoined the brigade before disaster struck. Those two companies found their way to Snodgrass Hill later in the day, but were not present for this first engagement.

24 Clark, *Opdycke Tigers*, 107; OR *30*, pt. 1, 636.

Colonel Emerson Opdycke (left), from an image taken later in the war.
Library of Congress

Now what? The Federals had stopped the Confederate advance and driven it back to the middle of the field, where it was reorganizing and exchanging fire with them—but it was not retreating. The forest and intervening heights to his right prevented General Wood from knowing about the opportune arrival of the 21st Ohio, but he could see the 5th Texas trailing Robertson's main line, turning to fire at the 74th Indiana in the woods off to the left before hurrying forward to join the brigade. Wood also noted that Harker's sudden appearance "seemed to take the enemy by surprise and disconcert his movements." All of these factors suggested to the aggressive Wood that the moment was ripe for a renewed attack. And who better to lead that attack than Opdycke and the 125th Ohio?[25]

This time Wood took a few more minutes to organize things. In a more coordinated movement, he sent the 64th and 125th Ohio forward to press the Rebels. Lieutenant Charles Clark of Company F, 125th Ohio, was only 19 but already a veteran who had demonstrated his military skills during his several months of service. Despite his youth, he was now in command of Company H because the rest of that company's officers were absent. The attack would remain vividly etched in Clark's mind for the rest of his life. The two regiments employed an unusual maneuver not taught in any of the drill books: "'Advance, firing.' In that movement," explained Clark, "the files doubled up, making four ranks, leaving intervals through which the rear rank passed, running rapidly forward a few paces, halting, firing and dropping to the ground to load, the next rank meantime passing still farther to the front to deliver its fire, and so on in succession."[26]

25 Ibid.

26 Clark, *Opdycke Tigers*, 107.

What Clark was offering was a detailed description of Brig. Gen. August Willich's patented attack formation—the one Willich had used to such good effect on September 19 in the woods near Winfrey Field. Where and how Harker's men learned the technique remains a mystery. What was not a mystery was the result: a methodical advance combined with a wall of fire that delivered a volley every 15 or 20 seconds while still sustaining a measured forward progress. If executed properly, "Advance, Firing" was a devastating technique—as Willich's men demonstrated the previous day and Harker's troops did so now, "breaking the Rebel line and causing them to fall back in confusion." To Sergeant Giles of the 4th Texas, this was "the meanest, most unsatisfactory place I struck during the whole war." All around him, "men [were] staggering and stumbling to the rear covered in blood, some swearing and some calling on God to protect them in their blind endeavor to find shelter from the storm of iron hail, [it] made me feel like the world was coming to an end then and there." Under this pressure, the Rebels broke again and fell back in a disorganized mass.[27]

Wood was positively jubilant—giddy with excitement and success. "See the Tigers go in!" he shouted admiringly while watching the 125th—unknowingly christening them with a nickname that would forever stick: "Opdycke's Tigers." A small thinly wooded copse of trees projected into Dyer Field between the Ohioans and Robertson's men, and as the 64th and 125th reached the fence bordering the southern edge of this open woodlot they halted and poured additional fire into the fleeing Rebels. "That was a glorious charge and if I live it shall be made official and go into history!" exulted Wood to the 125th's adjutant, E. G. Whitesides. "Our view southward was now wholly unobstructed," wrote Company F's Lieutenant Clark. The Buckeyes could see Robertson's broken command retreating, but behind them the fields were alive with other Rebel regiments maneuvering to face them.[28]

27 Clark, *Opdycke Tigers*, 107; Lasswell, *Rags and Hope*, 203. There is no obvious connection between Willich's brigade and any of Harker's regiments. Where the 125th Ohio picked up the drill remains unknown, and Clark does not say whether or not Harker's entire brigade was trained in the tactic or if only the 125th Ohio used it. It is possible that Harker, a young, forward-thinking officer, observed Willich's men training in it and decided to adopt the technique himself.

28 Richard A. Baumgartner and Larry M. Strayer, *Ralsa C. Rice, Yankee Tigers: Through the Civil War with the 125th Ohio* (Blue Acorn Press, 1992), 65; Entry for September 20, E. G. Whitesides Diary, AHEC; Clark, *Opdycke Tigers*, 107. From here on, the 125th took the nickname of "Opdycke's Tigers" as its own. Today, this copse is a considerable thicket, about 100 yards

Unfolding before Clark's eyes was one of the most fateful moments of the battle of Chickamauga, though he would not know it until years later. Riding among Robertson's broken men was Maj. Gen. John Bell Hood who had just ordered Brig. Gen. Joseph Kershaw to change front to the right and support Robertson. Hood intended to rally Robertson's brigade (formerly his own) and met the brigadier at the southern edge of North Dyer Field. Hood was conferring with Robertson when a bullet struck him in the upper right thigh, shattering his femur. Stunned, Hood slipped from the saddle into the arms of men he had led since he was a colonel. The superstitious Texans took note of the fact that Hood was not riding his favorite roan, "Jeff Davis." The men considered him invincible so long as he was mounted on "Jeff." When Hood was forced to ride another horse at Gettysburg because "Jeff" was lame, fragments from a shell that exploded above him ripped into his arm early in the fighting. Here in North Georgia, "Jeff" was wounded in the previous day's fighting and once again unable to bear his master. This time Hood would lose his leg.[29]

Union artillery was also playing on the reforming Rebel line, inflicting additional losses. One of these unfortunates was Capt. Robert Bassett of the 4th Texas's Company G. The Texans were rallying in the timber when a Yankee shell struck the fork of an oak tree about 20 feet off the ground, splitting the tree in two. One of the falling limbs crushed Bassett's shoulder so severely that he subsequently died.[30]

Hood's fall was a damaging blow to the Confederates. General Longstreet was still back near the Brotherton farm, having ceded tactical control of the attack to his trusted subordinate. Now that Hood was out of action, no one was sure who should take charge. An already difficult command situation had just become much more chaotic. Confederate brigades were drifting all over the field as it was. As noted earlier, Perry and Coleman had just passed behind and through the retreating Texans to the relative safety of the trees east of Dyer Field, both commands essentially directionless after storming Mendenhall's

wide, and obstructs the view southward from Harker's original line. At the time of the battle it was smaller in dimension and much more open. It was probably used as a daily fuel source for the Dyers. No account of this part of the fight mentions it being an obstruction to either movement or visibility.

29 Hood, *Advance* and *Retreat*, 63-65.

30 Lasswell, *Rags and Hope*, 204.

gun line. Benning lacked orders after being pushed back by the 105th Ohio's reckless charge. With Hood being carried off the field, Robertson felt he had no chance of successfully renewing his attack. "Having failed to get the co-operation of the only forces in reach," he complained, "I formed my brigade in the timber and awaited orders." Curiously, he said nothing in his report about Kershaw's and Humphreys's two fresh brigades even then wheeling into position behind him.[31]

Hood's last act hurled Kershaw's brigade directly at Harker's line. Kershaw's command was larger than most. With five regiments and a battalion, South Carolinians all, it numbered 1,596 officers and men. Kershaw's regiments formed from left to right as follows: 2nd South Carolina, 3rd South Carolina Battalion (also known as James's Battalion) and the 3rd, 7th, 15th, and 8th regiments. The brigade occupied at least 400 yards of frontage, but maneuvering to the front had spread the regiments out until their line overlapped Harker's Federals on both flanks. Because of the absence of division commander Maj. Gen. Lafayette McLaws, Kershaw was temporarily in charge of the division (which included Brig. Gen. Ben Humphreys's Mississippi brigade) but he also decided not to cede tactical control of his South Carolina brigade to its senior colonel. Chickamauga was his first test of combat as a division commander. Numbering 1,226 men, Humphreys's four Mississippi regiments would extend Kershaw's line left (eastward) another 300 yards—if they could deploy alongside quickly enough to join in the advance.[32]

Joseph Brevard Kershaw was 41 that third September of the war. The South Carolina lawyer served as a lieutenant in the Mexican War, though without seeing combat; he was struck down by fever and returned home a physical wreck. After he recovered he entered politics and served as a state legislator. John Brown's 1859 raid on Harpers Ferry, Virginia, prompted Kershaw to join the state militia. He supported secession, served in the state's secession convention, and volunteered with part of his militia regiment to go to Virginia in May 1861. There, Kershaw was promoted to brigadier general in February 1862 and assumed command of the brigade that would bear his name for the next two years. Kershaw was 5'10" tall, with striking blue eyes and a deep commanding voice. By the fall of 1863, the South Carolinian and his men were veterans of all the Eastern Theater's combats except Chancellorsville. At

31 *OR* 30, pt. 2, 512.

32 Powell, "Numbers and Losses," CCNMP.

Gettysburg, the brigade took a fearful pounding from Union artillery during the July 2 fight south of the Peach Orchard, losing 649 out of 2,183 officers and men.[33]

Initially, Kershaw advanced through Brotherton Field around 11:45 a.m. As he crossed the La Fayette Road, Longstreet warned him about the ongoing threat to his right flank, where considerable fighting was still raging around the Poe farm. In response, Kershaw shifted Col. John W. Henegan's 8th South Carolina a bit to the rear. The brigade continued west several hundred yards into Dyer Field, where Kershaw met General Hood (just minutes before Hood's wounding) and received instructions to turn 90 degrees to the right. All the while, a steady flow of men fell through their ranks on the way to the rear. Watching Perry's Alabamians falling back, men in the 15th South Carolina called them cowards. Stung by the accusation, one of the Alabamians fell in with the 15th to continue the fight. On the brigade's left flank, John Coxe in the 2nd South Carolina saw Sugg's nine captured artillery pieces rumble past driven by Union prisoners—a clear sign of victory. According to Coxe, it was about noon when "we heard from a party of jubilant officers that the center and right of the Federal army had been smashed. . . . [W]e raised a great Rebel shout."[34]

Shortly after Kershaw changed front one of Evander Law's staff officers brought word that Hood was down. The first complications of that loss arose almost at once. The staffer suggested that since he was senior, Kershaw should take command of the two brigades on his right (Robertson and Benning) as well as his own force. This debate was underway when Bushrod Johnson rode up seeking support for his men, then halted south of the Vittetoe farmstead. Johnson wanted to press the Yankees up the Dry Valley Road and seize the high ground to the northwest. Kershaw thought little of this idea since he still had to deal with Federals in his front and (based on Benning's discomfiture) to his right. When the two generals were unable to settle on a plan, Johnson demanded a comparison of date of rank to determine who held seniority. Kershaw had the advantage, which settled the question. The South Carolinians would move against Wood and Harker off to the north; Johnson would have to

33 D. Augustus Dickert, *History of Kershaw's Brigade, with a complete roll of companies, biographical sketches, incidents, anecdotes, etc.* (Elbert H. Aull Co., 1899), 86-87; John W. Busey and David G. Martin, *Regimental Strengths and Losses at Gettysburg* (Longstreet House, 1986), 281.

34 *OR* 30, pt. 2, 503; "Dear Mother," September 20, 1863, David Crawford Letters, University of South Carolina, Columbia, SC; John Coxe, "Chickamauga," *Confederate Veteran*, vol. XXX, no. 8, (August, 1922), 293.

find support elsewhere. This "seemed to satisfy him," reported Kershaw. However amicably the issue was resolved, the incident just minutes after Hood fell demonstrated just how much his guiding presence would be missed.[35]

At this point Hood's assistant inspector-general, Maj. Edward H. Cunningham, made the germane suggestion that perhaps someone should go to Longstreet and let the wing commander sort things out. A relieved Kershaw agreed and asked Cunningham to ride and tell General Humphreys to bring his Mississippians up on his right. Kershaw's earlier change to front north had left Humphreys's brigade directly in Kershaw's rear still facing west. Kershaw also understood Johnson was going to advance on the left, with or without the desired support, in an effort to make a concerted attack on the new Union line.[36]

Spurred by a sense of urgency, however, Kershaw felt that there was no time to wait for Humphreys or Johnson. He ordered his brigade to advance immediately. The Mississippians would have to catch up as best they could. He did pick up some support when a substantial part of the 1st Arkansas Mounted Rifles of Coleman's brigade joined him. After losing contact with Coleman, Lt. Col. Daniel Reynolds and his Arkansans fell in on Kershaw's right, adding perhaps 100 men to his line. The enemy about 800 yards ahead appeared strong, one continuous line emerging from the timber east of the "cove [Glenn-Kelly] road" to run atop the knoll where Robertson had come to grief, and back into the woods again on the west side of the field. Three salient points leap out from Kershaw's terse description of the Federal position: First, he could not make out the staggered nature of Harker's line, where the 64th and 125th Ohio projected about 250 yards farther south; Second, he made no mention of any Union artillery, despite the presence of Schultz's and Church's nine guns that had been the bane of Confederate movements through Dyer Field the hour previous; Third, the Yankees appeared to be insolently challenging him by waving their flags "ostentatiously" at his oncoming line.[37]

By this time the field had grown strangely quiet. Lieutenant Clark of the 125th Ohio remembered "only a desultory firing by skirmishers . . . between us and their main body." A paralyzing uncertainty now gripped the Federals. Were

35 *OR* 30, pt. 2, 461, 503.

36 Ibid., 503.

37 Entry for September 20, Reynolds Diary, UARK; *OR* 30, pt. 2, 503.

Lt. Gen. John Bell Hood. Hood's fall in North Dyer Field came at an extremely inopportune time for the Confederates.
Library of Congress

the oncoming troops friend or foe? "Those moving battalions did appear to wear blue, dusty blue," added the Buckeye, "[and] we had never seen a Confederate clothed otherwise than in butternut or gray." Similar thoughts ran the length of the Union position. Up near the top of the knoll, Harry Allspaugh also described the approaching uniforms "[as] a kind of blue." Debate erupted in the 58th Indiana; some of the officers thought the approaching battle line, "dressed in dark clothing," might well be Federal, but Colonels Embree and Buell thought otherwise. The Hoosiers had never seen Rebels in anything but "regulation butternut," while these troops were "dressed in dark clothing, and with battle flags somewhat like ours. They came up in good order, bayonets fixed, and guns at 'right shoulder shift.'" Marcus Woodcock of the 9th Kentucky thought they "exactly resembled Federal soldiers;" he remembered that the "Lieut. Col." (he must have meant Embree) initially identified them as Yankees and ordered the line not to fire. From his elevated position on the knoll, Embree had a clear view of the unfolding scene. There were "four regiments dressed in dark uniform and carrying dark red flags immediately in our front," he recalled. "Another regiment moved . . . against the right flank of the [58th] . . . concealed by the hill and brush."[38]

38 Clark, *Opdycke Tigers*, 107-108; Entry for September 20, Allspaugh Diaries, University of Iowa; Hight, *Fifty-Eighth Regiment*, 192; Noe, *A Southern Boy in Blue*, 210; *OR* 30, pt. 1, 664. The "dark red" flags were especially confusing to the Federals. General Bragg's Army of Tennessee did not carry the now-familiar Rebel battle flag at Chickamauga, which was mostly used in the Army of Northern Virginia at this time. Instead, the Army of Tennessee used corps flags of various patterns that were mostly blue. General Longstreet's men, with their Army of Northern Virginia pattern flags, were an unusual sight on the field.

XIV Corps commander George Thomas was also present. A short time after sending Wood back south to help Brannan, the corps leader decided he had better ride and see things for himself. Thomas was still expecting Sheridan's division to arrive from this quarter, and had earlier sent Captain Kellogg to see what was keeping the Irishman. "I met Kellogg returning," wrote Thomas, who said "he met a large force in an open cornfield . . . advancing cautiously." Those troops had fired on Kellogg, but he still thought they could be Sheridan's men. Thomas found Harker in an agony of indecision. The colonel did not want to fire on a Federal line, but if the approaching troops were Confederates, he risked slaughter in his own command. For want of a better solution, "orders were given . . . to keep the flags well up" (thus accounting for Kershaw's observation of the enemy flags waving "ostentatiously"). Thomas, in his typical pragmatic fashion, noted that if they shot at the Federals, Harker would have to fire back.[39]

The presence of Harker, Wood, and Thomas on this line did little to prevent the chaotic nature of the battle from returning once the fighting began anew. During the lull between Robertson's repulse and Kershaw's advance, the Union line grew weaker when the right flank atop the knoll evaporated. The first time Schultz's battery was ordered to leave, John Brannan's timely intervention returned the guns to the fight. Brannan was elsewhere when an officer (likely one of Negley's aides) now arrived with new orders for Schultz to depart. Captain Church followed with his wreck of a Michigan battery. Church could only move one gun, since nearly all of his horses were out of action, so he abandoned two more guns atop the knoll. "I then moved what I had left of my battery to the rear." All of this was happening just a few hundred yards from where Thomas and Wood were discussing Kershaw's approach, and yet neither general was aware of the departure of their artillery support.[40]

Deeper in the woods to the right of the now-denuded knoll, the officers of the 21st Ohio were also dissatisfied with their position. Since the 21st could not see over the crest of the knoll to the east face, where Buell's ad hoc formation and Harker were deployed, they felt alone. The 21st was subject only "to a scattering fire" from the enemy here—skirmisher work—but Lt. Silas Canfield approached Lt. Col. Dwella Stoughton to tell him he was worried the officers might "lose control" of the regiment if they lingered too long in this spot.

39 *OR* 30, pt. 1, 252, 694-5; Clark, *Opdycke Tigers*, 107.

40 Entry for September 20, Sturges Diary, AHEC; *OR* 30, pt. 1, 414.

Stoughton also felt exposed and the Ohioans climbed up the hill behind them and took up a position on the right flank of Brannan's new line. Their departure left the 58th Indiana vulnerable to a flank attack from the right.[41]

The loss of the artillery and the 21st Ohio substantially reduced Wood's firepower. Wood's line now consisted only of Harker's four regiments, Buell's agglomeration of a regiment and a half, and stragglers from the 17th/31st Ohio, which Embree described as "about 40 or 50 men . . . under command of a captain." Wood still had perhaps 1,600 men, but his line ended just short of the crest of the knoll. When the artillery rumbled away, Colonel Buell shifted the 58th Indiana a little farther west, but the Indiana men could not see very well into the woods beyond their right. A flanking force could use the timber and ravines to infiltrate the Federal rear, and Brannan's line back atop Snodgrass Hill was too far away to fire on the blind spot.[42]

Kershaw's men, meanwhile, continued their steady advance through the field. About 400 yards from the Union line, the South Carolinians scaled a fence and reformed on the far side. Kershaw ordered bayonets fixed, and instructed Lt. Col. Franklin Gaillard's 2nd South Carolina, on the brigade's left, to move west into the trees to turn the Union right. Then the general moved to the right down the brigade line until he reached the color guard of the 3rd South Carolina Battalion. He did so on foot, for he and his staff officers were still without mounts—a serious problem about to become even more so. Pointing across the field at a set of Union colors, Kershaw told the 3rd Battalion's color-bearer, "I want you to march directly to that Federal flag."[43]

Lurching into the double-quick, the South Carolinians rapidly closed with the Federals, who mysteriously (to the Rebels, anyway) were still not firing. Several Confederates took special note of the Union flags so prominently displayed, and a trio of men in the 2nd South Carolina wrote about the last stage of the advance. In a letter home two weeks after the battle, Lieutenant Colonel Gaillard recalled, "as we passed the wounded [of Robertson's brigade] . . . they would say 'press them boys, press them. They will give as quickly as Yankees in Virginia.' As we were changing front to meet [those Federals] they seemed to

41 Canfield, *History of the 21st Regiment*, 116.

42 *OR* 30, pt. 1, 664.

43 Ibid., pt. 2, 503-504; James Edward Caldwell, *Recollections of Events of the Civil War*, http://gen.1starnet.com/civilwar/caldwelj.htm, accessed 11/03/2013. These were probably the colors of the 65th Ohio.

think we were wavering . . . so they waved their flags defiantly at us." From amid the ranks in Company I, Cpl. Reginald H. Screven recalled Rebel "sharpshooters in the field firing upon the enemy's line [who were] waving [the] Stars and Stripes." Sergeant Dubose Egleston of Company A also took note of the enemy banners: "we had a splendid view of the U. S. Colors about three hundred yards off. . . . I expected a shower of grape and balls every second, but when we advanced they gave way before us."[44]

Federal uncertainty as to the identity of the marching troops evaporated when the approaching line erupted with a full volley. Kershaw claimed his men fired first when about 100 yards from the Union line—fatally close in Civil War combat. In reality, given the staggered nature of the Union position and Kershaw's efforts to send troops out to the flanks as well as directly at the Yankees, the distance varied considerably depending on what part of Wood's line was struck. At some point during Kershaw's advance, Opdycke ordered his 125th and the 64th Ohio to fall back on the main line, connecting with the 3rd Kentucky's left. On Wood's orders, Opdycke's skirmishers remained along the advance line "with a view of annoying and delaying the progress of the enemy." These few Buckeyes fired and fell back as the South Carolinians closed the final yards—which Sergeant Egleston mistook as the entire Federal line retreating.[45]

Back on the main line, the Union right flank gave way first. The 58th Indiana suffered under the initial Rebel fusillade, but managed to return fire "in a vigorous manner."[46]

These Hoosiers were trading rounds with Kershaw's men to their front when Gaillard's 2nd South Carolina struck their right flank. From Gaillard's perspective, his sharp attack succeeded brilliantly. "The whole line then moved on in splendid style, not faltering a minute, and with not much loss drove them from their position and took every piece of artillery they had," he reported.[47]

44 "Dear Maria," October 5, 1863, Franklin Gaillard Papers, UNC; Entry for September 20, Reginald H. Screven Diary, South Carolina Historical Society, Charleston, SC; "Before Chattanooga, Sept. 27th, 1863," Dubose Egleston Letter, Ruffin, Roulhac and Hamilton Family Papers, UNC.

45 *OR* 30, pt. 2, 504; Ibid., pt.1, 637.

46 Hight, *Fifty-Eighth Indiana*, 193.

47 "Dear Maria," Franklin Gaillard Papers, UNC. The artillery referenced by Gaillard consisted of the two pieces Captain Church had to abandon, and so by this time were not actively part of the fight.

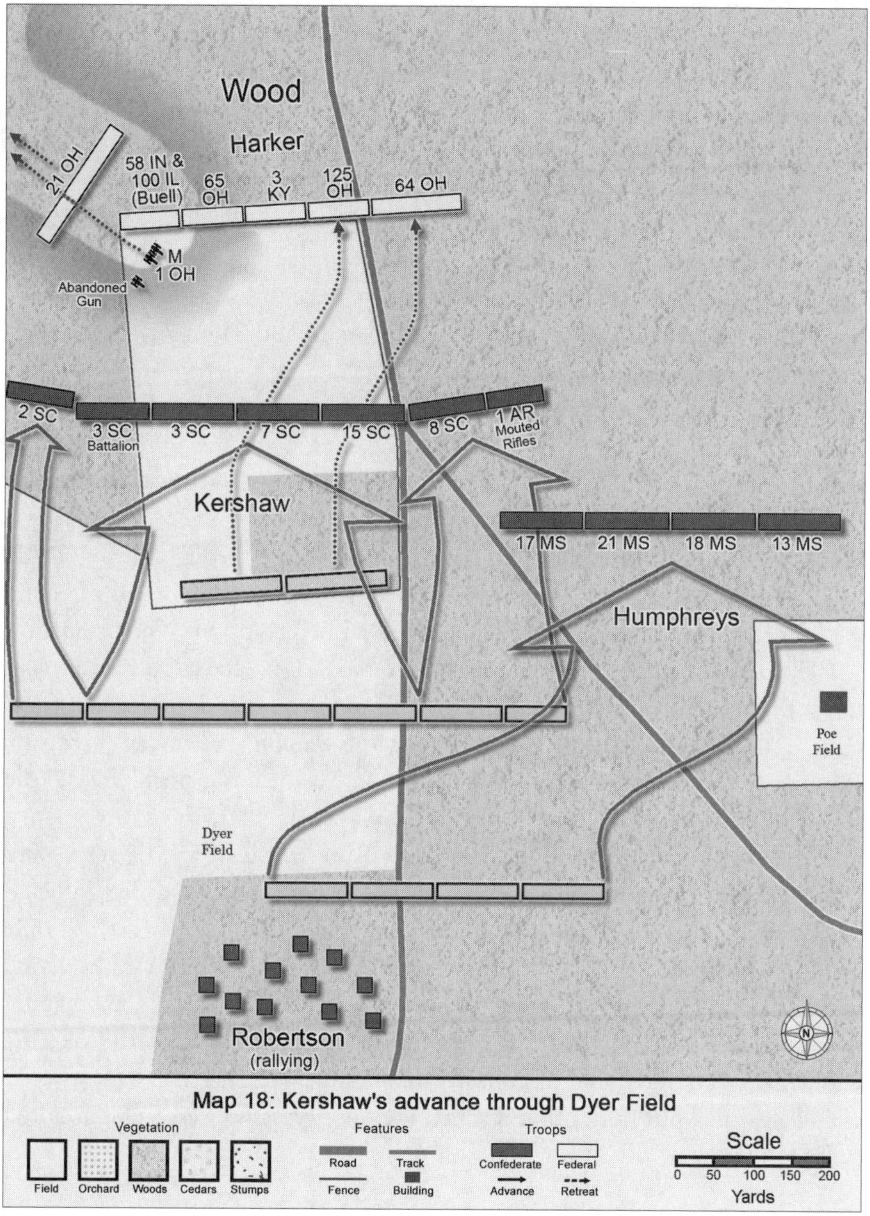

Map 18: Kershaw's advance through Dyer Field

So far, the 58th Indiana had managed to maintain unit cohesion under trying circumstances, throughout the initial breakthrough and during the difficult retreat across Dyer Field. This new attack against their front and flank simultaneously was simply too much. With Gaillard's appearance, the Hoosiers fell apart. "The position became untenable," explained its historian. "The regiment fell back again and rallied on the colors, on a hill to the left and rear of our former position. In this movement a part of the regiment became separated . . . [and] could not be gotten together for some time." Sergeant Holmes of the 100th Illinois, integrated into the 58th's line, also recorded the fateful moment: "Another Rebel regiment advances with the red flag flying, dressed in our uniform. Some of us open on them, and others say 'don't do it, they are our men.' While paying attention to this regiment, up comes a division [the 2nd South Carolina] on our right to flank us, so we have to 'skedaddle' again."[48]

Alongside the Hoosiers, the 31st Ohio remnant fragmented yet again. "[W]e do not fire upon them until they charge, then it was too late," Harrison Allspaugh scribbled in his diary. In 1883, he added a postscript alleging he had pleaded with the officers to commence firing, and, when they refused, left the ranks to open fire on the approaching Rebels on his own initiative. He claimed he and the men who joined him "did effective work" for a short time before it was "every man for himself, as we fell back tree to tree through the wood." If true, Allspaugh's memory suggests the pressure of the moment was affecting discipline, an understandable lapse but one that helped doom Wood's line.[49]

Harker's right flank regiment, the 65th Ohio, was posted at the tree line just down the slope from Buell's rapidly disappearing command. It later fell upon Capt. Thomas Powell of Company E, the ranking surviving company commander, to describe what happened next: "We held our position until the regiment on the right . . . broke in confusion, thus enabling the enemy to take possession of the hill. Our right being thus flanked, we suffered a severe fire from the enemy and were forced to fall back." The crossfire inflicted devastating losses on the Buckeyes. Major Samuel C. Brown, who had only assumed command the day before when Lt. Col. Horatio Whitbeck fell wounded, was cut down here, as was the senior company commander (unnamed in Powell's report), leaving Powell in charge. Unable to hold, the regiment broke, retreating in considerable confusion. The 65th Ohio would eventually rally, but not until it reached the Snodgrass house several hundred yards to their rear.[50]

48 Hight, *Fifty-Eighth Indiana*, 193; Woodruff, *Fifteen Years Ago*, 291.

49 Entry for September 20, Allspaugh Diary, University of Iowa.

50 *OR* 30, pt. 1, 704. In July 1864, Powell would eschew command to become the 65th's Chaplain.

With his line unraveling, Harker initiated a fighting withdrawal with his remaining regiments. Still wrestling with the question of the uniform colors, he had ridden to the left and forward of his advanced line to get a better view. By the time he returned, the issue was nearly settled: Buell was gone, the 65th Ohio was breaking, and the 3rd Kentucky was in distress. Colonel Henry Dunlap ordered the Kentuckians to change front "by file to the right at a double quick," but before they could accomplish that maneuver, the Bluegrass men took a "galling fire from two sides of a right angle triangle. . . . [U]pon this ground I lost about 80 officers and men." The Kentuckians shattered. Captain George W. McClure, who led Company K, was holding the regiment's left flank. He remembered General Wood being directly behind the 3rd Kentucky when the moment of retreat arrived. Wood had just lost his horse—his second mount of the battle—and was still suffering from that first fall the day before. "The brigade was just then driven back," related McClure. "General Wood ran back afoot and made good speed but . . . being young and muscular, [I] outran and passed him." That Wood could keep up at all, given the fact of the hernia he suffered that Saturday in the first fall, was altogether amazing. To Sgt. John Wesley Hubbard of Company A, only chaos reigned: "Our men was giving away. They ran through us [and] tangled up our regiment so that we were forced to fall back about a mile." The 3rd also retired to the vicinity of the Snodgrass cabin.[51]

The collapse of Harker's right wing left the 64th and 125th Ohio equally vulnerable. The 3rd's departure left Opdycke's own right dangerously exposed. Kershaw, however, was attempting to orchestrate the movements of seven units (including the impromptu attachment of the 1st Arkansas Mounted Rifles) across more than 700 yards of frontage, trying to envelop both Union flanks simultaneously—and he was attempting this on foot. Gaillard's 2nd South Carolina succeeded in turning Harker's right, but the 8th South Carolina, charged with doing the same to the Union left, was not as successful. In fact, all the regiments comprising Kershaw's right wing (in order, the 7th, 15th, and 8th South Carolina) were slow in coming up, first delayed by the aggressive presence of Opdycke's skirmishers, and then trading volleys with Harker's left

51 Ibid., 695, 700; "Dear Sir," Anonymous Letter to H. V. Boynton, October 9, 1893, 3rd Kentucky file, CCNMP; Betty J. Gorin, *"Morgan Is Coming!" Confederate Raiders in the Heartland of Kentucky* (Harmony House Publishers, 2006), 375. For Wood's injury, see Powell, *A Mad Irregular Battle*, 485.

wing. This delay allowed the 64th and 125th Ohio regiments to retain a greater measure of unit discipline while retreating.

Initially, Opdycke focused his attention on the threat approaching his front. "The terrible grandeur of this advance is beyond the reach of my pen," he admitted. "The whole vast mass seemed moved by a single mind; their step was proud, and in perfect order." Soon both sides were locked in a bloody musketry duel, and both suffered heavy losses. In the 125th, three color bearers fell in quick succession. When Cpl. John Warman lofted the flag, a ball shattered the shaft leaving him clutching only the ragged standard. The retreat of Dunlap's Kentuckians followed, exposing Opdycke's men to a wicked crossfire. About that same time, the 64th Ohio decided to retreat, their commander believing that Harker's brigade was "almost surrounded." Within moments Opdycke was alone: "The regiment to my left [the 64th] fled, and soon after, the one posted on my right [the 3rd] retired." In the ranks of the 125th, Opdycke's steadying influence proved invaluable. "[Then] my Co. A arose, and faced to the rear. I caught their eyes and said 'back to your posts until I order you away!" Opdycke held the regiment to its work a few minutes more, but with both flanks exposed it was increasingly difficult to hold on. Losses mounted. At one point Lieutenant Clark told his colonel, "'They can kill us, but never whip us.' I need not tell you, I felt proud of the 125th Ohio," Opdycke boasted to his wife.[52]

The newly christened Tigers had done all they could. "I looked back for aid, but none was to be seen," recalled the colonel, and "then I retired my regiment." Clark admitted, "we did retreat before [Kershaw] to a stronger position, but the retrograde movement was conducted with obedience to orders, and . . . in perfect order." The Tigers also withdrew toward the Snodgrass cabin, where the rest of the brigade was reforming. As they did so, the 64th and 125th Ohio regiments crossed paths. The 125th had started out as the center-left regiment, but when it reformed on the ridge it was holding the extreme left flank, with the 64th on its right. The only note Opdycke took of this switch was in remarking that during the retreat, "some regiment dashed obliquely through my right wing, and caused a little confusion." Despite the

52 Longacre and Haas, *To Battle for God and the Right*, 100-102; Clark, *Opdycke Tigers*, 110; Charles G. Brown, ed., *The Sherman Brigade Marches South: The Civil War Memoirs of Colonel Robert Carson Brown* (Charles G. Brown, 1995), 49. Opdycke's sequencing of the action here is interesting. He claims that the 64th Ohio retreated before the 3rd Kentucky gave way, but given the rest of the brigade descriptions of this fight, it seems likely that the 3rd departed first. It is possible that Opdycke only noted the 3rd's departure after he saw the 64th moving.

mishap, the 125th served as the rear guard, giving ground only grudgingly, "halting two or three times, facing to the rear and firing on the enemy directly south of us." The Tigers finally stopped "perhaps 200 feet" from the Snodgrass cabin.[53]

Kershaw's brigade was disrupted by its own success, and the reasons why are instructive and worth discussing in detail. Kershaw's travails began when he elected not to wait for Humphreys to come up on his right, but decided to attack immediately. Also, as noted, Kershaw was trying to fill two command slots at once: as a first-time division commander in McLaws's absence, while still exercising direct command of his own brigade instead of following normal protocol and yielding that duty to Colonel Nance. Back in August, when McLaws was temporarily absent, Kershaw had done just that, but in the heat of combat Kershaw did not want to leave his brigade in another's hands. The result was the unraveling of his broad attack.[54]

Then, as his line advanced, Kershaw lost contact with the right half of his command due to its lagging pace. Attempting a double envelopment across such an extended front proved too ambitious. The 7th, 15th, and 8th regiments drifted too far eastward. Being still afoot, Kershaw and his staff were unable to effectively communicate with the various pieces of the brigade on the move. The decision to send the 8th South Carolina even farther to the right in order to replicate the 2nd South Carolina's flanking move on the left also proved unwise. The 8th had more ground to traverse if it were to turn Harker's left, and the Union skirmishers in the woodlot slowed the 8th's advance considerably. Not only did the 8th not outflank the Yankees, but the regiment drifted so far eastward that it completely missed the fight. At some point during this movement the 1st Arkansas Mounted Rifles also left the line in search of its parent brigade.[55]

Once the South Carolinians closed with the enemy, more disruption set in. Near the center of Kershaw's line in the ranks of the 3rd South Carolina, Pvt.

53 Longacre and Haas, *To Battle for God and the Right*, 100-102; Clark, *Opdycke Tigers*, 109; "Dear Sir," February 12, 1909, Charles T. Clark to Ezra E. Carmen, 125th Ohio Website, http://home.earthlink.net/~nhaldane/ctc-letter.html, accessed 10/22/2012.

54 Mac Wyckoff, *A History of the Third South Carolina Infantry, 1861-1865* (Sgt. Kirkland's Museum and Historical Society, Inc., 1994), 131.

55 *Charleston Daily Courier*, October 24, 1863; Entry for September 20, Reynolds Diary, UARK. Kershaw might not have even known the Arkansans were there, since he failed to mention their participation in his report.

James E. Caldwell recalled "four Federal flags waving defiance" until his regiment dipped out of sight while moving through a swale. When it reappeared, the 3rd took the first Federal fire—probably from the Union 3rd Kentucky, even then being outflanked—and "as we rushed forward, our regiment crowded us and threw our company into confusion. Here [Pvt.] B. M. Lovelace was shot through the jaw and fell. I stepped around him, I thought our company might stop[.] I sprang forward and shouted, 'forward boys.' I don't know that anybody heard me, but forward we all went." Lieutenant Augustus Dickert agreed. "As the regiment reached the brow of the hill . . . my company and the other color company, being crowded together by the pressure of the flanks . . . became for a moment a tangled, disorganized mass." Similar confusion disrupted the ranks of Gaillard's 2nd Regiment and the 3rd Battalion.[56]

Once in the trees north of Dyer Field, things became more confused. By the time the brigade entered the timber, Kershaw's line was much too long to take in at a glance, and moving through the brush only further disrupted it. Colonel Nance's 3rd South Carolina, already crowded, was now further discomfited by the tree cover. All in all, it is hardly surprising Kershaw's attempted double envelopment did not come off as intended.[57]

The length of Kershaw's line more than doubled during the advance and broke into three distinct fragments. The 8th South Carolina's drift eastward created a 300-yard gap between it and the 15th South Carolina. In an effort to maintain contact on its right, the 15th also shifted right, dragging the 7th South Carolina on its left along with it. This in turn opened another 300-yard gap between the 7th and Nance's 3rd South Carolina. By the time the last of Harker's men were seen off, Kershaw's brigade was scattered across a front at least 1,000 yards long, with two brigade-sized gaps in the line, and with several regiments effectively reduced to little more than armed mobs.[58]

With Harker driven back, the Confederates could now see their next challenge. The first intimation of what lay ahead arrived when Nance's men crested the knoll near Church's two abandoned guns. "I suffered considerably

56 Caldwell, Recollections, *http://gen.1starnet.com/civilwar/caldwelj.htm*, accessed 11/03/2013; Dickert, *History of Kershaw's Brigade*, 279.

57 Wyckoff, *Third South Carolina*, 139.

58 *OR* 30, pt. 2, 504, 508. Kershaw noted that when Humphreys came up, his four Mississippi regiments came into line between the 8th South Carolina and the 15th South Carolina.

by a fire delivered from the high ground in the woods beyond the field," observed Nance. Chasing after Wood's Yankees carried Kershaw's men to the foot of yet another imposing slope, crowned with another line of blue-coated infantry. Kershaw called a halt to reorganize his broken brigade and wait for General Humphreys. [59]

John Brannan watched the arrival of the South Carolinians from the top of Horsehoe Ridge. The Federal division commander had succeeded in rallying a new Federal line there. Taking it would be no easy matter.

59 Ibid., 507.

Chapter Sixteen

Retreat to Horseshoe Ridge:

Sunday, 12:00 p.m. to 1:00 p.m.

Horseshoe Ridge—also known as Snodgrass Hill—is the most famous landmark on the sprawling Chickamauga battlefield. Amidst the mostly flat timbered bottomland comprising the valley of West Chickamauga Creek, its abrupt slopes (a spur of the even loftier Missionary Ridge) dominate the field. Both terms "Horseshoe Ridge" and "Snodgrass Hill," however, are misleading. The final Union position on this sector of the field included several different features: hills, ravines, and two partially partly wooded narrow ridges. In general, Horseshoe Ridge has come to collectively embrace all of these features, but it is important to fully grasp the geography of this part of the field in order to understand the fighting that took place there.

Writing in 1911, Archibald Gracie was one of the first to systematically examine the official records and veterans' accounts to better understand this geography and the complicated action that unfolded there on September 20. Frustrated by the loose terminology his research uncovered, early in his book Gracie warned readers to beware "of the pitfalls of nomenclature." He then set about to standardize the names of the various features that together comprise the Union final line, and later writers have retained his labels.[1]

1 Archibald Gracie, *The Truth About Chickamauga* (Morningside Press, 1987), 33.

By Gracie's system, Snodgrass Hill proper refers to the open ridge running northeast from the Snodgrass cabin. In 1863, this ridge was cleared and covered by a large cornfield belonging to George Snodgrass, an 1860 immigrant from Virginia. The cornfield was in fact much larger than the ridge itself, extending well to the north, west, and southeast; meaning that troops stationed on the open ridge had extensive fields of fire as well. Snodgrass was still expanding the field, which included a number of dead standing trees along the northern edge that had been "girdled" but not yet felled. The Snodgrass cabin and other farm buildings sat on the ridge at the south edge of the cultivated land.[2]

For Gracie, Horseshoe Ridge began with a prominent hill rising 200 yards to the south of the cabin, where the modern road ends in a parking loop. Pragmatically, Gracie labeled this next feature Hill One. Hill One is about 50 feet higher in elevation than the farmstead.

From there, Hill Two lies 250 yards to the west, its crest about 20 feet higher than Hill One, and is the highest piece of ground on Horseshoe Ridge. The small Snodgrass family cemetery adorned the crest of Hill Two in 1863. Another 250 yards farther west and slightly to the south is Hill Three, at about the same elevation as Hill One. Beyond Hill Three is a longer and lower ridge running another 600 to 700 yards west by northwest until it rises to join Missionary Ridge proper. About halfway along this ridge is another spur that shoots off south toward the Vittetoe house and ends in an abruptly sloped, elongated hill parallel to the main ridge. Major General Bushrod Johnson's Confederates occupied this extension during the afternoon of September 20. Since Gracie never named this last feature, for the sake of clarity and consistency I have chosen to label this elongated height as Vittetoe Hill. Gracie assumed history would eventually provide more evocative names than Hills One, Two, and Three, but subsequent historians have accepted his prosaic nomenclature.[3]

Keep in mind that these hills all represent points on the same long ridge. The slopes are steep, with narrow draws separating each hill. There were four such ravines or draws, the first starting west of Hill One and the last just west of Vittetoe Hill. None of these features have formal names. Following Gracie's

2 Gracie, *The Truth About Chickamauga*, 33-34. Girdling was the act of making a circular cut all around the trunk deep enough to cut into the cambium layer, thereby killing the tree.

3 Gracie suggested a new name for Hill One—"Gracie Hill" after his father who had fought there. The name never stuck. The exact location of the Snodgrass cemetery has since been lost.

convention, this work labels them Draws One, Two, Three, and Four (from east to west). In 1863, except for the open field around Snodgrass Hill, Horseshoe Ridge was timbered, but the trees were mature and well-spaced. The commander of the 2nd South Carolina, Lt. Col. Franklin Gaillard, described these woods as "a growth of heavy [large] oak timber and very little underbrush." Collectively, the features comprising this tangled ridge complex—the "last Federal stronghold"—made it an exceedingly difficult place to attack.[4]

* * *

The first Federal troops to occupy Horseshoe Ridge that morning were from Maj. Gen. James S. Negley's division. As described earlier, by 11:00 a.m. Negley held the ridge with Col. William Sirwell's brigade and three batteries of artillery. Sirwell's force included 1,729 men in the 37th Indiana, 21st and 74th Ohio, and 78th Pennsylvania. Two of the three batteries were also from Negley's division—G and M of the 1st Ohio—with the third being Lt. Frank Smith's four commandeered Napoleons in Battery I, 4th U.S. Regulars, of General Brannan's division.

Major General George Thomas wanted Negley on Snodgrass Hill in order to secure the XIV Corps's right flank in Kelly Field. However, Negley never fully understood Thomas's intent, and Negley's troop placements atop Horseshoe Ridge reflected his confusion. Both the guns and the infantry were redeployed multiple times between 11:00 a.m. and noon. According to Battery M's Capt. Frederick Schultz, he "changed position several times" until he ended up on the knoll overlooking Dyer Field.[5] Smith's Napoleons dropped trail directly in front of the Snodgrass cabin. Shortly after these guns were placed, Sirwell's infantry arrived and was posted on the open ridge behind Smith's battery facing generally southeast toward Poe Field. Colonel Sirwell was one of Negley's peacetime neighbors, a fellow native of Pittsburgh and another longtime militia soldier. Sirwell raised the 78th Pennsylvania in late 1861 and had served with Negley thereafter. At six feet Sirwell was tall for the era, broad of shoulder, and limited his facial hair to a bushy mustache. He'd done well in

4 "Dear Maria," Camp near Chattanooga, October 5, 1683, Franklin Gaillard Papers, UNC; Gracie, *The Truth About Chickamauga*, 33.

5 *OR* 30, pt. 1, 383.

previous fights and especially at Stones River, where his men captured a Rebel battery and two enemy flags.

As the minutes ticked off, Sirwell's infantry front diffused. The large 21st Ohio (539 officers and men) took up a position near Schultz's battery, while the 74th Ohio and 78th Pennsylvania occupied other portions of the hill complex farther west, though they left no definitive accounts of these intermediate positions. The 37th Indiana, Col. William D. Ward commanding, remained in direct support of Smith in the cornfield virtually at the doorstep of the Snodgrass cabin. Once they settled in, however, all of these units faced south or southeast, not north or northeast, as they would need to do if they were to support Thomas's right.

While his command was deploying, Negley enjoyed a panoramic view of the battle. When he first reached Snodgrass Hill he could see, off to the northeast, much of the final moments of Maj. Gen. John C. Breckinridge's attack and the struggle near the McDonald house. A short time later the battle smoke rising above the trees to his front (due east) indicated heavy fighting along the length of Thomas's Kelly Field line, where Cleburne's Confederates were making no headway. Sometime later, directly below him along the Glenn-Kelly Road, Negley watched Tom Wood's men heading north in response to General Rosecrans's soon-to-be infamous order. Wood, in turn, took note of the presence of artillery (Smith) and a brigade of infantry (Sirwell) atop Snodgrass Hill. Shortly after Wood marched north (around noon) the situation dramatically worsened. Standing in the Snodgrass farm lane, the 21st Ohio's Capt. Isaac Cusac recalled the moment: "In front of us severe fighting was going on at this time three or four hundred yards to the southeast. We could see the Federal troops moving to the rear and we expected to fight . . . . We threw down the fence . . . and piled the rales so as to protect us from the bullets of the enemy."[6]

The first signs of collapse appeared soon thereafter when stragglers and wounded men poured out of the woods from the southeast from Brotherton and Poe fields. To Maj. James Lowrie of Negley's staff, "it became evident that some disaster had happened to portions of General McCook's and General Crittenden's corps. A large number of fugitives came up through the ravines and over the ridge. Batteries were dragged up with all the haste that horses and men could exert. Some of these did not stop on the ridge; others sought

6 Ibid., 1020; "Mr. E. A. Carman," March 13, 1909, Isaac Cusac Letter, MMS 1404, BGSU.

positions and prepared again for action. One corps battle-flag," continued the major, "went past without an officer or escort. Division and brigade battle-flags and regimental colors were hastily carried to the rear."[7]

Not everyone was running away. John Brannan's division might have been scattered and driven back with heavy loss, but Brannan was not yet ready to admit defeat. When it became clear the fight in Poe Field was hopeless, he fell back to the next logical place to make a stand: Horseshoe Ridge. The hill mass also drew routed men from Wood's and Van Cleve's divisions. Negley's force of infantry and artillery served as a magnet for other disordered Federals. All of these forces coalesced into two general groups: one under Negley's direct supervision on Snodgrass Hill, and a second formed by Brannan on Hills One and Two. Brigade (and even regimental) order was largely gone, with units often splitting into multiple fragments, some rallying here with Negley and others there with Brannan. It was not uncommon for half of a regiment to reform with another group thinking the other half lost, only to be reunited the next day. Despite this breakdown, most of the troops had not lost their will to fight.

Colonel John Connell's experience typified this confusion. Connell, who led Brannan's First Brigade, holding the division's right in Poe Field, was the first to break when Wood's departure exposed his flank. Connell made repeated efforts to rally the men, an "apparently vain and painful task" until he reached the Snodgrass farmstead. There, he found Lt. Col. Frederick Lister with the bulk of the 31st Ohio and Maj. Benjamin F. Butterfield "with a squad" of the 17th Ohio, both from his command. Much of the rest of the brigade was rallied by its former commander, Col. Moses Walker, about a quarter-mile to the southeast. Walker was technically still under arrest, a fact he ignored in this moment of crisis. Connell's fragment numbered no more than 350, mostly Ohioans from the 17th and 31st, with a few Hoosiers from the 82nd thrown in. Negley rode up and took charge of Connell's detachment. Walker's portion of the brigade, somewhat smaller, numbered between 200 and 300 men.[8]

Brannan's artillery also made for the high ground. Captain Josiah Church's 1st Michigan battery, it will be recalled, fell back to go into a new position alongside Schultz's guns on the knoll overlooking Dyer Field, only to meet

7 *OR* 30, pt. 1, 339. Lowrie did not specify which corps flag went by, but it could only have been the XXI Corps.

8 *OR* 30, pt. 1, 410. Connell's numbers include all the troops he was able to rally by the time he reached Rossville later in the day. He likely had fewer in the ranks here on Snodgrass Hill.

additional disaster when that position was overrun by Joseph Kershaw's South Carolinians as earlier described. The five surviving pieces of Lt. Marco Gary's Battery C, 1st Ohio Light, also of Brannan's division, fetched up on Snodgrass Hill. Despite having lost only one gun, Gary's battery was a wreck. Fully one-quarter of its horses were down. Also missing was one caisson and parts of two more, together with many killed, wounded, and missing artillerists—which left the Ohio outfit "badly disabled." Gary noted in his report that he "moved with the troops of Major General Negley's command" for the rest of the day.[9]

Thus far, all these stragglers had come from the southeast. When that wave died down, however, men began streaming in from the northeast. The first to arrive was what was left of Capt. Lyman Bridges's Illinois battery, battered from the McDonald Field fighting. Only three of Bridges's six guns escaped. The trio of pieces went into position beside Lieutenant Smith's four guns. About this time, Capt. James S. Wilson of John Beatty's staff found Negley and conveyed Beatty's urgent request for support. Beatty, it will be recalled, was struggling to stabilize the Union right south of the McDonald house to stop Breckinridge's assault toward Kelly Field. Negley had no troops to give, and sent Wilson back with orders for Beatty to fall back to Snodgrass Hill. Caught up in the middle of a full-blown crisis on Thomas's left flank, Beatty rightly ignored Negley's order until he could "explain to [Negley] the necessity of maintaining the line."[10]

Beatty's brigade was later overrun and broke into two pieces. The 15th Kentucky and 104th Illinois fell back south while the 42nd and 88th Indiana were driven due west about 1,000 yards up the slopes of Missionary Ridge, before turning south to try and find either their brigadier or division leader (Negley). Hoosier George Kirkpatrick of the 42nd Indiana recalled the Rebels captured several officers and "one hundred twenty four [enlisted men] of the regiment." Kirkpatrick escaped to fall in with Smith's gunners at the Snodgrass cabin. Neither Indiana regiment fully reformed, for Rosecrans met some of these same men on his ride to Rossville. The tale they told was of Negley's division being routed. It was untrue, but Rosy had no way of knowing that.[11]

Despite the wreck that was his brigade, John Beatty's efforts were instrumental in repulsing Breckinridge's Rebels. Leaving the 15th and 104th in

9 Hendrick, "Chickamauga," *National Tribune*, November 5, 1891; *OR* 30, pt. 1, 427.

10 *OR* 30, pt. 1, 369, 375. See Chapter 6 for more detail of Beatty's fight with Breckinridge.

11 Francis M. Carlisle Autobiography, http://www.42ndindiana.com, accessed 11/3/2013; Kirkpatrick, *Experiences of a Private Soldier*, 31.

charge of Col. Marion Taylor of the 15th, Beatty assumed command of a disparate force including Col. Tim Stanley's brigade and, for a time, Col. George Dick's brigade of Horatio Van Cleve's divison. Negley, however, never grasped the nature of the ongoing crisis at the northern end of Kelly Field. When his first order for Beatty to fall back, conveyed through Captain Wilson, failed to bear fruit, Negley dispatched the order a second time with Major Lowrie.[12] When Beatty later sought Colonel Taylor, he learned to his dismay that Taylor and the two units (15th Kentucky and 104th Illinois) had also disappeared. They were not there because Lowrie had found them first and ordered them back to Snodgrass Hill. "Colonel Taylor obeyed the order without consulting Beatty, for which he was afterward sorry," observed the 104th's historian William Calkins. Taylor "was a brave man [who] "had simply erred, thinking he must obey the Major General commanding." In doing so, however, he put those troops out of reach of their brigadier for the rest of the day.[13]

During Taylor's journey back he met Captain Bridges, who was looking for some manpower to help him save his guns. After Breckinridge was repulsed the Federals recaptured the ground where his cannon were sitting, but Bridges had no means of drawing them off. He had originally appealed to Beatty for help, and the brigadier ordered his ordnance officer, Lt. Joseph Atherton, to find some men for the task. Atherton, formerly of Company A, 15th Kentucky, passed this appeal to Taylor, who in turn gave Bridges a detail of 30 men under the command of Company I's Capt. James Allen.[14]

Allen and Bridges proved industrious. Somewhere they found limbers enough not only to drag Bridges's three guns off, but also two more pieces from among the various cannon that had been fought over on the 19th and which now lined the La Fayette Road. With their five rescued guns in tow, Taylor led the whole force a half-mile west and rejoined Negley. Though both the Kentucky and Illinois regiments were battered, together they added roughly 400 muskets, though desperately short of ammunition, to Negley's strength.

As if things weren't confused enough, another regiment wandered into Negley's sphere of command: Col. Louis Waters's 84th Illinois. If the 105th Ohio's strange odyssey against Benning's Georgians in Poe Field takes the blue

12 See chapter 7.

13 Jenkins, *The Battle Rages Higher*, 182-183; Calkins, *One Hundred and Fourth Regiment*, 138.

14 Jenkins, *The Battle Rages Higher*, 182-183.

ribbon for the most misplaced Federal unit on the battlefield, the 84th, part of Col. William Grose's brigade (John Palmer's division, Tom Crittenden's XXI Corps), has a strong case for second place. Grose, it will be recalled, was in reserve on the morning of the 20th in Kelly Field. When Breckinridge's Rebels burst into the field's northern quarter, Grose's men were drawn into that chaotic fight and fared badly. At one point, wrote its historian, they "were obliged to affect a hasty retreat [and] fell into considerable confusion." During that "considerable confusion" the 84th lost touch with the rest of its brigade.[15]

During the retreat, explained Colonel Waters, the regiment ran into a dense thicket. Waters tried to ride around it one way while most of the regiment went another. The result was a regiment scattered in the timber west of the La Fayette Road, in the same area Beatty was rallying various units. Waters eventually found some of his men and posted them in the woods near Beatty, but many others were lost for the rest of the day. Private Christopher Wetsel was among the latter. "[The] regiment . . . did not get back together until after knight," wrote Wetsel in a letter home, three days later. Wetsel recorded that Waters at some point set off to find Grose, but as was common that day, Waters had no luck. When the colonel tried to return to the 84th, he discovered that his men were also gone. During Waters's absence, his brother and adjutant, Charles E. Waters, assumed command. Adjutant Waters encountered one of Negley's couriers, who sent the survivors up to Snodgrass Hill. Eventually Colonel Waters, still bereft of most of his men, managed to rejoin Grose's brigade, but the bulk of the 84th Illinois would march back to Rossville with Negley.[16]

While Negley was unwittingly stripping Thomas's left flank of troops about as fast as the big Virginian could dispatch them northward, Confederate Brig. Gen. Daniel C. Govan's attack hooked around the Federal left. Govan's movement came well after Breckinridge's failed assault. Beatty still had Stanley's men on hand, and had scrounged up George Dick's brigade as well. Unfortunately, Dick's line skedaddled early in the action. Beatty and Stanley, heavily outnumbered and bereft of their last support, felt they had no recourse but to fall back on Negley's position.[17]

15 Simmons, *84th Reg't Ill. Vols.*, 97.

16 "Dear Wife, Parents and Family," September 23, 1863, Christopher Wetsel Letters, Western Illinois University, McComb, IL; *OR* 30, pt. 1, 787.

17 See Chapter 7.

Fortunately for the stability of Thomas's northern flank, Govan's attack stalled of its own accord. The Rebel brigade fragmented and Govan found himself outflanked in turn. Instead of trying to cut their way back to friendly lines, three of Govan's regiments, led by Lt. Col. John E. Murray of the 5th Arkansas, moved west and then north to circle back out of danger.[18]

Meanwhile, back on Snodgrass Hill, some Hoosiers from the 42nd and 88th Indiana finally reported in. With them came word of a strong force of Rebels on their heels—an allusion to Breckinridge's earlier effort. They were mistaken, of course; Breckinridge had turned south, as had Govan's men. Somehow, however, some of these Indianans must have also seen something of Colonel Murray's retreat, and misinterpreted it as an offensive movement. Negley interpreted this report as describing a new threat, "a strong column of the enemy, who pressed forward rapidly between me and the troops on my left." One of the stragglers added a worrisome detail: "they had counted 7 stands of [enemy] colors across the road in that direction." If accurate, seven enemy flags would mean that at least a strong brigade, maybe even an entire division, was now threatening to cut Negley off from Thomas's embattled line in Kelly Field.[19]

It is likely these reports conflated Breckinridge's and Murray's movements. Colonel Murray's force was a far cry from seven regiments, and the Arkansans were seeking a safe path of retreat, not mounting a new attack. It was a still considerable force: several Rebel regiments apparently moving to potentially envelop Negley's left at a time when the Union right and center were already routing. Even worse, "reliable information" reached Negley that "the enemy's cavalry was moving from our right to our rear." The Pennsylvanian was beginning to feel surrounded.[20]

While Negley was sending aides hither and yon to round up strays, he also sent riders to Rosecrans asking for orders and support. Army headquarters was to the south, in the middle of the unfolding crisis, so Negley sent two officers by separate routes to accomplish the mission. As mentioned previously, Capt. Alfred Hough and Lt. William Moody made the trip. Moody returned first,

18 *OR* 30, pt. 2, 265.

19 Ibid., pt. 1, 330, 343.

20 Ibid., 331. The "enemy cavalry" mentioned here are unidentified, if they indeed existed at all. No large force of Confederate cavalry was operating on Negley's right. Perhaps someone saw elements of Longstreet's or Hood's headquarters escorts.

describing a difficult and ultimately unsuccessful journey: "The woods were literally filled with disorganized bodies of troops. The enemy's shot and shell were coming thick and fast, their infantry rushing forward with yell after yell. Across the open field I could see General Rosecrans, alone, his staff and escort, with drawn sabers, endeavoring to check the avalanche of panic-stricken men." When he reached Rosecrans, Moody reported, the army commander informed him there was no help to give. Hough reined up a few minutes later, bearing the same dismal message.[21]

And what of Thomas? In his report, Negley simply stated that he was "unable to communicate with Thomas." Months later at a formal inquiry, Hough's and Moody's testimony detailed their efforts to reach Rosecrans, but no officer described trying to find George Thomas at this time. According to Capt. Joseph C. Hill, a member of Rosecrans's staff, he was the only officer sent by Negley to communicate with the XIV Corps commander, but not until much later in the day. Hill made two efforts to find Thomas, the first at an unspecified time, and the second between 3:30 and 4:00 p.m. Both efforts were made from Rossville, well after Negley left Snodgrass Hill. Captain Hill was not even with Negley during these critical minutes on Horseshoe Ridge, but was instead leaving the field with Rosecrans; he first joined Negley at Rossville. There is no record James Negley sent anyone to find General Thomas while both men were still on the battlefield.[22]

Why didn't Negley seek out new orders from Thomas before he decided to depart? At this critical juncture, Brannan was rallying troops on Hills One and Two and Wood was with Thomas heavily engaged in Dyer Field. Negley was only a few hundred yards from the XIV Corps commander, with no intervening Rebels between him and the Virginian. A short while later both Thomas and Wood joined Brannan on Hill One without any difficulty. If Negley had waited a few minutes longer, Thomas would have come to him on the high ground. When Col. Emerson Opdycke's 125th Ohio retired, it withdrew to the same ground held by Negley only minutes before. Moreover, Charles Harker's brigade should have been perfectly visible to Negley throughout most of its fight with Brig. Gen. Joseph Kershaw's South Carolinians. Men in the 21st Ohio in Sirwell's brigade, from their initial position in the Snodgrass farm lane,

21 Ibid., 349.

22 Ibid., 331, 1022-1024.

could see all the way to the Poe cabin. Harker's presence in North Dyer Field contradicts Negley's assertion, made in his report and at his court of inquiry, that there were no other formed bodies of Federal troops on the field. Finally, it was Thomas, not Rosecrans, who ordered Negley to assume his current position atop Snodgrass Hill. Thomas was his immediate superior. Negley should have made every effort to reach Thomas, but did not.

Negley's report, submitted on October 9, described his movements during this fateful period of time and offers clues as to his thinking. With the collapse of the right, Negley rode to where he had earlier posted Schultz's battery out on the knoll overlooking Dyer Field. "I . . . rode forward alone to the crest of the hill. . . . The smoke was so dense and the firing so heavy that I failed to see the enemy on the crest until I confronted his line within 100 feet of him. Before they could seize my horse or take direct aim," he continued, "I turned and rode back amidst a shower of balls." Negley returned to Bridges's battery at the gallop, "300 yards back," to find them "also actively engaged."[23]

The troops who nearly killed or captured Negley were probably Kershaw's men, who had just seized the knoll and were even then moving to outflank Harker's line. Negley didn't specify the exact timing of this personal reconnaissance, but the fact that he was "alone" indicates Schultz's battery and the 21st Ohio were already withdrawn. The sudden encounter with enemy troops from such an unexpected quarter may have sufficiently further rattled Negley to conclude that Thomas's line had also given way, or was at least cut off by swarming Rebels.

John Brannan could be a tenacious fighter. As his line in Poe Field fell apart, flanked from the south by successive waves of Confederates (Bushrod Johnson's and Benning's troops), Brannan looked for both support and a place to make another stand. He thought he found both about 800 yards to the rear, where Negley held Snodgrass Hill. In Brannan's words, Connell's brigade was "much exposed, [and] broke with considerable disorder." Croxton was down with a wound, and only part of his command was able to conduct a fighting withdrawal to the new position. Colonel William Hays assumed command and brought the 4th Kentucky, 10th Kentucky, and 14th Ohio back to Horseshoe Ridge, but the 10th and 74th Indiana missed the retrograde movement and went instead to Kelly Field. Brannan accompanied Hays's three regiments and

23 Ibid., 335.

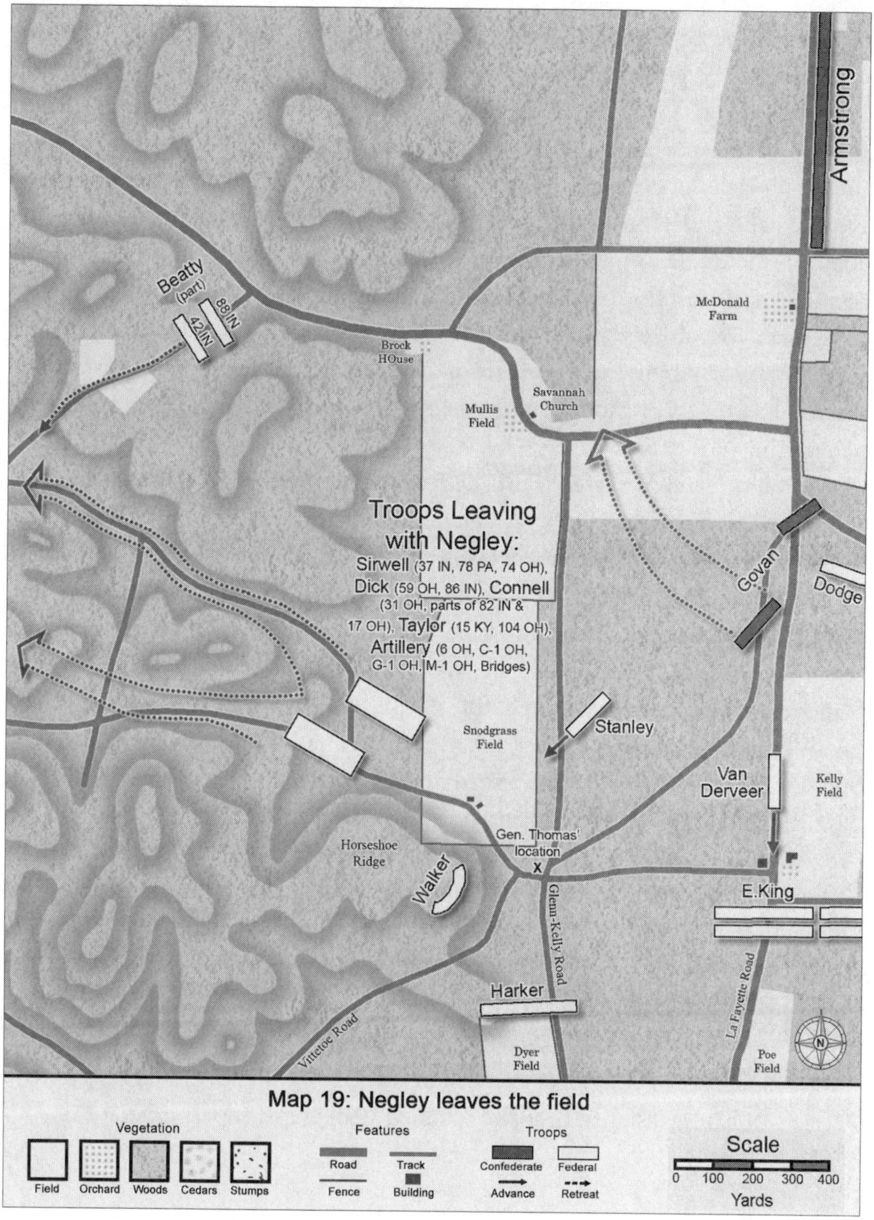

Map 19: Negley leaves the field

reported that the withdrawal was "accomplished with wonderful regularity under such circumstances."[24]

24 Ibid., 402.

In reality, Croxton's (Hays's) retreat was more disorderly than Brannan remembered. Sergeant Richard Boyle of the 10th Kentucky recalled that back in Poe Field, when the brigade formed the right angle facing south, that change of front to confront Benning's Georgians caused "considerable confusion." Boyle found himself in charge of a company of about 40 men, a mixed bag of Kentuckians and Hoosiers from several of Croxton's regiments, holding the apex of the angle. When the time came to retreat, Boyle lost track of his regiment and marched his band north until he met Brig. Gen. John Turchin, of Maj. Gen. Joseph Reynolds's division. Turchin ordered Boyle to fall in, but Boyle "refused, as [his] men were from several different regiments." Instead, he marched farther west and eventually found part of the brigade in a declivity behind the Snodgrass house.[25]

Captain Israel Webster, with the main body of the 10th Kentucky, also recalled the experience: "As we came out of this trap we were marched over a small hill, [the knoll where Schultz was posted] on the top of which were a few pieces of artillery supported by some infantry. We passed over the hill, descended into the valley, halting for a short rest, and if possible, to gather our scattered forces." Another Kentuckian, James Mills, thought they reached "'Snodgrass Ridge' at or a little before 12 M."[26]

When he crested Snodgrass Hill, John Brannan was doubtless relieved to find a formed body of troops already there in the form of Sirwell's brigade. According to Colonel Sirwell, "here I was solicited by General Brannan to leave a regiment to support one of his batteries." The 21st Ohio was close at hand so he tapped it for the assignment. The Buckeyes moved to the right onto Hill One, where they spotted the familiar face of Colonel Walker, their erstwhile (and technically still under arrest) former brigade commander. After a short spell with him, the 21st marched down toward the knoll and their confrontation with Jerome Robertson's Texans.[27]

Colonel Moses B. Walker was a man without a job that Sunday afternoon. Because of his legal status, Brannan retained Walker as a supernumerary aide on

25 Boyle, "Chickamauga," *National Tribune*, January 10, 1907. Written 43 years after the fact, Boyle's "refusal" of Turchin's order rings a little false, but the diversity of men in his small band clearly shows the confusion of the moment.

26 Webster, "Chickamauga," *National Tribune*, July 2, 1891; "Dear Sir," Letter from James T. Mills to Gen. E. A. Carmen, March 4, 1909, 10th Kentucky file, CCNMP.

27 *OR* 30, pt. 1, 385.

his division staff during the fight rather than have an experienced and capable officer sit out the action in the rear. Walker's moment had come. The rout seemed complete, and Union troops were flying everywhere, including—to his shock—members of his own brigade.

"Seeing the emergency" Walker later wrote, "I disregarded my arrest and putting myself at the head of such troops as I could induce to obey my orders, I immediately formed a new line upon the hills." The ad hoc nature of Walker's line was reflected in its make-up, for it contained units from several brigades. The anchor was Lt. Frank Smith's Battery I, 4th U.S. Artillery, which Negley had placed earlier in front of the Snodgrass cabin. Walker's polyglot command extended from Smith's right up onto Hill One—"about fifty men from 17th Ky Inf headed by the brave Col. Stout, the 21st Ohio Inf commanded by Lt. Col. Stoughton, a part of the 17th Ohio commanded by Col. Ward, a part of the 82nd Ind. commanded by Col. Hunter, a part of the 10th Ky Inf. comd. by Col. Hays, [and] a part of the 31st Ohio commanded by its line officers." In all, Walker collected parts of six regiments from four brigades, from three different divisions.[28]

Unfortunately, Walker had gathered no more than 250 men to defend Hill One. Except for the 21st Ohio, which would only remain on Hill One a short time, the rest of the units were fragments of a larger command. For example, Col. Morton Hunter recalled that while his 82nd Indiana was falling back, he sent the regimental adjutant (his brother Alfred) ahead to a fence line with 40 men to establish a rallying point. This detachment was commandeered by Negley and lost to Hunter for the remainder of the fight. Hunter only had 200 men at the start of the fight that morning, and he lost at least 90 of them in Poe Field. The additional loss of 40 more left the 82nd Indiana with perhaps 70 men—less the inevitable stragglers. The 31st Ohio was even more scattered. Sergeant Allspaugh and some others fell in with the 58th Indiana. Connell, Colonel Lister, and the regimental colors reformed alongside Negley's men. This left no more than a handful of Buckeyes from the 31st to fall in behind Walker. Despite these paltry numbers, Brannan rode up a few minutes later and, delighted with Walker's work thus far, immediately released him from arrest and ordered him to "continue the command."[29]

28 Walker Report, NARA.

29 Hunter, *History of the Eighty-Second Indiana*, 78-81; Walker Report, NARA.

Other units began to coalesce around Walker. In addition to his own 10th Kentucky, Colonel Hays added the 4th Kentucky and 14th Ohio regiments. In the 14th, B. B. Jackson remembered they "had to give back to a small mountain" where, he added, "we held the Rebels in check the entire day." The 14th Ohio's Lt. Col. Henry D. Kingsbury reported that only "the major and several other of the officers, with what men they could rally, remained on the hill to the right" and out of his direct observation for the balance of the battle. As for Kingsbury himself, his report leaves his whereabouts unclear, but it is likely he fell back with Connell and Negley. He was not present on Hill One. The 4th Kentucky did not file a report, but years later Lt. Granville West remembered the regiment accompanied Brannan back to Hill One and joined the line.[30]

Sam Beatty's brigade was one of the most scattered Federal formations on the battlefield that morning. Neither Beatty nor division commander Horatio Van Cleve was present; both were trying to rally some of their troops behind Mendenhall's gun line, where they collected no more than 100 muskets. Colonel Stout and the bulk of his 17th Kentucky found their way to Walker. Lieutenant DeWitt Downing, serving alongside the 17th in the 9th Kentucky, also of Beatty's brigade, remembered his regiment conducting a series of intermediate stands and retreats until he reached Walker's line, a "high hill where we done our last and best fighting." Here, Col. George Cram of the 9th Kentucky "formed the remainder of the regiment and counted off and behold[,] we only had 40 or 50 men present." Lieutenant Marcus Woodcock was not among them. Somewhere in the chaos he became separated from his comrades, failed to notice Walker's budding line, and fell back even farther to the wooded hollow behind Hill One. Another member of the brigade, diarist James M. Nash of the 19th Ohio, wrote that as his own unit reached Walker, they "rallied in squads at different points on the crest of [the] hill." The 19th was short their commander, Lt. Col. Harry G. Stratton, who along with 75 to 100 other men of the 19th ended up in Negley's portion of the line near the Snodgrass cabin. The 19th Kentucky began the battle with 384 men, suffered at least 50 casualties on September 19, and lost track of another 100 soldiers during the retreat from Poe

30 "Beloved Wife and Family," September 27, 1863, B. B. Jackson Papers, BGSU; OR 30, pt. 1, 425; Granville C. West, "Personal Recollections of the Chickamauga Campaign," *MOLLUS*, vol. 45, 429.

Field. Accounting for stragglers, perhaps the regiment added between 100 and 200 additional bayonets to Walker's strength.[31]

Sam Beatty's last regiment, the 79th Indiana, had much the same experience. Colonel Frederick Knefler reported that his efforts to rally the men "were utterly unavailing in the confusion." Knefler remained with Beatty and Van Cleve, leaving the field via the Dry Valley Road. Captain Daniel Howe's Company I followed Howe's stepfather, Lt. Col. Samuel P. Oyler, back to Hill One, where Howe offered a colorful description of Walker's growing quilt-work of a line: "There were colonels without regiments, captains without companies, and men without officers, all gathered promiscuously together." According to Oyler, his fragment of the 79th was nothing more than "five or six of the officers . . . and thirty or forty of the men." By the time Oyler arrived, he estimated Walker's force to number 700 to 1,000 men.[32]

While these bits and pieces of regiments streamed in Brannan rode the length of the burgeoning line, exhorting here, rallying there. At one point he ranged far enough forward to dramatically order Schultz's cannon back into position, as described earlier. A bit later, when he witnessed Harker's men coming up to engage Robertson's Texans in North Dyer Field, Brannan deemed his left flank reasonably secure. Not so his right. Walker's reorganized line ended somewhere short of the crest on Hill Two—and there were Confederates already much farther west than that. If those Rebels turned and attacked north, they would enter the fight from Hill Three and atop the long ridge beyond, easily overlapping Walker's line. Finding men to reinforce his right was now John Brannan's top priority.

Sometime between 12:30 and 1:00 p.m., Brannan and Negley came face-to-face for their first and only time that day. Each man came away with a very different impression of the encounter. According to Brannan, he found Negley leading a column of troops westward up the ridge behind Walker's line and exclaimed, "General Negley, I am very happy to see you with troops, as I am very hardly pressed and want assistance." "Certainly, I'll do all I can," replied the Pennsylvanian. Brannan asked Negley to go into line to his right,

31 "Dear Parents," September 25, 1863, DeWitt Clinton Downing Papers, Western Kentucky University, Bowling Green, KY; Noe, *A Southern Boy in Blue*, 210; Entry for September 20, James M. Nash Diary, WRHS.

32 *OR* 30, pt. 1, 812; Daniel Wait Howe, *Civil War Times 1861-1865* (The Bowen-Merrill Company, 1902), 189; "My own dear Lucy," September 21, 1863, Samuel Oyler Letters, Daniel Wait Howe Papers, InHS.

James S. Negley (right), the first defender of Snodgrass Hill and Horseshoe Ridge. After his decision to withdraw, Negley never held command in the Union army again.
Generals in Blue

"which was on another ridge, with a small ravine between." Brannan also reiterated his request for the loan of the 21st Ohio. (Sirwell had loaned out the 21st earlier, but the two division commanders confirmed that decision now.) With that, Brannan turned back to his own front, satisfied that Negley had "pledged himself to hold my right and rear."[33]

Negley's description was at odds with much of Brannan's. Negley thought Brannan only wanted one regiment, so he "ordered the 21st Ohio . . . to his assistance." In Negley's mind, nothing else was asked for or offered—certainly there was no discussion of extending Walker's line onto Hill Three. Negley hotly denied that any "pledge" was ever given, and even called the idea "incredible." He also denied ever agreeing to hold the ridge Brannan described. By the time the two generals met, Negley was convinced further resistance was useless, and was already leaving the battlefield. Worse, he did not tell Brannan of his decision to depart. He also neglected to inform several of his own officers, as subsequent events would demonstrate.[34]

Two factors proved instrumental in Negley's decision to retreat. The first was Rosecrans's word that no help was forthcoming. The second was the report of those seven enemy flags moving around his northern flank. However soberly he might have reached this decision, in executing it he proved quite sloppy, and even a bit panicky. None of his three brigade commanders were informed of his decision. Stanley and John Beatty were still caught up in the struggle in Kelly Field and so were not present, but Colonel Sirwell was certainly close by. Sirwell had just posted the 74th Ohio in support of Schultz's battery when he discovered Negley had taken the rest of his brigade and departed west through

33 *OR* 30, pt. 1, 402, 1041. Negley makes no mention of Sirwell's role in lending the 21st Ohio.

34 Ibid., 330, 1044-1051.

the timber. When Sirwell returned to where he had left the 74th Ohio, he discovered it, too, was gone—ordered away by one of Negley's aides almost as soon as Sirwell put it into position. Alone and no doubt frustrated, Sirwell set off to try and find his command, which he eventually caught up with at Rossville.[35]

Sirwell's last two regiments, the 37th Indiana and 78th Pennsylvania, also endured some confusion. At 11:00 a.m., Col. William D. Ward's 37th Indiana was posted just behind the Snodgrass cabin, tasked with supporting Smith's (and later Bridges's) cannon. Over the course of the midday, Ward watched as first the 21st Ohio departed to help Brannan, and then as Sirwell led the 74th Ohio off to the right a bit later. Ward was on foot, having sent his horse and servant to the rear earlier that morning for safekeeping during the move northward.[36]

For the next hour or so Ward and his Hoosiers watched the battle unfold, suffering through a noisy but mostly harmless artillery barrage as Smith and Bridges threw shells into the distant Rebel ranks somewhere near Poe Field and received an erratic return fire. Enemy shells knocked splinters off trees, "but hurt no one seriously." The regiment was deployed behind the crest of the open ridge when Negley rode up and ordered Ward to shift somewhat to the left. They did so, crossing "a little hill, and formed in an open woods." Here according to Sgt. (and later, regimental historian) George H. Puntenney, the men of the 37th could clearly see Harker's fight, giving lie to Negley's assertion that no other troops were present: "Union troops on our right and a little in advance were in a cornfield, and the dust raised . . . by rebel bullets striking the ground among them, reminded one of the dust raised sometimes by a dashing summer rain."[37]

Ward and his command were certain they were going to be in the thick of the fight any minute. Instead, they were moved again, this time back up the hill to their original position, where "a Union battery [Smith's] was firing very rapidly. To Puntenney, this place seemed like a veritable hell: "the blue smoke

35 Ibid., 385.

36 Entry for September 20, William D. Ward Journal, DePauw University. Ironically, both Ward's black servant and his mount would be captured in the subsequent rout of the Union right flank.

37 Puntenney, *History of the Thirty-Seventh*, 57. This "little hill" was the shoulder of Hill One, and they were placed facing southeast, looking down at the low ground east of Hill One.

from the cannons' mouths made it difficult to see, and the roar was simply deafening." Suddenly, added Puntenney, "An officer rode up on a fiery steed flecked with foam and inquired 'What Regiment is this?' On being told, he ordered us to charge over the point of the hill and capture a Rebel brigade. From the ranks, Pvt. Rufus Henderson retorted, 'I don't want any Rebel brigade.'"[38]

Doubtless to the private's dismay, Ward did not question the order: "I halted, fronted, and rectified the line, and gave the order 'Forward! Guide Center double quick!' but before the word March could be given an aide of General Negley rode up and ordered me to move off by the right flank and follow the General." The division was leaving the field. Henderson and his comrades were probably relieved when they turned to follow the aide back to Negley.[39]

The identity of the officer ordering this charge remains unanswered. Sergeant Puntenney had his suspicions: "It was at that time, and is yet believed by many of us . . . that man was a rebel officer." Ward's quick acceptance of the command, however, makes that scenario unlikely. Ward never specified the man's name, and he accepted his authority without question. It is possible the officer was John Brannan, who was very active on the ridge at midday. Brannan, however, was trying to build a defensive line, not launch an attack. It might also have been Tom Wood in an effort to help the embattled Harker. Assuming he had secured another horse, Wood could have ridden to an unknown regiment and demanded it come to his support. Wood, however, makes no mention of this in his report, which is otherwise quite detailed. Wood was among the generals most angry with Negley for the manner of his departure, and would have no reason to obscure this kind of incident. Indeed, it would help him make a better case against Negley. Nor does this mystery officer appear to have been John Beatty, despite the fact that he was approaching Snodgrass Hill by this time. Beatty also makes no mention of such an incident in his otherwise descriptive report and memoirs.[40]

It is very possible the mystery officer was an overwrought Col. George Dick. After his force routed at Govan's approach, Dick and a portion of his

38 Ibid., 58.

39 Entry for September 20, William D. Ward Journal, DePauw University.

40 Puntenney, *History of the Thirty-Seventh*, 58.

brigade attempted to move back south. He hoped to retrace his steps down the Glenn-Kelly Road and locate General Van Cleve, who Dick and others presumed was still, according to Lt. Col. Granville Frambes of the 59th Ohio, "in the place we left in the morning." By now, of course, Van Cleve was gone, swept away by the tide of Confederates who now blocked Dick's way.[41]

Dick's own report is vague on the course of events after he left Stanley's men. Lieutenant Colonel Frambes offers a little more detail, noting how the rump of the brigade (which now only included the 59th Ohio and 86th Indiana) moved to the right some distance and eventually formed "in line under cover of the hill" and subsequently supported Brannan for a time. If Dick's and Frambes's reports are reasonably accurate as to timing and location, both put Dick in the right place to encounter Ward and his Hoosiers.[42]

There is one more piece of potential evidence to suggest Dick's role on that part of the field. Colonel Marion Taylor was leading his own 15th Kentucky and the 104th Illinois back to Snodgrass Hill during this same timeframe. Where they came to rest is unclear. Taylor did not file a report, and the report filed by the 104th's commander, Lt. Col. Douglas Hapeman, does not cast much light on the matter. A diary kept by Capt. William Strawn, commanding Company F of the 104th Illinois, however, provides more detail. According to Strawn, Taylor's demi-brigade came to rest on "the hill directly south of the Snodgrass house [Hill One]." There, Taylor had an encounter with a man Strawn identified as General Van Cleve, who insisted "Taylor must lead a charge through the cornfield [Dyer Field] against the rebel flank."[43]

This officer could not have been Van Cleve, who was at that time nearly 1,000 yards away trying to rally Sam Beatty's men—but it very well could have been Colonel Dick. His brigade was part of Van Cleve's division, and he may have identified himself in that way. If so, his words during the heat of battle could have been misinterpreted if overheard by men in the ranks. In any case, Taylor ordered the men to fix bayonets (most were out of cartridges) and both regiments started down the hill to the south. They didn't get more than 30 feet, however, before Maj. James Lowrie appeared again. A charge was out of the

41 *OR* 30, pt. 1, 833.

42 Ibid., 834.

43 Jenkins, *The Battle Rages Higher*, 184.

question, Negley was retreating to protect a long train of wagons and artillery, and Taylor was needed to form the rear guard for the movement.[44]

Dick made no mention of trying to organize a counterattack, though he did insist that he supported Brannan for a considerable period. Colonel Frambes added that the 59th Ohio and 86th Indiana "did good service in aiding Brannan . . . until we were completely outflanked on the right" and cut off from Brannan's part of the line. Eventually Dick observed Negley's retreat, mistook it for "the greater part of our army falling back," and followed suit, "gathering as many stragglers from the Twenty-First Corps as possible." Dick wasn't ordered away by Negley directly, but he may as well have been.[45]

Back at the Snodgrass cabin, the 37th Indiana's departure, described above, left Sirwell's last regiment all alone behind the guns. Commanding the 78th Pennsylvania, Lt. Col. Archibald Blakeley watched in surprise as Bridges's battery abruptly limbered up and left. Colonel Blakeley's orders were to support the battery, so its wordless departure left him both perplexed and without a mission. Blakeley put Maj. Augustus B. Bonnaffon in temporary charge of the regiment while he searched for someone who could tell him what was going on. Blakeley rode back to his Pennsylvanians empty-handed and decided to follow Bridges's guns as best he could. After marching about 1,000 yards to the west, the 78th stumbled upon General Negley, apparently all alone. Negley posted Blakeley's 78th in a ravine and, after ordering the colonel to "prevent the enemy at all hazards from breaking through," disappeared once again. Blakeley and Bonnaffon rode forward to get a better understanding of their position and, to their dismay, spotted off to the south what looked like an entire Confederate division moving west across the open fields. The overly aggressive Bonnaffon urged a charge, but Blakeley wisely demurred. One of Thomas's staff officers rode by a short time later, discovered the abandoned regiment, and told Blakeley the only way to safety was "to strike for the Dry Valley Road."[46]

Most of the motley collection of troops Negley took off the field with him received word to retreat in a similar haphazard fashion—if they got word at all. Connell's fragment of Brannan's division, Colonel Taylor with the 15th

44 Ibid., 185.

45 *OR* 30, pt. 1, 824, 834.

46 Ibid., 1066-1067. Blakeley and Bonnaffon likely saw Bushrod Johnson's men moving west toward the Vittatoe Road, for Johnson's division of Rebels were the only Confederates in that area at that time.

Kentucky and 104th Illinois, together with the 42nd and 88th Indiana (all of John Beatty's brigade), and Bridges's battery (Negley's division) got orders to leave. By contrast, Smith's 4th U.S. Battery (Brannan's division) was never ordered away and remained throughout the fight. Schultz's guns (Negley's division) and the 74th Ohio (Sirwell's brigade) were ordered away without the knowledge of Harker's men. Adjutant Alfred Hunter and his advanced detachment of the 82nd Indiana (Connell's brigade) met General Negley and were ordered away despite protest. Conversely, Major Hammond's 100th Illinois (Buell's brigade) seems to have just followed the general crowd off the field. According to Hammond, after he lost sight of the 58th Indiana during the retreat from Harker's Knoll, he "attached" himself to Negley's line and "eventually fell back with them . . . to a point near Rossville." Captain Marco Gary's Battery C, 1st Ohio (Brannan's division), initially ordered by Brannan to join Negley, also fell in with the general retreat. The wayward 84th Illinois (Grose's brigade) departed the field, much to Colonel Waters's later disgust. The regiment, he fumed with no little sarcasm, "had been ordered to Chattanooga to guard a train."[47]

Negley's column was swelled en route by the addition of at least some of the guns from Mendenhall's artillery line. Captain George Swallow of the 7th Indiana Battery—one of the few to escape Mendenhall's disaster— reported that his five surviving guns retreated under Negley's direction, as did most of the other guns that escaped the clutches of Bushrod Johnson's onrushing Confederates. When the final numbers were tallied, Negley withdrew between 2,000 and 2,500 infantry and possibly as many as 42 artillery pieces (though some of these guns, such as those rescued by Colonel Taylor, were not combat-capable). This force was more than twice as strong as the scratch line Brannan was feverishly cobbling together. Negley's departure robbed the Federal defense of badly needed artillery and bayonets at a critical time.[48]

Perhaps the worst blow of all would not be felt until much later. In addition to the troops and artillery, Negley took with him a sizable portion of the XIV Corps's ammunition trains. The withdrawal of the wagons infuriated General Thomas, though he remained circumspect in reporting the blunder, noting only that "my . . . trains [were] unfortunately . . . ordered to the rear by some

47 *OR* 30, pt. 1, 660, 787.

48 Ibid., 836. Negley's count of 42 cannon was likely actually 42 artillery vehicles, including caissons and limbers in that total. About half seem to be actual guns.

unauthorized person." The loss, while not immediately fatal, would have important consequences later in the day.[49]

Confusion reigned among these XIV Corps trains. They might well have been lost entirely if not for the presence of Nadine Turchin, the wife of the general. Against all orders, Nadine was still with the army, riding with General Reynolds's division ammunition train that day. She and her husband shared everything (including acerbic opinions about the proficiency of American armies). She was probably as competent a soldier, via her husband's tutelage and the expedient of practical experience, as most of the officers on the field. As the various divisional trains merged into one massive column, she suppressed at least one incipient panic by drawing her pistol and halting the formation until order could be restored. At another point she overrode a panicked officer's hasty order to burn the wagons lest they fall into enemy hands. She brought "confidence out of disorder, moving on the wagons that had stopped . . . shamed [stragglers] to order, and not a few induced to return to the front," recalled Sgt. John T. Booth of the 36th Ohio's Company G. "Mrs. Turchin had made up her mind to take the train to a place of safety and she did. The result of her pluck and good common sense . . . was that not a pound of ammunition was lost."[50]

Most of Negley's aides later testified that Negley's demeanor during this retreat was calm and collected. Captain Hough thought him "cool and self-possessed." Outside of his staff, however, opinions were less charitable. Ambrose Bierce, then a lieutenant and topographical engineer on Brig. Gen. William B. Hazen's staff, encountered Negley in the woods behind Horseshoe Ridge about this time. Bierce, whose topographic duties had given him a pretty good sense of the lay of the land, offered to guide Negley back to "glory or the grave," but his offer was rejected "a little uncivilly." Lieutenant Eben Sturges, serving in Schultz's artillery, was similarly disgusted. Sturges recorded in his diary that Negley's division had become scattered "through [Negley's] own bad management," and in a letter to his family similarly confessed, "I think Negley managed miserably." Colonel Ward of the 37th Indiana, who spent most of the day under Negley's direct command, offered no description of Negley during

49 Ibid., 253.

50 John T. Booth, "Chickamauga: A Campaign Unrivaled in the Annals of War, Part III," *National Tribune*, October 16, 1890.

this period, but he did praise Jefferson C. Davis of the XX Corps, who Ward found at Rossville reorganizing routed units.[51]

Fortunately, there were other troops available to hold Snodgrass Hill. Harker's brigade, after retreating in the face of Kershaw's attack, was coming into line amid the stubble of the Snodgrass cornfield. Harker reformed facing southeast just behind the crest. The 3rd Kentucky and 125th Ohio formed the left and right, respectively, of his first line, while the 65th and 64th Ohio fell in behind them. The brigade was resupplied with ammunition here, and despite its depleted ranks, steeled itself for the next action. Several men noted General Thomas's mounted presence nearby watching the deployment. Harker's regiments had taken a pounding in Dyer Field, losing an additional 250 men there. Fewer than 1,000 bayonets remained in line holding 150 yards of frontage. There was also some good news: Companies A and C of the 3rd Kentucky, previously cut off from the regiment and busy rallying stragglers with Walker, rejoined their regiment here.[52]

As far as George Thomas was concerned, Snodgrass Hill was now the key point on the field, and he took a personal interest in making sure it was defended with resolve. "This hill must be held," he barked to Harker, "and I trust you to do it." "We will hold it or die here!" Harker replied. Taking no chances, Thomas next rode to Colonel Opdycke, still mounted on Barney, and whose 125th Ohio was now the left flank regiment of the entire Horseshoe Ridge line. Thomas reiterated his instructions: "The position must be held." Turning to the regiment, Opdycke informed his men: "I am willing to die for my country, right here, and I hope you are all with me!"[53]

Harker was still forming when John Beatty rode up looking for both Negley and his own wayward brigade. By this time, both had left the field. Despite his action-packed morning, Beatty's adventures were far from over. His own troops might be gone, but plenty of Federals needed rallying. "I found abundant opportunity to make myself useful," he wrote. "Gathering up

51 *OR* 30, pt. 1, 1034, see also 1008, 1013, and 1023 for similar descriptions; Ambrose Bierce, "A Little of Chickamauga," *Ambrose Bierce's Civil War* (Gateway Press, 1956), 35; Entry for September 20, Sturges Diary, AHEC; Letter to "Dear Folks," October 2, 1863, Sturges Papers, AHEC; William D. Ward, Unpublished Recollections, p. 142, DePauw University.

52 *OR* 30, pt. 1, 695; Clark, *Opdycke's Tigers*, 113; Anonymous Letter to H. V. Boynton, October 9, 1893, 3rd Kentucky file, CCNMP; Clark, *Opdycke's Tigers*, 113; *OR* 30, pt. 1, 700.

53 Hinman, *The Story of the Sherman Brigade*, 429; Longacre and Haas, *To Battle for God and the Right*, 101.

scattered detachments of a dozen different commands, I filled up an unoccupied space on the ridge between Harker . . . and Brannan."[54]

Some of the men Beatty rallied were from Dick's brigade—the same unidentified command he unsuccessfully called on during the fight against Daniel Govan's Rebels earlier. In the ranks of the 44th Indiana, Sgt. Fred Banta recalled that after the retreat from Kelly Field the regiment fell back "into an open field . . . just to the left of an old log cabin . . . where we were attached to Harker's brigade." These men rallied by Beatty belonged primarily to the 44th and 13th Ohio, now under the direction of Lt. Col. Simeon Aldrich of the 44th. The 13th was rendered all but leaderless during the brief fight against Govan's men, losing both Lt. Col. E. M. Mast and Maj. Joseph T. Snider in almost the same instant. Reduced in numbers and under the command of a captain, Aldrich posted them in line behind Harker.[55]

Among the last troops to appear on Snodgrass Hill were those of Stanley's brigade, following in Beatty's wake. Colonel Stanley's three regiments reached the ridge in a moment of relative calm, retiring slowly in the face of Govan's advance until that pressure abated. Then, said Stanley, also feeling alone and without orders, "I withdrew my command and took position next to some log buildings on the brow of the hill, near the Rossville Road." Collectively, the 11th Michigan, 18th Ohio, and 19th Illinois now numbered roughly 900 men, their strength welcome indeed. Stanley's force arrived just as the first shots from Kershaw's South Carolinians started to tell among the Federal defenders on Hills One and Two.[56]

54 Beatty, *Citizen-Soldier*, 340.

55 Fred Banta, "The Twenty-First Corps at Chickamauga," *National Tribune*, May 24th, 1883; OR 30, pt. 1, 824; Commissioners, *Indiana at Chickamauga: 1863-1900, Report of Indiana Commissioners, Chickamauga National Military Park* (Sentinel Printing Co., Printers and Binders, 1900), 189; "Dear Friends at Home," September 24, 1863, Clark-Williams Family Papers, OHS.

56 *OR* 30, pt. 1, 379.

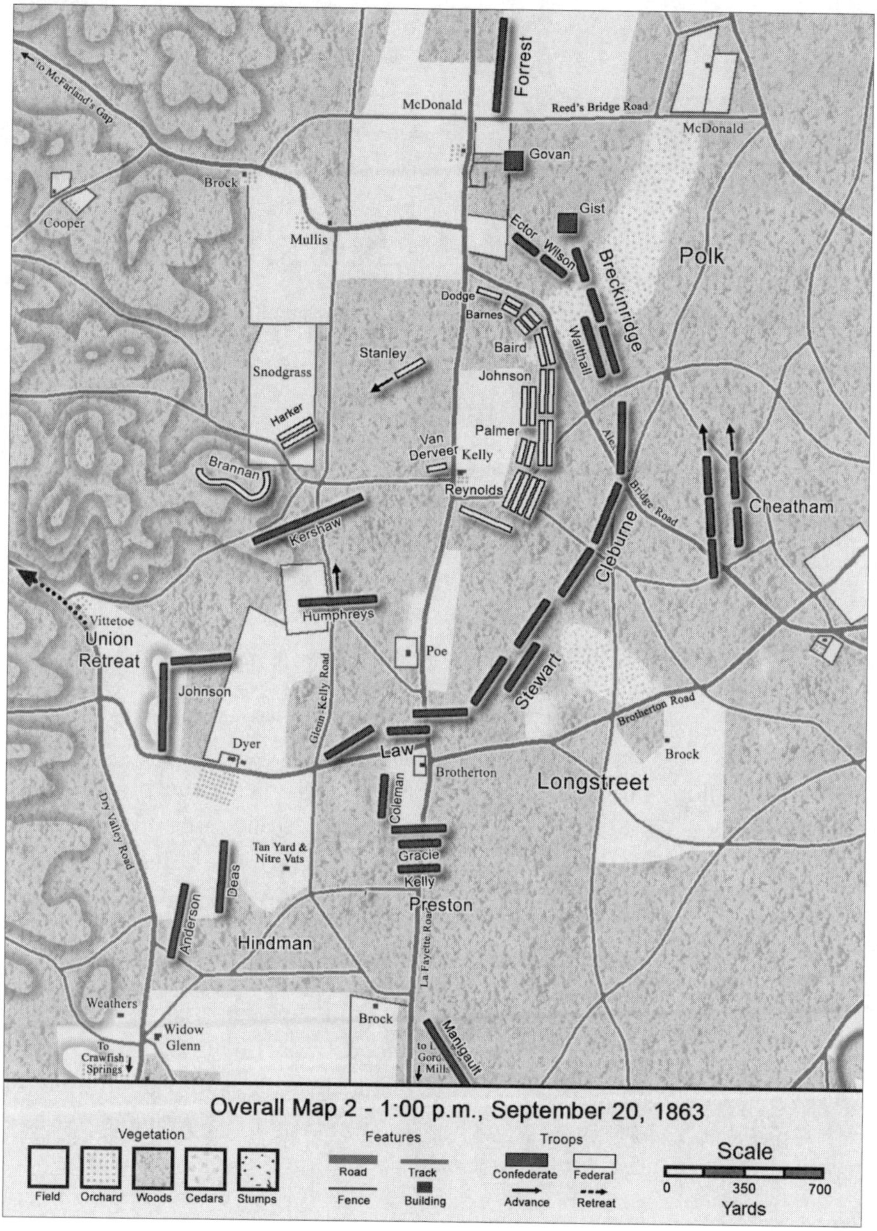

Overall Map 2 - 1:00 p.m., September 20, 1863

Chapter Seventeen

Kershaw's First and Second Attacks:

Sunday, 1:00 p.m. to 2:00 p.m.

Joe Kershaw's South Carolinians had thus far suffered comparatively few casualties, especially among the leftmost regiments. Union confusion over uniforms allowed the Gamecocks to close upon the enemy before facing incoming fire, and in some cases they got in the first volley. Flanked by the 2nd South Carolina, the collapse of Charles Harker's line precluded extended musketry duels except, perhaps, with the 125th Ohio. Things were about to change.

Kershaw intended to reform his line, wait for Ben Humphreys to come up with his brigade on his right, and together mount a coordinated assault against the new Federal position atop Horseshoe Ridge. Intent on pursuing a retreating foe, however, some of Kershaw's troops plunged headlong into an impromptu attack with barely a pause. Leading the 2nd South Carolina, Franklin Gaillard reported that he and his men "followed up and met their second line at the summit ridge strongly posted. As we approached this we were met with a very destructive fire." The 2nd was attempting to storm Hill Three, occupied in the nick of time by 21st Ohio of Sirwell's brigade.[1]

1 "Dear Maria," October 5, 1863, Franklin Gaillard Papers, UNC.

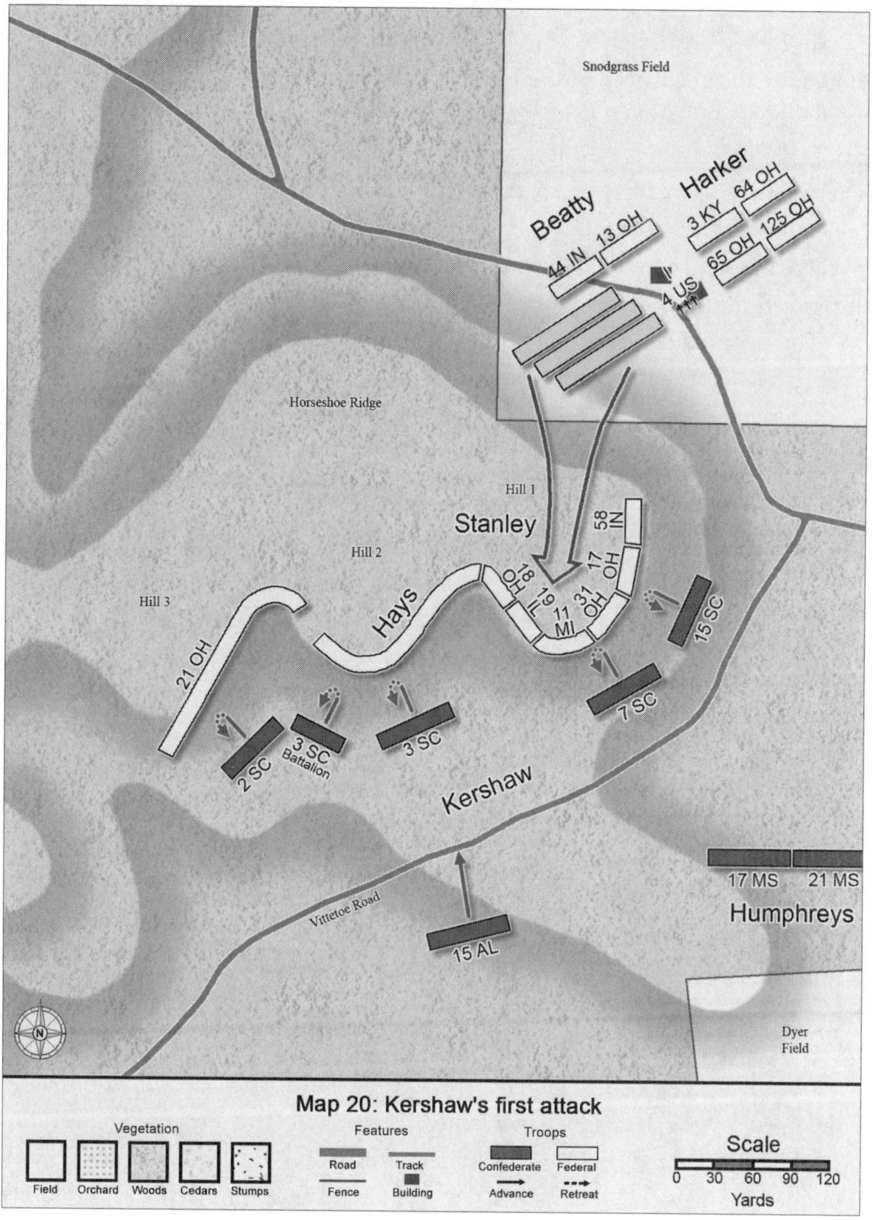

Map 20: Kershaw's first attack

When the 21st Ohio retreated from what would later become known as Harker's Knoll, at the north end of Dyer Field, it first came to rest on the crown of Hill Two, the highest point of Brannan's burgeoning new line. While there, Sgt. John Bolton of the 21st remembered "heavy columns of the enemy could be distinctly seen through the sparsely timbered woods moving towards us."

These Rebels overlapped the 21st's right flank by a good margin. An unidentified staff officer (probably sent by General Brannan) ordered the 21st to shift to Hill Three. There, the regiment lined the crest "facing southward [and] adapting itself as best it . . . could to the irregularities . . . of the ground." The Ohioans also scraped together some brush and deadwood to serve as breastworks. Back on Hill One, as the ranks of Col. Moses Walker's force swelled, Brannan extended the line onto newly vacated Hill Two. The men filed into position just minutes before the South Carolinians arrived.[2]

The commander of the 21st Ohio's Company D, 20-year-old Lt. Wilson J. Vance, would remember this moment for the rest of his life. The initial clash was "a sharp encounter—that first brush—and a stubborn one." The five-chambered Colt revolving rifles provided a nasty surprise for the South Carolinians. "At first the charging Johnnies, reaching the proper distance and receiving a volley from the regiment, returned the same and then started on the keen jump, expecting to reach us before we could reload. Before they had advanced ten paces . . . they would get another volley, and while they were pondering upon this circumstance, still a third; then they would scarcely get their backs turned . . . [to retreat] before the fourth would catch them, and [then] on a dead run, the fifth came singing about their ears." Facing this unexpected hail of lead, Rebel John Coxe recalled reaching the crest of the hill only to discover the Federals "were protected by fallen timber. They launched a withering fire . . . from behind the logs, and . . . we withdrew."[3]

About 150 yards to the east, the two 3rd South Carolinas—one a battalion and the other a full regiment—were climbing Hill Two. Unlike Gaillard's 2nd, these two units were considerably more disrupted by the fight for Harker's Knoll. Gaillard's men had the advantage of appearing on a vulnerable Union flank, but James's Battalion and Nance's 3rd regiment faced Buell and Harker's men directly. The battalion moved through Draw Three and up the southwest face. With Nance's 3rd Regiment scaling the southeast face, both commands converged on Walker's newly planted Federals. After taking note of the crowding that ruined the 3rd's regimental formation, Pvt. James Caldwell was wounded in the woods below Hill Two by a shell fragment that so bruised his knee he could no longer bend it. Unable to keep up, the hobbled soldier sought

2 Canfield, *History of the 21st Regiment*, 142.

3 Wilson J. Vance, "On Thomas' Right at Chickamauga," *Blue and Gray*, vol. 1, no. 2, (February 1893), 90; Coxe, "Chickamauga," 293.

shelter behind a tree, where he "was wounded [again] with the brass tubing of a percussion shell," which finally took Caldwell out of the fight for the day.[4]

Colonel Nance reported his 3rd South Carolina advanced only about 100 yards before Kershaw called a halt. Some of his men refused to stop. Blue-clad Harry Allspaugh of the 31st Ohio remembered South Carolinians following him all the way to the crest. "As we fell back through the wood we poured a constant fire on the enemy. . . . We finally occupied a knoll of the ridge, lying down in line and firing on them as they appeared." That fire stopped even the most diehard of Nance's men, and once the Rebels fell back Allspaugh found he had fallen in with men of the 17th Ohio. Identifying himself, Allspaugh told them "my regiment was broken up, but I was going to stay, and if I was killed to report me to my company."[5]

Kershaw's three right-hand regiments did not join this attack. The 7th and 15th South Carolina both "obliqued to the right," opening up a considerable gap between the 7th and the 3rd. Back in Dyer Field, the 7th faced off against Opdycke and the 125th Ohio, taking a more significant punishment than the rest of Kershaw's command. Especially telling was the loss of both Lt. Col. Elbert Bland and Maj. John S. Hard, the only two field officers present. Bland "fell . . . in the first moment of . . . triumph" while leading the 7th across Dyer Field. With Bland and Hard down, the 7th fell into disarray and halted in the timber short of the open line of Snodgrass Hill, as did the 15th. Opdycke's fighting retreat taught both regiments a bit of caution when pursuing presumably beaten Yankees. Kershaw's last regiment, the 8th South Carolina, drifted so far to the right that another gap of several hundred yards opened between it and the 15th. The 8th did not come into contact with any Federals at all, moving into the timber between Snodgrass Hill and Kelly Field.[6]

4 Caldwell, *Recollections*, http://gen.1starnet.com/civilwar/caldwelj.htm.The 3rd South Carolina Battalion was also called James's Battalion after a previous commander, though at Chickamauga it was commanded by Capt. Joshua M. Townsend.

5 *OR* 30, pt. 2, 507-508; Entry for September 20, Allspaugh Diaries, University of Iowa.

6 *OR* 30, pt. 2, 504; Anonymous, "Lieut. Col. Elbert Bland Late Commander of the 7th Regiment S.C.V.," Daniel Augustus Tompkins Papers, DU. Bland was well regarded by the men of the 7th, who keenly felt his loss. A doctor by training, Bland served in the Mexican War and in the initial stages of the current struggle as regimental surgeon before deciding that a combat role was more to his liking. Just before the move to Georgia, Bland contemplated resigning, still troubled by a wound received at Savage Station during the Seven Days' Battles in late June 1862. The regiment petitioned him to stay.

Trailing Kershaw was Brig. Gen. Benjamin G. Humphreys, leading a brigade into action for the first time. A Mississippi planter, lawyer, and legislator by profession, his education included a year-long stint at West Point before being dismissed for his involvement in a cadet riot. He entered the war in May 1861 as a captain in the 21st Mississippi, and by that fall was a colonel, in charge of the regiment. His brigade commander, fellow Mississippian William Barksdale, was an imposing figure, an able brigadier loved by his men. After Malvern Hill, Lee wrote that Barksdale "displayed the highest qualities of a soldier—seizing the colors himself and advancing under a terrific fire." Humphreys led the 21st in all of General Lee's battles through Gettysburg, where he inherited brigade command when Barksdale fell mortally wounded on July 2, 1863. Chickamauga was Humphreys's first real challenge in brigade command. "A humiliating sense of my incompetency painfully oppressed me [in trying to fill Barksdale's boots]," admitted Humphreys.[7]

Thus far all Humphreys had to do was follow in Kershaw's wake. When the South Carolinians changed front to the north, an officer Humphreys misidentified as Bushrod Johnson ordered Humphreys to follow suit and advance on Kershaw' right. The Mississippians marched north through Dyer Field, where Humphreys discovered Kershaw's "success had produced a panic on my front. I found they [the Federals] were 'skedaddling' instead of bristling their bayonets." Humphreys's line followed along behind the South Carolinians for some time, firing where possible. When the 8th South Carolina drifted far to the right, Humphreys's Mississippians unwittingly filled the gap between the 8th and the 15th. Once they did, he and his men caught their first glimpse of the blue line forming atop Snodgrass Hill.[8]

The Mississippians halted about 350 yards south of the 125th Ohio's new position at the Snodgrass farm, formed from left to right as follows: 17th, 21st, 13th, and 18th Mississippi. The brigade occupied a bit more than 300 yards of frontage, and easily filled the gap between the 15th and 8th South Carolina. Enemy lead began to pick through the ranks manning the left side of the line. Now taking fire, the 17th Mississippi swung toward the northwest to more

7 Ezra J. Warner, *Generals in Gray: Lives of the Confederate Commanders* (Louisiana State University Press, 1991), 145; Benjamin Humphreys, "History of the Sunflower Guards," John F. H. Claiborne Papers, UNC.

8 *OR* 30, pt. 2, 509; Benjamin Humphreys, "History of the Sunflower Guards," UNC. Humphreys must have mistaken Major Cunningham for Johnson.

squarely engage the Federals. The rest of the brigade tried to follow suit, but the maneuver was raggedly executed, leaving the 17th to face the brunt of Harker's fire alone. One month after the battle, 15-year-old Mississippi Pvt. John W. Flynn recounted the moment to his father: "We went into the woods at double-quick and got within about one hundred yards of the enemy. . . . We were going too fast for another part of our line." Sergeant John S. McNeely watched this advance from the ranks of Company E, 21st Mississippi. "The two right regiments were very little exposed," he explained, but "the left regiment [the 17th] was the most exposed and returned the fire."[9]

Private Flynn described a punishing enemy fire that tore apart the 17th: "[E]very man took his tree and pitched in . . . [but] it appeared that the trees did not do us much good. Nearly all of the boys that I saw fall were behind trees." The curving Union line allowed some Yankees to sweep the Mississippians with a deadly crossfire, including canister from Smith's battery. The Confederates concentrated on silencing Smith's guns. Flynn recalled firing nearly 30 rounds here and claimed he and his comrades "killed most of [the] gunners," but in fact the Federals got the best of this exchange. Flynn's recollection of friendly losses was closer to reality. The private thought nearly 100 of his comrades fell here—a higher loss in the 17th than in the rest of the brigade combined. Flynn was not far mistaken, for the 17th officially reported 12 dead and 76 wounded out of the 338 men engaged. From the 21st, some distance to the left-rear, Sergeant McNeely watched this slaughter with growing frustration. The 21st Mississippi had not yet opened fire, "for we were all expecting the order to charge at doublequick—but it never came." The brigade seemed paralyzed with indecision. McNeely's comrades in the 21st suffered an additional 50 casualties just waiting for Humphreys to act.[10]

Atop the hill, meanwhile, Harker's brigade was fighting in a calm and steady manner. Charles Harker had managed his command with great skill, especially during the retreat, and he was up to the task facing him now. Harker rotated his front and rear regiments, bringing them up to fire and then falling back to

9 Humphreys Brigade Tablet, CCNMP; Letter of John William Flynn to his father, October 20, 1863, NYHS; Gracie, *The Truth About Chickamauga*, 245. Gracie identifies this man as Capt. J. S. McNeily, but there is no one by this name and rank in the unit. There are three different versions of McNeely (McNaily, McNeilly) in the Consolidated Service Records, but they all refer to Sgt. John Seymour McNeely.

10 Flynn Letter, October 20, 1863, Gilder-Lehrman CollectionNYHS; *Memphis Appeal*, September 28, 1863; Gracie, *The Truth About Chickamauga*, 245.

load—a tactic that required tremendous discipline and confidence to successfully execute. When the Mississippians appeared in the trees below, Opdycke yelled "Attention, battalion! Right dress! Forward, march!" Cresting the ridge, the 125th now had a "good view" of their targets, "and within a few paces, he gave the orders, in deliberate succession, 'halt; ready, aim, fire!'" Captain McClure, alongside the 125th Ohio in the 3rd Kentucky, related "the 65th Ohio and the 3rd Kentucky occupied alternately the same front . . . and passed over each other to their slight line of works on the front and delivered their fire by volley and [then] retired to reload." "We was on the crest of a hill," remembered Cpl. Andrew Tousley of the 64th Ohio, "& had two lines of battle & the first line would go to the top of the hill & fier & then fall back under the cover of the hill & load & the 2 line would go up & fall back in the same manner." Tousley found this effort exhausting. "For my part" he continued, "I never worked harder in my life for the sweet [sweat] just roaled alf from us But we held them."[11]

Humphreys rode forward through the ranks of the 21st to get a good look at the Yankees who were punishing his command with such crisp, accurate volleys. From below, the Federals appeared to be "strongly entrenched," reported the brigadier, and "a slight reconnaissance satisfied me that to attempt to attack [would cost] one half of my brigade." Humphreys left a skirmish line in place and ordered his men to fall back. He also sent an aide to find General Longstreet to report what he had found, that he could not successfully attack without artillery, and that he needed further instructions. While waiting for Longstreet's reply, Humphreys "conceal[ed] the brigade behind trees, logs, etc." Unfortunately, he did not inform Kershaw of his circumstances despite the fact that Kershaw was just a couple of hundred yards to his left waiting for word that Humphreys was up and ready to attack with him. Humphreys never explained why he bypassed Kershaw to communicate directly with Longstreet.[12]

"Hold [your] position without advancing," replied Longstreet through a courier. He would send "a division to attack [the Federals] on the left and right." This was the response Humphreys was hoping for, but it was not what his

11 Clark, *Opdycke Tigers*, 113; Anonymous Letter, October 9, 1893, 3rd Kentucky file, CCNMP; "Dear friend Minnervia," October 12, 1863, Andrew Tousley Letter, Nina Ness Collection, Bentley Historical Library, UMich.

12 Gracie, *The Truth About Chickamauga*, 245.

brigade desired or expected. "My brave boys wanted to charge the hill—begged and importuned," recalled the brigadier. Sergeant McNeely agreed, recalling that "the men were keyed up to the highest tension, and would have gone over the enemy's lines as we did at Gettysburg." Of course, the brigade lost nearly 600 of its 1,600 men in that Pennsylvania fight, so perhaps Humphreys's caution was well-founded. Leaving the skirmish line behind as a screen, the Mississippians moved south 400 yards to the vicinity of a blacksmith shop Longstreet had designated as the "landmark" for the brigade's new position. There, Cpl. James B. Boothe of Company F, 21st Mississippi, was struck by the comparative silence of the new location, for "no enemy was in sight or hearing." Humphreys's brigade was out of the fight for the rest of the day.[13]

Humphreys's advance and subsequent retreat occurred without Kershaw ever realizing his looked-for support had come and gone. About this time, an unexpected arrival further confused matters. Colonel Oates and his wandering band of gypsies, the 15th Alabama, arrived and slid into place between and among Kershaw's men.

By September 1863, Oates was a troubled man. He had always been quarrelsome. He left home at 16 because of an abusive alcoholic father, and fled Alabama a year later to avoid arrest when he believed he had killed a man in a fight. After some years he returned and when war came, Oates—by this time a practicing lawyer—raised a company in what would become the 15th Alabama. Seniority disputes and backroom politicking led to a long-standing feud with fellow officer Alexander G. Lowther. Even after Oates was promoted to colonel in April 1863 and given command of the 15th, Lowther, who proved adept at avoiding combat and repeatedly wrangled long leaves of absence, still connived to replace him. Oates was a better commander than the frequently absent Lowther, but Gettysburg marked a turning point in William C. Oates's demeanor toward both the war and his men.[14]

13 *OR* 30, pt. 2, 509; Gracie, *The Truth About Chickamauga*, 245-246; J. B. Boothe, "The Tallahatchie Rifles – 'Cap' Houston," *Confederate Veteran*, vol. XXXII, no. 12 (December, 1924), 459.

14 Glenn W. LaFantasie, *Gettysburg Requiem: The Life and Lost Causes of Confederate Colonel William C. Oates* (Oxford University Press, 2006), 8-13, 72-74, 145-146. The story of Oates's quest for rank and his struggles with Lowther make for a convoluted tale. To complicate matters, unknown to Oates at the time, though he was nominated for full colonel, the Confederate Congress failed to act on the appointment and for some time he technically remained a captain, a fact that would give him additional trouble later. Eventually he was confirmed as colonel.

At Gettysburg, Oates and his regiment separated from the brigade and fought on the far right of the army in a desperate struggle on the slopes of Little Round Top against Joshua Chamberlain and the 20th Maine. This storied encounter cost both Oates and the 15th dearly, taking the life of Oates's younger brother John and several of his boyhood friends. The months that followed were marked by depression and a hardening in Oates's attitude toward his command as he became more argumentative and independent-minded. His performance at Chickamauga, especially on the 20th, raised fresh questions concerning his ability to effectively command the regiment.[15]

On the morning of September 20, Oates and the 15th lost contact with the rest of General Law's Brigade early during the first advance. While Col. William Perry and the brigade were joining Bushrod Johnson for the attack on Mendenhall's gun line, Oates drifted nearly 800 yards off course and found himself behind Zach Deas's brigade. As described, Deas's fellow Alabamians were engaged with Phil Sheridan's Yankees when Oates's 15th Alabama emerged from the woods behind Deas's line and, in their haste to join the fight, fired a volley into the rear of one of the Alabama regiments.

Deas's men managed to take the hill, kill Union Brig. Gen. William Lytle, and all but rout his brigade. While Deas's brigade, along with the rest of the division, pursued the fleeing Federals west, Oates and the 15th Alabama climbed the hill. Oates later described finding Lytle's body—he was but one of many Confederate officers to do so—and dragging the dying Federal into the shade. Oates allowed the 15th a few minutes to rest. One company was detailed to haul two abandoned Union guns back to the La Fayette Road to ensure credit for their capture went to the 15th.[16]

It was only after all this that Colonel Oates actively sought to locate his own brigade. He marched the regiment back down the eastern slope of Lytle Hill to the open pits of the tan yard along the east edge of Dyer Field. By this time Perry's, Robertson's, and Benning's brigades had all fallen back to the vicinity of Brotherton Field, so Oates did not encounter a soul from his own division during this trek. He did, however, run into Bushrod Johnson, who was still looking for support. "He [Johnson] could not tell me anything of Law's Brigade

15 Ibid., 125-126. It is possible that Oates was suffering what the military today calls Post-Traumatic Stress Disorder, or PTSD.

16 Oates, *The War Between the Union and the Confederacy*, 258; William C. Jordan, *Some Events and Incidents During the Civil War* (The Paragon Press, 1909), 52.

and the sequel proved he knew as little . . . about his own," sneered Oates. In fact, Johnson had a pretty good grasp of the unfolding situation, far better than Oates himself understood things. Johnson ordered Oates north across Dyer Field toward Horseshoe Ridge in the hope his Alabamians would support his own two brigades, whom Johnson said were "hard pressed." Accounting for detachments and earlier losses, Oates probably still had nearly 300 men in the ranks (the 15th opened the battle with 373 officers and men), which would comprise a sizable reinforcement for Johnson's undersized command, much battered by two days of hard fighting.[17]

The 15th moved across Dyer Field in the wake of Robertson's and Kershaw's advance. Oates recognized Lieutenant Colonel Bland's corpse near the northern boundary of the field. Working their way through the timber, Oates found himself amidst Kershaw's brigade, filling a gap between the 3rd and 7th South Carolina regiments.[18]

What happened next borders on the bizarre. With Federals atop the ridge and regiments of South Carolinians clinging to cover on either flank, Oates decided an immediate attack was in order. He made no effort to report to Kershaw. Instead, he advanced up the slope of Draw One with his 15th Alabama considerably ahead of the two South Carolinian regiments. "I went to Colonel Nance . . . and requested him . . . to move . . . up . . . and connect with my left," wrote Oates. Nance, who had no idea who Oates was or under whose authority he was acting, sensibly refused. Oates next tried to pull rank and order Nance up the hill. Nance—who was senior to Oates by nearly a year— again refused, rightly recognizing the Alabamian had no authority here. The rebuffed and now-angry Oates "bestowed upon him a few encomiums" and went back to the 15th.[19]

17 Oates, *The War Between the Union and the Confederacy*, 259; Laine and Penny, *Law's Alabama Brigade*, 370. Given that Oates had almost immediately become separated from his own brigade, wandered incoherently over the battlefield with his regiment, and at one point so lost control of his command that they shot fellow Alabamians in the back, his criticism of Johnson during this brief encounter seems wholly unjustified. It was certainly not Johnson's job to keep track of Law's brigade.

18 Oates, *The War Between the Union and the Confederacy*, 259-260. Kershaw mistakenly reported that Oates fell in between the 7th and 15th South Carolina regiments; see *OR* 30, pt. 2, 509, Laine and Penny, *Law's Alabama Brigade*, 172, and footnote 103, 391. Oates specifically describes an encounter with Nance of the 3rd South Carolina, which would have been very unlikely had he been on the right of the 7th South Carolina.

19 Oates, *The War Between the Union and the Confederacy*, 259; Wyckoff, *Third South Carolina*, 41.

South Carolina Brig. Gen. Joseph B. Kershaw (right) was doing double duty on September 20, acting as both a brigade and division commander.
Battles and Leaders

Oates spread his men out in a single line, extending the 15th across most of the ground he wanted Nance to help cover. Once that was finished, he moved off to the right to try his luck with the 7th South Carolina, where Capt. Elijah Jeremiah Goggans of Company M was now in charge. Once again Oates tried to order Goggans up the slope. The captain also refused, on the "pretext," as Oates put it, that Kershaw had personally placed the 7th in this spot. The disgusted Oates decided the moment called for a little public oration. Climbing upon a log, Oates harangued the South Carolinians, appealing to state pride (and no doubt stinging their personal honor) until one unknown captain stepped forward and said that he would take his company up the hill. At last, Oates was getting the movement he looked for. He turned and went back up the hill, the captain and his company following. With that, the whole of the 7th South Carolina joined in, though it remains unclear whether it did so because of injured pride or because its members believed the advance was being made under orders.[20]

Under orders to attack it most assuredly was not, and Kershaw later specifically rebuked Oates on this very point. At the moment the 7th South Carolina went forward, Kershaw, who was still on the left side of his extended brigade waiting for word from Humphreys, took Oates's impromptu assault as the signal for the general advance. This impression was bolstered by the swell of fighting marking the 17th Mississippi's engagement. Taken together, both

20 Robert S. Seigler, *South Carolina's Military Organizations during the War Between the States: The Midlands* (The History Press, 2008), 170-171; Oates, *The War Between the Union and the Confederacy*, 259. Goggans had been unofficially promoted to major after the battle of Sharpsburg and was apparently serving in that capacity along with Major Hard at this time.

events convinced Kershaw the entire line was moving, and so he ordered the left wing of his brigade into action.[21]

While waiting for the order to go forward, Private Coxe reflected on the 2nd South Carolina sheltering in the Vittetoe Road. "The battle was raging to the left and right, and for awhile we enjoyed a nice breeze passing through the woods." Autumn leaves falling from the trees around him prompted Coxe to compare "these falling leaves to the falling men." Then came the attack order, and Coxe charged with "the hope of breaking up and capturing their line at the top [of Hill Three.]" According to a Charleston newspaper correspondent, "the 3rd, 2nd, and James's Battalion again dashed forward, and at some points gained the crest of the hill." If so, the objective was held but briefly. Coxe didn't recall reaching the top: "we were met with such a terrific fire . . . from behind log fortifications, that we . . . were compelled to fall back." Sergeant Dubose Egleston, however, remembered the 2nd coming within inches of success. "We reached the crest of the hill but were so broken, we could not hold it. Had our support been in its place we would have had no further trouble. . . . I was on the hill myself, but it was too hot to stay there long."[22]

One of those lost here would be keenly missed. Sergeant Richard Kirkland of the 2nd South Carolina was shot through the chest during the retreat. Kirkland was a solid soldier who had first come to Kershaw's attention in Virginia on the cold night of December 13, 1862. There, Kirkland sought permission to help wounded Federals in front of his position along the stone wall at Fredericksburg. His act of bravery and mercy earned him the sobriquet, "The Angel of Marye's Heights." Kirkland went on to fight well at Gettysburg, and made acting Third Lieutenant for his company, though he was still officially only a sergeant. Kirkland was hit while taking one last shot. He waved off two comrades who tried to carry him down the hill: "I'm done for," he said, "tell Pa I died right."[23]

21 *OR* 30, pt. 2, 504.

22 *Charleston Daily Courier*, October 24, 1863; Coxe, "Chickamauga," 293; "Before Chattanooga," September 27, 1863, Dubose Egleston Letters, UNC. Not surprisingly, given how long after the fact it was recorded, Coxe's account mixes up the order of these attacks. He described the Union 21st Ohio charging the 2nd South Carolina first, and getting repulsed. Then he recalled making this second attack. Colonel Nance's report notes that the Rebels charged first, and the Federals counterattacked.

23 Mac Wyckoff, *A History of the 2nd South Carolina Infantry 1861-65* (Sergeant Kirkland's Museum and Historical Society, Inc., 1994), 59-61; William D. Trantham, "Wonderful Story of

Kershaw's attack order unleashed Colonel Nance's 3rd South Carolina up Hill Two. Heavy fire dogged the 3rd from the start, and it only managed to get "within about 50 yards of the enemy's line. Here the fire . . . was very deadly." The 3rd lost 166 men on this day of combat, a large number of whom fell in this effort. Nance's effort lacked support on his right. Despite Oates's grand oration and posturing, his own impromptu attack (with his Alabamians and the 7th South Carolina) had quickly deteriorated into a confused mess.[24]

Goaded into the movement, the nearly leaderless 7th broke in the face of overwhelming Union fire. "My Seventh South Carolina Regiment ingloriously fled," recalled Oates with his usual charm. However, his Alabamians were no less prompt in flight. Turning away from the 7th, Oates remembered, "I saw my regiment start down the hill. I ran among the men, yelling 'halt, halt, men!'" His command soon rallied, and with one company of the 7th returned and clawed their way to very near the summit. Oates claimed they reached the top and broke the Federal line, but he was mistaken. Draw One forks about 150 yards north of the Vittetoe Road, splitting into a 'Y' with narrower ravines running off at angles to the northeast and northwest. Between them a tongue of land rises abruptly, projecting forward from the saddle connecting Hills One and Two. This small spur deceived Oates into thinking he had gained the crest of the main ridge, but the 15th Alabama was still well short of the actual summit or of driving off the Federals. The new position exposed Oates's flanks to a dangerous enfilade fire.[25]

"The regiment immediately on my right, [the 15th Alabama]" Nance complained, "(and which had already obliqued much too far to the right . . .) veered still farther. . . .With my right flank thus exposed and my line terribly thinned . . . I found it impossible to advance further." Worse, Gaillard's 2nd South Carolina and James's Battalion were not making any progress on Nance's

---

Richard R. Kirkland," *Confederate Veteran*, vol. XVI, no. 3, (March, 1908), 105. Kirkland's body was recovered and taken home to Camden, South Carolina for burial.

24 *OR* 30, pt. 2, 508.

25 Oates, *The War Between the Union and the Confederacy*, 262. Oates claimed the 15th Alabama reached the summit of Hill Two and forced the Yankees to retreat. No Union account supports this version of events, nor does Nance's report, which was penned within days of the battle. In his memoir, Oates admitted his own report was lost, and his description of events depended upon memories four decades old. Like Coxe, Oates seems to have muddied the sequence of some of this fighting. What Oates is probably recalling is the repulse of a limited Union pursuit down the hill after his own charge, which is clearly described in a number of contemporary accounts.

left. Kershaw's entire effort ground to a halt. Both Nance's Gamecocks and Oates's Alabamians clung to the slope of the ridge, trying to return fire as best they could, but clearly with no hope of going any farther.[26]

Things were not going well from the Confederate perspective, but the Federals atop the ridge recalled the ferocity of these uphill assaults, and how close the Rebels came to taking both Hills One and Two. Henry Davidson of the Union 10th Kentucky was one of Hill Two's defenders. "We hurriedly threw up a small breastwork of logs and rails," he wrote home, "and now the whole rebel horde rushed on us thinking to achieve an easy victory, again & atain they charged us, again & yet again they are driven back." During the 3rd South Carolina's first effort, Union Captain Webster remembered that 20 or so "strays" had mixed in with his Company I of the 10th Kentucky. To Webster's disgust, they "sprang as one man to the rear, and went scampering down the hill." As for his own men, Webster had no doubt of their determination; Company I stayed put and shot back as fast as they could load.[27]

On Hill Three, the 21st Ohio played a critical role in the defense of Horseshoe Ridge. The fight was mostly unfolding to their left-front, since the 21st's line extended farther west than did Kershaw's formation. Buckeye Sgt. John Bolton stepped into Sgt. Maj. Blakely's shoes after Blakely was killed, which allowed Bolton to roam the length of the 21st's position. "The battle became general along our part of the line, that is, immediately after the first charge had been repulsed; the firing . . . was rapid, and the deafening rattle of musketry was kept up with greater or less severity from this time on, and only at intervals of short duration would firing cease for a few moments. The enemy charged us repeatedly with a determination bordering on desperation . . . but with the aid of the Colts rifles they were repulsed each and every time." Bolton also remembered Colonel Walker and the 31st Ohio (or what there was of it) having a desperate time on the 21st's left. Walker's line "was forced back by overwhelming numbers, [but he] succeeded in rallying his men and again retook his position. [When] his color bearer fell back . . . Walker grasped the colors . . . and calling on his men to follow him he succeeded in regaining his position."[28]

26 *OR* 30, pt. 2, 508.

27 "My Dear Aunt," Letter of February 19, 1864, Henry G. Davidson Papers, ALPL; Webster, "Chickamauga," *National Tribune*, July 2, 1891. Perhaps these fleeing stragglers were the Federals Oates thought he saw retreating.

28 Canfield, *History of the 21st Regiment*, 142-143; John H. Bolton Papers, OHS.

Harry Allspaugh, one of those 31st Ohioans fighting in Walker's line, vividly recalled the desperate—and close—nature of the struggle. Like most of Horseshoe's defenders, Allspaugh and his comrades piled up whatever they could find for protection, but, he admitted, "more than once they drove us from behind our works. [W]e reformed and drove them out again until the ground on their side of the slope was covered with their dead and we had to drag the dead back out of our way on our side. Some times we were fighting hand to hand, firing across the piles of rails . . . and then clubbed muskets . . . decided the possession of the railpiles. At one time, through a hole in a partially decayed log . . . I saw the gray uniform of some poor fellow and stuck my musket through the opening and fired, with my enemy less than a hand's breadth away."[29]

On Hill One, Col. Morton Hunter at the head of the 82nd Indiana recalled that at "about 1:00 o'clock the enemy made the most determined and furious attack upon us that I ever saw . . . which we repulsed with great slaughter." Lieutenant Colonel Henry Davis, supervising the left wing of the 82nd, was the latest to be deceived by the color of the uniforms sported by the South Carolinians. When Hunter's regiment split into fragments after the desperate fight in Poe Field, Davis and his portion wandered for some time until stumbling across Hunter just before Kershaw attacked. The oncoming regiment "displayed no flag and were dressed in blue," recalled Davis, so initially he withheld fire. "[W]hen within 30 paces of our line they opened fire on us; not until then did [I] fully believe that the front line of the enemy weren't friends." Once all doubts were dispelled, the Hoosiers returned one deadly volley after another. The 82nd fired "almost as one man, and gave the enemy such a tremendous shock that they ran pell-mell." Private Benjamin Mabrey of Company K recalled the fearful slaughter in a letter home. "We layd thick in piles as they came up. We pord the boolets in them thicker than hale. There was a constant roring of musketry all the time. It was the hardest fight there ever was."[30]

Kershaw's remaining two regiments, the 15th and 8th South Carolina, comprised what amounted to the brigade's right wing. Kershaw, however, was still too far to the left to exercise effective control over these two regiments, and

29 1883 Addendum to entry for September 20, 1863, Allspaugh Diaries, University of Iowa.

30 Hunter, *History of the Eighty-Second Indiana*, 69; Davis Letter, CCNMP; Sutton, *Benjamin Benn Mabrey*, 81.

Col. Timothy R. Stanley (left) was wounded shortly after his arrival on Hill One.
Miller, Photographic History

so saw nothing of their fight. The brigade's extended frontage, Kershaw's own lack of suitable horseflesh, and his efforts to exercise both brigade and divisional command simultaneously were all conspiring to rob his brigade of tactical coordination. Neither regiment filed an official report, and few personal accounts have survived from the 8th and 15th to document their activity. Combat losses offer a clue as to the relative intensity of their engagement. While the 2nd and 3rd South Carolina suffered 44% and 48% losses, respectively, the 15th lost 21% (or 71 of its 343 officers and men). The 8th, which ended up on the east side of Humphreys's brigade, lost 13% (or 28 out of 215 engaged). The 15th came into action on the east face of Hill One, just to the left of the much-abused 17th Mississippi facing Harker's deadly volleys out on the open portion of Snodgrass Hill. Like the Mississippians, the 15th South Carolina must have taken damaging fire from the Federal defenders. John Belue, a member of the 15th's Company F, was shot here twice in rapid succession: "We [crossed] several lines of breastworks, drove them back a mile or more to a hill where the enemy had a strong position," remembered Belue. "Fighting a while I received a leg wound through the hip in a few minutes another on top of the head."[31]

Luckily for the scratched-together line of Union defenders, reserves were now close at hand, including Colonel Stanley's three regiments, which hastened to ensure that Hill One remained crowned in Federal blue. Stanley was wounded in the shoulder shortly after placing his three regiments in support of Lieutenant Smith's guns of the 4th U.S., so brigade command devolved upon

31 Powell, "Numbers and Losses," CCNMP; Entry for September 20, John Belue Diary, Winthrop College, Rock Hill, South Carolina.

Col. William L. Stoughton of the 11th Michigan. Seeing Walker's patchwork force of Federals struggling to hold Hills One and Two, Stoughton responded with alacrity. "I at once ordered the Eleventh Michigan and Nineteenth Illinois to their support. These regiments advanced at the double-quick and charged the enemy." Michigan Pvt. James Martin was among those rushing to the rescue: "When the [Union] line began to waver . . . we were ordered forward our regiment in the advance[,] we opened on them and fought for about fifteen minutes and repulsed them." Even subtracting the losses suffered against Adams's and Govan's Confederates earlier in the morning, the two Federal regiments still numbered nearly 600 bayonets—too much additional firepower for Kershaw's exhausted and disjointed command to overcome. The first attack against Horseshoe Ridge was a failure.[32]

The Rebels fell back in considerable disorder. Kershaw, still supervising the left wing, pulled those men back as far as the Vittetoe Road along the base of the ridge. There, remembered John Coxe, the 2nd South Carolina got in a little payback. When the Rebels fell back, Sergeant Bolton and the rest of the 21st Ohio surged forward after them. Some of the Buckeyes went too far and ran straight into the muzzles of the reforming 2nd. From the road bed, Coxe exulted, "Our officers commanded us to hold our fire until they got within short range . . . they [got] within twenty yards . . . [and] before they visualized our presence, we rose up as one man and poured into them such a volley." Kershaw witnessed some of this effort, reporting that "the enemy soon advanced, but by a cool, deliberate fire [was] quickly repulsed."[33]

While Coxe and the 2nd were fending off overzealous Ohioans, Colonel Nance, whose men were still clinging to the slope just below the crest, reported his desperate circumstances to Kershaw. The brigadier directed the 3rd to fall back "behind a small ridge just in front of the fence running which ran along the northern side of [Dyer] field. . . . Here the line was reformed. . . . I directed my men in the lull that then ensued to bring forward the rails from the fence . . . [and] make a rude breastwork." Once his men were out of range, noted Kershaw, "I determined to hold the enemy until reinforcements arrived."[34]

32 *OR* 30, pt. 1, 380-381, "Dear parents," September 24, 1863, Martin Letter, Bentley Historical Library, UMich.

33 Canfield, *History of the 21st Regiment*, 143; Coxe, "Chickamauga," 293; *OR* 30, pt. 2, 504.

34 Coxe, "Chickamauga," 293; *OR* 30, pt. 2, 504, 508.

Nance's retreat, coupled with the earlier retirement of the bulk of the 7th South Carolina, put Oates in an even tighter spot. All alone now, the 15th Alabama clung to the throat and sides of Draw One, their line so thin the men of Oates's left-hand companies were reduced to a single rank with each man "one or two paces apart." While walking the line to inspire his men and ensure no one broke for the rear, Oates took special note of the death of one young Alabamian, a 16-year-old cross-eyed lad named Tommie Wright who was industriously loading and firing one minute, then shot in the head the next.[35]

Not everyone was inspired by example. Oates also came across "one of the largest men in the regiment" cowering behind a tree insisting he was sick. When a stern prompting proved inadequate to return the man to the firing line, Oates tried harsher measures: "I . . . struck him over the head with my sword and knocked him down, cutting his head a little. . . . He then took his place in the ranks and fought as well as any of his comrades. I heard no more of his sickness." Years later, Oates recounted his theories about leadership in battle. "All the newspaper talk during the war about 'gallant leaders' was the veriest bosh. One good driver was worth six 'gallant leaders.' The latter generally accomplished little else than to get themselves shot." The 15th Alabama remained in place for about an hour, huddled behind whatever small shelter its members could find, and some distance ahead of Kershaw's main line.[36]

On Hill One, the defending Federals had orders not to pursue. John Beatty took charge here. Finding Colonel Stoughton "immediately after this charge," Beatty ordered him to hold Hill One with the 11th Michigan and 19th Illinois. Private Martin and his comrades "then fell back a few rods under cover of a hill out of reach of their sharpshooters." Michigander Lt. Borden C. Hicks recalled that, "After the first repulse of the enemy our lines were reformed, and we got together rails and logs, and made our position more defensible." James Fenton in the 19th Illinois dismissed these works as "flimsy," noting that they were constructed of "rails and trash merely to conceal the men, as a bullet would go through them anywhere." Flimsy they may have been, but they would prove their worth over the course of the long afternoon.[37]

35 Oates, *The War Between the Union and the Confederacy*, 262.

36 Ibid., 263.

37 *OR* 30, pt. 1, 381; "Dear Parents," Martin Letter, UMich; Hicks, "Personal Recollections of the War of the Rebellion," vol. 31, 530; Entry for September 20, James Fenton Diary, ALPL.

Kershaw finally received word from Ben Humphreys, now back at the blacksmith shop, who reported that his line had tested the Federal defenses and "that he could make no further advance." Rather than go investigate the Mississippian's circumstances personally, Kershaw directed Humphreys to hold where he was and protect the South Carolinians's right flank. The 7th, 15th, and 8th South Carolina fell back to about the same general line, curving along the foot of Horseshoe Ridge out of sight of the main Union defenses.[38]

The next Confederate attack would require considerably more men and better tactical finesse if it was going to succeed.

38 *OR* 30, pt. 2, 504.

Chapter Eighteen

Glass Mill and Crawfish Spring:

Sunday, Dawn to 2:00 p.m.

Union Brig. Gen. Robert Mitchell faced a complex task that Sunday morning. The general progression of the Army of the Cumberland's movements was to the north, driven by General Thomas's continued concern about his left flank and the absolute necessity of keeping open the path of retreat into Chattanooga. General Rosecrans's orders to Mitchell, however, were "to hold Crawfish Spring at all hazards." For Mitchell and the cavalry, that meant not only securing the Union hospital complex immediately around the spring and the Gordon mansion, but the extensive picketing of the important crossings at Lee and Gordon's and Glass's mills. Additional pickets guarded the gap between Mitchell's troopers and the right flank of Alexander McCook's XX Corps. At dawn, McCook's right flank was a few hundred yards south of the Widow Glenn's. As the day advanced, however, that gap widened as the army inched its way northward. Mitchell was also still waiting for the last elements of the army (Colonel Post's infantry brigade of Jefferson Davis's division, and Colonel Watkins's cavalry brigade) to reach him from the south, which further complicated matters.[1]

Divisional hospitals for the XX Corps and XXI Corps, as well as for Negley's and Reynolds's commands of the XIV Corps, were located at Crawfish Spring now a couple of miles south of the scene of the worst fighting.

1 *OR* 30, pt. 1, 893.

First light revealed a pitiable scene. Despite the logistical difficulties, all of these hospitals were now swamped with wounded. "The ambulance trains were worked very steadily until midnight," reported the army's chief medical officer, Glover Perin, "when almost all of the wounded accessible had been removed." The battlefield, Perin continued, was "about four miles distant . . . [and] our loss in wounded on Saturday afternoon was very severe, being, as near as I could estimate, about four thousand five hundred." Most of those men were carried to Crawfish Spring, where every available means of shelter was pressed into service, since "the night was very cold." Once those shelters were full, the remaining unfortunates "were arranged in rows near each other, and lines of campfires were built at their feet."[2]

These hospitals were never intended to be more than temporary aid stations. Earlier in the campaign, Perin issued orders for military hospitals to be established at Stevenson and Bridgeport, which connected by rail to permanent facilities at Nashville, Louisville, and points north—in all, beds for 12,000 men. A new, specially designed five-car hospital train linked these forward hospitals to the permanent facilities, all of which represented a significant leap forward in the care of the wounded since the battle of Stones River. First, however, the wounded had to be stabilized for travel. Several thousand were awaiting transportation, but in Perin's estimation, at least 1,500 were so seriously injured they could not be moved at all.[3]

At dawn, Mitchell's only available cavalry was Col. Edward McCook's division. Colonel Archibald Campbell's brigade contained three regiments: the 2nd Michigan, 9th Pennsylvania, and 1st Tennessee, all together 1,348 sabers. Colonel Daniel M. Ray's brigade included the 2nd and 4th Indiana, 2nd Tennessee, and 1st Wisconsin Cavalry, or 1,532 effectives. Colonel McCook's only artillery support was the Chicago Board of Trade Battery and two guns from a section of Battery D, 1st Ohio Light Artillery. Knowing the Confederates could cross West Chickamauga Creek at any number of points, Mitchell ordered McCook to deploy his 2,900 troopers along a front spanning five miles.

2 Joseph K. Barnes, *The Medical and Surgical History of the War of the Rebellion: Appendix to Part I* (Government Printing Office, 1870), 267.

3 David A. Rubenstein, *A Study of the Medical Support to the Union and Confederate Armies During the Battle for Chickamauga*, Master's Thesis, U.S. Army Command and General Staff College, Fort Leavenworth, KS, 1990, 23.

The 9th Pennsylvania Cavalry of Campbell's brigade took up position at and north of Lee and Gordon's Mills, its left tying in with Colonel Wilder's pickets near Viniard Field. Pennsylvania Capt. Thomas McCahan of the 9th simmered with anger as he rode out to take up his position. "We have heard that the Rebels stripped our wounded boys—took everything they had," he fumed. He also noted the 9th's pickets, Companies L and M, "were scattered, I suppose 2 miles" with the rest of the regiment's 397 troopers backing up that line in reserve.[4]

Another of Campbell's regiments, the 2nd Michigan, was still tied up at the other end of Mitchell's line at Glass Mill. Instead of relieving the Wolverines, Mitchell chose to leave them in place, which created a problem for Campbell, who could not possibly exercise effective command over such a divided brigade. Accordingly, Mitchell ordered Colonel McCook to reinforce the 9th with the 1st Wisconsin (384 officers and men) on the 9th's right flank, place the 2nd Indiana Cavalry in reserve to the immediate rear of Lee and Gordon's Mills, and to take personal command of all three regiments.[5]

Colonel Campbell and the 1st Tennessee, augmented by the 4th Indiana from Colonel Ray's brigade, were ordered into divisional reserve on "the crest of [a] ridge, one mile to the rear and right of Crawfish Spring." Together these two regiments contained nearly 1,000 troopers—one-third of Mitchell's entire force. The general wanted them ready for any contingency.[6]

These dispositions left the 476 troopers of Colonel Ray's own 2nd Tennessee Cavalry in place at Crawfish Spring to provide immediate protection for the hospitals. "It was a bright, beautiful day," recalled Lt. John Andes of the 2nd, "when nature had just begun to put on the sear and yellow leaf of autumn. There was considerable frost that morning, and some ice. The sun rose grandly over the eastern hills, and all nature seemed to be at peace." This also left Colonel Ray to do little more than supervise his own regiment. Circumstances had effectively bypassed him as a brigade commander.[7]

4 Entry for September 20, Thomas S. McCahan Diary, Historical Society of Pennsylvania, Philadelphia.

5 *OR* 30, pt. 1, 895.

6 Ibid., 900.

7 Charles S. McCammon, ed., *Loyal Mountain Troopers: The Second and Third Tennessee Volunteer Cavalry in the Civil War, Reminiscences of Lieutenant John W. and Major Will A. McTeer* (Blount County Genealogical and Historical Society, 1992), 64.

Several miles farther south, the commander of Mitchell's Second Division, Brig. Gen. George Crook, with Col. Eli Long's brigade, was camped at Pond Spring. This powerful force included the 2nd Kentucky, as well as the 1st, 3rd, and 4th Ohio, the whole numbering 1,846 men. The day before, these troopers toiled their way out of McLemore's Cove from Daugherty's Gap. Early Sunday morning, Mitchell ordered Crook and his men to join him at Crawfish Spring, which they reached about 10:00 a.m. There, Mitchell ordered Crook to report at once to Glass Mill to reinforce the 2nd Michigan. Fighting had touched off there again at dawn; that now seemed to be the most threatened point.[8]

Like so many other men on the field, a Wolverine quartermaster sergeant named Henry M. Hempstead spent a difficult night. Not only was it "cold [and] chilly," recalled Hempstead, but a painful boil on his face had kept him awake. The regiment was quietly roused well before first light. "We stood to horse until after daylight, but a thick fog obscured everything and no sound indicated a renewal of the strife." That inaction ended "as soon as the fog lifted." Companies C and M slipped forward, dismounted, to the banks of West Chickamauga Creek, where the night before they had skirmished with a similar force of Rebels belonging to Company D of the 8th Texas Cavalry. The Rebel troopers sent forward to picket the mill the night before were still there, but this time it was the Wolverines who prevailed. "After a hot skirmish we drove them from the mill," Hempstead scribbled in his diary, "and leaving a picket at the ford we fell back to the edge of a cleared field." Once there, having managed a bit of breakfast, Hempstead caught up on some sleep, warmed by a cook fire and the rising sun. His nap was destined to be a short one.[9]

The Texans had plenty of support. Major General Joseph Wheeler's entire cavalry corps was camped less than three miles away at Dr. Anderson's, where the Glass Mill Road joined with the State (La Fayette) Road. So far Wheeler had contributed little to General Bragg's battle plan, but that was about to change. During the night, Bragg sent new instructions to Wheeler. The orders included the familiar admonition to guard all the crossings over the Chickamauga and protect General Longstreet's left flank, with the added directive "to attack the enemy at every opportunity." When word arrived that Company D had been driven from the mill on the evening of September 19, Wheeler reacted aggressively, dispatching Col. Thomas Harrison's entire brigade (of Brig. Gen.

8 *OR* 30, pt. 1, 893.

9 Entry for September 20, Henry M. Hempstead Diary, Bentley Historical Library, UMich.

John Wharton's division) to take back the crossing. The balance of Wharton's command, a brigade under Col. Charles Crew, together with all of Brig. Gen. William T. Martin's division soon followed. In all, Wheeler's Corps numbered 6,870 officers and men. Taking into consideration the detachments allocated to guard other crossings, Wheeler was committing almost 6,000 men to this fight.[10]

Colonel Harrison easily seized the mill back from the Wolverine picket guard. Thereafter, Harrison deployed Capt. Benjamin F. White's Tennessee battery atop a little hill on the east side of the creek and proceeded to shell Companies C and M, whose men were busy eating breakfast, and sent the rest of the 8th Texas forward to attack. "We retreated rapidly across the fields to the center of the plantation," confessed Sergeant Hempstead, "when sheltered by the house, cabins and corncribs . . . with the aid of our support, the 3rd Batt. we checked our pursuers." Now it was the 2nd Michigan's turn once again. Reinforced, the Wolverines drove the Texans back to the mill, where the Rebels rallied under the cover of White's guns. Harrison committed the rest of his brigade to the fight as each regiment arrived, his numbers eventually telling on the embattled Wolverines. By midmorning, what had begun as a picket squabble escalated into a serious action.[11]

Mitchell was delighted to see George Crook. The 2nd Michigan was hard-pressed and needed help, he explained, but Mitchell was loath to commit his existing reserves. He had only sent Lt. Nathaniel Newell's Section of Battery D, 1st Ohio Light Artillery forward to counter White's guns. Fortunately, things were still quiet farther north where the 1st Wisconsin and 9th Pennsylvania watched the creek. This, in turn, allowed Mitchell to send Crook's entire force to help the 2nd Michigan. Mitchell instructed Crook "to take post at once in front of the fords of the Chickamauga and hold that point at all hazards." Crook dispatched his troopers forward as they arrived, Col. Thomas P. Nicholas's 2nd Kentucky Cavalry in the lead.[12]

Major Leonidas S. Scranton, commanding the 2nd Michigan, was relieved when Nicholas trotted up. With one of his battalions still covering the ford at Bird's Mill a mile to the south, Scranton knew he was facing long odds. By 10:00

10 *OR* 30, pt. 2, 521.

11 Entry for September 20, Henry M. Hempstead Diary, Bentley Historical Library, UMich.

12 *OR* 30, pt. 1, 918.

a.m., Scranton reported, his men fell back "to a more secure position," leaving Harrison's Rebels in uncontested control of the Glass Mill crossing. When Newell's Ohio guns arrived, Scranton had them support another effort to drive the Confederates back across the ford, only to meet with another failure. The Michiganders were falling back from this latest effort, flanked and outgunned, when, noted Scranton, "we were met by other regiments moving forward to form on our left."[13]

Henry Hempstead described the collapse of this last attack. "Looking down through the fields we saw a host of the enemy come charging out of the woods. Our Company C on our left crumbled and finally broke for the woods. Our battery retreated. . . . [B]eing in command of the left . . . [I] reported to Capt. [Thomas W.] Johnson that we were being nearly surrounded. . . . [O]n looking to the rear [we] saw the enemy swarm into the woods." With that, Hempstead, Johnson, and the rest of Company M also legged it rearward, slipping the noose just in time. Here, Hempstead found Colonel Nicholas's Kentuckians deploying. Lieutenant Colonel Elijah S. Watts, second in command of the 2nd Kentucky, recorded that Colonel Long "commanding brigade, placed himself at the head of our regiment and filing to the right by a road leading to a ford. . . . We soon halted and formed line." Watts waited while the three Ohio regiments of Eli Long's brigade deployed. Hempstead, who apparently expected these reinforcements to immediately counterattack, was destined to be disappointed. Instead, he told his diary with evident sarcasm, "our 'brave' Kentuckians had after short resistance fled in confusion."[14]

The arrival of Long's men induced a temporary lull, during which Crook arrived and assumed overall command. The respite gave Crook a chance to survey his assigned position. He didn't much like what he saw. Woods obscured much of his view, including a distant "juniper thicket" that masked Chickamauga Creek. When he asked a Wolverine officer where the creek actually was, the man replied, "he'd be damned if he knew." This was hardly comforting. Despite his unfamiliarity with the terrain, Crook did his best to establish a defense. He deployed "two lines of skirmishers, one mounted and the other dismounted." Crook brought with him another two guns, a section of

13 Ibid., 902.

14 E.S. Watts Report, August 17, 1889, Office of the Adjutant General, Union Battle Reports, RG 94, Box 56, NARA; Entry for September 20, Henry M. Hempstead Diary, Bentley Historical Library, UMich.

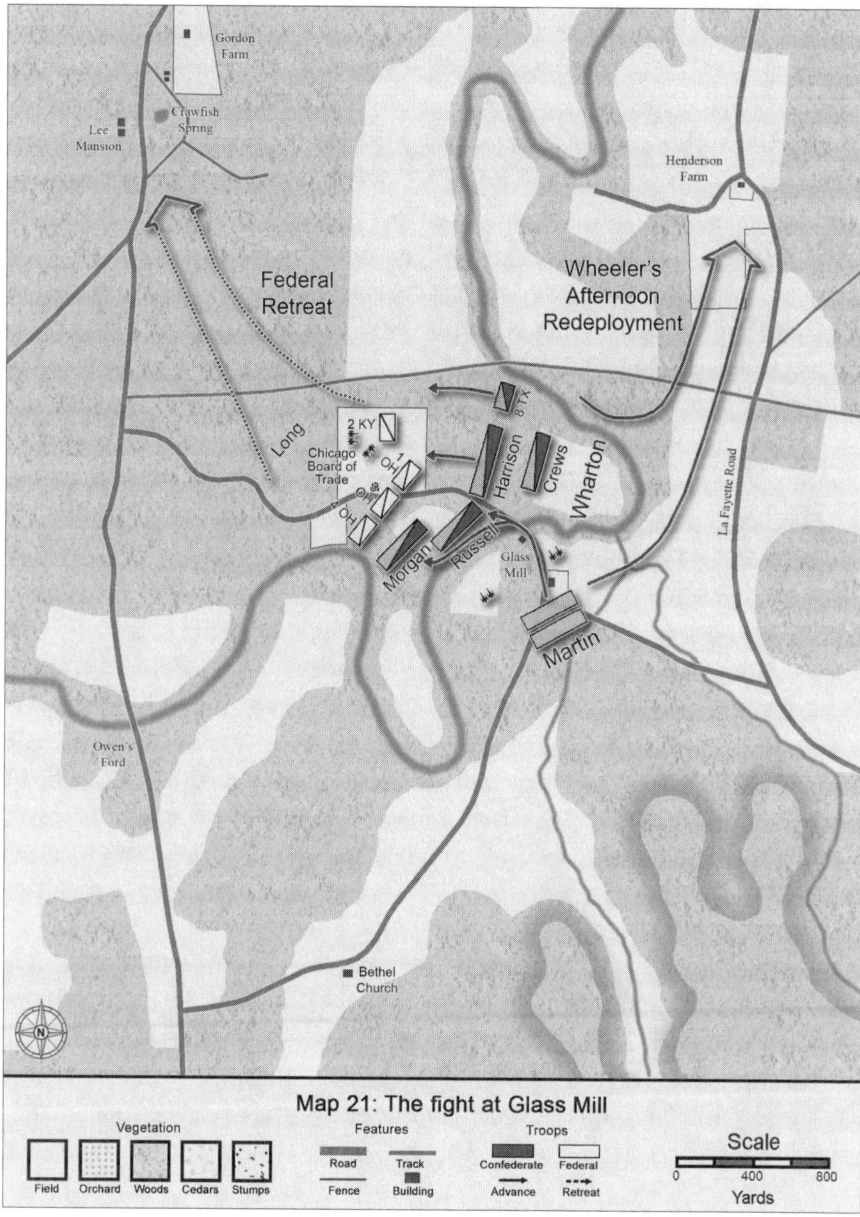

Map 21: The fight at Glass Mill

the Chicago Board of Trade Battery. Despite misgivings about the vulnerability of his artillery in the current position, he ordered the pair of Board of Trade pieces to open fire on the juniper thicket.[15]

15 Martin F. Schmidt, ed., *General George Crook: His Autobiography* (University of Oklahoma Press, 1946), 105-106.

Years later, Lieutenant Colonel Watts described Crook's dispositions thusly: "The 1st Ohio, 3rd Ohio and 4th Ohio dismounted and went into line on our right and advanced skirmishers." Then, noted Watts, "at this point the 2nd and 4th Mich Cavalry passed back from our front. They had been on guard at the ford, but the enemy effected a crossing in spite of them." Once the Board of Trade's guns were moved up the road and positioned on a small rise, Watts and his fellow Kentuckians went into line on the left of the artillery. "The ground in front of us was an old cornfield, ascending slightly from the river; and perpendicular to our left flank was a piece of woodland."[16]

Hempstead and the 2nd Michigan now departed, headed back to Crawfish Spring to refit. Of the 16 dismounted men Company M took into action that dawn, noted Hempstead, three were seriously wounded, one was missing, and "of the other twelve . . . all but four carry marks of the enemy's bullets either on their bodies or on their clothing. Several were slightly hit but none disabled." It had been a tough morning.[17]

By this time Joe Wheeler was on the scene and took personal control of the fight. He reinforced Harrison with Wharton's other brigade under Col. C. C. Crews, comprised of Malone's Alabama Regiment and the 2nd, 3rd, and 4th Georgia regiments. Either Wheeler or John Wharton also pulled the 8th Texas off the line and stationed the remounted Texans on the Confederate right. The 8th was Wharton's old regiment, with a reputation for hitting hard and one of the few Rebel units that still carried sabers. With those arrangements made, Wharton's entire 4,400-man division advanced. Will Martin's two brigades followed and deployed on Wharton's left once there was space enough to accommodate them.[18]

While Wheeler made his arrangements, which consumed a considerable amount of time, both sides peppered away with artillery. Union Sgt. John Chapin of Company K, 1st Ohio Cavalry remembered the Rebel cannon fire as particularly ineffective: "Not a man of the regiment was that day hit by shot or shell. . . . Their firing was too high and went over our heads." Chapin later estimated this barrage lasted about three hours, but, he admitted, he could have

16 Watts Report, NARA. Watts was mistaken about the presence of the 4th Michigan Cavalry, which was with Col. Robert Minty.

17 Entry for September 20, Henry M. Hempstead Diary, Bentley Historical Library, UMich.

18 R. F. Bunting article, *Rome Tri-Weekly Telegraph*, November 27, 1863.

been wrong. "It hardly seemed like fifteen minutes, so interesting was the occasion." Things were about to become even more interesting.[19]

Lieutenant George Guild, adjutant and later historian of Lt. Col. Paul F. Anderson's 4th Tennessee Cavalry, remembered this moment: "While standing in line . . . we noticed a staff officer ride up to General Wharton. . . . We were ordered to dismount and advance towards a battery that was shelling us. . . . [T]he order was received with cheers, for the men were chaffing to go forward." Not everyone was eager to go in, but only the incautious made that fact known. As they dismounted, the men counted off by fives, with every fifth man intended to hold the horses. In Company D of the 4th, Pvt. John K. Womack recalled that as the count progressed, a "trooper who was number five shouted very distinctly 'bully.'" Lieutenant Colonel Anderson overheard the comment, and "said very clearly through his nose: 'Let 'Bully' go into the fight and number four hold horses." With that business disposed of, the Rebel line advanced.[20]

Because of the shortage of cavalry carbines in the South, large numbers of Wheeler's advancing men carried infantry muskets, and they often fought in closed-rank formations using infantry drill. As a result, many Federals mistook the Confederate dismounted cavalry for a line of infantry. Sergeant Chapin would describe them as "Longstreet's men, and they advanced in three perfect lines of battle." Wharton's line struck Long's dismounted skirmishers head-on while the 8th Texas tried to work around the Union right flank. The action quickly developed into a prolonged firefight. "A strong brigade of the enemy's infantry advanced," wrote a similarly mistaken Colonel Watts, "covered by a heavy skirmish line. . . . The advance . . . was deliberate and steady, the skirmishers firing as they came, and our regiment responded, checking the skirmishers until they were lost in the main line . . . general firing . . . [now] opened all along both lines, the 2nd Kentucky pouring a galling fire into them, as did also the board of trade battery."[21]

19 William L. Curry, *Four Years in the Saddle: History of the First Regiment Ohio Volunteer Cavalry. War of the Rebellion 1861-1865* (Freedom Hill Press, 1984), 283.

20 Undated clipping, 4th Tennessee Cavalry (CS) file, CCNMP; J. K. Womack, "Chickamauga as I Saw It," *Confederate Veteran*, vol. XXV, no. 2 (February, 1917), 74. Womack's reminiscence is quite interesting. More typically, a cavalry regiment used one man in four as horse-holders. Either the 4th Tennessee deviated from the manual here or Womack's memory had slipped a bit.

21 Curry, *Four Years in the Saddle*, 283; Watts Report, NARA.

Tennessee Private Womack was on the receiving end of that fire, and he didn't like it much. "We slowly marched toward the enemy . . . [until] the command 'charge!' came in distinct tones. All went forward with a rush. I could still see the long black hair of Captain [James R.] Lester which seemed to quiver from the Minie balls that filled the air around us. I shall never forget how the enemy," he continued, "concealed behind trees and logs, poured a volley of leaden hail into us . . . cartridge boxes were shot off, men were wounded right and left." From the ranks of Crews's brigade, advancing alongside Harrison's line, a private named William Thompson of Company B, 3rd Georgia Cavalry, informed his family that during the fight, "I took four deliberate fires at the old Star Spangle Banner it fell three times but whether it was me or not I don't know."[22]

Martin's pair of brigades were now across the creek. Once there, Wheeler ordered Martin to dismount his troopers and extend Wharton's line southward to threaten the Union right flank. "Colonel [John T.] Morgan, who was then commanding the first brigade," reported Lt. Col. Tyra H. Mauldin of the 3rd Alabama Cavalry, ordered "[me] to take my Reg't—on foot—across the bridge to support a battery then in position on the left of the road." With Martin's entry into the fighting, Rebel numbers began to tell. The Federals, with only 900 men and a section of artillery on the field, now faced several thousand Confederates. The Union cavalry wisely elected to retreat before they were surrounded.[23]

The 8th Texas cavalry had by this time succeeded in turning Long's left flank. "Meanwhile the Rangers are across [the creek]," wrote Texan Robert F. Bunting, "and charging through a lane and across a camp of the enemy, they boldly dash up upon his lines. . . . They press him on his flank so heavily that he is compelled to flee for safety. Here the fighting was stubborn." A Federal Buckeye lieutenant named James Thompson and his comrades of the 4th Ohio Cavalry were on the receiving end of this charge. "The rebels began to show themselves advancing in regular order & in three columns & as they were pressing us very hard the order was given to fall back," wrote the lieutenant, "but as soon as they saw us giving way [their] Cav[alry] charged us & every

22 Womack, "Chickamauga as I Saw It," 74; "Dear Ma & Pa," September 24, 1863, William N. Thompson Letter, 3rd Georgia Cavalry file, CCNMP.

23 3rd Alabama Cavalry Report, William T. Martin Papers, Briscoe Center for American History, University of Texas at Austin. Hereafter UT.

Lt. Col. Valentine Cupp (left) was mortally wounded during the morning fight at Glass Mill.
W. L. Curry, History of the First Ohio Volunteer Cavalry

fellow tried to save himself. . . . Everything skedaddled until [we] got through a skirt of woods."[24]

It was at this point in the fighting that several things went wrong all at once for the Yankees. General Crook, watching the action near the Union guns, suddenly realized his flanks were being turned and tersely ordered the gunners to "get the battery out of here." Crook watched in horror as, in what looked to be a bid to buy time, a portion of the 1st Ohio Cavalry mounted and formed up as if to launch its own charge into the oncoming Rebel horde. The reckless order—seemingly given by Colonel Long—would result in a massacre if it was carried out. With no time to lose, Crook galloped to the regiment and personally countermanded the foolhardy command—but not before the newly mounted men suffered severely from Rebel fire. Among the fallen was Lt. Col. Valentine Cupp, the 1st Ohio Cavalry's commander. Cupp was borne to the rear, mortally wounded.[25]

Someone had indeed blundered, but it wasn't Colonel Long. In fact, the order Long issued was never intended to be a real attack. Either Long's courier garbled the message, or Cupp misunderstood its intent. Long intended the mounting of the Buckeyes as a feint to give the Rebels pause, not the prelude to a full-fledged charge. When he heard the order, Sergeant John Chapin of Company K was convinced the regiment was riding to its slaughter when Crook thundered up: "'The order was, prepare to resist the charge! That was quite different, and I felt much easier," confessed Chapin. Crook's hasty arrival

24 R. F. Bunting article, *Rome Tri-Weekly Telegraph*, November 27, 1863; Entry for September 20, James Thompson Diary, 4th Ohio Cavalry file, CCNMP. The camp Bunting referred to was likely the early morning bivouac site of Hempstead and his fellows in the 2nd Michigan.

25 Itinerary of Second Division, Cavalry Corps, George Crook file, CCNMP; Anonymous, *Proceedings of the Thirtieth Annual Reunion, 1st O.V.V.C.* (n.p. 1909), 18.

stopped the charge, but it also threw the 1st Ohio into considerable disorder. Not everyone got the word to halt. From the Union right flank, the mesmerized Lieutenant Thompson of the 4th witnessed "some of the 1st Ohio charg[ing] them with the saber but with little effect." Checked and repulsed, the 1st Ohio fell back.[26]

The departure of the guns and the retreat of the Buckeye 1st regiment left the 2nd Kentucky to confront the onrushing Texans. Before the 8th Texas could close, however, the Kentuckians fell back in disorder. Captain James Hawley of the 2nd Michigan was serving as acting inspector-general on the corps staff. He was present when Lieutenant Colonel Watts's Kentuckians broke. Hawley rode among the Bluegrass troopers in an attempt to rally them for a countercharge, but was shot out of the saddle by a hail of gunfire: "6 balls passed right throw [through] him," observed Michigan Pvt. John Wesson.[27]

With both flanks imperiled, the Union artillery skedaddled, and the bulk of the 1st Ohio Cavalry still trying to recover from its near-fatal charge, the last of the 1st Ohio's dismounted men also headed rearward. Lieutenant William L. Curry was one of the last to leave the field. Curry was convinced he would be killed or wounded in this fight, but thus far remained unscathed. When the main body of the 1st Ohio fell back, it took Company K's animals with it. Curry managed to procure a wounded man's mount, though both "the saddle and horse [were] covered with blood." Curry worked to get his men safely away. "The balls were still cutting the brush and trees on every side," he noted. "A strong line of dismounted cavalry of the enemy was sweeping up through a cornfield in our front. Our squadron was soon in imminent danger of being cut off and captured. We moved to the left and rear, and formed on the second line."[28]

Having taken heavy losses, Long's entire brigade fell back toward Crawfish Spring, taking up a new line close to the Gordon mansion. Colonel Cupp was carried into the house for care, though little could be done for him and he died that night. Not all of the Federal wounded were able to be retrieved, and many fell into enemy hands. Some Rebels commenced to reaping the spoils. John Wyeth of the 4th Alabama Cavalry watched in disgust as a callous Texan

26 John Chapin, "At Chickamauga," *Reunions of the First Ohio Volunteer Cavalry* (Landon Printing Co., 1891), 16; Entry for September 20, Thompson Diary, CCNMP.

27 "Dear Uncle," October 18, 1863, John Wesson Letters, WMU.

28 Curry, *Four Years in the Saddle*, 358.

stripped the boot from a Federal officer wounded in the foot. The Texan insisted the boot come off intact instead of being cut away to minimize the wounded man's pain. "You reckon I'm going to spoil that boot?" spat the Texan contemptuously.[29]

The Glass Mill fight ended sometime between noon and 1:00 p.m. Crook might have been in a great deal more trouble had Wheeler undertaken an immediate pursuit. In the flush of victory, however, Joe Wheeler received new orders—in fact, two conflicting sets of orders which gave Wheeler pause. Instructions from both James Longstreet and Braxton Bragg arrived nearly simultaneously, both directing Wheeler and his cavalry to ride north. Longstreet wanted Wheeler to bring his troopers forward to assail the Union mob retreating up the Dry Valley Road, a perfect target for marauding cavalry. Bragg, however, directed Wheeler to strike the Federals at "Gordon's Mills," which Bragg still believed marked the Union right flank. These conflicting directives left Wheeler on the horns of a complicated dilemma, but in either case he would have to break off the direct pursuit of Long's beaten men. For George Crook, the Confederate high command's intervention could not have come at a better time.[30]

While Union and Confederate troopers fought over the crossing at Glass Mill, General Mitchell cast a worried eye to the south. He was hoping to hear from the last two Union brigades moving out of McLemore's Cove. On the night of the 19th, Col. Sidney Post's men were still atop Lookout Mountain at the head of Stevens's Gap escorting the last of McCook's XX Corps trains. Early that morning McCook ordered Post "to move forward to the battlefield by way of Crawfish Spring, and to send all the trains by the Mountain Road to Chattanooga." Post complied, leaving his provost guard to escort the wagons and moved his four regiments down the mountain and into the cove.[31]

It was a nerve-wracking march. By midmorning the sounds of the distant battle were fully audible. Post rounded up locals to serve as guides, and pressed them for alternate routes to the army should he encounter the enemy in force. Rebels were in the vicinity in considerable numbers. Some of these men were

29 John A. Wyeth, *With Sabre and Scalpel: The Autobiography of a Soldier and Surgeon* (Harper, 1914), 248.

30 *OR* 30, pt. 4, 675. General Bragg's earlier order has not been found, but Bragg references it in a second dispatch he sent to Wheeler at 5:00 p.m. on September 20.

31 *OR* 30, pt. 1, 507.

patrols from Martin's division, which was still active in the cove. Others belonged to the 6th Battalion, Georgia State Cavalry, a home-guard unit called into service in August for local defense. However, not every local was interested in a fight. "Citizens in butternut jeans were plentiful on the roadside," noted Lt. Chesley A. Mosman of the 59th Illinois. "They were unquestionably Rebel soldiers who had found it too warm over on the [battle] field and skulked off throwing away their guns . . . but we are in no condition to care for them and as there is no visible evidence of their being Rebel soldiers we let them go." Besides, Colonel Post didn't want to be slowed down by any encumbrance. "Post wants a share of the battle," thought Mosman, despite being assigned as train guard.[32]

By the time Post's infantry column reached "the Ringgold Road," his men had been skirmishing with Confederates for some time and now "found the enemy apparently in considerable force." "We soon formed to give battle," recalled Lt. Leroy S. Mayfield of the 22nd Indiana, "expecting to fight our way through the rebel army . . . knowing at the time that [we] were cut off . . . and that we were at their mercy." Instead of a standup fight, however, the affair continued as a running skirmish, and the brigade pushed its way forward to Crawfish Spring, where it arrived at 1:00 p.m.[33]

Mosman recalled they almost had another fight as they arrived at Crawfish Spring—this time with their own men. "We run on to Gen. Robert B. Mitchell with two divisions of cavalry drawn up to charge us," recounted the lieutenant, "when he discovered by our brigade flag who we were." Once everyone's bonafides were established, "joy was engraved in every countenance—us at our delivery from the enemy, the cavalry at the appearance of assistance."[34]

Mitchell was certainly pleased to add Post's 1,100 infantry to his available strength, but the news he exchanged in return wasn't good. Contact with the main army had been lost, he explained, the courier lines swept aside; aides could

32 Arnold Gates, ed., *The Rough Side of War: The Civil War Journal of Chesley A. Mosman 1st Lieutenant, Company D, 59th Illinois Volunteer Infantry Regiment* (The Basin Publishing Co., 1987), 83. Six of the seven companies comprising the 6th Georgia State Cavalry were recruited in Walker County, with Company E hailing from Pond Spring. As for the civilians Mosman saw idling by the side of the road, some of them were paroled prisoners from the captured Vicksburg garrison.

33 *OR* 30, pt. 1, 507; John D. Barnhart, ed. "A Hoosier Invades the Confederacy: Letters and Diaries of Leroy S. Mayfield," *Indiana Magazine of History*, vol. 39, no. 2 (June, 1943), 161.

34 Gates, *Rough Side of War*, 84; Barnhardt, "A Hoosier Invades the Confederacy," 161.

no longer come and go. Mitchell's last contact was via Col. Gates Thruston (McCook's chief of staff) about noon, when Thruston delivered McCook's order to close farther to the north. Since then, however, the 9th Pennsylvania Cavalry's pickets reported only Rebels in that direction. Mitchell could not simply abandon the overflowing field hospitals. He had already begun preparing to evacuate the wounded as best he could, but that effort would take considerable time. For the moment, all he and Post could do was hold their ground and hope for the best.[35]

The last force making its way out of the cove was Col. Louis D. Watkins's brigade of Colonel McCooks's division, comprised of the 4th, 5th, and 6th Kentucky Cavalry. Watkins began his morning even farther south than Post. In the predawn hours of September 20, Watkins departed Valley Head, Alabama, for Stevens's Gap. His column included a hodgepodge of army detritus including the last of the cavalry trains, 400 sick Federals turned over to him by Colonel Post on September 18, and four captured Rebel officers.[36]

By Mitchell's estimation Watkins was at least a day behind. Late on the 19th, Mitchell sent a dispatch to Stevens's Gap, which was where he expected the Kentuckian to be by the end of the day's march. Mitchell wanted Watkins to "bring up to-night your entire brigade, excepting one battalion to be left at Stevens' Gap . . . [which] is expected to hold the gap at all hazards." Mitchell was expecting Watkins and his men to appear shortly behind Post's infantry. So far, however, neither Watkins nor word from him was to be had.[37]

Mitchell was being too optimistic. The cavalry commander perhaps assumed Watkins had departed a day earlier, for as noted, as night fell on the 19th Watkins's men were still at Valley Head. Unencumbered and riding hard, Watkins might have pushed his troopers fast enough to cover the entire distance to Crawfish Spring on September 20, but that would have meant abandoning the trains and the sick. Watkins's march must have been fraught with anxiety, for as one young Kentucky cavalryman noted, "we heard very heavy cannonading all day, but could not tell how the fearful conflict was progressing." When they halted at Stevens's Gap, some eight miles from

35 Post's reported strength was 1,239 officers and men, but at least 100 formed the provost guard that escorted the trains back to Chattanooga.

36 *OR* 30, pt. 1, 914-915.

37 Ibid., 917.

Crawfish Spring, they still had no knowledge of what had become of the Army of the Cumberland.[38]

Despite the storm of battle raging all around them, neither the 9th Pennsylvania nor the 1st Wisconsin (at Lee and Gordon's Mills) saw much action that morning. That didn't mean they passed an entirely quiet forenoon, however. For one thing, they could clearly hear the growing intensity of the infantry fighting off to their north. "At 11 o'clock a.m. the ball opened," penned Thomas McCahan. "I suppose 300 pieces of artillery opened all at once. We could feel the ground quiver under us." McCahan had charge of the 9th Pennsylvania's pickets, and placed his troopers carefully. He paid special attention to Lee and Gordon's Mills. Here, he noted, "the creek was narrow but the banks steep. . . . On the rebel side was an old stone mill full of rebels. Directly opposite on our side [was] a log house and two smaller houses about 15 ft apart connected by a roof. I dismounted 2 of our boys, they left their horses back [and] crept up to these houses. I went with them [and] stationed one in each house." These two privates, Oliver Ball and William Thompson, were to give warning if the Rebels attempted to cross. However, McCahan cautioned, "I instructed them to do no shooting and keep under cover."[39]

Despite McCahan's injunction, sporadic picket firing marked much of the morning. With Wheeler's main body busy at Glass Mill, however, none of this other skirmishing proved serious. The 1st Wisconsin reported two men missing, reputedly wounded and captured, on the 20th. Diaries and letters from within the regiment show a marked concern not for themselves, but for what was happening to the main army farther north. "We moved our line back, and in a little while back again," explained Wisconsin Sgt. Maj. Charles P. Goodrich to his wife four days later. "We hardly knew what it meant, but feared what proved to be the truth, that our men were being driven back."[40]

38 "Young Soldier," *Louisville Daily Journal*, October 9, 1863.

39 Entry for September 20, Thomas S. McCahan Diary, Historical Society of Pennsylvania, Philadelphia.

40 *OR* 30, pt. 1, 912; Richard N. Larson, ed. *Sergeant Major Charles Perry Goodrich: Letters Home to Francis Bowen Goodrich in Cambridge, Wisconsin from her Husband, Charles Perry Goodrich, Sergeant-Major in the First Wisconsin Cavalry 1862/1865.* (Published by the Author, 1990), 84.

Chapter Nineteen

Command Decisions:

Sunday, 1:00 p.m. to 2:30 p.m.

By 1:00 p.m., James Longstreet's initial attack had shattered all opposition and was driving from the battlefield in wild disorder the bulk of the Federals facing him. The hole created by Tom Wood's departure greatly aided this success, but the rapid collapse of Jeff Davis's command and Phil Sheridan's rout demonstrated that the entire Union right throughout the morning was dangerously vulnerable to exactly the sort of massed attack Longstreet planned and executed—gap or no gap. Now that the Union troops were in flight, what next? A series of tactical options open to Longstreet pulled his limited forces in divergent directions.

Some historians view Longstreet's role during this time as either passive or, at best, guiding with a light hand. One of his harshest critics is Peter Cozzens. Writing in 1992 in his influential study of the battle, Cozzens charged that "from 1:00 and 2:30 p.m., Longstreet was content to play the role of bystander. He issued no orders of consequence to his generals, who were left to muddle through as best they could." If true, this was a damning charge. There are valid reasons to criticize Longstreet on September 20, but passivity is not among them. In order to better understand Longstreet's decisions during this critical period, we first need to examine the situation as he knew it at the time.[1]

1 See James R. Furqueron, "The Bull of the Woods: Longstreet and the Confederate Left at Chickamauga," in R. L. Dinardo and Albert A. Nofi, eds., *James Longstreet: The Man, The soldier,*

Longstreet's rightmost division under A. P. Stewart was committed early because of General Bragg's hasty overreaction to the confusion in General Polk's Right Wing. Stewart's men were soundly repulsed by John Brannan's Federals before 11:00 a.m., and played no role in the subsequent successful assault. Even as late as 1:00 p.m., Stewart's men remained combat-ineffective. Success came in the center, where Bushrod Johnson led the First Corps into and through Tom Wood's newly vacated position at Brotherton Field. Johnson's men drove all the way to the Vittetoe house, nearly a mile deep into the Union vitals, capturing many prisoners and cannon. However, once there his small force was unsupported and left increasingly vulnerable to the threat posed by the budding Horseshoe Ridge line. Any further advance along the Dry Valley Road only increased this risk. Evander Law's division fragmented during its effort to deal with that same threat, a situation complicated by Law's lack of direct involvement. Wheeling to the north disrupted Law's line and cost considerably in casualties, especially in Jerome Robertson's and Henry Benning's brigades, each of which suffered overall losses greater than 40%. Some regiments lost more than half their number and devastating leadership casualties to boot. These Texans, Georgians, and Arkansans were simply fought out. Less hard hit were William Perry's Alabamians, who joined Johnson's advance in storming Mendenhall's gun line; confusion, however, and not casualties, left Perry rudderless.

Except for Colonel Oates's 15th Alabama, which was intermingled with Joe Kershaw's brigade line at the foot of Horseshoe Ridge, Law's entire division was hors de combat. On Saturday, September 19, Law took 3,957 officers and men into action. Saturday's losses (and stragglers) reduced this figure to no more than 2,500 by the morning of the 20th. When Law took stock of his division around 1:00 p.m., he discovered his command had been whittled down to no more than 1,700 effectives. Robertson and Benning were still capable of defensive action, but offensive tactics were out of the question.[2]

Coming into action on Law's heels, Kershaw was pulled even farther northward, pursuing Charles Harker's Federals to Snodgrass Hill. Now aligned along the Vittetoe Road, Kershaw's line of battle came to rest nearly a mile

---

The Controversy (Combined Books, 1998), 137-141, for a more detailed survey of this historical criticism. Cozzens, *This Terrible Sound*, 454.

2 The 1,700 figure does not include the 15th Alabama (300 strong), which was fighting with Kershaw.

northwest of the spot where he first crossed the La Fayette Road. Both Johnson and Kershaw were calling for reinforcements. Their initial attacks thinned and disrupted their ranks, leaving only skeletal formations to exploit the victory won thus far. In fact, of the eight brigades comprising Longstreet's "grand column," only three were still at the forefront.

Bushrod Johnson had the brigades led by Cols. John Fulton and Cyrus Sugg well in hand, though each was so reduced that they together numbered no more than 1,500 men. His third, under Colonel Coleman (McNair), had retreated all the way back to Brotherton Field and was, for the moment at least, out of the fight. Kershaw still had his South Carolinians in action, but Ben Humphreys's men had disengaged at Longstreet's directive.

Kershaw had also suffered significant losses, and had effectively lost control of Humphreys's command. Even including the impromptu addition of Oates's men, Kershaw had no more than 1,500 bayonets still engaged. Humphreys, who entered action with nearly 1,300 men, lost 155 during the brief engagement against Snodgrass Hill but, as we have seen, was not inclined to risk his brigade further in what he perceived to be a fruitless and bloody frontal assault.

On Longstreet's left, Thomas Hindman's division also needed time to reorganize. Hindman's three brigades had routed five Yankee brigades, though not without substantial cost. Colonel Wilder's unexpected Federal riposte had badly disrupted Arthur Manigault's command, posing a threat not just to Hindman's flank but to the rear of Longstreet's entire column. Fortunately for the Rebels, Wilder lacked support. Although the Hoosier colonel briefly contemplated cutting his way through to join General Thomas, common sense prevailed and Wilder instead moved to cover the retreat of the Federal right wing. The Confederates, however, had no way of knowing if Wilder was acting alone or whether his appearance was the precursor to a much larger attack. Manigault's retreat forced the rest of Hindman's command (Zach Deas and Patton Anderson) to pull back. By 1:00 p.m. the entire division was reforming and awaiting orders in south Dyer Field.

Once the assault began, Longstreet and Simon Buckner initially followed Hindman's axis of advance, moving west behind Patton Anderson's support line. By the time they reached the La Fayette Road (somewhere south of Brotherton Field), the two generals could already see some of the fruits of their success. Buckner staffer Maj. Henry Foote remembered "that the Federals had been driven back . . . and some guns captured. As we sat our horses on the road, General Buckner told Major [Samuel C.] Williams, our chief of artillery, to haul the guns to the rear." Once those spoils were accounted for, the command group rode north along the road into Brotherton Field, the scene of Johnson's breakthrough. By the time they reached the Brotherton cabin, Law's division and General Hood were already engaged in Dyer Field. While at the cabin, Longstreet witnessed Benning's repulse up in Poe Field. Benning, recalled Longstreet, "lost his hat in the melee, and [his] brigade disappeared under the steady crushing fire so quickly that he was a little surprised." Stumbling up to the wing commander, the agitated judge-turned-brigadier blurted, "General Hood is killed, my horse is killed, my brigade torn to pieces, and I haven't a man left." Kershaw's men just then "burst through the brush . . . in cheerful, gallant march" and Longstreet pointed them out to the distraught general. Their appearance brought Benning back to "his usual hopeful, courageous confidence," wrote Longstreet. After helping Benning regain his composure, Longstreet set him to reorganizing his survivors. Longstreet also took the opportunity to warn Kershaw about the threat to his right flank.[3]

By this time it was nearly noon. Longstreet's wing had been heavily engaged for about an hour, and the battle had progressed well as it rolled west. The command party left Brotherton Field and rode west again, toward the Dyer house, emerging from the intervening trees in time to witness the very last of Johnson's success against the Union gun line assembled by Mendenhall. "This attack forced [the enemy] from that part of the field . . . in disordered retreat," noted Longstreet with evident satisfaction. Federal resistance on the right, however, was even then drawing General Hood's attention.[4]

It was at this point Longstreet decided to forego Bragg's original plan to turn and drive south, and decided instead to swing his entire command to the right and move north. General Polk's wing, reasoned Longstreet, "had failed of the progress anticipated." Except for some cavalry, there were no Federal commands of consequence to turn south against. Any Yankees still in action were to Longstreet's north. In order to strengthen this blow, Longstreet ordered Hindman to move up and support Johnson, extending the latter's flank to the west, if necessary.[5]

3 Foote, *Recollections of the Chickamauga Campaign*, 11-12; Longstreet, *From Manassas to Appomattox*, 448. Longstreet was probably conflating events here, as Hood likely had not yet been wounded.

4 Ibid.

5 Ibid., 449; *OR* 30, pt. 2, 289.

There was a third option. Instead of turning south or north, Longstreet could continue west with an immediate pursuit up the Dry Valley Road to finish off the Federals fleeing in that direction. The current tactical situation made that option impractical. To accomplish anything of real note, the Confederates would have to push all the way through to Missionary Ridge and beyond, probably for several miles as far as Rossville. The threat to Longstreet's right increased, however, with each westward step. If the troops reforming on Horseshoe Ridge were ignored long enough, Thomas could reconstitute them and launch a counterattack that could potentially cut off a suddenly overextended Rebel force. Therefore, any pursuit would, of necessity, be limited to a secondary mission so long as a significant Union presence remained on Horseshoe Ridge. Pursuit westward was also a job best suited for cavalry. Longstreet would soon endeavor to bring up mounted troops for that very reason; at the moment he had none at hand.

The threat from the north was not Longstreet's only concern. While witnessing Johnson's success, Longstreet took note of "a discouraging account . . . from General Hindman, that . . . his left and rear had been struck by a formidable force of cavalry . . . [and] forced back in considerable disorder." This "formidable force," of course, was Colonel Wilder's lone command, but Longstreet was not privy to this information. All he knew was that the Federal threat was substantial. Therefore, a wholesale shift north would potentially expose the entire rear of the Left Wing to attack. Longstreet's stopgap solution was to commit a brigade from William Preston's reserve division to guard that flank. Colonel Robert C. Trigg's brigade of one Virginia and three Florida regiments had already been tasked to support Manigault, as needed. Now Trigg would cover Hindman's flank.[6]

A better solution was to call up Confederate cavalry to both counter the Union mounted threat to Longstreet's rear and provide pursuit capabilities up the Dry Valley Road while the infantry dealt with the Federals gathering on Horseshoe Ridge. Joe Wheeler's corps, operating just a couple of miles to the south, was the obvious source for this help. (At that time Wheeler was engaging Crook at Glass Mill, though Longstreet was unaware of that action.)

Did Longstreet have the authority to order Wheeler forward? The answer to that question remains unclear. By 1905, Longstreet thought he did and mentions doing exactly that in his memoirs. The only surviving written order

6 Longstreet, *From Manassas to Appomattox*, 449; *OR* 30, pt. 2, 303, 431.

from Longstreet summoning Wheeler north, however, was drafted at 5:09 p.m.—much later and near the end of the battle. In 1891, Thomas Claiborne of General Buckner's staff had a different recollection of this event. "I said to Genl. L[ongstreet] why not send for Wheeler," claimed Claiborne. "He has several thousand cavalry, and here is a good place to use them. 'I don't think I have the right to send for them,'" objected the wing commander. Longstreet's uncertainty about the extent of his authority over Wheeler resulted from Bragg's hasty restructuring of his army in the middle of the battle. It was never made clear to Longstreet whether or not Wheeler's cavalry was part of his command. In fact, it wasn't. Bragg was also sending orders directly to Wheeler about this time, which strongly suggests Longstreet's sphere of responsibility did not include Wheeler's corps.[7]

Whether or not Longstreet had the authority to do so, or if Claiborne's suggestion were the cause, in fact Longstreet did ask Wheeler for help. The situation on the Dry Valley Road cried out for cavalry, and so Longstreet sent for some.

Colonels Wharton and Martin were driving General Crook, Col. Eli Long, and the rest of the Ohioans from the field at Glass Mill when Wheeler received Longstreet's missive, and also new orders from Bragg instructing the cavalryman "to move my available force to Lee and Gordon's Mills and attack the enemy [there]." Both of these conflicting messages to Wheeler arrived sometime in the early afternoon—the one from Longstreet, sent at Claiborne's suggestion (which was probably verbal), and Bragg's dispatch—instructing him both to come to Longstreet's aid and capture Lee and Gordon's Mills. Wheeler chose to follow Bragg's orders and subsequently took the mills. He then overran the Union field hospital complex at Crawfish Spring. Longstreet received only a token cavalry regiment, and that support only much later that afternoon.[8]

Without help from Wheeler's cavalry, Preston's three-brigade division was the only force available to draw upon to protect the flank and rear, and that mission fell primarily upon Trigg's command. When Longstreet proposed

7 Longstreet, *From Manassas to Appomattox*, 449; *OR* 30, pt. 4, 675; "Dear Gen:" April 16, 1891, Thomas Claiborne Letter, CCNMP.

8 *OR* 30, pt. 2, 521; ibid., pt. 4, 675. The 2:00 p.m. order does not survive, but is mentioned in the 5:00 p.m. order from Bragg. Ibid., pt. 2, 521. See also Longstreet, *From Manassas to Appomattox*, 450.

shifting Preston's other two brigades northward to join Hindman in support of the attack against Horseshoe Ridge, however, Buckner objected. These brigades were the only remaining reserves in the Left Wing, argued Buckner. Committing them would leave the Rebel flank "in the air" and vulnerable should Trigg not be sufficient to stop whatever Federals still lurked in that direction. This argument convinced Longstreet. The big Georgian was loath to commit the last of his force until he saw how the next phase of the fight developed.[9]

While these decisions were being made, Longstreet and Buckner were also surveying the new Rebel circumstances. The day so far had been "hot and dry and dusty," Longstreet recalled, and during this ride they "could see but little of the enemy's line, and only knew of it by the occasional exchange of fire." Longstreet began this excursion from somewhere near the Dyer house. He rode north with Buckner and his group of officers probably along the ridge where Bushrod Johnson had recently triumphed over Mendenhall's line of guns, following in Kershaw's wake. Since neither Johnson nor any of his men mention seeing the wing commander at this time, Longstreet's entourage probably did not venture as far west as the Vittetoe house. Nor is it likely it reached as far north as the Vittetoe Road, which marked Kershaw's front line. Instead, the small group skirted the timber at the north edge of Dyer Field and entered the woods just east of the Glenn-Kelly Road. It was here Longstreet encountered General Humphreys and designated the blacksmith shop as the rally point for his Mississippians. Continuing east, the party soon ventured beyond the Confederate skirmish line and nearly stumbled into the rudimentary breastworks thrown up by Joseph Reynolds's Federals.[10]

From here the group turned south once again, crossing back into friendly lines somewhere in Poe Field. The Poe cabin was still ablaze. Both Buckner and Longstreet noted Poe Field as offering one of the few useful artillery positions on the battlefield. Buckner thought a line of guns firing north through the open field could bring enfilade fire on the Yankees holding the east side of Kelly Field. Three cannon were already engaged there: a Napoleon and two 12-pound howitzers comprising Capt. James F. Culpepper's South Carolina Battery. An 1854 Citadel graduate, Culpepper had been unable to keep up with Coleman's

9 Longstreet, *From Manassas to Appomattox*, 449.

10 Ibid., 450. Today a cannonball pyramid marks Longstreet's headquarters near the site of the Dyer house.

(McNair's) brigade, to which he was normally assigned, and so made himself useful in Poe Field. What he likely never knew was that he and his guns had nearly been overrun by the 105th Ohio, which had charged south across this very ground only a few minutes before the South Carolinians dropped trail.[11]

Buckner decided to reinforce Culpepper. Major Felix Robertson's reserve artillery battalion was nearby. Robertson's guns had been on the southern end of the battlefield the previous day, scattered behind Buckner's battle line near Hall's Ford; none saw action. "About midnight," recalled artillerist William R. Talley of Capt. M. W. Havis's battery, "a courier rode up to where Captain Havis was lying" and handed him orders to shift northward. The next morning, noted Talley, the battery was assigned to support Kershaw's brigade. Robertson had so far found no place to make himself or his gunners useful. Now he sent Havis's and Capt. Thomas Massenburg's batteries, all Georgians, to reinforce Culpepper. Both units were understrength and had only five pieces between them: two Napoleons, one bronze James rifle, and two 10-pound Parrotts. Still, combined with Culpepper's metal, they could deliver considerable firepower into Kelly Field.[12]

Leaving Poe Field, Longstreet ordered Buckner to shift Preston's remaining two brigades (Kelly and Gracie) northward. Leaving one battery and a regiment in place near the Hunt house to protect Confederate field hospitals and trains, the rest of the division marched up to Brotherton Field. There, they formed in two lines facing north "across the Chattanooga [La Fayette] Road in front of the Brotherton's house." Here they could be committed northward or move west to block any renewed Federal incursions from the flank or rear. It was now about 2:00 p.m. With his survey complete, James Longstreet halted at the Brotherton house, where lunch was waiting.[13]

11 *OR* 30, pt. 2, 358. For details on the 105th Ohio, see chapter 11.

12 William Ralston Talley Autobiography, CSI; Havis, Massenburg, and Culpepper Tablets, CCNMP. Neither Robertson nor any of his battery commanders filed reports that survived to make it into the *OR*. Culpepper's report was lost along with the rest of Evander McNair's brigade reports when that command was transferred back to Mississippi on September 23, 1863. As a result, my conclusion that Robertson sent Havis and Massenburg in response to a call from Buckner is reasoned conjecture. A more well-documented commitment of artillery at this location occurs later (about 5:00 p.m.), and confuses the issue of when and where the Rebel artillery first came into action in Poe Field. Culpepper's Tablet says he was in action "about noon," while Massenburg and Havis say they went into action "soon after noon."

13 *OR* 30, pt. 2, 415.

Far from being a bystander, between 1:00 and 2:00 p.m. Longstreet made an important reconnaissance and several significant decisions that would affect the rest of the battle. This survey of the field took him very nearly to the forefront of his own fluid battle lines, but also gave him a better understanding of how the fight developed than any other senior commander on the field had—certainly better than either Polk or Bragg understood things. This aggressive style of command was characteristic of James Longstreet; a similar reconnaissance in the Wilderness nine months later almost killed him.

The first and most important decision stemming from this ride reoriented his entire wing northward in order to break the new Union line forming on Horseshoe Ridge. His next decision—where should that blow land?—was almost as critical. Kershaw's and Humphreys's reports make it clear their attacks faced heavy and perhaps insurmountable opposition, and that even if successful would come at a high price. Bushrod Johnson was proposing to turn the new Union flank rather than attack it directly. Accordingly, Longstreet dispatched Hindman's three brigades to reinforce Johnson's flanking effort, not Kershaw's frontal attack.[14]

One detail Longstreet overlooked during his reconnaissance was the gap in General Thomas's defenses between Horseshoe Ridge and the preexisting Kelly Field line. This span included about 800 yards of undefended ground which lay between Harker's left flank atop Snodgrass Hill and Joseph Reynolds's right. A powerful blow delivered into this gap may well have duplicated the Union disaster of the morning. Fortunately for George Thomas, the intervening terrain was wooded and thus largely concealed the vulnerability from Rebel observation.

Why didn't the Confederates find this chink in the Federal armor? In fact, some did. The 8th South Carolina moved into this area when it drifted too far to the right during Kershaw's first attack. Unfortunately, that regiment did not file a battle report and no other source records what its members did or saw while there. Kershaw, who remained on the left of his overextended brigade during this part of the fight, apparently received no useful information from the 8th. Word of its uncontested advance did not filter up the chain of command.

Some of Humphreys's Mississippians also brushed through this gap. Humphreys's brigade fronted 300 yards during its advance up the Glenn-Kelly Road. Only the 17th Mississippi on the brigade's left ran into serious opposition

14 Longstreet, *From Manassas to Appomattox*, 450-451.

when it came under intense fire from Harker's brigade and the 4th U.S. Artillery on the high ground near the Snodgrass cabin. The 21st Mississippi suffered similarly when it tried to go to the 17th's support, but as their subsequent casualty reports attest, the 13th and 18th Mississippi on the brigade's right faced very few Federals. Instead of investigating (or even noting) this lack of pressure on his right, however, Humphreys remained focused on the furious opposition squaring off against his left. Humphreys left both Longstreet and Kershaw with the impression that a solid blue wall confronted his line. This was true enough in Snodgrass Field, but there was no Federal force facing Humphreys in the timber. Even an aggressive skirmish line pushed forward here would have revealed the gap. Instead, Humphreys fell back. When Longstreet rode through the woods east of the blacksmith shop he was 600 yards south of this gap, too far south to personally view the Federal forces (or lack thereof) to Humphreys's front.

A certain amount of limited Federal activity here may have confused the Confederates operating here. As noted, the 10th and 74th Indiana of Col. John Croxton's brigade never reached Horseshoe Ridge. They were last engaged with Jerome Robertson's Texans in Dyer Field, and when they retired, came to rest near the southwest corner of Kelly Field. These 400 Hoosiers would have only partially filled the yawning gap in question, but their skirmishers might have misled either Humphreys's Mississippians or Kershaw's 8th South Carolina. Additionally, Ferdinand Van Derveer's brigade was at this time resting near the Kelly barn (also in the southwest corner of the field) after its hard fight against General Breckinridge's troops. Van Derveer counted about 1,100 bayonets. While none of these elements were linked up with Harker's men, their presence in the smoke-shrouded woods could well have deceived the already-wary Rebels, and concealed any potential Union vulnerability. A determined Rebel push in this sector would have quickly revealed the weakness, but Kershaw's focus on his own left flank, coupled with Humphreys's lack of aggression, left the gap both undiscovered and unexploited.[15]

Longstreet's lunch at the Brotherton house figures large in the lore of Chickamauga. To some, the interlude strikes a discordant note: the prominent commander and his companions enjoying a convivial picnic in the midst of such carnage. In fact, having set major movements in motion with his orders to Generals Hindman and Preston, Longstreet had little left to do but wait. And as

15 Shaw, *Tenth Regiment Indiana Volunteer Infantry*, 234; *OR* 30, pt. 1, 430.

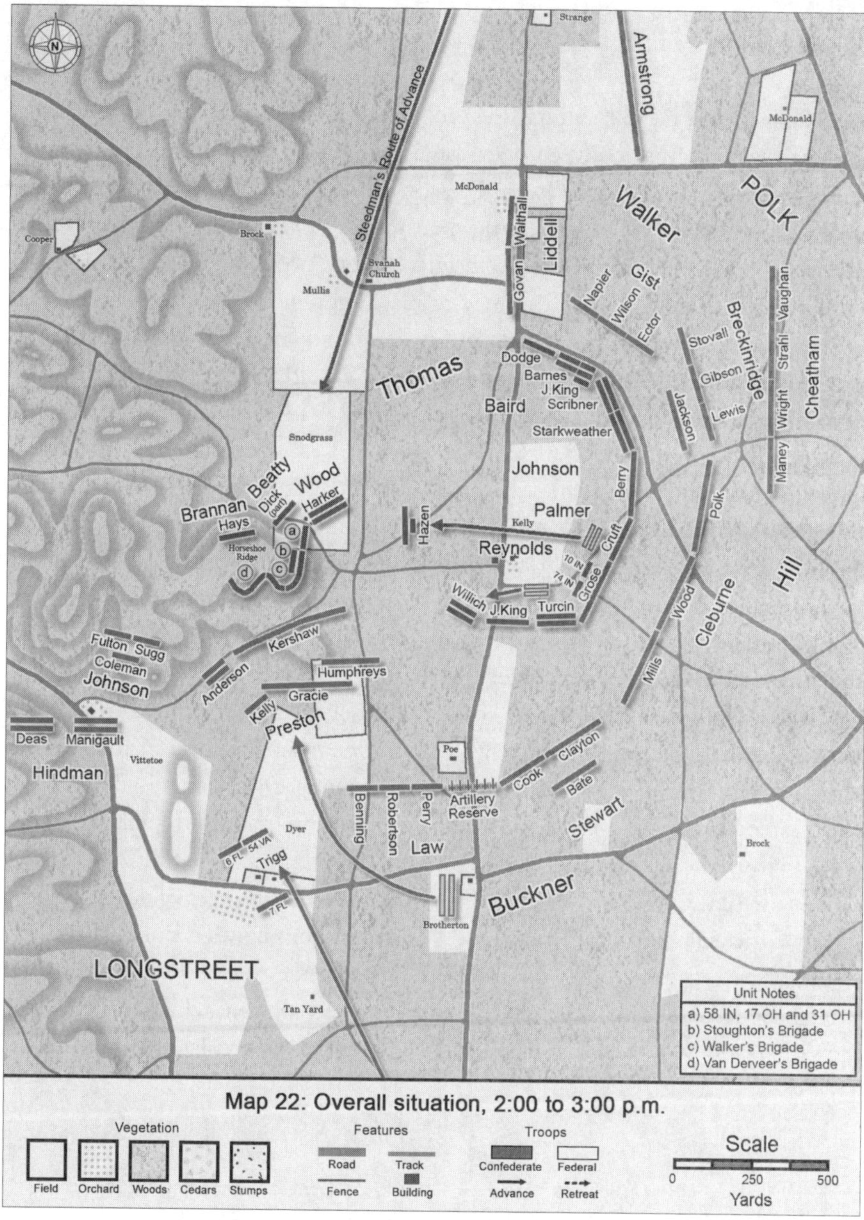

Map 22: Overall situation, 2:00 to 3:00 p.m.

the wing commander, Longstreet needed to do so in a convenient location, one quickly and easily accessible to couriers and staff officers. The Brotherton house, sitting as it did at the junction of two major roads, was ideal for this purpose. The lunch, while welcome, was simply the result of an old soldier's practical understanding that rations, like rest, should be grabbed whenever possible.[16]

While everyone was eating, Preston's two brigades filed into place nearby, their arrival punctuated by an occasional Federal artillery round dropping in their midst. Major William Owen, Preston's chief of staff, found "Longstreet and Buckner, seated on a log, eating their lunch." Owen was a familiar face to the Eastern Theater arrivals. Just a month earlier Owen had been serving as an officer with Longstreet's artillery in Virginia. When he received an offer to join Preston's staff, Owen approached Longstreet for advice. The general urged him to take the transfer, assuring Owen that they "would meet again." Earlier that morning, before the attack began, Longstreet had shaken hands with the younger man and reminded him of that promise. Now, outside the Brotherton house, Longstreet hailed the passing major and asked to borrow some pipe tobacco. The big Georgian's mood was ebullient. "They have fought their last man, and he is running," Longstreet thundered. In response to additional queries, he added that "a few are holding out upon the ridge up yonder, not many though." Then, with the offer of some new artillery pieces to re-equip Preston's batteries eagerly accepted, the general turned back to other business.[17]

In his memoirs, Longstreet recalled another incident from that lunch. By now Major Robertson's artillery was in action near the Poe house, and Federal guns were answering back with increasing frequency. One such missile wreaked small havoc among the picnickers when a piece of shrapnel ripped through a book in the hands of a mounted courier and struck Lt. Col. Peyton T. Manning. Observing Manning "gasping, it was supposed, in the struggles of death, friends sprang forward to look for the wound." In fact, Manning was choking on a bite of sweet potato. Once that obstruction was removed he resumed breathing, though he remained dazed and contused by the fragment, which never broke the skin. Even with these interruptions, the lunch probably lasted no more than

16 Longstreet, *From Manassas to Appomattox*, 451; Milton P. Jarnigan Reminiscences, TSLA. To Longstreet, the meal of Nassau bacon and sweet potatoes was a bit of a delicacy. "We were not accustomed to potatoes of any kind in Virginia," explained the general, "and thought we had a luxury." The "luxury" came courtesy of Capt. Milton P. Jarnigan of General Buckner's staff. Captain Jarnigan reached the battlefield on September 19 with a large sack of the tubers and generously shared his starchy horde with his friend Col. Thomas Ruffin and the rest of Buckner's staff.

17 Owen, *In Camp and Battle*, 264, 281.

30 minutes. Before he was finished eating, Longstreet was summoned to meet General Bragg.[18]

Their meeting, which likely occurred about 3:00 p.m., offers a study in contrasts. A little while earlier Major Owen glimpsed Bragg along the La Fayette Road. Owen thought the army commander seemed oddly downcast. "He looks pale and careworn, his features rendered more haggard by a white Havelock he wears over his cap and neck." Longstreet remembered that Bragg was "some little distance in our rear of our new position." The wing commander gauged Bragg's mood as not only pessimistic, but obdurate and unwilling to listen. Given the changed tactical circumstances brought about by the breakthrough at Brotherton Field, Longstreet argued for a revision of the plan: let the Right Wing stand on the defensive, he insisted, and give him some of Polk's men to pursue the Federals retreating up the Dry Valley Road. Bragg would hear none of it. "There is not a man in the Right Wing who has any fight in him," replied the gaunt army commander. Bragg's answer astounded Longstreet. Years later when he described the exchange to D. H. Hill, Longstreet confirmed that it was then he realized Bragg "thought . . . the battle was lost."[19]

According to Longstreet, Bragg refused to make any changes, or indeed, make any decisions at all. No additional reinforcements would be given to the left, nor could Longstreet expect that fighting would be renewed on Polk's front. After a few additional minutes of fruitless discussion, Bragg ordered Longstreet back to his lines and then rode away in turn, informing everyone present that if "anything happened his headquarters would be at Reed's Bridge and to communicate with him there."[20]

* * *

To many of his fellow soldiers, Maj. Gen. George H. Thomas seemed imperturbable. The stocky framed 47-year-old boasted an outward demeanor described by biographer Francis McKinney as "deliberate, mature, grave [and]

18 Longstreet, *From Manassas to Appomattox*, 451.

19 Owen, *In Camp and Battle*, 280; Longstreet, *From Manassas to Appomattox*, 451-452; Hill, "Chickamauga: The Great Battle of the West," 659. In a footnote, Hill quotes Longstreet's letter of July 1884.

20 George Ratchford, "Gen. D. H. Hill at Chickamauga," *Confederate Veteran*, vol. XXIV no. 3, (March, 1916), 121.

unostentatious." Brigadier John Beatty once characterized Thomas as "tall, heavy, sedate. . . . [He] puts on less style than . . . [others] and is a gentlemanly, modest, reliable soldier." Thomas had been a fixture in the Army of the Cumberland since the formation of that command in the fall of 1862.[21]

Tight situations were nothing new to Thomas. At Stones River, Bragg's men overwhelmed Alexander McCook's Right Wing and almost collapsed the entire Federal position. With the Union line bent back upon itself like a folded pocketknife, the Federal officers gathered for a nighttime conference. Many of those present counseled retreat. Thomas's reputed answer on this question was characteristically blunt: "I know of no better place to die than right here." The Federals stayed put, and two days later Bragg was the one to retreat. Thomas's theories on war matched his personality. Noted McKinney, "as Thomas condensed it, any unit no matter how small could nearly always save itself from annihilation if it would stay in its circle and fight . . . being cut off and surrounded was nothing to cause terror." Now, on a bloody Sabbath afternoon in late September in North Georgia, Thomas had ample opportunity to prove the validity of his thesis.[22]

As the fighting in Kelly Field dwindled to desultory sniping around midday, Thomas rode toward the army's right to see what was keeping his promised reinforcements from arriving. As earlier noted, there he encountered Tom Wood, witnessed the extent of the Union disaster on the right, and had a hand in the debate over the identity of Kershaw's South Carolinians. For the next several hours his attention would be fixed almost completely on the defense of Horseshoe Ridge, and particularly on Snodgrass Hill. He established a small headquarters on the back of the slope behind the Snodgrass cabin so he was readily available to the men defending the new line. Captain James Stinchcomb of the 17th Ohio (Connell's brigade) was one of those who had just escaped the hell of Poe Field. "Gen. Thomas was all over, unmoved—the same Thomas, cool and calm," confirmed the officer. A number of observers also recalled a dramatic moment when Thomas ordered Opdycke's 125th Ohio to hold the flank. An anonymous correspondent for the Cleveland Herald (writing under the name "VICTOR") tried to convey that drama to the folks back home:

21 McKinney, *Education in Violence*, 209; Beatty, *Citizen Soldier*, 236.

22 John Lee Yaryan, "Stone River," *MOLLUS*, vol. 24, 175; McKinney, *Education in Violence*, 208.

"[When] Gen. Thomas had said, 'this position must be held,' we could but die, we must not yield . . . [We] held our own."[23]

Like every other officer on the ridge, Thomas was busy building a new line to stop the Rebels. Colonel Morton Hunter, leading his battered 82nd Indiana onto Hill Two, was accosted by one of Thomas's staff officers who asked how long the Hoosiers could hold the hill. Hunter replied that he could hold as long as his ammunition held out, but he needed more. "He made no reply," recounted Hunter, "but rode away. In about fifteen minutes . . . fourteen men came up, carrying fourteen boxes of ammunition."[24]

Via General Wood, Thomas confirmed Harker's retreat to Snodgrass Hill. He also dispatched Captain Kellogg back to Kelly Field to inform Joe Reynolds that the "right had been turned, and the enemy was in his rear in force." Thomas was painfully aware of the yawning gulf between Wood's left and Reynolds's right, but for the moment had no one to fill that hole. Reynolds would simply have to refuse his right flank and hope for the best. Fortunately, shortly after 1:00 p.m., Kershaw and Humphreys were repulsed and another lull settled over the battlefield.[25]

During all this Thomas must have wondered what happened to Negley with his powerful artillery reserve and supporting infantry. If so, he made no mention of seeing Negley during this time or trying to locate him. Thomas arrived near Dyer Field sometime between 11:30 a.m. and noon. While his personal presence was noted in a number of places between Dyer Field and Hill Two, his principal location seems to have been at the Snodgrass cabin, a central location from which he could observe most of the ensuing action. Negley was at this same location until at least noon. Negley left the field before 1:00 p.m., probably just before Kershaw's first ragged attack climbed the slopes of Hills One and Two. Certainly George Thomas was aware that at least some of Negley's men were still in action, for he noted the presence of both Beatty and Stanley. He also made use of several members of Negley's staff when they

23 "Letter from Captain Stinchcomb," *Lancaster Gazette*, October 8, 1863; "Letter from VICTOR," *Cleveland Herald*, October 7, 1863, as quoted in Richard A. Baumgartner, *Yankee Tigers II: Civil War Field Correspondence from The Tiger Regiment of Ohio* (Blue Acorn Press, 2004), 29, 97. "VICTOR" was most likely Hezekiah Steadman, a noncommissioned officer and later captain of Company K, 125th Ohio.

24 Hunter, *History of the Eighty-Second Indiana*, 68.

25 *OR* 30, pt. 1, 252.

returned from various missions to find their chief gone. Perhaps Thomas simply assumed Negley was caught up in the rout. However, sometime after 1:00 p.m. Lt. Ambrose Bierce arrived on scene. Unable to locate his own brigade under George Hazen, which was then on line near Kelly Field, the future writer of the macabre reported to Thomas. He may well have related his encounter with Negley just a short while earlier, of offering to lead Negley back to the fighting and Negley's refusal. In his report, Thomas did not see fit to level any direct criticism at his senior subordinate. Thomas, however, would specifically praise every division leader who fought under his command on either the 19th or 20th of September except Negley, who passed unmentioned.[26]

In contrast to Longstreet, who requested reinforcements from Bragg and received none, Thomas desperately needed more men, but had no one to request them from. Fortunately for the XIV Corps leader, Union reinforcements were coming of their own volition.

Colonel Ferdinand Van Derveer had good instincts. Like John Beatty and Timothy Stanley, once Breckinridge's troops retreated Van Derveer found himself without orders. When he first entered the fight at Kelly Field, there was no time for any instruction other than "charge." After he drove back Marcellus Stovall's Confederates, Van Derveer had no further contact with his division commander John Brannan or with George Thomas—the last man to give Van Derveer orders. Van Derveer halted his brigade in the vicinity of the Kelly barn, where he took stock of his heavy losses and cared for his wounded. When the fight opened on Saturday, September 19, the 87th Indiana, 2nd Minnesota, and 9th and 35th Ohio fielded a total of 1,643 men in the ranks. Now, after two days of heavy fighting, these regiments probably numbered just over half that, or perhaps 900 muskets.[27]

Near the Kelly barn, Van Derveer was joined by Maj. Robert Kelly and his small fragment of the 4th Kentucky from Croxton's brigade. Kelly, who was no relation to the property owner, provided the first inkling that all was not well with the rest of the Union army. Van Derveer placed Kelly's scrap of a regiment on the right of the 35th Ohio where, shortly afterward, another motley group of Croxton's command joined him: 40 more men and three officers from the 4th Kentucky, and Lieutenant Colonels Taylor and Baker of the 10th and 74th

26 *OR* 30, pt. 1, 252-256.

27 Ibid., 430.

Indiana, respectively, each with a handful of men from their particular units. Kelly's fragments added perhaps as many as 150 men (drawn from nearly every regiment of Croxton's five-regiment brigade) to Van Derveer's force. Soon thereafter, another of Thomas's aides found Van Derveer and added more detail to Kelly's tale. A third of the army was in rout, he explained, and Brannan had retreated to Horseshoe Ridge and was even then under heavy attack. Lacking orders to the contrary, Van Derveer moved to the sounds of this new gunfire.[28]

The XIV Corps aide led Van Derveer due west through the intervening belt of timber to a cluster of seven mounted officers gathered near the Snodgrass cabin. Minnesotan Lt. Jeremiah Donahower of the 2nd regiment recognized several, including Generals Thomas and Brannan. Thomas rode forward to meet the new arrivals and welcomed Van Derveer with an urgent inquiry: "Glad to see you Colonel! What condition is your brigade in?" According to the regimental historian of the 9th Ohio, Van Derveer offered a laconic reply: "All in line save our dead and wounded." According to Lt. Col. Judson Bishop of the 2nd Minnesota, Thomas told him "that 'he was glad to see us in such good order.' We did not then know how many troops he had seen in disorder during the day," continued Bishop. To Lieutenant Donahower, who was listening from the ranks, Thomas was all business. "Colonel, I want you to hold the hill," Thomas instructed Col. James George, the commander of the 2nd Minnesota, referencing Hill Two. "We will, General, until we are ordered away or are mustered out," replied George. Brannan wanted Van Derveer to replace the troops on Hill Two because many of the men there were running out of ammunition.[29]

Major Kelly soon discovered that Colonel Hays of the 10th Kentucky was on Hill One in command of the rump of Croxton's brigade "a few hundred men" strong, including another "40 or 50" men of the 4th Kentucky. Kelly rejoined Hays there. With these arrivals the reconstituted 4th Kentucky now

28 Ibid., 1062; Bishop, *The Story of a Regiment*, 108; *OR* 30, pt. 1, 430. Bishop does not identify the aide, but Captain Kellogg had been sent to update Joseph Reynolds of these circumstances at this time, and it is very likely that Kellogg also found Van Derveer. The two commands were not far apart.

29 Donahower, "The Chattanooga Campaign," 136, MinnHS; Grebner, *We Were The Ninth*, 143; Bishop, *The Story of a Regiment*, 108; Donahower "The Chattanooga Campaign," 136; *OR* 30, pt. 1, 430.

numbered a respectable 125 men and swelled Hays's ranks to nearly 500 bayonets.[30]

As Van Derveer's brigade and the other troops moved to reinforce Thomas's line, more infantry was spotted heading toward Horseshoe Ridge. Their unexpected appearance was one of Thomas's most uncomfortable moments of his entire career.

Major General Gordon Granger was another officer chafing at his orders and lack of information. Granger's Reserve Corps numbered only 5,894 officers and men, but his missions were varied. General Rosecrans left the Reserve Corps at Rossville to defend the direct route to Chattanooga. However, Granger was also instructed to hold his command ready to move south if called upon. "You must help us in the fight tomorrow by supporting Thomas," Rosecrans wired to Granger at 8:10 p.m. on September 19. At 11:45 p.m., Rosecrans sent a second wire to Granger: "Do you think the enemy will still attempt to turn our left flank again tomorrow? . . . [W]hat sort of pass is Rossville to defend?" Granger was expected to help Thomas where possible—but not at the expense of exposing Rossville. Moreover, with the entire Union army sidling left, the support Rosecrans expected Granger to provide was in the nature of reaching out to Thomas's left flank as the Federals gradually closed up to the north. These were wide-ranging instructions for a three-brigade command several miles from the scene of the action. Beyond these few dispatches, Granger had only limited information from the battlefield about the extent of the fighting.[31]

Fortunately for the Federals, Col. Robert Minty's cavalry brigade was also available. Following Granger's orders of the night before, at first light on the 20th Minty pushed his troopers forward on Brig. Gen. Walter Whitaker's left flank as far as Missionary Mills on Chickamauga Creek. No Rebels were to be found, nor were any encountered when Minty advanced "a strong patrol . . . through Chickamauga Station and Graysville."[32]

That same morning Granger moved Col. Daniel McCook's brigade south to McAfee Church, a couple of miles north of the McDonald house on the road to Ringgold. From there, McCook could support Minty's cavalry or Whitaker's

30 *OR* 30, pt. 1, 1062.

31 *OR* 30, pt. 3, 741.

32 Robert H. G. Minty, "Minty's Saber Brigade: The Part They Took in the Chattanooga Campaign, Part II," *National Tribune*, March 3, 1892.

This image looks north from Horseshoe ridge near the Snodgrass cabin—near where Thomas made his headquarters. Note the lack of trees and the cleared fields. The postwar buildings in the distance are part of Fort Oglethorpe. Many of these structures still stand today, just north of the modern visitor's center. It was across these fields that Gordon Granger's men approached Thomas's position. *Library of Congress*

infantry, still defending the Red House Bridge over the Chickamauga, or move south to link up with Thomas. Granger retained Col. John Mitchell's brigade, of Brig. James Steedman's division, his reserve of last resort.[33]

James Steedman, the next senior officer present at Rossville, was in many ways the antithesis of Gordon Granger. Correspondent William Shanks portrayed Steedman as a headstrong political general who owed his military career to his dominance of Ohio Democratic conventions in the decade before the war—political influence that made him "the power in the party." In camp Steedman was anything but a disciplinarian. Drinking, gambling, and even women of questionable morals could usually be found at his headquarters. Like many successful politicians, however, Steedman had the common touch and

33 *OR* 30, pt. 1, 854.

proved popular with the men. Sergeant George E. Dolton in Battery M, 1st Illinois artillery, usually abhorred drunkenness and had trouble in his unit with that sort of frivolity. His impression of Steedman, however, overlooked such tales of revelry. "To hear him talk you would say he was a common farmer," related Dolton to his wife. "He dresses very plainly. His voice is mild, gruff. He can crack a joke at any time & is not afraid to talk & shake hands with a private."[34]

The general proved himself in combat, a trait that forgave much. He could also be headstrong to the point of recklessness, willing to seize the initiative at any opportunity. Steedman's motto, wrote an admiring Shanks, was "never, under any circumstances, take any body's advice, nor refuse any body's information." Years later Steedman would endeavor to parlay these traits into greater military fame than he deserved by attempting to take sole credit for the march to join Thomas; his partisans wrote Granger out of the picture entirely. That fight, however, was still in the future.[35]

Granger fretted as he listened to the sustained roar of combat three miles to the south. "Why the —— does Rosecrans keep us here?" he demanded of Maj. Joseph S. Fullerton, his chief of staff. "There is nothing in front of us now. There is the battle!" For the better part of an hour Granger waited in vain for orders that never arrived. Finally, Granger decided to move without them. Fullerton warned his boss that doing so could "bring disaster to the army and [Granger] to a court martial." "There's nothing in our front now but rag-tag, bobtail cavalry," shot back the general.[36]

Granger sent word to Colonel Minty, ordering the cavalryman to shift his brigade southward in order "to take possession of the Rossville and Ringgold

34 Shanks, *Personal Recollections*, 258; David S. and Jeanne T. Heidler, eds., *Encyclopedia of the American Civil War*, 5 vols. (ABC-CLIO, 2000), vol. 4, 1856; Theodore A. Dolton, ed., *The Path of Patriotism: Civil War Letters of George Edwin Dolton* (Booksurge LLC, 2005), 75. George Dolton was a teetotaler who was often critical of his fellow soldiers for drinking or visiting prostitutes, but he seemed to like Steedman in spite of the general's loose reputation.

35 Shanks, *Personal Recollections*, 279. For a complete description of this tale, see John M. Morgan, "Old Steady: the Role of General James Blair Steedman at the Battle of Chickamauga," *Northwest Ohio Quarterly*, vol. 22, no. 2 (Spring, 1950), 73-94.

36 J. S. Fullerton, "Reinforcing Thomas at Chickamauga," *Battles and Leaders*, 4 vols. (Thomas Yoseloff, Inc., 1956), vol. 3, 666. Fullerton's warning of a courts-martial was overstated, but Granger was taking a risk. His orders clearly gave him enough latitude to move to join Thomas of his own volition, but any negative consequences from doing so would clearly redound to him.

The same view as in the previous image (p. 461), taken from the road in front of the modern reconstruction of the Snodgrass house. The monument and cannon represent Battery I, 4th U.S. Artillery. Note the solid wall of trees limiting visibility northward. If the trees were not there, we could see the same buildings of old Fort Oglethorpe in the distance. *Harvey Scarborough*

Road." Minty moved with alacrity, and once in place sent another patrol forward to Red House Bridge. Before reaching the bridge, the patrol reported back that "Gen'l Scott, with his brigade [of Confederate Cavalry] was on the west side of the Chickamauga. This I considered an encroachment on our territory, and at once attacked and drove him across the bridge to the east side of the creek." That dust-up, however, would not distract Granger from his larger objective.[37]

With Minty on his way, Granger ordered Steedman to move his division south, leaving McCook's brigade to safeguard Rossville. For most of the men in Steedman's 10 regiments this was their first opportunity to engage in a real battle. Fear mingled equally with anticipation. Sergeant Major Charles Partridge, later the historian of the 96th Illinois, wrote that "we were 'spoiling for a fight,' half in hopes that they might be spared the dangers of the battle, and half in fear lest they might not share in its honors." Similar excitement simmered in the ranks of the uninitiated 22nd Michigan, which had been in service for a year. "I remember lots of the boys used to say we will never get to the front where there is any fighting to do," recalled Sgt. Marvin Boget of the 22nd. "Always kept back in the rear like a cows tail." That was about to change. In Mitchell's

37 Minty, "Minty's Saber Brigade," *National Tribune*, March 3, 1892.

brigade, Sergeant Dolton was filled with foreboding. The night before, "just as the fighting ended," Dolton watched as "a large flock of carrion buzzards came sail[ing] slowly around over the battleground. I have seen no sight in the war that made me feel half as bad as did those birds," he wrote to his wife. "It seemed as if some awful calamity o'erhung us." Now Dolton and his comrades were heading into the heart of that same "awful calamity."[38]

Having made up his mind, Granger set a fast pace for his Reserve Corps. General Whitaker's brigade led Steedman's division, with the 96th Illinois in the van. Whitaker was a prewar Kentucky lawyer and politician with Mexican War experience, further seasoned by combat at Shiloh as colonel of the 6th Kentucky. Whitaker's men set off in full panoply, with silk banners unfurled for battle. To Sergeant Major Partridge, the movement was pure pageantry. "It was a splendid sight as those battalions moved across the fields . . . on that beautiful Sabbath morning, their colors kissed by the breezes and their muskets gleaming in the bright September sun. The troops, having been in reserve, were under strict discipline, exceptionally well drilled, and their swords and muskets all as bright and clean as though they were moving out for an inspection instead . . . of a battle." The noise of the distant fight was by now "a continuous roar" which, to John Beach in the 40th Ohio "seem[ed] so much like an appeal for help." The march was conducted mostly at the double-quick, or close to a run. The column followed the La Fayette Road until it reached Cloud Church, were the men ran into that "rag-tag" Rebel cavalry.[39]

As he drew near the church, Whitaker reported "rebel mounted infantry drawn up in line of battle ready to intercept our progress." The church was also the site of John Brannan's field hospital, established on Saturday morning when everyone thought it would be safely behind the lines. That sense of safety proved illusory, and by Sunday morning the hospital was in no-man's-land between Thomas's and Granger's positions. During the morning fighting, the hospital was shelled by the 5th Company of the Washington Artillery of New Orleans. Advancing as part of Breckinridge's attack, the battery went into

38 Charles Partridge, *History of the Ninety-Sixth Regiment Illinois Volunteer Infantry* (Brown, Pettibone and Company, 1887), 175; Marvin Boget Letter, 22nd Michigan file, CCNMP; Dolton, *The Path of Patriotism*, 77.

39 Ezra J. Warner, *Generals in Blue: Lives of the Union Commanders* (Louisiana State University Press, 1991), 556; Partridge, *Ninety-Sixth Regiment Illinois*, 175; John Sanders Memoir, 84th Indiana file, CSI; John N. Beach, *History of the Fortieth Ohio Volunteer Infantry* (Shepard & Craig, Publishers, 1884), 44.

action near the McDonald house to fire at the retreating mass of John Beatty's brigade. Lieutenant Joseph A. Chalaron, a member of the Louisiana battery, observed what he thought was a concentration of Federals "around a large white house (Cloud's) on an eminence, some 700 yards off" and opened fire, dropping shells among the wounded. Chalaron retreated soon thereafter with the rest of Breckinridge's command. By the time Whitaker arrived the hospital was in the hands of General Forrest's troopers. "About eleven o'clock a line of rebel skirmishers were seen to emerge from a wood about four hundred yards distant," recorded the 35th Ohio's Surgeon, Dr. A. H. Landis, "followed by a large force of Forrest's cavalry. All the ambulances we had were loaded with wounded and sent to Chattanooga, and many of the slightly wounded were sent on foot. The enemy continued to advance until they ascertained it was a hospital, when a squad of them rode up, and for the first time we were in the hands of the rebels."[40]

Two regiments from Brig. Gen. Frank Armstrong's mounted division held the area around Cloud Church while the rest of Armstrong's troops served nearby, screening Breckinridge's right flank or waiting in reserve. Backing them up was Brig. Gen. Henry Davidson's brigade of Brig. Gen. John Pegram's division, resting after its engagement of the 19th. (Colonel John Scott's brigade was still at Red House Bridge, skirmishing with Minty.) Forrest supported these troops with the three artillery batteries assigned to his corps, Tennesseans all.[41]

Heading up Steedman's column, the 96th Illinois renewed the advance. The Rebels fell back in the face of the Union infantry and Whitaker's men recaptured the field hospital, which by now presented a distressing sight. "Hundreds of wounded were laying about without attention," recalled Beach. To his horror, Whitaker also discovered the body of a good friend, Maj. Richard Rockingham of the 6th Kentucky. Rockingham was wounded in Brock Field on the 19th, and while lying helpless in the hospital was killed by a shell burst fired by the Washington Artillery.[42]

40 *OR* 30, pt. 1, 862; Chalaron, "Vivid Experiences at Chickamauga," , 278; Thelma Hudson, *A History and Biographical Cyclopedia of Butler County, Ohio: with illustrations and sketches of its representative men and pioneers* (Western Biographical Publishing Company, 1882), 222.

41 *OR* 30, pt. 2, 525; John Watson Morton, *The Artillery of Nathan Bedford Forrest's Cavalry* (R. Bemis Publishing, 1995), 121.

42 Partridge, *Ninety-Sixth Regiment Illinois*, 178; Beach, *History of the Fortieth Ohio*, 45; *OR* 30, pt. 1, 862.

Steedman began deploying his men in the open fields around Cloud Church, preparing for a fight. At one point the 96th, threatened by mounted cavalry, formed a hollow square. Battery M, 1st Illinois Light Artillery, moved to a hill southeast of the recaptured hospital, where its members noticed a column of enemy cavalry in the distance. When Granger rode by the gunners asked if they could open fire. Granger, however, thought the troopers were Federals and led Battery M through another strip of timber into an open field, where Forrest's artillery opened on them. The battery unlimbered and returned fire. For the Illinois cannoneers, the fight had suddenly taken on a more personal dimension. A rider at the head of another party of Confederate cavalry was mounted on a gray horse that someone recognized from a fight near Triune, Tennessee, on June 11, where the battery had fired its first shots of the war in anger. Sergeant Dolton mistakenly identified the distant rider as Col. James W. Starnes of the 4th Tennessee Cavalry, the same officer who had led the probe at Triune. Whoever it was, it could not have been Starnes, for he was killed on June 30, 1863.[43]

An impatient Granger, meanwhile, returned to Steedman to inquire about the delay. The Rebel troopers, insisted the corps commander, "are nothing but rag-a-muffin cavalry." Forrest's artillery, however, was more of a threat. By this time 12 guns were deployed in line about a half mile east of the La Fayette Road. Any troops using the road would have to run a gauntlet of Rebel shells. Moreover, the road led directly to the Kelly Field line, which at the moment was relatively quiet. The solid roar of battle was coming from the southwest, perhaps a mile south of the Mullis farmstead. "Convinced [Forrest's men represented] only a large party of observation," recalled Major Fullerton, Granger decided to continue on, changing course to the west to detour around the exposed portion of the road. To help screen the movement, Granger sent Fullerton back to bring up Colonel McCook's brigade to defend Cloud Church.[44]

Granger's appearance along the La Fayette Road had an important effect on the Confederates, though no Federal knew it at the time. Lieutenant General D. H. Hill construed Granger's appearance as an assault aimed at his own right

43 Charles A. Partridge, "The Ninety-Sixth Illinois at Chickamauga," *Transactions of the Illinois State Historical Society for the Year 1910*, vol. XI (1910), 75; George E. Dolton, *Capsule History Battery M 1st Illinois Light Artillery*, CCNMP; Dolton, *The Path of Patriotism*, 77.

44 Cozzens, *This Terrible Sound*, 442; Fullerton, "Reinforcing Thomas," 666; *OR* 30, pt. 1, 855.

flank, which was still in considerable disarray after his failed attacks that morning. "A heavy pressure upon us when first disordered might have been serious," admitted Hill. With this new threat "giving every indication of a flank attack, preparations were made to meet it." Forrest deployed more of his men as skirmishers, more artillery was brought up, and Hill asked General Polk for reinforcements. Polk responded by ordering Frank Cheatham's division to his support. Of overriding importance was the fact that any thought of the Rebel Right Wing renewing its attack was shelved.[45]

Instead of moving against Hill, Steedman's infantry resumed their trek to find Thomas, this time angling southwest. The march was hot and dusty, conducted at speed and under some level of fire for most of the way. Even though the column detoured to the west in an effort to avoid the Rebel troopers, they were still exposed to Confederate shellfire. Young Tennessee artillerist Capt. John Morton and his battery were in the thick of this fight, supported by the guns of Capts. A. L. Huggins and Gustave Huwald. Most of Forrest's guns were older, smaller, and too light for service in the line, but were still useful for cavalry operations. The Rebel ordnance initially totaled 12 pieces, only two of which could be considered modern: a brace of 3-inch Rodman rifles in Morton's command. The rest included four 6-pound smoothbores and two 12-pound howitzers of Mexican War vintage, a pair of mountain howitzers, and two 2.5-inch "mountain rifles." All four of the latter pieces were scaled-down versions of larger guns. Despite the antiquity of their hardware, the Confederate gunners served their pieces well. As the action progressed, Forrest appealed for additional support from Breckinridge, who dispatched a section of Cobb's Kentucky battery to help. However, noted Cobb, these two guns, commanded by Lt. Frank Gracey, arrived toward the end of this duel and fired only "a few rounds."[46]

While the infantry pressed on, Battery M engaged in an unsuccessful artillery duel with Forrest's more numerous cannon. "Our fire in reply did not appear to have any effect," remembered Sergeant Dolton, but "some of their shells . . . would strike just in front of our guns, and ricocheting, pass far to the rear. A number passed through the columns of our infantry, which . . . was hurrying past the rear of our position." Dolton's fellow artillerist, Pvt. Samuel

45 Ibid., pt. 2, 144.

46 See Tablets for Morton's, Huwald's, and Huggins's batteries, Reed's Bridge Road, CCNMP; *OR* 30, pt. 2, 216.

Patten, thought the Rebel cannon were beyond the range of the battery's four "twelve pound Napoleon guns," leaving only the "Rodmans of the center section" able to return fire with any accuracy.[47]

In the 89th Ohio (Whitaker's brigade), Pvt. Thomas Doughman of Company G described the effect of this fire: "The first shell dropped some distance in front of us, the second coming nearer. The Colonel [Caleb H. Carlton] gave [the] command, 'forward, double quick, right oblique into [the] woods!' to avoid [the] shell fire." Colonel Nelson Trusler, heading up the 84th Indiana of the same brigade, reported that "for a considerable portion of the distance my regiment marched under the fire of the enemy." Partridge remembered a Rebel battery opening on them "not more than four hundred yards away." Despite the range and intensity of the fire, losses were few, but the danger loomed large in the men's minds. Private Thomas O'Dell of the 78th Illinois described his memory of the experience: "we came in range of the enemy's guns and were kept under fire some 2 hours hurrying part of the time in double-quick." Sergeant Edward Murray of Company C, 96th Illinois, also recalled that run. Murray was writing in his diary when "General Whittiker came dashing through the bushes and with an oath wanted to know where the Colonel . . . was. . . .[W]e all got into line and he gave the command 'march double quick' and off we went on a run . . . about a mile. . . . The dust was just awful."[48]

Granger took a moment to indulge himself here. As an old artilleryman, he could rarely pass up the opportunity to play again at being a gunner. The Rebels now had the range, and shells were falling all around Battery M. Orderly Sergeant Edwin C. Gillette had just dismounted when one shell passed

47 Dolton, *Capsule History of Battery M,* CCNMP; Online transcript of letter describing the battle of Chickamauga, September 23, 1863, Samuel Patton letters, Cowan's Historical auctions, Lot 259, November 20, 2012. http://cowanauctions.com /auctions/item.aspx?Itemid=3852. Accessed 12/06/2013, copy in author's possession. Samuel's last name is spelled "Patten" in the rosters, which is the spelling I use here. A Napoleon's range was about 1,600 yards; that of a 3-inch rifle, 2,000. Forrest's older and smaller guns, with effective ranges of 1,000 to 1,200 yards, would have been badly outclassed if Patten's estimate of the distance were accurate. Other evidence suggests that the distance was closer.

48 Thomas J. Doughman Recollections, BGSU; "September 28, 1863," Nelson Trusler Report, 84th Indiana Infantry file, Indiana Adjutant-General's Records, Indiana State Archives; Partridge, *Ninety-Sixth Regiment Illinois*, 178; Donald Odell Virdin, *The Civil War Correspondence of Judge Thomas Goldsborough O'Dell* (Heritage Books, 1992), 97-98; Edward Murray, *A Soldier's Reminiscences*, 25, Pamphlet in Lake County Discovery Museum, Wauconda, IL. As noted above, most Rebel accounts suggest the range was closer to 1,000 yards.

completely through his animal, spraying gore everywhere and testifying to the accuracy of the enemy's fire. Dolton recalled "that Gen. Granger dismounted and sighted one of the guns . . . and nearly lost his head by a shell from the Rebels." Granger had no better luck than the battery's regular artillerists, and after a few rounds gave up the exercise. "He ordered us to limber up and follow him, for 'he had work for us to do,'" recalled Dolton. The battery hastened to follow the rest of its division. Private Patten nearly lost his own head here, just as the guns were limbering to leave. "My back was turned towards the rebel battery," he remembered, "when someone called my name in a quick warning tone. I instantly dropped flat on the ground, while the shell whistled directly over me. I raised my eyes in time to see it in its rapid flight to the rear—and turning, I saw where it had touched the brow of the hill close behind me."[49]

Some Federal participants found the experience darkly comical. Watching the green 89th Ohio traverse the most exposed portions of the route, Lt. Edward Scott in Company G observed that "the shells made the boys dodge considerable. It was rather amusing to see them. They would be going along on the 'double-quick' when a shell would come howling along just above them and down they would go, flat on the ground as it passed, then jump up and trot along on the 'double-quick' again. No one was hurt, although some of them came pretty close." Scott's comrade, Sgt. Jesse McClave, recorded the moment later that night: "I shall ever remember this day. We marched for miles in line of battle over broken ground sometimes under fire of batteries, sometimes on the double quick. We had a very hard time."[50]

As they drew near the main fight, Steedman's troops were exposed to all the sights that marked the wake of a great battle—many of them glimpsed by these men for the first time. Captain William Boyd, commanding Company C of the 84th Indiana, recorded those ghastly scenes in his field journal. "A rapid march of three miles through dusty lanes & over a low range of hills brought us in full view of . . . 'the dread field of battle.' All around us were sickening signs of a contest. The dead and wounded were lying in every direction, mingled with all

49 "Dear Sir & Comrade," George Dolton to Col. A. McMahan, February 3, 1890, Sullivan Collection, BGSU. See also Dolton, *The Path of Patriotism*, 77; Dolton, *Capsule History of Battery M*, CCNMP; Samuel Patton letters, copy in author's possession.

50 Entry for September 20, Diary of Edward Scofield Scott, as quoted in Bryan P. Weaver and H. Lee Fenner, *Sacrifice at Chickamauga: A History of the 89th Ohio Volunteer Infantry Regiment* (Moyweave Books, 2003), 103; Entry for September 30, Diary of Sergeant Jesse McClave, 89th Ohio website, http://www.89thohio.com/Mcclave/mcclave02.htm, accessed 5/19/2012.

the implements of war. . . . [F]rightened women and children hastened through our lines." Sergeant Murray of the 96th recalled the steady stream of wounded "going to the rear. Some . . . had their coats off [and] I could see where the ball had entered; their shirts were covered in blood. Others were limping along, while some seemed as though there were nothing the matter only they wanted to get out of the fight. One of these men, "a great big fellow," observed Murray, passed too close to the oncoming column. "General Stedman asked him where he was going and he said to the rear. 'No you don't,' said [Steedman]; 'you get right back into the ranks here and march right back.'"[51]

Even more upsetting were the dead and those unfortunate wounded too injured to escape the battlefield. Murray recalled with horror those men caught in the flames of the ground fires: "their clothes were burnt and the flesh crisping. Some had been wounded and crawled under a log for safety, but the leaves were all afire about them. I thought it was a terrible sight. General Whittiker rode by and he says, 'we will soon be there boys and give them H—.' He was a profane man."[52]

Another of the raw regiments hustling along here was the 78th Illinois of Mitchell's brigade, its members also keyed up by the prospect of approaching combat. Formed in August 1862, the unit had spent the past year in the rear guarding bridges and feuding with its colonel, William H. Benneson. A prewar attorney from Quincy, Illinois, Benneson soon found that the reality of military life did not match his naive illusions. A lackadaisical officer more often absent than present, Benneson was deeply resented by the rest of the command. The backbone of the 78th was in its other field officers: Lt. Col. Carter Van Vleck (another lawyer), and Maj. William Broaddus. A mechanic in civilian life, Broaddus at 39 was older than many of his fellow soldiers. He also had combat experience with the 16th Illinois and soon became the 78th's drillmaster. A petition drawn up by the 78th's company officers finally forced Benneson's resignation on September 2, 1863. None of the men in the ranks wanted to go into their first serious action under Benneson's questionable leadership, and

51 Entry for September 20, William A. Boyd Journal, University of California at Berkeley. Murray, *A Soldier's Reminiscences*, 25. The civilians Boyd encountered were probably locals who had taken refuge in the hollows behind the Snodgrass house, fleeing once again as the battle drew near.

52 Ibid.

now they would not have to; Van Vleck led them across the fields toward battle.[53]

Granger moved the division into Snodgrass Field about 1:30 p.m. By this time his column had lost much of its parade-ground appearance that had so impressed Sergeant Major Partridge. The march "was pretty hard on the men," admitted Lt. Edward Scott. "It was very dusty, quite warm, and no water, and they got scattered considerable while on the 'double-quick.'" Years later, Cyrus Pomeroy, also in the 96th, remembered the dust above all else: "ankle deep in the road," he wrote, "and being light as feathers, it rose in clouds so [thick] it was hard to discern a horse from a man a few feet distant." For the moment, however, the column could halt and let the stragglers catch up. Granger had finally found George Thomas.[54]

For Steedman's men of Granger's corps, reaching Thomas meant a brief respite. For Thomas, however, their arrival meant the end of the minutes of intense anxiety spent observing the unannounced and unlooked-for column. Granger had dispatched an aide to find Thomas to inform him of the approach of his Reserve Corps, but the messenger never arrived.

Granger's arrival on Snodgrass Hill is one of the most dramatic scenes of the battle. It has been described many times, and most of those descriptions draw heavily upon William Shanks's singular account of the incident recorded in 1866. According to Shanks, the first harbinger of this unlooked-for arrival was "a heavy cloud of dust in the distance" that drew Thomas's eye. Approaching from the northwest, "it might be the enemy, or it might be . . . Granger." Thomas had last communicated with Granger at 8:00 a.m., when he was still trying to shorten the distance between his own left flank and Granger's position. If these troops were Rebels, Thomas could only assume his other flank had been turned and the rest of the army was doomed. If they were Federals, his stand on Horseshoe Ridge could continue and the army might yet be saved. Shanks claimed that "the doubt . . . excited [Thomas's] nerves to an unusual degree." Thomas rarely showed much outward emotion, but now small quirks manifested his degree of strain. "The greater the tension the more

53 See Steve Raymond, *In the Very Thickest of the Fight: The Civil War Service of the 78th Illinois Volunteer Infantry Regiment* (Globe Pequot Press, 2012), 6-7, 12, 101-103, for details of the 78th's difficulties.

54 Weaver, *Sacrifice at Chickamauga*, 103-104; Cyrus Watson Pomeroy G.A.R. Questionnaire, Chicago History Museum.

Thomas fussed with his beard. Now it was standing out from his face at all angles." One of the officers watching the dust plume rising into the sky speculated that it might be enemy cavalry, already known to be on that flank. With the experience of long army service, Tom Wood dismissed that idea. "The dust rising above them ascends in thick misty clouds, not in spiral columns, as it would if the force was cavalry," Wood observed. Soon enough, the column came into view, proving Wood correct. Foot soldiers were approaching.[55]

John Beatty was also close at hand, holding impromptu command over that segment of the line adjacent to Harker. Like every other commander, Beatty's eye was drawn to the approaching force as "we saw way off to our rear the banners and glittering guns of a division coming toward us, and we became agitated by doubt and hope. Are they friends or foes?" Lieutenant Bierce's observation mirrored Beatty's: "What I saw was the shimmer of sunlight on metal: lines of troops were coming in behind us! The distance was too great, the atmosphere too hazy, to distinguish the color of their uniform, even with a glass." Now that the approaching troops could be observed directly, Thomas's agitation only increased. His hands shook as he raised his field telescope. After a minute, he turned to his staff and the other officers gathered around. "Take my glass, some of you whose horse stands steady—tell me what you can see." Looking through his own field glass, Shanks replied that he thought he saw the U.S. colors floating among the arrivals. "Do you think so? Do you think so?" demanded an impatient Thomas.[56]

Soon the column was close enough to dispatch a rider and end the uncertainty. Thomas sent Capt. Gilbert Johnson, who had been left behind when General Negley quit the field, and Lieutenant Bierce galloping out to ascertain once and for all the allegiance of the tramping infantry column. The riders were to wave their hats if the newcomers were friendly. More moments of mental agony ensued until Johnson reached the column and signaled with his hat: Granger was here. Thomas rode out to meet the Reserve Corps commander while Granger and Steedman rode forward to see where they were

55 Shanks, *Personal Recollections*, 68. Shanks wrote by far the most detailed description of the incident, and virtually all authors thereafter have drawn on his account. *OR* 30, pt. 1, 139; McKinney, *Education In Violence*, 249.

56 Beatty, *Citizen Soldier*, 341; Bierce, *Ambrose Bierce's Civil War*, 35-36; Shanks, *Personal Recollections*, 69. Bierce records that he was the first to see Granger's column and drew Thomas's attention to it, but the dust cloud would have been obvious to everyone long before any troops could be discerned.

needed. Thomas and Granger shook hands shortly before 2:00 p.m. Less Dan McCook's detached brigade, Granger's arrival added 3,819 desperately needed bayonets to Thomas's beleaguered line.[57]

While their commanders conferred, the men of the Reserve Corps caught their breath. Wood's men were no less happy to see them than Thomas. The new arrivals halted near Opdycke's 125th Ohio, with the Tigers delighted to note the presence of fellow Buckeyes. Two of Mitchell's regiments, the 113th and 121st Ohio, had friends in the 125th. More significantly, Lt. Col. Henry Banning, now in command of the 121st, had until the previous March been second-in-command of the 125th. A capable officer, Banning was transferred to the latter regiment to improve that command's discipline and training. He and Opdycke hailed each other warmly, while Banning was "greeted by cheers" from his old comrades.[58]

That visit was destined to be cut short. Initially, Steedman's troops seemed the ideal force to fill in the gap between Horseshoe Ridge and Kelly Field, but then, word came down the line of a new threat to Thomas's right. The new arrivals would go into action there.

57 W. H. Yoe, "Chickamauga," *National Tribune*, November 21, 1889; Beach, *History of the Fortieth Ohio*, 46; Bierce, *Ambrose Bierce's Civil War*, 36; Fullerton, "Reinforcing Thomas," 667.

58 Clark, *Opdycke Tigers*, 114.

Chapter Twenty

Johnson vs. Steedman:

Sunday, 2:00 p.m. to 3:00 p.m.

Bushrod Johnson's busy morning of combat and maneuver wasn't going to let up any time soon. A large portion of the Army of the Cumberland was on the run, and others were defending the high ground atop Horseshoe Ridge. Johnson was enough of a general to know those defenders had to be swept away quickly before their line could harden, and the best way to do it was to turn their right flank.

While Fulton's and Sugg's brigades harassed the retreating Federals near the Vittetoe house, Johnson beseeched assistance from any officer he came across. When none of his aides returned with help or even the promise of it, a frustrated Johnson ordered his men shortly after noon to hold their current position "at all hazards" and "galloped off in person in search of support." His journey brought him in contact with first General Kershaw and later Colonel Oates, but, as noted, neither encounter yielded the results he wanted. Additionally, the exasperated Johnson sent Capt. W. T. Blakemore off to find Coleman's (McNair's) command.[1]

Matters then took a turn for the better. Riding east on the Dyer Road, Johnson met Hindman and Patton Anderson, riding west on the same lane. As Johnson soon discovered, one of his many aides had already found and

1 *OR* 30, pt. 2, 460.

informed Hindman of Johnson's circumstance. Better yet, Hindman passed along Longstreet's latest orders to Johnson. After a quick conference Patton Anderson's brigade was detached to support Johnson's right, filling the gap between Johnson's division and Joe Kershaw's embattled left. Hindman's other two brigades under Generals Manigault and Deas would move farther west to prolong Johnson's left.

These dispositions would take time. As the ranking officer, Hindman took charge of the overall effort. He wisely ceded tactical control over the fighting to Johnson, who believed speed rather than complete preparation was of the essence—there was simply not enough time to wait for Deas and Manigault to get into position on the far left. His men would be rested, their ammunition replenished, and their canteens refilled by the time Anderson arrived. And when he did, he would attack.[2]

Lieutenant William Harder of the 23rd Tennessee recalled that "at 2:00 p.m. [Fulton's brigade] wheel[ed] to the right and advanced to the first ascent." As it did so, Fulton's men stumbled upon an unusual sight. Passing the Vittetoe cabin, Tennessee Cpl. Elijah Wiseman of the 17th remembered "the ladies of the house came out meeting us, waving their aprons and bonnets. We were almost worn out, but managed to give them a few cheers." By Sunday afternoon, Hiram Vittetoe had had his fill of Yankees. Wagons, caissons, and an abandoned Napoleon made a wreck of his yard. His fields were trampled flat, his animals scattered or killed, and his fences all destroyed for firewood or barricades. His family's plight moved Wiseman's commander, Lt. Col. Watt Floyd, to indulge in a bit of poetic license. For the past two days, noted Floyd, Vittetoe's wife and three daughters hid under the floorboards to avoid the "insults and dangers of the vandal foe." Now, Floyd effused, they ran out "shouting as I had never seen women shout before. Tear[s] of joyful sympathy started from many a soldier's eye," inspiring implied vows of "we will save you or die." Major Kleber M. Van Zandt, commanding the 7th Texas, also remembered the "women . . . rushing out, shouting and clapping their hands." Years later, back for the 1913 reunion, Van Zandt recalled meeting one of the daughters, who wanted to "thank him for driving the Yankees away."[3]

2 Ibid., 304, 460.

3 Harder Reminiscences, TSLA; Wiseman, "Tennesseans at Chickamauga," 205; *OR* 30, pt. 2, 482-483; Myres, *Force Without Fanfare*, 103-104.The Vittetoe name is variously spelled, the most common alternate versions being Viditoe, Vittitoe, or Vittatoe. For consistency, I have used the

In Sugg's brigade, Pvt. W. J. Davidson of the 41st Tennessee didn't get to meet any girls. Davidson was a skirmisher posted to protect the brigade's right flank. While everyone else got to rest, he was stuck with "this duty, though very tired and thirsty." When Johnson ordered the command forward "we advanced, cautiously, from tree to tree." Just 200 yards north of the cabin, the steep slope climbed more than 100 feet to Vittetoe Hill. Here, Johnson took a few moments to realign Sugg's formations, thrown into disorder by the upward scramble. The height was also an effective artillery platform. Its crest was about 150 yards wide and paralleled the main portion of Horseshoe Ridge 200 yards farther north. Johnson ordered up the nine guns of Capt. S. H. Dent's and Lt. William Everett's batteries and unlimbered them here. He also finally shifted two of Sugg's regiments—the 7th Texas and 50th Tennessee—back to Sugg's control; both units had fought under Fulton's direction since first stepping off that morning. Johnson was completing these arrangements when Patton Anderson's men came up on his right as expected. Johnson still lacked support on the left, where neither Deas nor Manigault had yet materialized.[4]

Johnson's spur was actually slightly higher than the main ridge, but a couple of steep ravines lay across the path to that next crest. Anderson's men, Mississippians all, were down in one of those draws deploying at the foot of Horseshoe Ridge where the Vittetoe Road angled abruptly southward from its generally western course. Both Johnson's and Anderson's men would face another rugged climb to reach their objectives.

Anderson's command bore the unusual nickname of the "High Pressure" brigade, reputed to have been bestowed at Shiloh by either Bragg or Albert Sidney Johnston. The exact origin remains murky. Like their commander, the men of the brigade were solid veterans, flushed with their recent success.[5]

Forming on the Vittetoe Road, Anderson's five Mississippi regiments and one battalion (the 7th, 9th, 10th, 41st, 44th, and 9th Battalion Sharpshooters) faced northwest at an obtuse angle to Johnson's line on the spur. Anderson's right was potentially at risk from the fire of the 21st Ohio occupying the western face of Hill Three. Anderson found he could not fit his entire brigade into the

---

spelling found in James Alfred Sartain, *History of Walker County, Georgia*, 2 vols. (Thomasson Printing and Office Eqpt. Co., Inc. 1972), vol. 1, 108.

4 W. J. Davidson, "Diary of Private W. J. Davidson," in Edwin L. Drake, ed., *The Annals of the Army of Tennessee and Early Western History*, 2 vols. (The Guild Bindery Press, n.d.), vol. 1, 367.

5 Mamie Yeary, comp., *Reminiscences of the Boys in Gray, 1861-1865* (Smith & Lamar, 1912), 717.

interval between Kershaw on his right and Johnson on his left. Only the 500 men of the 10th and 44th Mississippi could find room to form the initial line. The remaining 1,000 infantry of the 7th, 9th, and 41st regiments formed a support line. Major W. C. Richards was ordered to take the 134 men of his 9th Battalion Sharpshooters forward as skirmishers, "with instructions to move forward and draw fire." Once Anderson was set, Johnson ordered the entire line forward.[6]

The 21st Ohio watched both Anderson's and Johnson's preparations with growing alarm. The Ohioans had spent the time since Kershaw's last attack improving their own position and dealing with Confederate sharpshooters. A round fired by one of these trigger-pullers shattered several bones in Lt. Col. Dwella Stoughton's left shoulder. One fragment that had to be removed was three inches long. "I think this will about use me up," moaned Stoughton as he was borne off. "These joint wounds are dangerous." His last words to Adjutant Silas Canfield were to think of the regiment: "I want you to see that the men do their duty, for they have a hard fight ahead of them." Major Arnold McMahan, who inherited command, remembered this time taken up with "heavy skirmishing" as Anderson's sharpshooters got down to business.[7]

During the lull, Ohio Capt. Henry Alban of Company F, out on the 21st's right flank, realized what was coming. Alban wanted to swing his line back to meet the new threat. Originally, the 21st Ohio deployed along only the southeast side of Hill Three. "The regiment was drawn diagonally across the brow of the hill," Alban recalled, "with the right wing on the face next to the enemy." This deployment allowed the 21st's right to savage Kershaw's flank, but also left them vulnerable to exactly the kind of movement Johnson now intended. The 21st "suffered terribly in the two previous charges," Alban admitted, "having lost fully half [our] numbers in killed and wounded besides the usual number of Skulkers." With his part of the line so depleted and exposed, Alban wanted to bend the line back around the curve of the hill so it faced southwest. McMahan agreed, sending word back to Alban to "use his own discretion." Companies A and F moved quickly. As they did so, the skirmishing swelled into a larger engagement. Vance remembered the movement was "made with coolness, the men facing the foe and fighting as

6 Anderson's Brigade Tablet on Vittetoe Road, CCNMP; *OR* 30, pt. 2, 318, 321-322, 328.

7 R. S. Mungen letter, *Hancock Courier*, October 2, 1863; Canfield, *History of the 21st Regiment*, 118; OR *30*, pt. 1, 389.

they slowly moved back, until they got into the new position, the right wing refused and formed at almost right angles with the left." On the spur opposite, the Rebel artillery opened, and the Ohioans replied as best they could.[8]

In later years, young Lieutenant Vance came to regard this moment as one of the pivotal events of the battle. In 1889, he "considered [this] movement [to be] the one that saved the army from utter destruction," and put himself forward as the man who first saw the need, though he gave full credit to Alban for ordering the redeployment. In 1893 Vance further embellished his tale, asserting that "the importance of doing something at once was so great" that there was no time to wait for orders from McMahan. While acknowledging that Vance was "brave and did his duty well for his age and experience," Alban dismissed the younger man's grandiose claims of credit and downplayed the nature of the crisis. A practical, no-nonsense man, Alban informed McMahan that "the enemy were forming on our flank[.] There was not an enlisted man in my company that could not have seen that and comprehended the remedy. In fact, it would have been a downright disgrace for a man commanding a company not to have seen it . . . and . . . know what to do." As to Vance personally, Alban added that he "was rather amused at first at his claims . . . but his insinuations and arrogance have become really annoying."[9]

Alban was too modest. While the solution was obvious, carrying out the movement was another thing entirely. Already at Chickamauga, a dozen or more Union regiments had come to grief trying to execute similar maneuvers in the face of the enemy. Brannan's entire line unraveled in Poe Field under very similar circumstances. A limited retirement had a way of morphing into headlong retreat under fire. That did not happen to these Buckeyes, who performed superbly under trying circumstances. Despite Vance's and Alban's later quarreling, they both earned their shoulder straps that afternoon.

The 21st's shift was aided by the careful nature of the Rebel advance. Johnson realized the terrain made a concerted advance difficult. He estimated that Fulton's left flank was about 1,000 yards distant from the main ridge, but Sugg's men were much closer "on account of its curvature to the south."

8 "Dear Colonel," Letter of H. H. Alban to Arnold McMahan, June 12, 1889, Sullivan Collection, BGSU; Canfield, *History of the 21st Regiment*, 118, 143; Vance, "On Thomas' Right at Chickamauga," 93.

9 Wilson J. Vance, "Chickamauga," *Cincinnati Commercial Gazette*, May 25, 1889; Vance, "On Thomas' Right at Chickamauga," 93; H. H. Alban Letter, BGSU.

Anderson's men were also within about 300 yards of the crest of their part of the ridge, but their path would take them largely across the front of the Ohioans instead of directly at the Union line.[10]

Accordingly, in an effort to keep all three commands aligned, Johnson's advance was cautious and slow. On the left, the 17th Tennessee halted for a time on the spur until the artillery could open fire. While stopped, noted Lt. Col. Watt Floyd of the 17th, "I kept flankers well out on my left, as an occasional shot from the enemy's sharpshooters indicated danger from that quarter." Moving again, he reported, "we received the enemy's fire before we had gone 100 yards." Who was doing this shooting? There were no formed bodies of Federal troops west of the 21st Ohio at this time. The troops who retired with Negley or up the Dry Valley Road should have been well gone by now. These men were almost certainly anonymous, unidentified stragglers doing their best to serve as a last desperate rear guard. If so, they were unsung heroes who rendered an immense service to George Thomas and the Federal cause. Fearing their presence, Floyd advanced only far enough to "make a standing fight, and halted again." Apparently, neither Johnson nor any of his subordinate s officers realized they overlapped the Union flank by a wide margin. Had they pressed rapidly forward with vigor, the Confederates almost certainly would have taken Horseshoe Ridge without too much difficulty, and completely outflanked the 21st Ohio. Instead, Fulton cautiously dispatched a mere skirmish line forward to the main ridge.[11]

Sugg was similarly guarded. While Dent's and Everett's guns unlimbered on the spur to "secure its possession . . . [s]kirmishers were thrown out to ascertain the position and strength of the enemy. He was found to be in heavy force on the same ridge on my right." Behind that skirmish screen, Sugg's brigade formed in two lines, four regiments up front and two behind. As Sugg advanced, the 21st Ohio opened a heavy fire on his right, disabling yet another regimental commander in this hard-hit command. Lieutenant Colonel James D. Tillman of the 41st Tennessee went down with a shoulder wound. Tillman, only 22, was a proven combat officer whose loss would be a blow to the entire brigade. Sugg later reported that the enemy "was driven back," but in reality was

10 *OR* 30, pt. 2, 461. Johnson overestimated the distance. In reality, Fulton was about 600 yards from the ridge, while Sugg was within 300 yards.

11 Ibid., 483.

observing Capt. Henry Alban's redeployment of Companies A and F, the 21st Ohio.[12]

If Johnson's men were feeling their way forward warily, Anderson's men hurled themselves headlong into action. Johnson later described the Mississippians's advance as "a gallant and impetuous charge." Just prior to the final push, Anderson recalled the sharpshooter battalion, pulling it back behind the brigade to act as a curb against straggling. Then the 10th and 44th Mississippi surged northwest up the ravine and soon discovered that, instead of hitting the Yankee line squarely, they exposed their right flank to the Ohioans. Lieutenant Colonel James Barr, whose 10th Mississippi was on the left and somewhat ahead of the 44th, remembered driving the Yankee first line back—in reality, Alban's retirement viewed from another perspective—and coming upon a second Union line deployed across his now-exposed left flank. If Barr was confused, he had ample reason to be. He was now in the middle of a swirling firefight, with bullets ripping through his ranks from what seemed like every direction. Barr was pivoting to the northeast to more squarely face the 21st Ohio when Sugg's rightmost regiments moved up from his rear and, if not actually shooting into the backs of his men, began firing in their general direction. Dent's artillery was also throwing shells over the heads of the embattled Mississippians. Matters were further complicated when Barr turned to his right to find the 44th Mississippi firing across his front.[13]

Colonel W. H. Bishop and his 7th Mississippi began the attack behind the 44th, but once there was enough space on the right, Bishop shifted his regiment up alongside the 44th to extend that flank. The 7th "succeeded in gaining a position within a few feet of the crest," and clung there, trading shots with the Ohioans while waiting for the 10th and 44th to reorient their fronts. Anderson's advance had ground to a halt.[14]

The 21st Ohio was hanging on by the narrowest of margins. Anderson's line outnumbered the Buckeyes three-to-one, and even with the benefit of terrain and the enhanced firepower of their Colt rifles, McMahan's men were hard pressed. Even worse, two Rebel brigades were working their way around

12 Ibid., 495. Ed Gleeson, *Rebel Sons of Erin: A Civil War Unit History of the Tenth Tennessee Infantry Regiment (Irish) Confederate States Volunteers* (Guild Press of Indiana, 1993), 246; *OR* 30, pt. 2, 496.

13 *OR* 30, pt. 2, 462, 328, 324.

14 Ibid., 322.

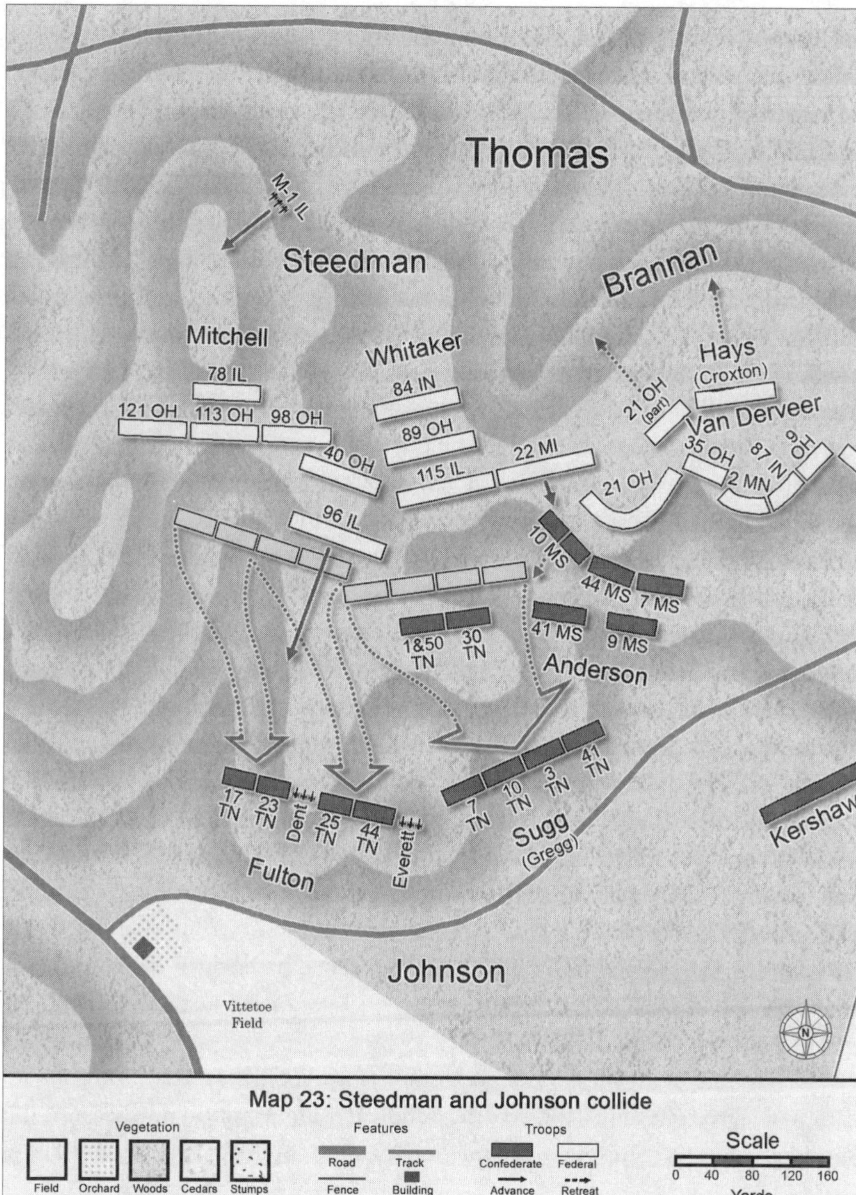

Map 23: Steedman and Johnson collide

the Union right essentially unopposed. No matter how cautiously Johnson pressed this advance, the 21st's position was doomed unless help arrived.

At least part of Johnson's caution was fueled by the fact that both Fulton and Sugg led seriously weakened brigades. Both had been engaged on September 18 and 19, and on this day had made repeated charges against Union positions and advanced several miles into the Federal rear. At the start of the morning they combined to field about 1,700 rifles. Losses and stragglers reduced that number to no more than about 1,200 men. As long as their advance remained unimpeded, they could again play a decisive role in the breaking of yet another Federal line.

Back by the Snodgrass farmstead, meanwhile, Generals Thomas and Granger conferred on their next move. Thomas had originally intended for Steedman to fall in on Wood's left and seal the gap between Horseshoe Ridge and Kelly Field. John Brannan, however, was alert to the fast-developing crisis on the right. Once the Rebel cannon opened, Brannan sent word that he needed help there immediately. Steedman's men were the only troops available to send. Fullerton recalled Thomas asking Granger if his men would be able to secure Brannan's right. "My men are fresh, and they are just the fellows for that work," snapped Granger, who anticipated a bloody job ahead. "They are raw troops, and they don't know any better than to charge up there."[15]

Thomas agreed, but pulled the 18th Ohio battery out of line behind Whitaker's brigade in the column to reinforce Harker's position. The 18th's commander was a 21-year-old captain named Charles C. Aleshire from Gallipolis, Ohio. That summer, Aleshire fell in love with Fannie Coldwell of Shelbyville, Tennessee, the daughter of a prominent Unionist family. The captain took his duties seriously; the newfound love would have to wait, and it would in no way soften his military demeanor. "Aleshire was a strict disciplinarian," recalled one of his men years later, so strict that one night his headquarters tent received "a terrific [and anonymous] bombardment of rocks" as a protest. However, with Miss Fannie now in the picture, Aleshire fretted that army life had coarsened him. Resolving to change, he decided to try and quit swearing. Now, as he told his mother, "when I get mad I just shut my mouth and grit my teeth."[16]

At Thomas's direction, Granger's chief of artillery, Col. James Thompson, commandeered Aleshire's Ohio battery and led it into position northeast of the Snodgrass house. The guns unlimbered next to Smith's Napoleons. Here,

15 John C. Smith, *Oration at the Unveiling of the Monument Erected to the Memory of Maj. Gen. James B. Steedman* (Knight & Leonard Co., 1887), 26; McKinney, *Education in Violence*, 249; Fullerton, "Reinforcing Thomas," 667.

16 "Dear Mother," Letter of September 4, 1863, Charles Aleshire Letters, Marshall University; C. C. Barton, "Bravest of Them All," *National Tribune*, July 16, 1903; "My Dear Mother," Letter of October 1, 1863, Aleshire Letters, Marshall University.

however, Aleshire found something to curse about, for Rebel small arms fire was already playing havoc with his men and livestock. "Bullets cannot be dodged," he explained, "[because] you never hear it whiz until after it has passed you. Shell may be dodged but seldom, and when you dodge them effectively, you must be watching the Enemys Battery from wherever they come. I never try to dodge any thing neither grape, canister, shell [n]or bullets, and if I should fall it will not be when dodging." There was space here for only four of his six pieces. "Double-shotted with canister," Aleshire opened fire within minutes of dropping trail. Because the right-hand section had no space to deploy, Aleshire ordered Lt. Albert S. Bierce to turn his guns around and rejoin Steedman's column on the way to reinforce Brannan.[17]

Ten Federal regiments hurried westward to help Brannan, as did Battery M and Bierce's section of the 18th Ohio, all marching or rolling along the low ground on the north side of Horseshoe Ridge. They moved in column of division, in a double line of regiments, as directed in Casey's *Manual.* Whitaker led the way, with the 96th Illinois still in front. Whitaker's two rear regiments, the 22nd Michigan and 89th Ohio, were not organic to his command. Both regiments had been left behind earlier in the campaign to conduct occupation duties, but during the general movement to the battlefield received orders to make for the front and temporarily attach to Whitaker's command. Colonel Heber Le Favour of the 22nd Michigan commanded the two orphaned units as a sort of demi-brigade under Whitaker's overall direction, at least in part because the brigade's line, with 1,300 men in the front rank, covered nearly 400 yards of frontage.[18]

Whitaker's men moved west through the fields and woods listening to the increasing intensity of the cannon and musket fire and watching the clouds of powder smoke rise above the ridge line off to their left. Their march carried them behind the embattled 21st Ohio, which from its position just below the crest on the south side of Hill Three was not directly visible to the new arrivals. Artillery fire dropped around them, over-shots from Dent's and Everett's Confederate batteries. Near the end of the march, Capt. William Boyd of the 84th Indiana caught sight of the enemy just then moving into place atop the ridge—"dusky columns of the Rebels were plainly visible . . . moving in the

17 Gracie, *The Truth About Chickamauga*, 406; "My Dear Mother," Letter of October 1, 1863, Aleshire Letters, Marshall University.

18 "My Dear Little Wife," Letter of September 15, 1863, Caleb Henry Carlton Papers, LOC.

same direction. It was just as visible that we were both approaching the same point."[19]

Major John Smith of the divisional staff was riding at Steedman's side. "We saw the enemy's line, which was pushing down the valley on our left, halt and front," recorded Smith. Steedman reacted quickly: the division must turn and attack. "Halt the first brigade," Steedman yelled at Smith, "front, and move up the hill on the double-quick." Smith galloped to Whitaker, while Capt. S. B. Moe was sent to Mitchell. Whitaker immediately formed his brigade for battle. Now, facing left, the front line consisted of the 96th Illinois on the right, the 115th Illinois in the center, and the 22nd Michigan on the left. In support, the 40th Ohio fell in behind the 96th; next came the 84th Indiana, and then the 89th Ohio. "Finally," noted Boyd from the ranks of the 84th, where he had a ringside seat, "the ball was opened on both sides presenting a sublime and dreadful spectacle."[20]

Lieutenant John W. Dove in Company G of the 115th Illinois watched as Steedman rode to the middle of the first line of Whitaker's brigade. "General Steedman riding very fast towards us," recalled Dove. "He passed the left of the regiment and rode on to the center." Halting in front of the 115th's color guard, Steedman waited for his staff to join him. As Captain Moe took careful note of the time, "Steedman's stentorian voice was heard above the roar of battle: 'Forward, the First Division! Double-quick, men, and give them h—l!'" The brigade surged forward. Steedman and his staff let the 115th pass around them and then followed up the ridge.[21]

Both Union and Confederate participants remembered the other side seizing the crest first. For most Confederates the stubborn defense made by the 21st Ohio, combined with the resistance put up by the anonymous stragglers, made it seem like the ridge line was already in Union hands. Johnson's advance had been so cautious and careful that only his skirmishers crested the ridge to look down on Whitaker's deploying battle line. Now the main lines of both sides were locked in a footrace to the crest. Perrin Cole of the 96th Illinois took

19 Entry for September 20, William A. Boyd Journal, UC Berkeley.

20 Smith, *Steedman*, 27; Partridge, *Ninety-Sixth Regiment Illinois*, 205; *OR* 30, pt. 1, 862-863; Entry for September 20, Boyd Journal, UC Berkeley.

21 J. W. Dove, "Chickamauga," *National Tribune*, March 13, 1884; Smith, *Steedman*, 27; I. H. C. Royce, "Iron Brigade at Chickamauga," *National Tribune*, December 31, 1908. Moe recorded the time as 1:10 p.m., which was almost certainly an hour too early based on the timing of other events.

note of the fact that the charge was made through "thin timber [of] large trees [and] no underbrush;" and even through the woods visibility was about two hundred yards, allowing the drama to be witnessed by all participants. Cole and his comrades could see Rebel skirmishers firing and falling back, heralding by their action the arrival of the main Confederate line. "Up the steep, corrugated ridge . . . across gullies and shallow ravines they rushed," remembered Sgt. Charles Partridge, also of the 96th. "A cheer was raised as the Confederate line came in full view, and in a moment every man . . . was yelling with all the voice he could command."[22]

Wild yelling spread from blue regiment to blue regiment until the entire division was in full voice. Lieutenant Isaac Royce of Company E, 115th Illinois, remembered it as the "Union Yell," a counterpoint to the overwhelming wave of sound known as the "Rebel Yell." If the Rebels were raising any clamor themselves, thought Royce, "we were making too much noise to hear it." The same roar heartened Lt. Robert Dilworth and his comrades in the 21st Ohio. "Then the Yankees charge," he recalled. "Just hear the chorus."[23]

Whitaker deployed his own skirmishers, but when the charge began they rejoined the main line almost immediately. "I shouted for the men to rally together as quickly as possible," recalled Capt. George Hicks of Company A, 96th Illinois. "By the time the company could be formed, our regiment with the rest of the brigade was abreast . . . and we resumed our place [in line.]"[24]

Mitchell's four regiments trailed Whitaker, and in the normal course of events would have formed on Whitaker's left. In his haste to confront the Rebels, however, Steedman halted Whitaker's brigade before it was fully beyond the 21st Ohio, leaving no room for Mitchell's regiments to form on the left. Mitchell's men kept moving west behind Whitaker and formed on his right in double line, with the 98th Ohio and 113th Ohio in the first line, left to right, and the 78th Illinois and 121st Ohio behind them. Within a short time Mitchell rethought his alignment and extended his front line by shifting the 121st up alongside the 113th, leaving only the 78th Illinois centered behind the line. This somewhat unorthodox deployment placed 771 of Mitchell's 1,124 men in the

22 P. P. Cole, "Wrote letter in Year 1863," *The Belleville Semi-Weekly Advocate*, September 21, 1910; Partridge, "The Ninety-Sixth Illinois at Chickamauga," 77.

23 Isaac Henry Clay Royce, *History of the 115th Regiment Illinois Volunteer Infantry* (Published by the Author, 1900), 128; Entry for September 20, Robert S. Dilworth Journal, OHS.

24 Partridge, *Ninety-Sixth Regiment Illinois*, 232.

Brig. Gen. Walter C. Whitaker (left), formerly of the 6th Kentucky, led his large brigade up the slope of Horseshoe Ridge and into a storm of fire. He was wounded in the stomach by a spent ball, and for a time relinquished command to Col. Thomas Champion of the 96th Illinois.
Miller, Photographic History

brigade front, leaving only 353 in support, but it increased the brigade's frontage to nearly 200 yards. Battery M, moving in "column of sections," followed behind, "receiving a broadside of bullets from the left and front" as it wheeled southward.[25]

Whitaker's front line scrambled up the hill well in advance of its own line of support; Mitchell's regiments lagged well behind Whitaker's advance. According to Captain Hicks, the 96th faced an "extremely hot fire . . . right up the ridge," and the combat intensified at the crest. Doctor Moses Evans, the 96th's surgeon, reported they met "a murderous fire of infantry and artillery at short range." Years later, Lieutenant Royce of the 115th Illinois described that moment at the summit: "As our lines rolled over the crest, the Confederates were in plain view . . . scarcely more than sixty yards distant. . . . We had the advantage, [since] every man presented a bright bayonet, while many of the Confederates . . . [lacked] that weapon." The Illinois troops "halted and gave them 'leaden hail.' Our fire was returned in the most terrible volleys."[26]

Private Samuel Patten observed this initial clash as a spectator, toiling along as he was with his fellows in Battery M. "Our men rushed forward with a shout," recorded Patten, to whom the horror of a pitched battle was something altogether new, "and when near the top of the hill, ran into an ambuscade of the enemy, whose columns in the form of a horse show [shoe] were concealed in the thick undergrowth." Ambush or no, Confederate fire scythed men out of the blue ranks. Whitaker and his staff, all mounted, were hard hit. Just two days earlier near Red House Bridge, Lt. George Pepoon witnessed his first man die in

25 *OR* 30, pt. 1, 867-868. Dolton, *Capsule History of Battery M*, CCNMP.

26 *Northwest Galena Gazette*, October 13, 1863; *Waukegan Weekly Gazette*, September 26, 1863; Royce, *History of the 115th Illinois*, 128; Entry for September 20, Isaac H. C. Royce Diary, InSL.

action. "It rather startled me," he confessed in a letter home to his sister. What was unfolding atop Horseshoe Ridge must have been rather more than startling, for men were now dropping all around him.[27]

Whitaker was struck in the stomach. "The effect was singular," wrote Captain Moe, who was with the general when the bullet found him. "It did not tumble him off his horse simply, but seemed to lift him right out of the saddle into the air. Supposing him killed or mortally wounded . . . [I] dismounted and went to him. The bullet had struck his sword belt, low down, had passed through it, and apparently . . . [penetrating] directly into the abdomen." Almost all stomach wounds were fatal, and Whitaker assumed his would be no different. Moe offered feeble reassurance, hoping that "it was not as bad as all that." Unbuttoning his coat and shirt, Whitaker attempted to give Moe a memorable final utterance, fitting for such a dramatic moment. "In the midst of these 'last words' the bullet dropped to the ground," explained the surprised captain. "The sight of it produced an immediate change in the mind of [the] General." Whitaker had been struck by a spent ball that badly bruised, but did not penetrate, his stomach. He was in no danger of dying, at least from this wound, but he was in considerable pain and set out for an aid station.[28]

Most of the rest of the staff were not so fortunate. "Gen. Whitaker had on Sunday morning six staff officers; two were killed on the field, two badly wounded, one taken prisoner. . . . I alone escaped uninjured," marveled Pepoon. "How I lived through that terrible storm . . . God only knows." One of the wounded was Capt. James Allen, "who was in the English army at the siege of Lucknow." One of those killed was Charles Aleshire's good friend Lt. Jerome B. Mason, who only that morning had a premonition of his own death when he told his orderly he would be shot. "Sure enough," Aleshire wrote, "he was killed while attempting to dodge a bullit. He was a brave fellow, I miss him much."[29]

27 Samuel Patton letters, http://cowanauctions.com/auctions/item.aspx?Itemid=3852, accessed 12/06/2013; "Dear sister Betsy," October 5, 1863, George Pepoon Letters, Northern Illinois University.

28 Beach, *History of the Fortieth Ohio*, 127; Partridge, *Ninety-Sixth Regiment Illinois*, 210.

29 "Dear sister Betsy," October 5, 1863, George Pepoon Letters; Partridge, *Ninety-Sixth Regiment Illinois*, 210; "My Dear Mother," October 1, 1863, Aleshire Letters. The siege of Lucknow was part of the Sepoy Rebellion of 1857 in British India, a fascinating action in its own right.

Steedman also went down when his horse was shot from under him and pitched the general headfirst onto rocky ground. Cut and bruised, Steedman "bled so freely" from his injured face that he "gave the appearance of having been badly wounded," recalled Sergeant Partridge of the 96th. Despite his "arms, hands, and face [being] severely torn, cut and bleeding, hatless, and with hair disheveled," Steedman was still full of fight and looked for another mount. For the moment, the Federal attack had been stripped of both its division and brigade commanders.[30]

The 22nd Michigan had an easier approach to the crest because at least part of the regiment was masked by the 21st Ohio's battle line. Wolverine Sgt. Marvin Boget never forgot the attack. "The 22nd was hustled into line and started for the front through woods and open fields, and a slashing of timber," he recounted to his grandson many years later. "While we were advancing the Rebel batterys was throwing shells and solid shot at us, but their aim was a little too high and the shot passed over our line." That soon changed. Cresting the ridge brought them into full view of the conflict and they merged with the embattled Ohioans. Severe fighting had swept so many men out of the 21st's ranks that to the Michiganders, the 21st appeared to be little more than a skirmish line clinging to the hill. The 22nd Michigan's left flank overlapped the 21st Ohio's right flank by a considerable margin, so many of the Wolverines were now charging through the ranks of these Buckeyes. "The Johnies were coming up the hill just as fast as we were, shooting and yelling at every jump. But when they met us at the brow," Boget explained with a boast, "back they went pellmell."[31]

One of those Wolverines cut a small figure. A private only four feet tall named Johnny Clem was serving as a regimental marker. He had turned 12 just the previous month, though when he formally enlisted as a regimental musician four months earlier he had lied and given his age as 13. John was wild to be in the war in 1861 at the age of just 10, but his father wisely refused his entreaties. Unable to garner parental permission, Johnny ran away from his Newark, Ohio, home several times until he was finally able to attach himself to the 22nd Michigan in the fall of 1862. The Michiganders adopted him as a mascot and before long the boy abandoned his drum for a cut-down musket and was now

30 Partridge, *Ninety-Sixth Regiment Illinois*, 210; Smith, *Steedman*, 28.

31 Marvin Boget Letter, 22nd Michigan file, CCNMP; Statement of William P. Hamilton, 22nd Michigan file, CCNMP.

serving in the ranks. Like the rest of the men in the regiment, he was going into action for the first time.[32]

Behind the 22nd Michigan, Lieutenant Bierce's section of the 18th Ohio battery had just caught up to the brigade. Bierce followed the 22nd Michigan "up the hill almost south of the [Snodgrass] house." Cresting the ridge filled the young artilleryman with dismay. The ridge was too narrow and steep to deploy any guns, and he had nothing to shoot at anyway because firing into the "almost hand to hand conflict" below him would kill as many Federals as Rebels. Bierce turned his section away and headed back down the northern slope and ultimately rejoined the rest of his battery.[33]

Bierce's abrupt decision, however, had unfortunate consequences. During his move up the hill, Bierce inadvertently slipped his guns between Whitaker's first and second lines, between which a considerable distance had opened. The 22nd Michigan, observed Col. Caleb Carlton of the 89th Ohio, was soon out of sight over the crest. A rising crescendo of "firing indicated that it was heavily engaged." Carlton halted his regiment in a "wooded ravine formed by spurs running northwest off the main ridge." The rest of Whitaker's support line on Carlton's right also went to ground, temporarily leaderless and without clear orders. After a few minutes of uncertainty, Carlton—mindful of Le Favour's request for the Ohioans to support the 22nd Michigan—decided to go forward anyway. It was just then that Bierce's gun section "came to the left about and moved rapidly to the rear." To avoid being run down by rumbling cannon wheels, Carlton moved his regiment rapidly by the "right oblique," a diagonal movement that shifted his unit out from behind the 22nd to a space between Whitaker's two center regiments, the front-rank 115th Illinois and the trailing 84th Indiana. The 89th halted just short of the ridge's brow. For the time being, Bierce's disruption took Carlton's men out of the fight, and left the 22nd Michigan bereft of any immediate support.[34]

32 A regimental "marker" was a person who went out to stand to mark the point where a movement would occur, such as the pivot point of a wheel. See also, Greg Pavelka, "Where Were You Johnny Shiloh?," *Civil War Times Illustrated*, vol. XXVII, no. 1 (January, 1989), 35-37. Pavelka does an excellent job of separating fact from fiction in examining the famous "Johnny Shiloh" Civil War legends concerning John Clem. Clem later claimed he had fought at Shiloh, Perryville, and Stones River, but the 22nd Michigan was not engaged in any of those fights.

33 Gracie, *The Truth About Chickamauga*, 406.

34 "Dear Colonel," August 8, 1889, Caleb H. Carlton to Colonel Arnold McMahan, Sullivan Collection, BGSU; Carlton Papers, LOC.

Meanwhile, out on Whitaker's right flank, the 96th Illinois summited the ridge opposite Bushrod Johnson's artillery spur. Brought up short by the sight of Fulton's and Sugg's Rebels, the 96th halted and, as Captain Hicks narrated, "brought our Enfield rifles into active play." The intense incoming fire proved no less dangerous for regimental officers than it had been for brigade staffers. Colonel Thomas Champion of the 96th lost his horse, Lt. Col. Isaac Clarke was mortally wounded with a shot in the chest, and, remembered Partridge, "all along the line wounded men were running to the rear, sometimes in such numbers" that it looked like "the line itself was giving way." The survivors immediately sought cover, flattening and struggling to return the withering Confederate fire.[35]

Fortunately for the 96th, Mitchell's brigade was coming up on their right to menace Fulton's flank. Sergeant John L. Erwin was elevated to command the 98th Ohio's Company F when its captain was wounded in the leg early in the advance. As the 98th crested the ridge, Erwin noted Whitaker's Federals heading for the rear in numbers so heavy he thought both the 96th and its supporting regiment, the 40th Ohio, had "given way." When the 98th engaged, noted Erwin "[our] fire must have been exceedingly destructive, as we were practically face to face with the enemy and . . . we were not troubled by a [return] fire in front." The advance up the ridge opened a gap in Mitchell's front between the 113th and 121st Ohio; Mitchell filled that hole with the 78th Illinois. With his entire brigade now formed in a single line, his frontage extended well beyond Fulton's left flank.[36]

Mitchell's men did not come away unscathed. As they moved to the front, noted Illinois Lt. Col. Carter Van Vleck, the "loss in wounded was severe." Tragically, Van Vleck's good friend Maj. William Broaddus was killed almost instantly when a bullet tore into his jawbone and ripped through his neck. Broaddus was extremely popular, so much so that after the fight the regimental officers drafted a resolution affirming his soldierly and patriotic qualities in an effort to comfort his widow. Resolutions to widows would have to wait, however, for there was still much fighting to be done.[37]

35 *Northwest Galena Gazette*, October 13, 1863; Partridge, "The Ninety-Sixth Illinois at Chickamauga," 77; Partridge, *Ninety-Sixth Regiment Illinois*, 233.

36 J. L. Erwin, "The Battle of Chickamauga," *National Tribune*, November 29, 1925; J. L. Erwin Memoir, 98th Ohio file, CCNMP; *OR* 30, pt. 1, 869.

37 *OR* 30, pt. 1, 869; "Resolution," Broaddus Papers, DU.

From the ranks of the 23rd Tennessee of Fulton's brigade, Capt. William Harder described the effect of Mitchell's fire: "We advanced a short distance up the [slope] when an overwhelming volley poured on us from the top, in a semicircle completely enfilading our line." The stunned Confederates halted and began to shoot back in multiple directions. General Johnson attempted to substitute bullets for men by directing Fulton's regiments to fire "obliquely to the left," which seemed to check the Yankees for the moment. The respite proved fleeting. Fulton's line could not deal with all the threats facing it, and his formation began to unravel. Major G. M. Crawford, commanding the 44th Tennessee, acknowledged that the Federal fire "became so severe and deadly that the regiment fell back 100 or 200 yards." To some, that retreat was more of a rout: "the men . . . fled over the turn of the hill to the rear," complained Harder, who suddenly found himself alone on his part of the line.[38]

Seeing Rebels in retreat, Colonel Champion ordered the 96th Illinois to charge. Captain Hicks reported the 96th responded with enthusiasm, "running and yelling and again driving the enemy." In doing so, however, the Illini angled to the right, charging along the relatively flat ground of the spur. This drift opened a gap of some 200 feet between themselves and the 115th Illinois, and carried the 96th Illinois directly into the muzzles of the two Rebel batteries—Dent and Everett. Champion's men drifted so far to the right they moved entirely across the front of the 98th Ohio to mask most of the 113th Ohio. And there, just a handful of yards short of the Rebel gun line, murderous blasts of artillery brought the charging Illini to a bloody halt. "We went forward in the face of an awful fire from the batteries and musketry," wrote Orson Young of Company D. "We went on until we were directly under the cannon mouth when we were so tired out that the whole line was compelled to stop."

Private Perrin Cole was knocked nearly senseless when a Rebel shell dropped a tree limb on his head, "which in turn dropped me." Men were falling all around him. Cole clearly heard a comrade utter, "there goes another one." "Not this time," barked Cole, scrambling back to his feet for a few short seconds before the regiment went prone once more as the men sought cover in an effort to make a stand. Private Cyrus Pomeroy of Company K remembered that he "held this advanced position until I had fired my gun nine times, not knowing that in front of us were seven massed batteries." The regiment, however, was rapidly disintegrating. Champion tried his best to hold the

38 Harder *Reminiscences*, TSLA; *OR* 30, pt. 2, 461-462, 493.

wavering line to its task yelling, "Don't move men! Keep where you are! Hold your position!"[39]

"There was a Rebel battery right in front of us, supported by infantry, and they poured galling fire into our ranks," recalled Sgt. Edward Murray of Company C, 96th Illinois. "Our lines were broken and the boys got behind logs and trees, as protection. The roll of musketry on both sides and the discharge of the cannon . . . was deafening. Then the officers, at the top of their voices, giving the word of command. It was a perfect pandemonium."[40]

Sugg's Confederates were also thrust back by the impetuosity of Whitaker's assault. Sugg had angled his line to face the 21st Ohio when the 115th Illinois and 22nd Michigan appeared. Their sudden arrival crumpled Sugg's right wing, flanked by the 115th's fire sweeping the length of Draw Three. Now Sugg's left was in jeopardy. He ordered the 3rd Tennessee, 50th Tennessee, and 7th Texas back to the Rebel gun line, where he intended to reform his entire brigade. Doing so, however, left the 10th and 30th Tennessee regiments exposed. Yet another regimental commander went down here. Colonel William Grace of the 10th, commanding both his own and the 30th, had his horse shot from under him. Grace hit the ground hard and aggravated a back injury from a similar mishap a year earlier. When he discovered the pain was so bad he could not rise, Grace lay helpless in the face of the oncoming Federals. Sharpshooters from the 10th Tennessee halted to screen their colonel until he could be rescued. Lieutenant Robert P. Seymour, one of the few officers still mounted, dragged Grace up over his own saddle to the cheers of the rest of the 10th, and doubtless the agonizing groans of his injured chief.[41]

Colonel Jesse Moore's 115th Illinois did not follow Champion's 96th Illinois in its charge to the right. Moore understood his mission at the brigade's center was to serve as a guide for both flank regiments in order to keep the main battle line intact. Unfortunately, neither flank regiment guided on Moore. The 22nd Michigan proved no less impetuous than the 96th. With Rebels tumbling

39 Partridge, *Ninety-Sixth Regiment Illinois*, 233; Henry Gayle to Gen. H. V. Boynton, April 30, 1900, 96th Illinois file, CCNMP; "Dear Parents," September 24, 1863, Orson V. Young Papers, Lake County Discovery Museum, Wauconda, IL; Cole, "Wrote letter in Year 1863," *The Belleville Semi-Weekly Advocate*, September 21, 1910; Pomeroy GAR Questionnaire, Chicago History Museum; Partridge, *Ninety-Sixth Regiment Illinois*, 234. The chaos of battle confused Pomeroy, who counted each individual Rebel gun as a "massed battery."

40 Murray, *A Soldier's Reminiscences*, 26.

41 *OR* 30, pt. 2, 496; Gleeson, *Rebel Sons of Erin*, 247.

back before them, the Wolverines gave chase, moving down into Draw Three at a leftward angle, drawn by the promise of rolling up the flank of an enemy brigade (Anderson). With the 96th moving right and the 22nd moving left, Whitaker's brigade front fragmented into its three component parts. A frustrated Moore halted his 115th Illinois near the crest, where Sgt. Frank Gates of Company K recalled "the bullets of our own and the enemy's guns . . . bark[ed] the trees and [tore] up the earth and gravel around us at a fearful rate."[42]

Given his circumstances, Moore decided to retreat. "Being hard pressed and much fatigued in connection with the front line," he reported, "I caused my regiment to fall back . . . and form in the rear of the second line." His calm description put a good face on the movement. In reality, the regiment, like the others in Whitaker's first line, was unraveling in the face of intense enemy fire and the exhaustion of their uphill charge. The 89th Ohio lay directly behind the 115th, still on the reverse slope of the ridge, and thus relatively sheltered. "Here came an Illinois regiment down the hill Pel Mel [sic] with the rats right behind," was how Ohio Pvt. Thomas Doughman recalled the withdrawal. "We were under a very hot fire here; the air above us seemed literally filled with missiles of all sorts. We had been lying here but a few minutes when the line in front . . . commenced falling back, and as the enemy continued driving them, retreated right over our Regiment," recorded fellow Buckeye, Lt. Edward Scott. Colonel Carlton lost his horse here, killed out from under him, but the uninjured officer immediately commandeered the mount of a corporal named Allen from Wilder's brigade, who for some reason happened to be nearby.[43]

Some distance ahead and to the 89th Ohio's left, the 22nd Michigan did not stop or even slow when it crested the ridge and moved partially through the 21st Ohio. Colonel Le Favour, who was still expecting the 89th Ohio to appear behind him, personally stopped to direct Carlton into a position to support his Wolverines. His decision left immediate command of the advancing 22nd to Lt. Col. William Sanborn. Whatever other leadership qualities Sanborn possessed, he was vocally ill-equipped to lead a regiment amid the tumult of combat. Sanborn "had a very poor voice, and when we reached the summit we did not

42 F. W. Gates, "Chickamauga" *National Tribune*, April 7, 1887.

43 *OR* 52, 83; Entry for September 20, Doughman Diary, BGSU; Weaver and Fenner, *Sacrifice at Chickamauga*, 104; Carlton Papers, LOC. Carlton gives no explanation for why or how Allen was there. Perhaps he was serving as a courier.

hear his orders to halt," recalled Lt. George W. Button. This impetuosity now proved costly. The Wolverines turned southeast into the ravine and pitched into the left flank of Anderson's Rebel line, but in doing so exposed their own right flank to Everett's Georgia guns and the small arms fire from parts of Sugg's reforming brigade.[44]

The unintended consequence of the 22nd's movement provided a brief respite for the beleaguered 21st Ohio. Lieutenant Vance remembered his relief when he spotted the approaching Michigan regiment. The Wolverines "came sweeping up, with ringing cheers and splendid courage," he recorded. "[T]hey swept on and over us, driving the enemy far back . . . [giving us] time to get our breath, re-dress our line, and prepare for more fighting." Captain John Atkinson of the 22nd's Company C thought his regiment drove the Rebels nearly half a mile, when in fact the Michigan men pushed them back perhaps 300 yards, sweeping southeast to a point near the Vittetoe Road at the foot of Hill Three.[45]

Patton Anderson's Mississippi brigade was already in some difficulty when the 22nd Michigan appeared. Lieutenant Colonel Barr's 10th Mississippi on the front-left was unraveling, beset by incoming fire from several directions, and much of it from friendly muzzles. On Barr's right, the 44th Mississippi's line lay at an angle to his own, laying a fire across his front that effectively precluded any farther advance. On the far right of the front line, Colonel Bishop's 7th Mississippi clung to the southern slope of Hill Three, unable to press ahead. Private Reuben Mills of the 44th remembered this as the worst place of the day: "It was here that my company lost 26 men in as many minutes," he mourned. And then the Wolverines appeared.[46]

The 22nd Michigan came up and over the crest, slamming into the exposed left of Barr's 10th Mississippi. Overwhelmed and "seeing my regiment nearly surrounded," Barr called for a retreat. His abrupt retirement pulled Colonel Sharp's 44th Mississippi back with him toward the road "in confusion." Bishop's 7th Mississippi knew nothing about the new threat on its left until both the 10th and 44th were scrambling rearward in near-panic down the hill. Major John C. Thompson of the 44th tried to stem the retreat, fearing his men

44 Gracie, *The Truth About Chickamauga*, 433, fn. 1.

45 Vance, "On Thomas' Right at Chickamauga," 93-94; John Robertson, comp., *Michigan in the War* (W. S. George and Co., State Printers, 1882), 424.

46 Anonymous, "The Autauga Guards in the Civil War," *Prattville Progress*, August 8, 1928.

This famous photograph shows Sgt. Andrew M. Chandler of Company F, 44th Mississippi, along with his servant Silas. Andrew was wounded in the right leg and ankle at Chickamauga and crippled for life. He probably fell here on Horseshoe Ridge, where the 44th Mississippi suffered its most serious losses of the day. *Library of Congress*

were "showing the White Feather." His efforts ended when a bullet to the head killed him instantly. The retreat was now a rout. At 73, Thompson was almost certainly the oldest casualty of the battle and may have been the oldest combatant on either side. He started the war as a private in the 44th Mississippi when it was still known as Blythe's Regiment. Wounded at Shiloh, Thompson recovered and was elected major. He helped lead his command up—but not back down—the forbidding slopes of Horseshoe Ridge.[47]

Having helped rout three regiments of Mississippians, the 22nd Michigan found itself in a great deal of trouble. Elated with their success, some of the

47 *OR* 30, pt. 2, 324, 327; *Montgomery Daily Advertiser*, August 6, 1905; W. H. Lee, "Major John C. Thompson of Mississippi," *Confederate Veteran*, vol. XVI, no. 11 (November, 1908), 588.

Brig. Gen. James B. Steedman (left) was a political general, unruly and undisciplined by West Point standards but outstanding in the field. When he was thrown from his horse and bleeding profusely, Steedman insisted his staff make sure the newspapers spelled his name correctly should he be killed

Battles and Leaders

Wolverines pursued the Rebels as far as the Vittetoe Road, only to share the experience of earlier counterattacks when rallied Confederates poured a fire into the ranks of overeager Federals. "[They] charged us once," noted Mississippi Lt. Otis Baker in the 10th, "but were repulsed with heavy slaughter." Worse than the Mississippians lining the road, however, was the raking fire delivered by Everett's cannon and Sugg's musketry. The 22nd Michigan followed the natural drift of the ravine, thus turning its formation roughly perpendicular to Johnson's line atop the spur. During this effort to reorient their line, the Wolverines were shot to pieces. Lieutenant Colonel Sanborn struggled to regain control of his headstrong troops as he followed his men down the slope. He was pushing his way to the front and calling on them to stop when enemy fire shredded his foot and ankle.[48]

Command of the 22nd Michigan passed to Company B's Capt. Alonzo Keeler because Colonel Le Favour was still well behind them trying to coordinate the other half of his demi-brigade. Keeler made his way to the colors hoping to rally the regiment, but he found only slaughter. Years later, Keeler could still recall the moment in terrible detail: "Color Sergt Philo P. Durkie . . . was struck in the breast by a grape shot. . . . Corporal Richard A. Stansell took the flag from [Durkie's] dying grasp . . . and gave his [own] life for the flag, a musket ball passing through his brain. Corporal Pearl Mitchell raised the flag amidst the storm of shot . . . that soon carried away his left arm. Corporal Jonathon Vincent . . . rushed for the flag and defiantly waved it in the face of the enemy. He fell severely wounded." Every man of the color guard fell here, killed

48 Sunday, September 20, T. Otis Baker Diary, Mississippi Department of Archives and History, Jackson, MS. Hereafter MDAH; Gracie, *The Truth About Chickamauga*, 432.

or wounded, leaving both flags in the hands of Capt. John Atkinson's Company C. The 22nd struggled to hang on, their time in action so far having been about 15 minutes. Of the 455 men who began the charge, remembered William P. Hamilton, nearly "one third of our brave fellows went down" during this fighting. "Death Reigned—my dear friend was killed. I am slightly wounded," wrote Pvt. John J. Snook that night. When Le Favour appeared, he ordered Keeler to withdraw the 22nd up the ridge and fall in behind the 21st Ohio. A grim carpet of mixed blue and gray dotted the southern slope of Hill Three.[49]

Fortunately for the 22nd, Caleb Carlton and the 89th Ohio were now at the crest, having weathered the passing storm of the 115th Illinois's retreat. With their front now clear, and using the rear slope of the crest as a parapet, Carlton's Buckeyes opened fire on Sugg's Rebels to prevent any similar riposte. Private Doughman remembered that Carlton sent the 89th's flags back out of sight behind the crest as the regiment engaged. "We proceeded to fight them laying down," he recalled. "Our colonel had already instructed us to shoot at the collar berars. . . . We succeeded in checking them." Carlton had little choice but to spread his ranks dangerously thin to fill the gap left by both the absence of the 22nd Michigan and 115th Illinois. Captain William C. Russell of Granger's staff joined Carlton on the ridge at the height of this engagement. When Carlton explained his actions thus far, recalled Doughman, Russell affirmed the colonel's decisions: "'Granger told Steedman to put you here, so you are where you are wanted,'" yelled back Russell. "As the captain was riding away he was killed, and four men of the 89th were sent to take his body to the rear." The captain's death left Granger deeply shaken. His loss, admitted the general, was "severely felt."[50]

After initially supporting the 115th Illinois, the 84th Indiana also shifted west and at some point held the ridge to Carlton's right, though only briefly. The 84th had just started to move down the south slope (somewhere between the 115th Illinois and the 96th Illinois) when, in Capt. William Boyd's words, "there were the enemy." Now "the fight became warm. Many [men] were falling

49 As quoted in Robert D. and Cheryl J. Allen, *A "Guest" of the Confederacy: The Civil War Letters & Diaries of Alonzo M. Keeler, Captain, Company B, Twenty-Second Michigan Infantry, including letters & diaries written while a prisoner of war* (Cold Tree Press, 2008), 57. This passage is taken from an undated but obviously postwar battle report found in the Alonzo M. Keeler Papers, Bentley Historical Library, UMich. Gracie, *The Truth About Chickamauga*, 432; Robertson, *Michigan in the War*, 424; Entry for September 20, John J. Snook Diary, Lester Mange Collection, WMU.

50 Doughman Recollections, BGSU; Carlton Letter, BGSU; *OR* 30, pt. 1, 856.

all around me. . . . The Rebels were [with]in a few feet of us & it appeared to me we were slaying them in fine style. I was busily engaged in directing the men to fire to the right when I suddenly discovered I was almost entirely alone." The realization mortified the blunt-spoken, no-nonsense Hoosier. "My first impression was that the 84th was routed and disgraced forever," admitted Boyd. "I followed them at my leisure, seeing no danger." Colonel Nelson Trusler admitted "the fire . . . became so heavy that my regiment fell back in immediate disorder." The 84th's retreat left a gap of "from one to two hundred y[ar]ds from the right of the 89th." This hole would give Carlton reason to worry for the rest of the afternoon.[51]

Once the 84th halted in the lee of the ridge, Captain Boyd worked to reconstitute the regiment. When he got word Colonel Trusler was doing the same thing a little to the right, Boyd dutifully ordered his fragment to rejoin Trusler's group. Half of Whitaker's brigade was busy reforming on the north slope of the ridge when the 84th joined the 22nd Michigan and 115th Illinois there. In the absence of higher command, brigade staffer Maj. John C. Smith was also trying to rally these men. Still mounted, Smith sent Lieutenants Pepoon and J. B. Hayes along the line of the 115th Illinois to reorganize that command. Into this drama strode General Steedman, bloodied and battered from his fall and still dismounted, but determined to reorder his troops. His demeanor mesmerized Major Smith. Steedman, he recalled, was "stern, angry, and defiant. . . . Hatless, and with hair disheveled, that magnificent form of his seem[ed] to tower giant-like above all the rest." The division commander seized the colors of the 115th and ordered its survivors back up the hill to the front line.[52]

As the 115th moved off, Smith rode up next to his division commander and offered up his horse as he dismounted. "General, if you should be killed and I survive you," asked Major Smith, "what disposition do you wish made of your body and effects?" Steedman brushed the staff officer's concern aside. "I shall not be killed. We shall both live through this battle, and whip Hell out of them yet!" With that, Steedman mounted the animal and was about to ride away when he yanked the reins and spun the horse around. "Yes, Major, I have a

51 Entry for September 20, Boyd Journal, UC Berkeley; 84th Indiana Report, Indiana State Adjutant General Records, InSL; Carlton Papers, LOC.

52 Carlton Papers, LOC; Smith, *Steedman*, 28. This is perhaps the first of several "flag incidents" involving Steedman seizing regimental colors to rally or lead a unit.

request to make. If I am killed . . . see that these damned newspaper reporters spell my name correctly!"[53]

All alone out on the spur, meanwhile, Colonel Champion's 96th Illinois could hang on no longer. On Champion's right, Mitchell's brigade had halted on the crest and remained there. Farther east on his left, the 115th Illinois and 84th Indiana were already gone. The 22nd Michigan, even then being shot to pieces in Draw Three, would soon follow. Champion and the 96th Illinois could not know the fate of the Wolverines, but the overall disintegration of Whitaker's front line was certainly apparent. By this time the 96th was again prone, facing what Captain Hicks remembered as "a fearful storm of canister . . . and showers of Minie balls." Describing their position, Pvt. Henry Gayle remembered that "the crown of the hill where we then fought was about the same as an ordinary street pavement, and the men laid flat, and rolled over to load." Recognizing the obvious, Champion ordered a retreat, urging his men to "Fall back. Keep to your colors! Don't scatter! Keep to your colors! Keep your line!" In his report, the colonel noted only that the regiment "fell back about 500 or 600 yards, and reformed."[54]

In reality, the 96th temporarily dissolved. "The brigade line was already badly broken," Captain Hicks recalled, "and we could not keep the regiment line intact." In Company H, Sgt. Michael Hileman was nearly left behind. Johnson's Confederates were shooting at them "with awful havoc," noted Hileman, when "Captain [Joseph L.] Pierce, upon looking around, saw our men retreating pell mell . . . 'God, Sergeant,'" shouted Pierce, "'look where the men are!' Then we turned in a hurry. . . . I expected every moment to be the last one for us on this earth. My left hand comrade was hit in the head by a shell, which completely opened it, spattering his brains and blood all over me. It was too horrible for words." The 96th Illinois broke into two distinct fragments, each headed in different directions. Led by Champion, one bit retreated diagonally to

53 Smith, *Steedman*, 28. There are two versions of this story. Joseph T. Woods, *Steedman and His Men at Chickamauga* (Blade Printing Company, 1876), 55, has this comment passing between Steedman and Granger. Both Smith's and Woods's accounts are potentially flawed, but Woods makes a greater effort to portray Granger as a kindly old fool. He wished to contrast Steedman's and Granger's demeanor, and this incident did so in dramatic fashion. Also, Steedman and Granger were not together much after the initial meeting with General Thomas, and it is unlikely this conversation took place there. Steedman's name was pronounced "Steadman," and like any smart politician, he was always concerned about getting it spelled right.

54 Partridge, *Ninety-Sixth Regiment Illinois*, 234; Gayle Letter, CCNMP; OR 30, pt. 1, 865.

the northeast, back down their path of advance toward the 40th Ohio. Hicks and the larger remnant fell back due north and commingled with the ranks of the 113th Ohio.[55]

Company C's Sergeant Murray did not retreat. Murray had just discharged his weapon and rolled over onto his left side to reload when "a ball struck me between the shoulders near the right side of the spine." The round paralyzed him from the waist down, "rendering me perfectly helpless while the battle continued." Private William B. Lewin, a neighbor from back home in Newport Township, tried to help his friend but was unable to lift his sergeant's "dead weight." The unfortunate Murray would spend the rest of the day sprawled between the lines, where he would be hit twice more and survive to tell the tale. The second round entered his "left shoulder, coming out near the elbow on the inside of the arm. . . . I shut my eyes and brought my canteen up to my face as a kind of protection for the balls were falling thick as a hail storm. Another ball hit me on the flesh part of my hip." For Murray, these were only the first hours of a very long ordeal.[56]

The 40th Ohio marked the left of Whitaker's support line, now bolstered by the arrival of the 98th Ohio (Mitchell's brigade) on its right. Colonel Champion and his portion of the 96th slipped between the two units and, like so much of Whitaker's command, set about the business of forming up. Champion was rallying his men when he discovered Whitaker was down, meaning he was now in command of the brigade. Sending word to Captain Hicks to take overall charge of the 96th, Champion rode off to take up his new duties.[57]

In the 40th Ohio, Sgt. Isaac Doan recalled a pattern that marked the regiment's first clash and set the tone for the rest of the day: "Our front line was driven back from the crest of the ridge, over the rear line which was lying some thirty yards down the northern slope. . . . [A]s soon as the front line passed over them [we] would leap to our feet, and with a yell and murderous volley . . . hurl them back as quickly as they came."[58]

55 Partridge, *Ninety-Sixth Regiment Illinois*, 234; Michael Hileman memoir, http://www.rootsweb.com/~usgenweb/sd/buffalo/hileman.html, accessed 3/11/2010.

56 Murray, *A Soldier's Reminiscences*, 27.

57 Partridge, *Ninety-Sixth Regiment Illinois*, 186.

58 Isaac C. Doan, *Reminiscences of the Chattanooga Campaign: A Paper Read at the Reunion of Company B, Fortieth Ohio Volunteer Infantry, at Xenia, O., August 22, 1894* (J. M. Coe's Printery, 1894), 6.

The 98th Ohio was lagging behind, recalled Sergeant Erwin of Company F, because part of the regiment "faltered for a moment when Capt. [Moses J.] Urquhart . . . was severely wounded in the right ankle" during that first advance. Adjutant Duncan Milner witnessed Urquhart's wounding, thought the injury would cost Urquhart his leg, and realized it was now his task to notify the next in command. Milner located Capt. Armstrong Thomas of Company H, next in seniority, but as Milner later related, he was conveying the news when "a bullet entered [Thomas's] eye . . . and he dropped dead at my feet. I then carried the orders to Captain [William C.] Lochary." While passing the 40th, another of Granger's staff officers was hit. Many years later, Pvt. William H. Smyth still recalled how the officer nearly fell on him when shot off his horse in front of Company H; Smyth never learned the man's identity. Adjutant Milner, scrambling back up the rear slope of the ridge, found the officer, whom he later mistook for the deceased Captain Russell. "I called some soldiers and with their assistance . . . laid him out right at the turned up root of a tree, took his field glasses, watch and papers from his body and left him there." Milner returned to the 98th Ohio, and there entered what he described as "the most terrific part of the conflict."[59]

Private Oliver Smith of Company G agreed. "Our regiment's first job was to drive the rebels off on a point where they had just forced our men from. We had one of the hottest places ever a regiment of men went into but we drove them back and gained the point," wrote the private. "When we first charged on them, our lines was only about twenty yards apart so you may know that it was a hot place."[60]

Farther to the right, Hicks and the bulk of the 96th Illinois ran completely through the 113th Ohio, badly disrupting that regiment. These Buckeyes had already been taking heavy fire from the Rebels to their left front. Artillery shells thrown at the 96th were also landing in their midst. Lieutenant Colonel Darius B. Warner, leading the 113th, remembered the Illinoisans bursting through his ranks, shouting "Retreat, Retreat!" "Then and there," he wrote, "I wished I

59 Erwin Memoir, CCNMP; Duncan C. Milner Reminiscences, "War Chapter," 21, Illinois Historical Survey, University of Illinois, Champaign; W. H. Smyth, "Holding Snodgrass Hill," *National Tribune*, September 14, 1922; In his postwar reminiscences, Milner identified this officer as Russell, but as noted above Colonel Carlton of the 89th Ohio places Russell's fall on his regimental front. At the time, it is unlikely that Milner knew the stricken officer's identity.

60 Letter of Private Oliver Smith, as quoted at: http://www.mojaveweblog.com/98thOVI/index.html, accessed 3/20/2010.

could die. My men wavered and fell back half way down the hill." To Ohio Sgt. Francis McAdams in Company E, it seemed that for "a brief time, the utmost confusion reigned." Quickly, however, Warner and the other officers rallied the 113th, narrowly averting an abject panic. Now the Ohioans went up the hill much more cautiously. The next day, Pvt. Jasper Hall described that moment: "We were ordered back to our old position where we had suffered so badly. We crept up to the brow of the hill and lay as close to the ground as we could." Skirmishers went forward, and quickly came back, driven in by Johnson's resurgent Rebels, "and again commenced another terrific conflict." This time, the 113th Ohio hung on.[61]

Behind these Buckeyes, Captain Hicks was rallying his company when a wild-eyed staff officer, sword in one hand and pistol in the other, appeared manifesting "intense excitement," explained Hicks. "Doubtless I was equally excited; probably we all were." The officer passed along the news that Whitaker was out of action, Colonel Champion had taken over the brigade, and Lieutenant Colonel Clarke had been mortally wounded. The upshot was that Hicks was now in charge of the 96th Illinois. Undaunted if perhaps a bit "excited," Hicks methodically set about reorganizing the companies, rounding up stray men, redistributing ammunition, and all the other myriad tasks needed to reconstitute his new command. Like so many of the brigade's regiments, both the color guard and the officers had been especially hard-hit. Still, Hicks recalled with pride, those still with the regiment "were doing splendidly." They would be needed again soon enough.[62]

Some of Bushrod Johnson's Confederates pursued the retreating 96th Illinois and brushed up against Jasper Hall and his compatriots in the 113th Ohio, but that advance was unauthorized, limited, and brief. Neither Fulton nor any of his four regimental commanders saw fit to single out this small movement in their reports. Instead, they noted, they halted and waited for the rest of Thomas Hindman's men to come up. Fulton's failure to take advantage of the significant disruption in Steedman's line can be easily explained: Mitchell's two right-most regiments, the 78th Illinois and 121st Ohio, reached

61 Darius Warner Letter, 113th Ohio file, CCNMP; Francis M. McAdams, *Every-Day Soldier Life, or A History of the One Hundred and Thirteenth Ohio Volunteer Infantry* (Charles M. Cott, Book Printers, 1884), 42; "Sunday, September 20," Jasper Newton Hall Diary, Creighton University, Omaha, NE.

62 Partridge, *Ninety-Sixth Regiment Illinois*, 236-237.

the crest and held it firmly. Their line extended the Union front well beyond Fulton's own left flank, and so threatened to envelop any renewed Rebel advance. The presence of these two regiments alone was fully sufficient to give Fulton, and by extension, Johnson's whole division, pause.[63]

Sergeant John J. Ramage in Company A of the 121st Ohio was proud of his regiment's position on what he regarded as the post of honor on the brigade's (in fact, the entire army's) right flank. "[A]fter we occupied the hill upon our first charge," he wrote years later, "our line was formed just at the crest of the hill," which, he added, the 121st held for the balance of the afternoon. Unlike Whitaker's men, these two regiments did not keep going once they moved just beyond the crest—though they would have but for General Steedman's timely arrival. After leaving Major Smith, Steedman arrived on the scene, busy bringing up Battery M of the 1st Illinois Artillery. The battery's Sergeant Dolton also found Steedman's persona riveting. "General Steedman," he wrote, "discovered what our infantry was doing, and, dashing after them at full speed, screamed out 'Halt! For God's sake, halt!'. . . . Forcing his way to the front, and catching the leading colors with one hand, his hat in the other, he managed to [stop] them." From the ranks of the 121st Ohio, W. A. Hill remembered the same moment: "his hat off, his gray hair streaming in the air," Steedman struggled to reverse the regiment's course. "Such was the ardor of our men," recalled Hill, "that it was hard to bring them to a halt, and although the officers repeated the command, we still moved forward. At last, however, we came to a halt and fell back to the top of the hill."[64]

As the infantry returned to the crest, Battery M unlimbered on their right, taking "a position commanding a gorge . . . through which the enemy were attempting to pass." The Illinois artillery added its fire to that of the Federal infantry, engaging Dent's and Everett's laboring gunners. Sergeant Dolton sensed that the Rebels would not come again, and a brief period of relative calm followed.[65]

It was now close to 3:00 p.m. Steedman's men had been in action less than an hour and during that time successfully blunted Johnson's flanking attack.

63 *OR* 30, pt. 2, 475-476, 483.

64 Letter of March 17, 1896," John J. Ramage, 121st Ohio file, CCNMP; Dolton, *Capsule History of Battery M*, CCNMP; W. A. Hill, "The 121st Ohio at Chickamauga," *National Tribune*, May 1, 1884. This is another of the many "Steedman and the Colors" incidents.

65 Dolton, *Capsule History of Battery M*, CCNMP.

The cost of keeping the Confederates off the high ground was heavy. Between one-quarter and one-third of those engaged had been killed or wounded. Combined, Steedman's 10 regiments lost between 500 and 800 men in perhaps 45 minutes. Bushrod Johnson's and Patton Anderson's losses were probably lighter because most of the Rebel line did not face close-range artillery fire, but their combined casualties were certainly substantial.

Steedman and his brigade commanders set about reorganizing the division, gathering up disordered regiments and bit of units, and cobbling together a solid Union line. Mitchell's brigade continued to occupy the right side, with the 121st Ohio on the extreme right flank. Battery M was divided; two sections moved a little to the rear to more squarely face the gorge earlier described, and to better command a hilltop off to the southwest, while a third section shifted east to lend more support to the infantry line. Next in line to the 121st Ohio's east was the 78th Illinois, followed by the 98th Ohio, moved to the right during or after the moment when the 113th Ohio gave way in an effort to close the resultant gap. The 113th Ohio was brought back into line to hold Mitchell's left flank.[66]

Whitaker's brigade was in greater disarray, and of its regiments, the 96th Illinois was in the worst shape. Before being informed of his elevation to regimental command, Captain Hicks had sent men off in search of water and ammunition. The former was in especially short supply. Soon enough, the men returned with more ammunition and by various means Hicks ensured everyone had ample rounds. He let the bulk of his men rest in the lee of the ridge. The 84th Indiana and 115th Illinois were similarly occupied. In the 84th Indiana, the sick and exhausted Colonel Trusler told the men he would have to relinquish command. Captain Boyd remembered leaving the colonel "safely ensconced between two trees." Boyd also took note of several stragglers. "One cowardly dog left our company before we went into the first charge, and now several others were shirking out of it," he penned with disgust. "Some slipped off unseen and others made themselves officious in taking away the wounded but took good care not to return." Isaac Royce of the 115th Illinois observed that his regiment was "ordered back behind the hill to rest. There was now another lull in the battle of a half hour's duration."[67]

66 Erwin Memoir, CCNMP.

67 Partridge, *Ninety-Sixth Regiment Illinois*, 235; Entry for September 20, Boyd Journal, UC Berkeley; Entry for September 20, Royce Diary, InSL.

For the moment Whitaker's front was held only by the 40th Ohio adjacent to Mitchell's brigade. A gap to the east some 200 yards separated the 40th from Carlton's 89th Ohio. Because it had not joined in that initial reckless charge, the 89th's losses were considerably fewer. Ohio Lt. John Scott remembered they lost 25 wounded in this first clash. Worried the Rebels would creep up on them unseen, the Buckeyes of the 89th spent some minutes firing blindly into the brush on the south side of the slope until General Steedman—yet again on foot—came up and ordered them to stop. Carlton vividly recalled the general's arrival and appearance: "General Steedman came to us from our right rear and I dismounted and showed him [our] position. . . . He was on foot without staff or orderly with his handkerchief wrapped around his hand. [I] asked him if he had any orders to give. He said 'No, only hang on to this position.' The General expressed his satisfaction and as he walked away . . . towards the 22nd Michigan, laughingly said 'I have my scratch of a wound and am fireproof for the rest of this fight.'"[68]

The 22nd Michigan, now also regrouped, took up a position on the 89th's right, holding the crest and west face of Hill Three. At roughly the same time, the 2nd Minnesota came into position on the saddle between Hills Two and Three, relieving some of Brannan's men. The presence of both of these units allowed Maj. Arnold McMahan to contract the thinned ranks of the 21st Ohio, leaving him to defend only the east face of Hill Three.[69]

As this fighting raged between Johnson's and Steedman's troops, an equally fierce action ignited along Hills Two and Three. In support of Patton Anderson's attack, Joe Kershaw's South Carolina brigade made one more effort to storm the heights in what would be their most determined assault of the day.

68 Weaver and Fenner, *Sacrifice at Chickamauga*, 104; Carlton Papers, LOC.

69 Bishop, *The Story of a Regiment*, 108; "The Chattanooga Campaign," unpublished manuscript, 137, Jeremiah C. Donahower Papers, MinnHS; Canfield, *History of the 21st Regiment*, 136. Some members of the 21st Ohio never believed any part of their regiment left the line at this time. The Minnesotans were convinced they took the 21st's place in line, while men in the 21st vehemently denied being replaced.

Chapter Twenty-One

Kershaw's Third Assault:

Sunday, 2:30 p.m. to 3:30 p.m.

When Patton Anderson's Mississippi infantry filed into position, Joe Kershaw watched them come up with evident relief. He had no idea, however, that these men from the Deep South were about to reprise the bloody role his own brigade had just experienced.

Kershaw explained that the Federals atop Hill Three might be vulnerable to a flank attack, and Anderson deployed and advanced accordingly. To my dismay, noted Kershaw, "raising a shout along their line, [the Federals] advanced their line of battle at a charge, driving back Anderson's Brigade in some confusion." The similarity to Kershaw's own effort earlier that day continued when the Yankees reached the Vittetoe Road and were repulsed. Watching the remnants of the 22nd Michigan scrambling back up the draw to their left, many South Carolinians believed the moment was now ripe for their own renewed assault. The attack that followed was more spontaneous than intentional. Certainly Kershaw did not order another effort up the hill. However, at least two of his regiments—the 2nd and 7th South Carolina, and possibly James's Battalion—went up the slopes yet again.[1]

It was 2:30 p.m. The Gamecocks had been "clinging to [their] enemy like grim death" for the past 90 minutes, draining away their ammunition and slowly bleeding away strength into the red Georgia dirt. To an aggressive regimental

1 *OR* 30, pt. 2, 504.

commander like Franklin Gaillard of the 2nd South Carolina, the status quo was simply unsatisfactory.[2]

The men of the 2nd regiment still held Kershaw's left, and so witnessed Anderson's failed attack. It was Gaillard's first real chance to observe Western Confederates in action. He was not impressed. "A brigade was then advanced upon our left but did not go much in advance of us before it fell to the ground and began to fire furiously from that position. The enemy, then encouraged, raised a shout . . . and began to advance. The brigade to our left, belonging to the Army of Tennessee, broke back at a run." Sergeant Dubose Egleston, also of the 2nd, was equally disdainful of these Mississippians. "These Western troops don't know how to fight Yankees," he announced. "They will . . . stand off and fire; the Yankees will fight them forever that way, the only way to do is to charge."[3]

When the 44th Mississippi broke, its retreat exposed the 2nd South Carolina's left flank. Gaillard, however, wasn't interested in retreat. While the 2nd "stood like a rock," he noted Lt. Ralph S. Brown of Company A urging the leftmost companies to cheer and call on the Mississippians to rally. Brown, a Scotsman living and working in Columbia when the war broke out, did not hesitate to join up. Gaillard regarded him as "a very fine officer." Brown's efforts worked, and Gaillard noted that for all their Western taint, the Mississippians rallied "promptly."[4]

By now the Wolverines of the 22nd regiment had lost formation and were suffering a punishing raking fire from Johnson's Rebels, which helps explain why from Gaillard's perspective the Yankees retreated so quickly. "In ten minutes we had them retiring," he wrote proudly, attributing the abrupt Federal retreat to his own fire. Anderson, not surprisingly, believed it was the speed with which his own Mississippians reformed. He also noted that by the time the Federals came charging down the hill "with some impetuosity," those Yankees were quickly seen off by counterattacking Mississippians. This riposte was brought up short when neither Colonel Sugg's men on Anderson's left, nor Kershaw's on his right, advanced in turn. Feeling alone and worried about

2 Dickert, *History of Kershaw's Brigade*, 275.

3 "Dear Maria," October 5, 1863, Franklin Gaillard Papers, UNC; "Before Chattanooga," September 27, 1863, Debose Egleston Letters, UNC.

4 "Dear Maria," October 5, 1863, Franklin Gaillard Papers, UNC; Wyckoff, *History of the 2nd South Carolina*, 164.

getting too far ahead of the rest of the Rebel line lest his men become the targets of more friendly fire, Anderson halted his troops a short distance up the slope.[5]

Sugg was not moving forward, but Anderson was mistaken about the South Carolinians. Gaillard's 2nd regiment was indeed moving up Hill Three again, and with *esprit.* When the Mississippians halted, however, they created the very condition for the 2nd South Carolina that Anderson feared would happen to his own troops: an exposed left flank subject to both enemy fire and errant friendly bullets.

This attack was Kershaw's most desperate of the day and culminated in brutal close-range fighting. Gamecock Reginald Screven of Company I, 2nd South Carolina, recorded his impressions later that night: "[A] third and terrible charge. Terrific fire, rifle bullets as thick as hail, crashing through trees human flesh and bones—saw one man's foot lying by him completely shot off." Private John Coxe agreed. "We were met by a heavy fire, but held our ground," he explained in a postwar recollection. "Many of our men fell here. . . . Soon after this we saw the brigade on our left began to fall back down the hill." According to Dubose Egleston, the 2nd was "the only reg't in the brigade to co-operate with an advance on our left. We were going up splendidly," he confirmed, "when our support deliberately came in behind & poured a volley into us; of course it broke us."[6]

Despite Kershaw's later assertion that all his regiments were involved, neither Nance's 3rd South Carolina nor James's Battalion made as strong an effort this time. Nance did not report any third assault, noting only that "an irregular fire was then kept up until at length" reinforcements arrived (a reference to the arrival of Brig. Gen. Archibald Gracie's brigade, still more than an hour away). Until Gracie's troops appeared, Nance's men were content to hold their position. Nance's failure to move also explains Egleston's assertion that only the 2nd South Carolina was ordered to "co-operate with an advance on our left." On Nance's right, Colonel Oates and the 15th Alabama also declined to go forward again up the slope. By this time, Oates may have been convinced the South Carolinians could not be counted upon and saw no point in making another charge. Oates also had a physical barrier blocking his path.

5 "Dear Maria," October 5, 1863, Franklin Gaillard Papers, UNC; OR 30, pt. 2, 318.

6 Entry for September 20, Reginald Screven Diary, South Carolina Historical Society, Charleston, SC; Coxe, "Chickamauga," 293; "Before Chattanooga," September 27, 1863, Dubose Egleston Letters, UNC.

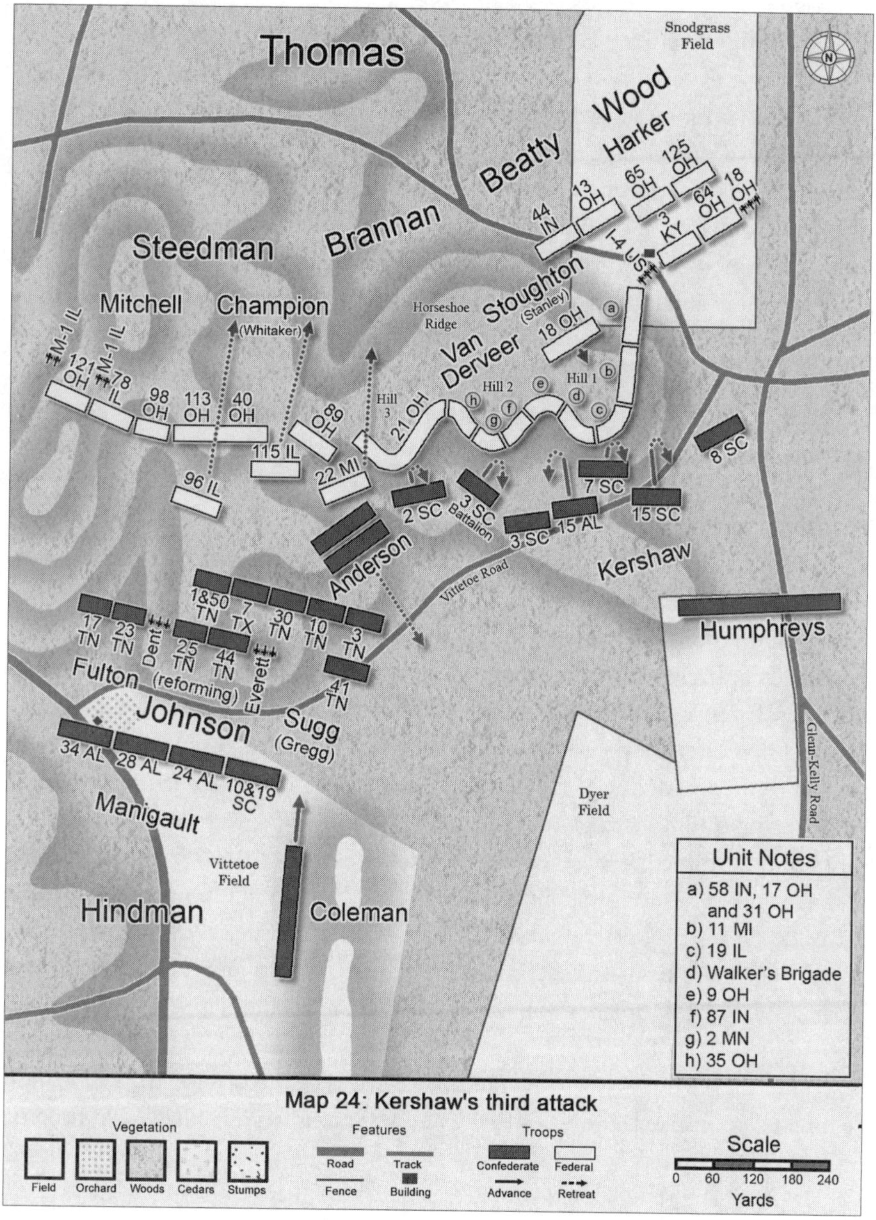

Map 24: Kershaw's third attack

The relentless musketry had touched off several ground fires between the Alabama troops and the Yankees. "[W]e were compelled to witness the horrid sight of seeing their wounded burned to death and [listening] to their awful shrieks within twenty yards of us with no means of relieving them," Oates recalled, "for the enemy kept up a constant fire from their works on the next hill."[7]

The situation was different on Oates's right. If he thought the South Carolinians of the 7th lacked fight, he misread their spirit as badly now as he had earlier. Here, the 7th launched its most determined attack of the day. This last charge, wrote Pvt. J. S. Gilbert a year later, was "a supreme effort to take possession of this position." Their effort carried the Gamecocks to the very crest of the hill and into the Federal defenses. Unsupported, they could not hold their gains, and hard fighting—some of it hand-to-hand— was required to repulse them.[8]

The 2nd and 7th regiments might have captured both Hills One and Three had they only faced Brannan's rallied fragments and the 21st Ohio, for many of the Yankees atop Horseshoe Ridge were out of ammunition, or nearly so. The crisis was especially severe among Brannan's men, most of whom had fired away their basic load twice over. "By this time the ammunition in the boxes of the men was reduced, on average, to 2 or 3 rounds per man, and my ammunition trains having been unfortunately ordered to the rear. . . . We should have been entirely without ammunition in a very short time," reported George Thomas. Every expedient was adopted. Henry Davidson of the 10th Kentucky recalled that once they scrounged all they could from their own casualties, they turned to the Confederate fallen: "Our men would run to a dead or wounded Rebel & take his cartridge box. . . . Several prisoners were taken, and their ammunition immediately given out to the men." Fortunately for the Federals, Granger brought along his division ordnance train in addition to Steedman's bayonets. Its timely arrival allowed for a limited reissue, averaging about 10 rounds per man. Equally welcome, Col. Ferdinand Van Derveer's brigade was now available to replace Col. Moses Walker's accumulation of exhausted defenders on Hill Two.[9]

Van Derveer's men were among Thomas's favorites. In fact, these regiments comprised Thomas's first Civil War command. He had been fond of

7 *OR* 30, pt. 2, 508; *OR Supplement*, vol. 6, 690. Oates's report is an 1868 reconstruction of his original report, lost during the war.

8 "Ensign Clark's Courage," J. S. Gilbert Letter, 7th South Carolina file, CCNMP.

9 *OR* 30, pt. 1, 253; "My dear Aunt," February 19, 1864, Henry G. Davidson Papers, ALPL. Normally, each man carried 40 rounds of ammunition in his cartridge box, with another 20 in his haversack. This constituted a basic ammunition load. Additional ammunition was usually issued when action was anticipated, such as on the morning of the 20th.

them ever since the Kentucky battle of Mill Springs in January 1862. Another of their former commanders was Brig. Gen. James Steedman. Van Derveer's veterans had more than held their own thus far. All in all, Thomas could not ask for a more reliable force to meet the needs of the moment. And he had plenty of needs.[10]

Over on Hill Three, the 21st Ohio was also short of ammunition and held (by Civil War standards) a huge frontage. Formed per the drill book, the 21st's 539 men should have occupied about 135 yards of frontage—a sizable distance even in a clear level field. By now, however, the 21st's formation was anything but parade-like, and its numbers had been reduced considerably. The Buckeyes had shifted position several times, repulsed two charges, and attacked down the slope at least once. When Capt. Henry Alban refused the regiment's right wing, he lengthened the regimental frontage yet again. The straight line distance from the western shoulder of Hill Three to the crown of Hill Two is about 350 yards. However, a defensive line following the military crest, snaking its way sinuously around the curving southern face of Hill Three, would be even longer. It is impossible to state with certainty the location of the 21st's flanks, but the left was somewhere on the western face of Hill Two, and the right curved far enough around Hill Three to obstruct the 22nd Michigan's movements. By 2:00 p.m., the 21st's line stretched across some 400 yards—equal to the frontage of a large brigade. According to Maj. Arnold McMahan, the regiment entered the fight that morning with "517 men with rifles and 22 officers," but now numbered no more than about 400.[11]

With no more than one man per yard, holding such an expansive frontage in the face of a determined attack would be nearly impossible. The added firepower of their Colt rifles certainly helped, as did the fact that Kershaw's brigade was similarly hyper-extended, exhausted, and thinned by heavy losses. William Hamilton of the 22nd Michigan recalled thinking the 21st Ohio was a skirmish line when he first set eyes on the Buckeye formation.[12]

10 Jack K. Overmeyer, *A Stupendous Effort: The 87th Indiana in the War of the Rebellion* (Indiana University Press, 1997), 29.

11 21st Ohio Monument, CCNMP; OR 30, pt. 1, 390. Reports of the 21st's engaged strength vary slightly. The military crest is defined as that place on the slope where a defender can see and fire at all of the ground in front of him, leaving no dead (i.e., unobserved) space where an enemy can hide.

12 Statement of William P. Hamilton, 22nd Michigan file, CCNMP.

However, the extra firepower of the Colt rifles was meaningless without bullets. The 21st's ammunition problems were exacerbated by the fact that their rifles chambered .56 caliber rounds, but the cartridges for Enfield and Springfield rifle-muskets were .577 and .58 caliber, respectively. When Capt. Silas Canfield noticed the ammunition shortage and caliber problem, he instructed Lt. Ara B. Spafford of Company C to send back for more Colt rounds. The reply was dismaying: "He said he had sent in every direction and could not find any that could be used in our guns."[13]

As was described earlier, it was at this juncture that Van Derveer's men came up behind part of the 21st. The 2nd Minnesota, it will be recalled, had halted briefly at the Snodgrass cabin while Col. James George conferred with General Thomas. Even then, the Minnesotans were already taking note of the 21st's troubles. "I saw the last field officer present of the 21st Ohio wounded & helped off his horse and a call was made for the ranking Capt. who mounted . . . & took command," recalled Pvt. H. M. Bayliss. "We were then told that that Regt was out of ammunition." Lieutenant Colonel Judson Bishop added that when the 2nd arrived "near the crest, we found a line of men there in our front—there was at the moment no firing except scattered shots." Despite their earlier rest and refit, Van Derveer's men were also low on bullets, though not nearly as bad off as the Ohioans. The Minnesotans had between 15 and 20 rounds per man. Half full cartridge boxes were better than empty ones, and these men were the only fresh troops available.[14]

Van Derveer noted in his report that the brigade "took position in one line on the crest," with the 35th Ohio on the right flank. Van Derveer's brigade had entered every other action during the battle in the suggested two-line formation, as prescribed in Casey's Tactics. Given the circumstances, it is likely Van Derveer repeated that process here during his approach. The space to be filled, however, was too large for just two regiments, so Van Derveer probably ordered the second line forward at this time to fill the space. Years later, Lieutenant Colonel Bishop described their final deployment with the 35th on the right, and the 2nd Minnesota, 87th Indiana, and 9th Ohio extending the line

13 S. S. Canfield to Col. A McMahan, June 7, 1889, Sullivan Collection, BGSU.

14 H. M. Bayliss to Arnold McMahan, July 1, 1889. Sullivan Collection, BGSU: J. W. Bishop to Col. Arnold McMahan, August 10, 1889, Sullivan Collection, BGSU; Judson W. Bishop, *Van Derveer's Brigade at Chickamauga* (n.p., 1903), 14. Bayliss might have seen Stoughton go down, but he was mistaken about the last field officer. McMahan was with the 21st Ohio until the end of the fight.

left. Today, this is how the monuments run, with that of the 35th Ohio proudly claiming the post of honor at the apex of Hill Two. Based on a careful computing of distance and available manpower, the 35th Ohio's stone should be farther west near the saddle between Hills Two and Three. The Minnesotans likely held the actual summit.[15]

The exact timing of Van Derveer's arrival is uncertain. Bishop placed it at 1:30 p.m., just before Steedman's men were dispatched to the right. Although that is likely a little too early, he and his comrades certainly arrived before Kershaw's third effort commenced. According to Frederick Kiel, historian of the 35th Ohio, Granger's men (Steedman) arrived shortly after Van Derveer reported to Thomas, and all three brigades were ordered into action together. Hoosier Cpl. Peter Keegan recalled that shortly after he and his comrades of the 87th Indiana entered the line, "Gen. Steadman [sic] with two brigades of the reserve corps came up, fresh and strong . . . and were soon hotly engaged."[16]

With roughly 275 men in the ranks, the 2nd Minnesota occupied no more than a frontage of 100 yards. Bishop later estimated the 2nd Minnesota "was large enough to occupy all the ground . . . covered" by that portion of the 21st Ohio he could see, though he did not realize at the time that he was only viewing that regiment's left wing. In writing to one of the Buckeye officers, he noted, "Our regiment halted a few paces in rear of the line already there and I learned from the officers and men *in front of us* that the regiment was the 21st Ohio and that [you] were out of cartridges, and noticed that they had revolving . . . guns." Bishop also recalled that the 2nd replaced the 21st "almost immediately after our arrival there & took your place in time to repulse an attack."[17]

15 *OR* 30, pt. 1, 435; Bishop, *Van Derveer's Brigade at Chickamauga*, 14. Henry V. Boynton commanded the 35th Ohio. Later he served as historian and chairman of the Chickamauga National Military Park. His judgment in matters concerning both his old brigade and especially his old regiment was less than objective. His efforts to ensure that the 35th Ohio monument sat alone at the crest of the highest hill on Horseshoe Ridge, directly in front of the observation tower later erected there, distorted the placement of markers on the rest of Horseshoe Ridge. Despite a number of challenges by veterans of other units, Boynton's version remained the official interpretation of the battle.

16 Bishop Letter, BGSU; Frederick W. Keil, *Thirty-Fifth Ohio: A Narrative of Service from August 1861 to 1864* (Archer, Housh and Co, 1894), 146; Entry for September 20, Peter Keegan Diary, InHS.

17 Bishop Letter, BGSU. Italics in original. Numbers are estimates. Van Derveer's regiments had likely suffered about 2/3 of their total casualties by now, with the heaviest single loss coming in Kelly Field that morning.

This simple statement would stir up decades of controversy. Many veterans of the 21st steadfastly refused to admit that they had ever been relieved, or that another regiment could have moved in front of them. Ohio Capt. Isaac Cusac of Company G recalled things quite differently. "Some time in the afternoon, a regiment, said to be the 2nd Minnesota, came in our rear and laid down and began firing over us, their balls passing very near our men. We feared they would kill some of our men. I requested those in the rear of my company to cease firing, or else raise up and fire," he wrote. "It has been claimed by some that the 2nd Minnesota relieved the 21st that evening, but that is not correct. There was no other regiment in front of the 21st that evening except . . . the 22nd Michigan, and that but a very short time." As late as 1909, Cusac was still crusading to make sure his regiment's reputation remained unsullied. Writing to park historian Ezra A. Carman, he insisted that "the 21st held this position for seven hours without being relieved by any other troops, notwithstanding reports to the contrary. The regt. that was sent to relieve us [2nd Minnesota] laid down in our rear for a short time and then moved away."[18]

Cusac was mistaken, but only in part. First, Captain Canfield contradicted Cusac when he noted that as the 2nd Minnesota and 35th Ohio came up, Canfield's portion of the 21st fell back "behind the crest and rested a brief space." His men also received some ammunition during this lull. Thereafter, Canfield's men rejoined the line with the rest of the 21st farther to the right, which explains Cusac's insistence that no other regiment held ground in front of the 21st: Cusac was in that part of the line never relieved.[19]

Before entering the fight, the regiment had emptied the division ordnance train of all boxes of .56 Colt cartridges. Virtually all of those rounds were now gone, and the cartridge boxes of their fallen comrades had been picked clean. Acting Sgt. Maj. John Bolton left the ridge to find any bullets at all that might serve, and soon returned with several cases of .577 Enfield rounds. These provided for the roughly one-third of the 21st carrying the English muskets, but left the men armed with Colt rifles unsupplied. Necessity being the mother of invention, the men soon discovered they could force the rounds into the chambers of the cylinder, but that firing them burst the barrels; by affixing

18 Isaac Cusac to Mr. E. A. Carman, March 13, 1909, Sullivan Collection, BGSU. Carman replaced Boynton on the Park Commission in 1905 upon Boynton's death, and after Carman's tenure as the historian of Antietam.

19 Canfield, *History of the 21st Regiment*, 136.

bayonets, however, the muzzles were reinforced just enough to prevent splitting. Soon all of the 21st had a limited—if not regulation—supply of cartridges.[20]

Captain John Mahony of the 21st Ohio offered up additional evidence of the shifting nature of his regiment's position. "I do not mean to imply that we changed our position," wrote Mahony, "but it always looked to me that we worked a little to the west of where we had [previously] been engaged." This bit of reshuffling left four regiments holding the line that, until then, the 21st occupied alone. The 22nd Michigan reformed on the crest to the 21st's right, the 21st itself held the crest and eastern shoulder of Hill Three; the 35th Ohio draped down the western shoulder of Hill Two, and the 2nd Minnesota atop the summit and eastern shoulder of Hill Two. Together they formed a formidable obstacle to Kershaw's attack.[21]

The rest of Van Derveer's regiments replaced men along Brannan's scratch line. The 87th connected with the Minnesotans's left, then came the 9th Ohio. Both units occupied the saddle between Hills Two and One. On Hill One, Col. Moses Walker viewed their arrival with relief: "Gen. Vandervere with his Brigade well in hand . . . by a judicious disposition . . . greatly strengthened my line." Among those troops now replaced were the men of the 10th Kentucky, including Capt. Israel Webster, who fell back behind the Snodgrass farm "just in the rear of where General Thomas was."[22]

The 82nd Indiana saw no such relief. Van Derveer's line wasn't long enough to cover its front, so these Hoosiers remained in line near the crown of Hill One. The 9th Ohio came into position on the 82nd's right, probably only minutes before the 7th South Carolina charged a third time. Colonel Morton Hunter watched the 9th deploy, noting with surprise that the Germans were not content to merely hold their part of the hill, but instead were preparing to charge themselves. "I told them," recalled Hunter, "that they had better stay on top of the hill and throw logs in their front and let the Rebels charge them." That wasn't the kind of warfare the 9th practiced.[23]

20 S. S. Canfield to Col. A. McMahan, July 18, 1889, Sullivan Collection, BGSU; Entry for September 20, Bolton Papers, OHS; Vance, "On Thomas' Right at Chickamauga," 93.

21 Canfield, *History of the 21st Regiment*, 138.

22 Walker Report, NARA; Webster, "Chickamauga," *National Tribune*, July 2, 1891.

23 Hunter, *History of the Eighty-Second Indiana*, 82.

Colonel Gustave Kammerling had already led his men in several spirited charges at Chickamauga, recapturing Lt. Hiram Burnham's battery of Regulars on the 19th, and spearheading the counterattack that cleared Kelly Field earlier that morning. Now, atop Horseshoe Ridge, Kammerling intended to do it once more. Before he could do so, however, the storm broke anew with the attack of the 7th South Carolina.

The Gamecocks of the 7th, still led by Capt. Elijah Goggans, struck just as the Union line to their front was shifting. As a result, they made surprising progress and, for a brief moment, drove the Federals from the crest. The focal point of this affair centered on the 7th's Palmetto flag, borne up the slope by Ensign Alfred D. Clark. Years later, Clark's good friend J. S. Gilbert vividly recalled that moment: "Our forces were making a supreme effort to take . . . this position, the last which the enemy occupied. Here Ensign Clark . . . was several paces in advance of the regiment with his flag so near the line of the enemy that their commanding officer . . . announced . . . that he would give a captain's commission to any man who would capture [it.]" For the briefest of moments the Union line had been ruptured, and a Rebel banner crowned the summit of Hill One.[24]

Ensign Clark's flag drew considerable attention from all quarters. John Beatty, still supervising this part of the line, was with some of the men withdrawn for resupply. "After a desperate struggle our troops were driven from the crest, and the enemy's flag waved above it," noted the brigadier. "The men were rallied, and I rode up the hill with them, waving my hat and shouting like a madman." To Pvt. Lewis Tripp in Company D of the 18th Ohio, one of Stanley's regiments, it seemed like "the hotest fight that ever was fought. . . . Their was the most musketry that I ever [heard.]"[25]

Lieutenant Colonel Charles H. Grosvenor, commanding the 18th Ohio, had just moved his men back into reserve when the Rebels struck. Reduced to merely 80 men, the 18th Ohio was distributing water when Grosvenor reported that "an order reached me . . . to come up to the top of the hill as rapidly as possible with whatever men I had." On the way Grosvenor met Beatty "swinging his hat and waving his sword and [he] cried out: 'Colonel Grosvenor,

24 Gilbert Letter, CCNMP.

25 Beatty, *Citizen-Soldier*, 340; "Dear Father, Mother and Sister," September 21, 1863, Lewis Tripp Letters, AHEC.

Lt. Col. Charles Grosvenor (right) led the 18th Ohio. He was impressed by the bravery of the 7th South Carolina's color bearer.

Miller, Photograhic History

there is a Brigadier General's commission for the man that will capture that flag!'"[26]

Clark and his standard combined to make a prominent target nearly impossible to miss. "At this moment [Clark] . . . received a mortal wound," recorded his friend Gilbert, "and as he fell he threw the flag backwards over his head [into] . . . the hands of his comrades." Several Federals on the receiving end of this charge also recorded their recollections of the event for posterity. General Beatty was close enough to see the whole thing. The Union watched with amazement as the Rebels "only saved their colors by throwing them down the hill." Also awed by Clark's bravery and sacrifice, Grosvenor also left a description of the event: "The South Carolina troops had climbed over the little wooden works . . . and were encountering a hand-to-hand fight. . . . I saw a young fellow with their flag, and I saw him indicate the receipt of a bullet. At the minute he did so, he turned partly around and threw his flag, saving it, over the works down the hill. . . . No one of the war showed greater courage." The 7th, together with its flag, went reeling back down the southern slope.[27]

Stanley's last regiment, the 19th Illinois, was still on the line atop Hill One. James Fenton recalled that by now the regiment was "mingled with the other men at the works or anywhere they saw a chance." Fenton himself was behind a "small tree . . . some six feet from the works, and . . . firing up the ravine in front of Snodgrass." He watched in amazement as "all at once in this last charge there was a panic and all the troops in the spur ran out. It was done so quickly that I

26 Gracie, *The Truth About Chickamauga*, 310-11.

27 Gilbert Letter, CCNMP; Beatty, *Citizen-Soldier*, 340; Gracie, *The Truth About Chickamauga*, 311.

had no time to run. . . . At the lower end of the spur a rebel color-bearer was waving a flag with a southern cross on it by a tree at the works."[28]

Fenton was sure the day was lost. Then his attention was drawn northward toward the reforming Federals: "I saw some flags at the open end of the spur and heard the voice of Capt. Bremner and others from different regiments calling the men to the colors from the works; and as soon as they had gotten over 100 in line (some of the 18th Ohio, some from the 11th Michigan, and fully half of the 19th Illinois) they charged in and retook the spur. The brave Johnnies rallied around their flag. . . . It was a mix-up for a few minutes—our officers using their revolvers. The rebel color bearer, as he dropped mortally wounded, threw his flag backward over his head and the enemy closed around it and took it away with them, leaving their dead and wounded and a few prisoners."[29]

Private Lewis Tripp of the 18th Ohio described this melee from the inside. Charging up to the crest, Tripp wrote, "I got thew all of the iron hail . . . that the Rebels could throw at me with out getting scratched. . . . The regiment was in 3 different charges . . . and we drove the Rebs each time. The fight was dreadful. [Here] we fought them almost hand to hand."[30]

Captain William H. Eckles, commanding Company G of the 14th Ohio, was also in the thick of things. "We held our ground," he informed his wife, "notwithstanding the enemy fought like incarnate devils. They . . . attempted to plant their colors on the very top of the low rails, hastily thrown together for a kind of defense; while some of them stuck the muzzles of their guns over and fired at our men. But their time was brief when they had once performed the daring deed."[31]

This was probably the moment Colonel Kammerling chose to order his 9th Ohio to charge. His German Buckeyes advanced with conspicuous valor, driving down the slope through Draw One and slicing into the flank of the 7th South Carolina. Every Federal with eyeshot along the line took note of the ferocity of the attack. Lieutenant Colonel Davis of the 82nd Indiana remembered the 9th's distinctive presence, with "commands all being given in

28 Entry for September 20, James Fenton Diary, ALPL.

29 Ibid.

30 "Dear Father, Mother and Sister," October 15, 1863, Tripp Letters, AHEC.

31 "Dear Wife," Letter of September 27, 1863, *Paulding Independent*, October 22, 1863.

the German language." Van Derveer proudly reported that the charge was very successful, "scattering [the enemy] like chaff" before returning to the top of the ridge. Morton Hunter, who had counseled Kammerling to remain on the high ground, told a somewhat different story: "Colonel Kammerling insisted on going, and I told him to go. The [Germans] . . . stayed about five minutes, and then came back. Colonel Kammerling, when he came back, remarked that the rebels were too d—d thick down there." Thick they were. The 9th's advance threatened the 7th South Carolina's flank, but also exposed its own right flank to a steady fire from Oates's 15th Alabama, as well as parts of the 3rd and 15th South Carolina, still in line along the Vittetoe Road. Though it undoubtedly helped break the 7th, like every other Union advance down the south slope, Kammerling's attack proved but a fleeting success.[32]

Kershaw's last two regiments did not join in this third attack. The Federal defenses opposing them were the strongest anywhere along the Horseshoe Ridge line. The four Napoleons of Smith's battery faced southeast and could sweep all the ground to their front. Sometime around 2:00 p.m., Smith's pieces were reinforced by four (and later all six) guns of Aleshire's 18th Ohio battery. The daunting firepower of up to 10 cannon and the disciplined volleys of Harker's infantry easily dissuaded the 8th and 15th South Carolina from another attempt.

Thomas, who spent most of his time near the Snodgrass house, observed much of this fighting. He did his best to lend the troops some of his own quiet confidence. At one point the general was sitting on his horse next to a large oak directly behind the 3rd Kentucky. Thomas noted the regiment's disciplined firing and informed Capt. George W. McClure that he felt safe behind the 3rd.[33]

Here, instead of headlong assaults, the Rebels contented themselves with trying to pick off the Federals from a distance. Private Charles Reed of the 125th Ohio fell wounded during the earlier retreat, shot through the hand and breast. As he lay exposed on the open slopes in front of the regiment, his comrade in Company H, Pvt. Peter Knapp, was sure Reed was dying and wanted to collect Reed's personal possessions for the family. As Knapp made his way forward, however, he was hit by a Rebel sharpshooter and sprawled unconscious near his friend. Both Reed and Knapp survived—Reed to be

32 Davis Letter, CCNMP; OR 30, pt. 1, 430; Hunter, *History of the Eighty-Second Indiana*, 82.

33 Anonymous Letter, CCNMP.

exchanged and mustered out due to disability in 1864, while Knapp spent the rest of the war as a prisoner.[34]

The 3rd Kentucky was similarly bedeviled by Confederates firing from a clump of trees. Thomas finally asked if there were any "good squirrel shooters" in the ranks and directed the Kentuckians to send out a detail to discourage the Rebels. Captain McClure recalled that he took several men and circled around behind the regiment to the right to gain a new and better angle on the sharpshooters. They killed one Confederate and drove off three others. While this *petit guerre* was being carried out, Kershaw's men were being driven back from their toeholds on Hills One and Three.[35]

This third effort to take the high ground proved to be Kershaw's last attempt. In the final estimation, it was a fitful one reflecting the brigade's weariness and heavy losses after hours in action. Despite the extreme valor and tenacity exhibited by the 2nd and 7th South Carolina, they were the only two commands in the brigade to fully commit to the charge. Perhaps, as Kershaw later reported, James's Battalion also joined in, but a lack of eyewitnesses leaves the matter unsettled. Nance clearly did not order his 3rd South Carolina to make the charge, nor did Oates and his 15th Alabama go forward. Sources are sparse among the 8th and 15th South Carolina, but they squared off against the east face of Hill One and the open fields of Snodgrass Hill—all heavily defended sectors. None of the Federals holding the line there reported repulsing any attack. The frustrated Colonel Gaillard noted that, bereft of any support, "I reluctantly had to retire my line to its original position. General Kershaw remarked to me that so gallant a charge ought to have been more successful." It was now approaching 3:30 p.m. The South Carolinians were fought out. If Horseshoe Ridge was going to end the day in Rebel hands, other troops would have to seize it.[36]

34 Clarke, *Opdycke Tigers*, 128.

35 "Anonymous Letter, CCNMP.

36 "Dear Maria," October 5, 1863, Franklin Gaillard Papers, UNC.

Chapter Twenty-Two

Hindman Assaults Horseshoe Ridge:

Sunday, 3:30 p.m. to 5:00 p.m.

Joe Kershaw's final attack was fading when Maj. Gen. Thomas C. Hindman's remaining two brigades under Zach Deas and Arthur Manigault arrived on Bushrod Johnson's left. Hindman's third brigade under Patton Anderson had a relatively short march to reach Johnson's right flank and so was engaged much sooner. Deas and Manigault, on the other hand, had much father to march and the terrain grew more rugged with each westward step. While Hindman was preparing to assault Horseshoe Ridge, he also cast one eye on his exposed rear. John Wilder's earlier attack rattled more than just Manigault's men. About 3:00 p.m., Hindman reported that Yankees "appeared on my left, capturing several men of my infirmary corps and others who had fallen out from fatigue."[1]

By this time, Johnson's brigades (Sugg and Fulton) had been repulsed by Granger's Federals under James Steedman. According to Johnson, after his men fell back to Vittetoe Hill, he set eyes on Manigault's brigade "advancing through the Vidito cornfield in the cove in our rear. As [his brigade] came up on the left of my line, Brigadier General Deas reported in person, having . . . swept

1 *OR* 30, pt. 2, 304.

the ridge west of the Crawfish [Dry Valley] Road." Johnson detailed a staff officer to direct Manigault and Deas where to form and then conferred with Hindman, who readily ceded tactical control to Johnson even though he was junior in rank. This was a sound decision because Johnson had the clearest grasp of the tactical situation. In addition, Hindman had begun the day ill before taking to the field and suffering a light wound earlier that afternoon. At some point during the fighting against either Jeff C. Davis or Phil Sheridan, Hindman was struck in the neck by a piece of shrapnel. The injury was not serious enough to force him to leave the field, but it did cause "much pain." There was one flaw in this new tactical arrangement, however: Johnson would be responsible for controlling six brigades from two different divisions across a mile of hilly, wooded terrain.[2]

Deas's Alabamians led the way westward. Even after their morning's losses, the five regiments and the sharpshooter battalion, which combined had originally totaled 1,932 men, now counted perhaps 1,600 bayonets. This was probably as many or more troops than could be found in both of Johnson's brigades combined. The terrain they traversed grew progressively worse, described by one as "a range of high, abrupt, and rugged hills . . . heavily timbered." Both Deas and Manigault moved up the Dry Valley Road past the Vittetoe house, though this time no one remembered meeting any pretty girls, for the women had fled to safer ground. Deas halted here. Johnson's guide either misjudged or misunderstood the plan and as Deas soon discovered, he had gone too far: his right was nearly 700 yards beyond Johnson's left. Instead of forming behind Deas in support, Manigault's troops would have to fill that gap. Unfortunately for the Rebels, the terrain here was the worst yet seen on the battlefield by men of either army. In front of Deas's Alabamians, steep wooded slopes climbed abruptly to a crest of 950 feet, considerably higher than the rest of Horseshoe Ridge.[3]

Manigault faced obstacles even more imposing. The South Carolina brigadier was happy to discover Captain Dent's long-lost Alabama battery already in place supporting Johnson. Dent's guns had become separated from the brigade all the way back in Dyer Field, and Dent had joined Johnson of his own volition. Manigault also found that his left flank regiment, the 34th

2 Ibid., 462; *Memphis Appeal*, September 23, 1863; *OR* 30, pt. 2, 305.

3 Powell, "Numbers and Losses," CCNMP; Tower, *A Carolinian Goes to War*, 99; Deas Brigade Tablet at Vittetoe Well, CCNMP; *OR* 30, pt. 2, 330.

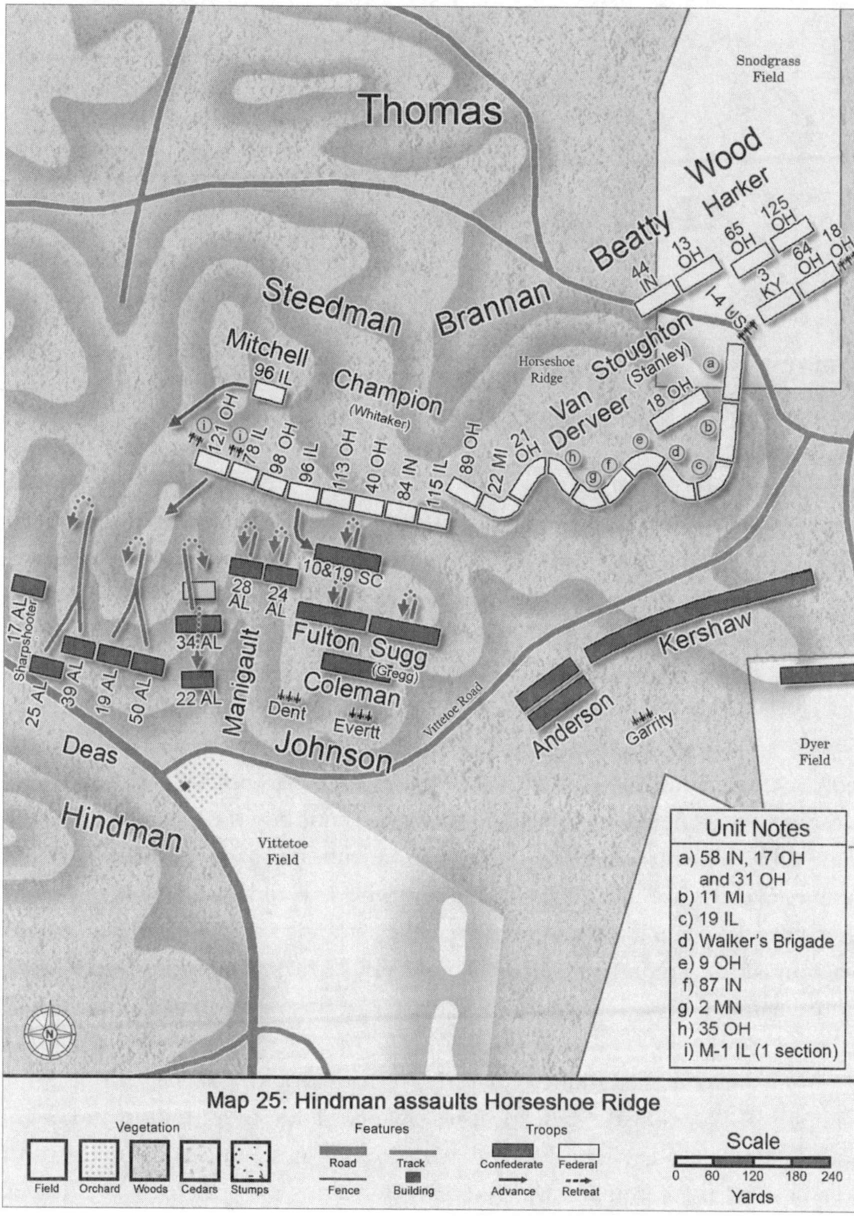

Map 25: Hindman assaults Horseshoe Ridge

Alabama, was still partially masked by Deas's line. Worse, his "center rested on a gorge between the ridge[s]" on his right and left. This steep-sided ravine was especially problematic, for it began at the Vittetoe house and ran northeast directly toward the Union line. As Manigault advanced, his flanks would drape atop the hills to either side trying to keep pace with the center more than 150

Maj. Gen. Thomas C. Hindman (left), shown here in civilian dress. The aggressive general left the tactical details of the September 20 assault to Bushrod Johnson.

Library of Congress

feet below. Exercising effective command would prove a considerable challenge.[4]

Both Johnson and Hindman believed their new position significantly overlapped the Federal right flank. In an effort to further exploit this advantage, Johnson added another complication by ordering Hindman's pair of brigades to execute a right wheel as they advanced. "Our instructions," Manigault remembered, "were to swing round to the right, my right being the pivot, and endeavor to close in the enemy or to . . . take him in flank." In theory , this was a sound plan. Keeping everyone properly aligned in this terrain, however, would be nearly impossible. Manigault faced the aforementioned gorge while Deas's Alabamians, as the outer edge of this grand wheel, would have to move faster to keep pace. Expecting them to keep up while climbing a slope so steep that Deas was forced to dismount and lead his horse up the ridge was asking a great deal. Coordinating this movement was bound to be at the least, daunting. In practice, it proved impossible.[5]

Johnson was determined that this effort would not fail for lack of manpower. Not only did he expect his own brigades under Fulton and Sugg, and Hindman's brigade under Anderson to join in, he also rode east to find Kershaw, whose command was re-organizing along the Vittetoe Road. Issues of rank forgotten, the South Carolinian gamely agreed to support Johnson's maneuver as best he could. In reality, Kershaw's men were unlikely to provide

4 *OR* 30, pt. 2, 343. Six of the 34th Alabama's 10 companies were behind Deas's line.

5 Tower, *A Carolinian Goes to War*, 99.

much help. Their overall casualties now approached 30 percent, with the hardest-hit units having lost nearly half their complement.[6]

Johnson was returning to his line when he received additional reinforcements. Evander McNair's brigade under Col. David Coleman reappeared after its long search for more ammunition. Coleman's brigade became separated during the confusion following the capture of the Union artillery line in Dyer Field, after which it headed rearward in search of a fresh supply of cartridges. Coleman had trouble finding Johnson's ordnance train. According to Lt. Col. Daniel H. Reynolds, his men of the 1st Arkansas Mounted Rifles resorted to the same measures the Federals were adopting on Snodgrass Hill: rummaging through the cartridge boxes of the fallen, friend and foe alike. No prisoner passed by their ranks without being stripped of his ammo. Coleman eventually fell back all the way to Brotherton Field before finding a full supply. His men also rested here a short time until one of Johnson's aides ordered them back to the front.[7]

With no place to insert Coleman into his front line, Johnson formed the new arrivals in support behind Fulton and Sugg, just below Dent's and Everett's guns. Leading Company F of the 4th Arkansas, Lt. John W. Lavender remembered his first glimpse of the brigade's daunting new objective: "This Hill was a very Strong Point. They Massed Their Forces on it. The Hill on the South East Side . . . was very steep and Rough. Our Forces being Massed at the Foot of the Hill we Prepared to attack them by Climbing the Hill in Mass." Johnson's men, observed Lavender, were deployed "four lines deep."[8]

Johnson formed his line with care, for he intended it to be his most serious effort of the day. He described his preparations in detail in his report:

> Our line, from left to right, was formed . . . in the following order, viz. Deas' Manigault's, Johnson's [Fulton's] Gregg's [Sugg's] and Anderson's, with McNair's [Coleman's] in rear of Johnson. Deas' Brigade occupied the brow of the steep spur which forms the north side of the gorge through which the Crawfish [Dry Valley] Road passes Missionary Ridge. Manigault's stretched across the ravine and extended

6 *OR* 30, pt. 2, 304-305; Powell, "Numbers and Losses," CCNMP.

7 Entry for September 20, Reynolds Diary, UARK.

8 W. L. Gammage, *The Camp, The Bivouac, and The Battlefield, Being a History of the Fourth Arkansas Regiment from its First Organization down to the Present Date; Its Campaigns and its Battles, With an Occasional Reference to the Current Events of the Times, Including Biographical Sketches of its Field Officers and Others of the "Old Brigade"* (Arkansas Southern Press, 1958), 91; Lavender, *They Never Came Back*, 82-83.

> up the side of the adjacent spur to the right, on which Johnson's and McNair's Brigades, with seven pieces of artillery, were posted. Gregg's Brigade was formed on a spur of some greater length, extending more toward the east, and separated in part from the main ridge by a hollow, with a piece of table-land at its head to the west. Anderson's Brigade was formed in two lines on the right. . . . The section of Dent's artillery with Gregg's Brigade . . . was now moved to the hollow on the right, ready to be run up by hand on the main ridge as soon as it should be carried.[9]

The only flaw in these arrangements, noted Johnson, was that "Kershaw's brigade was somewhere on the right of, but not connected with, Anderson's [men]." Not counting Kershaw, Johnson's force numbered about 5,300 men. Each of his own three brigades (Sugg, Fulton, and Coleman) counted about 500 troops still with the ranks. Of Hindman's men, Anderson numbered about 1,000; Deas,1,200; and Manigault,1,600 muskets. With his preparations complete, Bushrod Johnson rode west and ordered General Deas to move out.[10]

Steedman's Federals made only minor adjustments to their line during the lull between Johnson's first repulse and the opening of his next grand assault. Nominally organized into two brigades, his men fought on the 20th in three distinct groups. The 22nd Michigan and 89th Ohio under direction of Col. Heber Le Favour formed one sub-command, holding the line just to the right of the 21st Ohio. General Walter Whitaker's remaining four regiments still held Steedman's center, though only the 40th Ohio was on the front line (the 96th Illinois, 115th Illinois, and 84th Indiana were still reforming, and in various stages of confusion and exhaustion). Colonel John Mitchell's regiments held the west end of the line, braced by the six guns of Battery M, 1st Illinois. Mitchell's men would bear the brunt of the next attack.

After losing about 200 men during the first collision, Mitchell's line numbered about 900 troops. With 235 rank and file, Lt. Col. Henry B. Banning's undersized 121st Ohio held Mitchell's right. Having originally come into action against Johnson's left flank, the 121st's losses were the lightest of any in Steedman's command. Still, Mitchell's line was stretched thin. On the extreme right, Orderly Sgt. John J. Ramage, leading Company A of the 121st was acutely aware of the lack of support to the west. "We were apprehensive that the enemy were moving around our right . . . on the right of a deep ravine,"

9 *OR* 30, pt. 2, 462.

10 Ibid.

recalled Ramage. Accordingly, he continued, "I took a squad of my men and moved . . . over the hill some fifty rods [to the right.] While . . . there the men saw . . . some Rebel skirmishers coming up over the hill. . . . Presently . . . on our left front a line of battle of the enemy were seen rising over the edge of the hill and [down] in the ravine. I then ordered my men to return to the company." Ramage had spotted Deas's Alabamians picking their way up the slope.[11]

Hoping to ensure more effective coordination this time around, Johnson gave "careful instructions to preserve the dress and the connection to the right" to each brigade in turn as he rode back east along his line. Thus began the "hardest fight of the day," wrote one Alabamian. "We were then ordered to take a hill so steep that our General had to lead his horse, and this will give some idea of how difficult a position we had to assault."[12]

Disrupted by geography, Johnson's plan fell apart almost from the start. From left to right, Deas's line included the 17th Alabama Sharpshooters, then the 25th, 39th, 19th, 50th, and finally the 22nd Alabama infantry regiments. A forbidding slope almost immediately in front of them proved to be the first difficulty. The 22nd Alabama promptly lost contact with Manigault's left, which as Deas later reported, stripped his brigade of "any support whatever," since there was no one on Deas's own left. The climb up the hill was difficult, but at least Deas's troops were mostly sheltered from Federal fire while doing so. When they drew near the top, a Union infantry line and the fire of at least four artillery pieces greeted them at close range. "[W]e met with such a terrible fire of musketry and grape that we were compelled to fall back," explained Col. J. G. Coltart, commander of the 50th Alabama. Lieutenant James H. Fraser, also of the 50th Alabama, described that same dreadful moment in a letter home to his father: "The ground was so steep that we could not go with a rush, until we reached the top of the hill. [There] we were met with a terrible volley . . . no more than 80 yards distant. The men could go no further, death reigned on every side."

For a few bloody minutes the Alabamians slugged it out with Mitchell's Yankees. Already exhausted from the morning's fight and fighting without artillery or any support on their right, Deas's troops were unable to reach or break the line. Colonel Samuel McSpadden of the 19th Alabama reported that

11 Powell, "Numbers and Losses," CCNMP; Letter of March 17, 1896, John Ramage to Chickamauga National Park Commission, 121st Ohio file, CCNMP.

12 *OR* 30, pt. 2, 462; *Mobile Daily Register*, October 4, 1863.

his regiment fell back briefly just below the crest, where it reformed to make a second effort. Similar disorder gripped Deas's other regiments.[13]

The Union fire was intense and unrelenting. According to George Dolton of Battery M, "we double-shotted our guns with canister and reserved our fire until they were at close quarters." In a letter, Dolton exulted, "As fast as our canister would mow them down, they would close up & advance. We must have piled them up." Each of Deas's regiments gamely renewed the attack on its own hook, a series of piecemeal affairs the Federals took as separate charges. Each attempt, however, did nothing except add to their casualties.[14]

Additionally, the Union right flank on the western side of the high ground now received some more help. Captain George Hicks and the 96th Illinois were resting some distance to the east on the lee side of the ridge when Deas's men stepped off to attack. The 96th was still there when the Alabamians appeared below the crest. Captain Seth Moe of Steedman's staff arrived, and, as he later recounted: "It was then discovered that the enemy's left overlapped our right, and to meet the condition thus presented [the 96th] at my suggestion, bore to the right." Acting on Moe's instructions, Hicks and the 96th now hurried forward to extend Mitchell's flank on the 121st Ohio's right. The 96th's unexpected arrival sparked considerable controversy. No Ohioan recalled the 96th's appearance at the time. In later years, the Buckeyes of the 121st Ohio would carefully guard their status as anchor of the right flank. The addition of a couple of hundred extra muskets from the 96th falling in on their right would cloud that claim. As a result, the Buckeyes would continue to dispute that the 96th ever appeared to bolster their flank.[15]

In reality, more than simple jealously over shared battle honors worked to hide Hicks's arrival. The situation was very confused, and several factors obscured the Illinoisians's appearance. The 96th came up the ridge from behind the 121st Ohio just as its commander, Lieutenant Colonel Banning, decided the

13 *OR* 30, pt. 2, 331, 334, 339; "Dear Pa," letter of September 26, 1863, printed in *Montgomery Daily Advertiser*, October 8, 1905, 17.

14 Dolton, Capsule History of Battery M, CCNMP; Dolton, *The Path of Patriotism*, 78.

15 John C. Smith, *The Right of the Federal Army at Chickamauga* (Knight & Leonard Co., 1894), 12; Partridge, *Ninety-Sixth Regiment Illinois*, 238-239. Moe mistakenly remembered Colonel Champion as still commanding his regiment. The placement of the 96th Illinois's monument on Horseshoe Ridge would generate a great deal of controversy, with other regiments hotly disputing the 96th's claims. For more detail on this affair, see David A. Powell, "The Battles for Horseshoe Ridge," *North & South*, vol. 8, no. 2 (March, 2005), 48-59.

moment called for a countercharge. Banning's Buckeyes thrust forward angling southwest, driving the already battered Alabama formations before them. This advance put the spine of the ridge between the Buckeyes and the 96th, which prevented the Ohioans from seeing Hicks's supporting movement.

The 121st, recalled Sergeant Ramage of Company A, "charged them, drove them back along the hill and out of the ravine." Several months later, fellow sergeant Abner Said got a chance to track the bloody wake of the regiment's attack. Sergeant Said was not present during the fight, but he accompanied a burial detail back to the battlefield in January 1864 to help identify the regiment's dead. While at their mournful task, Said's comrades described what happened: "the men, in talking of the battle, showed me the places where they charged up the hill, where they held the ridge . . . and [where] the regiment charged down the spur and in the ravine where there was desperate slaughter, and we found many of the bodies of the 121st in that ravine." The 22nd Alabama bore most of the fury of this countercharge. With the 22nd's senior officers all dead or wounded, the regiment was in the hands of Capt. Harry T. Toulmin. It was Toulmin's misfortune to be in charge during the 121st's counter blow. According to Toulmin, his regimental color-bearer "fearlessly rushed to the front and in advance of the line, [where he] was literally riddled with balls." Next, he continued, Federal fire threw the Alabamians "into confusion, in which the loss [of] the colors was not discovered until too late." Members of the 121st Ohio triumphantly bore the 22nd's flag back to their own lines, and eventually sent it to Ohio as a trophy.[16]

Captain Hicks witnessed this attack. Years later he even remembered joining it. In fact, he and the rest of the 96th Illinois probably did little more than deliver parting shots into the mass of fleeing Rebels. Illinois Pvt. Cyrus Pomeroy was wounded about this time. "[W]e heard the wild Rebel yell as they began a charge. . . . Then came the order from our commander, 'fix bayonets; forward, right oblique, double-quick, march!' Soon we were on the right of our battery and had driven the enemy back," wrote Pomeroy, "[and] with the

16 Ramage Letter, CCNMP; Letter of March 17, 1896, Abner Said to Chickamauga National Park Commission, 121st Ohio file, CCNMP. *OR* 30, pt. 2, 337. Letter of March 17, 1896, J. S. Gill to Chickamauga National Park Commission, 121st Ohio file, CCNMP. Said had been a prisoner and returned to the regiment shortly after the battle. The identity of this color bearer remains a mystery. Toulmin identifies him only as "Private Braswell." Unfortunately, the only Braswell listed in the compiled service records for the 22nd Alabama was named Thomas, and he was killed at Shiloh. Two other men had similar names—Pvts. Joseph M. Bracewell and Elseylus Brazile—but their records are too sketchy to make a determination.

eleventh load in my gun, while advancing in the shelter of a tree to reply to a rebel who had just fired toward me I felt the sharp sting of a bullet. . . . It had passed through my left leg about six inches above the joint." Fortunately, no bones were broken and Pomeroy hobbled his way to the rear.[17]

During this first move to the right one more fracturing occurred, which only helped to confuse things. At this time, the 96th Illinois broke into two pieces and would fight that way for the rest of the action. The split was triggered by Colonel Champion's return, resuming control of his regiment because Colonel Whitaker had similarly returned to take up the reins of brigade command. Hicks spotted Champion, but assumed he was still acting brigade commander. Champion, however, apparently did not see Hicks. While Hicks was following Captain Moe to the right, Champion was reasserting his authority over the regiment's left. As a result, the three left-hand companies (B, G, and K) split off on Champion's order and hustled leftward. As Moe later put it, "in the confusion of the moment two or three companies of the 96th were so badly intermingled with the . . . Second Brigade that they did not move to the right . . . and consequently were separated from the regiment."[18]

While Banning's enthusiastic Buckeyes were finishing off the 22nd Alabama, Hicks placed his portion of the 96th into line alongside the two rightmost guns of Burton's Battery M, who were at that moment also busy punishing Deas's troops. The 96th moved up onto the crest in time (as noted above) to witness the 121st Ohio's charge, and lent a hand by rounding up a number of stray Rebels overrun by Banning's enthusiastic Ohioans. As Banning's men returned to the main Union line, Hicks noticed a "little hill, heavily timbered [where] the men were allowed to scatter themselves . . . taking position behind trees . . . [maintaining] a slow, irregular fire upon the enemy." Hicks took the additional precaution of detaching two more companies and sending them farther to the right as a flank guard. By 4:00 p.m., the 96th Illinois was operating in three distinct elements scattered the length of the divisional line.[19]

17 Pomeroy G.A.R. Questionnaire, Chicago History Museum.

18 Partridge, *Ninety-Sixth Regiment Illinois*, 238; Gayle Letter, CCNMP; Smith, *The Right of the Federal Army*, 12.

19 Partridge, *Ninety-Sixth Regiment Illinois*, 239; 96th Illinois flank marker, Horseshoe Ridge, CCNMP. These two companies are tentatively identified as A and D.

The overly-complicated nature of Johnson's plan was now readily apparent. From left to right, Arthur Manigault's line included the 34th, 28th, and 24th Alabama regiments, with the combined 10th/19th South Carolina holding the right flank. Numbering about 1,600 men his line stretched more than 400 yards. Manigault's movement began about the same time Deas's men stepped off, but Manigault's line advanced fitfully. According to Col. Newton N. Davis of the 24th, the line "moved forward upon the slope of a hill, where it was ordered to halt . . . to await the movement of some troops on the left." This pause of several minutes was intended to give Deas time to wheel his line to the right as Johnson ordered. Unfortunately, Manigault's line was slow in restarting, and Deas's troops pressed forward alone, leaving the latter brigadier to feel, justifiably, that he had no support on this flank. The combination of the rough terrain, Johnson's overly-complex plan, the Federal efforts atop the crest, and Manigault's tactical problems all meant that Deas's line was bloodily repulsed before Manigault had much of a chance to come into action.[20]

When Manigault finally resumed his advance, things began to go badly all at once. Major John Slaughter, commanding the 34th Alabama on Manigault's left, detailed the problems: "The regiment had moved forward . . . some 50 or 60 paces up the hill when they were met by the right regiment of Deas's brigade [22nd Alabama] falling back in disorder . . ." Deas's stampeded men crashed through the 34th, completely disrupting Slaughter's formation. Roughly half of the men of the 34th rallied and continued up the hill, where they would fight alongside the 28th Alabama, next in line to their own right, for the rest of the action. The remainder, however, fell back to "the top of the opposite hill" and remained there the rest of the day.[21]

On the right of the 34th Alabama, Lt. Joshua Calloway in the 28th Alabama was struggling up the hill, all the while impressed by the awful din. "A thousand thunderstorms all turned loose together could not equal the noise," he wrote his wife. "We were now ordered forward and when we got half way up the hill they opened on us with great fury. . . . But we moved steadily on till we got in about twenty yards where we halted and went regularly to work. Here commenced a scene that beggars description, and God forbid that I should ever have to witness such another. The carnage was awful. Men were shot down all around

20 *OR* 30, pt. 2, 346, 353.

21 Ibid., 353.

me. I was indeed in the very midst of death. We fought them thus close I suppose about ten minutes when, as if by command, our whole line gave way and we went down the hill like a gang of sheep."[22]

Some of the Federals facing Calloway's regiment included the 98th Ohio. With only seven companies in the fight, the 98th began the action with just 181 men, and combat losses from the initial clash whittled down that number considerably. The 28th Alabama, by contrast, entered the day's fight back in Brotherton Field with 626 men. Although its casualties had also been high, its ranks included the impromptu reinforcement of at least half of the 34th Alabama. Here the combined Alabamians likely still had at least 400-500 men in the ranks as they traded volleys with fewer than 150 Federals. The Alabamans, however, were worn down by their mad scramble and had just seen Deas's men on their left break in wild confusion.

The Ohioans of the 98th did not lack for pluck. Captain Armstrong Thomas, already these Buckeyes's second commander that day, ordered a charge just as the Alabamians faltered. The 98th responded with enthusiasm. Captain David Roach provided the details: "We made another charge upon them, driving them the second time from their position. Here we sustained the loss of Captain Thomas and a few men killed, with several wounded. With this, the men seemed somewhat confounded; but Captain [William C.] Lochary immediately took command and the regiment was ordered to fall back over the crest." The 98th lost two more leaders in quick succession during the retreat. Lochary fell first, killed on the field, and then Adj. Duncan Milner was hit almost as soon as he took up the reins of command. Once he returned to the crest, Captain Roach found himself in charge—the fifth commander in less than two hours, and the fourth in less than 30 minutes.[23]

The fight now deteriorated into a confused mess. Men on both sides described the seesaw nature of the contest. The 28th Alabama rallied and made a second try, this time, according to Calloway, advancing "again within about fifty yards of our former position." A Federal private named Oliver Smith fighting in the ranks of Company G, the 98th Ohio, recounted a similar cut and thrust: "After we drove them back, we soon discovered them flanking us but we soon changed our position and repulsed them again, but they . . . rallied and advanced again, and again we drove them back, but all of this was not without

22 Hallock, *The Civil War Letters of Joshua K. Calloway*, 137.

23 *Stuebenville Weekly Herald*, October 21, 1863.

loss on our side." Alongside the 98th, the 113th Ohio gave ground under this same pressure. Private Jasper Hall of the 113th recorded his distress at seeing a comrade fall at his side, shot in the back. "He was no coward," insisted Hall, worried that his friend's wound would be misinterpreted. "He staggered a few steps and stopped. . . . [I] laid the poor fellow down and hurried on."[24]

The Alabamians failed to exploit even this fleeting success, however, because as Calloway explained, "the Regt on our left gave way again and the Yankees swung round into their place giving them a complete crossfire on the 28th [Alabama]." According to Confederate Col. John C. Reid, "twice did we reach the summit of the hill in close proximity to the enemy, and as many times forced by weight of numbers, canister, shell and grape shot, to retire." Reid's advance was also checked by the sudden appearance of Colonel Champion and the three companies of the 96th Illinois, arriving to bolster the 113th. Apparently Champion joined his small detachment to the 113th, for as Henry Gayle of the 96th Illinois's Company G recalled, they "struck another command, and moved with them a distance to the right."[25]

On Manigault's right, the 10th/19th South Carolina fared no better. "We moved upon this position about 3:30 o'clock, and were several times repulsed, but not discouraged," reported Col. James Pressley. His terse account conveys nothing of the desperate nature of the fighting. Felix G. De Fontaine, a newspaper correspondent with the army, fleshed out the story, including the near-loss of the colors: "During this stubborn resistance . . . the flag of the 10th South Carolina was . . . captured . . . and its bearer, Sergeant Glysson was killed, but the regiment rallying promptly in this emergency, the Federals were in turn attacked and the colors recaptured."[26]

The 10th/19th faced the 40th Ohio on Whitaker's right. The Buckeyes entered the battle with 537 men, making it Whitaker's largest regiment. By this time it still fielded at least 400, or about the same strength as the 10th/19th,

24 Hallock, *Letters of Joshua K. Calloway*, 137; Letter of Private Oliver Smith, as quoted at: http://www.mojaveweblog.com/98thOVI/index.html. Accessed 3/20/2010, copy in author's collection; Entry for September 20, 1863, Jasper Newton Hall Diary, Creighton University. The Smith letter was originally posted on a website dedicated to the 98th Ohio and maintained by Dan Walker. That site has since disappeared.

25 Hallock, *Letters of Joshua K. Calloway*, 137; *OR* 30, pt. 2, 349; Gayle Letter, CCNMP.

26 *OR* 30, pt. 2, 355; *Charleston Daily Courier*, October 17, 1863. While the colors were indeed recaptured, De Fontaine failed to note that it was not done so by the 10th/19th. Instead, the 17th Tennessee recovered the lost banner.

which had been whittled down some after its fight with Sheridan back near Lytle Hill at the south end of the battlefield, around midday. The 40th was not without its troubles. During the first attack, Lt. Col. William Jones was discovered hiding behind a tree. He was marched at gunpoint to Steedman, who ordered him off the field in disgrace, leaving a major to fill his command shoes. Still, this setback did little to dampen the 40th's ardor. Watching his fellow Buckeyes with admiration at the head of his 113th Ohio, Col. Darius Warner acknowledged that "the 40th Ohio came to our support and charged over the hill in splendid style, driving the enemy before them."[27]

This bloody and exhausting give and take shattered Deas's and Manigault's brigades. Manigault later admitted that "towards the latter part of the fight there was scarcely any order preserved, and no defined line. Regiments and companies were inextricably mixed up, and it resembled more a skirmish on a grand scale than the conflict of a line of battle." With this chaos came the loss of command control. Newspaperman De Fontaine agreed, observing that "the different regiments became mixed with each other, and here and there the faint hearted were stealing to safer positions in the rear; still," he insisted with patriotic exaggeration, "there was no thought of defeat. Men fought from behind trees and coverts, loading and firing while they dodged from point to point, but always gaining ground." Lieutenant Calloway of the 28th Alabama was more forthright: "there were a good many laying back and skulking behind trees under the hill." Whatever anyone wrote, there was no denying reality: both Deas and Manigault had been repulsed all along the line. For the moment, at least, their men had had enough of combat.[28]

Throughout this attack Bushrod Johnson and his staff watched with mounting frustration. Johnson's brusque report, penned a month after the fact, dedicated only a few lines to Hindman's contribution. His men, Johnson observed, participated in "a most obstinate struggle." Once repulsed, he added, they "did not again enter the fight." The clipped description reflects Johnson's anger and frustration with the performance delivered by Deas and Manigault.

27 Woods, *Steedman and His Men*, 59; Darius Warner Letter, 113th Ohio file, CCNMP. The regimental history is silent on Jones's conduct on September 20. However, it lavishes no praise on him, either. He is only listed as commanding the regiment from September 1 to November 1, 1863. He resigned "on account of disability" on February 28, 1864. Beach, *History of the Fortieth Ohio*, 151.

28 Tower, *A Carolinian Goes to War*, 100; *Charleston Daily Courier*, October 17, 1863; Hallock, *Letters of Joshua K. Calloway*, 137.

In January 1864, Johnson asked one of his aides, Lt. George Marchbanks, to submit a more detailed follow-up report. "According to the best of my recollection," Marchbanks wrote, "I delivered the order [to advance] to General Deas. I do not recollect his reply, but the troops were not advanced immediately. I was sent back with the same instructions two or three times." Then, when they finally entered the fight, they "had scarcely gotten under fire when they began running back—one, two, and three together—until finally both brigades gave back in utter confusion." Marchbanks helped rally the men. Instead of returning to action, however, Deas informed the stunned lieutenant "that he and General Manigault had had a consultation, and that . . . they thought it would not be best to put these troops in the same place, 'that they would not stand,' or words to that effect." According to Marchbanks's damning conclusion, "I do not think these two brigades were under fire over twenty minutes."[29]

Marchbanks was being unfair. There is no doubt both brigades fought stubbornly and for longer than 20 minutes, and that both suffered severe losses here. However, neither unit fought well on Horseshoe Ridge. Massive straggling from previous combat and the exhausting hill climb thinned their ranks and they were repulsed by half their number. Manigault's earlier assessment that the division had slipped to "third-rate" status had merit.

Federal leadership was crucial in holding the ridge. Steedman turned in a magnificent performance. His presence was felt everywhere, and often at the critical point of action. He was personally involved in keeping the Federal line from breaking during crisis after crisis. One memorable trick Steedman used repeatedly was to ride or walk up to a regiment's color guard and seize one of the flags. This stirred the men's sense of possessiveness and unit pride. As the primary means of guiding and directing a regiment during combat when verbal orders passed unheard, the colors also were an immediate way to catch everyone's attention. Once he had drawn every eye, Steedman rallied or steadied a regiment, as needed. He didn't always get possession of the banner, however. J. Batchelor of Company I, 78th Illinois, recorded what happened when the general reached his regiment: "Steedman commanding our division walked along the line encouraging the men . . . taking the colors and walking forward with them. He came to Thomas Edmonson, our Color Sergeant, [and] asked him for the flag. [Edmonson] refused to give it . . . saying 'I can carry it

29 *OR* 30, pt. 2, 462-463, 470.

anywhere.' 'Then,' [retorted Steedman] 'step out two paces. . . . Men, rally on your colors,' and they did." After the battle, men from almost every one of the division's 10 regiments recalled an incident of this sort within their ranks, stories that would reverberate and grow with the telling in G. A. R. halls and regimental reunions during the years to come.[30]

On the division's right, Mitchell handled his four regiments well, if without Steedman's flair for the dramatic. Mitchell's men were fortunate in that they initially climbed the ridge largely unopposed and did not plunge recklessly down the other side, as did Whitaker's troops. Nor, unlike Whitaker, was Mitchell wounded and forced to leave the field for a time. This continuity of command helped maintain the stability of the Union right. Farther east along Steedman's line, however, matters were almost as confused as they were within Rebel ranks.

As noted earlier, Whitaker was just now returning to the fight. When first struck, he made his way back to an aid station behind the Snodgrass cabin. Captain Webster, whose own 10th Kentucky had just been relieved from its position on Hill Two, recognized him. "I heard a familiar voice, and looking around saw Gen. W. C. Whitaker riding towards Gen. Thomas," recalled the captain. "After paying his respects to the General, he called for a surgeon. He had been wounded in the charge over the hill by a bullet, which struck him in the thigh. He did not dismount." While being treated, Whitaker excitedly described the attack and "the hot place they found on the rebel side of the hill. 'We gave them H___!'"[31]

At least one observer believed Whitaker benefited from a more informal sort of doctoring. George Dolton of Battery M, 1st Illinois artillery, wrote years later that when he "saw General Whitaker that day, he was under the influence of something that made him reel considerably in his saddle. I do not think . . . when he rode to the rear, he could tell where his command lay. He wanted my men to fix bayonets on their cannon, when they told him they were out of ammunition." Was Whitaker drunk when he returned to the line? Dolton's accusation is the only evidence suggesting that he was inebriated. It is possible

30 Entry for September 20, John Batchelor Diary, ALPL.

31 Webster, "Chickamauga," *National Tribune*, July 2, 1891. Whitaker was not only a prominent Kentucky general, but also a state senator, making him a highly recognizable figure among the Kentucky regiments in the Army of the Cumberland. Whitaker actually received a blow to the stomach, not the thigh. Jack D. Welsh, M.D., *Medical Histories of Union Generals* (Kent State University Press, 1996), Kindle edition location 9548, states only that Whitaker was "wounded on the right side of his abdomen."

that personal admiration or state loyalty prevented Whitaker aide Lieutenant Pepoon or fellow Kentuckian Captain Webster from mentioning any sign of intoxication. Other witnesses, however, went out of their way to praise Whitaker. Captain George Hicks of the 96th Illinois claimed Whitaker and his staff "endeared themselves to every member of the brigade by their heroic bearing" during the fight. General Thomas, who saw at least as much of Whitaker as did Dolton, thought well enough of the Kentuckian that on November 30, 1863, he recommended Whitaker for promotion to major general "for the gallant and obstinate defense . . . in the battle of Chickamauga."[32]

On the other hand, there are reports of Whitaker being intoxicated in other circumstances. Six weeks after the battle, Assistant Secretary of War Charles H. Dana had an opportunity to observe Whitaker at Brown's Ferry outside Chattanooga on November 1, 1863. The next day Dana telegraphed his boss, Secretary of War Edwin M. Stanton and reported that "Brigadier General Whitaker [was] drunk and disorderly in public." What effect Dana's charges had is unclear. Whitaker was not promoted to major general as Thomas recommended, but he did continue to command brigades in combat through the end of the war during the Atlanta and Tennessee campaigns. He was finally brevetted to two-star rank in March 1865 for his service at Atlanta.[33]

Certainly Whitaker was excited, as reflected in Webster's recollections. In this era, an officer's "coolness" under fire was much admired. Displaying excitement or agitation was often disparaged. The bruising to his abdomen probably made it very difficult to ride comfortably, which may explain his unsteady seat. Whether he was intoxicated remains an open question. Drunk or not, Whitaker's reappearance did little to restore order to his line. He arrived just as Deas and Manigault were being repulsed, but Bushrod Johnson's division was not yet fought out. Sugg's and Fulton's brigades, with Coleman in support, were now aimed directly at Whitaker's command.

32 "Dear Sir & Comrade," George Dolton to Col. A. McMahan, Feb. 3, 1890, BGSU; George Pepoon to Sister Betsy, October 5, 1863, George Pepoon Letters, Northern Illinois University; *Northwest Galena Gazette*, October 13, 1863; *OR* 31, pt. 3, 201. How did Dolton happen to see Whitaker? His battery was mainly supporting Mitchell's brigade, and Whitaker's command was several hundred yards father to the left. It is possible Dolton's "eyewitness" testimony is actually hearsay, gleaned from others right after the battle and, by 1890, metamorphosed into a memory of direct observation by age and time.

33 *OR* 31, pt. 3, 55; Warner, *Generals in Blue*, 556.

Whitaker soon discovered he retained control over only about one-half of his brigade. He believed the 22nd Michigan and 89th Ohio had been loaned to General Brannan and were now beyond his authority. About one-half of the 96th Illinois had already departed to support Battery M. This left the injured general with the 40th Ohio, 84th Indiana, and 115th Illinois. At the moment he returned, the 40th was driving off part of Manigault's command, unsupported and out in advance of the rest of the Federal line. Both the 84th and 115th were sheltering behind the crest where they had come to rest after the first charge. They were the only formations Whitaker had at hand to help the Buckeyes of the 40th stop Johnson's approach.[34]

In Johnson's front line, Confederate Lt. Col. Watt Floyd and his 17th Tennessee held the left flank of Fulton's brigade. Floyd had watched hopefully when Hindman's men first arrived and moved into the attack. If all went well, Floyd and his men might finally be done fighting for the day: "I thought that if we could hold the hill until they came up, the remnant of my regiment would get some rest." The collision between the 10th/19th South Carolina (Manigault's brigade) and the 40th Ohio, however, deflated his optimism. "I soon learned that I was mistaken." The South Carolinians "started off well," Floyd noted, "[but] when they advanced about 50 yards they received . . . fire . . . and fell back."[35]

With the rest of his planned attack dissolving into bloody ruin, Johnson ordered his own men forward. Fulton's four small regiments replaced the 10th/19th South Carolina, while Coleman's brigade marched out of reserve to extend the left of Floyd's 17th Tennessee, trying to fill in the gap left by Manigault's 24th and 28th Alabama regiments. In the 25th Arkansas, one of Coleman's regiments, Pvt. Jones C. Moore also watched as the 10th/19th South Carolina recoiled: "In less time than it takes to tell it they came back in double quick and made no halt until they got down, jumping over us, when that gallant hero, General Johnson, shouted: 'Arkansas boys, forward!'" Moore vividly recalled Johnson's horse rearing and Johnson wildly waving hat and sword in encouragement.[36]

34 The 22nd and 89th, still operating under Le Favour's command, were never assigned to Brannan, but Whitaker mistakenly thought otherwise.

35 *OR* 30, pt. 2, 483.

36 Ibid.; J. C. Moore, "McNair's Arkansas Brigade," *Confederate Veteran*, vol. XIV, no. 3 (March, 1906), 124.

Despite Johnson's theatrics, bold charges and countercharges were now largely a thing of the past, at least for this fight; replaced by slow and careful advances, met by stubborn defense. Lieutenant Colonel Floyd led his Tennesseans to "the summit of the hill and got . . . into line. Here we had a long and desperate struggle." The 40th Ohio fell back, losing the Palmetto flag it had captured just minutes earlier. Adjutant Alexander R. Greigg of the 25th Tennessee recovered the 10th South Carolina's banner when a retreating or fallen Ohioan dropped it, and carried the standard back to the grateful Gamecocks. Leading the 1st Arkansas Mounted Rifles, Lt. Col. Daniel Reynolds mistook the South Carolinians for Fulton's men: "An attack was made on our lines and Johnson's Brigade broke & attempted to leave the field, and were stopped by our brigade. We were at once ordered forward to drive back the enemy soon yielded a short distance and contested the ground stubbornly. . . . Here the contest was terrific for nearly an hour."[37]

With the 40th Ohio retreating and the Union center again imperiled, Whitaker sent his last two regiments into the fight. The 84th Indiana moved with speed. "In the second charge we again passed over [the] ridge and partly down the opposite side," noted Capt. William Boyd. The Hoosiers were ordered to fix bayonets, "after which we stood for some time." That position proved a hot one, and the men of the 84th were less than pleased with their stationary exposed position. Having already left Col. Nelson Trusler back behind the ridge, too sick and too winded to continue, there was also some confusion about who was now in charge. "Many officers became restive and Capt. [George] Carter . . . swore, wanting to know who was to command us. Looking towards me he asked if 'some of you ranking captains could not take command.'" Boyd's sarcasm got the better of him: "I pointed to where a clump of trees had got between the Major [Elias Neff] and the enemy and said 'There is the Major, Captain.'" Carter, his anger thoroughly aroused, shouted "Major, what in the Hell are you going to do with this regiment!" The shamed Neff emerged from his clump of "hateful trees" and led the unit back over the crest to where the 84th could use the brow of the hill as shelter.[38]

37 *OR* 30, pt. 2, 483, 491; "Sept. 20," Reynolds Diary, UARK.

38 Boyd Journal, UC Berkeley. Boyd claims that in this movement, the 84th fell back over the 96th Illinois. If so, these were either wounded men still lying there from earlier, or the three companies acting under Colonel Champion's direction. The bulk of the 96th was on the far right flank under Captain Hicks's command.

The 115th Illinois used the lull not only to rest and get water, but to gulp down a hasty lunch of hardtack and raw salt pork. With the action again heating up, however, they returned to the fight. The 115th crested the ridge between the 89th Ohio and the 84th Indiana. They found the same ridge top no less naked than did the 84th. "It was necessary for our line to be on the crest to do effective work," explained Lt. Isaac Royce, "but being there exposed it not only to the murderous fire of the enemy in front, but an equally destructive fire from the slopes . . . to the right and left. It must not be supposed that our lines were dressed as on parade. . . . Each man handled his gun in his own way. . . . Sometimes the whole line lay close to the ground, loading and firing without rising. . . . At other times the men would step back . . . from the crest, load their pieces, and then step briskly forward."[39]

The 84th Indiana and 115th Illinois blunted Bushrod Johnson's attack. Facing stalemate atop the ridge, the Confederates looked for help. "During this awful struggle," reported Lieutenant Colonel Floyd of the 17th Tennessee, "hundreds were skulking behind trees to our rear. Myself and several officers of our brigade went back . . . and tried to rally these men—we succeeded in rallying enough to increase . . . our fire smartly." Floyd also proudly noted that none of the stragglers he collected were from Fulton's brigade, but neither were they all from Hindman's division. On October 13, 1863, for example, Sgt. John M. Knowles of Sugg's 1st Tennessee Battalion was convicted of leaving the ranks to "then and there pillage and plunder" a silver watch and 65 dollars from the body of his comrade in Company B, Pvt. Francis W. Wilkinson.[40]

The 23rd Tennessee's commander, Col. R. H. Keeble, was also furious at these malingerers. Echoing Lieutenant Marchbank's disgust, Keeble noted that he and "every other field officer of the brigade begged and besought a brigade which was skulking behind trees in our rear to come forward and give but one volley. Alas! They heeded not the call."[41]

With Fulton and Coleman seemingly checked, Union Col. Thomas Champion decided to make one more effort at clearing the slopes of the ridge to his front. As described previously, when Whitaker returned to assume

39 Royce, *History of the 115th Illinois*, 129, 132-133.

40 *OR* 30, pt. 2, 483; Records of Military Court, Longstreet's Corps, Museum of the Confederacy, Richmond, VA.

41 *OR* 30, pt. 2, 486. The skulking "brigade" referred to was in fact a large mass of men from all six of Hindman's and Johnson's brigades engaged here.

command, Champion went in search of his 96th Illinois. He reappeared with his de-facto three-company battalion, and, unbeknownst to Whitaker, fell in alongside the 113th Ohio. Witnessing Manigault's precipitate retreat, Champion realized the moment was ripe for an attack of his own. "We . . . again charged the enemy," he reported, "driving him down the ridge running nearly parallel with our first line nearly half a mile." The 113th Ohio did not follow, choosing instead to let Champion and his handful of Federals plunge recklessly into the midst of Fulton's entire brigade. Worst of all, the diagonal nature of their advance meant that Champion's forlorn hope was exposed to a raking fire from their friends in the 84th Indiana and 115th Illinois in passing. Not surprisingly, Champion soon felt "compelled to retire," but he remained convinced that he came within an inch of complete success. After the battle, regimental surgeon Dr. Moses Evans wrote that "our officers seem sanguine that with 500 more men we could have driven the enemy completely from the field."[42]

Private George Butler in the 96th's Company G was wounded here. "We fought over the ground until 4:00 p.m., when we had to retreat. It was about this time that I was shot," recalled Butler. "I tried to get up, but seemed to be numbed all over. . . . I was finally able to sit up . . . and found I was hit in my left foot. I took off my shoe and stocking and found a ragged hole in the side of my foot. The bullet did not go through but seemed to be just under the skin on top of the foot. I took my knife and was about to cut it open." Just before Butler embarked on this bit of impromptu field surgery, however, "one of my company came up and said 'don't do it.' The Rebs were close up, but he got me on my feet and we started for the rear." Butler next hitched a ride on a passing artillery caisson, who took him to a small house (perhaps the Brock or Mullis cabins, each about a mile north of the fighting) where he spent "the most lonely night" of his life, expecting Rebels to appear at any moment. The next morning the private hobbled another half-mile on a makeshift pair of crutches until he finally found Union troops and an ambulance ride back to Chattanooga.[43]

Farther to the right the 89th Ohio didn't make a charge, but fought aplenty. Sergeant William J. McKell of Company D noted that Confederate enthusiasm seemed to be waning: "In fifteen or twenty minutes after the first charge, we

42 *OR* 30, pt. 1, 865; *Waukegan Weekly Gazette*, September 26, 1863; *OR* 30, pt. 1, 865. Champion used the same phrasing in his official report.

43 George Butler Reminiscences, 96th Illinois file, CCNMP.

received another; the rebs having to fall back as before; after sustaining our fire from five to ten minutes. They were longer now in coming up," he noted, "and when they made the next charge it was with the same result." This time the 89th did not get off as lightly. A number of men were killed and wounded in this action, one of whom troubled the sergeant a great deal. Eighteen-year-old Pvt. John Dillman was a fun-loving, good natured youth, well-liked by the rest of Company D. He was gripped by a premonition that he would be killed in the first fire of the coming battle, however, and superstitiously threw away his playing cards during the approach march. When the 89th crested the ridge the first time, Dillman bolted in panic. A little later McKell was surprised and heartened to see a shame-faced Dillman return: "At the second charge he took his place in line, using no caution to protect himself, but standing out in the open in full view of the rebels, loading and firing his gun. A ball struck him in the centre of the forehead with a dull thud. He raised his eyes, looked wildly about, and fell like a log."[44]

Johnson's Confederates had been in heavy action three days running, and thus far had driven the Federals from every position. They had fought magnificently, but this last obstacle proved to be too much. They had repeatedly sought help in taking the ridge, only to be disappointed each time. Now their ranks were too thin and their energy too sapped to drive any farther and the effective collapse of Hindman's division left them again unsupported. It was five in the afternoon; daylight was on the wane. But the Federals opposing them were in little better shape, and a last opportunity for victory still beckoned if the troops to seize it could be found.

44 Watt P. Marchman, "The Journal of Sergt. Wm. J. McKell," *Civil War History*, vol. 3, no. 3 (March, 1957), 316-318.

Chapter Twenty-Three

All Quiet in Kelly Field:

Sunday, 1:00 p.m. to 4:00 p.m.

In the fields around the Dyer house and on the slopes of Snodgrass Hill, the afternoon had been filled with desperate combat. In stark contrast, the Kelly Field sector of the Union line witnessed no serious action after the last of the Confederate attacks by Leonidas Polk's Right Wing (The Confederate Reserve Corps) fizzled out around noon. This quiescence on the Union left allowed XIV corps commander George Thomas to turn his full energy and attention to defending Horseshoe Ridge, where Joseph Kershaw, Bushrod Johnson, and Thomas Hindman were doing all they could to seize that key position. What were Generals Leonidas Polk and D. H. Hill doing all this time?

By midday, all of the troops in the Confederate Right Wing had been in action except four brigades (totaling only about 4,000 men) belonging to Maj. Gen. Frank Cheatham's division. D. H. Hill's Corps had suffered severe losses, losing roughly one-third of the 9,200 men who saw action. Major General William H. T. Walker's Reserve Corps was in even worse shape. Its morning's losses, combined with Saturday's bloodletting, pushed the overall casualty rate to a staggering 40%. Brigadier General States Rights Gist's just-arrived command offers a stark example of a hard-hit brigade. Overall, the brigade lost 336 men, or 24% of its starting strength, but that figure includes some late-arriving elements that missed that initial bloodbath. The 24th South Carolina's casualties topped 47%—all coming within one gruesome half-hour.

If the fight was to be renewed against the Union left, all of these men would need time to rest, reorganize, and recover their nerve.[1]

All along the Confederate Right Wing, regiments and brigades fell back out of range and into the sheltering timber. The resultant deployment facing Thomas's XIV Corps position can only be described as haphazard. At the south end of Polk's line, where Polk's left met (and was partially overlapped by) A. P. Stewart's division of Longstreet's Left Wing, Maj. Gen. Pat Cleburne's division straddled Alexander's Bridge Road 400 to 600 yards east of the main Union line. Brigadier General James Deshler's brigade (now under Col. Roger Mills) came to rest on the division's left. Dissatisfied by Brig. Gen. S. A. M. Wood's performance, Cleburne stuck Wood's brigade in the division's center so he could keep an eye on its commander. Cleburne's last brigade under Brig. Gen. Lucius Polk held Cleburne's right. Lucius Polk's right flank, however, did not connect with Brig. Gen. John K. Jackson's (of Cheatham's division) left flank—the next command in line to the north. Each of Cleburne's brigades had taken heavy losses, but believed they had also inflicted significant damage to the Union men on their front. Lucius Polk, for example, optimistically reported that when his brigade fell back, the Federals "were too much hurt to" pursue. In fact, the Yankees couldn't recall an easier fight, or one in which they'd suffered fewer casualties. They had no intention of foolishly abandoning their defenses, sending out instead a skirmish line to give warning of the next assault.[2]

John K. Jackson was in a precarious position. His brigade was dispatched to fill a gap between Brig. Gen. Edward C. Walthall's brigade (of Brig. Gen. St. John Liddell's division) and Polk's brigade. By the time Jackson reached the front, however, both Polk and Walthall had retreated to rejoin their respective divisions. Their retreat left Jackson's 900 men clinging to a slight ridge about 200 yards from the Union line, and at least 200 yards in advance of Polk's brigade, meaning both of Jackson's flanks were exposed. The brigadier was especially worried about his right, so he placed Maj. Richard Whitely's 2nd Battalion Georgia Sharpshooters there in an effort to grope northward to connect with the now-departed Walthall. Jackson's command was the only

1 Cheatham's division, which was held in reserve, actually included five brigades; but Brig. Gen. John K. Jackson's brigade was committed to action in order to help fill the earlier gap between Breckinridge's and Cleburne's divisions of Hill's Corps, leaving only four of Cheatham's formations out of the morning's combat.

2 Polk put the figure at 400 yards, while Col. Benjamin Hill of the 35th Tennessee estimated the distance at "half a mile." *OR* 30, pt. 2, 177, 183.

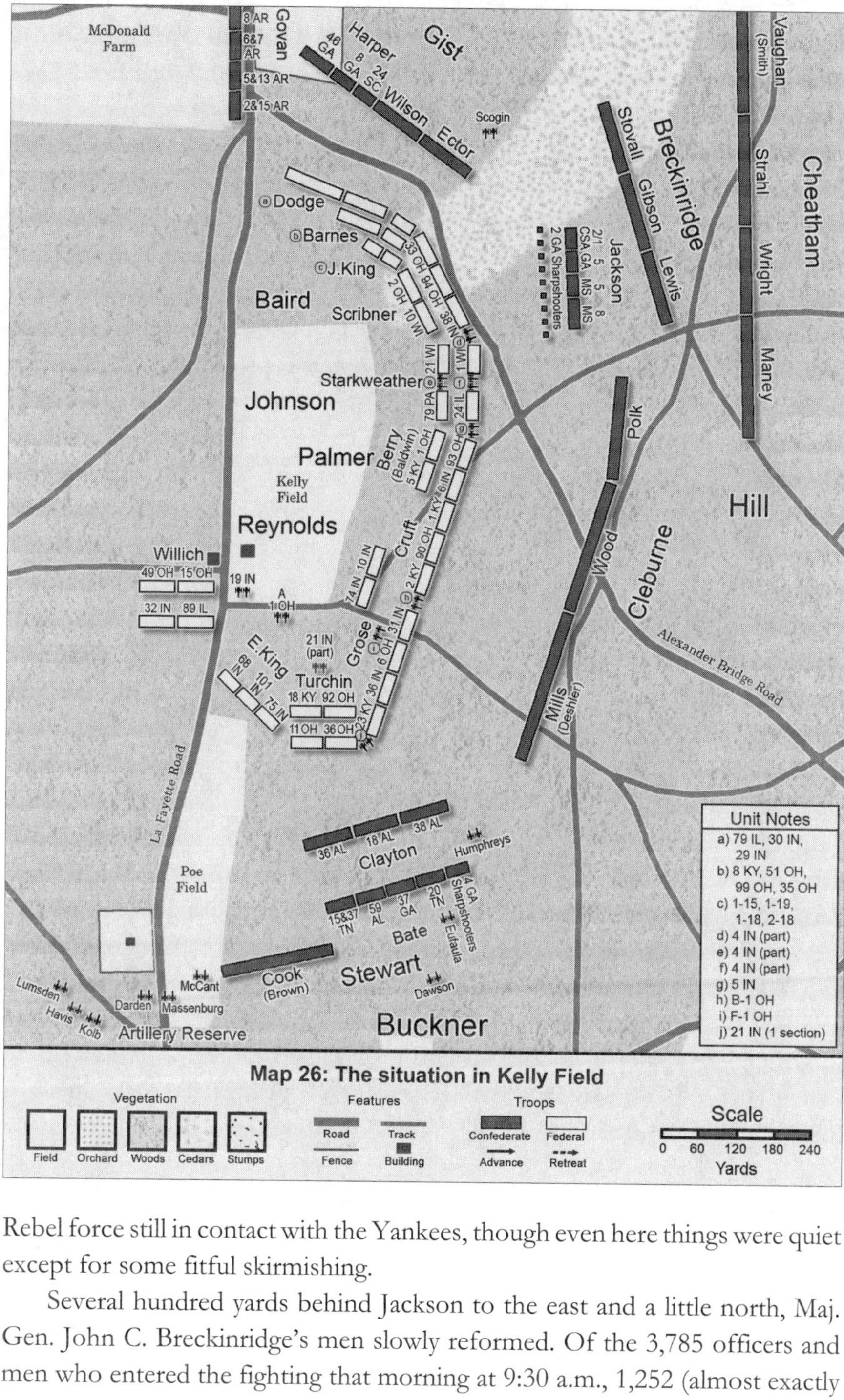

Map 26: The situation in Kelly Field

Rebel force still in contact with the Yankees, though even here things were quiet except for some fitful skirmishing.

Several hundred yards behind Jackson to the east and a little north, Maj. Gen. John C. Breckinridge's men slowly reformed. Of the 3,785 officers and men who entered the fighting that morning at 9:30 a.m., 1,252 (almost exactly one-third) were killed, wounded, or missing within 90 minutes. "The troops . . . rallied without trouble," recalled Capt. John Ellis of the 16th Louisiana. "They were not panic-stricken or demoralized, but angry, for they saw they had been sacrificed and defeated through the incompetency of someone high in command." The three brigades once more formed in a single line, with the fallen Ben Helm's Kentucky Orphans (now under Col. Joseph Lewis) on the left, Col. Randall Gibson now heading up Brig. Gen. Dan Adams's Louisianans in the center, and Brig. Gen. Marcellus Stovall's regiments on the right.[3]

William H. T. Walker fully appreciated the Louisianans's anger. Indeed, his own fury had not abated a whit. As he set about reconstituting his Reserve Corps, Walker's first concern was to rally Gist's shattered command. Colonel Claudius Wilson's and Brig. Gen. Matthew Ector's small brigades provided a covering force, slowly withdrawing a few hundred yards until they were just out of contact with the Federals. Like Lucius Polk, Gist mistakenly believed he had given as good as he got: "The enemy did not venture beyond their works, so severely had they suffered," he reported. Wilson's and Ector's men fell back alongside Gist's survivors, now commanded by Lt. Col. Leroy Napier of the 8th Georgia Battalion, thrust into that role when Col. Peyton Colquitt fell. All three brigades formed a single line, with Wilson in the center, Napier to his right, and Ector on his left. The entire division probably mustered no more than about 1,600 men. All three brigades faced southwest, opposite that part of the Federal line now secured by Dodge's and Barnes's brigades.[4]

St. John Liddell had a more difficult time reforming his command. Liddell had personally accompanied Daniel Govan's brigade across the La Fayette Road, and witnessed Govan's complete disorganization during its subsequent retreat. After "a circuitous *detour* to the right," Liddell ordered Govan to gather his Arkansans in the timber behind Gist's line, north of Breckinridge, and went to look for his other errant brigade under Ed Walthall. He found the Mississippians resting after their confusing, unsatisfactory effort to assault the Union line at the 4th Indiana Artillery salient. Liddell instructed Walthall to move "by the right flank some 400 yards." Govan joined him there. Finally

3 Ellis Diary, LSU; *OR* 30, pt. 2, 200.

4 *OR* 30, pt, 2, 246. It will be recalled that when Walker was elevated to command the Reserve Corps, Gist assumed command of his division when he arrived because he was the division's senior brigadier. Colonel Colquitt assumed command of Gist's brigade, and was killed in action.

reconstituted between Gist and Breckinridge, the division now numbered about 2,400 troops.[5]

By 1:00 p.m., except for the popping of light skirmish fire, the Kelly Field sector was quiet. General Bragg had no intention of letting that quiet persist. At 2:00 p.m. he ordered Right Wing commander Lt. Gen. Leonidas Polk "to again assault the enemy in his front with his whole force and to persist until he should dislodge him." Unfortunately for the Confederates, however, D. H. Hill and Polk were still playing out their tragic comedy of blunders. Like so many other directives issued by Bragg in the past fortnight, this order, too, was ignored.[6]

D. H. Hill, who had never showed much enthusiasm for attacking in the first place, had by now reverted to a mulish and defensive mindset. To Hill, Gordon Granger's appearance with his Union Reserve Corps pushing south along the La Fayette Road, driving in Forrest's cavalry, and recapturing the Union field hospital at Cloud Church, looked very much like a Union effort to turn his own right flank. Hill appealed for support. Given Granger's initial moves this was not an unreasonable conclusion, and in response Polk turned to Ben Cheatham.

Hill's request arrived when Polk was instructing Cheatham to move up, replace Cleburne's division, and renew the attack. When Polk received word that Federals were turning Hill's flank, however, the wing commander sent Cheatham (who was still without Jackson's brigade) to reinforce Hill's right. At 2:00 p.m. Cheatham's four brigades began sidling northward. According to Cheatham, he was ordered to move to "the extreme right." The march, estimated Brig. Gen. George Maney, covered "about the distance of a mile." Cheatham's brigades came to rest behind Breckinridge's line about 800 yards east of McDonald Field, with Cheatham's right flank resting on the Reed's Bridge Road. The division would sit there for the next couple of hours, bothered only by the occasional stray artillery round.[7]

Hill's right was also anchored by the 14 guns of General Forrest's three batteries of artillery, augmented by the section of Capt. Robert Cobb's guns under Lt. Frank P. Gracey, all supported by Brig. Gen. Frank Armstrong's cavalry division. The guns were arrayed astride the Reed's Bridge Road on the

5 Ibid., 253, 275.

6 Ibid., 34.

7 Polk, Bishop and General, vol. II, 260; OR 30, pt. 2, 79, 96.

east edge of the cedar glade, with good fields of fire into both McDonald's and Cloud's fields, should a Union attack materialize there.

By the time Cheatham's men moved into position, Granger's Federals were long gone, having diverted their march south by southwest. The threat to Hill's flank had dissipated, and there was now no good reason why Polk and Hill could not execute Bragg's earlier order. Indeed, Cheatham's move strengthened their chances for success. His redeployment placed four of the five divisions in Polk's Right Wing (Cleburne excepted) on or north of the Union left flank, which was as vulnerable to being turned now as it was earlier that morning. With John Beatty gone, heading back to Snodgrass Hill, taking with him his own and Stanley's troops, the Union flank was even more susceptible to being turned and crushed. As Daniel Govan's noontime movement so aptly demonstrated, the Union left flank ended in the woods north of Kelly Field and short of the La Fayette Road. A strong force could cross that lane and turn south into the rear of Kelly Field without much opposition. Breckinridge and Walker had taken a severe beating, but augmented with Cheatham's fresh troops the entire force still counted roughly 12,000 men. Unfortunately for the Confederates, nothing of the sort occurred. Harmony of command was required, but with Polk, Walker, and Hill all at odds and refusing to listen to each other, a harmony there surely was not.

Braxton Bragg, meanwhile, summoned James Longstreet to their 3:00 p.m. meeting somewhere near the Brotherton house, shortly after Longstreet's famous lunch of bacon and sweet potatoes. According to Longstreet, Bragg was angry and depressed, unaware of (or perhaps uninterested in hearing about) Longstreet's success and unable to do more than brood over Polk's failures. It was likely Polk's inaction that prompted Bragg's snarling comment about the lack of fight in the Right Wing. Whether Bragg also informed Longstreet of this ongoing insubordination is unknown; Longstreet made no specific mention of it. Polk's disobedience, however, was uppermost in Bragg's mind. After leaving Longstreet, Bragg "dispatched a staff officer to General Polk urging a prompt and vigorous execution of my written orders." Nothing happened.[8]

According to Polk's son and biographer, the problem for this inaction rested with D. H. Hill, who "was very much opposed to executing [the attack] as ordered. . . . The order to advance was given to Hill at 3:30, and had to be twice repeated before he moved." Earlier, Hill's delay might have been justified.

8 *OR* 30, pt. 2, 34.

Granger's potential threat to Hill's flank was real, and offered a valid reason to wait. Hill's next excuse, however, had much less merit.[9]

At some point that afternoon Hill remembered there was a gap between the divisions of Breckinridge and Cleburne, a chasm used by the Yankees to enfilade Helm's and Gist's assaults with disastrous results. Polk's dispositions were faulty, and Hill refused to advance until that gap was plugged. Supposedly the hole had been filled by Jackson's brigade, but as earlier noted Jackson's line was not long enough to cover the entire gap, especially after Lucius Polk's men retired. By this point in the afternoon, Hill was exhibiting a very poor grasp of the dispositions of his own command. Most significantly, he thought Jackson's men were still "far to the rear," and dispatched several officers to look for those troops in the wrong place. The aides returned empty-handed, grumped Hill, with "staff officer after staff officer having in vain been sent to find [Jackson.]"[10]

Brigadier General St. John Liddell was a witness to this friction. After his division's disjointed advance and sharp repulse, and while his troops were reassembling, the general reported in and found D. H. Hill and W. H. T. Walker conferring. A short time later, remembered Liddell, "General Polk rode up suddenly in cheerful spirits. Upon being asked by someone how goes it on the left, answered, 'Oh, merrily, merrily. Now let us arrange things for you.'"[11]

Polk's rekindled good spirits did nothing to alleviate Hill's ill temper or Walker's ongoing exasperation. If anything, Polk's inexplicable cheeriness served to further irritate both generals. Liddell watched the ensuing fuss with dismay:

> Affairs were still discussed rather angrily. General Hill asserted that a gap in his line was not filled up. General Hill said to Polk, 'come with me and see.' Polk declined, but ordered some staff officer to examine and make a report to him. The dispute still continued. Walker joined in and complained to Polk [that due to] Hill's disposition of his command . . . he now had no command. I [Liddell] rode up to General Hill and told him I regretted these disputes. Something must be done, and I was ready to obey his orders no matter what they were. Hill, however, walked off towards the skirmish line, apparently angry at something said by Walker. Walker saw this and remarked, "the man is mad, and in a mad fit will expose himself to the sharpshooters and will get

9 Polk, *Bishop and General*, vol. II, 263.

10 *OR* 30, pt. 2, 144.

11 Hughes, *Liddell's Record*, 145.

> killed." He then loudly called Hill to come back, apparently much troubled. Hill shortly afterwards returned, reserved and tired of discussion.[12]

Captain William W. Carnes also observed this contretemps. Carnes's battery was so damaged on Saturday, September 19 that it had to be temporarily disbanded. He began that Sunday morning in temporary command of Capt. William L. Scott's Tennessee battery due to Scott's absence, sick, in La Fayette. When Scott heard the distant rattle of combat on the 19th, however, he rode back to join his men and reached the field Sunday morning. His arrival displaced Carnes, who reported to Polk for new duties. Thus far Carnes had spent the day conveying dispatches for the bishop-general, and was now ready for his next assignment.

Carnes arrived near the end of the argument with updated word from General Cleburne's front. Electing not to interrupt, he "dismounted and awaited General Polk's pleasure as to receiving my report." Spotting him, Polk "rose from the log on which [Hill and Polk] sat . . . I heard him say to General Hill, with considerable warmth of manner, 'Well sir, I am sorry that you do not agree with me, but my decision is made and that is the way it shall be done.'"[13]

This last was Carnes's public version of the story, recounted in 1883. Many years later in a more private memoir, Carnes added a coda to that episode. "With that [Polk] turned away from General Hill, and as he approached me I heard him say, 'that is the most pig-headed General officer I have ever had to deal with.'" If true, whatever good cheer Polk recovered since his last confrontation with Hill had again thoroughly evaporated.[14]

While the Confederate brass were quarrelling, there was some movement on the Federal side of the line as well, of a minor nature. When Thomas departed Kelly Field at midday to find Sheridan, he left no one specifically to take charge in his absence. After all, he only intended to be gone long enough to bring up more troops. In fact, he would be gone the rest of the afternoon. Major General John M. Palmer was the senior officer remaining in Kelly Field, but he was not officially informed that he should take command of the troops stationed there.

12 Ibid.

13 William W. Carnes, "Chickamauga: A Battle of Which the Half Has Not Been Told," *Atlanta Constitution*, April 5, 1883.

14 William W. Carnes Memoirs, Carnes Battery file, CCNMP.

Thus far the Union line had held admirably, at least when assailed head-on; there was little reason to rearrange things now. The most significant changes in deployment unfolded on the flanks. Joseph Reynolds, who had watched his line nearly swept away by the rout in Poe Field and lost at least one regiment (the 105th Ohio) in that tempest, undertook major redeployments. Both of Reynolds's brigades changed front from east to south, with the right of Col. Edward King's brigade thrown back until it faced a bit southwest. Brigadier General John Turchin placed the 11th and 36th Ohio in his front line, with the 92nd Ohio and 18th Kentucky in support. Four fieldpieces from Capt. William W. Andrew's 21st Indiana battery were also "in front" with the other "two in the reserve."[15]

Colonel King found he could not afford the luxury of a reserve. Harris's 19th Indiana artillery, now skippered by Lieutenant Lackey, formed alongside Turchin's right, and then, extending in a single line angled back to the northwest came the 75th, 101st, and 68th Indiana. Having witnessed Brannan's collapse firsthand, some members of the 68th were convinced they were surrounded. "The Rebs closed in around us," reminisced John Beals, "and the only chance was to cut [our way] out." For the moment, however, no cutting was needed. Despite the precarious nature of their position, no Confederates appeared to menace their exposed flank. Instead, more Federals arrived.[16]

Sometime between 2:00 and 4:00 p.m., one other Union brigade would move to strengthen the Union southern flank. After participating in the repulse of Breckinridge's attack that morning, Brig. Gen. August Willich cast about for something to do. His brigade was in the second line of defense and clearly not needed to help hold the breastworks. Division commander Richard Johnson had no specific instructions for him, so Willich moved his men across the La Fayette Road to a position near the Kelly barn, facing south and extending King's flank.[17]

Exactly when Willich took up this line remains unclear. The German made no mention of Col. Ferdinand Van Derveer's troops, who had occupied this same ground until their move to Snodgrass Hill sometime shortly after 1:00 p.m. Instead, when Willich's skirmishers went forward, they returned bearing

15 *OR* 30, pt. 1, 474-475.

16 68th, 75th, and 101st Indiana position markers, in tree line south of Kelly Field, CCNMP; John Beals to Comrade J. H. Gray, December 8, 1896, John Beals Letters, InHS.

17 *OR* 30, pt. 1, 540.

prisoners and reported that "a whole brigade of Longstreet's corps was about 500 yards in my front, concealed and quietly lying down." That brigade was Humphrey's Mississippians, fallen back to the blacksmith shop at Longstreet's direction sometime after 2:00 p.m. Probably Willich did not move his brigade into position until shortly after 3:00 p.m. Once there, he was sure trouble was brewing, for he could see and hear the distant movements of Rebel infantry to his south as the Confederates redirected their own forces toward Horseshoe Ridge.[18]

At the north end of Kelly Field, Brig. Gen. John King's Regular brigade still anchored Brig. Gen. Absalom Baird's divisional left. Behind them, extending the line back toward the La Fayette Road lay only two more small brigades. Colonel Sidney Barnes's men, it will be recalled, had rushed here earlier at Thomas's personal direction. Their timely arrival helped scatter Govan's Arkansans, and after that action, they fell in on the left of the Regulars. Barnes placed his command in the standard double line formation, with the 8th Kentucky and 51st Ohio in front and the 35th Indiana and 99th Ohio in support. Barnes offered up this reserve line for General Baird's use if needed, to be commanded by Col. Peter Swaine of the 99th, but for the moment things were quiet. The 99th and 35th busied themselves building a reserve breastwork in rear of the main position.[19]

Barnes's deployment left Col. Joseph Dodge's three regiments in their semi-isolated position on the line's extreme left, facing north, just where they had been all morning. Dodge's left ended more than 200 yards short of the La Fayette Road—an entire brigade frontage. With Thomas gone, no other Union senior officer in Kelly Field realized just how vulnerable the northern flank remained. Fortunately, neither did the Confederates. General Palmer was focused not on the Kelly Field position, but on the sounds of battle emanating from the west directly to his rear. With Kelly Field quiet, the swells and roars of battle coming from Horseshoe Ridge were fully audible. That roar and rumble played on the fears of all four Union division commanders still holding Thomas's original line.

18 Ibid. The War Department Tablet marking this position places Willich's arrival at 4:30 p.m., which would be much too late, since by then the Union army had begun to withdraw from Kelly Field. Willich's own report suggests that he was in position for some time before that retreat began.

19 Kevin B. McCray, *A Shouting of Orders: A History of the 99th Ohio Volunteer Infantry Regiment* (Xlibris, 2003), 249-250.

About 3:30 p.m., Palmer heard Thomas Hindman's attack going on and decided he needed to do something. Since his own line had held so easily that morning, "repulsing" the Rebels with "great slaughter," Palmer decided he could spare Brig. Gen. William B. Hazen's brigade for other duties, reasoning his remaining two brigades should be enough to hold the line. Hazen's 9th Indiana, 6th Kentucky, and 41st and 124th Ohio numbered now just about 1,000 men. The 6th Kentucky's officers were hard hit and the regiment had to be split up, with pieces attached to the other three commands. Still, the brigade was rested and ready to fight. All in all, Hazen was an excellent candidate for an open-ended mission fraught with potential disaster at its conclusion.[20]

Hazen was also worried about ammunition, but his careful leadership limited the problem. He had taken care to restrict his men's fire by controlled volleys, which better regulated consumption, and cautioned his colonels to engage sparingly. This discipline paid off. Noting (with perhaps a touch of irony) "the feeling that our ammunition was gone was like a leaden weight in the breasts of many," and also that by mid-afternoon none of the regiments in the brigades around Hazen's men "appeared to have any." Hazen took stock and discovered that his brigade "still had 40 rounds per man," a fact that Hazen attributed to the superb fire discipline instilled by his own training and the use of controlled volleys rather than allowing his men to simply fire at will. Promptly Hazen set off to find Thomas. A brief flurry of action erupted when Hazen moved out and Col. William Grose's brigade moved up to fill the line. Spotting this activity, Rebel skirmishers launched a foray. Hazen halted, ready to rush back to the breastworks, but the threat was minor and almost immediately Palmer ordered him to proceed.[21]

From his brigade's position in Kelly Field, Hazen's route retraced the path blazed earlier by Van Derveer, passing Willich's command near the Kelly barn and crossing the same belt of timber unoccupied by either army. By this time these woods were alive with stragglers and sharpshooters. Uncertain of what he might meet, Hazen deployed the 9th Indiana and 41st Ohio in front, with

20 *OR* 30, pt. 1, 715, 763. Palmer remembered that he ordered Hazen to go, while Hazen recalled that he asked for and was granted permission to make the move. See John M. Palmer, *Personal Recollections of John M. Palmer: The Story of an Earnest Life* (The Robert Clarke Company, 1901), 183; and Hazen to Benson H. Lossing, August 23, 1866, William Palmer Collection, WRHS.

21 *OR* 30, pt. 1, 763-764; Hazen, *A Narrative of Military Service*, 132.

several companies extended as skirmishers, and plunged into the gloom. The 124th Ohio brought up the rear.[22]

Commanding Company B of the 124th, Capt. George W. Lewis came to regret a decision he made here. For the past several hours, he explained, "we had no water and the air was thick with a sulphurous smoke that created an intense thirst." When Pvt. George Benton volunteered to take the company's canteens and find water, Lewis refused. "I am afraid you will never come back." "I will come back, Captain, or I will be a dead Benton." At that point "I made a mistake," admitted Lewis. He let Benton go, loaded down with the company's canteens. Private Benton was never seen again, yet another of the faceless missing and presumed dead, likely later buried in an unmarked grave in the Chattanooga National Cemetery. The decision haunted Lewis for the rest of his life. Years later, while visiting the man's family, he discovered they still held out some hope that Benton might yet be alive. Watching Hazen's men depart, Palmer might well have understood Lewis's reservations; for all Palmer knew of the larger battle, he might be consigning the whole command to a fate similar to Private Benton's.[23]

The Confederate attacks had abated, but for most of the Federals in Kelly Field the afternoon was a busy one. Sergeant August Bratnober of the 10th Wisconsin, Col. Benjamin Scribner's brigade, remembered the lull allowed him and his comrades to strengthen their works. "At intervals when we were not being attacked," he noted, "gradually we put in logs crosswise to protect ourselves from a flanking fire and by three o'clock we had intrenched ourselves so well that we had no trouble to drive them back." Similarly, Lt. John Johnston of the 79th Pennsylvania, Brig. Gen. John Starkweather's brigade, recalled using more than just trees and brush to strengthen their works. During the height of the fighting that morning, Lieutenant Johnston asked Col. Henry Hambright if his men could shed their knapsacks so they "could load and fire lying down much more rapidly." Hambright agreed that indeed they could. "Every knapsack was unslung in a minute and placed against our little barricade as an additional defense."[24]

22 *OR* 30, pt. 1, 764, 767.

23 George W. Lewis, *The Campaigns of the 124th Regiment Ohio Volunteer Infantry with Roster and Roll of Honor* (The Werner Company, 1894), 68.

24 August Bratnober Diary Extracts, 10th Wisconsin file, CCNMP. Johnston, "At Chickamauga."

Ammunition and water were on everyone's mind. In Scribner's brigade, Lt. John Otto of Company D, 10th Wisconsin, recalled when the combat ended and it became "singularly still and quiet." Some of the precious water was used to clean fouled muskets by pouring the liquid down the muzzles and "violently shaking" the weapons. Otto dispatched two "trusty men" with the company canteens to find more water, "men who I was sure would return." Unlike Private Benton, they did, the canteens now full. Just as other Federals were doing atop Horseshoe Ridge, Otto also sent details out among the dead and wounded to "rob their cartridge boxes [and see] if their bullets would fit our rifles." Some men, "especially the younger ones," even went to sleep.[25]

General Starkweather's stentorian voice had turned raspy, strained by his efforts to be heard above the din of battle. He had also suffered a severe wound to his ankle, but refused to leave the field. Instead, he went "limping along behind the lines with a stick together with Colonel [Harrison] Hobart [of the 21st Wisconsin.] They spoke to and encouraged the men with good assurances, with which they themselves probably did not feel."[26]

Not content to merely await the next attack, shortly after 2:00 p.m. Starkweather decided to push his skirmish line forward and probe the Rebels. Lieutenant John Johnston reported to the brigadier with Company G of the 79th, along with a company from the 21st Wisconsin under an officer Johnston remembered only as "Lieutenant Lacount." Placing Johnston in overall command, Starkweather instructed him to deploy his force across the front of the brigade and push forward. Moving out smartly, Johnston soon had his little command properly arranged. "Cautioning the men to keep under cover as much as possible and to keep their eyes and ears wide open, we moved briskly forward and were soon where the rebel line had been an hour before. The dead were scattered thickly around us, some of them roasted and burned to a crisp."[27]

Ignoring their grisly surroundings and the entreaties of the many Confederate wounded, Johnston pushed his men forward to the crest of the next rise. He moved down the length of his line, supervising the placement of his little force until he reached the left flank, where he found a captain from

25 John Henry Otto Memoir, 259, WHS.

26 John M. Johnston, "At Chickamauga."

27 Ibid. Johnston was likely mistaken. There is no Lieutenant Lacount named in the muster rolls of the 21st Wisconsin.

Scribner's brigade doing the same thing. Noting that his own line was some distance east of the other, Johnston asked the captain to push his own right flank forward until it linked up with Johnston's. He was completing these arrangements when word passed down the line that Rebels could be seen forming on the far side of a field.[28]

Johnston's line had brushed up against John K. Jackson's advanced skirmishers. While their comrades back on the main defensive lines rested or worked on their fortifications, each side's opposing skirmishers began a deadly game of cat and mouse in the woods. "The rebel skirmishers have a great advantage over our own," noted the Pennsylvanian. "In their gray uniforms they can scarcely be distinguished in the woods . . . and their butternut suits agree with the 'sere and yellow leaf.' Our bright blue uniform, on the contrary, stands out in bold relief."[29]

For the better part of an hour, each party angled for advantage. Suddenly Johnston got word that Scribner's pickets were retiring and he scurried over, only to find the other force was already gone. Johnston would have to conduct a fighting retreat with his own line, or risk being cut off. The lieutenant had long since eschewed an officer's sword for the much more practical Enfield rifle, of which he had a "fine" example, and "filled my pockets with excellent cartridges (manufactured by neutral John Bull for the 'Emperor of China.')" He could barely see the enemy, until one rebel, "as gray as a louse" came close. Letting fly a round, Johnston reloaded and ordered his men to fall back. They did so, tumbling back into the works, expecting a full attack to follow on their heels. When no Rebel assault materialized, Starkweather ordered Johnston and his men back out again, this time instructing him to go no farther than the foot of the hill just below the main line. Thus the *petite guerre* went on here as well.[30]

Shortly after 10:00 a.m., Gen. Leonidas Polk sent Lt. William B. Richmond off with a dispatch for General Bragg. He never saw the young officer again. At some point during this skirmishing the Confederate lieutenant was struck down in front of the 4th Indiana salient. Richmond was a Polk family friend, an earnest and energetic young man highly regarded by his peers. A British soldier, Lt. Col. Sir James Arthur Lyon Fremantle of Her Majesty's Coldstream Guards

28 Ibid. Johnston only identified this man as Captain "W."

29 Ibid.

30 Ibid. Literally, *petite guerre* is French for "little war." In nineteenth century terms, it was used to describe the fighting between outposts, skirmishers, or irregular forces.

visited the Army of Tennessee that summer and met Richmond among Polk's entourage. Both Richmond and fellow staff officer Henry C. Yeatman, gushed Freemantle (who was sympathetic to the Confederacy), were "excellent types of the higher class of southerner. Highly educated, wealthy, and prosperous . . . they have abandoned all for their country. . . . No staff officers could perform their duties with more zeal and efficiency than these gentlemen."[31]

According to Polk, Lieutenant Richmond was feeling "unwell" on September 20 and when Polk heard the young man had reached Bragg's headquarters and was resting there, "we did not feel uneasy." Later in the day Richmond improved enough to attempt a return ride. He was looking for General Polk when he blundered into Federal skirmishers.

Captain Joseph Patton commanded Company A of the 93rd Ohio, Col. Philemon Baldwin's brigade, and also led the regiment's company of the officially disbanded (but unofficially still very much in existence) light battalion. "We were very much annoyed by sharpshooters," recalled Lt. Col. William H. Martin of the 93rd, and so Martin sent out 10 men from each company. Among them went Captain Patton and his men, armed with their lever-action Henry rifles. Private David Kinsey of Company K spotted Lieutenant Richmond on his way back to Polk and brought him down. The bullet "enter[ed] his head just below the right eye and [came] out at the back of his head shattering it very much." Kinsey and several comrades crept forward to investigate the fallen officer's corpse.[32]

The Yankees found "two maps" showing the positions of both armies, "a silver scabbard and sword, presented to Col. M. B. Richmond by the ladies of (I think) Charleston; a fatigue cap, with a pass pasted in the top on the inside" allowing Richmond to move through friendly picket lines, and, most promising of all, "a scrap book with the following written on the fly leaf: The finder of this body, by delivering it to _____, of Clarksville, Tenn., will receive $500 in gold."

Unfortunately for the fortunes of Kinsey and his comrades, there was no time to secure the body, for Rebel skirmishers were active all around. The

31 Walter Lord, ed., *The Fremantle Diary, Being the Journal of Lieutenant Colonel James Arthur Lyon Fremantle, Coldstream Guards, on his Three Months in the Southern States* (Little, Brown and Company, 1954), 136.

32 William H. Martin, "Death of Colonel Richmond," *National Tribune*, October 1, 1891; Leonidas Polk to "My Dear Wife," September 21, 1863, Gale-Polk Family Papers, UNC. Martin was mistaken concerning Lieutenant Richmond's rank.

trophies and papers were taken back to Colonel Martin, who passed the maps up the chain of command. The other souvenirs were retained by the men.[33]

No one at Polk's headquarters learned of Richmond's demise until Lt. Henry Yeatman found him the next morning, September 21st, covered in blood and dust a short distance from Polk's camp established on the night of the 20th. Yeatman reported that his friend's body had been stripped of all valuables, leaving Richmond clad only in "boots, pants, & a shirt. . . . We were all deeply grieved at his loss and melancholy death," mourned Polk.[34]

Meanwhile, the stress of the day was wearing on Union Maj. Gen. Joseph J. Reynolds. Thus far, Reynolds had performed ably under trying circumstances on both the 19th and especially on the 20th. On the former, he faced off disaster in Brotherton Field, and did so again when forced to turn his flank in Poe Field earlier this Sunday morning, when Brannan's line broke. He had also sent the 105th Ohio into what everyone assumed would be death or certain capture in order to buy critical time with which to forge a new defense. By Sunday afternoon, however, Reynolds's nerve was beginning to fail.

"About this time," wrote Maj. Gen. John Palmer, "the commander of one of the divisions near my own, approached me and said that I was now the ranking officer on the field, and that I ought to order a retreat. . . . He said the right and center of the army were defeated, and no doubt Rosecrans and Thomas were killed or in the hands of the enemy. At the moment the prospect did appear gloomy," continued Palmer, "and I was inclined to apprehend that matters were as bad as he supposed them to be." Palmer, however, refused to completely give in to pessimism. He was also a politician, with a keen understanding of public perception: "I had rather be killed and be d—d," Palmer retorted, "than be d—d by the country for leaving the battlefield under such circumstances." Palmer never identified this officer, but others were less circumspect. It was Joe Reynolds.[35]

Sometime shortly before his departure to Snodgrass Hill, Hazen caught part of this conversation. Hazen remembered the details slightly differently, but the gist was the same. "Quite a number of general officers were congregated discussing the condition of the fight," recalled Hazen, "among them two major

33 Martin, "Death of Colonel Richmond."

34 Leonidas Polk to "My Dear Wife," September 21, 1863, Gale-Polk Papers, UNC.

35 Palmer, *Personal Recollections*, 183-184.

Maj. Gen. Joseph J. Reynolds (right). By about 4:00 p.m. on September 20, the division commander's nerves were beginning to fray.
Miller, Photographic History

Generals, Reynolds and Palmer; and it was urged that it was necessary to have a general commander of our four divisions [in Kelly Field.] Reynolds, the senior, declined positively to assume it, remarking that it would only be assuming a disaster which was certainly impending." This was damning stuff indeed. For a professional soldier to shirk his responsibilities this way was appalling: "The command of the whole really rested on him . . . and his refusal to exercise it, was, in my opinion, an inexcusable and most serious neglect of duty."[36]

Hazen was mistaken in one regard: Palmer, not Reynolds, was the senior man. Still, Reynolds's nerve was clearly fraying, and those around him knew it. Palmer at least understood that an abrupt retreat from Kelly Field now would certainly spell disaster unless it could be carefully coordinated with those troops defending Horseshoe Ridge to the west; to do otherwise would expose Thomas and whatever other forces were with him to destruction. Whatever the risk, Palmer would stay. Thus rebuffed, and with his personal morale still at an ebb, Reynolds rode back to his command.

Fortunately for John Palmer and all the other Federals in Kelly Field, back at the Snodgrass cabin George Thomas was receiving information concerning Rosecrans's whereabouts and the state of the rest of the army, all of which would help the big Virginian decide what to do next.

36 Hazen, *A Narrative of Military Service*, 131.

Chapter Twenty-Four

Rossville and Horseshoe Ridge:

Sunday, 2:30 p.m. to 4:30 p.m.

During the early hours of Sunday afternoon, George Thomas remained in complete ignorance of what had happened to Generals Rosecrans, McCook, and Crittenden, and the rest of the army. Beyond the limits of his lines, confusion and chaos reigned. That particular fog began to dissipate by mid-afternoon. Couriers were finally finding their way to Thomas with news, rumors, and eventually, orders.

The first to reach him was Lt. Col. Gates P. Thruston, General McCook's chief of staff, shortly after 3:00 p.m. Thruston had had a trying day before he reached Thomas. McCook's staffer, it will be recalled, was on his way back after delivering a dispatch to Brig. Gen. Robert B. Mitchell, commanding the Union cavalry when disaster overtook him. Caught up in the collapse of Phil Sheridan's division, Thruston encountered the 39th Indiana and guided the Hoosiers into action. Then, with a gaggle of Rebel prisoners in tow, he and his escort trotted up the Dry Valley Road in search of McCook.

Thruston never found his boss, who by then had been led astray by Mr. McDonald. Nor did he come across Maj. Gen. Tom Crittenden, who had also left the field via the Dry Valley Road just a few minutes earlier. Instead, Thruston encountered Sheridan and Jeff C. Davis marching what was left of their divisions toward Rossville while trying to decide their next course of action. Neither man was in good humor. Sheridan, recalled Thruston, was "furious . . . *swearing* mad." The Irishman had also "lost faith," and neither general was sure what to do next. Everyone could still hear the sounds of battle raging off to the east. The latest crescendo marked Gordon Granger's and Thomas Hindman's renewed engagement. Since that roar meant *someone* was still fighting, Thruston offered to ride to find General Thomas, determine the state of affairs, and report back "as soon as possible."[1]

Thruston departed. Davis and Sheridan had only just found one another. Brigadier General William Carlin, who was present before Davis arrived, described Sheridan's worries. Little Phil "told me that we were cut off from Thomas and that he did not know the extent of the disaster," recalled Carlin. "He said he was hesitating between two courses—one was to go across the mountains to Bridgeport and the other was to go to Rossville and . . . [try] to communicate with Thomas. The latter course he pursued." Most of Davis's division—Col. Hans Hegs's brigade now under Col. John Martin, Carlin's own command, the division flag and staff—fell in with Sheridan along the way; Carlin assumed temporary command of the division and placed himself at Sheridan's orders. Augmenting the whole column were "eight guns, forty-six caissons, and a long ammunition train . . . found in a state of confusion behind the Widow Glenn's."[2]

The combined column moved through McFarland's Gap to the Xzanders G. McFarland farmstead about three miles south of Rossville on the west side of Missionary Ridge, where another substantial gathering of troops was found. The nucleus of this budding force was Col. John G. Parkhurst and his 9th Michigan provost guard. Parkhurst's regiment of stragglers had grown into a brigade-sized force. Jeff Davis was also there, having come up and assumed command from a relieved Parkhurst. Present as well was Maj. Gen. James Negley, who had come in from the east with his amalgam of a command. Davis's and Parkhurst's straggler contingent numbered about 3,000 men. Negley's force amounted to perhaps 2,500 to 3,000; Sheridan's strength added another 2,000 or 2,500 troops. All told, the entire grouping massed near 8,000 men and perhaps a half-dozen effective batteries.[3]

Negley, the senior man, assumed command. Parkhurst outlined what he knew: Generals Rosecrans and Crittenden had both passed up the road through Rossville and gone to Chattanooga. Rumors placed McCook at or headed for

1 Thruston, "The Crisis at Chickamauga," 665.

2 Girardi and Hughes, *Carlin Memoirs*, 104; Sheridan, *Memoirs*, vol. 1, 284.

3 *OR* 30, pt. 1, 264, 953. Parkhurst placed this point as three miles beyond McFarland's Gap. It was probably not nearly that far west, as others put the subsequent meeting closer to the gap.

that same place, though no one present had actually seen or spoken to the man since Carlin's last encounter with him.

Also present was Lt. Col. Arthur Ducat of Rosecrans's staff, along with much of the army headquarters group and the 15th Pennsylvania Cavalry. Ducat had been busy. He was among the first to arrive at the McFarland farm in his effort to overtake Rosecrans after becoming separated from him on the battlefield. McFarland's was "the first open space at the forks of the road" where troops could be rallied. Once there, Ducat "resolved to go no farther." Lieutenant Colonel Calvin Goddard, also of Rosecrans's staff, agreed to ride on in the hope of locating the army commander while Ducat worked to organize the growing stream of stragglers into something resembling a military force.[4]

Ducat called for volunteers from the staff to help with this task. Several stepped up. At Ducat's direction, Capt. Abraham B. Garner deployed his Company K of the 15th Pennsylvania Cavalry across the road to "stop all men armed, and send them to the line we were forming." At first, admitted Ducat, this proved a difficult task, but after the first thousand, "they did so cheerfully." Not so with everyone. Brigadier General Horatio Van Cleve came upon Ducat's ad hoc brigade but, thoroughly dispirited, kept on going. When Parkhurst arrived, he combined his own straggler detachment with Ducat's force (this was the command Crittenden declined to lead, but which Davis accepted). Once Negley and Sheridan joined up, Ducat estimated the entire force at "between 10,000 and 12,000 men." Although almost certainly an overestimate, it was by any reasonable measure a substantial force.[5]

What this budding grouping lacked was leadership. Tom Crittenden's decision to ride on instead of halting to take command of what was soon to be a de-facto army corps was his worst of the campaign, both from a personal and a professional standpoint. No longer could he use as an excuse that he did not know if Rosecrans had survived, for Parkhurst and Ducat both informed him the army commander and Garfield were unharmed and on their way to Chattanooga. In Crittenden's absence the duty fell to Negley, who, as noted, was the senior officer present. In other circumstances Negley might have exercised a firm hand, but both his health and his grasp of the overall situation were tenuous, at best. Crittenden was not ill, and, having spent much of the morning in Rosecrans's presence (at least before the rout) should have had a

4 Ibid., 52, 80.

5 Ibid., 81.

much better understanding of the Army of the Cumberland's dispositions than did Negley. Crittenden, for example, knew how much of the army had been sent to reinforce Thomas. He should have stayed. With Crittenden's absence, a leadership vacuum developed.

By the time the official reports were written everyone understood careers teetered on the brink, and great care was taken in the penning of those missives. Negley, who left the field with an organized force, had the most to explain. Writing on September 26, he reported that on Sunday afternoon he first found Parkhurst, who relayed Crittenden's earlier order to slowly fall back on Rossville. Negley claimed he found this instruction "inexpedient; [instead] the troops must be immediately reorganized and prepared to march to the front." On October 9, Negley elaborated by adding that after he ordered the troops to "return to the front," he heard that General Thomas might still be holding out, "and rode back to communicate with him if possible." Major James Lowrie, who rejoined Negley at McFarland's farm, agreed: "General Negley told me he would leave these troops in command of General Davis, and he would go back and attempt to reach General Thomas."[6]

General Davis made no mention of Negley making any such decision. William Carlin did, though only conditionally. According to Carlin, he and Negley met on the road just before reaching McFarland's house. "General Thomas is out there about two miles and still fighting," announced Negley. "If you will go to him with your command, I will support you." Negley wasn't ordering Carlin back into the fight, explained the brigadier; he was only offering to follow if Carlin chose to return of his own volition. Carlin declined. He was too junior to take such a weighty decision on his own, and besides, he was still acting under Sheridan's direction. Instead, Carlin "referred him [Negley] to that officer." Captain Joseph Hill of Rosecrans's staff affirmed that Negley did make at least one such attempt, but to no avail. According to the captain, when they tried, they met Rebels "not more than 500 yards" away and turned back.[7]

Shortly after 3:00 p.m. (at roughly the same time Thruston was reporting to Thomas) Sheridan, Negley, Davis, and Ducat all met in the Xzanders McFarland house. Mr. McFarland, his slaves, his four teenage daughters, and his animals were absent, having departed southward a few days earlier to avoid

6 Ibid., 331, 335, 339.

7 Girardi and Hughes, *Carlin Memoirs*, 105; *OR* 30, pt. 1, 1022.

rampaging Federals. His wife Lucy, a servant, and his three younger sons, however, were still at home. Two older sons were in Rebel service, both members of the 1st Confederate Regiment in John Jackson's brigade. The house, as might be expected, was filling up with wounded.[8]

As also might be expected, the meeting was an unhappy one. The need for decisive leadership was glaring. The still-pessimistic Sheridan wanted to retreat to Rossville. Davis argued they should stay put and defend the gap, which was an obvious back door to both Rossville and Chattanooga. Negley, who as the senior man should have been in charge, couldn't decide what to do. These arguments were interrupted by the return of Gates Thruston, arriving sometime between 3:30 and 4:00 p.m. Unlike Negley, Thruston managed to reach Thomas and so offered the first reliable news of that officer.

Like Thruston's other missions that Sunday, his most recent ride was suitably adventurous. Still escorted by the same detail of the 2nd Kentucky Cavalry, he rode to the sound of the guns. Rebels forced them to circle to the north, but by about 3:00 p.m. finally reached the Snodgrass house, which was also overflowing with wounded. After listening to Thruston's account, Thomas immediately sent the colonel back to the Dry Valley Road with the idea of bringing both Sheridan's and Davis's men up to connect with Steedman's line.[9]

Thruston met no Rebels on his return ride, but he did have to contend with Union troops thronging the road and narrow gorge of McFarland's Gap. As he fought his way through the ranks, he repeatedly inquired after both Sheridan and Davis. All he received in return were wisecracks: "Some old trudger in the ranks called out: 'we'll talk to you, my son, when we get to the Ohio River!'" After some jostling and delay, Thruston was finally pointed toward the McFarland house and the meeting unfolding inside.

Thruston's news didn't seem to help much. Negley aide Alfred Hough observed that the generals "could come to no agreement for common action. After a conversation they each decided to go to General Thomas independently." Sheridan, whom Thruston thought was still "lacking faith," decided to play it safe. The division commander announced he would take his

8 Chickamauga campaign roadside markers, "The Xzanders G. McFarland House and McFarland Gap," http://chickamaugacampaign.org/pdfs/TheXzanders.pdf, accessed 2/18/2012. Note that Xzanders was also sometimes spelled Xander or Xanders by participants in the campaign.

9 *OR* 30, pt. 1, 253.

division to Rossville, and from there move back south along the La Fayette Road to rejoin Thomas's left. This was a considerable distance, probably at least six miles, and could not be done quickly. It was also contrary to Thomas's intent, as relayed by Thruston. Sheridan was supposed to come back into the fight on Thomas's right, which was then fighting for its very life; his left remained unengaged.[10]

Negley, wrote Thruston, "was vacillating," and eventually compromised. He would follow Sheridan—but only as far as Rossville. There, explained Negley, he would defend the gap in case of further disaster. Jeff Davis, the most aggressive of the trio in Thruston's eyes, "ordered a right-about at once, and marched briskly to the front." Colonel Ducat remembered Davis's decision a little differently and reported only that Davis was going to remain in place along the Dry Valley Road to serve as the rear guard. Ducat may have had the better memory, for while Davis did push a ways back south along the Dry Valley Road, he did not attempt to rejoin the battle. Carlin recalled that this move was made slowly, even more so after they left the road and deployed to push through the woods.[11]

Meanwhile, back at the Snodgrass cabin, Thomas received a second messenger in the form of army chief of staff James A. Garfield. The high-level staffer and future American president arrived within a few minutes of Thruston—so close that Thomas later reported the two men traveled together, but this wasn't so. Garfield rode up with two members of the 15th Pennsylvania Cavalry and Capts. William B. Gaw and John D. Barker of Thomas's own staff. Gaw accompanied Garfield when the latter left Rosecrans, while Barker encountered the group en route. With the precision expected of an army chief of staff, Garfield placed his arrival at 3:35 p.m.[12]

In 1880, "Garfield's Ride" became a centerpiece of his campaign for the presidency, so much so that other witnesses later marveled at the mythology that sprouted up around the tale. In fact this mission, as noted by Garfield's most reliable biographer, historian Theodore C. Smith, "although a creditable

10 Thruston, "The Crisis at Chickamauga," 665; Robert G. Athearn, ed., *Soldier in the West: The Civil War Letters of Alfred Lacey Hough* (University of Pennsylvania Press, 1957), 149; Thruston, "The Crisis at Chickamauga," 665; *OR* 30, pt. 1, 1022.

11 Thruston, "The Crisis at Chickamauga," 665; *OR* 52, 81; Girardi and Hughes, *Carlin Memoirs*, 105.

12 *OR* 30, pt. 1, 141, 253; Thruston, "The Crisis at Chickamauga," 665.

display of courage, involved no unusual risk." It helped that with Gaw's presence, Garfield had a dependable guide. After leaving Rosecrans, Garfield and his party set off for Rossville. Catching word of General Negley's presence to the south, Garfield sent Negley an order instructing him to "cover the retreat of the trains." Once through the Rossville Gap, the party turned south, where it met with Captain Barker. Returning from army headquarters just before the rout, Barker preceded them up the Dry Valley Road and into Rossville; he was now also headed back to the field. After a short while they bumped into a Confederate skirmish line, dodging a few scattered shots before they rode on. When the party arrived at the Snodgrass cabin, the men brought General Thomas "the first reliable information" of what had happened to the rest of the army.[13]

Within 10 minutes, Garfield was able to perform the same service for Rosecrans. When Garfield asked how Thomas was faring, the big Virginian answered that, "We have repulsed every attack so far, and we can hold our ground if the enemy can be kept from our rear." Composing a hasty dispatch for Rosecrans outlining the army's condition, Garfield noted that "Thomas has Brannan's, Baird's, Reynolds, Wood's, Palmer's and Johnson's Divisions still intact after terrible fighting." He also reported that "Granger is here . . . [and] Sheridan is in with the bulk of his division, but in ragged shape." All in all, this was heartening news. Seven of the army's ten divisions were still fighting, and an eighth (Negley's) was guarding Rossville. Only Davis and Van Cleve were unaccounted for. It seemed the army was still intact, if battered. Garfield also offered a degree of optimism: "I hope General Thomas will be able to hold on here till night, and will not need to fall back farther than Rossville: perhaps not any. . . . I think we may in the main retrieve our morning disaster. I never saw better fighting than our men are now doing. The rebel ammunition must be nearly exhausted. Ours is fast failing. If we can hold out an hour more it will be all right. Granger thinks we can defeat them badly to-morrow if all our forces come in." This message had to be hand-carried to Rossville, backtracking Garfield's previous precarious route, but from there it could be telegraphed

13 Theodore Clarke Smith, *The Life and Letters of James Abram Garfield*, 2 vols. (Yale University Press, 1925), vol. 1, 342-343; *OR* 30, pt. 1, 141, 253, 1028; Cozzens, *This Terrible Sound*, 468-469. It is not known if Negley received this order before or after the conference at McFarland's farmstead, but it did confirm Negley's own decision to retreat toward Rossville. Garfield claimed a battalion fired on them, but one member of the escort recalled only a single shot. In any case, the party was forced to detour to the west, just as Granger had done earlier.

directly to Chattanooga. When it arrived near 5:00 p.m., it doubtless buoyed Rosecrans's spirits, given the size of the disaster previously assumed by all.[14]

Ammunition shortages had been an intermittent problem since mid-afternoon, most notably among the men of the 21st Ohio and Brannan's scratch line, all of whom had been engaged since midday. By 3:30 p.m., however, the problem was spreading to the rest of the line. The cartridge boxes of Steedman's regiments were also emptying quickly. Sergeant Isaac Doan of the 40th Ohio remembered how thankful he was that "there was no Joshua present to stay the downward course of the sun . . . for night found us with empty cartridge boxes, though many borrowed largely from . . . the unresisting dead." Doan personally "fired eighty rounds from [his] breech-loading carbine, and the . . . chamber became so hot I could not bear my hand on it." Lieutenant Edward Scott reported much the same in the 89th Ohio: "Our men were nearly half killed or wounded and our ammunition nearly gone; in some companies, entirely gone, and they were taking the cartridges out of the boxes of the killed and wounded."[15]

Steedman's reserve ammunition had already filled the cartridge boxes of Brannan's and Wood's men. In better circumstances both divisions should have had their own supply to draw upon. Brannan's train, however, was now in the hands of the Rebels, captured during the retreat. Wood's wagons were "carried off by the rout from the right" and thus beyond reach. Negley's wagons went with him when he departed, leaving Stanley's brigade with no more chance to resupply than the rest of Thomas's force.[16]

Although furious that his trains had been ordered off the field "by some unauthorized person," Thomas was not yet ready to quit the fight. In addition to Granger's supply, already distributed, an unknown additional quantity of bullets was located about this time. Soon after Garfield's arrival, Thomas sent

14 McKinney, *Education in Violence*, 252; *OR* 30, pt. 1, 141; Rosecrans, "Chattanooga Campaign." Garfield was wrong about Sheridan, of course, but Thomas had just met with Thruston and had every reason to believe the Irishman's three brigades would be joining Steedman's right when this dispatch was written. Curiously, Garfield did not mention Jefferson C. Davis. Though Thruston told Thomas that both Davis and Sheridan were at McFarland's farm, Davis was somehow omitted from Garfield's report.

15 Doan, *Reminiscences of the Chattanooga Campaign*, 6; Weaver and Fenner, *Sacrifice at Chickamauga*, 105. The 40th was armed with Springfield rifled muskets at this time. Doan's carbine was likely another example of arms secured for the short-lived "Elite Battalions."

16 *OR* 30, pt. 1, 406, 639.

his artillery chief, Maj. Walter E. Lawrence, "to notify the different commanders that ammunition would be supplied to them shortly." Barker and Captain Kellogg were tasked with overseeing its distribution. However, its issue was only a stopgap measure. Too many units were warning they soon enough would have to hold their ground entirely on the points of their bayonets.[17]

Thomas's resolve was remarkable. He struggled to maintain a rock-solid imperturbability in the face of immense crisis, despite momentary displays like that exhibited during the uncertain moments of Granger's appearance. As related by Thomas biographer Francis F. McKinney, George Thomas was "ever mindful of the influence upon the men of his own attitude and that of his staff. Once he sent word to Brannan . . . 'that his is my old division and that they will hold their position.' Another time he called back one of his aides who was dashing off with a message and told him to ride leisurely, as he did not want to get the troops excited. At one crisis of the battle . . . another aide who had started on an errand turned back to Thomas, saluted, and asked, 'General, after delivering your order, where shall I report to you?' 'Here, sir, here,' replied Thomas impatiently." While moving to the right James B. Steedman overheard a similar exchange. In that version, as related by biographer Freeman Cleaves, Thomas sent an aide to Harker with instructions. "Where shall I find you, General, when I return? Enough had been said of retreat that day. Thomas glared at the officer and thundered: 'Here!'"[18]

In addition to solid leadership confidence and a trickle of fresh ammunition, another unexpected reinforcement appeared about this time, sent from the southern end of Kelly Field. Thomas had not visited that part of his line since before noon, when he rode to the right and discovered the Rebel breakthrough. Since then, he had made no demands on the troops there. They, however, had not forgotten him; now another brigade was coming to his support.[19]

These troops belonged to Brig. Gen. William Hazen, dispatched by General Palmer to reinforce the beleaguered Thomas. Hazen's men had to traverse the wooded no-man's-land between Snodgrass Hill and Kelly Field,

17 Ibid., 253; Thomas B. Van Horne, *The Army of the Cumberland* (Smithmark Publishers, 1996), 275.

18 McKinney, *Education in Violence*, 251; Freeman Cleaves, *Rock of Chickamauga: The Life of General George H. Thomas* (Greenwood Press, 1974), 172.

19 MicKinney, *Education in Violence*, 253-254.

Brig. Gen. William B. Hazen (right), asked Maj. Gen. John M. Palmer around 3:00 p.m. to let him take his brigade and join General Thomas. Kelly Field was quiet at this time, but everyone could hear heavy combat to the west on Horseshoe Ridge. Palmer agreed, and Hazen appeared on Harker's left flank sometime around 4:00 p.m.
Library of Congress

with no knowledge of what awaited them in the dark of the trees or on the far side. "The movement was made cautiously but rapidly, the brigade constantly in readiness for any misfortune," Hazen reported. Contact was soon made, but only with "some scattered Confederates in the woods, and a Confederate skirmish line was struck obliquely, but no other force was encountered." To Capt. Amasa Johnson of the 9th Indiana, it seemed that the "thicket of timber . . . [was] filled with rebel sharp-shooters. It looked as if we were certain of being captured, but we drove the rebels before us." The march, wrote Hazen, required "a sharp skirmish all the way." Indeed it was so, for the journey produced nearly a dozen casualties along the way. The 9th Indiana had one man injured, the 6th Kentucky lost six more, and the Buckeyes of the 41st reported "several" losses. It was close to 4:00 p.m. when Hazen's brigade emerged from the gloom into Snodgrass Field, where the new arrivals saw the 125th Ohio engaged with the next Confederate attack—delivered by William Preston's division of Buckner's Corps, representing Longstreet's last reserves. Without hesitating, Hazen's men pitched in.[20]

Preston's commitment opened a new phase of the fighting for Horseshoe Ridge. By this time in the afternoon, James Longstreet's troops were having

20 Robert L. Kimberly and Ephraim S. Holloway, *The Forty-First Ohio Veteran Volunteer Infantry in the War of the Rebellion 1861-1865* (W. R. Smellie, 1897), 53; Johnson, *Ninth Indiana Regiment at Chickamauga*, 4; Hazen, *A Narrative of Military Service*, 132; *OR* 30, pt. 1, 769, 772, 776.

trouble coordinating their blows. Scattered by their earlier successes, each subsequent attack contained considerably less striking power. After John Bell Hood's fall, only Bushrod Johnson seemed focused on mounting a coordinated effort among multiple divisions. Generals Law, Kershaw, and Hindman each committed one brigade at a time, or allowed their commands to be moved off in divergent directions. The silence along the Kelly Field line, while the gray wave stumbled and crashed against Horseshoe Ridge, was especially helpful for it allowed Thomas the time to concentrate his presence and energy on the threat to the high ground, rather than divide them between two simultaneous battles a mile or more apart. Equally fortuitous was the lack of Rebel effort in the gap between the two sectors, which Hazen's troops had just traversed.

Simply put, Thomas did not have enough troops to fully man his entire line. He intended for Granger to fill that hole between Kelly Field and Horseshoe Ridge, but then Brannan reported the developing threat to his right. Thomas dispatched Steedman to help Brannan, where the new arrivals saved the ridge and the day, but he also fully understood the gift he was being given by Confederate inconsistency. When Steedman asked him how the fight was progressing, Thomas replied almost angrily, as if military blunders, even when made by his opponents and redounding to his favor, irritated him: "The damned scoundrels are fighting without any system!" Hazen's reinforcement was further evidence of this lack of a "system." The quiescence in Kelly Field gave Palmer the confidence to send Hazen to succor Thomas—just in time to break up another Confederate attack.[21]

Longstreet was finally coming to realize that more than just a few Yankees were "holding out over yonder." Near four o'clock, when it became obvious there would be no help from Polk's Right Wing, Longstreet summoned his last reserve. Confederate Brig. Gen. William Preston was a man thoroughly immersed in the antebellum Southern aristocracy. His father was a hero of the Revolution, one who took his reward for service in the form of a land grant on the banks of the Ohio River at the site of modern-day Louisville, which subsequently made the Prestons one of the wealthiest clans in Kentucky. William was born in 1816, graduated from Harvard, studied law at Yale, and settled into life among the Kentucky elite. He married Margaret Wyckliffe, daughter of another of Kentucky's richest scions, and served in the U.S. Congress for a session. His own connections to prominent men were many,

21 Shanks, *Personal Recollections*, 64.

Brig. Gen. William Preston (right) of Kentucky led a division in Simon Buckner's Corps. He was an experienced politician, diplomat, and a member of one of the Blue Grass State's oldest and richest families. Like so many others, he turned soldier when the war came.
Miller, Photographic History

including his cousin John C. Breckinridge. His wife's connections eventually reached into the White House. Her close friend Mary Todd married a gangly Illinois lawyer named Lincoln. When the Buchanan-Breckinridge ticket was elected in 1856, Preston was appointed minister to Spain, where one of his duties was to try and negotiate the purchase of Cuba.[22]

Preston's military credentials were not extensive. During the Mexican War he served as lieutenant colonel of the 4th Kentucky for the 10 months of that regiment's service, but saw no action. Preston's brother-in-law, however, was Albert Sidney Johnston, whose son was both named for and raised by William Preston while Johnston was serving in Texas. When President Davis appointed Johnston to command the Western Military Department, Preston joined him as an aide-de-camp with the rank of colonel. Preston cradled the dying Johnston in his arms when he was struck down at Shiloh on April 6, 1862. In addition to his service with Johnston, Preston supplemented his military education with extensive military reading. He was promoted to brigadier general a week after Shiloh and given a brigade, which he would lead at Corinth, Stones River, and during the Vicksburg campaign.[23]

Preston proved a capable officer, with his most significant combat experience coming at Stones River. His brigade was engaged on both

22 Peter J. Sehlinger, *Kentucky's Last Cavalier: General William Preston, 1816-1887* (Kentucky Historical Society, 2004), 12, 33; Peter J. Sehlinger, "Preston, William" in David S. and Jeanne T. Heidler, eds. *Encyclopedia of the American Civil War*, 5 vols. (ABC-CLIO, 2000), vol. 3, 1561.

23 Sehlinger, *Kentucky's Last Cavalier*, 55, 132-133, 166; Charles P. Roland, *Albert Sidney Johnston: Soldier of Three Republics* (University of Texas Press, 1987), 338.

December 31, 1862, and January 2, 1863, suffering 30 percent casualties. His own conduct was considered conspicuously brave. In the spring of 1863, Preston replaced fellow Kentuckian Humphrey G. Marshall in command of a division in Simon Buckner's department. Preston followed the fortunes of that command, joining General Bragg when Buckner's troops were re-designated as an infantry corps in the Army of Tennessee.[24]

Lieutenant William Miller Owen, the recent transplant from Virginia, joined Preston's staff and was quickly impressed with his new commander. "General Preston himself is a most interesting traveling companion as well as polished gentleman," wrote Owen, "a handsome, large-framed man [who] has the appearance of what we can imagine a French marshal should have been in the wars of the first Napoleon. He is chock-full of anecdote . . . but what interests me most is the story of his life at the Spanish court. . . . [He] spent each year, in keeping up a grand establishment, fifty thousand dollars over and above the government salary. How he astonished the Dons!" Despite all that high living with tales of French chefs and multiple attachés, Owen found Preston common enough on campaign. With everyone willing to "partake of our slice of bacon and dip our crackers in the grease, [Preston] would give a sigh of satisfaction and say 'Ah! Owen, this is just as good. Now we are greased for another day.'"[25]

The troops Preston brought with him to Bragg's army, while not new to the service, were still inexperienced in battle. Typical was the 54th Virginia. Raised in late 1861, for two years they served in the mountainous border regions of Virginia, Kentucky, and Tennessee. Their sole combat experience stemmed from a skirmish at Middle Creek, Kentucky on January 10, 1862. Middle Creek dignified as a battle by early 1862 standards, but by mid-war hardly merited a footnote, for the entire Confederate force lost 62 men out of the more than 2,000 engaged. With one exception, none of the 14 regiments comprising Preston's command earned any significant battle honors. Only the 5th Kentucky had "seen the elephant," suffering a punishing 134 casualties at Shiloh. For the rest, combat was a horror yet to be fully experienced.[26]

24 *OR* 20, pt. 1, 679, 811-813; Sehlinger, *Kentucky's Last Cavalier*, 143-144; Stickles, *Simon Bolivar Buckner*, 217.

25 Owen, *In Camp and Battle*, 269-270.

26 Joseph H. Crute, Jr., *Units of the Confederate States Army* (Derwent Books, 1987), 389; *OR* 10, pt. 1, 621.

Preston's three brigade commanders were young, but talented. Brigadier General Archibald Gracie, Jr. was a successful Mobile resident, a transplanted New Yorker who moved to Alabama with his father in the 1850s to make his fortune in King Cotton. Educated in Europe before graduating from West Point in 1854, Gracie served two years on the frontier before deciding he was a businessman instead of a soldier. He quickly rejoined the ranks when war came, this time on the side of his adopted South. Like Owen, Gracie also enjoyed Preston's company. Years later, members of the division suggested Preston and Gracie were especially close. "Gracie is a rising young general, devoted to his profession," Owen observed. "He is justly proud of his brigade of young soldiers, most of whom have never yet been under fire. They will do good work."[27]

Gracie's command tenure was not untroubled. Comprised of non-slaveholding mountaineers with little sympathy to the larger cause, these men often made for reluctant Rebels. Lieutenant Colonel Bolling Hall, Jr., the commander of the Alabamians of the 2nd Battalion, Hilliard's Legion, faced an ongoing morale problem. "A good many desertions have been going on lately from the Legion," he wrote in May 1863. "Twenty four of mine started but I caught eight of them and now have them in ball and chain awaiting trial." One of the prisoners was an older man who was caught urging desertion in "broad daylight." Bolling's brother Crenshaw Hall noted with some alarm that "the men say the officers are afraid to shoot them. . . . If we had a few more Braggs perhaps desertion would not occur so often." When asked to leave their native valleys, where at least they could justify their service as defending home and hearth, to join Bragg in Georgia, many refused to go.[28]

The spate of desertions hinted at a larger problem: disloyalty. Many of these men were not just unenthusiastic about secession, but still true to the Union. Across the Appalachian south various secret societies sprang up to encourage desertion and even outright mutiny. Buckner's department was one such hotbed. Just a few months after the battle of Chickamauga in December 1863, for example, 70 men were arrested for mutiny in an Alabama brigade serving

27 Archibald Gracie IV to Col. Harvey E. Jones, August 23, 1907, ADAH; Owen, *In Camp and Battle*, 274. Gracie's family also flourished back in New York. The Gracie Mansion, which now serves as the mayor's residence, was the family estate.

28 Charles T. Jones, Jr., "Five Confederates: The Sons of Bolling Hall in the Civil War," *Alabama Historical Quarterly*, vol. 24 (1962), 173.

near Mobile. An investigation revealed that the revolt was instigated by men transferred from the battalions of Hilliard's Legion and other troops from Gracie's brigade just after Chickamauga. The 2nd battalion was singled out as specifically affected by this treason.[29]

Another of Preston's brigades had similar troubles. It was comprised of four regiments—the 65th Georgia, 5th Kentucky, 58th North Carolina, and 63rd Virginia—and commanded by Col. John J. McMahon of the 63rd. As in Gracie's command, desertion was a problem, with the worst of it centered in the 63rd, a conscript unit raised only that spring. Captain Thomas B. Hampton, who commanded Company B, observed on September 16 that "our regiment has deserted at a tremendous rate. . . . I am heartily ashamed of all such cowards." Hampton was not exaggerating. Between the time the regiment was alerted for movement on August 22 and its arrival in La Fayette on September 14, no fewer than 150 men had left the ranks—more than double the casualties the 63rd would sustain in the coming fight. One former commander labeled the Virginia regiment as the "worst regiment in the army of Western Virginia." Colonel McMahon, a Presbyterian minister with limited military experience, proved wholly inadequate at both regimental and brigade command. McMahon, wrote historian Jeffrey Weaver, "refused to enforce military discipline" and was relieved. This fortuitous opening was Col. John H. Kelly's opportunity. Reassigned from his place at the head of the 8th Arkansas in Maj. Gen. Patrick Cleburne's division, Kelly assumed control of the brigade on September 13, just a few days before the Chickamauga fighting opened.[30]

John Kelly was a rising star in the Rebel army. A member of the Class of 1861, he resigned from West Point before graduation to follow the South. He accepted a lieutenant's commission and a position on Maj. Gen. William J. Hardee's staff, transferred soon thereafter to line duty, and led regiments at Shiloh and Stones River, where he picked up an arm wound. By age 22 he was colonel of the 8th Arkansas and recognized as a man destined for higher responsibilities. Taking up his new duties only a week before the fight left Kelly

29 Georgia Lee Tatum, *Disloyalty in the Confederacy* (University of Nebraska Press, 2000), 64-65.

30 "Camp near Fayette, Geo," September 16, 1863, Thomas B. Hampton Letters, UT; Jeffrey C. Weaver, *63rd Virginia Infantry* (H. E. Howard, 1991), 10-13, 34; Jeffrey Weaver, "58th North Carolina Infantry, Confederate States Army," http://nc58thinf.tripod.com/id1.html, accessed 1/31/2015 . McMahon had previously only served as an aide to Maj. Gen. John B. Floyd, and was present at the Fort Donelson debacle in February 1862. McMahon didn't even revert to command of the 63rd Virginia upon Kelly's transfer, choosing instead to simply leave the army.

with little chance to make much of an impression on his men, but his competence and courage on other fields made him an excellent choice for the job.[31]

Preston's third brigade commander was also a military school graduate, though not a West Pointer. Robert C. Trigg of the 54th Virginia rose to brigade command as a colonel that summer when Buckner reorganized his department in Eastern Tennessee. The 1848 graduate of the Virginia Military Institute was practicing law in his hometown of Christianburg, Virginia, when the sectional rift convinced him to raise and captain a local militia company a full year before the firing on Fort Sumter. He and his men fought at First Manassas as part of the 4th Virginia in the soon-to-be famous Stonewall Brigade. Trigg left the 4th soon thereafter to raise the 54th from his home county. Unlike the 63rd, the 54th was a volunteer regiment, but Trigg still faced disciplinary problems. In July 1863, "nearly all of Company G went AWOL," got drunk, and visited a brothel—a dereliction of duty so flagrant it drew departmental commander Simon B. Buckner's attention. The company commander was cashiered and the rest of the men court-martialed. In late July when news of the defeats at Gettysburg and Vicksburg reached the civilian populace, darker rumors circulated. A private in the 54th received a letter from home informing him that nearly "Two hundred and fifty" deserters a week were passing through Floyd County, Virginia, and "there has bin a good many left from the fifty-fourth." No blame seems to have been attached to Trigg, however, who was officially confirmed in brigade command on September 1, 1863. As late as December, well after Chickamauga, Maj. Gen. Samuel Jones requested Trigg be returned to southwest Virginia because he was "an officer of great merit."[32]

Veteran or novice, motivated or unenthusiastic, Preston's men were about to get their chance at the Federals. His division represented Longstreet's carefully hoarded final reserve, and he now called upon them to finish the job of storming Horseshoe Ridge and driving the rest of the Union army off the field.

Gracie's and Kelly's brigades were halted in the fields around the Brotherton house enduring the occasional stray Federal artillery round when orders arrived. Kelly lacked the services of the 65th Georgia, which was still supporting Capt. William C. Jeffress's Virginia battery near Hunt Ford. In

31 Terry L. Jones, "John Herbert Kelly," in Davis, ed., *The Confederate General*, vol. 4, 2-3.

32 Anonymous, "Col. Robert C. Trigg of Virginia," *Confederate Veteran*, vol. XVII, no. 2 (February, 1909), 65; Jeffrey C. Weaver, *54th Virginia Infantry* (H. E. Howard, 1993), 67, 70-71.

addition, Colonel Wilder's earlier Union attack that had so disrupted Manigault's brigade of Hindman's division was still on Buckner's mind; at 2:30 p.m. the corps commander sent Colonel Trigg and two of his four regiments—the 1st Florida (Dismounted) Cavalry and 7th Florida infantry—back south along the La Fayette Road in response to yet more reports of enemy cavalry operating near Lee and Gordon's Mills.[33]

Preston's waiting men found the spectacle of a major battle rather daunting. Captain J. T. Gaines of the 5th Kentucky recorded his impressions: "Fences were burning along the border of the woodland in which we stood [and] before us was a magnificent battle scene. Away to the right . . . we saw flag after flag marking the positions . . . of our men. Couriers and aids were dashing here and there. The attack on Snodgrass Hill had already begun." Gaines's attention was firmly fixed on that struggle. "A fierce fight was raging somewhere in the front. Clouds of smoke rose above the tops of the trees, and a pandemonius of sounds issued from among them. The crash of artillery and the rattle of small arms . . . mingled with the cheers of the men engaged in the death grapple."[34]

About 3:30 p.m. it became apparent to Longstreet that the troops so engaged were "not strong enough for the work," so he "ordered General Buckner to move Preston forward." Captain Gaines, still watching from the ranks, perhaps sensed their moment had arrived all too soon. "Soon men bleeding from wounds came pouring out of the forest. Men with litters came out bearing others who were more desperately hurt. The first attack had evidently failed."[35]

Preston immediately recalled Trigg and all but one of his regiments, but hurried forward with Gracie's and Kelly's brigades into Dyer Field without waiting for Trigg's troops to arrive; they would have to catch up. John Dyer, the son of the owner, rode at Preston's side providing the courtly Kentuckian with a "most accurate and valuable description of the local topography." Using young Dyer's information as a guide, Preston placed Gracie in a single line at the northern end of the field with his left resting on the summit of Harker's Knoll and his right extending to near the Glenn-Kelly Road, essentially duplicating

33 *OR* 30, pt. 2, 431, 442-443.

34 J. T. Gaines, "Recollections of Chickamauga," Confederate Veteran Papers, DU.

35 *OR* 30, pt. 2, 289; Gaines, "Recollections of Chickamauga," DU.

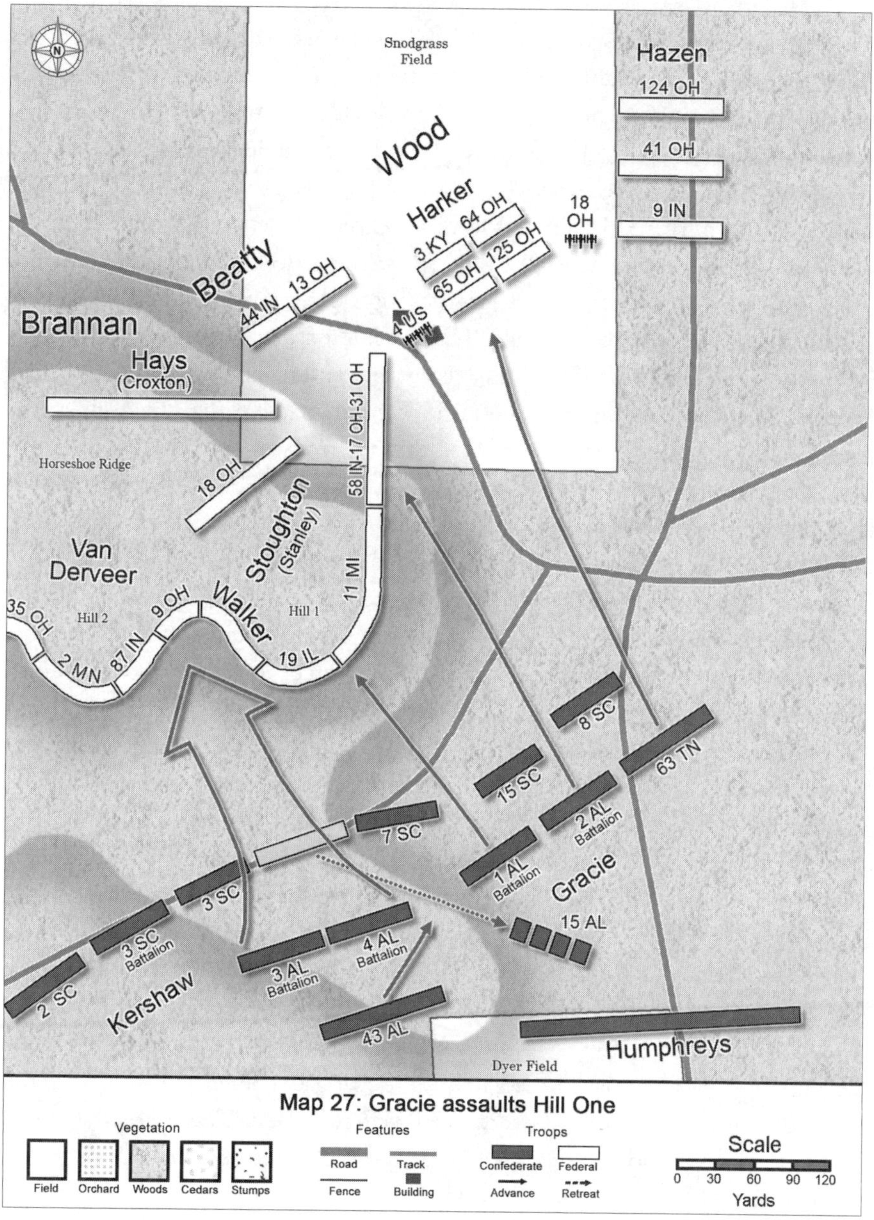

Map 27: Gracie assaults Hill One

Kershaw's advance of about 2:00 p.m. Kelly was ordered to extend Gracie's left into the woods behind Patton Anderson and Bushrod Johnson.[36]

36 *OR* 30, pt. 2, 415.

Preston intended to wait until both brigades were aligned before sending them forward, but events outpaced him. General Kershaw, who was still actively directing affairs on his part of the field, took charge of the new arrivals. "I determined on an attack," he wrote, "combining all our forces: McNair's . . . Gracie's, Kelly's, Anderson's, [and] my own." Kershaw's intentions were laudable, and mirrored Bushrod Johnson's earlier efforts, but his intervention had just the opposite effect. "[W]hile [I] was engaged in bringing Kelly into position," reported Preston, "Gracie's brigade disappeared in the woods, advancing against the battery hill." The bewildered division leader watched as the large brigade advanced without his orders, and dispatched an aide to find out why Gracie was moving. When he learned that Kershaw had given the order, the frustrated Preston lamented that this movement was "premature," but circumstances could now not be helped. Preston ordered Kelly to hasten forward as Gracie's flank support, and anxiously awaited the outcome.[37]

Gracie's command was large, weighing in at 1,927 rank and file. In addition to the 43rd Alabama and 63rd Tennessee, the bulk of his brigade included the four infantry battalions of Hilliard's Legion. In the early stages of the war, some ambitious officers attempted to recruit integrated formations of all arms. Several such legions were raised, and Col. Henry W. Hilliard's command was among the largest, originally numbering 3,000 men. Raised in the summer of 1862, Hilliard commanded his oversized formation in East Tennessee until he resigned in December 1862, frustrated that he had not been promoted to brigadier. No one was sorry to see him go. The cavalry and artillery components were stripped away, leaving the four infantry battalions on their own.[38]

These six commands made for a lengthy battle line of roughly 650 yards. The 63rd Tennessee took the right flank, and in order from right to left came the 2nd Battalion, 1st Battalion, 4th Battalion, and 3rd Battalion of the Legion. Colonel Young M. Moody's 43rd Alabama advanced on the left. This line became unwieldy almost immediately as the brigade moved up the timbered hillside in an attempt to pass through Kershaw's men. The 43rd first broke formation when Moody discovered his path was blocked by "the brigade on our left [Kershaw.]" Gracie ordered the 43rd to halt, let the rest of the brigade forge

37 Ibid., 415, 505.

38 Bruce S. Allardice, *Confederate Colonels: A Biographical Register* (University of Missouri Press, 2008), 196. The cavalry force was merged into the 10th Confederate Cavalry, now serving in Brig. Gen. Henry B. Davidson's brigade, while the artillery became Kolb's Alabama battery.

ahead, and then fall in behind. One Alabamian remembered the 43rd was ordered to lie down while the rest of the brigade moved into the attack.[39]

On the other flank, the 63rd Tennessee was also experiencing difficulties. Major John A. Aiken led the Tennesseans, 400 strong, through Humphrey's Mississippians. Initially formed in column of companies, Aiken deployed the 63rd into line once past Humphrey's troops, coming under "a heavy fire of musketry." Doing so, however, disconnected the 63rd from Gracie's main line, opening a sizable gap between it and the 2nd Battalion on its left. Aiken now found his command all alone on its first battlefield taking heavy fire, all while facing the strongest part of the Union line opposite Harker's blue-clad veterans and the Federals holding the east face of Hill One.[40]

As the Tennesseans stepped into range, Col. Emerson Opdycke's 125th Ohio resumed its disciplined volleying. This was the moment when Hazen's Yankees emerged from the trees at the eastern end of Snodgrass Field. Hazen recognized Opdycke, who had served under him as a junior officer, mounted and directing the 125th's fire. "I found him firing by volley with great rapidity—a species of tactics he had been taught when a captain in the 41st Ohio Regiment," bragged Hazen. Ever the tactician, Hazen noted the technique in approving detail: "The [125th's] position was admirable, being [on] a little crest at the south side of the field at the Snodgrass house. The men, alternating by companies, would advance up to this crest to deliver their fire, and then fall back a few yards for shelter and to reload." Opdycke remembered the fire from Rebel sharpshooters was more hazardous to him than the fire of the raw Tennesseans. These sharpshooters, he wrote his wife, "sent special compliments to Barney [Opdycke's horse.] One ball cut through my blouse, some grazed Barney, warming his nose, and ears, which insult he resented, prancing about and shaking his head."[41]

Hazen immediately brought his men into line alongside and added their fire to Harker's. Captain Charles Clark of the 125th recalled Hazen's men joined them "about 3:30 or 4 o'clock . . . the right regiment of that brigade, the 9th Indiana, halted first immediately in the rear of our regiment, and at the beginning of the next assault fired over us." The rest of Hazen's men fell in

39 *OR* 30, pt. 2, 423; "Gracie's Brigade," *Mobile Advertiser and Register*, October 14, 1863.

40 *OR* 30, pt. 2, 429.

41 Hazen, *A Narrative of Military Service*, 132; Longacre and Haas, *To Battle for God and the Right*, 101.

alongside, "massed in column of regiments," and lay prone. As the 63rd Tennessee struggled to move forward, Hazen's lead unit "sprang to its feet, delivered its volley, and went down again to reload." The remaining regiments followed suit with devastating effect. "The slope was strewn with Confederate dead and wounded, but not a man could reach the crest," recorded the 41st Ohio's regimental history.[42]

Lieutenant Colonel Simeon Aldrich and his wayward 44th Indiana watched this display of firepower with awe. Aldrich belonged to Col. George Dick's badly fragmented brigade, originally of Horatio Van Cleve's division, the XXI Corps. While most of Dick's men left the field with General Negley, the 44th and a small portion of the 13th Ohio fell in behind Harker, determined to lend a hand where they could. "We repulsed the enemy three times with great slaughter. They finally abandoned the ground," reported Aldrich. Of Harker's men, he marveled, "I never saw troops handled better or fight more determinedly."[43]

Facing the fire of parts or all of 10 Union regiments (even if many of those units were mere shadows of their previous strength), it is no surprise the Tennesseans failed to make any headway. While some of this Union attention was drawn away by Hilliard's 2nd Battalion attacking Hill One, most of it was directed at the perfect target presented by the 63rd Tennessee—a line of men in gray alone in the open cornfield. Hazen's arrival and contribution added a damaging crossfire to the deadly mix, the lead balls slicing into the 63rd's right flank. Still, the Tennesseans were nothing if not game. Unable to advance but unwilling to retreat, Major Aiken sent word of his predicament to General Gracie and appealed for help.[44]

Bolling Hall's 2nd Battalion first came under fire and took early casualties about 250 yards from the Federals. The first fire caused a moment's difficulty, soon corrected. Reaching the foot of Hill One, however, the battalion's 281 officers and men halted again. They fought for some time, slugging it out with the Yankees atop the hill. According to battalion adjutant Crenshaw Hall, "the fighting was hard and much to our disadvantage, and some confusion

42 "Dear Sir," February 12, 1909, Charles T. Clark to Ezra E. Carmen, 125th Ohio Website, http://home.earthlink.net/~nhaldane/ctc-letter.html, accessed 10/22/2012; Kimberly and Holloway, *The Forty-First Ohio*, 53.

43 *OR* 30, pt. 1, 828.

44 Ibid., 2, 429.

prevailing, a retreat was made for a short distance." The officers set about rallying the command for another try.[45]

These Alabamians faced Stanley's brigade, now under Colonel Stoughton of the 11th Michigan. In describing this fight, Wolverine Pvt. James Martin noted, "we then fell back a few rods under cover of a hill, out of reach of their sharpshooters [and] there we made a high breastwork on the brow of the hill. . . . In a short time they massed their force and attacked us again. We held them at bay for over an hour." Alongside the 11th, Cpl. J. Henry Haynie of Company D, 19th Illinois, remembered that the hillside was a ghastly mess. "Bullets splash red mud—the earth had been made mire by human blood—into our faces."[46]

While Gracie's command was coming to grips with the Yankees, Col. William C. Oates of the 15th Alabama, still hanging on in the middle of Kershaw's extended line, was finally ordered out of action. True to form, his departure caused one final disruption. "It was getting late in the afternoon," Oates recalled, "when Law's Adjutant General came up and said he had been hunting us for two hours. . . . He told me to withdraw, and that Gracie's brigade was going into action. . . . As we moved out we passed Gracie's brigade going in, in echelon of battalions, as handsome as a command ever moved to such perilous work. It had never been in battle, and the ranks were very full." Oates may have admired Gracie's men as they passed, but Maj. John D. McLennan, commanding Gracie's 4th Battalion, spoke less flatteringly of Oates: "We had gone but a short distance when we were ordered to lie down in order that Kershaw's brigade might retire. Being under a telling fire, the withdrawing of this brigade necessarily caused some confusion and partly broke my lines, which I could not afterward perfectly restore."[47]

45 Powell, "Numbers and Losses," CCNMP; *OR* 30, pt. 2, 425.The 2nd Battalion's strength is usually given as 238 men, a figure cited in the report as the "total" engaged. The report also records 260 "aggregate" engaged. Both figures, however, are for enlisted men only. See Tabular Report, Wyckliffe-Preston Papers, University of Kentucky, Lexington.

46 "Dear Parents," Martin Letter, Bentley Historical Library, UMich; J. Henry Haynie, *The Nineteenth Illinois: A Memoir of a Regiment of Volunteer Infantry Famous in the Civil War of Fifty Years Ago for its Drill, Bravery, and Distinguished Services* (M.A. Donahue, 1912), 225.

47 Oates, *The War Between the Union and the Confederacy*, 264; *OR* 30, pt. 2, 427. Oates's "in echelon" phrasing suggests Gracie's regiments were not aligned straight, but staggered at different intervals. Likely he was seeing the effects of Moody's halt and the disruption his own departure initiated. McLennan mentions "Kershaw's brigade," but the only unit leaving the line at this point is Oates's 15th Alabama. All of Kershaw's South Carolinians remained deployed along the line of the Vittetoe Road.

Alongside the 4th, the 1st Battalion also struggled with Yankee fire. At 250 yards the fire became "furious," remembered Adjutant John Massey. Lieutenant Colonel John H. Holt fell at nearly the first volley with a shattered leg, leaving Capt. George W. Hugeley in command. Most of the other company commanders were soon down as well, rendering the battalion nearly leaderless; an anonymous member of the 1st Battalion noted that only Captain Hugeley "and perhaps one other" remained unscathed.[48]

Pressing forward, the inexperienced Alabamians caught their first glimpse of the Union defenses, which to these green troops appeared daunting indeed. According to Private Davis, "the enemy was securely posted behind their well constructed breastworks. They had three lines of breastworks on a hy hill . . . constructed [so] that three brigades could operate on us at the saim time. Their works . . . form[ed] the sircul of a half moon so [they] cros fierd on us from both sides and in front." Once again, the natural curvature of the several hills and draws made direct attacks difficult. In their effort to come to grips with the enemy lining the summit of each hill, Gracie's regiments channeled themselves into individual advances, each subject to a crippling enfilade fire.[49]

McLennan's 4th Battalion, which with 243 officers and men was the smallest formation in Gracie's command, pressed to within 40 yards of the crest of Hill Two. The battalion, noted McLennan, was already facing "a murderous fire" from the front when "a heavy fire . . . poured into us from the left." The 4th Battalion could go no farther, with "fire pouring upon me from the front, right and left. . . . To advance farther without support," he explained, "would have been reckless in the extreme." The 4th Battalion was moving up Draw One, the same path the 15th Alabama followed earlier, and was experiencing a murderous flanking fire from the 2nd Minnesota's left wing atop Hill Two.[50]

Now holding Gracie's extreme left, Lt. Col. John. W. A. Sanford led his 3rd Battalion directly at the 2nd Minnesota. With McLennan's battalion in trouble to his right, Sanford paused while the 4th rallied, and then renewed the advance

48 Anonymous, "The First Battalion Hilliard's Legion at Chickamauga," *Montgomery Advertiser*, May 5, 1907; *OR* 30, pt. 2, 425; Anonymous, "The First Battalion." *Montgomery Advertiser*, May 5, 1907.

49 "Chattanooga, Sept 26, 1863" Davis Letters, ADAH. The exact identity of this man remains a mystery. There were at least six men named Davis in the 1st Battalion engaged at Chickamauga, three of whom survived unwounded. The letter writer could be either E. L. Davis of Company C, R. E. Davis of Company D, or Richard E. Davis of Company B.

50 *OR* 30, pt. 2, 427.

together. Sanford claimed he gained the crest of Hill Two and held it through the ensuing firefight, but in all likelihood the 3rd Battalion only reached a level shelf on the forward slope, not the actual crest. Nor was it able to keep aligned with the 4th Battalion. Both units went to ground, pinned down and exchanging fire with Van Derveer's Federals, but unable to do more.[51]

General Gracie's men had reached an impasse. Units were stopped all along the disjointed brigade line, clinging to the bloody slopes and enduring a heavy fire. The 3rd and 4th Battalions wrapped around the eastern and southern slopes of Hill Two, facing the 2nd Minnesota and 87th Indiana from Van Derveer's brigade. The 1st Battalion was trapped in Draw One, facing the west face of Hill One. The 9th Ohio raked its left flank, while the 82nd Indiana savaged them head-on. Hall's 2nd Battalion grappled with the 11th Michigan and 19th Illinois on the southern face of Hill One. Lastly, the beleaguered 63rd Tennessee was still suffering under Harker's and Hazen's disciplined killing volleys. Only Colonel Moody's 43rd Alabama, which had been forced out of line and was now moving up behind the 1st and 2nd Battalions, remained unengaged.

Despite his good intentions, Kershaw's coordinated attack never materialized. He expected three of his regiments to join Gracie's assault, but none of them had much fight left in them. Private Screven in the 2nd South Carolina recorded the reality: "I was anxious for the line to charge the enemy still further, but no they were contented to remain where they were and fire at long range. . . . We were relieved in the levying of the charge by some other regiment who rushed over us but when they got to the front. . . . They lay down and commenced firing, so Col. Gaillard called for the 2nd Regt to fall back." John Belue of the 15th South Carolina had an unfortunate front row seat for the 63rd Tennessee's engagement. Wounded earlier, Belue lay exposed under Union fire all afternoon: "[D]uring the evening two other Brigades came up just on the ground where I lay and ingaged the enemy most desperately[,] my only shelter being a small tree."[52]

With Gracie stalled and Kershaw's men going nowhere, Kelly's brigade moved up to take its turn. With only three regiments and 874 men, fronting

51 Ibid., 426.

52 "September 20, Sunday" Reginald Screven Diary, SCHS; J. Edward Lee and Ron Chepesiuk, eds., *South Carolina in the Civil War: The Confederate Experience in Letters and Diaries* (McFarland and Co., 2000), 142.

perhaps 200 yards, Kelly's line was less than one-third as long as Gracie's. Placing Maj. James M. French's 63rd Virginia in the center, Kelly sent Col. John B. Palmer's 58th North Carolina to the right and Col. Hiram Hawkins's experienced 5th Kentucky to the left. The 5th regiment was one bright spot in Kelly's new command. This was a proven outfit without the morale problems found amongst the conscripts of the 58th North Carolina or 63rd Virginia. It also bore an unusual nickname. Unlike most other Kentucky Confederates, recruited in the wealthier Bluegrass, the 5th was largely drawn from eastern Kentucky. One staple of nineteenth century mountain life was the use of ginseng, a root so prevalent in some areas it was used as barter currency. In no time at all, the men of the 5th were dubbed "Sang Diggers" by their fellow Kentuckians in the Army of Tennessee.[53]

With Gracie already engaged, Preston ordered Kelly to hurry, obliquing to the right in an effort to close up on and support Gracie's left flank. Years later, Colonel Palmer of the 58th North Carolina recalled that Kelly solicited General Hindman's advice here, which apparently proved unhelpful. "Unfortunately," Palmer remembered, "instead of forming us on a line with the balance of the division, and parallel with the position we were to charge, we were moved through the timber at a considerable angle."[54]

Kelly's men found rough going. "The enemy was posted on a heavily wooded ridge . . . [and] the approach to him was over a succession of hills with intervening depressions, each hill to the front being somewhat more elevated." They also had to pass through Anderson's Mississippians. Anderson's formations had largely dissolved by now, the men fighting as individuals from any cover they could find. Captain J. T. Gaines remembered that as the "Sang Diggers" approached, he could see the Mississippians "falling or rather straggling back in little groups." One Mississippi captain tried to reform his command when he spotted the new arrivals. He also had advice for Gaines: "don't stop when you sight them but give a yell and rush them." All of this happened under a steady, long range Federal fire. "The brigade," Kelly

53 *OR* 30, pt. 2, 441-443, 447; Ed Porter Thompson, *History of the Orphan Brigade* (Lewis N. Thompson, 1898), 226. In his battle report, Colonel Kelly lists only 852 engaged. However, the tabular strength statement found in the Wyckliffe-Preston Papers indicates the strength "actually under arms and carried into action" for each regiment in the division, and that is the number noted.

54 *OR* 30, pt. 2, 441; John B. Palmer, "The 58th North Carolina at the Battle of Chickamauga," *Our Living and Our Dead*, vol. 3 (1875), 454-455.

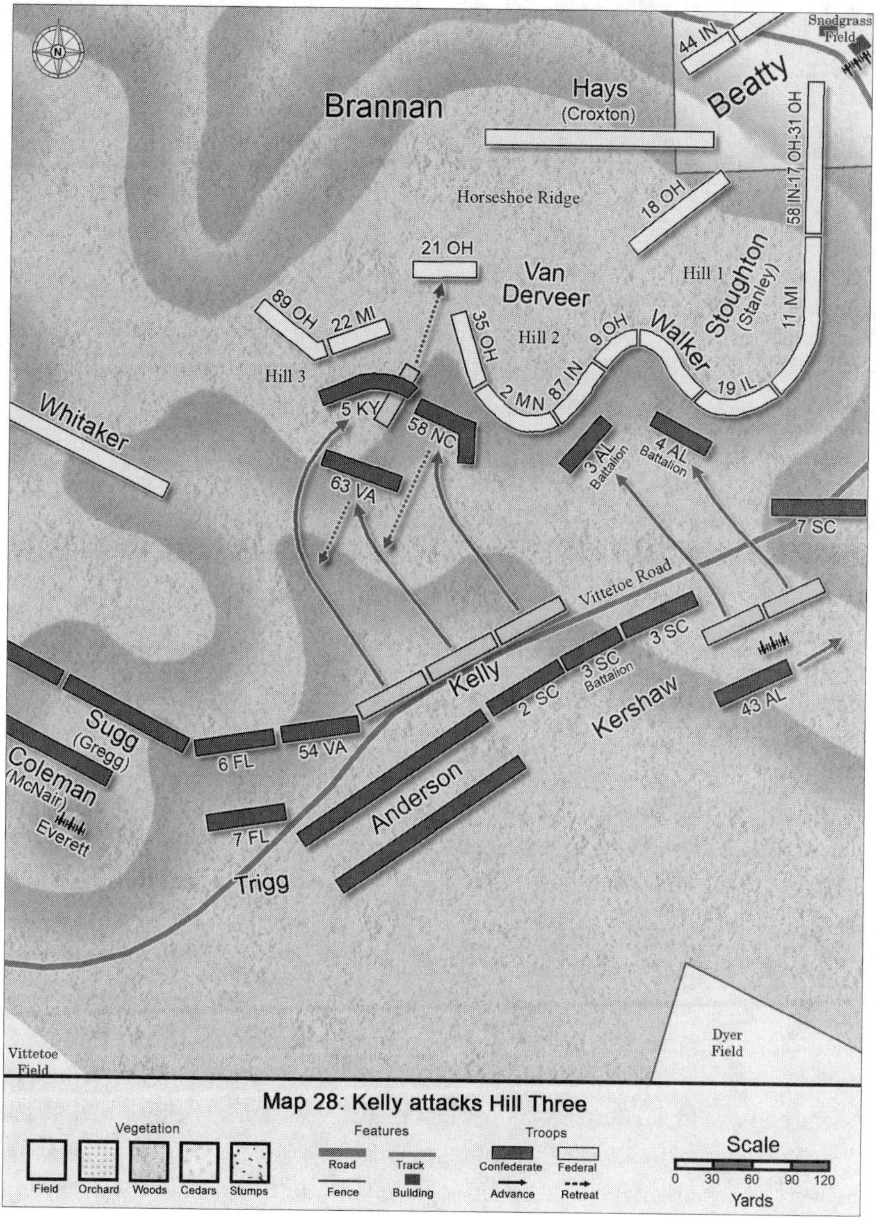

reported, was "under fire of the enemy" for the last "300 or 400 yards" of the advance.[55]

55 Gaines, "Recollections of Chickamauga," DU; *OR* 30, pt. 2, 441.

Still advancing northeast in search of Gracie's elusive left flank, Kelly's line reached a point opposite Draw Two. As elsewhere, the Federal line there followed the curve of the crest. Kelly's right was approaching the 2nd Minnesota's right, his center facing the 35th Ohio, and his left squared off against the 21st Ohio and perhaps some of the 22nd Michigan. Just as the Alabamians in Hilliard's battalions discovered, the farther up the draw they moved, the more crossfire they suffered. The 58th North Carolina experienced this unpleasant reality first.

Colonel Palmer led his regiment steadily forward until he stumbled on the main Federal position. With the blue line meeting his own at an angle, his right flank was much closer to the enemy than his left, perhaps as near as 10 or 12 yards. The Federal volley that followed was devastating. "My major, the captain and 1 lieutenant of my left flanking company, 2 lieutenants in the center, and my adjutant had been wounded. My Lieutenant Colonel and two company officers had been killed on my extreme right. Two thirds of my right flanking company, which was exposed to a most galling crossfire . . . [were] killed and wounded," reported Kelly. Witnessing this advance, Jeremiah Donahower of the 2nd Minnesota recalled that the North Carolinians's "heroism was grand: they drew [our] admiration . . . as they forged onward . . . only to receive a decimating fire." The Tar Heels brushed up so close to the Union line that a dozen Rebels surrendered to the Minnesotans rather than hazard retreat, and entered the Federal line in front of Companies D and E.[56]

The 58th's problems were compounded by the fact that in the middle of this withering fire, Colonel Kelly sent word to Palmer to cease firing. Kelly mistakenly thought Palmer's troops were shooting at elements of Gracie's command. Palmer momentarily obeyed, with some two-thirds of his men checking their fire. The men on the right wing, fully aware their opponents were Yankees, never stopped pulling their triggers. The damage, however, was done, and the 58th faltered. On the right of the 58th North Carolina, Lt. Col. Edmund Kirby exhorted, "Push them, men, push them!" just before being struck dead. The North Carolinians lost 65 men in this first effort. Palmer soon ordered his men to resume firing, but "a longer continuance in this position was beyond

56 *OR* 30, pt. 2, 445; Jeremiah Donahower Papers, MinnHS.

human endurance." The Tar Heels fell back, seeking shelter from the relentless Union fusillades.[57]

Palmer's retreat exposed Major French's 63rd Virginia to similar treatment. At first French thought victory was within his grasp. "When within 15 paces of the enemy," he reported, "my regiment was halted and poured a deadly fire into his ranks. The enemy gave way." French was about to order a charge when Kelly's confusing order to cease fire reached him as well. "This mistake gave the enemy time to rally," lamented French, and whatever opportunity beckoned was lost. With the 58th gone, a brutal flanking fire scourged the right side of the Virginia line. Captain Thomas Hampton, leading Company B, took a hit here. "I was slightly wounded on the outside of my thigh," he wrote, reassuring his wife that the ball cut a gouge "only . . . its' thickness in depth and about 3 inches long." As the 63rd settled into a steady exchange of fire with the rallied Yankees, Hampton limped away to the field hospital, his battle finished.[58]

Atop Hill Two, Lt. Col. Judson Bishop of the 2nd Minnesota disagreed with French's assessment. As far as he was concerned, the only ones who gave way wore gray or butternut. "Picking their way over and among their fallen comrades who already encumbered the slope by hundreds, they came bravely and steadily on," wrote Bishop. "As however they approached nearer, and the firing in their faces grew hotter . . . they seemed to lose the reassuring touch of elbows, and as the vacancies rapidly increased, they began to hesitate . . . then they halted and commenced firing wildly into the tree tops, then turned and rushed madly down the slope, carrying the second line with them."[59]

Kelly's last regiment, the 5th Kentucky, met with the most success. The 5th crossed the Vittetoe Road somewhere near where it curved southward, and then turned northeast. The angled advance of the Kentuckians brought them up the southwest face of Hill Three. According to Colonel Hawkins, his men not only reached the crest but swept right over it, driving the Federals before them, all while under a heavy crossfire from Yankees to their left and right. Captain Gaines recalled that as the 5th "came in sight of the enemy we gave the fox-hunter's view halloo and broke into a run." The 5th charged up through

57 Palmer, "The 58th North Carolina," 455; *OR* 30, pt. 2, 445.

58 *OR* 30, pt. 2, 447; "Jestin Dear Wife," September 24, 1863, Hampton Letters, UT. French faced the 35th Ohio. Hampton would go on to fight through the war only to be killed on March 19, 1865, at Bentonville in North Carolina.

59 Bishop, *Van Derveer's Brigade at Chickamauga*, 17.

and amidst some of Anderson's Mississippians scattered along the hillside trading shots with the 21st Ohio. This fact worked in the "Sang Diggers'" favor, thought Gaines, who noted the Yankees "were not able to give us a volley because they were firing at will at the time."[60]

In fact, the Federals's problems were more serious than just a lack of fire discipline. Once again the 21st Ohio was desperately short of ammunition. To Adjutant Canfield the situation was now ominously familiar. Nearly 10 months before at Stones River, the 21st ran out of ammunition and was outflanked. The retreat that followed deteriorated into complete confusion. Canfield was determined to prevent a similar disaster atop Horseshoe Ridge. Moving down the line, he instructed the company commanders to pull the men out individually as each fired his last rounds, and gather them in a depression to the rear. The regiment could "form there and march together to the rear" in search of more cartridges. The Buckeyes of the 21st slowly melted away before the Kentuckians, and "when our line was not stronger than a skirmish line," recalled Captain Canfield, "I ordered up the regiments in reserve." These "reserve regiments" were in fact part of Van Derveer's right wing, in line to the 21st's left. From their position on the southwest face of Hill Two, the 35th Ohio and one-half of the 2nd Minnesota could now turn and fire at Hawkins's Kentuckians. Judson Bishop wrote that the 5th Kentucky's "advance was only broken up when their foremost men were within ten paces of our line." Facing this new fire, and without support from the rest of Kelly's brigade, the "Sang Diggers" fell back in turn.[61]

From Colonel Hawkins's perspective, the 5th was dangerously exposed, alone amidst the enemy line and about 80 yards in advance of the rest of Kelly's men. Captain Gaines also explained that by the time they crested the ridge, the 5th was badly fragmented. "It happened that fallen timber had divided our regiment and we reached the summit some distance apart. Our Senior Captain, [Joseph] Desha, took command of three companies and put us in position to resist attack from the enemy. He sent me to report to Col. Hawkins and ask him to bring the left wing to join us. I found them about 200 yards away across a depression in the ridge." Hawkins decided he had to halt and consolidate. Once reunited, the regiment fell back to greater cover and began a protracted firefight

60 *OR* 30, pt. 2, 443; Gaines, "Recollections of Chickamauga," DU.

61 Canfield, *History of the 21st Regiment*, 74; S. S. Canfield to Col. A McMahan, June 7, 1889, BGSU; Bishop, *The Story of a Regiment*, 110.

with those Federals who were barely discernable on the far side of the hill. Gaines later claimed the Kentuckians repulsed numerous Union counterattacks and eventually fired away their entire ammunition supply, but no Union regiment had the strength or sufficient ammunition to drive the 5th completely off the crest of Hill Three. Rebel possession of this part of Hill Three further divided the Union defensive line, partially isolating the 22nd Michigan and 89th Ohio.[62]

This second withdrawal of the 21st Ohio has only added to the subsequent historical confusion concerning the movements of these Buckeyes. As noted earlier, some of the 21st disputed that they were ever relieved, while others recalled this passage of lines happening when Van Derveer's regiments first came up behind the 21st. Still others in the 21st vividly recalled this last retreat about 5:00 p.m. Additionally, the accounts of Van Derveer's brigade make it clear that far from being in reserve, they were in the thick of the fight from early in the afternoon, repulsing several attacks.

Despite the apparent contradictions, all these accounts offer accurate, if incomplete, views of what happened. Van Derveer's men did come into line about 2:00 p.m., and did relieve a part of the 21st's line at that time. Resupplied with scrounged Enfield rounds, the 21st took up a much shorter line atop Hill Three, connecting with the 22nd Michigan and 89th Ohio on their other flank. Confirming this, Bishop stated that "an hour later we heard that they [the 21st] had got ammunition from Granger . . . and taken places on the right of our brigade."[63]

The second incident occurred when the Rebel 5th Kentucky appeared on the scene. Because the Rebels approached at an angle from the southwest, the 21st naturally fell back directly away from the "Sang Diggers" to the northeast, passing through the 2nd Minnesota and 35th Ohio on Hill Two. Here the 21st executed Canfield's plan of individuals falling back through Van Derveer's ranks and down into the ravine behind Hill Three. This might have been the end of the 21st Ohio's role in the battle, had McMahan been allowed to march

62 *OR* 30, pt. 2, 443; Gaines, "Recollections of Chickamauga," DU. It might not have been quite 200 yards, but the 5th Kentucky did traverse the length of Hill Three along its long axis. If the bulk of the 5th reached the spot where its marker now stands in the saddle between Hills Two and Three, this is a reasonable guess.

63 Bishop, *Van Derveer's Brigade at Chickamauga*, 15.

his regiment away as originally intended. His command was destined to play out one more part, however, though not a happy one.

Ideally, assuming an effective Federal defense here, the 5th Kentucky should have experienced the same flanking problem that brought Anderson's Rebels so much grief earlier in the battle. The 22nd Michigan and 89th Ohio defended the western side of Hill Three, with the rest of General Whitaker's line beyond them on the spur. Colonel Le Favour's line should have been able to fire at the Rebels from their position, or even launch another counterattack into Hawkins's exposed left flank. There are four reasons why the Yankees failed to do so.

The first was the lack of unified command. Whitaker provided no direction here, for he was busy elsewhere along the line and assumed Le Favour's 22nd Michigan and 89th Ohio had been loaned out to Brannan. Le Favour still regarded himself as a demi-brigade commander under Steedman, leaving the 22nd Michigan initially in the hands of Lt. Col. William Sanborn and subsequently, Capt. Alonzo Keeler.[64]

McMahan and the 21st Ohio were apparently operating without any senior direction at all. After Brannan sent them to the right, the Buckeyes received no additional instructions the rest of the day. Van Derveer was holding his own front, and after initially replacing the 21st Ohio's left wing, had only a vague understanding of events happening west of him. Thus, within a span of no more than 400 or 500 yards, these five regiments operated as three independent elements, with no single officer in charge.[65]

The second reason was the terrain. Because of the rise and fall of the ground, the bulk of Hill Three blocked any direct line of sight between Van Derveer's position on Hill Two and Le Favour's line. Hawkins's Rebels advanced through what amounted to a blind spot with regard to both Van Derveer's and Le Favour's positions. Only a strong force atop the crest and the southeast face of Hill Three could see the 5th Kentucky coming forward. Once the 5th swept the hilltop and used the south crest as a parapet, it was sheltered from incoming fire from the northeast and the northwest. After the 21st could no longer hold the hilltop, the integrity of the Union line was lost. The outthrust mass of the hill worked to shelter portions of the Rebel approach.

64 Robertson, *Michigan in the War*, 421.

65 Bishop, *Van Derveer's Brigade at Chickamauga*, 15.

The third reason was visibility. It was now 5:00 p.m. The sun would not set until 6:30 p.m., but the late afternoon light was already being blocked by various hills and the woods. Far worse than waning daylight was the thick, choking smoke. The discharges of thousands of muskets and some two dozen cannon filled the air with powder smoke, augmented by ground fires kindled by muzzle flashes that had been burning since mid-afternoon. Two hours earlier, Jeremiah Donahower observed the ravines in front of his position were filling with smoke from those small fires burning near the Confederate wounded. A little later, Sgt. John Bolton in the 21st Ohio described the same phenomenon: "The dry leaves in our front caught fire towards evening and the smoke from their burning, in connection with that from the musketry and artillery fire, very materially added to the darkness and gloom."[66]

The fourth reason the Federals failed to fire into the Kentucky flank or counterattack was the now-standard lament: no bullets. The 22nd Michigan and 89th Ohio had no more ammunition than did McMahan's Ohioans. Colonel Le Favour sent word of his plight to Whitaker. His answer was not encouraging: "You must use your steel." Against a Rebel enemy fully supplied with 80 rounds per man, Le Favour's nearly bulletless band could achieve little.[67]

The 5th Kentucky may have actually seized Hill Three, but there was still an entire Union line clinging to the rest of Horseshoe Ridge. The bulk of William Preston's Rebel division had been soundly repulsed and was now struggling to reform at the foot of the slope amidst the detritus of the many previous attempts. Were there enough men left to make one last effort to capitalize on the 5th Kentucky's localized success?

66 Jeremiah Donahower Papers, MinnHS; Canfield, *History of the 21st Regiment*, 144.

67 Robertson, *Michigan in the War*, 424.

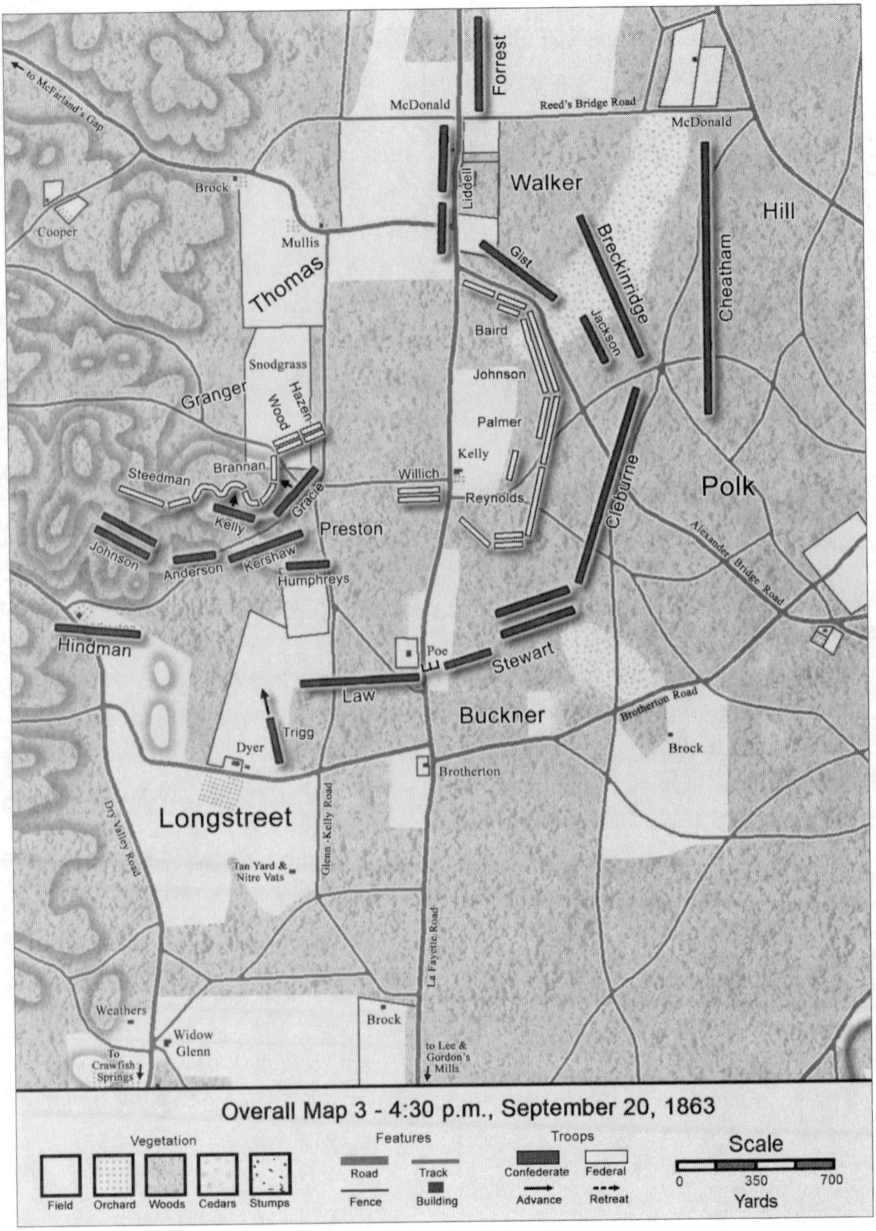

Overall Map 3 - 4:30 p.m., September 20, 1863

Chapter Twenty-Five

Turchin's Charge:

Sunday, 4:00 p.m. to 6:00 p.m.

By the time he arrived at the Brabson house on the afternoon of September 20, William S. Rosecrans was beyond exhausted. The general was barely capable of dismounting, let alone taking charge of the chaotic and highly fluid situation. After some rest, however, the commander of the Army of the Cumberland revived sufficiently to at least begin to take stock of his circumstances.

Rosecrans's first order of business was to address the command vacuum left behind on the Chickamauga battlefield. About 4:15 p.m., he drafted the following order to his XIV Corps commander, George Thomas:

> Assume command of all the forces, and with Crittenden and McCook take a strong position and assume a threatening attitude at Rossville. Send all the unorganized forces to this place for re-organization. I will examine the ground here and make such dispositions for defense as the case may require and join you. I have sent out ammunition and rations.

The timing of this directive is significant. Rosecrans wrote this before he received his chief of staff James Garfield's much more upbeat assessment, sent from the Snodgrass cabin at 3:45 p.m. Had the field telegraph still been connected all the way to the battlefield, the transmission of each message would have required only a few minutes to reach him. Instead, each dispatch had to be hand-carried to or from Rossville. As a result, Garfield's and Rosecrans's missives crossed paths. Lacking full knowledge of General Thomas's actual circumstances in the field, Rosecrans had little choice but to err on the side of caution.[1]

Later, when reputations and careers were at stake, much would be made of the idea that Thomas should have disregarded the order to retreat to Rossville, and that by issuing it, Rosecrans snatched defeat from the jaws of victory. General Granger, for one, urged Thomas to stand fast. Thomas's own intentions, however, were more in line with those of his army commander. While immediate retreat was impossible, as Thomas himself acknowledged: "it would ruin the army to withdraw it now. This position must be held until night." Once the dark came, however, Thomas knew he needed to fall back. Garfield sided with Granger and urged Thomas to hold on at least through the next day. In 1870, Garfield informed Rosecrans that "Gordon Granger will tell you that both he and I strenuously urged Thomas not to retire on Rossville."[2]

When they met with Thomas to urge him not to retreat, however, remains unclear. According to Garfield, neither he nor Granger was present when Thomas first received Rosecrans's 4:15 p.m. instructions, and their protests came only after Thomas had already decided on an overnight withdrawal. In his official report, Thomas reiterated that he was "determined to hold the position until nightfall, if possible," but added that preparations for an eventual retreat began almost immediately. When he learned of Rosecrans's orders, Garfield immediately understood the political costs of such a move. By holding its ground, the Union army would escape the taint of a rout "worse than Bull Run," and could claim a tactical stalemate against overwhelming odds. Conversely, if it left the Rebels in sole possession of the battlefield, the scope—and the political fallout—of the defeat would be greatly magnified. "I will only say that it was won and then abandoned," mourned Garfield five days after the battle, "giving

1 *OR* 30, pt. 1, 140, 256-257. When Brig. Gen. George B. Wagner was placed in charge of the Chattanooga garrison on September 10, 1863, he established his headquarters at the residence of an attorney named Reese Brabson at 407 E. 5th Street, a two-story brick mansion with an imposing portico. After the battle of Chickamauga, the Union headquarters was moved to the Thomas Richardson house at 321 Walnut, which was considerably less exposed to Rebel shellfire during the subsequent quasi-siege to follow. Note that the order to Thomas was originally mistimed as 12:15 p.m. General Rosecrans later noted that he did not arrive in Chattanooga until at least 3:40 p.m., and the order was written about one-half hour later.

2 Michael Hendrick Fitch, *The Chattanooga Campaign, with Especial Reference to Wisconsin's Participation Therin* (Democrat Printing Co., State Printer, 1911), 118; Glenn Tucker, *Chickamauga: Bloody Battle in the West* (Press of the Morningside Bookshop, 1981), 359; Smith, *James Abram Garfield*, vol. 2, 855.

the enemy an opportunity to follow and injure us, but he was too much crippled to do so."[3]

Garfield might have understood the political implications, but he overlooked tactical reality. Thomas, who more fully understood the precarious nature of his position, never gave the idea of standing fast serious thought. It simply wasn't practical. It was by now apparent that Braxton Bragg had been heavily reinforced from all across the Confederacy. Would another of General Lee's infantry corps from Virginia show up tomorrow? Or perhaps more of Joseph E. Johnston's brigades? Moreover, Thomas's current "line" was anything but, and was in fact little more than a disjointed mess. Thomas knew Rebel cavalry extended beyond his northern flank, controlling the La Fayette Road between the McDonald house and Rossville. There was also a half-mile gap between Kelly Field and Snodgrass Hill, and it was anyone's guess how long that would continue to go unnoticed by the Confederates. Bragg could cut off the back door to Rossville by merely moving in force up the Dry Valley Road, which was inadequately defended (as reported by Thruston) by remnants of Davis's and Sheridan's divisions. A coordinated Rebel assault could simultaneously turn both of Thomas's flanks and pierce his undefended center. This was no place for what was left of the army.

There was also the ammunition crisis. As early as 3:00 p.m., the lack of cartridges plagued units on a localized level, and by 5:00 p.m. those localized shortages were fast becoming epidemic. Entire brigades and divisions were running low, or had already depleted their stocks. The most serious shortages were in Granger's Reserve Corps, whose men had already given away their extra rounds. Bayonets could only replace bullets for so long. The Confederates were also experiencing sporadic ammunition shortages, primarily among Bushrod Johnson's men, but their problem was far less widespread, as evidenced by the volume of fire maintained by Archibald Gracie's and John Kelly's brigades. Moreover, the Confederate ordnance trains were still close by, ensuring that butternut cartridge boxes would be refilled by morning. The Yankees had no such guarantee.

George Thomas was intimately aware of all these factors. In all likelihood he would have ordered a nighttime retreat of his own volition, orders or not.

3 Smith, *James Abram Garfield*, vol. 2, 855; *OR* 30, pt. 1, 253; Frederick D. Williams, ed., *The Wild Life of the Army: Civil War Letters of James A. Garfield* (Michigan State University Press, 1964), 297.

Edward A. King (left) of the 68th Indiana commanded Reynolds's Second Brigade. He was struck down about 4:00 p.m. near the southern end of Kelly Field.

Indiana at Chickamauga

Rosecrans's instructions simply confirmed what needed to be done. However much his innate pugnacity and stubbornness might have wanted to hang on until nightfall and retreat under cover of darkness, he had run out of time.[4]

In a carefully argued timeline, historian Archibald Gracie made a strong case that Thomas knew the game was up and was preparing to retreat even before Rosecrans's instructions arrived. Once that order reached him approximately 4:30 p.m., noted Gracie, "every division commander received orders for withdrawal [from Thomas] at 5:00 p.m. or earlier," with the first, to Joseph Reynolds, sent off within a few minutes. "[T]here is no doubt in my mind that at this particular time," Gracie concluded, "[Thomas] saw the impossibility of holding his position any longer."[5]

The retreat would begin in Kelly Field. General Reynolds's division would leave first and so lead the way for the rest of the army. A few minutes later

4 Biographer Francis McKinney also argued that Thomas had already made up his mind to retreat when Rosecrans's orders arrived, but had independently elected to wait until dark. McKinney, *Education in Violence*, 254. See also Thomas's official report in *OR* 30, pt. 1, 253.

5 Gracie, *The Truth About Chickamauga*, 95-97. Archibald Gracie IV was the son of Archibald Gracie the Confederate Brigadier. The younger Gracie visited Chickamauga, following his martial father's footsteps, and took issue with the official park interpretation of the battle, as told on the various blue and red War Department Tablets that dot the battlefield. The *Truth About Chickamauga* was the first of two planned volumes, this one dealing with the Union side of the fighting on Horseshoe Ridge. Gracie was returning from a European vacation on the *Titanic* when that famous ship sank. His health was shattered and he died a few months later. His projected second volume never came to fruition. Gracie's timeline also makes some attempt to rationalize all the time discrepancies given in the various official reports. He argues convincingly that Thomas was consistently about one hour off on all the times given in his report.

Thomas departed Snodgrass Hill to personally direct Reynolds out of his position, leaving Granger in charge of what was effectively the army's right wing—Steedman's, Brannan's, and Wood's divisions, plus assorted other fragments. Garfield, his mission to find Thomas concluded and for the moment without any duties, made himself useful among the ranks of Harker's men, whom he had personally led the year previous, and who were delighted to see their former commander.[6]

If Thomas caught wind of Reynolds's earlier failure of nerve, he made no mention of it, either verbally or in his report. He was probably unaware of Reynolds's lapse, for he did not ride directly to find Reynolds. Instead, Thomas made for the northern end of Kelly Field, expecting to meet Reynolds en route in order to "point out to him the position where I wished him to form line to cover the retirement." While still in the timber west of the Kelly clearing, Thomas ran into two soldiers hunting for water. "They informed me that there was a large force of rebels in these woods, drawn up in line and advancing towards me." If correct, this could be a disaster, for it meant that Rebel infantry (and not just cavalry) had once again blocked the La Fayette Road.[7]

Reynolds's division consisted of only two brigades, those of Edward King and John Turchin. Turchin was a worried man. The brigadier's command rested uneasily on the southern flank of the Kelly Field line, and Turchin prowled its length like a caged animal. Night couldn't come too soon for the Russian, but unlike his division commander, Turchin entertained no thoughts of despair. Instead, he intended for the Confederates to pay dearly for their success. At one point, Lt. Col. Douglas Putnam of the 92nd Ohio asked what they should do until nightfall. "Do?" roared Turchin in reply. "This brigade stays right here until we are all cut to pieces, that's what we'll do!" Thus far the enemy had shown little inclination to force Turchin to live up to that desperate pledge.[8]

All afternoon the fighting bypassed Reynolds's men. The tumult of furious combat could be heard all around, but only skirmish fire and intermittent artillery fell among the Yankees here. The sniping and cannon fire was mostly from the south, where Majs. Felix Robertson's and Samuel C. Williams's reserve batteries still banged away. Even desultory fire could be deadly. Colonel

6 *OR* 30, pt. 1, 253, 638; Smith, *James Abram Garfield*, 343, 345.

7 *OR* 30, pt. 1, 253.

8 John T. Booth, "Turchin's Brigade Cut Their Way Through the Rebels," *National Tribune*, October 16, 1890.

Edward King, a brigade commander in Reynolds's division, had remained on his horse throughout the day in an effort to set a conspicuous example for his men. He had done so thus far unscathed. Shortly after 4:00 p.m., however, his movements just behind General Palmer's line drew the eye of a Rebel sharpshooter. "I well remember our men begging Colonel King to dismount and not expose himself needlessly," recollected Sgt. Henry C. Woods of the 19th Indiana battery, "as several shots had been fired at him while sitting on his horse."[9]

Ironically, King was just in the process of heeding those warnings when he was finally struck. Brigadier General Thomas J. Wood, who was married to King's niece, later described her uncle's passing, relaying details supplied to him by General Reynolds. While afoot, "King walked to the front to look out for movements of the enemy," wrote Wood, "when he was shot. . . . The ball struck him just above the right eye, passed through his brain, and of course, killed him instantly." Senior officers were often accorded better treatment than the rank and file, even in death, and King's case was no exception. Reynolds ordered the brigadier's corpse removed from the field, borne on a limber belonging to the 19th Indiana battery. His remains were carried to Rossville, where he was buried in a temporary grave that night. It was not until the following January that King's body could be recovered and shipped home. Brigade command fell to Col. Milton Robinson of the 75th Indiana.[10]

Ammunition shortages were almost as much of a problem here as they were on Snodgrass Hill. Kelly Field was still jammed with a panoply of cannon, limbers, and wagons. The encircling infantry had taken to referring to this area as "the bullpen." Few of those wagons, however, had any ammunition, and the corps trains, it will be recalled, had been ordered off the field. Fortunately for the 68th and 101st Indiana of King's (now Robinson's) brigade, a couple of spare boxes were found. Lieutenant Colonel George W. Steele of the 101st Indiana remembered that his own unit and the 68th Indiana got one box each. "The scramble by each man for his share of it was greater than I ever saw . . . for rations, notwithstanding that we went through the siege of Chattanooga." Each box of ammunition held 1,000 rounds, and even after deducting for losses, stragglers, and officers, the two regiments still had a combined strength of at least 500 muskets; four cartridges apiece would not go far. The fact they were

9 High, *Sixty-Eighth Indiana*, 96.

10 Commissioners, *Indiana at Chickamauga*, 200.

Kelly Field and Cabin. This view looks east from the La Fayette Road from behind the Union line. The pyramid monument visible in the slight break in the tree line is where Edward King was shot. The empty field in the foreground was jammed with all sorts of equipment in September 1863. *Harvey Scarborough*

issued at all, however, would have important consequences for both regiments later in the day.[11]

When Thomas's retreat order arrived, it was probably greeted with relief by both Reynolds and his subordinates. The movement was promptly executed and came off well, disturbed by nothing more than the aforementioned skirmish and artillery fire. Turchin's works were on fire again in several places, which created an impromptu smokescreen that shielded the movement from Maj. Gen. A. P. Stewart's Confederates. Both brigades (King's now under Robinson and Turchin's) first moved west, crossing the La Fayette Road near the Kelly cabin, and then north once in the woods on the far side of the field. From there, they marched in double column of regiments until they met George Thomas.

As King's and Turchin's men tramped past the Kelly barnyard, they also passed August Willich's brigade. Willich's soldiers were deployed facing south, moved there, it will be recalled, at Willich's own discretion sometime after 3:00 p.m. Willich's presence extended Reynolds's right flank and filled part of the gap that still yawned between the Kelly and Horseshoe lines. Like Turchin,

11 "My Dear General," George W. Steele to H. V. Boynton, June 7th, 1895, 101st Indiana file, CCNMP. A "bullpen" was where cattle were held prior to slaughter. Period slang had come to use it to describe a prison, jail, or a holding cell.

Willich was equally fretful. His line faced into part of Poe Field, and his men caught their share of Confederate shells from Robertson's and Williams's guns. This bombardment convinced Willich that he was about to be attacked. "I called the attention of General [Richard W.] Johnson several times to the approaching thunderstorm," reported Willich. The German's own attention was drawn to Reynolds's departure, which as far as Willich was concerned came at the absolute worst possible moment. "Just when it was on the point of breaking forth, one or two of our divisions . . . left this portion of the battlefield under higher orders, each regiment cheering as they left, which . . . did not at all cheer us."[12]

Thomas met Reynolds before his columns reached McDonald Field. Ahead were Rebels. They must be driven away or the rest of the troops in Kelly Field would be left without a viable means of escape. These Confederates consisted of Edward Walthall's and Daniel Govan's brigades of St. John Liddell's battered division. Liddell had recently assured D. H. Hill that he would obey the corps commander's orders, no matter what—a pledge he now regretted having made. Around 4:00 p.m. "General Hill ordered me to move straight forward and occupy the Chattanooga [La Fayette] Road," wrote Liddell. "I requested . . . support . . . on the left, as I was satisfied from personal observation [earlier] . . . that I would be enfiladed. This he said he would give me, and I moved off at once." Liddell deployed his two brigades in a single line, with Walthall on the right (north) and Govan to the left (south), with each brigade's artillery in reserve. In addition to the expected threat to Govan's left, when his men moved into the open space of McDonald Field, they spotted Yankees about a half-mile to the northwest crowning a distant hill.[13]

These distant troops comprised Col. Daniel McCook's brigade, nearly 2,100 infantry and the six guns of Battery I, 2nd Illinois Light Artillery. As described earlier, McCook's men had been left here by Granger to keep Forrest's cavalry away from the rear of his Reserve Corps as it moved south to join Thomas. The significant force of Rebel infantry moving into McDonald Field made for an inviting target, and Battery I began dropping shells among Govan's men. Liddell quickly rode back to bring up his own guns. The division commander found artillery Capt. Charles Swett and outlined the problem: "We

12 *OR* 30, pt. 1, 541. Reynolds's men did not cheer, having been instructed to keep quiet. Therefore it was likely Palmer's men who followed who made the noise.

13 *OR* 30, pt. 2, 253.

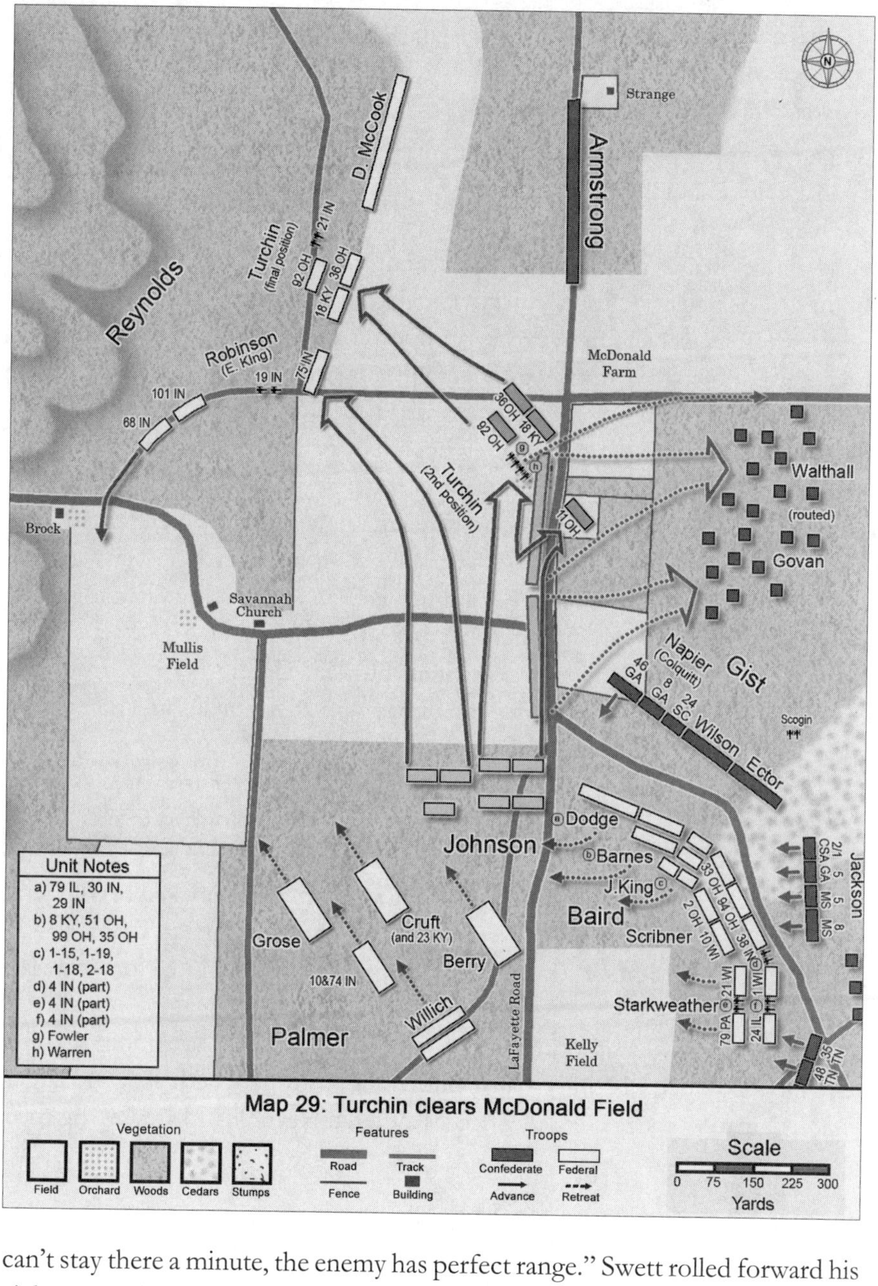

Map 29: Turchin clears McDonald Field

can't stay there a minute, the enemy has perfect range." Swett rolled forward his eight guns, placing Capt. William Fowler's Alabama battery and his own Warren (Mississippi) Light Artillery, led by Lt. Harvey Shannon, on an open knoll just north of the McDonald house near Edward Walthall's right flank. Gunners on both sides set to their business with a will. Despite his exposed position, Swett was determined to hold fast. "I will tell you when to leave," he cautioned Shannon.[14]

"Here in the open," noted Illinois battery commander Capt. Charles Barnett, "our gun[s] fire with great rapidity, and deadly execution. Shot, shell, minnie balls and every kind of missile fall like hailstones on the dead leaves at our feet." "The rebel batteries tried to silence us, but they found that they had more on their hands than they had calculated," bragged a bugler named William Putney. "The position of the battery was well protected by the sharpness of the ridge, while the rebel guns were in an open field Northwest of McDonald's house, with no cover." Putney estimated that at one point the guns were firing as fast as three rounds a minute. At that rate, things got a little hectic. The "Number Two" man on one of the guns was a private called "Buffalo" Tom Finnell, whose job was to load the piece. At one point Finnell lost track of whether or not his gun had fired, and when the sergeant of the piece called for a fresh load, "Tom refused, saying 'there's a load in her already.'" The sergeant insisted, so Tom complied, but then immediately ran back some yards to safety, protesting "Krist gud, boy, touch her off aizy! Touch her off aizy or she'll boorst!" It turned out Finnell was right, but she didn't "boorst" from the double load, and immediately the crew leapt to re-sight their gun and resume the contest. Both shells and canister flew thick and fast.[15]

The Union gunnery fire was deadly effective. Swett later estimated as many as four Union batteries were firing on him, while he could only get seven of his eight guns into action in reply. Lieutenant Shannon thought they were dueling with five Union batteries, and later mistakenly reported he knocked two Federal guns out of action. Shannon freely admitted the Confederates were badly overmatched. In fact the Union artillery involved never amounted to more than Barnett's six pieces.[16]

The artillery threat occupied so much of Liddell's attention that he neglected to watch his other flank, but it was from the south that the larger Union threat loomed. George Thomas ordered Reynolds to deploy his two

14 Charles Swett, "A Brief Narrative of the Warren Light Artillery," http://www.perryvillebattlefield.org/html/ms-swett-charles-cs.html, accessed 5/28/2012.

15 Entry for September 20, Charles Barnett Journal, Clements Library, UMich; William G. Putney, Thaddeus C. S. Brown, and Samuel J. Murphy, eds. Behind The Guns: The History of Battery I, 2nd Regiment, Illinois Light Artillery (Southern Illinois University Press, 1969), 63.

16 *OR* 30, pt. 2, 257, 270-271.

brigades in line facing north perpendicular to, and to the left of, the La Fayette Road. Turchin's brigade was now perfectly placed to crush Govan's left flank—an opportunity tailor-made for the aggressive Russian who liked nothing better than a good charge.[17]

Reynolds was less sanguine. Some veterans would later assert the division commander raised the possibility of surrender because he believed they were by now entirely surrounded. According to Pvt. Henry H. Adney of the 36th Ohio, General Turchin dismissed the idea out of hand. "I never surrenders, I cut my vay out," retorted the Russian. Sergeant Alfred Phillips of Company E of the same regiment recalled a similar sentiment: "I not surrender; I take my brigade and charge right out of this." Reynolds acquiesced. "All right General," he replied to Turchin, "you can try it." Thomas either overheard this exchange or heard of it, for while Thomas's report mentioned nothing of this concerning Reynolds, he did see fit to specifically praise Turchin with evident satisfaction.[18]

Moving through the ranks of the 18th Kentucky, Turchin told the men what he expected of them. "When I say charge, you not charge in then charge back again, but go right through them, G__ D___ 'em." The brigade was formed with the 36th and 92nd Ohio in front (the former regiment just west of the La Fayette Road), and the 11th Ohio and 18th Kentucky in support. Colonel Robinson (King's brigade) placed his three Hoosier regiments (the 68th, 75th, and 101st) in a single line on Turchin's left. Thomas also rode among them, and by some accounts ordered each regiment into the fight as it deployed, without waiting for word from the brigade commander. "Go at once," he told Lt. Col. Douglas Putnam, commanding the 92nd Ohio, "every minute is precious." With what can only be described as reckless abandon, the entire force surged forward.[19]

The attack caught the Confederates by surprise. "A volley from the rebels' first line, not three rods away, passed harmlessly over our heads," recalled Phillips. "Ours did considerable execution . . . . I glanced down the line and saw

17 Turchin made sure his men received extra training in the use of the bayonet, as the 19th Illinois (his first command) noted, and Turchin himself demonstrated his fondness for the charge the previous night, September 19, when he counterattacked to bolster Grose's brigade along the Brotherton Road between Brock and Brotherton fields.

18 Civil War Career of Henry Harrison Adney, http://worldconnect.rootsweb.ancestry.com/cgi-bin/igm.cgi?op=GET&db=thezubers&id=I12495, accessed 5/24/2012; Alfred R. Phillips, *Fighting with Turchin* (privately printed, 1924), 118; *OR* 30, pt. 1, 253-254.

19 Phillips, *Fighting with Turchin*, 119.

it spring forward with unanimity; no flinching there; no stragglers marred the symmetry of our formation." Phillips also saw General Reynolds, who seemed to have recovered at least his spirits, "riding about the center of the line, cheering it on and setting an example. It was a moment that converts any man into a hero."[20]

This rapid descent against his exposed left bewildered General Liddell. "The enemy left his works and escaped from the field," recalled the flustered Confederate, "but in doing so he struck my left flank and captured over one hundred men. . . . The thing was done so suddenly that it was incomprehensible. The enemy, passing my left flank in overwhelming numbers, took with him all of my men within reach." Govan's Arkansans bore the brunt of this fresh disaster. "Under this heavy and galling fire, no other alternative was left but to withdraw the brigade as speedily as possible to save it from annihilation or capture," admitted the brigadier. "The brigade retreated in considerable confusion."[21]

Only Govan's northernmost regiments had time to react. The men of the 5th/13th Arkansas had been lying down somewhere near the La Fayette Road, taking what shelter they could from Union cannon fire. The regiment's Lt. Col. John E. Murray was more alert than his superiors. When he spotted Reynolds's Yankees deploying in the woods to the south, he tried to warn the rest of the brigade but could not get anyone to listen to him. Murray's men were on the brigade right, with the 8th Arkansas next on line on Murray's left. When a swell of firing broke out to his left, Murray discovered the brigade's other regiments were no longer in position. Murray tried to induce Maj. A. Watkins of the 8th to change face to the south to meet the advancing Federals head-on, but Watkins was unwilling to do so without orders from someone higher up the chain of command. The frustrated Murray spurred his horse to find either Govan or Liddell, but instead met Lts. J. L. Bostick and W. S. Sawrie, both of Liddell's staff. He was explaining the situation to them when the trio spotted the rest of Govan's command moving into what Murray assumed was a position to resist Reynolds's assault. He rode back to the 5th/13th just in time to watch the entire brigade, his own regiment included, bolt for the rear.[22]

20 Ibid.,120.

21 Hughes, *Liddell's Record*, 145-146; *OR* 30, pt. 2, 260.

22 *OR* 30, pt. 2, 265.

Walthall's men fell back in no better order. "The enemy struck our line on the left flank," recalled Pvt. Robert A. Jarman of the 27th Mississippi. Jarman and the rest of Company K were deployed as skirmishers, and so had a better view of the unfolding disaster than most. The Federals "engaged only one regiment or part of a regiment at a time, and from our position . . . nearly three hundred yards in front, we could see the [enemy] brigade [in reality, Reynolds's whole division] beating back [one] regiment [after another]. We held our position until our regiment broke to the colors, when began a race with us only equaled . . . on some famous race course, we were so hotly pursued. When we crossed the road all pursuit seemed to stop."[23]

The sudden rout of the Rebel infantry forced Liddell's artillery into an equally abrupt departure. Heeding Swett's forceful command to remain in position until told to leave, Shannon stubbornly waited for the captain's word to retreat. It never arrived. "On reaching the foot of the hill," Shannon reported, "a line of Federal skirmishers . . . within 30 yards of us . . . killed off the wheel horse in the leading gun, thereby causing the piece to upset and breaking the pole." The Yankees swarmed over the downed piece, capturing it and several members of its crew. As his remaining three gun tubes thundered away, Shannon sought help to recapture his lost piece. Riding among the milling mass of Govan's command, he found Capt. T. J. Fletcher of the 5th/13th Arkansas, who agreed to render assistance. The only bright spot in this sudden stampede were in the actions of Captains Fletcher and A. B. Washington, who, along with Lt. William Jones, rallied a number of Arkansans and rushed back to save Shannon's and Fowler's artillery.[24]

Fowler's battery, meanwhile, was suffering a similar fate. Fowler had the fourth highest percentage of casualties (18%) of any of the Rebel batteries engaged at Chickamauga. He lost 26 of his 142 officers and men, including six killed, 18 wounded, and two missing; in addition to 27 horses. About half of his losses were suffered on September 19, and the rest fell here. Fowler, too, had to temporarily leave one gun on the field, but it (together with Shannon's) was soon recaptured as a result of Captain Fletcher's rescue mission. Fletcher and his impromptu company—just a handful of men—fought their way back into McDonald Field, a success accomplished with surprising ease. As it turned out,

23 Robert A. Jarman, *History of Company K, 27th Mississippi Infantry*, 18-19, MDAH.

24 *OR* 30, pt. 2, 265-266, 271.

Turchin's men were not interested in burdening themselves with prisoners or artillery trophies during their effort to escape the field.[25]

In fact, Turchin's brigade was just about as badly disrupted by its sudden success as Liddell's command was by its rout. Buckeye Sergeant Phillips reached the McDonald house during this assault, where he "came upon some men who were arguing with twenty-five or thirty prisoners." Hoping that their own troops would soon arrive to free them, the balking Confederates were refusing to go with their captors. "I told the men to shoot them or make them move on," recorded Phillips brusquely. The Confederates must have given in at that threat because no one was shot, but Phillips didn't wait to debate the situation further. Men from both sides were now dangerously intermingled. A little farther on, Phillips saw Sgt. Ambrose King, also of Company E, 36th Ohio, get shot in the face. "Sergeant King had his mouth open, giving vent to his feelings, when a bullet entered it, passing through his cheek and carrying with it some teeth. He had hardly recovered from the shock when a rebel demanded his gun. [King] answered 'yes, damn you,' and plunged his bayonet through him."[26]

Initially, neither Col. Daniel McCook's infantry nor Barnett's battery had any way of knowing what this new development signified. Large parts of the field had been set aflame by the cannonade, and it was becoming hard to distinguish friend from foe in the growing gloom of the smoke-shrouded dusk. Govan's movements were at one point mistaken by Colonel McCook as an effort to turn his own brigade's right (southern) flank, which of course could not be allowed to happen. That threat was countered by the 125th Illinois, but McCook's men expected to be assaulted by a full horde of Confederates at any moment. As a result, for much of the way forward Turchin's men suffered shelling from Barnett's guns. One of these friendly rounds killed General Turchin's horse. "On foot he labored on, lamenting his fate," noted Sergeant Phillips. "He could not run and was assisted to the top [of the hill held by McCook's men] by Lieutenant [Isaac C.] Phillip of Co. 'F'."[27]

After clearing McDonald Field, Turchin and the bulk of his brigade veered northwest in an effort to reach McCook's line. It was soon thereafter that they

25 Ibid., 271, 287.

26 Phillips, *Fighting with Turchin*, 121.

27 Entry for September 20, William B. Galway Journal, InSL; Phillips, *Fighting with Turchin*, 122.

were finally recognized as fellow Federals. There, noted Bugler Putney with some amusement, "the Union men did not stop running . . . finally turning up into our line. . . . General Turchin was with the detachment that came into the battery. His horse having been killed in the charge . . . he had to take it afoot, and when he reached our line he was so badly exhausted that Lieutenant McDonald was obliged to hold him up."[28]

Joe Reynolds was not with them. The division commander and about 150 men (those closest to the La Fayette Road) had continued moving straight ahead and so missed the swing northwest. This party included the colors of the 36th Ohio, Lt. Col. Hiram F. Devol (who had inherited command of the 36th after Col. William Jones's death), Col. Philander Lane of the 11th Ohio, and a mingling of others from the 11th, 36th, and 92nd Ohio regiments. "Turchin gave the command to move by the left flank, intending to join Thomas," recalled Robert Adney of the 36th. He was about to follow suit when he "heard a man on horseback on the [La Fayette] Road shouting loudly and waving his hands for the men to come [in]." The mounted officer was General Reynolds. "Under his orders, the little squad of men . . . started north on the [La Fayette] Road."[29]

Reynolds apparently misunderstood Thomas's intent. Thomas wanted Turchin to clear McDonald Field so the Federals could fall back to Rossville via McFarland's Gap. Reynolds's division was not strong enough to reopen the entire length of the La Fayette Road as far as Rossville, nor would a subsequent retreat up that road have been practical. Any Yankees doing so would have been under constant threat from their right as they moved, and might well have been cut to pieces by Forrest's cavalry. As a result, falling back through McFarland's behind Missionary Ridge was a much safer move.

Reynolds would not realize his mistake until his small force reached the crossroads near Cloud Church, where his nerve once again failed him. He halted the group and together with a couple of others conducted a quick personal reconnaissance. To their dismay, Rebels appeared to be all around them. Alarmed, Lt. Col. Hiram Devol watched as the general, in an apparent panic, "removed his shoulder-straps, saying we would have to surrender." Reynolds also "gave us positive orders not to fire when the enemy came upon

28 Putney, Brown, and Murphy, *Behind the Guns*, 64.

29 Rob Adney, "Account of the Battle of Chickamauga," 36th Ohio file, CCNMP. There were at least three Adneys in the 36th Ohio.

us, as it would only exasperate him to kill us in our tracks." His words appalled the troops. "If men ever swore both loud and deep it was here. They swore they would die fighting rather than surrender." At this point, everyone stopped paying any attention to their division commander.[30]

Colonel Lane would later report only that at this juncture, the group "marched by the left flank and joined General Granger's command, where we found our brigade." As befitting an official report, Lane's explication was a masterful piece of understatement. Others were not so circumspect. As Sergeant Phillips wrote it up, "it was almost dark when General Reynolds and Colonel Lane . . . came up with the colors. Then a scene that would bankrupt the language to describe ensued. The Thirty-Sixth had its colors, the Eleventh had its colonel, and the division its commander." Phillips further described Reynolds being mobbed by relieved men, "shouting, laughing, shaking hands, dancing in delirium of joy, utterly heedless of the shells that flew over our heads." Corporal John H. Soule of the 36th even came back leading a horse, taken after he emptied the saddle of one of Forrest's troopers, "which he presented" to the recently de-horsed Turchin.[31]

When word of Reynolds's actions on the road circulated, however, the mood soured. "The indignation was intense when we told them that Reynolds had ordered us to surrender," recounted Rob Adney. "Captain Curtiss, Turchin's adjt. gen., almost choked with rage. He said 'boys we have all had hell for 2 days. I had two horses shot under me, and came out afoot, but when any G-d D—n man tells you that you have to surrender, don't you believe him. You don't have to surrender[!]' and then the boys roared."[32]

As would be expected, Turchin was very critical of Reynolds's behavior, especially his misunderstanding of Thomas's intent:

> A major general declaring that he did not know that there were any other roads leading from our position to Rossville, except the La Fayette to Chattanooga Road, while fighting two days in a position which covered those *other roads* . . . shows one of two things: either that he was grossly ignorant of military matters, or that he was

30 Margin note by John Booth in Hiram F. Devol, *Biographical Sketch* (Hudson Kimberly, 1903), 38; Rob Adney, "Account of the Battle of Chickamauga," 36th Ohio file, CCNMP.

31 *OR* 30, pt. 1, 480; Phillips, *Fighting with Turchin*, 124. Turchin claimed the animal was an unwounded artillery horse taken from one of the Rebel batteries. Turchin, *Chickamauga*, 151-2.

32 Rob Adney, "Account of the Battle of Chickamauga," 36th Ohio file, CCNMP.

inexcusably indifferent to what surely interested not only the major generals but also every intelligent private in the army, namely, how our army could reach Chattanooga.[33]

George Thomas and the deceased Col. Ed King's three Hoosier regiments under Milton Robinson followed along with Turchin as best they could. Robinson's trio of regiments didn't get far before the big Virginian found other work for them. "I posted [Robinson] on the road leading through the ridge to hold the ground while the troops on our left and right passed by," reported the XIV Corps commander. Thomas was referring to the road that entered McFarland's Gap via the Savannah Church, passing by the Mullis and Brock houses about 1,000 yards west of the McDonald farmstead. This route would serve as the primary means of escape for the bulk of the troops from both Kelly Field and Horseshoe Ridge. At the Mullis house, where the road climbed into hillier terrain, Robinson deployed his men and waited for additional orders.[34]

With them, at least for a time, were both the 19th and 21st Indiana batteries, though the former was in rough shape. The stresses of two days of combat had heavily damaged the 19th's guns. Lieutenant Robert S. Lackey reported that the axle broke on a three-inch Ordnance rifle: "in coming off the field we lost the 3-inch rifle by the axle coming entirely off from the axle bed, making it impossible to bring it any further." The gun was abandoned in the road west of the McDonald house. Additionally the axle straps snapped on one of his Napoleons.[35]

The rout of his men, coupled with the escape of thousands of Federals, enraged the mercurial Liddell. His entire division had bolted to the rear and was reforming in the woods about 400 yards to the east, and he had nearly lost both of his batteries. When he encountered his artillery commander, Captain Swett, shortly after the cannon escaped, Liddell "exclaimed, 'My God! Where is the artillery?' Being told it was out, he was greatly relieved and said, 'I told you we couldn't stay there a minute.'" Swett recalled that "the old gentleman seemed to be very angry with someone, probably Gen'l Hill."[36]

33 Turchin, *Chickamauga*, 152.

34 High, *Sixty-Eighth Indiana*, 97; *OR* 30, pt. 1, 254.

35 *OR* 30, pt. 1, 479.

36 Charles Swett, "A Brief Narrative of the Warren Light Artillery," http://www.perryvillebattlefield.org/html/ms-swett-charles-cs.html, accessed 5/28/2012. Swett was 35 years old; Liddell, 48.

Turchin's successful charge cleared the way for the rest of the army to fall back to Rossville. George Thomas and John Turchin might have opened the door to escape, however, but there was still the matter of extricating the remaining Union troops from Kelly Field. That task would prove to be more difficult than it appeared, for Braxton Bragg was mistaken: the men of the Confederate Right Wing did have some fight left in them after all.

Chapter Twenty-Six

End Game in Kelly Field:

Sunday, 5:00 p.m. to 7:00 p.m.

Though Reynolds's men had to fight their way out through McDonald Field, their departure from the south end of the Kelly Field line was much easier. The same would not be true for the remaining Federals in this sector of the battlefield. The Rebel Right Wing still had a role to play in the battle of Chickamauga. In order to examine this final action, however, we must set the clock back a couple of hours and explore what was happening with those same Confederates earlier in the afternoon.

As noted, at about 2:00 p.m. Maj. Gen. Simon Bolivar Buckner lifted his binoculars and examined what looked to be a good position for artillery at the southern end of Poe Field. As a result of that interest, the Georgia batteries of Capts. Minor Havis and T. L. Massenberg, as well as Capt. James F. Culpepper's South Carolina battery were all engaged here for some time, but by 3:00 p.m. those guns ran low on ammunition and departed to find more. They were not replaced, and a lull resulted. The three batteries of Maj. Gen. A. P. Stewart's divisional artillery remained in the vicinity, deployed in the woods east of Poe Field, though they lacked a clear line of sight into the opposing Union lines. Other than throw occasional blind shells toward the Yankees, there was little else Stewart's gun crews could accomplish.

James Longstreet was not content to let things stand. At 4:00 p.m., when he sent William Preston's division into the fight against Horseshoe Ridge (see Chapter 24), he also turned some attention to renewing the battle in Poe Field.

Hoping to support Preston, Longstreet ordered A. P. Stewart back into the fight. In order to support Stewart's renewed effort, Buckner directed his chief of artillery, Maj. Thomas K. Porter, to round up whatever guns he could find and deploy them back in Poe Field.[1]

This turned out to be a plethora of cannon. Havis's and Massenberg's artillery (of Maj. Felix Robertson's reserve battalion), their limber chests now replenished, were ready to reengage. So too was Capt. Culpepper's South Carolina battery, Culpepper having given up on trying to locate his own brigade, which was now fighting under Col. David Coleman out on Horseshoe Ridge. In addition, Capt. Rueben Kolb's Alabama battery, Capt. Putnam Darden's Mississippi battery, and Capt. Robert McCant's Florida battery were at hand. All three commands belonged to Maj. Samuel Williams's battalion of artillery, part of Buckner's corps, though thus far they had had little to do. Within a short time Porter amassed a formidable gun line across the southern end of Poe Field.[2]

Between them, Havis, Massenburg, and Culpepper had earlier managed to bring only eight guns into action. Porter's new line totaled 17 additional pieces: 12 from Williams's batteries and another five tubes belonging to Capt. Charles Lumsden's Alabama battery. While all 25 guns were not engaged simultaneously (there wasn't enough space in Poe Field for all of them at once), they still represented the single largest massing of guns achieved by Bragg's army on the Chickamauga battlefield. The pieces rolled into position just minutes after Joe Reynolds departed with Turchin's and Robinson's brigades in their effort to break out northward, and so witnessed the tail end of that movement. The Confederate gunners opened a rapid fire that rained shells into Kelly Field more or less indiscriminately. Simultaneously, Stewart's infantry moved up under cover of this bombardment to provide infantry support.[3]

1 *OR* 30, pt. 2, 358.

2 Culpepper belonged to McNair's brigade of Bushrod Johnson's division, but fell behind early in Johnson's advance and never caught up. At this time, McNair was back with the rest of Johnson's men out near the Vittetoe House, forming for their next assault on Whitaker's Federals. Simon Buckner's Corps was particularly rich in artillery, what with William's battalion, the three batteries belonging to each division, and the informal presence of Robertson's reserve battalion, which had been attached to Buckner at the beginning of the current operation and had marched with him since leaving Rock Springs on September 18.

3 See tablets for Lumsden, Kolb, Darden, Massenburg, Culpepper, McCants, and Havis, Poe Field, CCNMP. Porter's 25 pieces equaled Mendenhall's deployment of cannon on the west side of Dyer Field at midday.

By this time Longstreet had little hope General Polk's Right Wing would resume the fight. After all, General Bragg had reissued attack orders at 2:00 p.m. to no obvious result. The army commander had spent much of the afternoon prodding Polk, who in turn poked ineffectually at D. H. Hill. By 4:00 p.m., the only tangible result of this effort was St. John Liddell's occupation of McDonald Field—a presence that proved all too temporary when Turchin struck the Confederate division's exposed left flank.

At long last, this Confederate inactivity was about to end. The Federal retreat, Longstreet's commitment of Preston, his orders to A. P. Stewart, and D. H. Hill's long-demanded assault would all occur nearly simultaneously, reigniting the fighting in Kelly Field that would end this time with much different results.

On D. H. Hill's front, another Rebel artillerist was working hard to bring his guns into action. Throughout the day the 4th Indiana Battery salient remained the cardinal danger point threatening any renewed attack against the Kelly Field line from the east or north, as the shattered brigades of Ben Helm, Lucius Polk, John K. Jackson and Ed Walthall each discovered in turn. Captain William Carnes experienced that gauntlet of fire firsthand several times as he went about his dangerous courier duties. Growing increasingly frustrated by D. H. Hill's stubborn refusal to attack, at 3:00 p.m. General Polk sent Carnes to find Pat Cleburne and order him to close up the gap that so bothered Hill. Carnes informed the division commander of Polk's instructions, and about 3:30 the two set off on a quick reconnaissance. Cleburne, wrote Carnes, "direct[ed] me to go with him to point out the left of the line upon which it was directed to form." Cleburne rode directly in front of the 4th Indiana's frowning redoubt, at much too slow a pace for Carnes's liking. It was here the captain realized the life of a staff officer "was by no means the sinecure" he and his fellow line officers supposed it to be. "I ventured to suggest that he was within shot range of their guns," recalled the staffer, but the implied warning fell on deaf ears. Only when Cleburne "was startled by the 'Zip!' 'Zip!' of the minie balls and the sharp rattle of infantry fire" did the general kick his mount into a canter. This was the same spot, Carnes later recalled, where Lt. William Richmond of Polk's staff was killed a few hours earlier.[4]

The dangerous scouting mission convinced Cleburne something would have to be done about the lethal Federal artillery salient. The division

4 Carnes, "Chickamauga," *Atlanta Constitution*, April 8, 1883.

commander turned to Capt. Henry Semple, the acting divisional artillery chief after Maj. Thomas Hotchkiss fell wounded in Winfrey Field on September 19th. His might be only a temporary promotion, but Semple intended to make the most of it.

Semple resented Hotchkiss. The captain was the senior artilleryman in Cleburne's division when Hotchkiss was promoted over his head for the position. Hotchkiss was merely a staff captain (Cleburne's ordnance officer) before being assigned to command Cleburne's artillery on a temporary basis just before Stones River. Hotchkiss proved his mettle in the new position, and in May 1863 was bumped to major and given the job permanently. This move proved unpopular with all three battery commanders in Cleburne's division, but it was Semple who took the most umbrage. Hotchkiss might be brave and an effective disciplinarian, but he was also "very illiterate, as his written orders . . . amply testify," complained Semple. "As far as I can tell, his acquaintances with the drill of Light Artillery is very imperfect, and . . . he is almost totally ignorant of the simplest hunches of mathematics." None of this mattered. Hotchkiss earned the job Semple regarded as rightfully his own with a gallant performance at Stones River. There was no reason to think it would not happen again. Cleburne favored Hotchkiss. Semple simmered.[5]

Hotchkiss was not a scientific gunner, as his straight-ahead, charge-'em-and-to-hell-with-the-consequences manner so aptly demonstrated in Winfrey Field the evening before. Semple, by contrast, was a canny veteran tactician. Close range was fine—if you could get there and deliver accurate fire without getting shot to pieces first—but what Hotchkiss failed to grasp was that artillery was most effective when it delivered a converging fire.

Semple intended to position the two 6-pounders and two 12-pound howitzers of Capt. James P. Douglas's Texas battery on a rise north and east of the 4th Indiana's bastion while Semple's own four Napoleons under Lt. Richard W. Goldthwaite took up station to the southeast on another suitable hill. At less than 300 yards the range would be deadly close. Semple's intent was to converge fire upon the 4th Indiana's position at nearly 90 degrees, which was almost textbook perfect. Once these eight guns had knocked out or silenced the Federal artillery, Lucius Polk's brigade would storm the Federal line. Semple prepared for that eventuality, as well. Lieutenant Thomas Key, commanding

5 Larry Daniel, *Cannoneers in Gray, The Field Artillery of the Army of Tennessee, 1861-1865* (The University of Alabama Press, 1989), 82.

Calvert's Arkansas battery, had orders to be ready to advance with Polk's foot soldiers, mimicking Hotchkiss's artillery charge of the evening before, rushing forward to unlimber his three remaining pieces (two 6-pounders and one 12-pound howitzer) at an exceedingly close range and blast the dazed defenders with double canister. Semple intended to go his rival Hotchkiss one better by combining calculation with courage to leverage the Yankees out of their thus-far impregnable position. When all was ready, Semple ordered his gun crews into action. The timing was even better than Semple could know, for his guns thundered to life at or near the same time Major Williams's pieces opened from Poe Field.[6]

The Rebel guns began their work after Joe Reynolds's division had effectively disengaged, but the Federal movement did not pass unnoticed. More than three decades later, Lt. Col. Moxley Sorrel of Longstreet's staff recalled seeing the move, though he misinterpreted it. Sorrel thought Union troops were arriving to reinforce Kelly Field, not abandon it. "A column of fours was seen marching across Gen. A. P. Stewart's front," he recalled. "If attacked, its destruction was certain." When Sorrel urged Stewart to attack, however, Stewart refused. As Longstreet's chief of staff, in theory Sorrel had the authority to direct troops in Longstreet's name as if the order came from the Wing Commander himself. In Virginia, noted Sorrel, this was common practice. Not so in Georgia, at least for men less than 24 hours on the battlefield. "He [Stewart] was there by orders," recalled Sorrel, "and could not move until he got [new] orders." The frustrated staff officer pointed out his nominal authority in his boss's name, but procedures commonplace in the Virginia army were not going to work here. Leaving word with Stewart to hold himself ready, Sorrel galloped off to find Longstreet, whose "thunderous tones need not be described" when Sorrel informed him that Stewart required a confirming order direct from Longstreet himself. The order was promptly issued, and Sorrel dashed back. Stewart would go in.[7]

Later, Stewart would only report that at "about 5:00 p.m. an order reached me by an officer of General Longstreet's staff to move forward upon the enemy," omitting any potential dispute with Sorrel. There is also good reason to think that Sorrel's memory might have played him false here, and not just about

6 See Semple's and Douglas's battery tablets, September 20 positions, CCNMP. Key's other 12-pound howitzer had been disabled during the morning fighting.

7 Sorrel, *At the Right Hand of Longstreet*, 201.

what the Federals were doing. Both Longstreet's and Buckner's official reports (written within just a few weeks of the battle, as opposed Sorrel's memoir, penned in 1905) make it clear that Longstreet decided to commit Stewart in support of Preston well before George Thomas ordered Reynolds's division out of Kelly Field. Who, then, were the troops Sorrel saw? We know they were not Federal reinforcements, for there were none to be had. The only large scale movement was William Hazen's, but that was behind Reynolds's line, not marching across A. P. Stewart's front. Nor does Sorrel make any mention of the Confederate artillery, which should have been going into position in Poe Field. The movement of 25 guns would have been easily noticeable. Even if Sorrel for some reason was not yet aware that Longstreet had ordered an attack, a quick inquiry directed toward either Major Williams or Major Porter would have illuminated him.[8]

If the incident happened as Sorrel described, Stewart likely had good reason to hesitate. Not only was Sorrel new to him, and perhaps not immediately recognizable, but Stewart had witnessed a similar incident nine months earlier at Stones River that did not turn out well. Stewart was a brigade commander at the time, and heavily engaged. Confederate Col. John A. Jaques rode up, identified himself as a member of Frank Cheatham's staff, and ordered one of Stewart's regiments (the combined 31st/33rd Tennessee) to retreat immediately. The Tennesseans obeyed, a move which triggered the retreat of Stewart's entire brigade—right in the middle of an attack. As Stewart later discovered, Colonel Jaques was not on Cheatham's staff, but instead had abandoned his own 1st Louisiana regiment in a panic during the height of the action, sowing disorder wherever he went. To Stewart, then, it seemed only prudent to be wary about obeying unknown field officers dashing up with dramatic new orders without first checking their bona fides—especially in the arrest-prone Army of Tennessee.[9]

Meanwhile, though McDonald Field was now clear, Thomas's evacuation plan hit another snag. Thomas sent a courier to each division commander conveying the retreat orders and how each division would pull out in turn. Unfortunately, those orders did not all arrive smoothly. The first Maj. Gen. John M. Palmer knew of any retreat was when he noticed Reynolds's line departing, thus exposing his own right flank. Alarmed, Palmer "rode to the rear,

8 *OR* 30, pt. 2, 364.

9 Elliott, *Soldier of Tennessee*, 71.

in order to learn the meaning of the movement." There, he met staff officer Capt. Sanford Kellogg bearing "orders to 'retire from the field.'" This directive stunned Palmer. Reynolds's men may have gotten off unscathed, but the sudden recent barrage of Rebel artillery shells meant any subsequent retreat would be, as Palmer reported, "one of those scenes that most severely tests the qualities of officers and men, and where the difference between well-drilled troops and the undisciplined is most perceptible."[10]

Palmer had no choice but to obey, and set about organizing his withdrawal. First out would be Col. William Grose's brigade. "Which way or where to retire was not an easy question to solve," thought Grose when he got word from Palmer, for "the enemy [were] fast approaching from right and left toward our rear, their artillery fire meeting." In order to minimize exposure to this fire, Grose determined to take his men straight back across the field west beyond the Kelly house, and then into the same woods Reynolds used as cover. From there, they would move northwest, tracking Turchin's earlier movement. Grose's 6th Ohio was the first regiment to vacate, followed by the 36th Indiana with the 23rd Kentucky bringing up the rear. Of the two remaining regiments in the brigade, the 84th Illinois was by this time but a fragment (Col. Louis Waters having become separated from most of his men earlier), and the battered 24th Ohio had already been broken up and distributed amongst the other units.[11]

Grose led them out with the brigade's flag at his side, determined to control the pace to make sure the withdrawal did not deteriorate into a rout. In this, he was not wholly successful. According to Maj. Gilbert Trusler, commanding the 36th Indiana, the men had to run a gauntlet of "concentrated fire from the enemy's artillery, who appeared to anticipate the movement." A fair number of Grose's troops broke formation, many of them dashing through August Willich's brigade just west of the Kelly cabin.[12]

Two other regiments joined Grose's withdrawal: the 10th and 74th Indiana of Col. John Croxton's brigade (Brannan's division). Both Hoosier outfits had finally come to rest behind Hazen's (subsequently Grose's) defensive works. No one in any authority paid much attention to either of these two commands, reduced by their two-day ordeal to no more than 443 rank and file, or a 40%

10 Palmer, *Personal Recollections*, 184.

11 *OR* 30, pt. 1, 782.

12 Ibid., 789.

loss. Lieutenant Colonel Marsh Taylor of the 10th commanded both units. Taylor provided few details of this movement, and even misidentified the division he followed off the field, reporting that he fell back with General Reynolds, though claiming to have done so in good order. Lieutenant Colonel Myron Baker of the 74th Indiana believed the 10th and 74th Indiana regiments were the last units to leave their part of the field, and that they "were the last organized bodies of infantry . . . [to depart] that ground." In all likelihood, both of these two regiments were among those that fell back through Willich's ranks into the sheltering woods, where they regrouped and headed north in Reynolds's wake. Somewhere during this movement, Capt. Orville Chamberlain of the 74th recalled meeting George Thomas, "accompanied by an orderly and by nobody else. . . . [He] expressed surprise at finding us there, and pointed out a direction for us to take."[13]

By the time it was the 23rd Kentucky's turn to leave the line, things looked beyond desperate. Just behind the Kentuckians was Battery M of the 4th U.S. Artillery, though without much ammunition. Lieutenant Francis Russell reported that someone had earlier ordered his caissons (originally posted 200 yards to his rear in the woods) off the field with Thomas's wayward ammunition train. When the retreat began, Russell was also ordered away. Lieutenant Colonel James Foy of the 23rd Kentucky watched the guns pull out, saw Rebels moving up on his right, and, when he looked to his left, spotted Brig. Gen. Charles Cruft's men (also of Palmer's division) falling back "in excellent order." It dawned on Foy that the 23rd seemed to be the only unit not retreating, and other than routed men, the field looked empty of organized units. Somehow Foy managed to locate Palmer and inquired "what was best to be done." The general directed him towards his brigade commander Grose, who had just halted the 6th Ohio and 36th Indiana in the distant wood line to help cover Cruft's movement. Foy fell back as directed, but could not immediately locate Grose or the other two regiments of the brigade.[14]

General Cruft, however, managed a perfect withdrawal. He recorded the receipt of Palmer's retreat order as precisely 5:12 p.m., and proceeded to

13 10th Indiana Report, Indiana Adjutant General's Records, Indiana State Archives; *OR* 30, pt. 1, 421; Orville Chamberlain to Gen. H. V. Boynton, November 26, 1895, 74th Indiana file, CCNMP. Chamberlain places this meeting with Thomas at the site of Hazen's breastworks, but that is much too far to the east.

14 *OR* 30, pt. 1, 795, 801.

execute it with equal precision. "The regiments were marched out from behind the breastwork," he noted proudly, "formed in line, and moving out separately, formed in column of regiments at long intervals, and marched across the field to our rear under a most severe artillery fire from two directions." "We were . . . at the mercy of Reb artillery in our rear and both flanks," agreed Pvt. Joseph K. Marshall of the 90th Ohio in reference to that "most severe" gunnery, but the Rebel aim proved erratic and the brigade did not suffer unduly. However, this did not mean that there weren't moments of horrific drama. One of those Confederate shells passed through the neck of Cruft's horse before exploding, its fragments injuring four men in the 31st Indiana. Though his mount was dreadfully mangled, Cruft survived this astounding incident without personal harm. Private Henry Eby, a member of Palmer's escort, never forgot the gruesome sight of Cruft's "fine horse lying on the ground dead with its head almost severed from its body." Palmer remained focused on watching "Cruft's troops [who] left the field as if on parade," he observed. "I saw the Rebels cross our late defenses, and, to my regret, a Rebel battery approached within four hundred yards."[15]

The unfolding scene mesmerized Palmer, who thought an impending slaughter was nearly upon them. He paused beside a dead standing pine tree, watching in expectant horror for the Confederate cannon to rip into Cruft's exposed flank. Suddenly, he found himself prostrate. "My horse sunk to the ground," he recalled, "and I fell at the foot of the tree." A shell had struck the pine, knocking his mount off its feet and showering both man and beast with "soft, rotten wood." The shaken division commander regained his feet, as did his equally shaken horse a few minutes later. It was the second time the animal had been so treated that day. Rather miraculously, neither man nor mount was seriously hurt. Once back in the saddle, Palmer heeded the near-fatal warning and made for the trees.[16]

Enemy infantry accompanied those guns. These approaching Confederates were Alabamians of Brig. Gen. Henry Clayton's brigade, A. P. Stewart's division. Once cleared to attack, Stewart deployed Brig. Gen. John C. Brown's

15 Ibid., 733; Entry for September 20, Joseph K. Marshall Diary, OHS; Entry for September 20, Henry F. Dillman Diary, Lilly Library, Indiana University; Henry H. Eby, *Observations of an Illinois Boy in Battle, Camp, and Prisons—1861 to 1865* (Published by the Author, 1910), 111; Palmer, Personal Recollections, 184-185.

16 Palmer, *Personal Recollections*, 185.

men (the brigade now led by Col. Edmund Cook of the 32nd Tennessee) to support the reserve artillery in Poe Field and advanced Clayton's troops, with Brig. Gen. William Bate's brigade in support. Staff officer Lt. Terry Cahal rode with General Stewart. "We again pushed upon the enemy and this time the attack being general along the whole line [we] carried the enemy's works," recalled the Rebel lieutenant. "With a shout, and cheer upon cheer, our gallant men leaped the breastworks, and pressed upon the flying foe." The lieutenant also observed Cruft's withdrawal. He identified these Federals as professionals because of the crisp precision of their movements. Cahal noted their opponents "consisted of a brigade of yankee regulars and some two or three other volunteer regiments of Ohioans." This time, recalled Capt. Ben Lane Posey of the 36th Alabama, there was no reckless dash like that of the morning. Instead, Clayton's regiments "moved forward in much better order, and kept together. The result . . . was highly successful." Clayton thought his troops advanced "with great spirit, the enemy fleeing across a large open field, upon the edge of which I ordered a halt, and the brigade continued to fire as long as the enemy could be seen."[17]

The battery that so concerned Palmer was Capt. McDonald Oliver's Eufala artillery. Normally attached to Bate, Oliver's four 3-inch rifles now accompanied Clayton. Seeing an opportunity, Oliver pushed his pieces forward through Turchin's abandoned and now dismantled breastworks to engage Cruft. The battery "opened a rapid and destructive fire upon the enemy, who was then retiring from the field." The chaotic situation, coupled with the spreading darkness, convinced Stewart to confirm Clayton's decision to halt so the Rebel gunners could fire into the Federal mass without fear of hitting friendly troops.[18]

The next Union formation slated to depart was Richard Johnson's division. By this time Johnson's men were parceled out all over Kelly Field. Willich was to the southwest, and what was left of Colonel Dodge's brigade was still squeezed into line at the northern end of the fought-over field. William Berry's (formerly Baldwin's) brigade was in line between Palmer and Baird. Both

17 "Dear Colonel," September 30, 1863, Cahal Papers, TSLA; "Clayton's Brigade at Chickamauga," *Montgomery Daily Advertiser*, October 23, 1863; *OR* 30, pt. 2, 403. There were Regulars on the field, but not here. Brigadier General John King's brigade, which included the 1/15th, 1/16th, 1/18th, 2/18th, and 1/19th battalions, were all still at the northern end of Kelly Field.

18 Eufala Battery tablet, Battleline Road, CCNMP.

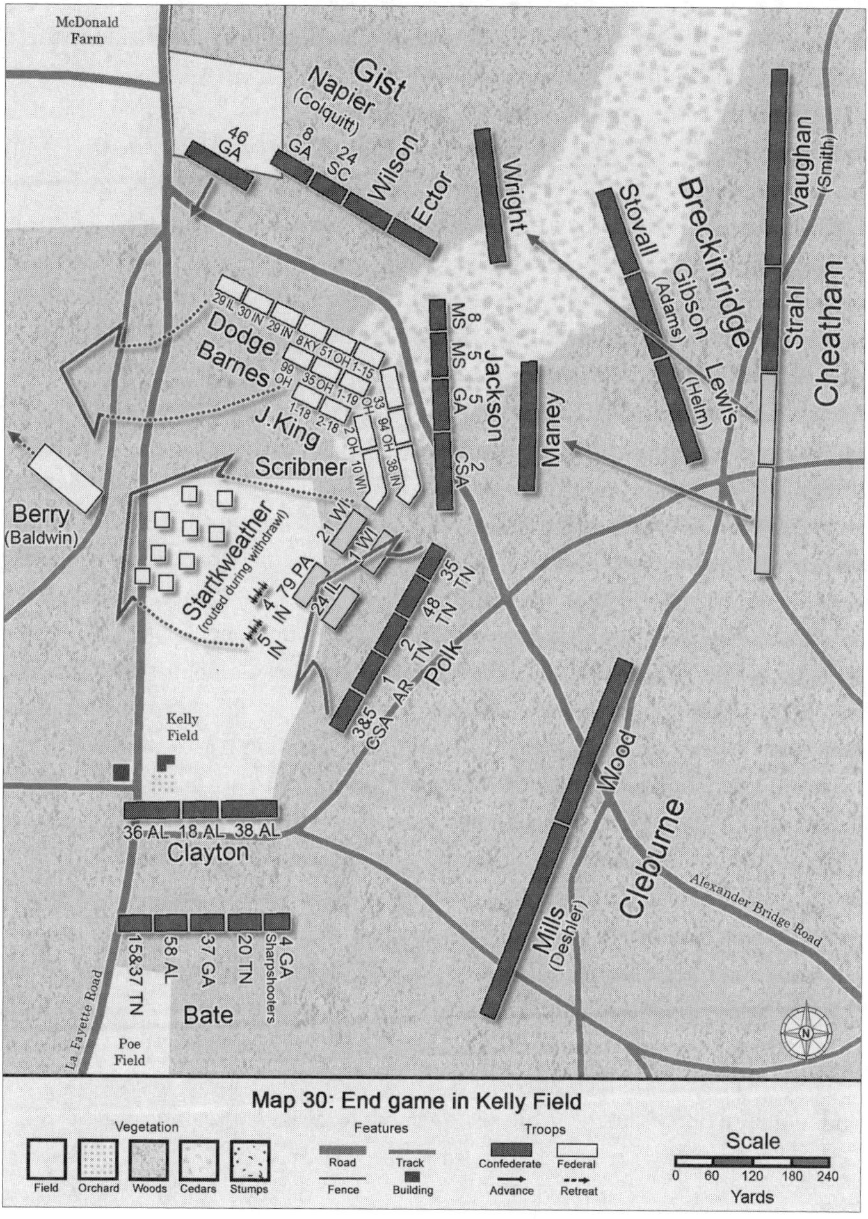

Reynolds's and Palmer's men benefited from the fact that the Confederates had remained relatively quiet when the directive arrived ordering them out of line. Not so for Johnson. "About 4:00 p.m.," he recalled, "we were again vigorously attacked." When the retreat order arrived (more timely than Palmer's copy, for Cruft's brigade was still in line on Berry's right), Johnson sent that courier riding back to inform General Thomas that a retreat at this time and under these circumstances might be "disastrous."[19]

The pressure against Johnson was coming from Patrick Cleburne's Confederates. At last, Leonidas Polk's Right Wing was back in the fight. Captain Semple's carefully placed guns went to work demolishing the 4th Indiana battery. When they opened fire, Hoosier Cpl. Joseph Haddock was almost overwhelmed by the experience. There was "the terrible roar of artillery, the shrill note of thousands of leaden messengers of death, the shrieks of the wounded, the commands of the officers fill the air," recalled Haddock, who then felt the "thud of a shell . . . as it strikes a limber full of ammunition, followed by the sudden explosion of the contents . . . [which sowed] consternation into our ranks." Commanding the 38th Indiana, Lt. Col. Daniel Griffin stood ready on the 4th Battery's left, recalling that it seemed as if the Rebels "hurled the grape around us in showers." Despite the ferocity of this incoming fire, the Confederates "were again handsomely checked with heavy loss."[20]

That check was more imagined than real. This time, neither Cleburne nor Brig. Gen. Lucius Polk had any intention of rushing headlong into the fight. In a much more measured advance, Polk's line paused well short of the Union barricades to let Semple's crossfire do its work, sending forward only a heavy skirmish line to prepare the way. One member of the 2nd Tennessee recalled that the men "went forward with alacrity and restored confidence," this time fighting "Indian style, from tree to tree, up to within fifty yards of the enemy." Lieutenant Thomas Key, leading Calvert's battery, pushed his pieces into this fight by hand, closing to within 75 yards, where he also opened a rapid fire. "A thick smoke from burning leaves hung over the field, and both sides were closer than either fully realized. The Federal artillery overshot, and was silenced long before their infantry retreated."[21]

Polk's line struck the seam between Brig. Gen. John Starkweather's brigade and William Berry's men. Johnson, meanwhile, was still waiting for his staff officer to return with updated word from Thomas on whether he should execute his retreat as ordered. That question was decided for him when Cruft

19 *OR* 30, pt. 1, 535.

20 Joseph C. Haddock, "Historical Sketch of the 4th Indiana Battery," 27-28, InHS; *OR* 30, pt. 1, 291.

21 Anonymous, "The Second Tennessee," 60.

departed, a move that abruptly exposed Johnson's right flank. As Cruft's regiments retired, Johnson saw Clayton's Confederates swarming into the southern edge of Kelly Field. Now there was no choice. "I barely had time to send word to my command to save them from complete destruction," admitted Johnson.[22]

The 6th Indiana and 5th Kentucky held the first and second lines of Berry's right flank, respectively. Both units were under new leadership. The 6th was in the hands of Maj. Calvin Campbell because Lt. Col. Hagerman Tripp had been badly wounded that morning. The Kentuckians were taken over by Capt. John Huston when, upon Baldwin's death, Berry rose to brigade command. New leadership notwithstanding, the order to fall back was smartly executed. According to Major Campbell, the retreat was conducted "under a heavy fire from the enemy's skirmishers," braced by Key's three cannon. Both regiments "left the field in good order." Campbell faced skirmishers from S. A. M. Wood's and James Deshler's Confederate brigades, two commands Cleburne did not initially send forward, but who did come up on Polk's left when the fighting intensified.[23]

The 1st and 93rd Ohio, Berry's remaining two regiments, also got away in good order. In fact, Ohio Private Levi Wagner of the 1st regiment thought he and his comrades were only leaving temporarily "to assist those on our left, as we had done twice before." No one remembered to have the men pick up their packs. As Wagner lamented, "we left all our extra baggage on the field for our enemies to enjoy." Private David Kinsey of the 93rd Ohio regretted one loss in particular. Kinsey could not forget Lt. William Richmond, lying dead just in front of the works and, most importantly, the promise of $500 in gold to the man who brought Richmond's body home. Kinsey went to his commander, Lt. Col. William H. Martin and asked if he could rescue the remains and his prize? Martin agreed, but before a detail could be rounded up to retrieve Richmond's corpse, "the order came to fall back, double-quick, and we did not get the body."[24]

22 *OR* 30, pt. 1, 536.

23 Ibid., 568.

24 Levi Wagner, "Recollections of an Enlistee, 1861-64," AHEC; William H. Martin, "Death of Colonel Richmond," *National Tribune*, October 1, 1891. In later years, Martin remembered asking George Thomas for permission to send Kinsey and a guard detail with the body to

The gun crews of Capt. Peter Simonson's 5th Indiana battery, in line just north of the 93rd Ohio, were beyond exhausted. Simonson had five guns in line, having lost one cannon the previous day. His ammunition usage had been nothing short of prodigious: his gunners fired more than 1,000 rounds during the course of the fight, or an average of 200 rounds per piece. The time to leave had arrived, but the battery suffered a final loss during its departure. "One of the guns was disabled by a cannon ball that struck the axle so the wheel would not turn," recalled an artificer named Daniel H. Chandler, so "the Capt. . . . ordered the traces cut, horses detached, took an axe himself & chopped the vent thus effectually ruining it & left it."[25]

Johnson would later attribute his successful withdrawal to August Willich, whose four regiments changed position to the left as Reynolds's men passed by, and then watched with growing worry as Palmer's troops also fell back. The German next ordered Capt. Wilbur F. Goodspeed's Battery A, 1st Ohio, to engage A. P. Stewart's advancing Rebels, paying special attention to the Eufala battery. Overexcited by the moment, Ohio gunner Henry M. Davidson was sure Battery A's effective fire "was sweeping down [Rebels] by hundreds" with every discharge, but in fact, Clayton reported only light losses at this point. Goodspeed's fire did send Clayton's infantry scrambling for cover, however, checking any deeper advance by Stewart's infantry into Kelly Field, which in turn provided Berry's brigade safe passage out of a potentially lethal trap.[26]

Berry's departure and Simonson's disengagement now left division commander Absalom Baird facing the same quandary Johnson had just dealt with: pressure from the front that made a withdrawal in the face of an aggressive enemy potentially suicidal, with a simultaneous threat from the flank that made staying put an equally lethal decision. Believing that "to fall back was more difficult than to remain," Baird was preparing to override the withdrawal order on his own authority when Palmer's departure rendered the question moot.

Clarksville, which was granted, though too late to be acted upon. Richmond's body would be found by some of Polk's staff the next day.

25 5th Indiana tablet, Battleline Road, CCNMP; Daniel H. Chandler, "Manuscript History of the Fifth Indiana Battery," Stones River National Battlefield. An artificer was a skilled worker, paid an extra stipend for his skills. Artificers were essentially the mechanics and technicians of the Civil War era. In the artillery, it was an umbrella term that included blacksmiths, woodworkers (to repair caissons and limbers) and leatherworkers.

26 Henry M. Davidson, *History of Battery A, First Regiment of Ohio Vol. Light Artillery* (Daily Wisconsin Steam Printing Office, 1865), 89.

Baird dispatched Capts. James W. Forsyth and Eugene Cary to order his brigades out of line.[27]

Baird was facing more than just a single brigade of Rebels. John K. Jackson of Cheatham's division was aligned on Lucius Polk's right. On Jackson's right, States Rights Gist's three brigades were similarly arrayed. Gist's division was very small. In addition to Matt Ector's and Claudius Wilson's already heavy losses, Gist's own brigade (under the deceased Col. Peyton Colquitt) had suffered brutally during its noon assault and was now led by Lt. Col. Leroy Napier of the 8th Georgia Battalion. Napier's lone reason for optimism was the arrival of the remaining six companies of the 46th Georgia, which added another 420 men to his combat power. At least Gist would have one fresh contingent spearheading the next attack when the time came.

At the moment, however, Jackson's men where leading the way. The 2nd Battalion, 1st Confederate held the brigade left, with the 5th Georgia, 5th Mississippi, and 8th Mississippi extending the line to the right. Major Richard Whitely's 2nd Georgia Sharpshooters (the Wildcats) were still screening the gap between Polk and Jackson on the brigade left. In response to new orders, Jackson advanced about 4:30 p.m. "The brigade, with the battery in the center, moved forward in splendid style about 100 yards," reported Jackson. Major James Gordon of the 1st Confederate described what happened next: "We passed over an open glade through a thick undergrowth, up a long slope to the crest of the hill, when the enemy opened a heavy fire of musketry and artillery."[28]

Semple's crossfire against the 4th Indiana salient had not yet done its work, and for the moment Jackson's line faced the same deadly enfilade from the Hoosier gunners that had so stymied earlier Rebel efforts. Major Gordon ordered his men to lie down and return fire, and the rest of the brigade followed suit. Captain John Scogin's Georgia battery of four guns unlimbered on Gordon's right and added its firepower. The prone infantry consumed ammunition at a rapid rate for at least 45 minutes, while the Federal line was coming undone piece by piece, executing Thomas's retreat. Jackson, of course, knew none of this. His line faced Col. Ben Scribner's and General Starkweather's brigades of Baird's division, which didn't seem inclined to go

27 *OR* 30, pt. 1, 279. James W. Forsyth later commanded the 7th U.S. Cavalry at Wounded Knee in 1890.

28 Ibid., pt. 2, 85, 88.

anywhere. Worried about his falling stock of ammunition, Jackson sent word back to Cheatham seeking reinforcements.[29]

Three things now happened at once. First, the Union artillery ceased to be a factor once Simonson pulled out and the 4th Indiana was silenced by Semple's crossfire. Second, Baird began his retreat, starting with Starkweather's brigade. Third, Lucius Polk decided the moment had come for a charge. This trio of events meant the Federals were in trouble.

Lieutenant John Johnston of the 79th Pennsylvania was still out in front of Starkweather's position with his skirmishers when Jackson's Confederates made their first appearance. "Lieutenant, they're coming!" yelled several of Johnston's men. A quick glance revealed a full battle line surging through the trees. "Knowing that my squad of thirty men had no business with that party . . . we 'double-quicked' to the works," recalled Johnston. After alerting Lt. Col. George Bingham of the 1st Wisconsin that the Rebels were attacking, Johnston fell in with his own regiment in Starkweather's support line. It was about then, recalled Johnston, that he fully understood the expression "hell's broke loose."[30]

Starkweather's men were standing off Jackson ably, so Lieutenant Johnston was much surprised when the brigade commander ordered the 79th Pennsylvania and 21st Wisconsin to fall back. What he did not know at the time was that Capt. Eugene Cary had arrived with Baird's order to retreat. Starkweather intended to retire his support line only as far as midfield, where he would halt and cover the retreat of the 24th Illinois and 1st Wisconsin in turn. This plan fell apart before it properly began. The 79th retreated as ordered, but Lt. Col. Harrison Hobart and the 21st Wisconsin did not. "The order . . . never reached the 21st," insisted Hobart. Starkweather, meanwhile, rode forward to supervise the disengagement of his first line. Private Edward Carl of Company D, the 24th Illinois, vividly recalled the general's arrival: "Hell! The 24th is fighting yet!" bellowed Starkweather. "24th, fall back to the line!"[31]

The remnants of the 4th Indiana battery also disengaged at this time, retreating across that same terrible fire-swept cornfield that tormented every Federal forced to cross it. The 4th had expended all its ammunition, taken a

29 Ibid., 80.

30 Johnston, "At Chickamauga."

31 *OR Supplement*, vol. 5, 84; Edward Carl, "Stories of the Civil War," *Kewaunee Enterprise*, January 10, 1908.

fearful pounding from Swett's artillery crossfire, and was about to suffer additional loss during the retreat. One of the battery's remaining guns, noted Pvt. Alfred Galpin, "broke down completely" here and had to be abandoned. Galpin endured a gruesome close call when, while running across the field he grabbed the hand of a fellow crewman named Stumpf to help him move faster. "[We] were making good time," noted Galpin, "when a case shot burst behind us and one fragment cut off Stumpf's right arm above the elbow. The loose arm dropped [while] I was holding the hand, which I immediately dropped."[32]

The traumatic event shocked Galpin so deeply that, instead of continuing along with his battery, he wandered the field almost like a lost soul. He wrote no more about poor Stumpf, but he did relate a strange interlude of scavenging on a field being crisscrossed by lead and iron. He found "a cedar canteen full of raw whiskey" on one dead Rebel, "and a C.S. belt and buckle from another. Next came a U.S. haversack with about one pound of sugar. . . . Further [sic] on I picked up a blanket," all while "balls [were] coming in from every" direction. Seeking cover, Galpin dropped into the straw of Kelly Field for a time, hiding there until after nightfall.[33]

The left flank of Lucius Polk's Confederate brigade reached the now-abandoned Union breastworks on Starkweather's right shortly after the 4th Indiana withdrew. Polk reported that after "observing . . . that the enemy's line wavered, I immediately ordered a charge." A member of the 2nd Tennessee recalled the movement as being considerably more spontaneous. "As the enemy's fire began to slacken, a charge was made on their works by individuals, quickly followed by the rest of the line." Private John Terry of Company K was one of the first to leap ahead. Colonel William D. Robison, commanding the 2nd, raced to catch up. Terry was already across the works when Robison reached them, which is the same time "a big Dutchman rose and fired in his

32 Entry for September 20, Alfred Galpin Diary, WHS.

33 Ibid. Neither Galpin nor Stumpf appear on the 4th Indiana roster. Galpin was originally detailed from the 1st Wisconsin. "Stumpf" cannot be identified. There is no man by that name on the battery roster. There was a recruit named Garrett Stump who joined the battery in May 1863, but Stump mustered out in 1865 when the battery was disbanded, with no indication he had been wounded, much less lost an arm in so traumatic a fashion. "Stumpf" was probably similarly detailed from another regiment in the brigade, though I have not been able to identify him. Galpin's diary was rewritten in the early 1900s (for example, he mentions the existence of the Heg monument, which was in place by the end of 1894) and it does not appear to be entirely in sequence. His battlefield foraging suggests he was temporarily disoriented by the shocking loss of his comrade's arm.

face, but missed." Brandishing his sword, the colonel made the Yankee his prisoner.[34]

From this new position Polk's Rebels poured fire into Starkweather's flank. The outflanked Federals tried to form around Hobart's 21st Wisconsin, its members still in their secondary defenses. Colonel John Colquitt, leading the 1st Arkansas, witnessed this same effort and reported that as his men "drove [the enemy] from his fortified position, he fell back to another line of breastworks . . . and made an attempt to check our advance." Polk quickly dispatched Col. Benjamin Hill's 35th Tennessee to Colquitt's support, since the Arkansans were running low on ammunition. Hill's Tennesseans arrived and added their fire to the storm. "I discovered the enemy wavering in the second line of fortifications and deemed this a favorable moment to advance."[35]

That Rebel advance was all it took to push Starkweather's unraveling command from "wavering" into a complete rout. Lieutenant J. C. McMullen of Company H, 1st Wisconsin, recalled that the brigade had to "fall back . . . under the most destructive fire we have known in warfare. The field was swept from all sides with grape and canister. In doing so we suffered more than at any other time during the day." The men broke under this punishment, and there was nothing Starkweather could do to stop them. He probably could no longer be heard above the din. Throughout the two days of conflict, General Starkweather had used his formidable voice to carry above the cacophony of battle, a sound that some in the brigade claimed was more recognizable to his men than a bugle call. By this time, on this Sunday afternoon, his overworked vocal chords gave out, a blood vessel ruptured in his chest, and a bloody froth appeared on his lips.[36]

A couple hundred yards to the north, the appearance of Capt. James Forsyth bearing instructions to retreat stunned Colonel Scribner. The brigade commander refused to believe the order was legitimate. "He [Forsyth] not having been announced on the general's staff, I was unwilling to obey," Scribner reported. Besides, Scribner could see columns of troops passing

34 *OR* 30, pt. 2, 177; Anonymous, "The Second Tennessee," 60.

35 *OR* 30, pt. 2, 179, 183-184.

36 Quiner Scrapbooks, Wisconsin History Digital Civil War Collection, 102-103, http://content.wisconsinhistory.org/cdm4/document.php?CISOROOT=/quiner&CISOPTR=18427&CISOSHOW=18135&REC=4, accessed 6/20/2012. Earlier in the war, Starkweather came down with bronchitis, which eventually devoloped into "chronic lung disease and had episodes of pulmonary hemorrhage." See Welch, *Medical Histories of Union Generals.*

behind him heading north, a move he mistook for reinforcements. Thus far his own men had repulsed every Rebel effort to drive him. Why retreat now? Dutifully, Forsyth rode back to General Baird for clarification.[37]

Before the captain could return, however, the answer as to why a retreat had been ordered became all too obvious. The troops passing to Scribner's rear were no longer in such good order, and Starkweather's line unraveled, exposing Scribner's right flank. While this was unfolding, Captain Cary returned to reiterate Baird's command to withdraw. Cary first found Lt. Col. Daniel F. Griffin of the 38th Indiana and informed him of the need to fall back. Griffin sent Cary on to Scribner. With both a legitimate order and a better understanding of what was happening, Scribner agreed to retire. His initial hesitation, while understandable, proved nearly fatal to his brigade.[38]

In the meantime, with his troops struggling to overcome the Union line, Lucius Polk was searching for reinforcements. Several hundred yards to his rear, Polk stumbled into Brig. Gen. George Maney's brigade of Cheatham's division. Polk explained his need and the urgency of the moment. "His command had gained a portion of the enemy's breastworks, but was engaged in front without support on either flank, adding that if I would advance it would relieve him," Maney reported. While Maney rode off to confirm the movement with Cheatham, Polk dashed back to his own line, hopeful of support.[39]

Maney quickly secured Cheatham's permission to advance. In fact, Cheatham had just received Jackson's plea for help as well, and was already thinking along the same lines. When Maney appeared Cheatham authorized the Tennessean to move at once. Adding to that effort, Cheatham ordered Brig. Gen. Marcus J. Wright's brigade into action as well, instructing Wright to move up alongside Maney's right flank. As Maney and Cheatham rode back to Maney's line, the senior Polk rode up. All three officers stopped directly behind the 1st Tennessee, where an apprehensive Sam Watkins watched them confer. The privates, not privy to the plans of the day, didn't hesitate to make inquiries. "'Say, General, what command is that which is engaged now?'" someone asked from the ranks. "General [Polk] kindly answers," observed Watkins, "'that is Longstreet's corps. He is driving them this way, and we will drive them that way,

37 *OR* 30, pt. 1, 288.

38 Ibid., 291.

39 Ibid., pt. 2, 96.

and we will crush them between the 'upper and nether millstone.' Turning to General Cheatham, he said, 'General, move your division and attack at once.' Cheatham, to give the boys a good send-off, says, 'Forward boys, and give 'em h—l.' General Polk also says a good word . . . 'Do as General Cheatham says, boys.' (You know he was a preacher and couldn't curse.)" With that, both brigades moved out quickly.[40]

The biggest threat to Baird's command, however, came not from his front but from his left; Rebels were again threatening to outflank Kelly Field from the northern end. Earlier, when St. John Liddell moved into McDonald Field, General W. H. T. Walker instructed General Gist "to support the advance of General Liddell's division." Now, even though St. John Liddell's two brigades (Govan and Walthall) had been rudely ejected from their advanced position by Turchin, Gist's division was still in position to accomplish something. Sometime after 5:00 p.m., in an effort to cover Liddell's abrupt retreat, Gist sent his own troops forward.[41]

The only real enthusiasm for an assault within Gist's ranks was found among the newly arrived companies of the 46th Georgia, posted on the extreme right flank of the divisional line. The 46th's keenness for the fight equaled that of their comrades in the 24th South Carolina and 8th Georgia battalion earlier that day before coming to grief at noon. Now led by Maj. Alexander M. Speer, the 46th—400 strong—moved quickly southwest. "In a little while our front line [Liddell] gave way," wrote a member of the 46th, "falling back in disorder, leaving three of their guns with the enemy. We were ordered to advance and charge. We did so with a shout heard all over the field. We drove the enemy in great confusion, recapturing the lost guns, besides a good many prisoners."[42]

Speer's 46th Georgia probably overlapped the Union left flank in any case, but even if it hadn't earlier, it did now. Colonel Dodge's Federals of Johnson's division—which should have been in position to cover Baird's flank—were gone. Dodge's departure meant Gist's men could advance unopposed directly into Kelly Field, much to the detriment of Baird's men.

40 Ibid., 80, 119; Sam R. Watkins, *Co. Aytch: Maury Grays, First Tennessee Regiment, or A Side Show of the Big Show,* ed. Ruth Hill Fulton McCallister (Providence House Publishers, 2007), 115.

41 *OR* 30, pt. 2, 246.

42 Anonymous, "Forty-Sixth Georgia Regiment," communicated to the Macon *Telegraph*, reprinted in the *Daily Columbus Enquirer*, October 1, 1863. The guns mentioned probably did not belong to Liddell, but instead were some of the abandoned cannon lining the La Fayette Road from the fighting on the 19th.

Dodge did not simply abandon his position. He retreated under orders, but now the confused nature of the Union command structure once again played havoc with the integrity of the Union line. Through the day, Dodge continued to report to Richard Johnson, who had not forgotten about him. "At about 5 o'clock, during a very severe attack," reported Dodge, "I received an order from General Johnson in person to withdraw my command, fighting the best way I could, as our whole line was to do the same." Dodge galloped to his command, still under the tactical control of Col. Allen Buckner of the 79th Illinois, to bring them out.[43]

The exact location of the brigade at this time remains unclear. Colonel Buckner would later describe his position as behind the front, supporting another line of infantry. Buckner had already received one order to retreat by an unidentified staff officer, but had refused to leave. His line was not under direct assault, Bucker noted, but the troops in front of him were being attacked. Lieutenant Colonel David Dunn commanded the 29th Indiana, holding the brigade right. According to Dunn, his men had built a line of breastworks "behind the Second Ohio" of Scribner's brigade. If true, Dunn's report contradicts Buckner's assertion of not being directly attacked. "The enemy came up in our front," noted Dunn, "and poured into us a very destructive fire of musketry and artillery." No one mentioned either Sidney Barnes's regiments or King's Regulars, who held the line between Dodge's right and Scribner's left, where the 2nd Ohio was positioned. In fact, Buckner's men were still on the front line, but because the Union line turned sharply here, bending at almost a 90-degree angle to the west, it appeared to them as if they were echeloned behind Scribner, the Regulars, and Barnes. It is likely Buckner and Dunn were describing the frontal attack against Scribner, which was happening to their right rear.[44]

Like most of the other troops on the northern shoulder of Kelly Field, Colonel Buckner had trouble believing the retreat order was real. "We would not retire until we heard from you," he informed Dodge in his report. Dodge's prompt arrival with instructions fresh from Johnson put to rest any doubts. "The order was passed along the line to each Regimental Commander to watch," wrote Dodge, "and when the Regiment on his right had gotten ten

43 *OR* 30, pt. 1, 556.

44 Ibid., 559-560.

paces to the rear . . . he should order his command back and reform on the [La Fayette] Road."[45]

Despite Colonel Dunn's recollections, each of Dodge's regiments disengaged without much trouble. The real confusion came when they joined the horde of retreating troops crossing the exposed ground of Kelly Field. "Rebel batteries were [continually] playing on us," recalled Dodge. As he watched, "a solid shot struck" the crown of a "large dead tree" and "killed four men by landing on them." Most of the troops were making for a large gap in the fence lining the road. Heading for that same gap, Dodge saw another shell strike the ground under the fence and detonate, scattering a covey of "eight or ten nicely dressed officers." In an instant the fence was gone and "the air was full of rails and cast iron." The officers seemed to vanish as well. "Talk about partridges disappearing in the leaves! These fellows beat all the partridges that ever existed." Naturally enough, "Regiments, Brigades and Divisions had become inextricably entangled," a situation that would not get sorted out for some time.[46]

More evidence Dodge's regiments were in the main line on the Union left and not in a supporting position is found in the report of Lt. Col. Charles H. Wood, commanding the 51st Ohio. The 51st was part of Barnes's brigade, which belonged to neither Baird nor Johnson. Barnes, it will be recalled, was attached to Tom Wood's division of the XXI Corps, dispatched to the northern end of the field by General Thomas hours earlier. Lieutenant Colonel Wood recorded that even though the overall retreat began from the right, Dodge's untimely withdrawal from his left exposed his own regiment and the 8th Kentucky to "a terrific fire of musketry and artillery" from the left, "completely enfilading" both regiments. At the time, Barnes was struggling to comply with Baird's newly arrived order to fall back. His brigade was divided, with the 8th and 51st on line alongside King's Regulars while the 35th Indiana and 99th Ohio were still in reserve behind Scribner's line. The 8th and 51st fell apart almost immediately, trying to retreat while under that enfilading fire.[47]

Fortunately for both units, that enfilading fire was not followed by an immediate assault. The Confederates doing that shooting belonged to Matt

45 Ibid., 559; Dodge, "The Story of Chickamauga."

46 Dodge, "The Story of Chickamauga."

47 *OR* 30, pt. 1, 847.

Ector's and Claudius Wilson's brigades, which, unlike their fellows in the 46th Georgia, were no longer willing to rush headlong into the teeth of Union defenses. Instead, they contented themselves with keeping up a good fire and advanced only after they believed the Federals were giving way. Wilson's Georgians only elected to cross the Alexander's Bridge Road after Barnes's men had already departed. "[We] advanced to the last charge, meeting, however, no enemy," Wilson reported.[48]

The Federal retreat here was one of the most chaotic movements of the entire three days of battle. Sergeant Israel Correll of the 51st Ohio, Barnes's brigade, recalled a near panic. "When the fighting lines on our right became broken, then commenced a scene of flight and disorder seldom equaled," lamented Correll in his diary that night. "They succeeded in rallying some of the regiments about a mile from the scene of the conflict, [but] the 51st were not together in a body as they were badly demoralized."[49]

Now the other half of Barnes's brigade left the line. Colonel Peter Swaine of the 99th Ohio noted that both his own regiment and the 35th Indiana fell back under his direction. Swaine made no mention of the actual retreat, but Hoosier Maj. John P. Dufficy of the 35th acknowledged that the withdrawal "was accomplished under a most destructive fire," and that "our line was reformed on hill in our rear." Swaine reported halting "on a ridge to our rear," from which point he could see "that a general rout had taken place from all the forces in our vicinity." Colonel Swaine set to work rallying men, claiming that the "color-bearers of some twenty regiments planted their colors" around him, and soon he collected "a force worthy to be led by one of much higher rank." After some time spent redistributing ammunition, Swaine had just decided to take the entire force back to Rossville when a bevy of senior officers arrived and took charge, confirming the retreat.[50]

48 Ibid., pt. 2, 249.

49 McCray, *A Shouting of Orders*, 250.

50 *OR* 30, pt. 1, 844, 849. Swaine did not identify any of these officers by name. The location of Swaine's rally point is of some interest. Historian Archibald Gracie asserted this point was the open portion of Snodgrass Hill "halfway between Snodgrass' house and [the] Mullis'" farmstead. Gracie, *The Truth About Chickamauga*, 99. If so, Swaine should have met a number of troops retiring in good order and a fair number of general officers, among them William Hazen, John Beatty, John Brannan, and possibly Gordon Granger. Captain Harrison Shuey, commanding Company F of Swaine's 99th Ohio, seemed to confirm Gracie's conclusion when he wrote that the 99th "was relieved by General Granger's men." Shuey, however, also

Dodge's retreat and Barnes's collapse left only two Union brigades in Kelly Field: Scribner's five regiments and John King's Regulars—and Rebels were closing in on both flanks. These last Yankees scrambled to get out. "In crossing the open field, very many were struck down," reported Baird. However, he continued, the division "reached the woods, west of the road, in as good order as could be expected." It was only there, thought the general, that the various commands started to unravel. "Uncertain which direction to take, and having no landmark to guide them," many men lost their regiments. "We had, during the day been fired into from every point of the compass," Baird explained, and the men simply didn't know which direction offered a safe retreat.[51]

Baird's report was overly optimistic. In fact, this final retreat fell apart right from the start. More than half of Scribner's command didn't even get the word to depart. Colonel Oscar Moore of the 33rd Ohio reported that a good part of his own regiment, along with parts of the 2nd Ohio and 10th Wisconsin, could not hear the order "over the din of battle" and as a result, none of these units fell back intact.[52]

Colonel Scribner began his movement on the brigade right, where the threat was the most urgent. He rode up to "Lieutenant Colonel 'Little Dan' Griffin of the 38th Indiana and yelled, 'Get your command away from here as soon as possible.'" Sergeant George G. Newman of Company K overheard the order and recalled, "we did get, you bet." Scribner turned his horse to lead them out, but somewhere crossing that hellish field, mourned the colonel, my "poor little grey horse had one of his legs shot off and carried me along for some time before I noticed it."[53]

Scribner's remaining regiments struggled to find their own means of escape. The 38th's retreat caught Maj. Rue Hutchins, commanding the 94th Ohio, by surprise. The 94th held the brigade center immediately left of the 38th Indiana, with the 33rd Ohio on the 94th's left. During this last attack, Major

described a Union counterattack "which drove the rebels back with tremendous slaughter, and again held possession of our old line." No such counterattack occurred there at that time. It is more likely Swaine met up with either Palmer or Johnson, both of whom where also retreating. If so, Swaine's rally point was probably closer to the Mullis farm than out on the open fields of Snodgrass Hill. In any case, it was only a temporary refuge. McCray, *A Shouting of Orders*, 250.

51 *OR* 30, pt. 1, 279.

52 Ibid., 296.

53 George S. Newman, "Chickamauga," *National Tribune*, October 16, 1884; "Dear Wife," September 21, 1863, Benjamin F. Scribner Letters, InHS.

Hutchins "felt confident of holding our position," at least until the 38th Indiana "gave way." Realizing the game was up, Hutchins had to repeat himself twice before his men understood it was time to go.[54]

Lieutenant James P. Mitchell of the 94th Ohio did not hear either order to retreat. The first he knew of the crisis was when "I saw my company [E] beginning to break away from the works and to fall back. I shouted to them to stand their ground but my commands were of no avail! I looked to the right and found all the troops had fled. My own company simply obeyed the impulse to flee also." Once the 94th's cohesion dissolved, it was every man for himself. Mitchell recalled "zigzag[ing] across that cornfield as fast as my short legs would carry me." The 94th suffered significant losses here, but as a whole suffered much less than the balance of the brigade's regiments because it managed to avoid heavy losses on the previous day. Virtually all of its 46 killed, wounded and missing were lost during this collapse, its overall loss rate running about 15%.[55]

Witnessing the collapse of the 94th Ohio, Adjutant Angus Waddle of the 33rd Ohio warned Colonel Moore that the 33rd was now in danger of imminent capture. Moore "was conscious of it," recalled Waddle, "but expressed his intention to remain in position until he had orders to vacate." Moore's delay proved unfortunate. Those orders, noted Waddle, "never reached us." When these Buckeyes of the 33rd finally retired, they did so as a confused mass, not as an organized unit. "The regiment was badly broken up," and Waddle, along with two others, soon found himself mingled within Willich's brigade. Willich ordered them to fall in with his troops. When Waddle pointed out that there were only three of them, and it hardly seemed worth it, Willich replied, "well dat is shoost dree more, fall in." Colonel Moore reported that "3 officers and about 75 enlisted men" disappeared here, presumed captured.[56]

King's Regulars had maintained an aggressive, active defense all day, shifting position as needed and even charging forward at opportune moments, such as during Col. Peyton Colquitt's (Gist's) assault. The exact deployment of King's men when the end came is uncertain. King probably had them arrayed in four lines. The 1/15th U.S. under Capt. Albert B. Dod, numbering roughly 200

54 *OR* 30, pt. 1, 298.

55 James P. Mitchell Reminiscences, 35, OHS.

56 Angus Waddle, *Three Years with the Armies of the Ohio and the Cumberland* (Scioto Gazette Book and Job Office, 1889), 53-54; *OR* 30, pt. 1, 296.

muskets, held the breastworks between Scribner's 33rd Ohio and the 8th Kentucky of Barnes's brigade. Dod's men replaced Capt. George W. Smith's 1/18th, which had begun the morning in that position. Smith and the 1/18th (also about 200 muskets) held the second line, supporting Dod. Behind Smith stood Major Dawson's combined battalions of the 1/16th and 1/19th, about 300 strong. Captain Henry Haymond's 200 men of the 2/18th U.S. comprised King's final reserve. His was a narrow but deep position, especially since some or all of the supporting lines had by now constructed additional breastworks to shelter themselves. With retreat now inevitable, General King intended for each line to fall back in succession, the one immediately behind covering for their comrades in front until all four battle lines were safely away. It was an admirable plan, and the right one under the circumstances. Unfortunately for King and his men, events beyond their control doomed it to failure.[57]

Dod's line fell back first. Like all of their comrades, the 1/15th was dangerously short of ammunition. A while earlier, while engaged in holding off Jackson's Rebels, Captain Dod noticed Sgt. John Marrs's Company E moving slowly back from the line on his order. Marrs's men were green, and none of them had seen real combat except for the sergeant leading them. Marrs was walking slowly backward, facing his men with his rifle at the right shoulder in an effort to keep them steady. Dod halted the company and ordered Marrs to move the men back to the line. "Marrs faced to the front, brought his gun down, saluted, and said, 'Does the commanding officer know we are out of ammunition?' I told him to go back and fix bayonets," wrote Dod. "Every man returned, Marrs to fall almost immediately."[58]

Dod now had to execute a similar retreat with largely unloaded weapons. "We resisted the enemy successfully behind our little stronghold until our ammunition became exhausted," recalled Lt. William Heilman, who was in command of Company C. "In falling back we discovered that we had been almost surrounded. My company was in the center and we hardly knew what direction to take." Once disengaged, the 1/15th's experience in crossing that bloody field was little different than those that had gone before—their path

57 Johnson, *That Body of Brave Men*, 413, shows only three lines: 1/15th, followed by the combined 16th/19th, and then both the 1/18th and 2/18th, similarly combined. However, the War Department tablet for the brigade clearly mentions four lines. Smith also reported that he held the second line alone (see OR 30, pt. 1, 320), which would put the 1/19th in the third line and Heymond's 2/18th at the very rear of the formation.

58 *OR* 30, pt. 1, 317-318.

strewn with the dead and wounded of other outfits, artillery rounds plowing the ground around them, and the battalion losing cohesion as it scrambled for cover.[59]

When the 1/15th fell back, Confederate Brigadier John K. Jackson caught wind of the move. Even better, butternut reinforcements were now at hand. Jackson ordered a charge. "The enemy were driven from their breastworks," he exulted, "and Brigadier General Maney's brigade coming up at this opportune moment, charged them [as well]." The two Rebel brigades became intermingled almost immediately, with many of Jackson's men plunging forward alongside Maney's people deep into the open field. Major Gordon of the 1st Confederate effused that Maney's Tennesseans "dashed forward together with such of our men who had ammunition, charging them from their works, driving them pell mell forward over hill and dale." Private Sam Watkins of the 1st Tennessee remembered how he and the rest of the regiment, "with one long, loud, cheering shout . . . press right up to their breastworks and plant our battle flag upon it. They waver and break and run in every direction." Watkins also took note that the moment was not without plenty of confusion within the Rebel ranks. General Maney ordered the men to quickly cease fire because he was worried Watkins and his comrades were firing on friends, and after a good look around Watkins admitted, "had not the Yankees been routed, we would have been butchered."[60]

There was also still the little matter of the next Federal battalion in line, Captain Smith's 1/18th, which took a few moments to deliver a volley into the surging Rebels and may have discouraged any continued offensive effort. Following King's order, Smith attempted to fall back, but affairs took an even more desperate turn.

As with many of Scribner's troops, some of Smith's men did not hear the command and did not realize the battalion was retreating. To make matters worse, the next two lines (the combined 16th/19th and Haymond's 2/18th) began departing simultaneously, threatened as they were with capture on both flanks. King's carefully orchestrated phased withdrawal deteriorated into a wholesale retreat.

59 Theophilus F. Rodenbough and William L. Haskin, eds., *The Army of the United States: Historical Sketches of Staff and Line with Portraits of Generals-in-Chief* (Maynard, Merrill & Co., 1896), 620.

60 *OR* 30, pt. 2, 85, 88; Watkins, *Co. Aytch*, 115-116.

The 16th/19th's departure was especially deleterious, stripping Smith's battalion of its closest support at the worst possible moment. Private Jacob Van Zwaluwenburg of the 16th was a 20-year-old native-born Netherlander. His family left Holland for Michigan, and his older brother joined the colors in 1861. Jacob followed suit the next year. By now, Zwaluwenburg was a veteran and knew a rout when he saw one. "A few of us managed to cross that fatal field, which was raked right and left by shot and shell, grape and canister," he wrote. "All order and formation seemed to be lost. It was every one for himself." The 16th/19th, already reduced to less than half its original strength as a result of losses suffered on Saturday, was halved yet again in this terrifying dash. By now, there were enough Rebels all around them that even some unwounded men were stumbling into enemy ranks and falling prisoner. Lieutenant A. B. Carpenter of the 19th dolefully noted that by the time his battalion had a chance to call the roll late Sunday night, only 45 men and three officers answered.[61]

His support gone, Captain Smith reported that his 1/18th conducted a stubborn fighting retreat across this same bullet-swept plain. When the survivors of the 1/18th intermingled with Haymond's 2/18th, Smith took command of both battalions. Then, reported Smith, the entire force "steadily and slowly followed their color, when, gaining the woods, they faced about, fired, and moved to the rear, where . . . I reported to the general of brigade." Smith would insist he conducted a tightly controlled and disciplined retreat, but it is obvious that, like everyone else, both battalions of the 18th ended up scattered.[62]

Captain Haymond's recollection of that same event offers an interesting case in point. As far as Haymond was concerned, the time had come for every man to save himself, since "to stay behind was certain capture[,] to retreat seemed certain death." The captain decided he would take "the latter, not fancying a sojourn in Libby Hotel. I made as good as time as I could, falling down several times on the way, which was perhaps fortunate for me. I saw men fall a long distance before me and the gravel was frequently dashed over me by canister shot but none struck me—I reached the road safely," he continued.

61 Johnson, *That Body of Brave Men*, 417; "Dear Uncle," September 29, 1863, A. B. Carpenter Letters, Yale University.

62 *OR* 30, pt. 1, 320.

"Capt. Smith . . . and myself collected what men we could and started for Gen. Thomas Hd Qrs."[63]

Not every member of the 18th retreated with Smith and Haymond. As noted, a substantial number of Regulars didn't hear Smith order them back, and small groups continued fighting at the works, or on other parts of the field after the bulk of the brigade was gone. Also mixed into this stew of confusion could be found men of the 10th Wisconsin, the last of Scribner's regiments to depart the line. Posted on the left of Scribner's second line, the 10th was exposed not only from the right as the rest of the brigade collapsed, but also from the left when King's Regulars retreated. The hardest blow and the heaviest loss was the fate of this unfortunate Badger regiment.

Wisconsin Lt. Col. John H. Ely led the 10th. Aware that the Regulars represented his flank support, Ely kept a careful eye on King's troops throughout the day. That morning, when some of the Regulars gave way in the face of General Breckinridge's attack, Ely rode over to help rally them. From that hour until battle's end, he exhibited a continued sensitivity to threats real and perceived from that quarter. Sometime after 4:00 p.m., with ammunition growing scarce, Ely sent Maj. Duncan McKercher off to find more bullets. By 5:00 p.m. McKercher had not yet returned. Ely had no way of knowing he would not be coming back. The major had set off heading south and west—away from any presumed enemy—but somehow passed into Poe Field without realizing he was no longer amongst friends. When he spied a group of officers clustered near some artillery pieces, McKercher headed in their direction. "An officer rode out to meet him. 'For God's sake, send us ammunition or a reinforcement!'" gasped the major. "'I will take your sword, sir.' was the reply. That," admitted McKercher, "made the situation . . . clear." The Union officer had fought his last battle. He would remain a prisoner until March 1865.[64]

Ely, of course, knew none of this. His eye was drawn to the 1/15th, retreating as directed, and then watched as Smith ordered his own 1/18th back. Unaware of Scribner's retreat order, Ely rode over once more to rally the Regulars when, recalled Badger Lt. Lucius Hinkley, "I saw [Ely] . . . whirl about and fall to the ground." The colonel was mortally wounded, and with

63 "Dear Pa," September 24, 1863, Henry Haymond Letters, Novarro College, Corsicana, TX.

64 Lucius Dwight Hinkley Papers, WHS.

McKercher already in Rebel hands, the 10th was leaderless. Command devolved onto Company B's captain, Jacob Roby, but events had now outpaced any officer's ability to control them.[65]

"We could see troops marching rapidly behind us, going to our left," remembered Sgt. Augustus Bratnober of Company F. "We still held the fort [breastworks] when suddenly we were charged from the left, where we supposed our own troops were. . . . [O]ur fire did not check them and we gave away and made for the rear, only to find that we were completely surrounded." Hinkley recalled how "most of our men went obliquely across the Kelly field to the south of west, where we suppose the main line of battle to be." To Bratnober all seemed chaos, with men falling around him as they ran. "It was every man for himself. . . . I ran to where our flag was being held up and supposed that I had escaped," added the sergeant, "when I found that all there were prisoners already, flag and all." Nearly the entire regiment was captured here. Captain Roby, one of the few to get away, reported that only three officers and 26 men answered roll call the next morning. The Badger regiment lost 211 of its 240 men, including 145 missing and presumed captured—a staggering 88% casualty rate.[66]

The Badgers might have gotten away had they not run south. According to Lieutenant Hinkley, "the attacking force was cautious, and if they followed us at all, they did it slowly and at a distance." Instead, the 10th fell captive to Mississippians from Ben Humphreys's brigade of Joe Kershaw's division. Hinkley spent the night as a prisoner near the spot where he was captured, with General Humphreys camped close by. It was not a convivial evening. "He told some of our officers that his plantation in Mississippi joined that of Jeff Davis and that the buildings had been burned by . . . Federal soldiers," recalled Hinkley. "Perhaps quite naturally his feeling toward us was decidedly bitter."[67]

These Confederates were indeed displaying considerable caution. Most attackers stopped at the first line of works, where they contented themselves with pouring fire into the backs of fleeing Yankees, unwilling to expose

65 Ibid. Ely lingered until his death in a Confederate field hospital on October 4, 1863.

66 Bratnober Diary Extracts, CCNMP; Hinkley Papers, WHS; *OR* 30, pt. 1, 299. The 10th's loss rate here is stunning, though it does include the losses from both days' fighting. By contrast, the 1st Minnesota at Gettysburg lost 215 of 252 men, for an 82% rate, but in a single day on July 2. Similarly, the 1st Texas at Antietam lost 186 of 226 engaged (also 82%) in the fighting on September 17, 1862.

67 Hinkley Papers, WHS.

themselves to the same torrent of bullets and shells now playing on the field from multiple directions. Any Rebel unit venturing into that storm risked being torn apart by their own cannon and musketry. Both Maney and Jackson reported that the Union defenders gave way before they reached the first works. Marcus Wright's brigade, maneuvering to come in on Maney's left, had a similar experience. "At this time the scene was one of the most animated and exciting that can be imagined," reported Wright. "The enemy, already daunted by the fierce ordeal through which they had passed . . . could no longer bear the trial, when the cheers of our reinforcing battalion were wafted to them on the evening breeze. They broke in hopeless confusion. . . . My brigade did not reach the position in time to fire but a very few guns."[68]

It was sometime after 6:00 p.m. when James Longstreet issued his next major order—a directive that might have more dramatically affected the outcome of the battle had it come earlier. Evander Law's division, now reformed, watched with great interest as the Confederate artillery positioned by Major Williams thundered away in Poe Field. Now Longstreet decided to send Law's men back into the fight, directing them to advance through the timber west of Poe Field, between the La Fayette and Glenn-Kelly roads, aiming to strike the Union flank somewhere near Kelly Field. Alabama Col. William Perry, commanding Law's own brigade, recalled that after the guns "ceased, I was ordered to form my command . . . perpendicular to the Federal line . . . and attack." Dutifully, Perry "advanced three or four hundred yards through a dense thicket, when the officer in command of my skirmish line reported that the enemy had retreated." Finally, Perry's line was moving into the very gap that had so concerned George Thomas throughout that long afternoon. Unfortunately for the Rebels, however, Perry's movement came too late. If Perry's men had been committed about 4:00 p.m., many more Federals would have been trapped in Kelly Field.[69]

The last Southern actors to step onto the bloody stage late that afternoon belonged to John Breckinridge's already battered division. When Marcus Wright's Tennesseans moved forward to renew the assault, they passed through the Kentucky Brigade, which was now under the command of Col. Joseph Lewis as a result of General Helm's mortal wound. Thus alerted that a new

68 *OR* 30, pt. 2, 120.

69 Perry and Johnson, "A Forgotten Account of Chickamauga," 56.

assault was underway, Breckinridge asked D. H. Hill for permission to "make another charge." It was around 5:00 p.m.[70]

To do so, Breckinridge first had to reorient his front, which was still facing due west toward McDonald Field. He directed Brig. General Marcellus Stovall and Col. Randall Gibson to move their lines forward in a left-half wheel until they fronted southwest—directly toward the final Union line. It was a complex movement, made all the more so by the lingering clouds of acrid bluish-gray smoke, the growing darkness, and a number of other Rebel units scattered in their path. "The movement forward was made slowly, carefully, and with all possible precision," reported Gibson. Both Stovall and Gibson moved through multiple lines of troops (including Wright's men, who had just passed through the Orphans a short while before) "who cheered us heartily." At one point Gibson's Louisianans jammed up with some of the Kentuckians. By the time Breckinridge's preparations were complete, most of the Federals were gone.[71]

But not all. Gibson's front faced the Regulars's position at the crook of the Union line, and scattered groups of Federals still lingered there. Confused and effectively abandoned during the last moments of the retreat, these troops—elements of both Smith's and Haymond's battalions of the 18th—put up a stubborn final bit of resistance. In 1865, shortly after the end of the war, several of the officers captured here wrote "reports about their experiences." Captain Tenodor Ten Eyck, Lt. Rufus Gates, and Sgt. Maj. Isaac D'Isaay of the 18th all missed Smith's order to fall back. Each man independently assumed command of the men in their immediate vicinity and tried to make a stand. Ten Eyck remembered another officer telling him he was now the senior officer on the field, that the group was "immensely out numbered," and that an immediate retreat was in order. However, continued the stubborn captain, "I had received no order to retire . . . and maintained my position under a heavy fire . . . until after sunset." Gates found the sergeant major and combined those two groups into a force the lieutenant estimated as about 130 strong.[72]

These handfuls of left-behinds couldn't stop the Rebels, of course, especially once Breckinridge, whose line swept around both Union flanks, entered the fight. The Yankees fell back as a group but quickly dissolved into

70 *OR* 30, pt. 2, 200.

71 Ibid., 217.

72 Johnson, *That Body of Brave Men*, 418-419.

individual efforts hell bent at escape. Most ended up as prisoners. Lieutenant Gates thought that "about 80" of his band fell into enemy hands. Ten Eyck's entire band was captured. Among the Rebel prizes were the colors of the 2/18th.[73]

Breckinridge's Confederates pressed as far west as the La Fayette Road, where they halted for the night. Large numbers of Union men were now in Rebel hands. Lucius Polk reported taking 200 prisoners, all Regulars, though he likely had a mix of Scribner's and Starkweather's men as well. None of Ben Cheatham's brigade commanders reported their captures in detail. Only Gibson of Breckinridge's command estimated his prisoner take at "probably, 300 or 400." As noted, many in the 10th Wisconsin were snagged in Humphreys's net of Mississippian bayonets, and some others were taken by A. P. Stewart's command. All told, the Federal prisoners lost here amounted to perhaps 1,000 men.[74]

Those Yankees who somehow managed to escape the flying lead and iron fell back via McFarland's Gap, moving across the large open fields west of the McDonald Farm (a route now open courtesy of Turchin's earlier charge). George Thomas met them there, amidst the men of Col. Milton Robinson's (formerly Ed King's) brigade. Questioning Robinson, Thomas made an important discovery. It turned out that two of Robinson's regiments, the 68th and 101st Indiana, had at least partially refilled their cartridge boxes. Robinson's Hoosiers, it will be recalled, had stumbled across some cases of ammunition during their retreat and doled out a quick re-supply as best they could.

Thomas initially halted Robinson's men in the timber on the west side of McDonald Field, but only temporarily. In fact, he had in mind other important work for them to do. As soon as other troops arrived to take their place, Thomas ordered Robinson to bring along both regiments and follow him. The big Virginian led them back south to Snodgrass Hill, where a similar scene of retreat was taking place, to help cover that movement. While the rest of the army filed northward past them towards the safety of Rossville, it seemed to the men of the 68th and 101st that they were headed back into the very center of the maelstrom.[75]

73 Ibid.

74 *OR* 30, pt. 2, 177, 218.

75 High, *Sixty-Eighth Indiana*, 97.

Chapter Twenty-Seven

The Retreat from Horseshoe Ridge:

Sunday, 5:00 p.m. to 7:00 p.m.

George Thomas departed Horseshoe Ridge to supervise the disengagement from Kelly Field before 5:00 p.m. He did so just as, or just after, Archibald Gracie's attack there subsided. Fighting was still underway in some quarters, but it was now limited in scope and scale and static, not the swelling roar that signaled Confederate reinforcements or a renewed serious assault. This relative lull later led many Federals to regard Gracie's effort as the last Confederate attack of the day. It wasn't. William Preston's Rebel infantry had one more effort left in them, and the ever-tenacious and ubiquitous Bushrod Johnson was not quite ready to give up.

General Johnson was still fighting gamely when Gracie's attack was winding down, but by this time his command had been all but wrecked. The division leader sent Lt. George Marchbanks back once again to try and wring support from Generals Zach Deas and Arthur Manigault, to no avail. An indignant Marchbanks returned to report that in Deas's opinion, "it would not be safe" to go forward without additional reinforcements. The frustrated Johnson had little choice but to settle for a compromise, and sent Marchbanks riding back to the pair of recalcitrant brigadiers with instructions to at the very least bring their brigades up close enough to the front replace Johnson's exhausted infantrymen so they could attempt one final attack against Union-held Horseshoe Ridge.[1]

While Marchbanks was seeking more troops, Johnson observed that a slow, creeping style of combat had superseded the earlier bloody charges and countercharges. "Over three hours passed in this conflict, in which officers and men toiled on and manifested more perseverance, determination, and endurance than I have ever before witnessed on any field," Johnson wrote in his report. "We had now slowly driven the enemy . . . up the gradual ascent about half a mile, to the coveted crest of the ridge, where they made the last desperate resistance."[2]

Johnson massed all three of his brigades for this last effort. Colonel David Coleman's (McNair's) brigade had come up an hour earlier to support Cols. Robert Fulton and Cyrus Sugg (Gregg). Each command, however, was a mere shell of its earlier self. Johnson lost 1,433 out of 3,755 men engaged, or 38% of his effectives. Far fewer than 2,300 men were available to take the fight to the enemy, however. Stragglers, skulkers, and the lightly wounded (who often went unreported) were missing from the ranks. During the various attacks and retreats, more men became separated, either by accident or design, and decided they had had enough of fighting for one day. Historian Peter Cozzens estimated that combined, Fulton and Sugg fielded no more than 800 men willing to go forward in one final effort—not an unreasonable figure. Coleman's troops, who had managed a breather in Brotherton Field and so missed the early action against Horseshoe Ridge, probably added no more than 500 additional bayonets. One small measure of encouragement was that not all of Thomas Hindman's men were out of the fight. Colonel John Reid led his own 28th Alabama and about one-half of the 34th Alabama back into action alongside Fulton's brigade—perhaps another 500 rifles. All told, Johnson fielded perhaps 1,800 men for his final push.[3]

Captain John Lavender of the 4th Arkansas left a description of this last attack: "We moved slowly up the Hill. When about 200 yards from the top the

1 *OR* 30, pt. 2, 464. While Deas and Manigault were subject to Bushrod Johnson's authority, assigned to his command earlier by Thomas Hindman, both appeared to regard Johnson's orders as suggestions rather than commands.

2 Ibid., 464, 470.

3 Powell, "Numbers and Losses," CCNMP; Cozzens, *This Terrible Sound*, 484; *OR* 30, pt. 2, 350-353.

Infantry opened a heavy fire on us but over shot and Done but little Damage. Our lines held their fire for some time. The Bushes and Brush was tolerable thick which added to the difficulty . . . but the Hill being very steep saved us from the heavy fire of the Enemy." Federal resolve cracked in the face of this late assault. "The Yankees [were] fighting with the courage of desperation, but about sunset they gave way, and fled in the utmost disorder." Lavender remembered a moment of hand-to-hand struggle until "our men had got on top of the Hill and give them such a Deadly Fire that they Broke Ranks and made a perfect stampede."[4]

Alabama colonel John Reid reported much the same: "At sunset we made one last desperate assault and drove them, routed, demoralized, from the field." To Col. R. H. Keeble of the 23rd Tennessee, whose regiment was also nearly out of ammunition, the break couldn't come soon enough: "It seemed that the enemy . . . fled in the wildest confusion."[5]

Brigadier General James Steedman's Federals simply could not hold any longer. Their organizational state was no less chaotic than Johnson's, but while the Confederates were down to their last handfuls of cartridges, the Yankees would have regarded a handful as a treasure beyond price. Virtually every Union weapon was unloaded or contained its wielder's final round. It was too much to ask of them to stand without cartridges. No single regiment broke first. Instead, a general retreat set in very quickly. Some units were ordered away, but most fell back of their own volition.

Private Augustus L. Yenner of the 121st Ohio, part of Col. John Mitchell's brigade, was all but overwhelmed by the day's events. "May the Lord grant that I never see another day like this Sabbath," he wrote in his diary. Amid "the dread and horrid scenes of Battle [we] fought till night [and] all our ammunition was gone." Thomas O'Dell, in the 78th Illinois of the same brigade recalled that the regiment's formation had long since vanished. "We took shelter as best we could, some behind trees and logs, and others upon the ground. I could not get any other shelter and I lay down—at this time shot and shell came in a perfect storm. I was struck and I went to the rear." O'Dell managed to hobble a short distance with the help of a comrade when, "near sundown," he was overtaken by the rest of the retreating Illini members of his regiment. Lieutenant Colonel

4 Lavender, *They Never Came Back*, 83-84; Gammage, *Fourth Arkansas Regiment*, 91. Given the Federal ammunition problems, one wonders how heavy that firing could have been.

5 *OR* 30, pt. 2, 350, 486.

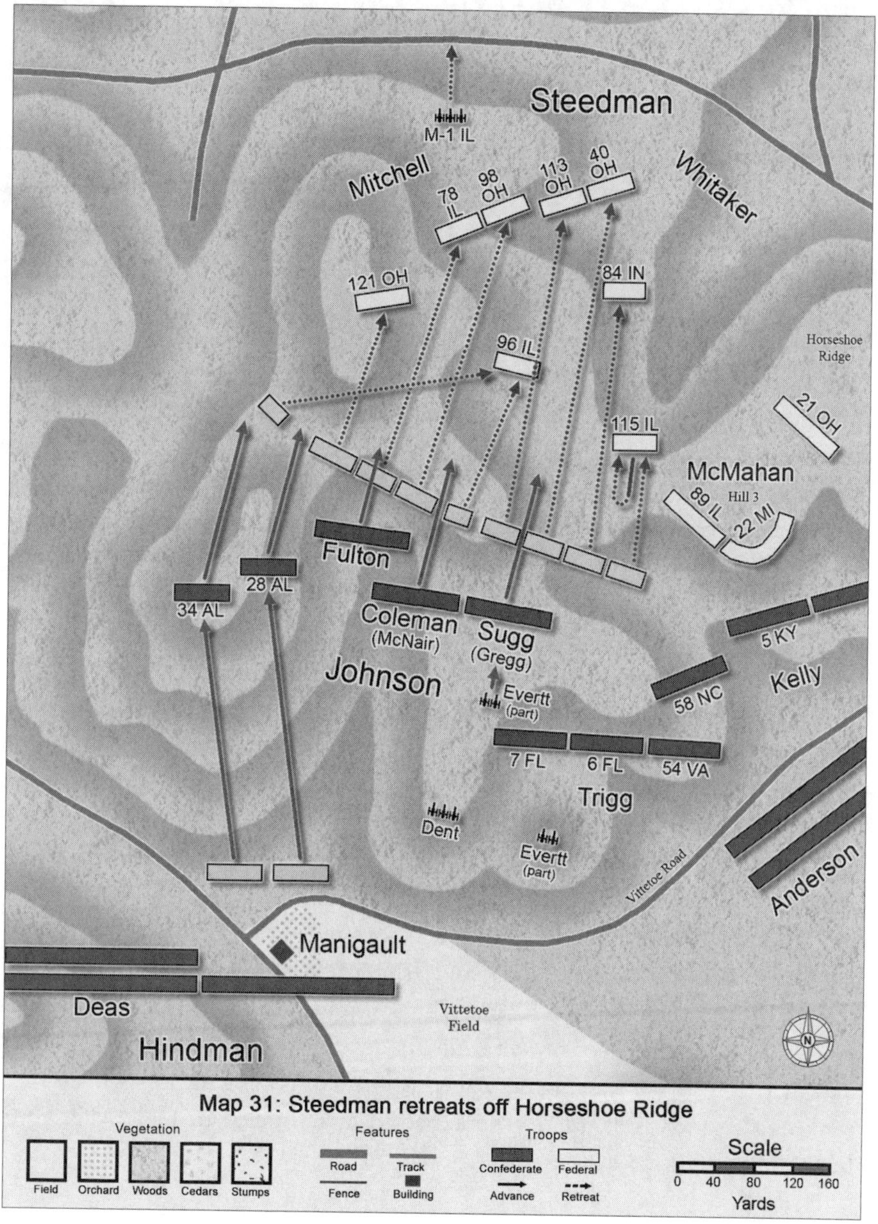

Map 31: Steedman retreats off Horseshoe Ridge

Carter Van Vleck, at the head of the 78th Illinois, reported that "an overwhelming force was thrown against our left wing, which left us no alternative but to retire or be overpowered and captured. . . . Our only salvation was in retreat." The 78th Illinois apparently had only a few rounds left. Its survivors fell back some 300 yards and resumed a limited fire to check any pursuit. The ammunition-less 98th Ohio joined the 78th here, fixed bayonets, and waited.[6]

Over in the ranks of the 84th Indiana of Whitaker's brigade, Capt. William Boyd remembered this last hour or so as the most difficult part of the fight—and perhaps the most confusing. After Hindman's men retired about 4:00 p.m., Boyd noticed a line of skirmishers, apparently dressed in blue, chasing after them. These mysterious skirmishers were not men of the 84th, however, and the Hoosiers suspected a Rebel trick. The 84th stayed put and the mystery soldiers disappeared into the smoke. That this movement, which was likely only the advance of a skirmish line from a neighboring Union regiment, sowed such thoughts in the ranks of the 84th reflects how little coordination there was between the Federal regiments by this stage of the battle. A short while later, some of the 84th's own officers threw the regiment into additional (and considerable) confusion. "Soon the Major and the Adjutant some distance in the rear of us [started] screaming 'fall back! The General says fall back!'" wrote a disgusted Boyd. "Each company did so at their own pleasure and in their own way." The order was a mistake. "We were soon ordered forward again at another point, and here was the bloodiest part of the conflict."[7]

Boyd believed this final fight lasted "for one dreadful hour," during which his company suffered nine casualties, more than the rest of the day combined. At dusk, the 84th was once again ordered to retreat, and it did so "in considerable disorder." In the midst of this movement General Whitaker appeared, accosted Boyd, and demanded to know "where my regiment was. I pointed it out to him, ascending an opposite hill. He expressed an emphatic disapproval and ordered me to plant the colors and gather all the men I could." Boyd rounded up about 30 souls and established a shaky line in the ravine behind (north of) Horseshoe Ridge. Whitaker returned a few moments later to tell the flag bearer "to hold myself ready for an attack at any time." Boyd's small (and by this time nervous) band waited in the gathering darkness while other Yankees streamed past them. The expected attack failed to materialize. For them, the fighting on that terrible day was finally over.[8]

6 Entry for September 20, Augustus L. Yenner Diary, WMU; Virdin, *Civil War Correspondence*, 98; *OR* 30, pt. 1, 869; J. L. Erwin, "Steedman at Snodgrass Hill," *National Tribune*, December 30, 1915.

7 Entry for September 20, Boyd Journal, UC Berkeley.

8 Ibid.

Just down the line from the 84th, Lt. Isaac Royce of the 115th Illinois, also of Whitaker's command, remembered that the ammunition crisis reared its head at 4:30 p.m. All the usual expedients were tried, including rummaging through discarded cartridge boxes and equalizing the supply among the survivors, but these stop-gap measures failed to alleviate the shortage in any meaningful way. The 115th was also more a mob than a formed unit. "Our lines were greatly thinned," recalled the lieutenant, "the men of various regiments were intermingled in many places." As a result, when Johnson's Rebels came again, "The most natural thing in the world occurred: [We] . . . began to retire from the hill."[9]

Royce described a stubborn, gradual retreat: "every man that could find a cartridge was using it to the best advantage. Even those without ammunition were but slowly moving to the rear. In this way the 115th Illinois had fallen back possibly 75 or 80 yards . . . when General Steedman came galloping along the line." Steedman confronted Col. Jesse Moore of the 115th and demanded to know why his men were giving way. Moore explained the lack of bullets and confirmed his men could hold the hill—if they were re-supplied. Steedman, of course, had no cartridges to give him. Undeterred, the general snapped, "Give them the bayonet, then." Dutifully, Moore ordered bayonets fixed and started his troops back up the hill. To everyone's surprise, Steedman promptly trotted to the front of the regiment, seized the colors from the shocked bearer, and "carried them a short distance in the charge, giving great enthusiasm to the men." With perhaps some allowable exaggeration, Royce remembered the 115th Illinois returning to the crest, recapturing it, and even driving the Confederates back down to the southern foot of Horseshoe Ridge. No Rebel account, however, recalls this impetuous charge. It is far more likely the 115th Illinois returned to the spine of the ridge, administered a brief check to the enemy, and "quietly dropped back from the crest of Snodgrass Ridge a little after sunset."[10]

9 Royce, *History of the 115th Illinois*, 133.

10 Ibid., 133-134. According to Royce, his men were fighting Preston's division. In fact, Preston's two brigades were engaged farther to the east, though Johnson's attack was timed to coincide with Preston's advance. Royce also provides yet another description of a Steedman "flag incident." Royce claimed that many writers incorrectly described Steedman's grabbing of a battle flag as taking place much earlier, but Royce himself was mistaken. In fact, the multiplicity of such descriptions makes it clear that Steedman used this trick repeatedly throughout the afternoon, usually to good effect.

The retreat of the 78th Illinois exposed the left flank of the 121st Ohio. Battery M of the 1st Illinois Artillery was still supporting these Buckeyes. Ordered back—by whom is unclear—the battery retreated under the cover of two quick rounds of double canister from each gun and joined Steedman's reforming men, "a strong line of infantry lying behind a low line of breastworks, hastily built by piling up stones." The 121st Ohio covered the battery's escape. "The whole line gradually gave way," wrote Capt. A. B. Robertson, and "it became necessary then for us to abandon our position, but still our boys reluctantly yielded." As they went, the men of the 121st "proudly taunted [the rebels] with the captured flag of the 22nd Alabama."[11]

On the far right flank, forgotten and now alone, remained the 96th Illinois. The Confederates did little to take advantage of the situation and Capt. George Hicks noted that a comparative silence settled on the line. "At length it grew so still," he recalled, "that I went out of the woods to see what was going on. One of my sergeants called out 'Captain! You're not leaving us?' 'Oh, no, I'll be back in a moment,'" Hicks replied. What he saw next alarmed him: "I discovered that the whole line was in motion, retiring leisurely, and that it was already some distance to the rear." Within a few minutes Hicks returned to the 96th and ordered it to follow suit. The "regiment" he rejoined had been whittled down to but 50-60 men, who together with Hicks soon stumbled into Col. Thomas Champion and another 30 or so men from the 96th. With fewer than 100 men and little semblance of organization, Champion herded the survivors into something of a rough formation: "Never mind your companies, boys," he instructed. "Get into line somewhere." The shredded colors were tied to the splintered staffs and the small band fell into line alongside them.[12]

By 6:00 p.m. Steedman's division had been driven in considerable disorder off of Horseshoe Ridge west of Hill Three. Initially, Steedman, Whitaker, and Mitchell made efforts to arrest the movement. Once it began, however, there was no stopping it. The Federals left behind hundreds of wounded, to the great anguish of many survivors. Captain A. B. Robinson of the 121st Ohio found it "indeed painful to leave that field, consecrated with our blood and endeared with our fallen comrades." Corporal John Patton of the 98th Ohio's Company B remembered the 98th's casualties "pleading" with their able-bodied fellows

11 Dolton, *Capsule History of Battery M*, 10; "Communication from Captain Robinson," *Marysville Tribune*, October 14, 1863. The 22nd's flag was not returned until 1972.

12 Partridge *Ninety-Sixth Regiment Illinois*, 239-240.

Col. Young M. Moody (right) led his 43rd Alabama up the slope of Hill One, hoping to salvage General Gracie's stalled attack.
Miller, Photographic History

"not to leave them behind." Some injured men hobbled or crawled away, a few were carried on limbers or by hand, but the bulk had to be abandoned atop the ridge.[13]

In conjunction with Steedman's retreat and the Confederate 5th Kentucky's success on Hill Three, the rest of Preston's division made a renewed effort against Hills One and Two. Masked during the initial advance and having fallen behind the rest of the brigade, Col. Young M. Moody's 43rd Alabama was Gracie's only uncommitted regiment. Gracie and Moody had worked together since early in the war, and despite being a decade older, Moody was something of Gracie's protégé. The two first met when Gracie was appointed major of the 11th Alabama on July 12, 1861. At that time Moody was a company commander in the regiment. In 1862, Gracie's military skills and West Point education won him the authority to return home and raise the 43rd, and he took Moody along as his second in command. Later, when Gracie was promoted to brigadier, Moody rose to full colonel and led the regiment. Now, early in the evening on Sunday, September 20, Gracie called upon Moody's 43rd Alabama to restart his stalled attack.

Moody marched his 43rd Alabama by the right flank behind the brigade until it was opposite the gap between the 63rd Tennessee and the 2nd Battalion. Moving the regiment abreast of the 63rd Tennessee, Moody attacked Hill One's southeast face. The angled nature of the 43rd's advance exposed the regiment to the same devastating fire that had earlier riddled the Tennesseans. Moody reported that soon after the outset of the charge he lost Lt. Col. John J. Jolly and "every company commander in the right wing." Initially it appeared the 43rd

13 "Communication from Captain Robinson," *Marysville Tribune*, October 14, 1863; John Patton Memoirs, LOC.

would have no better luck than the 63rd. An anonymous Alabamian reported that "the enemy were pouring a terrific fire into us from three sides, and a battery only a few hundred yards [away] was . . . pouring grape into us by the bushel." Major Aiken led the 63rd forward again in a vain effort to support Moody's right, but the Tennesseans faltered almost immediately. Moody noted that the 63rd's retreat "caused some confusion" and forced the 43rd to retire as well.[14]

Gracie met his old command when its members tumbled back down the hill, where he and Moody rallied them. Gracie realized the futility of moving back under the guns of Harker and Hazen's Federals. The next effort would come farther to the left where the curve of Hill One might mask some of the effect of that terrible fire. This approach worked better. "Changing front forward on the tenth company," Moody reported, "and charging up to the enemy's works on the hill, and with the Second Battalion . . . we succeeded in holding them."[15]

Lieutenant Colonel Bolling Hall's 2nd Alabama Battalion was still huddled at the foot of Hill One. The Alabamians hurled themselves back up the hill in conjunction with Moody's advance. Hall had almost reached the crest when a bullet struck him in the thigh. His brother Crenshaw, the battalion Adjutant, charged on. Bolling was the second Hall brother to fall that day: His younger sibling Tom, who together with brother Jim was serving in the 24th Alabama of Zach Deas's brigade, was badly wounded about 90 minutes earlier. Captain W. D. Walden of Company B succeeded Colonel Hall and led the battalion into the Union lines, where he was also cut down. This left Crenshaw Hall in charge. The latter Hall reported, with evident satisfaction, that "the enemy fiercely opposed our entrance. [Their] effort was useless—the works were carried, the enemy driven before us in confusion."[16]

This new Rebel lodgment proved precarious. The 11th Michigan's Pvt. James Martin remembered the Alabamians planted their colors on the rail pile serving as the Federal breastwork, forcing the Yankees back about 25 yards—but could not advance any farther. The crown of Hill One was a no-man's-land laced with fire. Gracie's men shot from the shelter of the rail pile

14 *OR* 30, pt. 2, 422; "Gracie's Brigade," *Mobile Daily Register*, October 14, 1863.

15 "Gracie's Brigade," *Mobile Daily Register*, October 14, 1863; *OR* 30, pt. 2, 422.

16 Jones, "Five Confederates," 182; *OR* 30, pt. 2, 425. Bolling Hall would recover, but Tom would not. He died on September 26, 1863, after an unsuccessful leg amputation.

while the 11th Michigan and 19th Illinois clung to the north side of the hill, firing back as best they could with what little they had left. According to J. Henry Haynie of the 19th, the Rebels only seized the point of the hill, having forced back "a part of the left of the 19th and the right of the 11th." Haynie insisted "there was no confusion in the ranks of the troops forced back, however, nor did they retire over one hundred fifty feet." In fact, both sides were thoroughly disrupted. The Rebels were stymied after losing so many officers and their formations were scrambled beyond repair, and the battered Yankees were unable to muster the effort (or the ammunition) to re-take their works. As a result, both sides fired and held on to what they had.[17]

Gracie's other three battalions were still in the fight, but not faring as well. A small portion of the 1st Battalion managed to get into the Federal line alongside the 2nd. The rest of the 1st Battalion was scattered across the southern slope and seeking cover—or at least its survivors were. The bulk of the 1st Battalion's manpower withered under a brutal crossfire during its approach against the southwestern face of Hill One. Adjutant John Massey described the scene: "The smoke soon became so dense that it was not easy to see far ahead. . . . Our line did not waver or fall back at any point; but it did not move forward as fast as it should." Wounded in the ankle, and with virtually all of his fellow officers down, Massey gamely tried to organize an advance. "For some time I received no orders from any superior officer. I knew we ought to go forward out of the slaughter pen in which we were being butchered every minute. I did my best to get the men to go forward at the double quick, but in the midst of such deafening roar it was impossible to make commands understood farther than a few feet. No courier, no adjutant, brought me any orders."[18]

Much to Massey's relief, into this mess stepped General Gracie, who urged the men onward. "For God's Sake," bellowed the brigadier, "have the men go forward! . . . I then ran from one end of our line to the other and repeated [the General's] order. When I had done this, I went in front of our line and waved the men to hasten forward." Massey was struck again, the bullet a spent one that passed through the rolled folds of his overcoat. It left a purple bruise and

17 "Dear Parents," September 24, 1863, Martin Letters, Bentley Historical Library, UMich; Haynie, *The Nineteenth Illinois*, 241.

18 Anonymous, "The First Battalion Hilliard's Legion at Chickamauga," *Montgomery Advertiser*, May 5, 1907.

knocked the wind out of him. After a few minutes of recovery, the indefatigable Massey was back at it, again urging the battalion upward. Within a few more seconds, however, he realized how few men were still with him: "Their thin line was leaving two thirds of the battalion lying wounded and dead behind them. Some of the gallant fellows were lying close to the breastworks." Private John Davenport, another member of the 1st Battalion, also witnessed Gracie's arrival. The general "flew from wing to wing between the fier of boath armeys, giving command and encurigen the men to deads [deeds] of graiter vallar[.] [I]n fact" he wrote, "all boath offersers and men dun ther hole deauty."[19]

The 1st Alabama Battalion suffered the heaviest losses of any of Gracie's units, surpassing even the unfortunate 63rd Tennessee with 167 killed, wounded, captured, and missing out of 281 engaged. It ceased being an effective force early in the attack.[20]

The two remaining battalions—the 3rd and the 4th—left only fleeting descriptions of this fight. Major John D. McLennan's 4th Battalion never got closer than 40 yards to the Union line. There, his men went to ground and returned fire for the entire duration of the action "until," as he noted, "our ammunition . . . [was] nearly exhausted." The 3rd Battalion laid claim to reaching and holding the crest of Hill Two, but its losses—the lowest in the brigade at 49 of 331 engaged—suggests it did not get nearly that far, and likely was pinned down on the slopes in front of the 9th Ohio and 87th Indiana. Certainly none of Van Derveer's Federals admitted to being knocked off the crest. By 5:30 p.m. Gracie's second effort reached its high water mark.[21]

Farther west, Kelly's brigade was in the same fix. The 58th North Carolina and 63rd Virginia sought cover in Draw Two, firing upward at Van Derveer's rightmost regiments. The 5th Kentucky was clinging to its precarious perch atop the southern crest of Hill Three, firing at a largely silent enemy across the way. Preston's raw division had thus far achieved the most success of any previous Confederate attack here, with parts of Hills One and Three under its control, but Preston had shot his bolt. Bushrod Johnson's men had done even better, and Steedman's men had been completely cleared off the ridge west of Hill Three, having retired at least 300 yards to the north. Combat sputtered to a

19 Ibid.; "My Dear Wife," September 26, 1863, John F. Davenport Letters, ADAH.

20 Powell, "Numbers and Losses," CCNMP.

21 *OR* 30, pt. 2, 427.

close on Johnson's front. His troops, however, were thoroughly spent and unable to exploit their success. Preston determined the time had come to commit his remaining brigade to complete the task.

The afternoon had thus far been one long frustration for Col. Robert C. Trigg. The enemy cavalry he had dispatched a pair of regiments to guard against were not Federals at all, but Joe Wheeler's Confederate troopers. Then, Simon Buckner ordered him to further divide his command by leaving one regiment to guard the La Fayette Road against any threat from the south, and bring the other back to rejoin the remainder of his brigade. Dutifully, Trigg led the 7th Florida northward, leaving behind the 1st Florida Cavalry. Trigg and the 7th had just tramped off when Preston's order arrived directing Trigg "to move rapidly to support . . . the division" in its attack against Horseshoe Ridge. Seeing no point in leaving an entire regiment behind to protect against friendly cavalry, Trigg took it upon himself to order everyone away. At Brotherton's, he discovered that Col. J. J. Finley had already taken the balance of the brigade (two regiments, the 6th Florida, and 54th Virginia) forward in response to the same Preston order. Instead of moving as a single command, the brigade was now divided into three pieces: Finley with the 6th Florida and 54th Virginia in the lead, moving northwest through Dyer Field towards where Kelly's brigade was engaged, Trigg and the 7th Florida coming up behind them in Brotherton Field, and Col. George Troup Maxwell a half-mile or so to the rear, moving up the La Fayette Road towards Brotherton's farm with his 1st Florida Cavalry (dismounted).[22]

When Trigg reached the scene of the fighting, he discovered Finley had already placed the 6th Florida and 54th Virginia on Kelly's left. Trigg extended this line farther west with the 7th Florida. With 1,265 men in the three regiments, Trigg's front spanned about 300 yards, partly masked by Johnson's men, who were themselves still engaged in their action on the ridge west of Hill Three. The 1st Florida Cavalry did not join Trigg or the rest of the brigade. Left to fend for themselves, Maxwell and the 1st lost track of Colonel Trigg. Writing

22 *OR* 30, pt. 2, 431. Trigg found only Rebel cavalry, but there was in fact a Union mounted probe in this area at the same time. About 3:00 p.m., Lt. Col. R. M. Russell took his 9th Pennsylvania up the La Fayette Road with orders to reestablish communication with the army. After traveling about two miles, Russell reported finding a Rebel brigade "strongly posted" blocking his path. Before he could explore further, he received orders to return to Crawfish Spring. Trigg mentions nothing about this encounter. See *OR* 30, pt. 1, 904-905, and Chapter 29 for more detail.

home a few days later, Lt. Col. William Stockton explained the confusion: "we were ordered to rejoin our brigade, but could not find it, in the mountains and woods as we moved forward to where a staff officer told us was our brigade. We found none of our own men but lots of Yankees on our flank."[23]

Upon leaving Brotherton Field, Colonel Maxwell and the 271 dismounted cavalrymen of the 1st Florida moved west and then turned due north along the Glenn-Kelly Road. When he finally met one of Preston's aides, Maxwell was ordered on straight ahead, where he soon found General Gracie near the foot of Hill One, "who informed me that his brigade had been twice repulsed." Gracie ordered Maxwell to make a third attempt. "It was hardly possible," protested Maxwell, "for my small regiment to do what his large brigade had failed to accomplish." Gracie acquiesced and the 1st Florida marked time while the brigadier rode off to rally his own men for a new effort. "We were ordered to lie down," noted Lieutenant Colonel Stockton, "and the balls whistled thick over us." The Yankee fire was largely ineffective, "not hitting more than fifteen of us," but one of the injured was Stockton himself: "One ball struck just in front of my face as I was watching the Yankee maneuvers and dashed the gravel into my eyes so sharply that I was blinded for a while." Maxwell later reported a total loss of one dead and nine wounded, but believed the count would have climbed much higher had they lingered, so exposed were they where Gracie had left them. Accordingly, he moved the 1st Florida back to the edge of the Dyer cornfield behind a fence along its northern edge. Effectively stripped from their brigade, these Floridians were unable to contribute anything else to the day's action.[24]

While Trigg was deploying the rest of his men, the gloom of evening deepened. It was now approaching 6:00 p.m. Gracie's riddled command, its cartridges now exhausted, was in the process of surrendering the precarious toehold on Hill One. John Davenport lamented that "we fought untell sunset when our aminshon [ammunition] gave out and our brigade was relieved by another brigade. If we onley had had a little more of that noisy kill dead we should have had the honer of capturing the enemey's brigade." Simultaneously, Colonel Moody ordered the 43rd to fall back "for want of ammunition, and my guns from frequent firing becoming unfit for use." Crenshaw Hall admitted

23 *OR* 30, pt. 2, 432; "My own darling Wife," September 21, 1863, Stockton Letters, Auburn University.

24 *OR* 30, pt. 2, 434; "My own darling Wife," September 21, 1863, Stockton Letters.

that "the hill was finally abandoned" by the 2nd Battalion, "but not until every cartridge was expended." One testament to the fury of the action here was the state of the 2nd Battalion's flag. Sergeant William H. Hiett wedged the staff upright amidst the barricade, where it then drew fire from every Federal in sight. The next day the Alabamians counted the holes and marveled at the total: the colors had been pierced 83 times. Three weeks later, when President Davis visited the army, Preston selected Maj. William Owen as an escort for Hiett and the tattered banner when it was formally presented to the Confederate president. Hiett, who had emerged from the fight with several close scrapes but no serious wounds, was promoted to second lieutenant on the spot.[25]

The 2nd's banner certainly drew the eye of a Wolverine private. According to James Martin, "they rushed on us and drove us back about five rods from our rail pile and planted their colors on top. . . . We fought them at the distance of five rods for an hour. We shot down their colors time and time again." Many Yankees were later adamant that they retook the hill, and held it at the close of the fight. However, recollections of this part of the action are particularly confusing. Colonel Stoughton, who replaced Col. Timothy Stanley when that officer fell wounded at midday, reported that it was during these final moments of the battle that he led the 18th Ohio's counterattack—and not earlier against Kershaw. Stoughton was clearly mistaken, because he also placed Brig. Gen. John Beatty in the midst of that fight, but by 6:00 p.m. Beatty was already gone. Beatty recalled that after the incident with the 7th South Carolina's colors a lull in the action developed, so he rode to the Union right to see how Steedman's troops were faring. Beatty stumbled upon his old friend Col. John Mitchell just as he was in the act of rallying a regiment. Beatty helped steady the line, and then rode back. "Returning to my old place," he recalled, "I find that disorganized bodies of men are coming rapidly from the left, in regiments, companies, squads, and singly." He had ridden into the human backwash that was the retreat from Hill One, just after Gracie's men gained their toe-hold.[26]

25 "My dear wife and Children," September 30, 1863, Davenport Letters, ADAH; OR 30, pt. 2, 423, 425; "Army Correspondence, Letter from Tennessee," 2nd Alabama Battalion file, ADAH; Owen, *In Camp and Battle*, 291.

26 "Dear Parents," September 24, 1863, Bentley Historical Library, UMich; *OR* 30, pt. 1, 381; Gracie, *The Truth About Chickamauga*, 312; Beatty, *The Citizen Soldier*, 341. Historian Archibald Gracie estimated that the timing of Colonel Stoughton's report is consistent, but also about two hours later than most other reports. The attack referred to by Stoughton, for example, occurred about 4:00 p.m., not 6:00 p.m.

Forty-six years later, Albert Cone of Company A, 19th Illinois (Stanley/Stoughton's brigade), described the difficulty of recalling accurately the exact sequence of charge and countercharge. From their place in reserve near the Snodgrass cabin, Cone recounted, "we moved forward and fell back some at times and our advance in all was somewhere between a quarter and a half a mile. . . . We were driven back some about four o'clock that afternoon and I don't think we regained—but we advanced and fell back and charged so much I do not now recollect all that we did do."[27]

Once Gracie's Confederates fell back, the Federals briefly regained undisputed control of Hill One. "[F]inally we rushed on them again and drove them down the hill," remembered Pvt. James Martin of the 11th Michigan. "In about a half hour longer they ceased firing and then attacked our left but were repulsed." Martin was probably mistaken about that last attack—it was more likely an incident of friendly fire. Private James Fenton in the 19th Illinois wrote that as Gracie's men withdrew, "we were feeling as though the battle was over for the day, but in about a half hour a volley came over us from our lines and Colonel [Alexander W.] Raffen sent Captain [James G.] Campbell and two men with him to tell them they were firing on their own men." Campbell and his escort returned with disturbing news: Col. Ferdinand Van Derveer's brigade, which had been holding firm on Hill Two all afternoon, was withdrawing.[28]

According to Van Derveer, his first inkling of trouble came when Brig. Gen. John Brannan noted that silence had descended on their right—the part of the field that had been occupied by Steedman's troops. Brannan "suspected all might not be right, and ordered me to place the Thirty-fifth Ohio across that flank to prevent a surprise." Accordingly, the Ohioans shifted from the southwest side of Hill Two to the northwest face, reorienting westward. In doing so, Van Derveer increased the gap between his brigade and the 22nd Michigan that had been left open when the 21st Ohio was driven back by the 5th Kentucky. Coupled with Steedman's retreat, this left Col. Heber Le

27 Albert Cone to E. A. Carman, March 1, 1909, 19th Illinois file, CCNMP.

28 "Dear Parents," September 24, 1863, Martin Letters, Bentley Historical Library, UMich; Entry for September 20, Fenton Diary, ALPL; OR 30, pt. 1, 403. General John Brannan reported Van Derveer's withdrawal as orderly, controlled, and free of enemy interference. In fact, it was a messy and confusing affair. Not everyone received the word to fall back, and some units were even ordered back into action while others were departing. These final scenes were to sow seeds of recrimination between Van Derveer and the men of the three abandoned regiments—21st Ohio, 22nd Michigan, and 89th Ohio—for years to come.

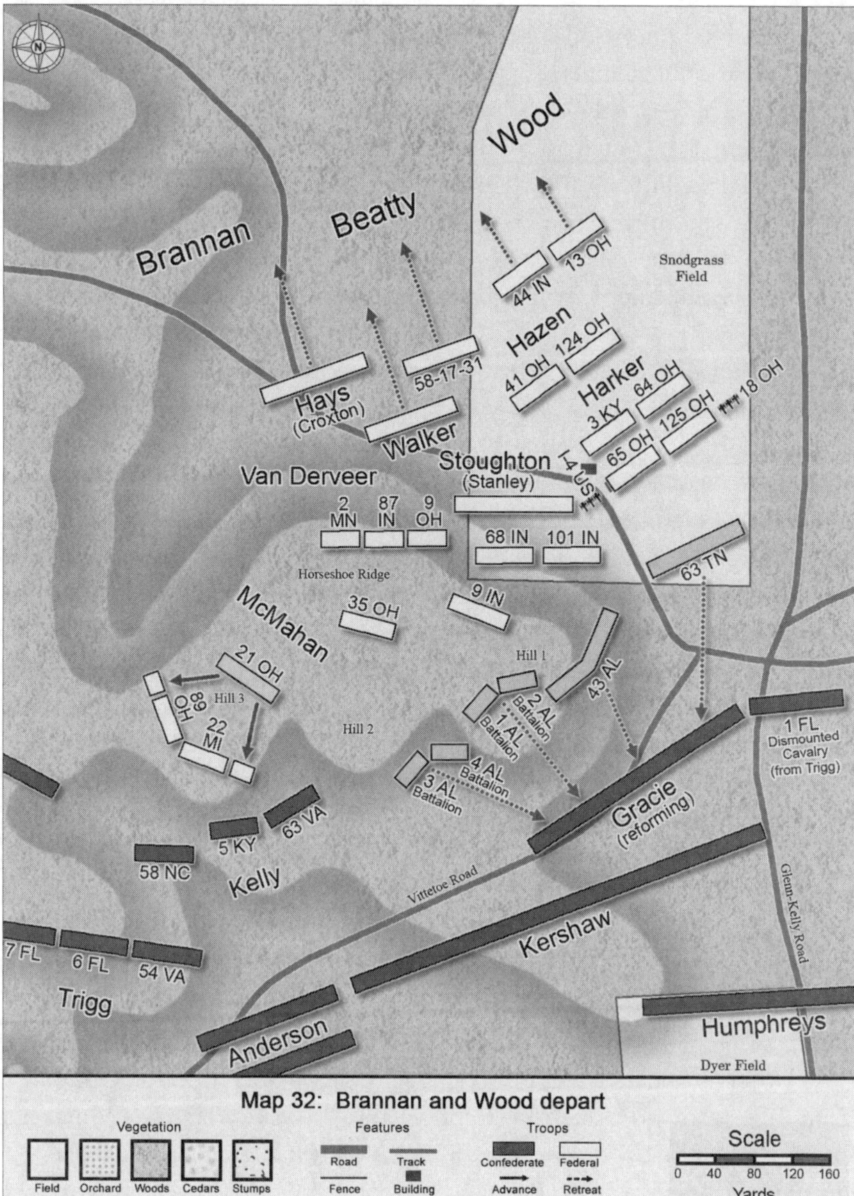

Map 32: Brannan and Wood depart

Favour's 22nd Michigan and 89th Ohio isolated just west of Hill Three, and the 21st Ohio still reforming behind the ridge somewhere off Van Derveer's right.[29]

29 Ibid., 430-431.

Van Derveer knew none of this. He thought all the Federals to his right had withdrawn without so much as a word of notice. With the 35th Ohio in place, he withdrew his other three regiments into the ravine west of the Snodgrass house, where they halted to await developments. This was the movement Captain Campbell of the 19th Illinois discovered and reported. Van Derveer and several of his officers conferred with Brannan about what to do next. While they did so, Brannan dispatched Col. Moses Walker to find General Thomas, "present his compliments, and receive such instructions as [Thomas] might see proper to give."[30]

Van Derveer's retreat triggered the final Federal withdrawal from Hill One. Initially, Stoughton fell back only a couple hundred yards to take up a new position north of the Snodgrass house. This force included not only Stoughton's three regiments but fragments of Brannan's command that had not withdrawn earlier (prominent among them Col. Morton Hunter's 82nd Indiana). Neither the official reports nor surviving personal accounts describe this movement in any detail, or differentiate it from the larger retreat to Rossville ordered a short while later. Colonel George Cram's report for the 9th Kentucky's actions is typical: "For a half an hour the firing was the most terrific I had ever heard, my men firing during that time 60 rounds of cartridges, and it was only when the last cartridge was expended that I ordered [them] to fall back. The enemy did not occupy the hill until the next morning. We moved off a short distance to the right, intending to rejoin the division." Because of their position on the left, Col. Charles Harker's men became the de facto rear guard for this retreat.[31]

Brigadier General Tom Wood remained with Harker's men all afternoon. As evening approached, he ordered the men to cheer. Harker's and Hazen's lines both responded with shouts "vigorous and prolonged; General Wood himself swinging his hat and leading the chorus." Then Harker's troops also shifted to a position behind the Snodgrass house. Colonel Emerson Opdycke's 125th Ohio and two guns from Capt. Charles Aleshire's battery (Whitaker's brigade) provided the covering force. Following suit, General Hazen encountered Brannan, Wood, and Van Derveer in conference. There, noted

30 Gracie, *The Truth About Chickamauga*, 177; Walker Report, NARA. Walker, it should be recalled, was the commander of Brannan's First Brigade, though for a good portion of the battle Walker was acting on Brannan's staff and Col. John Connell led the brigade.

31 *OR* 30, pt. 1, 814.

Hazen, "General Brannan asked for a regiment to take post on his right, and I sent the Ninth Indiana." Hazen also left a skirmish line forward at the "edge of the field," alert for any renewed Confederate effort, but the fighting in this sector was apparently over.[32]

Not so elsewhere. By now, the retreat from Kelly Field that coincided with a renewed attack by Leonidas Polk's Right Wing (which had been inactive all afternoon, as described earlier) was well underway. By about 6:00 p.m., Polk's Rebels possessed all of the Kelly Field line and broke out with an immense cheer. The shouting spread like wildfire south and west through the ranks of General Longstreet's men. Ambrose Bierce heard the yell and described the effect it had on those occupying the dark gloomy woods: "Away to our left and rear some of Bragg's people set up 'the rebel yell.' It was taken up successively and passed round to our front, along our right and in behind us again, until it seemed almost to have got to the point whence it started. It was the ugliest sound that any mortal ever heard." To others of Hazen's brigade, the sound "meant disaster, more or less, to the divisions that had stood all day as the left of the army."[33]

Sometime after 6:00 p.m., Col. Moses Walker returned from his mission to find General Thomas with both orders and a pair of infantry regiments. The staff officer had found the XIV corps commander "about a half mile in rear of the line" near the McFarland's Gap Road. The general sent Walker back to Horseshoe Ridge with instructions to commence a general retreat to Rossville.[34] Even in retreat, Thomas still exuded calm. Adjutant Angus Waddle of the 33rd Ohio, who had fallen in with another unit when he lost track of his own regiment, took heart when he caught sight of Thomas's demeanor. "The old hero was as we had often seen him on parade. Dismounting from his horse, he directed an orderly to gather some corn from a field just at hand, and while the horse was feeding, dispatched . . . members of his staff with orders." In addition to instructions, Thomas also sent the 68th and 101st Indiana regiments from Col. Ed King's (Robinson's) brigade of Maj. Gen. Joseph Reynolds's division with Walker. The two Hoosier commands still carried ammunition, a

32 Hinman, *The Story of the Sherman Brigade*, 430; Gracie, *The Truth About Chickamauga*, 316; Hazen, *A Narrative of Military Service*, 132; Kimberly and Holloway, *The Forty-First Ohio*, 53.

33 Bierce, *Ambrose Bierce's Civil War*, 37; Kimberly and Holloway, *The Forty-First Ohio*, 53.

34 Walker Report, NARA.

commodity in short supply on Horseshoe Ridge, and were loaned out to help cover the retreat.[35]

Walker returned to the Snodgrass cabin just after Hazen offered up the 9th Indiana. His arrival was timely, and the two new regiments were welcome support. Private John Beals of the 68th recalled that he and some of his comrades "crawled over the regiments that lay there and laid down facing the south west . . . with orders to shoot anyone coming from the direction of the enemy not more than fifty yards distant."[36]

Conspicuous by his absence at this gathering was Gordon Granger. Somewhere en route to rejoin Brannan, Walker encountered both Granger and Steedman and informed them of Thomas's orders. Steedman was several hundred yards to the west and north reorganizing his battered division. Walker did not specify where he met Granger, but it was not at the Snodgrass house, nor was he with Steedman. Major John C. Smith, of Steedman's staff, reported that the last time Steedman and Granger met on the field was 4:00 p.m., when Steedman rode to the Snodgrass house to check in. None of the officers grouped with Brannan mentioned seeing Granger at this juncture. It is possible Granger left to find Steedman. If so, Granger's intent in doing so remains unrecorded and, based on Smith's account of the day, unsuccessful. Granger himself reported only that he received Thomas's orders to retreat at 7:00 p.m., and that "they were promptly carried out."[37]

In fact, all of Granger's actions after joining Thomas at 2:00 p.m. are cloaked in some level of mystery. He did not accompany his troops to the far right flank, choosing instead to remain with Thomas at the Snodgrass house. There, he once again indulged in his fascination with cannon. Granger personally directed Aleshire's 18th Ohio battery into position, and then "engaged in fighting, firing, and almost loading" one of Aleshire's pieces. When Capt. William Russell's wounded horse trotted up, the empty saddle covered with blood, Granger ignored it until he realized it was Russell's horse. Russell was a favorite, and now Granger was oblivious to all else. According to

35 Waddle, *Three Years*, 54; High, *Sixty-Eighth Indiana*, 97. Walker remembered that Col. Oscar F. Moore of the 33rd Ohio also volunteered to join this movement with a small fragment of his regiment. No accounts from anyone in the 33rd recall making such a trip, however. Moore's 33rd Ohio was one of General Baird's regiments, and became badly scattered crossing Kelly Field.

36 Beals to J. H. Gray, February 19, 1897, John Beals Letters, InHS.

37 Walker Report, NARA; Smith, *Steedman*, 28; *OR* 30, pt. 1, 856.

newspaper reporter William Shanks, Granger forgot the cannon, forgot to send another aide to carry the order that Russell had apparently not delivered, and ordered several of his escort to find Russell's body. When they returned, a crying Granger exclaimed to Thomas, "By G-d, General, he was the best soldier I ever knew!" In a few minutes the tears subsided and he returned to firing the cannon.[38]

Thomas's departure for Kelly Field at 4:30 p.m. left Granger as the ranking commander. His last recorded order was to Brannan sometime around 5:00 p.m. In response to Brannan's worries about the lack of bullets, Granger instructed that the Federals should "fix bayonets and go for them."[39]

By this time Granger was nearly a mile and a half away from the Snodgrass cabin, off to the north. He was back on the same hill overlooking Cloud Church where he had ordered Burton's Battery M, 1st Illinois Light Artillery, into action briefly at midday. This time the hill was occupied by Col. Daniel McCook's brigade and Capt. Charles M. Barnett's Battery I, 2nd Illinois Light Artillery. According to one of McCook's aides, "about 6 o'clock, General Granger came up and ordered Barnett's battery to give the enemy a 'salvo.'" Thomas's own report casts some additional light on Granger's doings. After Thomas sent Moses Walker back to Horseshoe Ridge with two regiments and instructions to commence withdrawing, and after observing the successful disengagement of General Palmer's division from Kelly Field, wrote Thomas, "I then proceeded to Rossville, accompanied by Generals Garfield and Gordon Granger." All three officers scouted the new ground at Rossville Gap and selected positions for the troops that would soon be arriving. While this was not an unimportant mission in its own right, given the jumbled nature of the Federal forces back on Horseshoe Ridge, overseeing the retreat there required someone more senior than Brannan. Granger, as a corps commander, was the obvious choice for that mission. He should have remained there until the last Union regiments were safely disengaged, instead of riding off to find George Thomas.[40]

Meanwhile, back at the Snodgrass house, Colonel Walker finally took stock of his personal circumstances. He was unable to dismount. "During the day," he explained, "I had received a buckshot or pistol ball in my right leg. My left

38 Shanks, *Personal Recollections*, 275-276.

39 Fullerton, "Reinforcing Thomas," 667.

40 Gracie, *The Truth About Chickamauga*, 254, 449.

knee had been cut by a minnie ball and a piece of shell had injured my left shoulder and spine. . . . So great had been the excitement of the day that I was not until now aware that I was seriously hurt." In fact, Walker was nearly paralyzed. There was still work to do, however, and he was not yet ready to quit the field. Shortly thereafter, Brannan rode up and directed Walker to take charge of the rear guard.[41]

By 7:00 p.m. almost all the Federals were gone. With the fighting over, General Beatty determined to try and find out what happened to his brigade. Later, after a fair bit of wandering that included almost stumbling into Confederates near the McDonald house, Beatty located Tom Wood, who informed Beatty that everyone was headed for Rossville. Beatty next found Colonel Stoughton, only to discover that "they had been appraised of the movement and were then on the road to the rear. The march to Rossville," recalled Beatty, "was a melancholy one. All along the road . . . wounded men were lying. They had crawled or hobbled slowly away from the fury of the battle, become exhausted, and lay down by the roadside to die."[42]

Back atop Horseshoe Ridge, Confederates fanned out to collect whatever spoils they could find. Suffering from multiple wounds and paralyzed from the waist down, Sgt. Edward Murray of the 96th Illinois provided good pickings. One Rebel, probably from Cyrus Sugg's brigade, "took [Murray's] cartridges and put them in his own [cartridge box] and leaving his old gun he took mine . . . it was getting quite dark." Shortly thereafter, Murray noted, "there was a big commotion among the Rebels. They captured a number of prisoners and a number of flags and were feeling very jubilant about it. They were making the woods ring with their hurrahs and the Rebel yell."[43]

Not every Federal had vanished. Several Union regiments had been left behind, either as rear guards or simply forgotten by their commanders. The final act on Horseshoe Ridge offered a dark comedy of errors and a heartbreaking conclusion for several hundred of its most stubborn defenders.

41 Walker Report, NARA.

42 Beatty, *Citizen Soldier*, 343.

43 Murray, *A Soldier's Reminiscences*, 28.

Chapter Twenty-Eight

Left Behind:

Sunday, 5:30 p.m. to 8:00 p.m.

By 5:30 p.m., only the 22nd Michigan and 89th Ohio remained in place along the original line of Horseshoe Ridge west of Hill Three. Both units were under Colonel Le Favour's direction, and neither was in contact on either flank with any friendly forces. Once he realized the Federals to his left and right were gone, Le Favour decided it was time to withdraw. The 22nd would lead the movement, followed by the 89th.

Le Favour's last contact with any superior officer was about an hour earlier when he dispatched the 22nd's adjutant, Lt. Louis Drake, to find someone in authority and inform him the regiments were dangerously low on ammunition. Drake returned without bullets but carrying Gordon Granger's stock answer: "They must use the bayonet."[1]

Despite Granger's exhortation and the absence of any additional orders, Le Favour's decision to fall back was consistent with his immediate superior's intent, though he did not know this when he decided to pull out. Thirty minutes earlier, General Steedman had dispatched an aide to find Le Favour and order him to rejoin the rest of the withdrawing division. As Lt. Edgar G. Spaulding, commanding Company C of the 22nd Michigan learned later, Steedman's

1 Gracie, *The Truth About Chickamauga*, 429. Le Favour, quoted in Robertson, *Michigan in the War*, 423, stated that he first sent word to Whitaker requesting ammunition. Whitaker replied, "you must use your steel." See also Carlton Papers, LOC.

Colonel Heber Le Favour (right) tried to lead the 22nd Michigan and 89th Ohio to safety.
The Truth About Chickamauga

courier "was cut off by the enemy and never reached us." This failure should not have been fatal, since the two regiments were departing anyway.[2]

It appeared as though fortune was smiling on Col. Heber Le Favour and his regiments, for there were no Rebels barring their route to safety. Moving with the 22nd Michigan, a short distance behind the hill Le Favour encountered Maj. John C. Smith of Steedman's staff. The major had just come from Steedman's right flank, where he and Capt. Seth Moe were supervising the retreat of Mitchell's brigade. According to Moe, Steedman intended "to hold our position until all on the left had withdrawn, then retire." It was a difficult task, for as we have seen, much of Steedman's division was already drifting northward, deaf to any orders to the contrary. Major Smith was working his way east in an effort to arrest this rearward drift, and found the 22nd Michigan heading for the rear.[3]

The staff officer was unaware Generals Brannan and Wood had already left with their commands, and was operating under the belief that the "hold" portion of Steedman's order was still operational. Accordingly, Smith used his authority as a general's aide and directed Le Favour to move his regiments back into place on the west face of Hill Three. The order stunned Le Favour. "Ammunition and reinforcements will be sent at once," insisted Smith, though where those might be found was not explained. Several of the 22nd's officers remembered this disheartening exchange. "We marched down the hill till halted by an officer on horseback in Federal uniform," recalled Lt. William B.

2 Robertson, *Michigan in the War*, 425; Gracie, *The Truth About Chickamauga*, 230. Captain John Atkinson of Company C, one of the few of the 22nd Michigan not captured that afternoon, wrote home with news on September 29 that Steedman's order had come "too late."

3 Smith, *The Right of the Federal Army*, 13.

Hamilton of Company F. "He said 'the orders are to hold the hill at all hazards; use the cold steel if necessary; reinforcements and ammunition will be here soon.' I heard no general officer's name mentioned as giving the order, though I stood within thirty feet and heard all that was said. The Colonel may have known him." Lieutenant Edgar Spaulding offered a similar version: "'Colonel, the orders are to hold that hill.' 'But my ammunition is completely exhausted,' replied Le Favour. 'Then the orders are to hold it at the point of the bayonet,' replied the aide." A Michigan lieutenant named George W. Button of Company A never knew Smith's name, but many years later he clearly recalled his looks: "He was quite a large man, dark and swarthy," wrote Button, "with black hair and beard."[4]

Given the recent and temporary attachment of the 22nd to Steedman's command, it is not surprising the rank and file did not recognize Smith, but Le Favour knew him. According to Smith, the two men were well acquainted, for Smith had accompanied Le Favour during a reconnaissance to Ringgold just three days earlier. Dutifully, Le Favour accepted Smith's authority and, without additional protest reversed the course of the Wolverines. Major Smith would later insist that his order was one of those harsh but necessary decisions required by war. Le Favour remained dubious. However, the order was given, and Le Favour obeyed.[5]

The men of the 22nd Michigan reoccupied their former position alongside the 89th Ohio, which hadn't yet moved. As they did so, Pvt. O. W. Tock managed a final act of comfort for a dying friend, Color Cpl. Richard A. Stansell of Company H. Earlier, Tock and another comrade had carried Corporal Stansell behind the lines and laid him near a tree. Now, when they passed Stansell on the way back to the front, Tock took a moment to collect the corporal's watch and other personal effects to send them to his soon-to-be widowed wife.[6]

Le Favour's entire to-and fro movement began and ended so quickly that the Rebels failed to notice the 22nd Michigan's departure or return. According to Captain Hamilton, they returned to the "identical spot we had just vacated ten or twelve minutes before." Everything transpired so swiftly the 89th Ohio

4 Smith, *Steedman*, 29; Gracie, *The Truth About Chickamauga*, 434-435.

5 Smith, *The Right of the Federal Army*, 14.

6 Gracie, *The Truth About Chickamauga*, 430.

did not have time to leave its position, and the Buckeyes barely noted the incident as a separate event.[7]

While Le Favour was marching with his Michiganders, the 21st Ohio experienced a very similar experience. After being driven off Hill Three, Maj. Arnold McMahan gathered the Buckeyes in the ravine behind Van Derveer's brigade. Lieutenant John Mahony of Company K recalled the position as being "under the crest of the ridge a few rods" where the 21st gathered "singly & in squads." Mahony's attention was drawn to two unknown mounted officers near a distinctive pair of trees, one of which sported "colored spectacles."[8]

The two officers were brigade commander Col. Ferdinand Van Derveer and one of his regimental leaders, Lt. Col. Henry Boynton of the 35th Ohio. Both were there to order the 21st Ohio back into the fight. Since the resulting exchange decided the fate of these Buckeyes, it was long remembered by everyone in that regiment. Van Derveer first came upon Captain Cusac, who wrote, "An officer rode up to me as I stood in front of the regt and ordered me to take the men on the line." Taken aback by both the tone of the order and the fact it originated from an officer he did not know, the captain replied, "Colonel, we have no more ammunition," to which Van Derveer snapped, "It does not make a G— D—- bit of difference. Have the men fix bayonets and hold that line." The angry Cusac retorted that Van Derveer needed see Major McMahan. Lieutenant Mahony, who was listening, intervened with a blunt observation: "it would be murder to take men in again." "It must be done, sir," the mounted officer emphatically replied. As McMahan recalled, "I was unwilling to order the charge, though I did not permit that fact to be known to the men." McMahan also recalled a less heated exchange, observing that Van Derveer did not seem "imperious, but kind and encouraging." Private Abel Comstock recalled his major's reply quite differently: "G-d D—n it, you rank me," snarled McMahan. "Boys, we will have to go back." Lieutenant William Vance also claimed to have witnessed the scene, and described it with more than a touch of melodrama. "'Take your regiment and make a charge and re-take the hill! We will rally and re-form and support you!' 'We have no ammunition—,' began McMahan, more in explanation than remonstrance. 'But you have your orders,'

7 Ibid., 436.

8 "Dear Sir," John Mahony to McMahan, July 23, 1889, Sullivan Collection, BGSU.

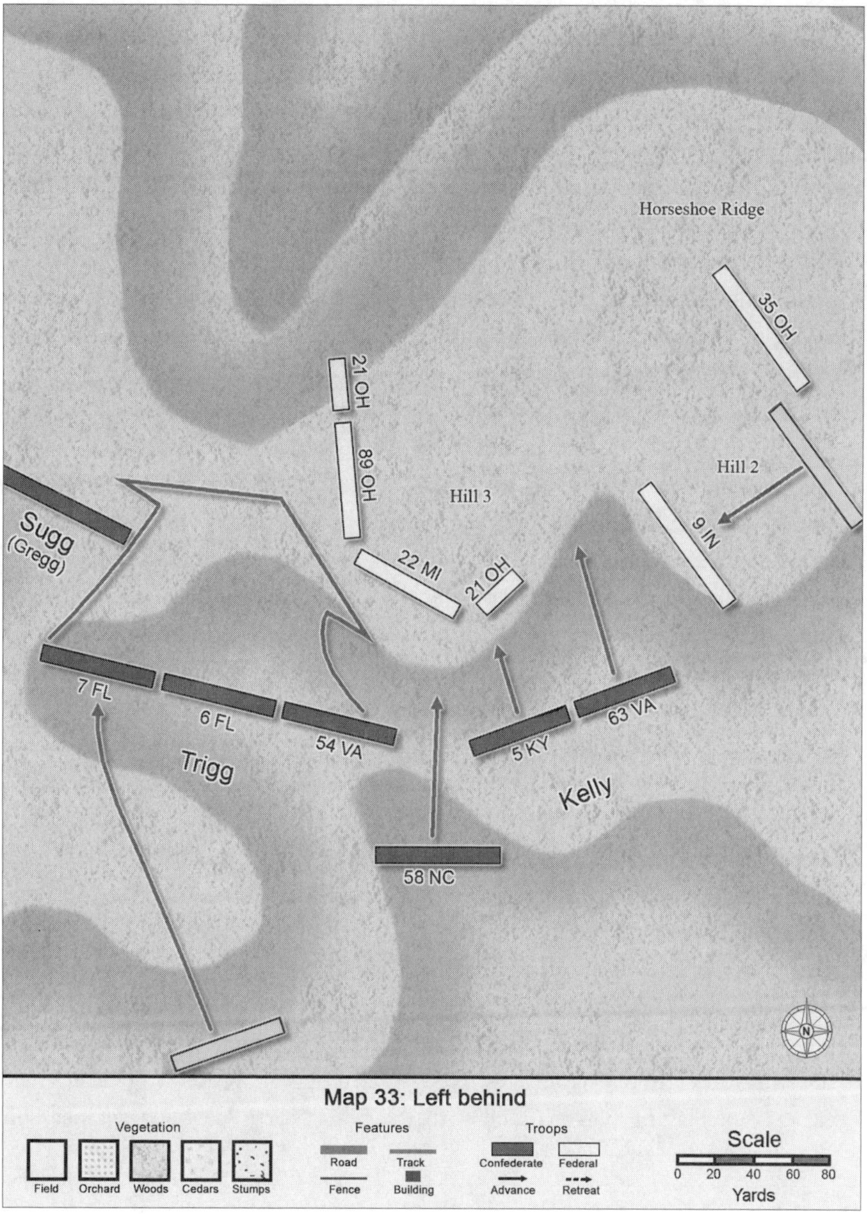

Map 33: Left behind

pompously responded the Colonel, as became a man seeking to . . . hide his chagrin at his own blunder." The 21st Ohio was going back into action.[9]

9 "Dear Sir," Cusac to E. A. Carman, March 13, 1909, Sullivan Collection, BGSU; Canfield, *History of the 21st Regiment*, 136, 146; "Dear Sir," John Mahony to McMahan, July 23, 1889,

The two mounted officers rode away. Like Le Favour minutes earlier, McMahan was also promised that reinforcements would be sent forward to support him as soon as they could be reorganized—a commitment that rang false as soon as the words were uttered. A final inventory of the regiment's cartridge boxes revealed that there were bullets enough for just one round apiece. With bayonets fixed and their last rounds chambered, the Buckeyes of the 21st regiment set off.

Nothing was destined to go smoothly for the regiment. McMahan marched the bulk of the command west behind Hill Three where, unbeknownst to him, the 89th Ohio was still holding the ridge. Instead of following McMahan, a confused Captain Cusac led two companies back up the slope to reoccupy their original position. The 22nd Michigan had yet to return, for Cusac noted that he struck the left of the 89th Ohio and then "went straight forward to the line . . . where the center of the 21st had been all that afternoon." McMahan, meanwhile, led the main body of the regiment "forward along the slope and at a charge gained the point of the ridge and took nine prisoners." During their advance they passed over ground littered with the dead and wounded of the afternoon's fight. One of these poor souls was Gilbert S. Robinson of the 115th Illinois. Earlier in the day, Robinson had assisted a wounded comrade to the rear. Unable to relocate his regiment, he fought alongside some stragglers for awhile until he was wounded. Lying near the crest, Robinson described the 21st as "a fragment of a regiment," one that "advanced without firing, in as perfect a line as if on dress parade. As the lines reached me two files dropped out to avoid stepping on me, and after passing resumed their place. There was no confusion, no fear displayed in this desperate charge." Once past Robinson, Confederates appeared out of the gloomy twilight of the evening.[10]

While Van Derveer was ordering the Buckeyes back to the front, Col. Robert C. Trigg's Floridians and Virginians were moving slowly forward to renew the Rebel attack; Col. John Kelly was redeploying his brigade for the same reason. Having had no luck with the 58th North Carolina against Hill

Sullivan Collection, BGSU; "Major McMahan's Response,"" McMahan Papers, Sullivan Collection, BGSU; Vance, "On Thomas' Right at Chickamauga," 96. As noted previously, other members of the 21st Ohio believed that Lieutenant Vance's account of September 20 was overly fanciful.

10 "Dear Sir," Cusac to E. A. Carman, March 13, 1909, Sullivan Collection, BGSU; Draft of letter, McMahan to Carlton, undated, McMahan Papers, Sullivan Collection, BGSU; G. S. Robinson, "Chickamauga," *National Tribune*, August 7, 1884.

Two, Kelly ordered Col. John Palmer to shift his Tar Heels from the brigade's right to the left in the hope of outflanking the Yankees through Steedman's now-vacated position. And so it was that Palmer's men collided with McMahan's portion of the 21st Ohio in an encounter that surprised both sides. The Ohioans fired off their last round and, deciding *en masse* that the bayonet was not enough to maintain their position, promptly fell back "in disorder, with [their] line broke," remembered Robinson. When Buckeye lead began flying, the North Carolinians scattered for the trees and vigorously pulled triggers for several minutes in a wholly one-sided firefight. Spooked by this ghostly encounter, the Tar Heels did not rally easily. Eventually, Palmer reported, "a second line was formed and another charge was attempted, with like results." This second charge must not have amounted to much, for by this time the bullet-less Ohioans had cleared off. When Palmer finally realized that no one was shooting back, he ordered his men to cease fire.[11]

While the 58th North Carolina was expending the last of its ammunition against an empty ridge line, brigade commander Kelly led the 5th Kentucky up the hill on Palmer's right (in what was now the brigade's center). The Kentuckians bumped into Federals somewhere near the top in an encounter that left the Confederates fuming with anger and both sides confused. "When I arrived at the base of the hill the enemy was heard to cry 'We surrender! We surrender!'" wrote Kelly. "I immediately stepped to the front . . . and called upon the officer who seemed to be in command and demanded that if he proposed to surrender he should lay down his arms. He came to the front and said 'wait a minute.'"[12]

Colonel Hiram Hawkins of the 5th Kentucky initially believed the line of unknown men was made up of fellow Confederates, perhaps some of Colonel Trigg's men, who were after all momentarily expected. In a postwar account, Colonel Hawkins remembered that he had stepped forward "on foot in front of the regiment, [and] demanded to know whose troops they were. They cried 'friends' [but] a soldier of the 5th, nearer the enemy, shouted 'They are Yanks! They are Yanks!' An [enemy] officer stepped to the front and cried 'We surrender,'" and then "immediately stepped back between his lines and fired a

11 *OR* 30, pt. 2, 441; G. S. Robinson, as quoted in "Dear Sir," George E. Dolton to McMahan, April 14, 1890, Sullivan Collection, BGSU; *OR* 30, pt. 2, 446.

12 *OR* 30, pt. 2, 441.

volley into our ranks." The clever ruse infuriated the Confederates. "They treacherously fired into us," complained Hawkins.[13]

The Yanks, of course, recalled things much differently. Earlier, Col. Caleb Carlton of the 89th Ohio (Whitaker's brigade) noted that during lulls, "men on both sides would, when the firing ceased, stand up, wave their hats and shout at each other, although the distance was too great to clearly understand what was said." Apparently some of the Rebels took this activity as a sign of surrender. Conversely, some of the Ohioans thought the Rebels were trying to surrender to them. One member of the 89th later told Carlton that he captured three supposed Confederate deserters who informed their captors that "the rebels were shouting that several hundred of them would come over if [the 89th] would not fire on them." Interestingly, wounded Gilbert Robinson of the 115th Illinois reported something similar: "A rebel ran in and gave himself up. Others were scattered over the sloping ground west of us. We thought they also wanted to surrender, and called to them to come in. They shouted to us in return—their number increasing. Soon we made out that they demanded our surrender. At about this time I first noticed a rebel line of battle across the ridge from 150 to 200 yards, west of us—[their] colors on the crest. . . . We opened fire on both sides."[14]

Captain J. B. Hall of the 17th Kentucky also witnessed the event. Somehow during the course of the afternoon Captain Hall and a small fragment of the 17th (which belonged to Sam Beatty's brigade, which by then had men scattered all over Horseshoe Ridge) found themselves fighting somewhere between the 21st Ohio and 22nd Michigan. At dusk, as Steedman's men withdrew, Hall recalled moving about 100 yards to the southwest. His description of the subsequent collision mirrored Robinson's. Moving "through the brush, we captured one of the advancing force and then saw a line in our front. We thought they also wished to surrender, and called on them to come in. They seemed to be of the same impression, and called on us to surrender. Both parties seemed then to realize the true condition, and a furious volley was fired from both lines."[15]

13 Hiram Hawkins Papers, Kentucky Historical Society, Frankfort, KY; *OR* 30, pt. 2, 444.

14 Carlton Papers, LOC; Robinson quoted in "Dear Sir," George E. Dolton to McMahan, April 14, 1890, Sullivan Collection, BGSU.

15 "Dear Sir," George E. Dolton to McMahan, April 14, 1890, Sullivan Collection, BGSU.

This meeting threw the 5th Kentucky and 58th North Carolina into confusion and effectively halted Kelly's second attack. Kelly dispatched men to the rear to bring forward more bullets while his men held their advanced position. During the lull he ran into Colonel Trigg and the 7th Florida; Trigg's 6th Florida and 54th Virginia were already in position on Kelly's left, and the 7th Florida was just catching up to the rest of his brigade. Kelly understood that even if the 58th North Carolina hadn't gained their flank, the Yankees were still vulnerable from that direction. Once apprised of the circumstances as Kelly understood them, Trigg agreed to connect his brigade with the 58th's left and cooperate in a joint advance "with the intention of swinging the whole force to the right." With Trigg in their rear and Kelly coming at them straight on, the Federals should be trapped. Trigg agreed and set off. Before the plan could be executed, however, a courier from General Preston called Kelly away to headquarters. The attack would have to wait.[16]

By this time Colonel Le Favour had moved the 22nd Michigan back into position. All of this Confederate activity drew Le Favour's attention. Leaving his regiment on the ridge, the Wolverine colonel descended the south slope to investigate and was promptly captured. When Col. Caleb Carlton of the 89th Ohio sought out Le Favour for a conference, he "was told he had walked out to reconnoiter the enemy in his front." Carlton had dismounted to light his pipe and wait for Le Favour to return when some of the Michiganders caught sight of Trigg's Rebels working around the flank. The alarmed Carlton remounted and rode back to his own regiment, where he met Major McMahan and most of the 21st Ohio falling back after their recent collision with Colonel Palmer's Tar Heels. To Carlton, the 21st seemed a mere fragment, "two or three small Co[mpanie]s with colors, probably a total of eighty or ninety men."[17]

Any support was a comfort, however, for as Carlton told McMahan years later, "as few as you were I was very glad to see you, for we had not seen anyone except rebels for some hours." Lieutenant Edward Scott of the 89th remembered that the firing had largely ceased, when "just at this moment, the Twenty First Ohio came down the hill and Col. Carlton told the major in command to go to our right, as he was afraid [the Rebels] were trying to flank us." McMahan complied by settling his troops in on Carlton's right, facing west

16 *OR* 30, pt. 2, 441.

17 "Dear Colonel," Carlton to McMahan, August 8, 1889, Sullivan Collection, BGSU; Carlton Papers, LOC.

and well down the northern slope of the ridge. By this time it was about 6:30 p.m. and very dark. With orders prohibiting retreat and hoping to see the reinforcements promised them by Smith and Van Derveer, the three Union regiments had no choice but to hold their ground as directed.[18]

Unaware that Colonel Kelly had been called away, Colonel Trigg placed the 7th Florida on the 54th Virginia's left and advanced. Trigg also discovered Bushrod Johnson's men atop Horseshoe Ridge to his west, but they declined to join in, having run out of bullets and endured more than their share of fighting for the day. By now it was so dark that the movement was more of a grope than a charge, but the poor visibility worked to Trigg's advantage. From the ranks of the 7th Florida, Sgt. Robert Watson of Company K observed that he and his fellow Floridians reached "the foot of the hill at dark. The enemy seeing us sent a man towards us to see whether we were their own men or not, with directions to fire if we were enemies but we took him before he could fire his gun, there for the Yankees took it for granted that we were their own men."[19]

Atop the hill, meanwhile, Lieutenant Scott of the 89th Ohio spotted the slowly approaching enemy. "A column of men had been seen to move along the hollow at the bottom of the hill we were on, but through the gathering darkness and smoke of battle we could not tell who they were," wrote the Buckeye officer. "By this time the firing had pretty nearly ceased. Soon the column in the hollow halted and gave the order 'front.'"[20]

The finale proved anticlimactic. "We then proceed[ed] to the top of the hill within about 50 yards of them and halted and took 30 prisoners," clamed Sergeant Watson of the 7th Florida, "when the Yankees opened a fierce fire on us. We soon silenced them." Whatever fire there was, it was certainly not "fierce." Lieutenant Scott remembered the helplessness felt by the Buckeyes: "It was impossible to tell who they were until they got within ten feet of us, when through the gloom we could see that their uniforms were gray. It was too

18 "Dear Colonel," Carlton to McMahan, August 8, 1889, Sullivan Collection, BGSU; Turchin, *Chickamauga*, 207. The 89th originally belonged to Turchin's brigade, and the Russian took an interest in how they came to be captured.

19 *OR* 30, pt. 2, 432; Entry for September 20, 1863, Robert Watson Diary, Florida State Archives.

20 Turchin, *Chickamauga*, 207. While not definitive, the evidence suggests Trigg placed the 7th Florida into an apparent gap between the 54th Virginia and the 6th Florida.

late then to do anything even if we had any ammunition." The men of the 89th began to lay down their arms.[21]

The situation was equally anxious and confused among the men of the 21st Ohio. The first prisoner Watson described turned out to be Captain Henry Alban, who, like Le Favour, stole forward down the slope to try and identify Trigg's approaching line. Ohio Sergeant John Bolton recalled Alban's departure and the uncertainty that followed: "Captain Alban stepped down the hill to see what troops they were, [and] when he was quietly taken prisoner, First Sergeant Celestine Crochard of Company D also stepped down to ascertain what troops were there, and was likewise taken prisoner." As the mysterious line neared, one of the Federals demanded to know who they were. "Jeff Davis's men," came the reply. As if the dark and battle smoke weren't disorienting enough, now this simple name confusion added to the mess. To Capt. Charles A. Vantine of Company I, "Jeff Davis's men" meant Federals from Union Brig. Gen. Jefferson C. Davis's division of Tom Crittenden's XXI Corps. Trigg's men, of course, were referring to the Confederate president. The mistake was understandable and readily apparent within a few moments—but by then it was too late.[22]

According to Sergeant Bolton, some Ohioans were unwilling to simply give up so easily after the day's grueling fight and tried to run. Unfortunately for them, they ran straight into the 6th Florida, which had worked around to the Union rear. The flight triggered a volley from the 54th Virginia (on the 7th's right) directly into the milling mass of intermingled Rebels and Yankees. Only a handful of the 21st escaped. Private H. H. Van Camp of Company C was one of those who bolted. Determined not to become a prisoner, Van Camp informed Major McMahan that he had "stayed all day, but would stay no longer." "Save yourself if you can," responded McMahan. With this permission, "about 12 or 15 of us broke over the hilltop." Bolton also chanced a run. He was still mounted, having ridden out earlier in search of the ordnance train, and his horse had thus far escaped injury. "I threw myself flat . . . and with spurs into the flanks of the old war horse 'Jim' rushed through their line of battle." Rebel bullets plucked at his clothes and his mount as they went, including one that

21 Entry for September 20, 1863, Watson Diary, Florida State Archives; Turchin, *Chickamauga*, 207.

22 Canfield, *History of the 21st Regiment*, 144; *OR* 30, pt. 1, 395.

grazed Jim's neck and another that pierced Bolton's hat, but that was the worst of it. Bolton and several others slipped away to safety.[23]

The rest of the 21st Ohio was not so lucky. McMahan, a number of officers, and about 100 others were captured. The regiment officially reported 243 total casualties, including 28 killed, 84 wounded, and 131 missing, but some of the wounded were also captured, and some of those missing were very likely among the dead scattered across the ridge. The next morning at Rossville, only 106 men with rifles were present to stack arms. The 89th Ohio was similarly depleted, reporting 253 total casualties, of which 171 were recorded as missing and presumed captured. Private William Kerns of Company H claimed that 177 men of the 89th fell into Rebel hands, a figure that certainly included some of the wounded.[24]

While the capture of the two Ohio regiments occupied Trigg's leftmost regiments, his 54th Virginia was accepting the surrender of the 22nd Michigan. Wolverine sergeant Marvin Boget remembered that "just at dusk our ammunition gave out, and the Johnnies had advanced on our right and left as we could tell by the yelling[.] Finally they closed in on us with guns pointing us in the face and a command to 'throw down your guns and lie down on the ground[.]' I tell you I wasn't long in obeying." The 22nd yielded up the single largest haul of prisoners. The outfit's recorded losses amounted to 32 dead, 96 wounded, and 261 missing, for a staggering 85% of its engaged strength.[25]

In addition to the prisoners, Trigg recorded the capture of five of the six Union regimental flags and a large haul of small arms. Men of the 54th Virginia captured the state and Federal colors of the 22nd Michigan, the Federal colors of the 89th Ohio, and the state colors of the 21st Ohio. The 21st's national colors fell into the hands of the 7th Florida. Private C. O. Bailey of that regiment wrote home a week later and described the captured banner as "a beautiful thing." A few clever Yankees managed to slip one of the 89th's flags

23 Entry for September 20, 1863, Watson Diary, Florida State Archives; H. H. Van Camp, "Chickamauga: The Stubborn Fight made by the 21st Ohio," *National Tribune*, September 4, 1884; John H. Bolton, "Chickamauga, September 20, 1863," Bolton Papers, OHS.

24 H. M. Provenmire, "Diary of Jacob Adams, Private in Company F, 21st O.V.V.I.," *Ohio Historical Quarterly*, vol. XXXVIII, no. 4 (October, 1929) 653; Addendum to Entry for September 20, 1863, William Kerns Diary, AHEC.

25 Boget Letter, 22nd Michigan file, CCNMP. As noted earlier, these kinds of losses place the 22nd Michigan in a rare and unfortunate category; of being among the hardest fighting regiments of the war, with the attendant lengthy casualty list.

out of the closing gray net. According to Trigg, Pvt. J. H. M. Moseley of the 6th Florida captured a Buckeye flag, but "while guarding prisoners to the rear he passed a small party of men" who claimed the colors as their own. "Being unable to distinguish these men in the dark and supposing them to be a squad detailed by me [Trigg] to receive the captured colors, he gave them up." Moseley's trophy was not seen again.[26]

Other booty consisted of 1,500 assorted rifles, including many Colts—a novelty for the Rebels. In honor of their capture, General Preston ordered that a number of the revolving rifles be distributed to regimental color guards in both Trigg's and Kelly's brigades to "commemorate . . . the great battle in which they were first engaged and achieved such brilliant distinction." Other, more informal exchanges also took place. Private Bailey recalled how he and his comrades "went in on Saturday with musket[s] and when we came [out] on Sunday we all had either springfields or enfields[,] we captured them all over the field." The butcher's bill for all this bounty proved miraculously small, at least on Trigg's part: seven casualties in the 6th Florida, nine more in the 54th Virginia, and an unrecorded (but similarly small) number in the 7th Florida.[27]

One more Union regiment played silent spectator to the surrender that unfolded on the west side of Hill Three. The all-but-forgotten 9th Indiana of General Hazen's brigade was still on Hill Two. Its commander, Col. Isaac Suman, was as nervous about remaining there as the men under his leadership. One of General Brannan's aides had led them forward earlier to cover the larger retreat, until they met Lt. Col. Henry Boynton and the 35th Ohio. Boynton's men were on the hill for roughly the same mission: to guard Brannan's retreat. Boynton ordered Suman to take his Hoosiers up to the crest of Hill Two. Suman balked at the idea, as did a number of his officers. "He is trying to work you, Colonel," cautioned Maj. George H. Carter. Suman agreed, telling Boynton, "I don't know that I ought to take orders from you." Angry whispers followed. The Hoosiers were "a lot of damned cowards!" snarled a frustrated Boynton. In later years, the 9th's regimental adjutant, Stephen P. Hodsden, remembered this accusation as the galvanizing moment that shamed the

26 "Dear Father," September 27, 1863, C. O. Bailey Papers, University of Florida; *OR* 30, pt. 2, 432.

27 Newspaper clipping, September 21, 1863, Gracie-Harper Correspondence, 58th North Carolina file, CCNMP; "Dear Father," September 27, 1863, C. O. Bailey Papers, University of Florida; *OR* 30, pt. 2, 437-440.

regiment into accepting Boynton's orders. Perhaps this was true. The presence of Brannan's aide, who was directed to lead them into position at the general's behest, probably had as much or more to do with it than did state or unit pride. In any case, the 9th Indiana moved forward.[28]

The Hoosier troops worked their way up the hill under the belief they were being deliberately sacrificed to buy time for the rest of the army to escape. They reached the summit of Hill Two and halted. The time of their arrival was after 7:00 p.m., perhaps closer to 8:00. It was certainly dark. There was no firing and everything was eerily quiet. Captain Amasa Johnson remembered thinking the battle was "over for the day" until his attention was drawn to "a singular noise to the right." It took him a moment to realize that Yankees and Rebels were intermingled there, with the Federals apparently being taken prisoner. The shocked captain hurried off to find Colonel Suman. Drawn in turn by "an unnecessary amount of talking," reported Suman, "I went over to see what it meant, and to my surprise, I found the enemy demanding our troops to surrender." Lieutenant Thomas Prickett of Company E watched the colonel as he went "over the ridge to see what was going on." Suman suddenly found himself in the middle of a Confederate line, with a Rebel officer pointing a pistol at him. The quick-thinking Suman informed his would-be captor that "I have already surrendered." Satisfied, the Rebel moved on and Suman slipped away in the darkness and confusion.[29]

When Suman did not immediately return, several other Hoosiers crept forward to investigate. Captain Thomas Madden of Company A sent Lt. Thomas Thompson to find the missing colonel. When Thompson did not come back, Madden ordered a sergeant and a corporal down the hill. They, too, failed to return. Just then, recalled Pvt. Byron Dunn of Company C, Lieutenant Thompson reappeared "greatly excited. His hat and sword were gone, and he reported that not more than twenty paces away the hill swarmed with Rebels." Like Suman, Thompson managed to escape in an unguarded moment, and returned in all haste to the 9th. The unnamed sergeant and corporal were not so lucky; both fell into enemy hands and ended up in Andersonville.[30]

28 Gracie, *The Truth About Chickamauga*, 175-176.

29 Johnson, *The Ninth Indiana Regiment at Chickamauga*, 4; *OR* 30, pt. 1, 769; "Dearest Matilda," September 24, 1863, Thomas Prickett Letters, InHS.

30 B. A. Dimm, "The Close of Chickamauga," *National Tribune*, May 2, 1907. There is no B. A. Dimm listed on the roster of the 9th Indiana, but there is a Byron A. Dunn, wounded at

Absent their commanding officer, members of the 9th Indiana sent Brannan's aide back to the general with word of the surrender. Brannan, in turn, sent orders back to Boynton's 35th Ohio to "hold the position." Boynton left his Ohioans and went forward to the 9th Indiana to see what was happening for himself.[31]

Colonel Suman, meanwhile, had rejoined his regiment. Captain Dyer B. McConnell of Company D recalled suddenly hearing the welcome voice of the colonel "right behind my men, saying 'March right out this way. . . . I am not going to surrender my regiment!'" Suman directed a pair of companies to face farther to the right, and then ordered them to fire a volley down the hill into the Confederates and newly captured Federals. After that volley, recorded Suman, "Our men ran one way and the Rebels ran another." During the withdrawal, Suman ran into Boynton, "who appeared to think it impossible that the enemy had gained that point." Recalling their earlier whispered confrontation, Colonel Suman scornfully recorded that Boynton "had but 30 steps to walk to convince himself, but he seemed not inclined."[32]

So much about the fighting at Chickamauga was confusing to the men who waged it, and even the Hoosier volley and immediate aftermath—which marked the end of the fighting on Horseshoe Ridge—triggered its own series of controversies. The Confederates found Suman's surprise volley a bit disconcerting but not especially lethal. "Just after we took the prisoners," noted Private Bailey, "we were fired into but no one in the [7th Florida] was hurt." According to Lt. Col. John J. Wade of the 54th Virginia, "a party of the enemy who lay concealed in a short distance from my regiment poured a volley into us, evidently with the intention of producing some confusion in order to affect the escape of the prisoners. Only 1 man was injured by this fire, and he was a mounted orderly of the brigade commander." The unlucky aide was James Chenault of the 54th, who had been detailed to serve on Colonel Trigg's staff.

Chickamauga and Nashville, whom I think to be the same man. Dunn never identified the two enlisted men, but the rolls of Company A, the 9th note that Sgt. Adam Keiste and Cpl. Asbury S. McCormick were both captured at Chickamauga; Keiste died in prison and McCormick lived to be mustered out on February 22, 1865.

31 Gracie, *The Truth About Chickamauga*, 325; *OR* 30, pt. 1, 392.

32 Dyer B. McConnell, "Address given at the 1891 reunion of the 9th Indiana," 9th Indiana file, CCNMP; OR 30, pt. 1, 769.

Wade was slightly mistaken. Chenault was not hit by any of the bullets from Suman's volley, but he did perish as a consequence of it.[33]

The Confederates thought the volley was yet another incident of friendly fire and moved to put a stop to it; Chenault was dispatched to figure out who was doing the shooting. Both Suman and Boynton reported that Chenault rode amongst them, but their recollections thereafter differ significantly. According to Suman, the mounted man identified himself as the colonel of the 35th Virginia of Simon Buckner's Corps, took the sword of one of the 9th's lieutenants, and was shot down in retaliation. The Hoosier lieutenant in question was probably Samuel Dustan of Company F, who later recounted the incident. "A mounted officer—at least he carried a revolver and sword—rode up the hill under the big tree where I stood. . . . He halted and asked 'who's command is this?' and on being told it was the 9th Indiana started to back off, but I had hold of his bridle rein," he continued, "and just then I heard the report of a gun close behind, and as the man fell forward I caught him. . . . [W]hen I asked who he was . . . he said General Twiggs or Briggs, or some name like that."[34]

In Boynton's version of the story, "a rebel general, believed to be General Gregg, here rode up and asked whose troops we were; at the reply 'Thirty-Fifth Ohio' he wheeled, but received a volley . . . which riddled him and his horse and raked the line of rebels." Writing just a few days after the battle, Cpl. Robert H. H. Tyner of the 9th Indiana remembered things this way: "They marched up and took two regiments up on our right prisoners. As they were retreating we saw them, and I went out in advance and hailed them. Their Col. advanced to within 20 paces of me and asked, 'who are you?' Seeing his gray uniform I did not answer, but demanded: 'what forces are those?' 'A part of Gen. Twiggs,' he answered." Tyner whipped his rifle up at the ready. "He wheeled his horse to run, and I pulled the trigger: my gun snapped [but did not discharge,] but several of the boys were watching and fired, bringing him to the ground. . . . He was shot in seven places."[35]

33 "Dear Father," September 27, 1863, C. O. Bailey Papers, University of Florida; *OR* 30, pt. 2, 439.

34 *OR* 30, pt. 1, 769; Gracie, *The Truth About Chickamauga*, 447.

35 *OR* 30, pt. 1, 436; "Dear Parents, September 24, 1863," *Marshall County Republican*, October 8, 1863. General Gregg had been badly wounded on September 19, so he could not possibly have been present.

Many years later, Capt. Angus McMillan provided a Confederate view of this incident. "I was in command of all the companies of the left wing of [the 6th Florida]. James Chenault was ordered to see who the men in the bushes were, when a party of Yankees asked who *he* was. When told, they said 'Damn him, shoot him.' They fired some shots, and he, being on horseback, was the only man wounded. This fire did not have any effect upon our regiment, which also fired upon the men in the bushes. [Then] there was an order not to fire. This order was given by Colonel Wade, who thought the firing was on our own men."[36]

One more Federal would claim a measure of fame from the incident. When the 9th Indiana's volley drew everyone's attention, a handful of the newly captured Yankees took advantage of the diversion to escape. One was young John Clem, the 22nd Michigan's 12-year-old former drummer boy. According to Clem, "a rebel colonel rode up and yelled at me 'Surrender, you damned little Yankee!' Raising my musket without aiming, I pulled the trigger and he fell from his horse, badly wounded." This show of resistance availed him not at all, and Clem was made prisoner along with the rest of the Michiganders. However, once the 9th Indiana opened fire, Clem escaped during the ensuing confusion. A Rebel guard ordered a number of the 22nd to lie down. "When order was restored and the order was given to march on, John and [one of the 22nd's Lieutenants] feigned death and later escaped." Clem's story was taken up by a correspondent for *Harper's Weekly*, which in turn fired the imagination of the nation and drew General Thomas's notice. Clem was promoted to sergeant and made one of Thomas' couriers. After the war he made the army a career, and despite failing the West Point entrance exam, managed a direct commission and retired in 1915 as a brigadier general.[37]

Regardless of how Chenault was killed, and by whom, those shots marked the last firing on Horseshoe Ridge. Both the 9th Indiana and the 35th Ohio

36 Gracie, *The Truth About Chickamauga*, 340.

37 Since no Confederate colonels from Trigg's or Kelly's brigades fell here, just who Clem shot, or if he shot anyone at all, remains open to speculation. It is probable that Clem witnessed the Chenault incident, and with the passage of time embraced it as his own. See Pavelka, "Where Were You Johnny Shiloh?," 40. Pavelka's account is an excellent examination of the various claims made by John Clem during the decades following the Civil War. Pavelka sorts the facts from the many fictions that still surround Clem to this day. Clem retired as a colonel, but received an automatic promotion to brigadier general. Later, an act of Congress gave him a second star. In later years he also claimed (almost certainly falsely) to have fought at Shiloh in April 1862, and so earned the sobriquet "the drummer boy of Shiloh."

retired, first back into Snodgrass Field and then on to Rossville. Suman reported that the 9th "fell back three miles and camped for the night." Boynton merely recorded that the 35th, "together with the troops on the hill . . . fell back to Rossville." As they did so, both units passed the 68th and 101st Indiana, still in line near the Snodgrass cabin. As Suman's and Boynton's men filed past, George Steele of the 68th recalled Boynton's final instructions: "We were directed to take position in your [Boynton's] front, and to wait until you had cleared the field, say ten minutes. . . . [W]e were to follow and to see that all troops able to travel should precede us." Guided by Captain C. A. Cilley, Van Derveer's topographic engineer, these two regiments were the last Federal troops to leave the field.[38]

More Federals might have made good their escape if not for the timely re-appearance of Kelly's brigade. It will be recalled that General Preston had called away Colonel Kelly just as Trigg was preparing to advance. Kelly's abrupt departure halted his men before they had taken more than a few steps forward. Colonel Hawkins of the 5th Kentucky took charge of his own regiment and Maj. James M. French's 63rd Virginia. While waiting for Kelly to return, Hawkins ordered his men to scavenge rounds from the cartridge boxes of the dead and wounded. They had just finished when "Colonel Trigg's mounted orderly came galloping" down the hill. "[We] have found the enemy," reported the rider, "and that if I [Hawkins] would move my two regiments forward we would capture them." Hawkins sent the courier back to inform Trigg that he was coming, and "moved rapidly to form junction" with the other brigade. Kelly's remaining regiment, the already rattled 58th North Carolina, did not initially participate because Col. John Palmer was awaiting Kelly's return and only belatedly discovered that Colonel Hawkins had moved forward without him.[39]

Hawkins's regiments reached the summit of the hill in time to witness both the capture of the three Union commands and the ensuing disruption caused by the 9th Indiana and 35th Ohio. "As the column commenced moving with the prisoners," reported Hawkins, "a volley was fired into our ranks, causing a good deal of confusion, it then being nightfall. Many of the prisoners scattered.

38 *OR* 30, pt. 1, 436, 770; "My Dear General," Steele to Boynton, June 7, 1895, 101st Indiana file, CCNMP; High, *Sixty-Eighth Indiana*, 102.

39 Hawkins Papers, Kentucky Historical Society; Gracie, *The Truth About Chickamauga*, 329; OR 30, pt. 2, 446.

Colonel Trigg's command moved off, leaving them. They would have made their escape had I not recaptured them."[40]

Once he realized the troops on both his left and right were moving forward, Colonel Palmer pushed his 58th North Carolina up the hill, conforming to the general movement by angling his line to the right as best he could. The effort netted about 20 Yankees. Shortly after, however, the 58th found itself alone once more when Trigg's men fell back between the 58th and Kelly's other two regiments. Palmer intended to collect the entire brigade and occupy Hill Three, but could find neither the 5th Kentucky nor the 54th Virginia, which had departed when Trigg fell back. Acting alone, Palmer led the 58th to the crest, secured the area, and began collecting the dead and the wounded.[41]

While Palmer was occupying Hill Three and Hawkins was busy rounding up wayward Yankees, Kelly returned to assume command. The fighting was by now clearly over. The unknown troops in the bushes were gone. With about one-third of his brigade already casualties, the darkness made any additional advance an exercise in futility. Kelly instead concentrated on securing the fruits already won. Besides, Kelly had a bone to pick with the Federal prisoners.

Colonel Carlton and Lt. Col. William H. Glenn of the 89th Ohio, both still mounted, also tried to escape in the confusion of Suman's volley. They were recognized as Federals and quickly seized, in part, thought Carlton, because he was still smoking his pipe. When order was restored, Carlton, Glenn, and Colonel Le Favour were brought before Kelly, who, according to Carlton, "after mentioning his heavy losses during the day and making some complimentary remarks in regard to our troops," accused them of pretending to surrender and then duplicitously firing into his ranks. Carlton was taken aback. "I didn't know of any of our command who had for a moment thought of surrendering." Both Carlton and Le Favour insisted to Kelly they were under the impression the Rebels were proposing to surrender to *them*. After a few

40 Ibid., 444. This was the second incident of taking fire after surrender to which Colonel Hawkins was party. The first took place a short time earlier when Colonel Kelly was rallying the brigade to go back up the hill, but before Colonel Trigg advanced. Most descriptions of these incidents merge them into the one event, taking place during the final surrender. Even Hawkins's papers conflate these events into a single instance, which Hawkins regarded as treachery. However, all of the *Official Records* reports for Kelly's brigade make it clear there were two encounters of this kind—one before Trigg advanced, and one after.

41 *OR* 30, pt. 2, 446.

Colonel Carlton (right), led the 89th Ohio.
The Truth About Chickamauga

minutes of debate, Kelly was apparently satisfied with this answer. In his report, the Confederate brigade commander blamed the incident on nerves, and that the fire was "drawn by an unauthorized shot from [their] ranks." With that settled, the matter of military courtesies could be observed. Lieutenant Edward Scott of the 89th, who was also present, recalled hearing Carlton ask Kelly, "Do you wish my sword, sir?" Kelly graciously declined, and sent the three officers to the rear.[42]

As it turned out, Carlton and Kelly were not only fellow West Pointers but enrolled at the academy at the same time (though not in the same class). It appears as though they did not recognize one another on the evening of September 20. Kelly was appointed in 1857, part of the Class of 1861, but resigned in December 1860. Carlton, an upperclassman, entered the academy in 1854 and graduated in 1859. Carlton's West Point status proved useful in affirming his honesty. In one of his trips to see General Preston, Kelly passed word of the false surrender incident up the chain of command. When the Union officers were brought before General Buckner, the Kentuckian demanded of Carlton (who, still mounted and carrying his sword, was mistaken as the senior officer) "to know if I had any excuse to offer for it. No explanation that I could make would satisfy him until one of his officers of Art[iller]y, an acquaintance of mine, informed him that I was a [West Pointer]. He did not seem to be satisfied with my statement that I knew about the circumstances of Col. Kelley's [sic] proposal [concerning the surrender] until he learned that I was a graduate."[43]

42 Carlton Papers, LOC; *OR* 30, pt. 2, 441; Weaver and Fenner, *Sacrifice at Chickamauga*, 106.

43 Carlton Papers, LOC; Jones, "John Herbert Kelly," 3; Francis B. Heitman, *Historical Register and Dictionary of the United States Army, from its Organization, September 29, 1789, to March 2, 1903*. 2 vols. (Olde Soldier Books, 1988), vol. 1, 282. In later years, Carlton recorded his Chickamauga

With their bona fides established, the Federal officers were treated as normal prisoners and eventually ended up in Libby Prison. After nearly two weeks of prison life, Carlton found the chance to sum up his emotions: "I received a couple of pretty sharp raps from spent bullets which in addition to loss of sleep, poor food, and general disgust renders me sore cross and very much dissatisfied with my situation." Doubtless he spoke for all those men taken prisoner on Horseshoe Ridge.[44]

In later years Maj. John C. Smith, the officer who ordered Le Favour back up Hill Three to cover the retreat in the first place, would insist that "the result was the loss of the two [really three] regiments but the saving of the division" and that "my order was afterwards approved by General Steedman." In reality, the sacrifice was probably not needed or warranted. If Smith had ridden just a bit farther east, he would have soon discovered that Brannan and Wood were already gone, leaving only their own rear guards still in place. Even the lack of firing from that direction suggested there was now little need for the mission. No one paid a greater price for the lack of command cohesion on Horseshoe Ridge than the men of the 21st Ohio, 22nd Michigan, and 89th Ohio.[45]

---

experiences several times in correspondence with various parties, but never mentioned Kelly as a fellow academy man.

44 "Dear Sadie," October 1, 1863, Carlton Papers, LOC.

45 Smith, *The Right of the Federal Army*, 14.

Chapter Twenty-Nine

Loose Ends: Crawfish Spring, Chattanooga, and Rossville:

Sunday, 2:00 p.m. to Midnight

While George Thomas and the remnants of the Army of the Cumberland were fighting for their lives against Braxton Bragg's attacking Confederates, Brig. Gen. Robert Mitchell waited anxiously for news at the Gordon house, some four miles south of Horseshoe Ridge. His had been an afternoon filled with gnawing uncertainty. His last communication with anyone in authority was hours earlier at noon, when Col. Gates Thruston arrived with orders to close up on the army's right, which was sliding its way north. About that time, Brig. Gen. George Crook's cavalry force at Glass Mill was beaten and fell back in disorder. It looked for a time like the next major fight would happen at Crawfish Spring. Inexplicably (to the Federals, at least) Joe Wheeler and his Rebel cavalry did not pursue their advantage. The arrival of Col. Sidney Post's brigade provided some welcome relief for Mitchell, bolstering his defense by the addition of another 1,200 infantry to his available force. The shifting fortunes of the fight farther north, however, which could be tracked by the ebb and flow of battle noise—first moving right to left, and then fading northward—suggested nothing good for the Union cause.

Wheeler's failure to follow Crook stemmed from a conflict of orders. Shortly after routing the Yankees at Glass Mill, Wheeler received two sets of instructions from two separate commanders. As noted in Chapter 18, General

Longstreet asked Wheeler to ride north and help him pursue the Yankees up the Dry Valley Road. At the same time, General Bragg wanted the cavalryman to move north a couple miles and capture Lee and Gordon's Mills. Wheeler decided to follow Bragg's instructions, which under the circumstances was understandable. Wheeler, however, seems not to have informed Longstreet.

Wheeler's next decision is less comprehensible. After his victory at Glass Mill, Wheeler had both of his divisions on the west side of West Chickamauga Creek. The fastest way to execute Bragg's orders was to ride north along the west bank and take the Union defenders at Lee and Gordon's in the flank. This movement would entail some risk by exposing Wheeler's own left flank to a Union counterattack from Crawfish Spring that could potentially trap him against Chickamauga Creek—if the Federals recovered enough to mount such an effort. Wheeler, however, had his full corps on hand. He could easily screen the enemy at Crawfish Spring with one division and strike toward Lee and Gordon's with the other. A means of escape was not out of the question if the need arose, for there were additional fords across the Chickamauga between the two mill sites.

Instead of the direct route, Wheeler elected for a more roundabout approach. He pulled his command back across the creek, retraced his steps along the Glass Mill Road almost through Wharton's campsites of the previous night, and turned north on the La Fayette Road to approach Lee and Gordon's Mills from the southeast. Years later, trooper Pvt. John Wyeth defended this move by claiming Wheeler wasn't aware of Longstreet's decisive success (which was probably true) or he would have simply turned north and rendered the entire argument moot. Wheeler never explained his reasoning.[1]

Wheeler's decision meant that his column of some 7,000 troopers would have to funnel through the choke points of the crossings not once but twice. Worse yet, if the Federals held Lee and Gordon's Mills in strength, the Rebels would have to force that second crossing under fire. The fights at both Reed's and Alexander's bridges on September 18 aptly demonstrated that such attacks were costly in both time and manpower. Fortunately for Joe Wheeler, Lee and Gordon's Mills was only manned by a Union picket line consisting of Capt. Thomas McCahan's detachment from the 9th Pennsylvania Cavalry, and the small outpost was even then preparing to fall back.

1 R. F. Bunting Letter, *Rome Tri-Weekly Telegraph*, November 27, 1863; Wyeth, *Sabre and Scalpel*, 248-249.

It was near 3:00 p.m. when Mitchell got word of what was happening with the army when one of XX Corps commander Alexander McCook's couriers reined in his mount with news. None of it was good. The aide explained the morning's disaster and also relayed McCook's verbal order "to fall back, [as] our right had been turned." This instruction, however, conflicted with General Rosecrans's injunction to hold Crawfish Spring at all costs. Mitchell was reluctant to order an immediate retreat. Instead, he split the difference. He dispatched a rider to call in Col. Edward McCook's horsemen from Lee and Gordon's Mills, but also instructed McCook to detach the 9th Pennsylvania and send it north along the Dry Valley Road in the hope of developing a clearer picture of what had befallen the rest of the army. As Lt. Col. Roswell M. Russell of the 9th explained, "I was ordered to push my regiment at a trot . . . and open communication, if possible, with General Sheridan." As for the rest of the order, noted Colonel McCook, he complied promptly "on a gallop."[2]

Mitchell also directed Col. Archibald Campbell to take the 1st Tennessee and 4th Indiana cavalry regiments, about 900 men in all, and ride west across Missionary Ridge. Their mission was to establish a blocking position in Chattanooga Valley and thus essentially hold the back door open so that Mitchell's force could safely retreat in that direction if circumstances turned out to be as dire as the XX Corps commander's communiqué indicated.[3]

Campbell's departure elicited a great deal of anxiety amongst the Federal wounded, many of whom believed his leaving was an ominous sign, and none of whom wanted to be captured. Many ambulances jammed with injured had already departed, but there were far more wounded men than wheeled vehicles to carry them. Corporal William Carter of the 1st Tennessee Cavalry recalled a heart-rending scene as his regiment prepared to move out: "Our boys began to dismount and place a wounded soldier in his stead, and in this way hundreds [more] could have been brought from the red field." Unfortunately, they would also impede the regiment if fighting was required. Many of these injured could barely (if at all) sit the saddle at a walk, let alone escape on foot, and no one knew what opposition the regiment might face on the distant side of Missionary Ridge. The regiment's commander, Lt. Col. James P. Brownlow, was having none of it.

2 *OR* 30, pt. 1, 893, 896, 904.

3 Ibid., 900.

Brownlow, continued Carter, "made all [of the wounded] dismount and return to the hospital."[4]

By this time Wheeler had reached Lee and Gordon's. Shortly after the 9th Pennsylvania Cavalry departed northward, Colonel McCook and the 1st Wisconsin Cavalry were abruptly called back towards the Mills. "Captain McCormick, of General Mitchell's staff," wrote Edward McCook, "overtook me and ordered me back to the right . . . as the enemy had attacked in force and were pressing us hard."[5]

The only force left behind to oppose any crossing were the two companies of the 9th Pennsylvania ordered out as videttes that morning. Captain McCahan, commanding Company M, recalled that the skirmishing began to pick up by mid-afternoon. The picket post at the Mills let Pvt. Oliver Ball do most of the firing, for as McCahan noted, "he was the best shot in our regiment with a carbine." Ball had already picked off three of the enemy when "a Rebel Major . . . [on] a snow white horse" appeared. The Federals remembered this man, for they had seen him on other fields riding in front of his own lines and often almost into their own. "He was so brave, no one would fire on him," continued McCahan. That was then, however, and this was now. "[As] he rode down to the edge of the creek Ball shot at him, he was seen to fall, throw[ing] his arms around the neck of his horse."[6]

These Rebels were but the precursor to Wheeler's main body. As his leading elements approached the Mills, Wheeler dismounted the bulk of his troopers and cautiously advanced them to the creek's eastern bank. Watching these men swarm forward in large numbers, McCahan knew he would soon have no choice but to retreat. "I held my men in line (skirmish) as long as I thought safe," but as the threat grew "I then rallied them" and fell back. "Shortly the rebels began to cross in force."[7]

Once opposition evaporated, the initially cautious Confederates relaxed their guard. At the millpond, some members of the 4th Alabama Cavalry tried

4 William Randolph Carter, *History of the First Regiment of Tennessee Volunteer Cavalry in the Great War of the Rebellion, With the Armies of the Ohio and Cumberland, Under Generals Morgan, Rosecrans, Thomas, Stanley and Wilson, 1862-1865* (Gaut-Ogden Co., 1902), 97-98.

5 *OR* 30, pt. 1, 896.

6 Entry for September 20, Thomas S. McCahan Diary, Historical Society of Pennsylvania. The Rebel major remains unidentified.

7 Ibid.

to keep their feet dry by crossing single file along the top of the dam. Alert to the havoc a single canister round could wreak on such a target, one of 4th's officers ordered everyone down into the water. Once across, however, Private Wyeth discovered "that we could have gone over . . . in perfect safety." The Mill buildings were abandoned, and the Federals were falling back to Crawfish Spring.[8]

It was at this juncture that the 1st Wisconsin thundered up, interposing itself between Wheeler's vanguard and the springs. The arrival of the Badgers set the stage for another large engagement, but for reasons that remain unclear, nothing happened. Wheeler later claimed his men "crossed the river, and vigorously assailed him. After a short time he commenced retreating in confusion." Federal accounts, however, differ. Wisconsinite Horace T. Persons claimed that while the regiment was "within a mile and a half of where the hard fighting was [here Persons is referring to the infantry battle off to the north] . . . [we] did not do much fighting [ourselves.]" This assertion was confirmed by the reports of the 2nd Indiana and 2nd Tennessee, both positioned to support the Badgers. Colonel Daniel M. Ray, temporarily commanding Edward McCook's brigade while the latter led the division, covered the action here in one terse sentence: "the brigade was formed in line near Crawfish Spring and continued skirmishing with the enemy until 4 o'clock, when we were ordered to fall back to Dry Valley." Losses in both regiments in the entire battle totaled only nine men: one killed, four wounded, and four missing. None of them fell on the afternoon of the 20th. Chaplain Robert F. Bunting of the 8th Texas Cavalry corroborated the relative lack of conflict. Bunting observed that while Lee and Gordon's Mills "had been a strong point," it was now deserted. "Crossing over the cavalry pressed forward, and although in hearing of the constant roar of small arms to our right and the booming of cannon, yet the country was clear, and for several miles we advanced to find that our left wing under Longstreet had driven the enemy before them."[9]

The reality was clear: it took Wheeler a very long time to cross and deploy both divisions. While he was arranging his men, General Mitchell was confirming his own worst fears. The 9th Pennsylvania's probe up the Dry Valley Road demonstrated that Sheridan and his infantry division had vanished

8 Wyeth, *Sabre and Scalpel*, 248-249.

9 *OR* 30, pt. 2, 521; "Dear Wife," September 30, 1863, Horace T. Persons Papers, WHS; *OR* 30, pt. 1, 907; R. F. Bunting Letter, *Rome Tri-Weekly Telegraph*, November 27, 1863.

somewhere into the North Georgia hills. In fact, the entire Union right flank was gone. The 9th's commander, Lieutenant Colonel Russell, found only Rebels: "Proceeding about 2 miles I found the enemy strongly posted upon the crest of a hill around which the road passed, and which his artillery completely commanded." Russell reported this information back to Mitchell and began deploying his men "for the purpose of forcing or turning" this Confederate line, when "I received orders from General Mitchell to return immediately."[10]

As described earlier, Russell's probe had one additional impact on the larger battle: "the enemy strongly posted upon the crest of a hill" were almost certainly Col. Robert Trigg's 1st Florida Cavalry (Dismounted) and 7th Florida infantry, which had been sent to this area of the field to investigate a report of Union horsemen. "I was ordered by General Buckner to move back on the Chattanooga Road with two of my regiments and one piece of artillery," reported Trigg, "and select a favorable position to resist the enemy's cavalry, which it was understood had passed to our rear and was moving on that road." Trigg never saw Russell's men (or if he did, mistook them for Wheeler's troopers), but he did run across some Rebel horsemen and concluded the report was in error. Neither the Pennsylvanians nor the Floridians exchanged shots. Russell's reconnaissance, however, fragmented Trigg's brigade during its subsequent attack against Horseshoe Ridge.[11]

Russell's information made it clear that McCook's corps was missing, but its location remained unknown. It fell to Colonel Campbell, redeployed to the far side of Missionary Ridge, to provide additional details: he relayed that the XX Corps was scattered, routed, and streaming back toward Chattanooga. Campbell deployed his two regiments in defensive positions, alert to Rebel pursuit from either the east or south. None materialized.[12]

While Mitchell waited, Colonel Post chafed. As far as he was concerned, it was his duty to find a way to report to General McCook, who would be deeply concerned about the safety and status of his corps trains. If the entire brigade couldn't join him, perhaps one man could. Captain Robert Hale of Company I, 75th Illinois, who was serving as the brigade provost-marshal, volunteered to try. According to the 75th's regimental historian, William S. Dodge, the effort

10 *OR* 30, pt. 1, 904-905.

11 Ibid., pt. 2, 431.

12 Ibid., pt. 1, 900.

"was deemed rashness by Mitchell, and was considered doubtful by Post; but so earnest was Hale to venture that both consented." Despite these concerns and the bloody chaos of the day, Hale not only succeeded in finding Alexander McCook but managed to return to Post with information about the extent of the Union rout and new orders instructing the colonel to remain with Mitchell. Delighted and impressed, Post sent him off again on a second round trip and later honored Hale with a special mention in his battle report.[13]

With Campbell's and Hale's information in hand, Mitchell realized that retreat was his only viable option. Russell was immediately recalled. Disengagement could prove tricky, especially if Wheeler pressed an assault. Neither side had a substantial numerical advantage over the other, however, especially with Post's infantry on hand. Lieutenant Chesley Mosman of the 59th Illinois, one of Post's men, noted the flurry of Union activity and concluded it meant there would be hard work ahead for him and his fellow foot soldiers. "Cavalry soon change position and we go into line for an attack that the cavalry report as momentarily expected. Well, don't that beat you," he groused.[14]

In later years, General Crook would exhibit a fair degree of contempt for his new corps commander. According to Crook, Mitchell was virtually paralyzed by the weight of the responsibility of his recently assumed command. "When I got back to where Gen. Mitchell was," charged Crook, "I found his cavalry, infantry and artillery all huddled together in this small field in a helpless condition. Gen. Mitchell came to me and said, 'General, you are a military man, I wish you would take charge and straighten things out and make the necessary dispositions.'" By his own account, Crook proceeded to do exactly that, setting things to rights and establishing a proper defense.[15]

No contemporary account bears out Crook's version of this story, or indicates that he played any greater role beyond his normal duties as commander of the Second Cavalry Division. Nor are his memoirs especially reliable for September 20. Crook's assertion that his men took charge of the rear guard, for example, is incorrect. His own report makes no mention of any such action, while other officers report their assumption of that role. In truth,

13 William Sumner Dodge, *A Waif of the War; or, the History of the Seventy-Fifth Illinois Infantry, Embracing the Entire Campaigns of the Army of the Cumberland* (Church and Goodman, Publishers, 1866), 95; *OR* 30, pt. 1, 509.

14 Gates, *Rough Side of War*, 84.

15 Schmitt, *Autobiography*, 106.

Crook—while an able soldier—could be as touchy as a society socialite snubbed at a soiree, and he resented the idea of a volunteer officer like Mitchell being his senior, especially in such a moment of crisis. If Crook manifested any outward signs of that resentment, Mitchell ignored them. In his own report, the corps commander wrote glowingly that Crook "deserves the gratitude of the entire country for the gallant manner in which he discharged his duty throughout the entire advance as well as on the battlefield at Chickamauga."[16]

After their retreat from Glass Mill around noon, Crook and Col. Eli Long spent a fair amount of time reorganizing Long's brigade, all the while expecting a renewed attack at any moment. After spending some time in line, mounted and "with drawn sabers," the Buckeyes of the 1st Ohio realized the Rebels were not coming and pushed their skirmishers back towards Glass Mill. There, recalled one of the Ohioans, "[we] took possession of the field, bringing off many of our wounded, including Colonel Cupp." From 2:00 to 4:00 p.m. the entire brigade remained in line covering the approach from Glass Mill until Mitchell ordered them to follow Campbell's command west toward Chattanooga Valley. Post's infantry and the remaining ambulatory wounded followed.[17]

These departures left five regiments of blue cavalry in the vicinity of the spring: Colonel Ray's 1st Wisconsin, 2nd Indiana, and 2nd Tennessee, along with the 2nd Michigan and 9th Pennsylvania of Campbell's command. Division commander Edward McCook took charge of this force. McCook reinforced the 1st Wisconsin with the 9th Pennsylvania, and tasked both units to act as the rear guard. Next to leave by 5:00 p.m. were Ray and the three 2nds (Indiana, Tennessee, and Michigan). The Federal rear guard probably vacated their positions between 5:00 and 5:30; leaving some 1,500 badly wounded men to the mercies of the Confederates. As if that wasn't grim enough, Maj. William A. McTeer of the 2nd Tennessee remembered that Rebel artillery shells ignited the dry grass and leaves, with the fires endangering some of the injured. "There was so much smoke it was impossible to distinguish a friend from a foe, twenty yards away," wrote McTeer. "The whole atmosphere was impregnated with the odor of gunpowder."[18]

16 *OR* 30, pt. 1, 894.

17 Anonymous, *First Ohio Cavalry Reunion Pamphlet*, 18, OHS.

18 Barnes, *Medical and Surgical History*, 267; McCammon, *Loyal Mountain Troopers*, 65.

The wounded were not completely abandoned. A number of surgeons and orderlies remained behind to care for them, and by doing so faced certain capture with them. Surgeon S. G. Menzies of the 1st Kentucky, in charge of the hospital for Palmer's division (XXI Corps), described a pitiable scene: "When the last of our vehicles left, the enemy's cavalry were within one-eighth of a mile of the hospital. About thirty men were left with four medical officers, who are doubtless in the hands of the enemy. . . . Ten men who died of their wounds were left at the hospital, unburied." Each divisional surgeon left a similar number of doctors and orderlies (a total of some 30 surgeons and roughly 200 men) behind to care for the gravely injured. Some volunteered, but most were simply ordered to remain. All hoped to be exchanged soon.[19]

Wheeler's men may not have pressed the Yankee rear guard, but as Surgeon Menzies recorded, they followed close enough to swoop in on the hospital complex within minutes of it being abandoned. The sight of the sprawling hospital complex staggered Lt. George Guild of the Confederate 4th Tennessee Cavalry: "The immense crowd of men tents, vehicles, etc., at Crawfish Springs caused us to believe at first that we had captured the whole Federal army. Dead men in rail pens for protection [from hogs and other animals] and wounded men in large circus tents were scattered about over acres of ground, with the accustomed retinue of hospital assistants and not a few shirkers from the fight."[20]

Assistant Surgeon Harry Goodale of the 21st Michigan was one of those who had remained behind. "The rebel cavalry commenced robbing the wounded of their haversacks and rations," recalled Goodale. "One soldier had a half-dozen of them coming out of a tent before I was aware of what they were doing. I took the haversacks away from him and returned them to the boys, and drove them out of the tent and had no further depredations in that line." Suitably abashed, the Confederates let Dr. Goodale continue his work until midnight, when "my physical endurance gave out."[21]

While Wheeler was assessing his prize, another courier from Longstreet galloped up with a second request for support. The fight for Horseshoe Ridge was still raging, and the exhausted Rebel infantry was gathering for a final push

19 Barnes, *Medical and Surgical History*, 280.

20 George B. Guild, *A Brief Narrative of the Fourth Tennessee Cavalry Regiment, Wheeler's Corps, Army of Tennessee* (n.p., 1913), 28.

21 Henry Goodale Recollections, Michigan State University.

against the equally worn-out Union defenders. As if to underscore the urgency of his need, a third message arrived 20 minutes later.[22]

The news once more placed Wheeler squarely on the horns of a dilemma. Longstreet's missives were important, and well within the bounds of the orders outlined by Bragg the night before. However, the retreating Federal cavalry column should be pursued as a matter of military course. In addition, Wheeler's capture of a large haul of prisoners and booty needed to be dealt with, with some of his men detailed to secure it all.

A curious passivity settled over the Rebel cavalry chief. He had begun the day aggressively enough by delivering a spirited attack against Long's Yankees at Glass Mill, but thereafter matters went awry. Even though his poorly conceived decision to approach Lee and Gordon's Mills in a roundabout manner was offset by the Union decision to abandon the crossing, Wheeler failed to launch a strong effort against the Yankees that afternoon and allowed Mitchell to slip away unscathed. He compounded his errors by dispatching northward but a single regiment, the 4th Tennessee Cavalry, to help Longstreet. This token effort arrived too late to accomplish anything significant, and the unit camped near Old Pete's headquarters that night "at the foot of Snodgrass Hill."[23]

Wheeler sent a similarly small force in pursuit of Mitchell. This tepid effort produced some additional skirmishing but no significant damage to the retreating Yankees. In his report, Wheeler claimed "the pursuit was continued till two hours after nightfall, when we retired to feed our horses." Lieutenant Colonel Russell of the 9th Pennsylvania reported a pursuit of a much different nature: "Shortly after leaving Crawfish Spring a body of Rebel cavalry made a dash upon my rear guard . . . but was instantly repulsed, and I proceeded without further annoyance." Wheeler's "pursuit" cost the Federals a grand total of four additional casualties, and so was hardly suggestive of any vigorous action.[24]

Wheeler's final decision of the day also proved unfortunate for Southern arms. Sometime after dark, the cavalry chief assigned Brig. Gen. William Martin's small division of just six regiments to guard the captured hospitals and

22 *OR* 30, pt. 4, 675; Longstreet, *From Manassas to Appomattox*, 453.

23 Guild, *Fourth Tennessee Cavalry*, 30.

24 *OR* 30, pt. 2, 178, 521; Ibid., pt. 1, 905.

establish a picket line in the direction of Rossville. His remaining (much larger) division under Brig. Gen. John Wharton, however, "re-crossed the Chickamauga that same evening for purpose of procuring forage," and ultimately returned to its old camps near Dr. Anderson's house some four miles to the rear. The mood of Wharton's troopers was ebullient triumph. "I will say here I never saw men in such high spirits," noted Pvt. Tom Coleman of the 11th Texas Cavalry. In the 8th Texas Cavalry, Chaplain Bunting recorded that the move back toward their camps of that morning was "for corn." Instead of preparing to renew the contest at first light on the morrow, Wheeler allowed his strongest division to retire miles to the rear and make camp. He would not be ready to mount any pursuit, vigorous or otherwise, at dawn.[25]

The retreating Yankees had a long night of riding (and marching, for Post's infantry) ahead of them. Mitchell's column fell back about seven miles into Chattanooga Valley before finally halting. It was a difficult movement, not because of Rebel interference (there was none), but because of the rough terrain and exhaustion of the troopers. In order to spur them on, regimental adjutant Orlando French rode back along the ranks of the 75th Illinois infantry, informing "the boys [of] the fix we were in—that we were cut off & that rebel cavalry were closely pressing our rear. That all who straggled & fell behind would be certain to fall into rebel hands and that we must make Chattanooga that night . . . now was the time for them to show their manhood and spunk. . . . [A]lmost every man was fired with new energy and came promptly up to mark."[26]

Lieutenant Mosman was bothered by a couple of Confederate deserters who fell in with the 59th Illinois infantry. "Two men of the 34th Alabama [Arthur Manigault's brigade] are here marching with us, though not under guard. They say they won't fight the yankees." The lieutenant remained skeptical. "They ought to be put under guard," he grumbled to his journal during one short break, "as they are probably spies who will leave us after dark."[27]

25 "Dear Parents and Home Folks," October 3, 1863, Thomas Coleman Letters, Western Historical Manuscripts Collection, University of Missouri, Rolla, Missouri; R. F. Bunting Letter, *Rome Tri-Weekly Telegraph*, November 27, 1863.

26 "Dearest Lydia," September 27, 1863, Orlando L. French Letters, University of Tennessee, Knoxville.

27 Gates, *Rough Side of War*, 84.

Shortly after leaving Crawfish Spring, Post's brigade came across several Union wagons loaded with rations rolling in the opposite direction. This was indeed a fortuitous find, for Post's troops were short on food. The wagons were promptly reversed, and about 9:00 p.m., recalled Adjutant French, the column stopped for a dinner issued from the newly acquired supply train. The break was a short one, and the entire column was soon back on the road stumbling through the North Georgia darkness. At the rear of the column rode the 1st Wisconsin, where its sergeant-major, Charles P. Goodrich, struggled with the little information he had to share with his men about their destination. "We marched that night, somebody knows where, I don't," he freely confessed to his wife. "The rebels followed us sometimes." One ugly rumor sweeping through the ranks of the trudging Badgers, no doubt triggered by the smoke from the grass fires visible as they departed, was that the Confederates had deliberately "burned the hospital, wounded and all, but," added Goodrich, "I do not believe it."[28]

The hospital remained intact, but plenty of things did burn that night. "As the army fell back fences, cotton gins, and other buildings were burned and kept a bright light along the route," wrote one eyewitness. The troops clomped and tramped along through most of the night. Infuriating delays slowed the movement. According to Lieutenant Mosman, the 59th Illinois infantry was delayed "two hours crossing a deep creek on logs" only to then proceed for another four agonizing miles. "The cavalry and infantry are marching alongside of each other and the dust is just awful, very deep and troublesome, filling our shoes, covering us all over and nearly blinding us. My nose bleeds profusely from the dust." Finally, Mosman noted with relief, "the column . . . halted and I lay down at 4 A.M. and was soon sound asleep."[29]

* * *

A dozen miles south in McLemore's Cove, Col. Louis Watkins and his Union Kentucky cavalry brigade spent their own uncertain night. Watkins's last instructions—sent by Mitchell the previous day—were to join the Cavalry Corps at Crawfish Spring. When the Federals abandoned that place, however,

28 "Dearest Lydia," September 27, 1863, Orlando L. French Letters; Larson, *Charles Perry Goodrich*, 84.

29 Anonymous, *First Ohio Cavalry Reunion Pamphlet*, 19, OHS; Gates, *Rough Side of War*, 84.

no one thought to send word to Colonel Watkins that Crawfish Spring was no longer in Union hands.

* * *

When night fell on September 20, another Federal column was also on the move, this one roughly a half-dozen miles north of Mitchell's men. About the time Mitchell ordered his troops to abandon Crawfish Spring, Maj. Gen. Philip Sheridan was departing Xzanders McFarland's house intent on rejoining General Thomas's left flank via Rossville. Sheridan's decision was, at best, problematic. Not only was he weakening the force left behind to defend the McFarland's Gap Road—the critical back door to Rossville, which in turn was the key to Thomas's entire fall-back position—but he was also doing exactly the opposite of what the XIV Corps commander expected Sheridan to do: pitch in and help General Steedman shore up the right flank of the Horseshoe Ridge line.

Sheridan remembered reaching Rossville about 5:00 p.m. Once there, he returned to the La Fayette Road. In addition to about 2,000 infantry, Sheridan's force included "sixteen pieces of artillery, forty-six caissons, one entire battery, and a portion of another . . . belonging to other divisions, which I had found in wild confusion and collected." In his memoirs, the general reduced that count to "eight guns" with the same number of caissons, and added "a long ammunition train . . . found in a state of confusion . . . behind the widow Glenn's" house earlier in the day. Leaving behind the excess artillery and the ammunition train west of Missionary Ridge, once through the hamlet of Rossville Sheridan bore right, his column moving through the eponymous gap before swinging back south toward Colonel Cloud's residence, and nearby Cloud Church. Another hour's march, he noted, brought him into contact with General Thomas. Sheridan also noted the temporary recapture of Brannan's and Baird's field hospitals (which he mistook for Rebel facilities). Despite his difficult journey there was little he could do there, explained Thomas, who went on to inform Sheridan that the Union lines "were too disorganized, and that it would be futile to attack; that all I could do was hold on, and aid in covering his withdrawal to Rossville."[30]

Sheridan accompanied Thomas back to Rossville, where a halt was finally called to allow the men some much-needed rest. The big Virginian, recalled the

30 *OR* 30, pt. 1, 581; Sheridan, *Memoirs*, vol. I, 284.

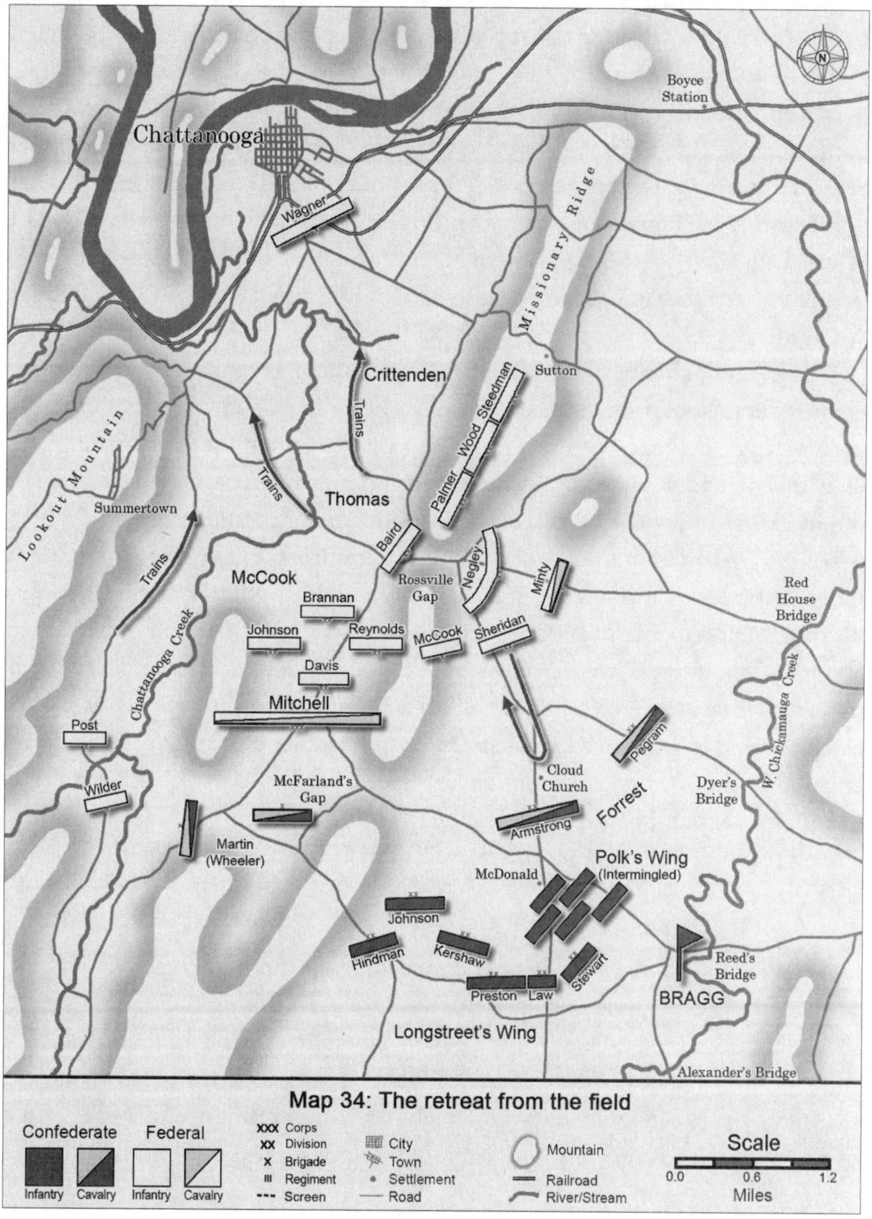

Map 34: The retreat from the field

more diminutive Sheridan, was "very much exhausted," so the two generals sat for a few minutes in virtual silence. When Sheridan rose to leave, Thomas roused himself enough to call for an aide fetch a nearby brandy flask, and each officer took a well-earned pull from it. With that, Sheridan excused himself and rode off to find a place to settle his men. The Irishman later remembered leaving Thomas "very tired, very hungry, and much discouraged."[31]

Sheridan's decision to move via Rossville later engendered controversy. Some charged that he never intended to rejoin General Thomas at all, and that Sheridan made up the entire episode in his memoirs. Two of Thomas's more vocal partisans, Henry Van Ness Boynton and Donn Piatt, accused Sheridan of as much in their joint biography of their Virginia-born hero published three decades after the battle. Piatt went so far as to dismiss Sheridan's conduct as "dastardly."[32]

These biting criticisms notwithstanding, there is no question Sheridan made a serious attempt to reach Thomas. Long before any accusations flew, Cpl. George A. Cooley of the 24th Wisconsin described the movement in his diary that night at Rossville. "We reformed and then had a hard march to the left of our army and back. We marched about 15 miles and camped about 8 o'clock." This attempt to return to the field became a point of pride for many in the division. Major George Sherman of the 36th Illinois, writing to his hometown newspaper nine days later, insisted that "we then went down a road going to Chattanooga, went to Rossville . . . and going back three miles towards the rebels' line . . . saved an ammunition train of fifty-seven wagons. We were broken up it is true, but demoralized, *never*." General Negley offered some corroboration of Sheridan's movements in a telegram sent from Rossville at 8:40 that evening. Sheridan, telegraphed Negley, reached "the meeting house [Cloud Church] 3 miles from this point," and "Forrest's cavalry harassed [him] all the way."[33]

Once back at Rossville, 21-year-old Pvt. James W. Riley, a member of Company E, 42nd Illinois, saw Sheridan making his quiet cold camp that night. The division commander was under a nearby tree busily arranging his "saddle for a pillow and saddle-blanket for a cover" when the general took note of Riley and his messmates boiling coffee. "I guess I must have been looking on wistfully, for in a little while they brought me a tin-cupful of the coffee and a small piece of hard bread, which I relished keenly," recalled Sheridan. "I gave

31 Ibid., 286-287.

32 Donn Piatt and Henry Van Ness Boynton, *General George H. Thomas, a Critical Biography* (Robert Clarke & Co, 1893), 481.

33 Entry for September 20, 1863, George A. Cooley Diary, WHS; "From the 36th," *Elgin Gazette*, October 14, 1863; *OR* 30, pt. 1, 144.

my cup of coffee and hardtack to General Sheridan," confirmed Private Riley, "for his cook was gone, so they said."[34]

Some time later, another visitor arrived on the scene from McFarland's Gap. About midnight, fellow Union division leader Jeff Davis stumbled across Sheridan and pitched his small camp alongside the Irishman's. Private Charles Dennis found both of them here sometime in the dead of night, having himself been summoned from Chattanooga by one of Davis's aides earlier that evening. After some fumbling about in the dark, Dennis found Davis and roused both generals in the process.

Dennis's efforts to wake him annoyed Davis, who hadn't seen Dennis since mid-afternoon when the orderly disappeared with the division's ammunition train. Dennis explained to the general that during the rout, he had been ordered back to Chattanooga by Rosecrans's chief of staff James Garfield, news that at least transferred Davis's anger away from Dennis and onto Garfield. The somewhat mollified Davis asked Dennis if had managed to find "anything to eat or drink during the day," recalled the aide, who replied, "I had been eating crackers dry." The general proffered "a half pint bottle of whisky that they had rustled up somewhere the day before . . . but I could see that it was about empty." Alarmed at Davis's generosity with such a scarce and valuable resource, "General Sheridan said he didn't think I needed any drink. 'We'll do the drinking and [Dennis] can do the spitting.'" Sheridan's words were but a jest, and Dennis managed at least a small swig of whisky.[35]

* * *

Chattanooga roiled with frantic activity through the afternoon, a chaos made even more feverish once news of the disaster trickled into town. Since the completion of the trestle bridge across the Tennessee River on September 18, the streets were constantly bustling with wagons coming and going. The bridge approaches were jammed with traffic waiting to cross, and everyone could hear the distant roar of battle. About midday Lt. John W. Marshall of the 97th Ohio, camped just outside the city as part of Brig. Gen. George Wagner's brigade,

34 Sheridan, *Memoirs*, vol. I, 287; C. W. Denslinger, ed., *Civil War Diary of James Wesley Riley Who Served with the Union Army in the War Between the States, April 22, 1861 - June 18, 1865* (n.p., 1960), 55.

35 Dennis Memoir, Hayes Library.

caught a rumor that "our troops are giving way." At 2:00 p.m., Marshall rode into town where he discovered that "all is uncertainty, but enough is seen to make us fear the worst." Among those he met were Lt. Joshua Fessenden and the survivors of Battery H, 5th U.S. Artillery, "entirely disabled, having lost more than half their complement of men and horses." A while later, the first stragglers from the rout appeared. "They say the day is lost and our forces are fleeing before the enemy," wrote Marshall. The lieutenant knew that early reports from skulkers were always to be treated skeptically, but a ride toward the front in search of more substantial news "fail[ed] to find anything positive."[36]

About noon, Sgt. Asbury L. Kerwood and his comrades in the 57th Indiana (Wagner's brigade) were ordered to move to the railroad depot. "Prisoners were arriving in large numbers," recalled Sergeant Kerwood, and the Hoosiers were needed to guard them. "Many . . . were from Longstreet's corps, late of the Rebel army in Virginia. These men were better clothed than . . . Bragg's army. They had always, till now, been used to victory, and were loud in their abuse of our men. . . . Some of them openly declared that before the sun set on Monday, Bragg would be in Chattanooga." A short while later, Kerwood was sent back to camp to round up the light duty men and employ them to guard the 57th's own camp, as much from the flood of blue-clad stragglers now pouring into Chattanooga as from any Rebel threat. "On going down Main street I found every foot of space crowded with teams, hurrying on toward the Pontoon bridge," wrote Kerwood. Dust choked everything, and panic was in the air. Alongside the wagons, men on foot thronged the sidewalks, "wounded, stragglers, and scattered musicians. . . . It was one constant rush towards the river." Every man who passed breathlessly past informed Kerwood that "we had better be getting on the north side of the Tennessee."[37]

More reports flowed in throughout the afternoon. Most of the news painted a gloomy picture. Both General Rosecrans and Assistant Secretary of War Dana arrived in town between 3:30 and 4:00 p.m., followed shortly by General Crittenden. Rosecrans was beyond exhausted, but after a short rest started issuing the orders outlined to Garfield earlier. NowLieutenant Marshall, the 97th Ohio, and the rest of Wagner's regiments fell in, drew extra ammunition, and moved to cover the main roads into town from the south.

36 Entry for September 20, 1863, John Wesley Marshall Diary, OHS.

37 Asbury L. Kerwood, *Annals of the Fifty-Seventh Regiment Indiana Volunteers* (W. J. Shuey, Printer and Publisher, 1868), 205-206.

Lines needed to be laid out and earthworks commenced to defend against what soon might become a siege.[38]

At 4:15 p.m., Rosecrans dispatched the order authorizing George Thomas to retreat to Rossville, if the Virginian thought it necessary. A second message, addressed to Garfield, instructed the Chief of Staff to "see General McCook [who had not yet reached Chattanooga] and other general officers. Ascertain extent of disaster." Rosecrans also directed Garfield to inform General Granger—whom Rosecrans thought was still at Rossville—"to contest the enemy's advance stubbornly, making them advance with caution. Should General Thomas be retiring in order, tell him to resist the enemy's advance, retiring on Rossville tonight."As previously described, the order to Thomas (and presumably the one to Garfield as well, though the latter lacks any indication of time sent or received) was sent before Garfield's Snodgrass Hill dispatch reached Rosecrans.[39]

What the army commander urgently required was more definite information before he informed Washington of the extent of the army's humiliation. About 4:30 p.m., McCook arrived in search of orders. "Wait a short time until I hear General Garfield's report . . . [which] will enable me to give more definite instructions to both you and General Crittenden," replied Rosecrans.[40]

That news arrived about 5:00 p.m. with Garfield's 3:45 p.m. dispatch: General Thomas was still in the fight, and much of the army was with him. Far from being routed, he was holding firm with no less than seven divisions (mistakenly counting Sheridan) and Granger's troops. The news surely lifted a heavy weight from Rosecrans's sagging shoulders. The army was not destroyed after all.

Shortly before 5:00 p.m., Capt. Joseph Hill rode into the city. Hill, it will be recalled, was with General Negley at McFarland's Gap and together they had tried to reach Thomas around 3:00 p.m. After Negley, Sheridan, and Davis settled on their course of action, they had sent Hill to Rossville (where Rosecrans was rumored to be) to report their decision to the army commander. Once at Rossville, Hill discovered Rosecrans had ridden on to Chattanooga,

38 *OR* 30, pt. 1, 60; Entry for September 20, 1863, Marshall Diary, OHS.

39 *OR* 30, pt. 1, 140.

40 Lamers, *The Edge of Glory*, 336.

and so he rode on as well. The news he carried served to further brighten Rosecrans's outlook, for it confirmed Sheridan's survival and the fact that Jeff Davis had eluded destruction. Rosecrans now confessed his own exhaustion. "I heard General Rosecrans order General McCook to lie down," testified Hill, "for, said General Rosecrans, I am nearly worn out and want some one with me to take command, if necessary to assist me." He offered similar advice to Crittenden: "He must take some rest, and be ready to return to the front," advised Rosecrans. While Crittenden was waiting with Rosecrans, Lt. Col. Lyne Starling discovered the XXI Corps headquarters wagons in town, and had the men commandeer a local house to act as Crittenden's headquarters. When he heard Rosecrans's injunction, Crittenden headed there to bed down. Now, finally, Rosecrans dedicated serious thought as to how best go about informing Washington of the day's events.[41]

Informing Washington was uppermost in Charles Dana's mind. While Dana did not arrive with Rosecrans, he did reach Chattanooga at roughly the same time. He must have stopped at Wagner's headquarters, now serving that same function for Rosecrans. Did he speak to the army commander? Neither Rosecrans nor Dana mention conversing at this time, but Dana did at least glean some basic facts: Rosecrans escaped via Rossville, and both McCook and Crittenden were also present. Dana left and headed for the army's telegraph office. He did not have a chance to read Garfield's 3:45 p.m. dispatch (though he and the courier bearing it probably passed in the street), nor was he present for Captain Hill's report. Had he waited a short time, Rosecrans's military future might have been much different.[42]

Sergeant Kerwood of the 57th Indiana met Dana shortly after he arrived at the telegraph office, perhaps while riding up the street. Dana left the sergeant with an odd impression, almost as if he were in charge of defending the town. "I . . . ascertained that the Assistant Secretary of War would undoubtedly use every possible effort to hold the place until reinforcements could reach us," wrote Kerwood. For his part, Dana was entirely focused on relaying his grim news: "The first thing I did . . . was to telegraph Mr. Stanton." Dana was still in a highly agitated state, and he later admitted that this mindset infected the dispatch created and sent: "Having made my way into Chattanooga through a

41 *OR* 30, pt. 1, 948, 978, 985.

42 Dana, *Recollections of the Civil War*, 117.

panic-stricken rabble, the first telegram which I sent . . . was naturally colored by what I had seen."[43]

"My report to-day is of deplorable importance," began Dana's missive. "Chickamauga is as fatal a name in our history as Bull Run." Dana then went on for several hundred more words, painting a picture of unmitigated disaster. In describing the Rebel breakthrough, Dana wrote that the Confederates "came through with resistless impulse. . . . Before them, our troops turned and fled. It was wholesale panic. Vain were all attempts to rally them . . . the road is full of a disordered throng of fugitives. Davis and Sheridan," Dana continued, "are said to be coming off at the head of a couple of regiments in order. Wilder's brigade marches out unbroken. Thomas, too is coming down the Rossville road with an organized command, but all the rest is in confusion." Dana estimated Union losses at "20,000, and may be much more," with 6,000 wounded abandoned to the Rebels. "Enemy not yet arrived before Chattanooga," he concluded. "Preparations making to resist his entrance for a time."[44]

Had Dana waited but an hour, giving himself time to calm down and also learn of Thomas's brave stand on Horseshoe Ridge, Granger's movements, and the rallying of Negley, Davis, and Sheridan at Rossville, his misinformed telegram would never have been sent. The army was far from destroyed, and the prospect of holding Chattanooga would have seemed much improved. Dana admitted as much in a follow-up telegram, sent that evening at 8:00 p.m.: "I am happy to report that my dispatch of 4 p.m. to-day proves to have given too dark a view of our disaster," he wired, again citing his own experiences with "the panic-stricken rabble." By then, however, the damage had already been done.[45]

The first of several dispatches from Rosecrans sped along the wires at 5:00 p.m. "We have met with a serious disaster; extent not yet ascertained," he wrote General Halleck. "Enemy overwhelmed us, drove our right, pierced our center, and scattered troops there." However, the department commander also noted Thomas's and Granger's stand, with "seven divisions." The army was still capable of a fight. Rosecrans also laid the foundation of what would become his standard defense in later years: "Troops from Charleston, Florida, Virginia, and all along the seaboard are found among the prisoners. It seems that every

43 Kerwood, *Annals of the Fifty-Seventh Regiment*, 206; Dana, *Recollections of the Civil War*, 117.

44 *OR* 30, pt. 1, 192-193.

45 Ibid., 193.

available man was thrown against us." Overwhelming Confederate numbers (as high as 150,000, by some estimates) explained the defeat, argued Rosecrans, along with the War Department's failure to inform the army commander of this vast concentration massing against him.[46]

Rosecrans sent a second missive to Maj. Gen. Ambrose Burnside in East Tennessee, informing him of the defeat and urging him, if he was "near enough to join us, to do so at once." If not, added Rosecrans, "let me know your exact position, and I will advise you what you had better do." Burnside would not even see this dispatch for several days, for on the strength of Halleck's earlier communiqués he was still moving against Jonesborough, well to the north and east of Knoxville, about 100 miles away from Chattanooga. Not until September 22 would any inkling of Chickamauga reach East Tennessee, and Burnside himself wouldn't even manage to return to Knoxville until the 24th. No help could be found for Rosecrans from that quarter.[47]

The evening of September 20 passed relatively quietly. Heartening news continued to flow into headquarters. Brigadier General James Spears reported in for orders. His brigade was still stationed south of town, where the Rossville Road crossed Chattanooga Creek. Rosecrans ordered Spears to remain there, "to halt all officers and soldiers below the rank of major-general, and to forward the wounded and transportation into Chattanooga." At 6:00 p.m. Colonel Wilder sent word of his successful disengagement and retreat. Over the next couple of hours more messages arrived from Rossville outlining the increasing Federal strength in that position as troops reported in and reorganized. At 8:40 p.m., Garfield sent another lengthy dispatch describing Thomas's retreat and Mitchell's successful evacuation of Crawfish Spring. Garfield urged Rosecrans not to give up hope. Far from facing defeat, he insisted, "I believe we can whip them tomorrow. I believe we can now crown the whole battle with victory. . . . I hope you will not budge an inch from this place, but come up early in the morning, and if the rebs try it on, accommodate them."[48]

McCook and Crittenden rested until nearly midnight. About 9:00 p.m., Colonel Starling reappeared at department headquarters, sent there by

46 Ibid., 142-143.

47 Ibid., 142; William Marvel, *Burnside* (University of North Carolina Press, 1991), 285.

48 *OR* 30, pt. 1, 884; Ibid., 144-145; Lamers, The Edge of Glory, 358-360. Lamers wrote that Granger brought Garfield's 8:40 p.m. dispatch to Chattanooga personally, but this seems in error.

Crittenden in search of an update. Starling waited for 90 minutes, but "there was no information of any importance." Later, Rosecrans summoned Crittenden back to headquarters, where he finally ordered both McCook and Crittenden to ride out to Rossville and take command of their men. General Thomas would exert overall command in Rosecrans's absence.[49]

Lieutenant Alfred Hough of Negley's staff also arrived in Chattanooga that night bearing dispatches, and later claimed to have glimpsed Rosecrans in an unguarded moment. "He looked worn and exhausted and was laboring under excitement, he heard my statement but in doing so showed the want of one requisite of a great military commander, firmness and self reliance under adverse circumstances," thought Hough. "He was evidently crushed under the weight of his disaster. . . . [H]is nervous temperament overbalanced all and exposed his one weakness." Unsettled by his commander's demeanor, Hough returned to Rossville.[50]

And thus ended the third (and most desperate day) of the battle of Chickamauga. The Army of the Cumberland had been decisively defeated—but not destroyed. Both sides had suffered heavily in the battle, and as the light faded across the smoke-shrouded woods and hills, uncertainty was the prevailing condition on both sides. The scope of any victory won by Bragg and the Army of Tennessee would only be gradually revealed, dictated in part by what came next.

Each army's casualties were severe. Exact numbers differ (especially on the Confederate side of the ledger), but the most widely accepted loss figures are 16,351 Federals and 18,454 Confederates. These break down to 1,644 killed, 9,262 wounded, 4,945 captured or missing Yankees, plus an additional aggregate of 500 losses amongst the cavalry, not broken down by category.

49 *OR* 30, pt. 1, 937, 941, 948, 958. Rosecrans later recalled that he gave McCook this instruction at 9:30 p.m., but Starling's testimony and that of Capt. Frank Jones (of McCook's staff) contradict this time estimate, noting instead that the summons came at midnight, Rosecrans's instructions were produced only after a considerable wait, and that it was "near daylight" before the two corps commanders reached Rossville.

50 Athearn, *Soldier in the West*, 150-151. In the margin notes of Hough's original hand-written autobiography, his son, Charles Hough, added an addendum to this story, related to him by his father but once, many years later. As Lieutenant Hough arrived, he "discovered [Rosecrans] crying, despairing, and even seeking spiritual comfort from the priest who was his confessor and who formed part of his bodyguard." There is good reason to doubt these details. Hough resented the later treatment of his own commander, Negley, which almost certainly colored Hough's memory. This passage also smacks of anti-Catholic prejudice, which was so common in that era.

There were 2,312 killed, 14,674 wounded and 1,468 captured or missing Rebels. Each side lost roughly 27% of their engaged strength over the course of the three days' fighting.[51]

* * *

Here also ends *Glory or the Grave*, volume two of *The Chickamauga Campaign*. The final act of the vast struggle for Rosecrans's bid to control Chattanooga, as well as the battle's aftermath and its repercussions, will be explored in the third and final volume of this trilogy, *Barren Victory*.

51 *OR* 30, pt. 1, 64, provides the Union losses. The Confederates never formally reported all their losses. The figure given here is that used by the National Park Service, found in the Chickamauga-Chattanooga National Military Park Visitor's Center. A more detailed analysis of both sides' losses will be found in volume three.

Index

David A. Powell graduated from the Virginia Military Institute (Class of 1983) with a BA in history. He has published numerous articles in magazines, and more than fifteen historical simulations of various battles. He is the author of *The Chickamauga Campaign: A Mad Irregular Battle: From the Crossing of Tennessee River Through the Second Day, August 22 - September 19, 1863* (Savas Beatie, 2014), the first of a three-volume study, as well as the author (with David A. Friedrichs, cartographer) of *The Maps of Chickamauga: An Atlas of the Chickamauga Campaign, Including the Tullahoma Operations, June 22 - September 23, 1863* (Savas Beatie, 2009). David's ground-breaking cavalry command study, *Failure in the Saddle: Nathan Bedford Forrest, Joseph Wheeler, and the Confederate Cavalry in the Chickamauga Campaign* (Savas Beatie, 2010), was awarded the Atlanta Civil War Round Table's 2010 Richard Barksdale Harwell Award.

David is currently working on other volumes for the Savas Beatie Military Atlas Series™ including the Chattanooga and Atlanta campaigns. He enjoys leading tours to Civil War battlefields in general, and the epic field of Chickamauga in particular. David is married and lives and works in Chicago, Illinois.